Women in Psychology

Women in Psychology

A Bio-Bibliographic Sourcebook

Edited by
Agnes N. O'Connell
and
Nancy Felipe Russo

GP

GREENWOOD PRESS
New York • Westport, Connecticut • London

150.922
W872

Library of Congress Cataloging-in-Publication Data

Women in psychology : a bio-bibliographic sourcebook / edited by Agnes
    N. O'Connell and Nancy Felipe Russo.
        p. cm.
    ISBN 0–313–26091–5 (lib. bdg. : alk. paper)
    1. Women psychologists—Biography.   2. Psychologists—Biography.
3. Psychology—Bio-bibliography.   I. O'Connell, Agnes N.
II. Russo, Nancy Felipe, 1943–   .
BF109.A1W65   1990
150′.92′2—dc20
[B]   89–25787

British Library Cataloguing in Publication Data is available.

Library of Congress Catalog Card Number: 89–25787
ISBN: 0–313–26091–5

First published in 1990

Greenwood Press, Inc., 88 Post Road West, Westport, Connecticut   06881
An imprint of Greenwood Publishing Group, Inc.

Printed in the United States of America

The paper used in this book complies with the
Permanent Paper Standard issued by the National
Information Standards Organization (Z39.48–1984).

10 9 8 7 6 5 4 3 2 1

CONTENTS

Part V: Appendices

ACKNOWLEDGMENTS

We wish to express our appreciation to the biographers for their cooperation and patience with our extensive editing during the many revisions, and the women they wrote about for their careers and contributions that shaped the field of psychology. We thank Thomas D. O'Connell and D. Allen Meyer for their comments on the manuscripts, their support, and their sustained assistance; Robert Kirschenbaum for reviewing our publications arrangements; and Edith Neimark, Richard Lore, and Albert Goss of Rutgers University for their enthusiasm and support for this project. Thanks also go to Ria Hermann for aid in collating recommendations for women contributors to be included in the book. Melinda Deacon, Celine Ennis, Mary Ann Griese, Julie Jones, Jan Lamoreaux, Brenda Lee, and Nora Villagomez gave invaluable help in collecting materials and manuscript preparation. Jane Little deserves a special commendation for her personal support and assistance throughout the project. Purchase of materials for background for this work was partially supported by a Minigrant from the College of Liberal Arts and Sciences, Arizona State University. This project was also partially supported by a Montclair State College Separately Budgeted Research Grant and by a Montclair State College Sabbatical Leave.

Agnes N. O'Connell
Nancy Felipe Russo

Part I

Overview

HISTORICAL AND CONTEMPORARY PERSPECTIVES

Agnes N. O'Connell and Nancy Felipe Russo

When we began our work examining the careers and contributions of women in psychology (Bernstein & Russo, 1974; O'Connell, Alpert, Richardson, Rotter, Ruble & Unger, 1978), little material focusing on women psychologists was available. Since that time, several books highlighting women psychologists have been published (O'Connell & Russo, 1980, 1983, 1988; Scarborough & Furumoto, 1987; Stevens & Gardner, 1982a, 1982b). A new subfield, the history of women in psychology, has evolved (Russo & Denmark, 1987), and the widespread participation, immense contributions, and impact of women in the field of psychology are beginning to be recognized and understood. Because the contributions of women and men in the evolution of psychology are interconnected, a full picture of the generation of knowledge in the field requires a perspective that integrates these contributions and their linkages. The new subfield, the history of women in psychology, provides an innovative vantage point for these examinations—examinations that are transforming the historical conceptualization of psychology itself.

This book—the first bio-bibliographic sourcebook on women in psychology—contributes to these examinations and transformations. The purposes of the book are both immediate and long-range. The immediate purposes are to document, evaluate, preserve, and make visible the diversity and excellence of women's contributions to psychology and society. The long-range purposes are to broaden the framework within which knowledge is sought and understood, and to serve as foundation and impetus for the integration of information about women's contributions into other works. We believe that achieving this latter goal involves a reconstruction of beliefs about the nature and scope of psychology and its contributions to Western thought.

This book is simultaneously an extension of and complement to earlier work (O'Connell & Russo, 1983, 1988) that provided a multilevel examination of the careers and contributions of women psychologists. Previous work used a combination of autobiographies with analyses of societal, professional, and personal factors to highlight women as role models, increase their visibility, and present a new vision of women's experiences in psychology and society. This book continues the effort to increase women's visibility, present a new vision of women, and offer a broader interpretive context to link their careers and contributions. It is also separate and distinct from our previous work and that of others focusing on women. This book combines a presentation of women as agents of knowledge, as ''knowers'' (Harding, 1987, p. 3), with an evaluative lens through which to view women's contributions to the evolution of psychology and society. For the first time, an assessment of women's past and present contributions and their impact on psychology and society are presented. While maintaining a clear focus on the scientific and professional contributions of these women, the chapters in Part II provide background information that links their individual experiences to the larger social and historical contexts. Selected bibliographies of the women's publications and of other sources of information about the women are also provided. The bibliographic resources in Part IV of this volume further advance access of readers to information about women contributors to psychology by providing sources of information about a larger group of remarkable women in the field.

Women have made major contributions to psychology since the inception of the field as a science in the late nineteenth century. This book is not intended to be comprehensive. Rather, the contributions and women included here were chosen as examples of the range of historical and contemporary achievements that have helped shape the many subfields of psychology.

The selection process for choosing the women included in this book was complex. Our first step was to develop a list of leading historical and contemporary women in psychology. The women included reflect the combined contributors identified in *Eminent Contributors to Psychology* (Watson, 1974), *A History of Psychology in Autobiography* (Lindzey, 1980, 1989; Murchison, 1930, 1932), *The Psychologists* (Krawiec, 1972, 1978), *Eminent Women in Psychology* (O'Connell & Russo, 1980), *Models of Achievement: Reflections of Eminent Women in Psychology* (O'Connell & Russo, 1983, 1988), the eight women starred for distinction in the first seven editions of *American Men of Science* and a sample of relevant women members of the National Academy of Sciences (Russo & O'Connell, 1980), prominent women in psychology listed in Gavin (1987), the *International Encyclopedia of Psychiatry, Psychology, Psychoanalysis, and Neurology* (Wolman, 1977), the *Biographical Dictionary of Psychology* (Zusne, 1984), additional minority women identified in *Even the Rat Was White* (Guthrie, 1976) and collegial recommendations; award winners recognized by the American Psychological Foundation (APF) and the American Psychological Association (APA), including APA's Committee on Women in Psychology; and a sampling of major office holders in national and international organizations, including APA presidencies and members of the Board of Directors. We then sent our list to individuals who had made ''steady and sustained contributions'' to the history of psychology as defined by election to Fellow status in the Division on the History of Psychology (Division 26) of APA. We asked those distinguished men and women to rate, on a scale from 1 to 10, the importance of including each woman in "a comprehensive, but highly selective, reference work of leading women in psychology." If a particular woman was unknown to the rater, NK (not known) was to be placed next to the woman's name. We also asked the History Fellows to add names and ratings of additional women that might be considered for biographical inclusion and to suggest potential biographers (including themselves). We received recommendations for seven additional women, and the names of potential biographers from thirty Division 26 Fellows. This list was then compared to another independently generated list (Gavin, 1987). Gavin's original list contained 600 female Fellows cited in the 1981 APA Directory. Her final list of prominent living women from the English-speaking world was based on the ratings of twenty-eight male and female Fellows. When these empirical lists were combined, duplications were noted and deleted. We made the final choices, keeping in mind historical periods, subfields, type of contributions, geographical locations, and accessibility of biographical information.

In conceptualizing the legacy of women psychologists, we used a broad definition, going beyond the norms and values of the traditional academic-based science of psychology to include examples of contributors to the professional practice of psychology and to public policy. The unifying criterion for our choices was a sustained record of achievements that have withstood the clarifying filter of time.

Limiting the number of women for chapter coverage to thirty-six proved to be an extremely difficult and painful task. Even beyond our full list of 185 women, cases could be made for inclusion of many, many more women who have contributed and shaped the field. To broaden the coverage of significant contributions beyond the thirty-six chapters and to increase access to other sources of information about women in psychology, we have included a chapter highlighting contributions of APA and APF award winners (Part III) and a chapter identifying the richest sources of information about women in psychology and providing sources of information for the full list of women (Part IV).

Thus, this book has five components that vary in depth of coverage of women identified for inclusion: (1) an overview chapter; (2) the thirty-six chapters with the most in-depth coverage; (3) a chapter summarizing the award-winning contributions of women as recognized by APA and APF; (4) a chapter of bibliographic resources that contains references to the most important books and other sources of information on women contributors to psychology and references to autobiographical and biographical information on 185 individual women; and (5) appendices containing a chronology of birth years; places of birth; and a listing by major fields for the thirty-six women highlighted.

Once our list was finalized, we recruited distinguished psychologists to prepare the chapters evaluating the contributions of the chosen women. We also prepared and sent to each biographer a "Guide to Preparation of Biography" that contained the following suggestions for inclusions:

- *Family Background*
  - Date and place of birth
  - Family of origin: father's name and occupation
                      mother's name and occupation
                      siblings
  - Early influences
- *Education*
  - Name, place (city, state, country), dates of attendance, major(s), and degrees earned for all educational institutions after high school
  - Significant influences, events, mentors, etc.
- *Career Development*
  - Major professional positions including institutions, title of position, and dates of employment
  - Significant influences, events, mentors, etc.
  - Awards and professional recognition, if any
- *Major Contributions and Achievements*
  - Describe in some detail important works and contributions
  - Explain in some detail main ideas, themes, etc., and their conceptual development
- *Critical Evaluations of Contributions and Achievements*
  - Refer to/cite/quote from published sources in assessing the *impact* of biographee's contributions and achievements
  - If the contributions are controversial or there is some debate about their importance, present a balanced representation of both sides
- *Integration of Personal and Professional Life*
  - If applicable, identify husband(s) by name and occupation, date of marriage(s) and how marriage(s) was (were) terminated or if it continues
  - Provide name(s) and birthdate(s) of children (occupation, if known), if applicable
  - Social and professional networks
  - Interests outside of psychology, hobbies, special institutional or ideological affiliations, etc.
- *Bibliographies*
  - In addition to the text and references include a listing of additional representative works by the biographee and a listing of additional representative works about the biographee, if appropriate.

Biographers were asked to give fullest coverage to the sections on major contributions and achievements and on critical evaluations of contributions and achievements. Although all contributions underwent intense editorial scrutiny, the specifics and variations in each woman's life and contributions and the individual styles of the biographers necessitated considerable diversity in the biographies. A balance was struck between uniformity across biographies and communication of the rich diversity of the experiences and contributions of the women.

The contributions of the thirty-six women covered in this book by biography span the field of psychology from its beginnings until contemporary times. Fourteen of the women represent the first generation of contributors, those born between 1847 and 1900, when the field was in its infancy; eight women represent the second generation, born between 1901 and 1915, when the field began to develop; and fourteen women represent the third and fourth generations, born between 1916 and 1945, when the field blossomed. Most are American-born, but also included are nine women born in Europe (Austria, Germany, Italy, Poland, and Switzerland) and Australia.

The women represent a wide range of subdisciplines, remarkable accomplishments, and varying lifestyles. Some came from professional families, some from poor and disadvantaged backgrounds. Their personal lives represent a cross section of the experiences and opportunities available to women in the late nineteenth century and in the twentieth century. They were single, married, married with children, and single parents. They worked alone, in collaboration with spouses in the field, and with colleagues. Their contributions, achievements, and leadership reached the highest standards of excellence in theoretical and applied domains and in academic, professional, institutional, and societal organizations.

The contributions of women psychologists are interwoven with the evolution of psychology, beginning with the field's early roots in philosophy, mathematics, and logic (Calkins, Ladd-Franklin). Their contributions are found in all subfields of psychology, the scientific to the professional, the theoretical to the applied. A sampling of the diversity represented here includes comparative and physiological psychology (Washburn); perception, learning, and cognition (Gibson, Goodnow, Inhelder, Ladd-Franklin), including Gestalt psychology (Henle); industrial psychology (Gilbreth); social psychology (Mayo, Sherif); humanistic psychology (Bühler); personality theory and psychoanalysis (Freud, Horney); and the history of psychology (Heidbreder, Henle, Sexton).

While the women in this book have made contributions in so many multiple areas that space precludes mentioning all of them after each example here, these highlights do illustrate the richness of the material to follow. Thus, women have made monumental contributions to the field of developmental psychology and basic conceptions of human development (Anastasi, Block, Gibson, Neugarten, Tyler), including cognitive development (Inhelder); the development of intelligence (Anastasi, Bayley, Clark, Goodenough, Thurstone, Wellman); and child psychology (Clark, Freud, Goodenough, Goodnow, Inhelder, Maccoby, Sears, Wellman). They have examined problems of human development, behavior, and interaction from infancy (Bayley, Gibson, Maccoby), to adolescence (Hollingworth, Inhelder), to adulthood and old age (Neugarten), from the gifted to the retarded (Helson, Hollingworth, Wellman). They have been particularly important in promoting an ecological, or more holistic view of human development, behavior, and interaction with the environment (Anastasi, Montessori, Wellman) in diverse subfields, from perception (Gibson, Henle) to motor development (Goodnow), to developmental and social psychology (Block, Jahoda, Maccoby, Mayo, Sherif, Wellman). They have focused on the self and meaning in human interaction (Bühler, Calkins, Horney, Sherif), and have made fundamental contributions to the understanding of personality and motivation (Bem, Frenkel-Brunswik, Helson, Horney, Spence, Strickland).

Women's contributions to psychology's evolution extend from basic science to the applications of psychology in diverse ways and with diverse issues, including those in government (Payton), education (Montessori), the teaching of reading (Gibson, Thurstone), and the effects of classroom conditions (Sears); industrial design and management (Gilbreth); unemployment (Jahoda); and prejudice, stereotyping, and discrimination (Bem, Block, Clark, Denmark, Frenkel-Brunswik, Helson, Hollingworth, Horney, Jahoda, Mayo, Payton, Strickland). In particular, the latter individuals have challenged psychology to understand all human experiences, including those of women and ethnic minorities and other groups underrepresented or disadvantaged in psychology and society.

Women have made fundamental contributions to clinical and counseling psychology in both theoretical and applied arenas (Frenkel-Brunswik, Hollingworth, Spence, Strickland, Tyler), including the development of personality theory and therapeutic techniques (Freud, Horney, Tyler).

Recognizing that their challenge to psychology's theories required the development of new methods and measurements, women made methodological innovations as well, including the paired comparisons technique (Calkins) and the visual cliff (Gibson); conjoint use of idiographic and nomothetic data (Helson); biography (Bühler); the Inventory of Life Satisfaction (Neugarten); laboratory use of doll play (Sears); and the choice pattern technique (Tyler). Some of these innovations were in psychometrics (Anastasi) and involved the development of scales (Bayley, Goodenough, Heidbreder, Spence, Strickland, Thurstone) that later came to be widely used.

Finally, the shaping of the field goes beyond scientific and applied work of individuals. Consensus must be built on issues relating to ethics and standards, accreditation, processes of peer review, publication, and public policy. In addition to the largest and oldest association of psychologists—APA, with its 70,000 members and its forty-five divisions representing subfield interests—there are numerous other regional and state associations; education and training, credentialing, and licensing organizations; and special interest groups (see VandenBos, 1989, for a listing). As the biographies here show, women have played critical leadership roles at various levels of organized psychology, including the presidency of the American Psychological Association (Anastasi, Calkins, Denmark, Spence, Strickland, Tyler, Washburn). Their leadership has built international bridges among psychologists (Bayley, Denmark, Sexton). Their presence has redefined the field.

To understand the immense, diverse, and often unrecognized contributions of such women is to obtain a new conceptualization of how psychology has evolved and what the psychological enterprise is and can be. Through the thirty-six biographies, the additional chapters, and the appendices, we hope that this book will serve as a point of departure for scholars and researchers as well as providing writers greater access to information that can give their readers a more complete and accurate picture of psychology's intellectual roots.

In addition to illuminating women's roles and experiences in shaping the field of psychology, the chapters in this book help us to explore ways in which knowledge in psychology has developed and been used. They help us to understand the impact of societal and historical context on the evolution of psychology and on the changing demographic trends in the discipline. They also help us to understand how the theories and applications of psychology and women's roles therein have reflected the larger societal and cultural contexts in which the psychological enterprise is embedded.

We hope that this book will be useful to historians of psychology who wish to reconceptualize their approach and integrate the contributions of women into their historical accounts; to scholars of women's history and the psychology of women; to psychology textbook authors who have yet to incorporate the contributions and activities of women psychologists into their works; to philosophers of science, feminist and nonfeminist, who have yet to appreciate fully how the contributions of women psychologists have served to shift the field's epistemological center and have shaped intellectual history; and to all psychologists and students of psychology who will be enriched and inspired by the quality and excellence of the field represented by the people in this book.

REFERENCES

Bernstein, M., & Russo, N. F. (1974). The history of psychology revisited: Or, up with our foremothers. *American Psychologist, 29,* 130–134.

Gavin, E. A. (1987). Prominent women in psychology, determined by ratings of distinguished peers. *Psychotherapy in Private Practice, 5*(1), 53–68.

Guthrie, R. (1976). *Even the rat was white.* New York: Harper & Row.

Harding, S. (1987). Introduction: Is there a feminist method? In S. Harding (Ed.), *Feminism and methodology* (pp. 1–14). Bloomington: Indiana University Press.

Krawiec, T. (Ed.). (1972). *The psychologists,* Vol. 1. New York: Oxford University Press.

Krawiec, T. (Ed.). (1978). *The psychologists,* Vol. 2. Brandon, Vt.: Clinical Psychology.

Lindzey, G. (Ed.). (1980). *A history of psychology in autobiography,* Vol. 7. San Francisco: W. H. Freeman.

Lindzey, G. (Ed.). (1989). *A history of psychology in autobiography,* Vol. 8. Palo Alto, Calif.: Stanford University Press.

Murchison, C. (Ed.). (1930). *A history of psychology in autobiography,* Vol. 1. Worcester, Mass.: Clark University Press.

Murchison, C. (Ed.). (1932). *A history of psychology in autobiography,* Vol. 2. Worcester, Mass.: Clark University Press.

O'Connell, A. N.; Alpert, J.; Richardson, M. S.; Rotter, N.; Ruble, D. N.; & Unger, R. K. (1978). Gender-specific barriers to research in psychology: Report of the Task Force on Women Doing Research—APA Division 35. *Journal Supplement Abstract Service: Catalog of Selected Documents in Psychology* (MS No. 1753) 8.

O'Connell, A. N., & Russo, N. F. (Eds.). (1980). *Eminent women in psychology: Models of achievement* [Special issue]. *Psychology of Women Quarterly, 5*(1).

O'Connell, A. N., & Russo, N. F. (Eds.). (1983). *Models of achievement: Reflections of eminent women in psychology*. New York: Columbia University Press.

O'Connell, A. N., & Russo, N. F. (Eds.). (1988). *Models of achievement: Reflections of eminent women in psychology, Volume 2*. Hillsdale, N.J.: Erlbaum.

Russo, N. F., & Denmark, F. L. (1987). Contributions of women to psychology. *Annual Review of Psychology, 38*, 279–298.

Russo, N. F., & O'Connell, A. N. (1980). Models from our past: Psychology's foremothers. In A. N. O'Connell & N. F. Russo (Eds.), *Eminent women in psychology* (pp. 11–54) [Special issue]. *Psychology of Women Quarterly, 5*(1).

Scarborough, E., & Furumoto, L. (1987). *Untold lives: The first generation of women psychologists*. New York: Columbia University Press.

Stevens, G., & Gardner, S. (1982a). *The women of psychology: Volume 1: Pioneers and innovators*. Cambridge, Mass.: Schenkman.

Stevens, G., & Gardner, S. (1982b). *The women of psychology: Volume 2: Expansion and refinement*. Cambridge, Mass.: Schenkman.

VandenBos, G. R. (1989). Loosely organized "organized psychology." *American Psychologist, 44*, 979–986.

Watson, R. I. (1974). *Eminent contributors to psychology, Volume 1: A bibliography of primary references*. New York: Springer.

Wolman, B. B. (Ed.). (1977). *International encyclopedia of psychiatry, psychology, psychoanalysis, and neurology*. Vols. 1–12. New York: Van Nostrand Reinhold.

Zusne, L. (1984). *Biographical dictionary of psychology*. Westport, Conn.: Greenwood Press.

Part II

The Women and Their Contributions

ANNE ANASTASI (1908–)

Virginia Staudt Sexton and John D. Hogan

In a career spanning almost sixty years, Anne Anastasi has developed and maintained a reputation that is known to psychologists in every corner of the world. Her work in psychological testing has changed the face of psychology and established her as the authority on the subject. Her research, which covers a broad range including trait formation, individual differences, the misuse of tests, statistical issues, and psychological aspects of creativity, has also explored the most basic questions, such as the manner in which research is conceptualized and conducted. Her books, which are known as models of clarity and synthesis, have become classics and are used extensively in the United States and throughout the world. As a result of her work, she has received accolades from peers, honorary degrees from five institutions, leadership roles in major psychological organizations, including the presidency of the American Psychological Association, and the National Medal of Science from the President of the United States. Not surprisingly, in a recent survey (Gavin, 1987), Anastasi was named the most prominent living woman in psychology in the English-speaking world.

FAMILY BACKGROUND AND EDUCATION

Anne Anastasi, the daughter of Anthony and Theresa Gaudiosi Anastasi, was born on December 19, 1908, in New York City. Her father, who had worked for the New York City Board of Education, died when she was one year old. Soon after his death, her maternal relatives became estranged from her father's family—his parents and sister were still alive—and she never met any of them.

Her immediate family consisted of her mother, her grandmother, and her mother's brother. Although both her mother and her uncle had been well educated in the classics and humanities, they had not been trained for the world of work. Her resourceful mother, however, taught herself bookkeeping, and before long she founded a piano factory. When that failed, she pursued several other jobs until she became the office manager of *Il progresso Italo-Americano*, one of the largest foreign newspapers in New York, a position she retained until her retirement.

Anastasi was first educated at home by her grandmother. The method was interactive, and the style was dramatic and glamorous for the somewhat isolated child. Her grandmother readily mixed the broad range of academic subjects with her own exciting youthful experiences.

Although there were few opportunities for peer interaction, the attention from the adults in her life was a constant. Her mother, no matter how tired, always had time to play the word games or role-playing games that the young girl enjoyed. Anastasi traced her distrust of authority figures and group stereotypes to lessons from her grandmother. Her interest in individual differences, she has written, may have been due to the conspicuous personality differences among the three major figures in her early life.

The boisterous activity of children from a nearby school convinced her grandmother that Anastasi should be educated at home. A regular public school teacher was hired who provided lessons every afternoon. The pleas of the teacher, Dora Ireland, for a more regular education for the child were ignored. Finally, when Anastasi was nine, it was agreed that she could attend the school at which Ireland taught, under the condition that the teacher escort her to and from school each day in a long subway ride.

The experiment was soon aborted. After two months in the third grade, the classroom teacher decided that the material was too easy for her new student, and Anastasi was transferred to a fourth grade class. Crowded, with the only vacant seat in the last row, the class became confusing, and she soon returned to studies at home. Only much later did it become evident that she could not see the blackboard at that distance. She needed glasses.

At the start of the new fall term, her family was willing to enroll her in the local school. She skipped two more grades, but after the sixth grade she advanced at the normal rate, thereby remaining with a group long enough to make some friends. She graduated from P.S. 33 in the Bronx at the top of her class and with the gold medal for general excellence.

The next move, to Evander Childs High School, immediately presented problems. Because of overcrowding in the regular building, the entering class was assigned temporary quarters. Facilities were meager, teachers were overworked, and classes were unsatisfactory. After two months Anastasi dropped out.

Following numerous family conferences, a family friend, Ida Stadie, came to the rescue. She convinced Anastasi that she should apply directly to college. She studied dozens of college catalogues and then decided on Barnard, in New York City. Since the college did not specify high school graduation as a requirement, Anastasi would submit results from the College Entrance Examination Board tests. To prepare for them, she enrolled in the Rhodes Preparatory School in Manhattan. After two years, Anastasi was admitted to Barnard in 1924 at age fifteen.

Anastasi was certain that her college major would be mathematics. The switch to psychology came about through two events, both in her sophomore year: a course with Harry J. Hollingworth, a stimulating and witty teacher, who for many years chaired the Psychology Department at Barnard; and the reading of an article by Charles Spearman on correlation coefficients. Spearman's article made her realize that she could pursue psychology and still remain faithful to mathematics. She changed her major to psychology.

In her junior year she was admitted to the honors program and enrolled in various courses, including graduate courses in psychology at Columbia and a psychology of advertising course in the Columbia School of Business Administration. She undertook a study of aesthetic preferences with Frederick H. Lund, then a Barnard instructor, which became her first publication (Lund & Anastasi, 1928). In 1928 she received her B.A. from Barnard at age nineteen. She was elected to Phi Beta Kappa and received a graduate fellowship awarded annually "to that member of the graduating class who shows greatest promise of distinction in her chosen line of work."

Anastasi was admitted to Columbia University to study for the Ph.D. in general experimental psychology, the only doctoral psychology program then available at Columbia. In a conference with A. T. Poffenberger, who chaired the Department of Psychology, she indicated that she wanted to complete the program in two years. She was told that this was possible but unlikely.

She had already taken a course with Poffenberger in the summer of 1928, and went on in her first year to take courses with Robert Woodworth, Carl Warden, Gardner Murphy, and H. E. Garrett, who later became her dissertation mentor. It was in one of his courses that she prepared her first paper on differential psychology. Garrett also provided the opportunity for discussions of the relative contributions of heredity and environment, with himself strongly on the heredity side, a position Anastasi found questionable.

Anastasi has described the summer of 1929 as a peak period of her psychological training, containing three unrelated but equally memorable experiences. First, she was given a summer research assistantship with Charles B. Davenport at the Carnegie Institution of Washington, in Cold Spring Harbor on Long Island. Her task was to assist in devising culture-free tests. Second, she took summer courses with Clark Hull and R. M. Elliott, both of whom she found intensely stimulating and who remained lifelong friends. Third, she attended the International Congress of Psychology at Yale, the first to be held in the United States, and attended by a glittering array of foreign participants.

By her second graduate year, she had completed the most basic courses and began to specialize. She took a course in intelligence testing (given at Randall's Island Children's Hospital under the title Clinical Psychology), a course on racial differences with Otto Klineberg, who had just returned from Europe with his comparative data on test performance, and neurophysiology and neuroanatomy courses at the Columbia Medical Center College of Physicians and Surgeons. The second year was also the time for completing a doctoral dissertation. One of several on the application of the tetrad technique done under Garrett's mentorship, her study identified a group factor in immediate memory for rote material (Anastasi, 1930).

MARRIAGE AND CAREER

While at Columbia, Anastasi met John Porter Foley, Jr., who was also working for a Ph.D. in psychology. They were married on July 26, 1933. Foley was from Indiana, and their two backgrounds complemented one another, sometimes generating new interests. One of these was art. They became frequent museum visitors, increasingly sophisticated in art, and eventually collectors.

Marriage served as a source for further professional growth. Foley, as an undergraduate at Indiana University, had been strongly influenced by J. R. Kantor. Anastasi met Kantor, read his works, and found that he began to influence her thinking. In addition, Foley, early in his career, worked in animal psychology, with which Anastasi had limited experience. This was also to influence her thinking in differential psychology, as was Foley's participation in several research projects with the Columbia anthropologist Franz Boas. In short, her marriage, as she has stated, gave her the benefit of two Ph.D.'s.

A year after her marriage she was diagnosed as having cervical cancer. The necessary radium and x-ray treatments left her unable to have children. She has described this illness as one of two critical factors in her life. (The other was the premature death of her father.) The cancer allowed her to remain childless without conflict or guilt, and she believes it formed a partial basis for her success.

The early years of marriage, from 1937 to 1942, were marked by geographic separation and frequent railroad travel. Jobs were scarce and universities were reluctant to hire husband and wife in the same department. Consequently, Anastasi taught at Barnard while Foley taught at George Washington University, in Washington. The dilemma was not resolved until Foley, whose interests had been increasingly turning to industrial psychology, accepted a position with the industrial division of the Psychological Corporation in New York City. They have remained in New York City ever since.

Anastasi was appointed Instructor of Psychology at Barnard in the fall of 1930, at an annual salary of $2,400. She remained there until 1939, when she became assistant professor and "chairman" of the new Department of Psychology at Queens College of the City University of New York. She was also the sole member of the department. By 1946 the department had grown to six, but bureaucratic demands and departmental infighting blocked any serious efforts at teaching and research. Four of the psychology faculty left that year, including Anastasi.

Her next position was at Fordham University where, in 1947, she was appointed associate professor of psychology in the Graduate School of Arts and Sciences, and professor in 1951. She remained at Fordham until her retirement in 1979, when she became professor emeritus and was awarded an honorary Doctor of Science degree. She continues to be active in writing papers, lectures, and books; the sixth edition of *Psychological Testing* appeared in 1988, with translation into Italian, Portuguese, Russian, Spanish, and Thai. (The first edition appeared in 1954.) She consults informally with Fordham faculty and students, continues to serve on committees, maintains an international correspondence, and shows no signs of slowing down, or wanting to.

MAJOR CONTRIBUTIONS AND ACHIEVEMENTS

Anastasi has written that her professional contributions are reflected largely in her publications. It is true that if she had done nothing else but write the book *Psychological Testing*, her name would be known to generations of psychologists and students of psychology around the world. However, her contributions are more diverse and can be divided conveniently into four areas: research, teaching, textbook writing, and organizational leadership.

Her research has followed a number of themes, although the range of individual papers is astonishingly wide. One major focus has been on the nature and measurement of psychological traits, with particular emphasis on the role of experience in trait formation. She began her investigation of trait characteristics with her dissertation in 1930, and by 1935 she was already engaged in a debate on the subject with the distinguished psychologist and psychometrician L. L. Thurstone. Her research on language development among black and Puerto Rican children, published in the 1950s, continued to look at the role of experience, and reached conclusions that remain interesting and provocative to this day. She carried this general theme into publications on intelligence and family size, age changes in adult test performance, and sex differences in psychological traits. Still another project was a series of publications on the role of experiential factors in the development of creative thinking in children and adolescents. The entire body of research eventually led to the emergence of major conceptual contributions.

A further focus of her writing and research has been test construction, evaluation, and interpretation, ranging from purely conceptual and statistical questions to problems of common misuse and misinterpretation. Far from taking an ivory-tower approach, Anastasi has been actively involved in projects sponsored by the College Entrance Examination Board and the U.S. Air Force, which required the development and validation of psychological instruments. She has also written extensively on misconceptions of ''culture-free'' or ''culture-fair'' tests and methodological problems pertaining to test bias, speeded tests, item selection, and coaching for tests. Further, she has written innumerable chapters in edited books on various aspects of testing, in addition to her own classic textbook. Finally, she has contributed a large number of reviews to the series *Mental Measurements Yearbook*, edited by Oscar Buros. With the publication of the eighth yearbook in 1978, she became the only contributor to have reviews in all volumes to date.

She and her husband have also produced a considerable body of work on various psychological aspects of art. Their avocational interest soon developed into the study of cultural differences in artistic expression, including children's spontaneous drawing and animal drawings by Indian children of the North Pacific Coast. They continued with various investigations of abnormality and art; several of the studies compared the artistic production of adult psychotics to that of normal control groups. Their work tended to debunk the notion of a relationship between artistic production and abnormality, and focused more on the causative factors of education, occupation, and sociocultural background. This work led to questions concerning the appropriateness of projective drawing tests in clinical assessment.

Another category of her publications could be called "isolated studies," those conducted simply to satisfy curiosity and fitting no general theme or pattern. Anastasi has identified a number of them (Anastasi, 1972), which include a study of the effect of shape on the estimation of area, methodological controls for the diary method, a study of fear and anger among college students, a factor analysis of the performance of dogs on certain learning tests, and a case study of a musically gifted "idiot savant."

A single measure of her impact can be seen in a recent publication by Lerner (1986). In a book devoted to theories and conceptions of developmental psychology, Lerner devotes an entire chapter (of twelve) to the discussion of an article Anastasi wrote more than three decades ago. This widely reprinted article (Anastasi, 1958b), based on her presidential address to the APA Division of General Psychology, is the centerpiece in Lerner's argument for development as an interactional phenomenon.

The title of this paper itself is instructive and holds the key to her proposal: "Heredity, Environment, and the Question 'How?' " In what Lerner called "a most lucid and well-considered treatment," Anastasi examines the nature-nurture controversy, the issue that many consider the most fundamental in all of developmental psychology. Her analysis is typically direct—psychologists have been asking the wrong questions and therefore cannot be expected to arrive at the correct answer. Nature and nurture never exist independently of one another; they are always inextricably linked in any behavior. Therefore, it is never correct to ask which one causes the behavior, or how much is due to either. The question can only be, How do they interact? The implications of that conclusion are breathtaking, as Lerner and others have pointed out. (See also Cravens, 1978.) A great deal of psychological research becomes meaningless because of the inability of the researchers to frame the research question properly.

In 1981, when Anastasi received the Distinguished Scientific Award for the Applications of Psychology, she was cited as

a major force in the development of differential psychology as a behavioral science, having illuminated the ways trait development is influenced by education and heredity, and the ways trait measurement is affected by training and practice, cultural contexts, and language differences. Her texts, *Differential Psychology* and *Psychological Testing*, being both integrative and probing, do not simply summarize the groundwork in these fields but provide impetus for further work. Ever watchful for misleading generalizations and misconceptions, she displays unusual perceptiveness in her timely emphasis on key issues and unusual critical acumen in her timely undercutting of spurious issues. (*American Psychologist*, 1982, *37*, 52)

The impact of Anastasi's textbooks has been enormous. Her major works, *Differential Psychology* (1958a), *Psychological Testing* (1988b), and *Fields of Applied Psychology* (1979), are considered classics and have been used in English and in many translations around the world. In the citation for the 1984 American Psychological Foundation Gold Medal Award, they were called "models of clarity, comprehensiveness, and synthesis" which "frame the very questions scientists in these disciplines ask and the manner in which research is conducted." *Psychological Testing* also appears as one of the frequently recommended books in surveys of reading lists for students in graduate departments of psychology (Solso, 1987).

In 1972 Anastasi became the first female president of the American Psychological Association (APA) in fifty years. Her work in professional societies, however, had begun long before that. Her first office in a scientific society was that of secretary of the Psychology Section of the New York Academy of Sciences a few years after her doctoral degree. In addition to APA, she served as president of the Eastern Psychological Association (1946–1947), the APA Division of General Psychology (1956–1957), the APA Division of Evaluation and Measurement (1965–1966), and the American Psychological Foundation (1965–1967).

Among her awards have been honorary degrees from a number of universities: University of Windsor (Litt.D., 1967), Villanova University (Paed.D., 1971), Cedar Crest College (Sc.D., 1971), LaSalle College (Sc.D., 1979), and Fordham University (Sc.D., 1979). The Educational Testing Service Award for Distinguished Service to Measurement was bestowed on her in 1977. She received the APA Distinguished Scientific Award for the Applications of Psychology in 1981, the American Educational Research Association Award for Distinguished Contributions to Research in Education in 1983, the E. L. Thorndike Medal for Distinguished Psychological Contributions to Education from the APA Division of Educational Psychology in 1984, and the American Psychological Foundation Gold Medal for lifetime achievement in 1984. In the summer of 1987, she was presented with the National Medal of Science by President Ronald Reagan. In view of all her accomplishments, it is fitting that her peers have rated Anastasi as the most prominent living woman in psychology in the English-speaking world (Gavin, 1987).

REFERENCES

American Psychological Foundation Awards for 1984 (1985). *American Psychologist*, *40*, 340–341.

Anastasi, A. (1930). A group factor in immediate memory. *Archives of Psychology*, No. 120.

Anastasi, A. (1958a). *Differential psychology* (3rd ed.). New York: Macmillan.

Anastasi, A. (1958b). Heredity, environment, and the question "How?" *Psychological Review, 65*, 197–208.

Anastasi, A. (1972). Reminiscences of a differential psychologist. In T. S. Krawiec (Ed.), *The psychologists* (pp. 3–37). New York: Oxford University Press.

Anastasi, A. (1979). *Fields of applied psychology* (2nd ed.). New York: McGraw-Hill.

Anastasi, A. (1980). (Autobiography). In G. Lindzey (Ed.), *History of psychology in autobiography* (vol. 7, pp. 1–37). New York: Freeman.

Anastasi, A. (1982). *Contributions to differential psychology: Selected papers*. New York: Praeger [especially chapter 1, for content and overview of research, and chapter 10 (pp. 229–238) for autobiography].

Anastasi, A. (1984). (Autobiography). In R. Corsini (Ed.), *Encyclopedia of psychology* (vol. 1, p. 60). New York: Wiley.

Anastasi, A. (1986). Focus on the psychologist. In R. Lerner, R. C. Kendall, D. Miller, D. Hultsch, & R. Jensen, *Psychology* (p. 388). New York: Macmillan.

Anastasi, A. (1988a). (Autobiography). In A. N. O'Connell & N. F. Russo (Eds.), *Models of achievement: Reflections of eminent women in psychology* (vol. 2, pp. 57–66). Hillsdale, N.J.: Erlbaum.

Anastasi, A. (1988b). *Psychological Testing* (6th ed.). New York: Macmillan.

Buros, O. K. (1978). *The eighth mental measurements yearbook*. Lincoln, Nebr.: Buros Institute of Mental Measurement.

Cravens, H. (1978). *The triumph of evolution*. Philadelphia: University of Pennsylvania Press.

Denton, L. (1987, October). The rich life and busy times of Anne Anastasi. *APA Monitor*, pp. 10–11.

Distinguished Scientific Award for the Applications of Psychology: 1981. (1982). *American Psychologist, 37*, 52–59.

Gavin, E. (1987). Prominent women in psychology, determined by ratings of distinguished peers. *Psychotherapy in Private Practice, 5*, 53–68.

An interview with Anne Anastasi (1975). In A. Davids & T. Engen, *Introductory psychology* (pp. III–1 to III–4). New York: Random House.

Lerner, R. (1986). *Concepts and theories of human development* (2nd ed.). New York: Random House.

Lund, F. H., & Anastasi, A. (1928). An interpretation of esthetic experience. *American Journal of Psychology, 40*, 434–448.

Solso, R. L. (1987). Recommended readings in psychology over the past thirty-three years. *American Psychologist, 42*, 1130–1132.

Additional Representative Publications by Anne Anastasi

Anastasi, A. (1936). The influence of specific experience upon mental organization. *Genetic Psychology Monographs, 18*(4), 245–355.

Anastasi, A. (1948). The nature of psychological "traits." *Psychological Review, 55*, 127–138.

Anastasi, A. (1956). Intelligence and family size. *Psychological Bulletin, 53*, 187–209.

Anastasi, A. (Ed.). (1965). *Individual differences*. New York: Wiley.

Anastasi, A. (Ed.). (1966). *Testing problems in perspective*. Washington, D.C.: American Council on Education.

Anastasi, A. (1967). Psychology, psychologists, and psychological testing. *American Psychologist, 22*, 297–306.

Anastasi, A. (1970). On the formation of psychological traits. *American Psychologist, 25*, 899–910.

Anastasi, A. (1972). The cultivation of diversity. *American Psychologist, 27*, 1091–1099.

Anastasi, A. (1981). Coaching, test sophistication, and developed abilities. *American Psychologist, 36*, 1086–1093.

Anastasi, A. (1981). Sex differences: Historical perspectives and methodological implications. *Developmental Review, 1*, 187–206.

Anastasi, A. (1983). Evolving trait concepts. *American Psychologist, 38*, 175–184.

Anastasi, A. (1983). Psychological testing. In C. E. Walker (Ed.), *Handbook of clinical psychology: Theory, research and practice* (Vol. 1, pp. 420–444). Homewood, Ill.: Dow-Jones Irwin.

Anastasi, A. (1983). What do intelligence tests measure? In S. B. Anderson & J. S. Helmick (Eds.), *On educational testing: Intelligence, performance standards, test anxiety, and latent traits* (pp. 5–28). San Francisco: Jossey-Bass.

Anastasi, A. (1984). Aptitude and achievement tests: The curious case of the indestructible strawperson. In B. S. Plake (Ed.), *Social and technical issues in testing: Implications for test construction and usage* (pp. 129–140). Hillsdale, N.J.: Lawrence Erlbaum Associates.

Anastasi, A. (1984). Traits revisited—With some current implications. In D. P. Rogers (Ed.), *Foundations of psychology: Some personal views* (pp. 185–206). New York: Praeger.

Anastasi, A. (1985). Psychological testing: Basic concepts and common misconceptions. In A. M. Rogers & C. J. Scheirer (Eds.), *The G. Stanley Hall Lecture Series* (Vol. 5, pp. 87–120). Washington, D.C.: American Psychological Association.

Anastasi, A. (1985). Reciprocal relations between cognitive and affective development—With implications for sex differences. In T. B. Sonderegger & R. A. Dienstbier (Eds.), *Nebraska Symposium on Motivation: Volume 32. Psychology and gender* (pp. 3–35). Lincoln: University of Nebraska Press.

Anastasi, A. (1985). Some emerging trends in psychological measurement: A fifty-year perspective. *Applied Psychological Measurement, 9*, 121–138.

Anastasi, A. (1986). Evolving concepts of test validation. *Annual Review of Psychology, 37*, 1–15.

Anastasi, A. (1986). Experiential structuring of psychological traits. *Developmental Review, 6*, 181–202.

Anastasi, A. (1986). Intelligence as a quality of behavior. In R. J. Sternberg & D. K. Detterman (Eds.). *What is intelligence? Contemporary viewpoints on its nature and definition* (pp. 19–21). Norwood, N.J.: Ablex.

Anastasi, A., & Cordova, F. A. (1953). Some effects of bilingualism upon the intelligence test performance of Puerto Rican children in New York City. *Journal of Educational Psychology, 44*, 1–19.

Anastasi, A., & Foley, J. P., Jr. (1938). A study of animal drawings by Indian children of the North Pacific Coast. *Journal of Social Psychology, 9*, 363–374.

Anastasi, A., & Foley, J. P., Jr. (1944). An experimental study of the drawing behavior of adult psychotics in comparison with that of a normal control group. *Journal of Experimental Psychology*, *34*, 169–194.

Anastasi, A.; Fuller, J. L.; Scott, J. P.; & Schmitt, J. R. (1955). A factor analysis of the performance of dogs on certain learning tests. *Zoologica*, *40*(3), 33–46.

Anastasi, A., & Levee, R. F. (1959). Intellectual defect and musical talent. *American Journal of Mental Deficiency*, *64*, 695–703.

Anastasi, A., & Schaefer, C. E. (1969). Biographical correlates of artistic and literary creativity in adolescent girls. *Journal of Applied Psychology*, *53*, 267–273.

NANCY BAYLEY (1899–   )

Lewis P. Lipsitt and Dorothy H. Eichorn

Nancy Bayley has been a giant among developmental psychologists, steadfastly enhancing our understanding of human development throughout the life course. The Bayley Scales of Mental and Motor Development, widely recognized as the best standardized measures of infant development, are used internationally. One of the first to discuss life-span development as a frame of reference for research, Bayley has documented change as well as continuity in intellectual, cognitive, and psychomotor development, and the effects of maternal behavior on offspring, using both naturalistic and experimental methodologies. She has been a pioneer in the rigorous measurement of intelligence in infants and young children, in the study of rate of physical maturation and its behavioral correlates, and in setting a model of multidisciplinary cooperation for the advancement of knowledge about human development. In recognition of her achievements, she received the G. Stanley Hall Award from the Division of Developmental Psychology of the American Psychological Association (APA), APA's Distinguished Scientific Contributions Award, and the Gold Medal Award of the American Psychological Foundation. Bayley was elected a Fellow of both the American Psychological Association and the American Association for the Advancement of Science.

FAMILY BACKGROUND, EDUCATION, AND CAREER

Nancy Bayley was born in The Dalles, Oregon, on September 28, 1899, the daughter of Prudence Cooper Bayley and Frederick W. Bayley. Her father headed the grocery department of a large department store in that city. Her mother cared not only for her own family, which included Bayley's two older siblings, Dorothy and Prudence, and two younger ones, Alfred and Katharine, but also assisted many families in the community both when they were in need and when the occasion was festive.

Attesting to the pioneering spirit of the family from which she came, Bayley's paternal grandparents sailed around Cape Horn to Victoria, British Columbia. Her grandfather was a member of the colonial government there, and her grandmother's father established coal mines. Her maternal grandparents traveled to the Northwest by covered wagon from the eastern part of the United States, where her Dutch ancestors had settled in the 1600s. En route to Oregon, these pioneers delivered a son in their wagon; their young daughter, Belle, made the entire trip. Years later, after being widowed, Nancy Bayley's Aunt Belle became a physician and drove an early model car over country terrain to make house calls. Among the babies she delivered were Nancy Bayley and her four siblings.

Sickly as a young child, Bayley did not attend public school in The Dalles until she was eight years old, when she entered the second grade. By age ten she had made up two grade levels, and then went on to complete high school. Intending to become an English teacher, she enrolled at the University of Washington. An introductory course with E. B. Guthrie kindled her interest in psychology, and she continued her studies, receiving the Bachelor of Science degree in 1922 and the Master of Science degree in 1924. During this period she had the opportunity to learn about both intelligence tests and the psychogalvanometer, and to serve as a research assistant at the university's Gatzert Foundation for Child Welfare. Her master's thesis, supervised by Stevenson Smith, involved the construction of performance tests for preschool children. Bayley earned the Doctor of Philosophy degree in 1926 at the University of Iowa (then the State University of Iowa) in Iowa City, where she had been offered a graduate fellowship following her master's work at Washington. For her doctoral dissertation she borrowed a new galvanometer from Carl Seashore, dean of the Graduate School and professor of philosophy and psychology, and did one of the first studies of children's fears utilizing the psychogalvanic skin response.

Bayley's first academic position was instructor, the usual starting rung in those days, at the University of Wyoming, where she stayed from 1926 to 1928. From this post she published, in 1926, the first of her almost 200 papers, chapters, and books. Throughout her career her research had continuity in its thematic core. Bayley devoted enormous time and effort to mental and physical growth, psychomotor development, the earliest mental functions that predict later intelligence, and environmental correlates of intelligence.

At the invitation of Harold Jones, Nancy Bayley moved to the University of California at Berkeley as a research associate in the Institute of Child Welfare (now the Institute of Human Development). There she initiated a major study of growth, beginning with healthy newborns, launching a career of over sixty years in which she carried out landmark studies not only of developmental regularities but of handicapping conditions as well. Today we know that program as the world-renowned and productive Berkeley Growth Study.

Although at Berkeley most of her career, Bayley held, at several periods between 1939 and 1951, concurrent research appointments in psychology and anatomy at Stanford University, and from 1947 to 1954 she taught a course on the assessment of infants and young children for the Department of Psychology at Berkeley. In 1954 she moved to the National Institute of Mental Health in Bethesda, Maryland, where she was chief of the section on child development of the intramural Laboratory of Psychology until her return to Berkeley in 1964. During this time she was importantly linked with the National Collaborative Perinatal Project for the study of cerebral palsy, mental retardation, and other neurological and psychological disorders, a large-scale study of 50,000 births begun in 1957. This project involved twelve centers throughout the United States and the eventual study, with support of the National Institute of Neurological Diseases and Blindness, of these 50,000 children from birth to eight years.

The Bayley Mental and Motor Scales were the instruments of choice for assessments at eight months of age of children in the collaborative project. With Bayley's expert guidance, normative data were collected with her newly revised scales on one-hundred children at each age level from one month to eighteen months of age. A large bank of data now exists on about 40,000 children born into the study who survived for their first eight months and were returned by their mothers for the eight-month Bayley tests, along with other psychological and medical assessments. Many of these study members, in their mid-twenties at this writing, are still participating in the follow-up studies carried out at Brown University and the University of Pennsylvania.

Bayley continued this work and the affiliation with the National Collaborative Project after returning to Berkeley in 1964 to serve as the first administrator of the new Harold E. Jones Child Study Center of the renamed Institute of Human Development. In 1968 she published the revised Bayley Scales and began the thirty-six-year recall of her growth study members. During this period she also became consultant to Sonoma State Hospital for a longitudinal intervention study of infants with Down's syndrome.

Nancy Bayley's relationship with her husband of many years, John R. Reid, whom she married April 27, 1929, was very important to her. They were married while he was completing his doctoral work in philosophy at the University of California, Berkeley, and both of them were employed at the Institute of Child Welfare.

ACHIEVEMENTS AND CONTRIBUTIONS

Awards and Honors

Bayley is a Fellow of the American Psychological Association (APA); her first APA meeting was in 1925 at Cornell University. She also holds Fellow status in the American Association for the Advancement of Science. She was initiated into Sigma Xi, the honorary scientific society, in 1926. She has been prominently involved in the affairs of the Society for Research in Child Development, from which organization she received a distinguished scientific contribution award in 1983, and of which she was president from 1961 to 1963. She also received the G. Stanley Hall Award for outstanding contributions to knowledge in the field of developmental psychology in 1971 from APA's Division on Developmental Psychology, which she served as president in 1953–1954. In

1953–1954 she was also president of the Western Psychological Association, and in 1957–1958 she was president of the Division on Adult Development and Aging of the APA.

As early as 1938 Bayley's work attracted national acclaim. She was cited by the American Educational Research Association for her 1933 monograph, *Mental Growth During the First Three Years*. She received the Distinguished Scientific Contribution award from the American Psychological Association in 1966, the first woman to be so honored, and the Gold Medal Award of the American Psychological Foundation in 1982 for her outstanding life's work in the behavioral sciences. In 1969 her own Institute of Human Development at Berkeley, on the occasion of its fortieth anniversary, honored Nancy Bayley for her distinguished contributions to the study of human development, and the California State Psychological Association similarly honored her in 1976.

Illustrative of her professional versatility, Bayley served as an examiner for the American Board of Professional Examiners in Professional Psychology—she is herself a diplomate in clinical psychology. She has been a representative from the Division on Developmental Psychology to the Council of Representatives of the American Psychological Association.

The stature of scientists may sometimes be assessed by the intellectual company they keep. Among Nancy Bayley's longtime professional associates can be found such stellar contributors to the field as Harold E. Jones, Mary Cover Jones, Earl Schaefer, Richard Q. Bell, Emmy E. Werner, Marjorie P. Honzik, and Harriet L. Rheingold.

Impact

The fourth volume of *Advances in Infancy Research* (Lipsitt & Rovee-Collier, 1986) was dedicated to Nancy Bayley in 1986, on the sixtieth anniversary of her first publication, which itself marked a significant advance in the field of child behavior and development. In the dedication message, it was said that Nancy Bayley has in fact been a pacesetter all her professional life. Virtually all developmental psychologists are familiar with her pioneering studies of infant development, including her assessments of behavior in infancy, which led to the best standardized measures of infant development, the widely used Bayley Scales of Mental and Motor Development. But few today are aware that Bayley carried out a landmark study of fear using the psychogalvanic skin response technique (Bayley, 1928). This research inspired numerous other studies and helped to generate technological advances in the development of electronic instrumentation for recording bioelectric responses.

Bayley's eclectic approaches and broad appeal as a contributing scientist are indicated by the fact that she has published with pediatricians, endocrinologists, anatomists, mathematicians, and psychologists of several different subdisciplines. Her paper with Mary Cover Jones in 1950, on the association of behavior with rate of physical maturation, followed in 1951 by her paper on the psychological correlates of somatic androgyny, pioneered a line of research still active today. Anatomists, physicians, and anthropometrists concerned with morphological maturation regard Bayley's work on physical development, the prediction of adult size, and the control of atypical growth, as well as her contributions to the understanding of rate of maturation as an indicator of developmental status, as outstanding.

In his landmark volume *A History of the Study of Human Growth*, James Tanner, an internationally renowned authority, devotes a major section of his chapter on North American longitudinal studies to Bayley's Berkeley Growth Study. He describes her contributions as "classic in their penetration and simplicity" and comments that the first paper on physical growth from this study "showed the style of scholarship that was to be the norm." Of his own widely cited paper on longitudinal growth standards (Tanner, Whitehouse, & Takaishi, 1966), Tanner states that "Bayley's seminal paper of ten years earlier lay at the base of it" and was "the first effort to produce standards for height which took into account an individual's tempo . . . a radical new departure in the whole approach to standards of growth" (p. 329). Tanner also credits Bayley with "the first set of correlations published which related infant size to adult size" and "a very important paper" examining the relationship between height and academic ability, which led to reinterpretation of hypotheses.

Bayley's broad impact is well summarized in the citation accompanying her Distinguished Scientific Contribution award from the APA:

For the enterprise, pertinacity, and insight with which she has studied human growth over long segments of the life cycle. With consummate skill in the use of available but imperfect instruments and with respect and sensitiveness for her subjects, she has rigorously recorded their physical, emotional, and social development from birth to middle life. Her studies have enriched psychology with enduring contributions to the measurement and meaning of intelligence, and she traced important strands in the skein of factors involved in child development. Her participation in a number of major programs of developmental research is a paradigm of the conjoint efforts which are essential in a field whose problems span the generations.

Nancy Bayley has steadfastly moved the field of developmental psychology toward an improved understanding of human development over the life span. She has called persistently for excellence in psychometric assessment at successive ages and for rigorous longitudinal methodology. At the same time, she has reported on change as well as continuity in IQ assessments, and on the maintenance rather than the decline of IQ throughout most of adulthood. She has also studied the influence of maternal behavior on offspring, both naturalistically and experimentally. If the field dares to ask vital questions about continuities in development, that is due in great part to Nancy Bayley's work and her commitment to that goal.

REFERENCES

Bayley, N. (1926). Performance tests for three, four and five year old children. *Journal of Genetic Psychology, 33*, 435–454.

Bayley, N. (1928). A study of fear by means of the psychogalvanic technique. *Psychological Monographs, 38*, 1–38.

Bayley, N. (1951). Some psychological correlates of somatic androgyny. *Child Development, 22*, 47–60.

Bayley, N. (1955). On the growth of intelligence. *American Psychologist, 10*, 805–818.

Bayley, N. (1968). Behavioral correlates of mental growth: Birth to thirty-six years. *American Psychologist, 23*, 1–17.

Jones, M. C., & Bayley, N. (1950). Physical maturing among boys as related to behavior. *Journal of Educational Psychology, 41*, 129–148.

Lipsitt, L. P., & Rovee-Collier, C. (Eds.). (1986). *Advances in infancy research* (Vol. 4, pp. xii-xv). Norwood, N.J.: Ablex.

Tanner, J. M. (1981). *A history of the study of human growth.* Cambridge, Eng.: Cambridge University Press.

Tanner, J. M.; Whitehouse, R. H.; & Takaishi, M. (1966). Standards from birth to maturity for height, weight, height velocity and weight velocity: British children 1965. *Archives of Disease in Childhood, 41*, 454–471; 613–635.

Additional Representative Publications by Nancy Bayley

Bayer, L., & Bayley, N. (1947). Directions for measures and radiographs used in predicting height. *Child Development, 18*, 85–87.

Bayer, L. M., & Bayley, N. (1963). Growth pattern shifts in healthy children: Spontaneous and induced. *Journal of Pediatrics, 62*, 631–645.

Bayley, N. (1932). A study of the crying of infants during mental and physical tests. *Journal of Genetic Psychology, 40*, 306–329.

Bayley, N. (1933). *The California First-Year Mental Scale.* Berkeley: University of California Press.

Bayley, N. (1933). Mental growth during the first three years: A developmental study of sixty-one children by repeated tests. *Genetic Psychology Monographs, 14*, 1–92.

Bayley, N. (1936). Growth changes in the cephalic index during the first five years of life. *Human Biology, 8*, 1–18.

Bayley, N. (1939). Mental and motor development from two to twelve years. *Review of Educational Research, 9*, 18–37, 114–125.

Bayley, N. (1945). The emotions of children. Their development and modification. *Childhood Education, 21*, 156–159.

Bayley, N. (1949). Consistency and variability in the growth of intelligence from birth to eighteen years. *Journal of Genetic Psychology, 75*, 165–196.

Bayley, N. (1954). Some increasing parent-child similarities during the growth of children. *Journal of Educational Psychology, 45*, 1–21.

Bayley, N. (1958). Value and limitations of infant testing. *Children, 5*, 129–133.

Bayley, N. (1963). The life span as a frame of reference for psychological research. *Vita Humana, 6*, 125–139.

Bayley, N., & Davis, F. C. (1935). Growth changes in bodily size and proportions during the first three years: A developmental study of sixty-one children by repeated measurements. *Biometrika, 27*, 26–87.

Bayley, N., & Espenschade, A. (1941). Motor development from birth to maturity. *Review of Educational Research, 11*, 562–572.

Bayley, N., & Jones, H. E. (1937). Environmental correlates of mental and motor development: A cumulative study from infancy to six years. *Child Development, 8*, 329–341.

Bayley, N., & Oden, M. H. (1955). The maintenance of intellectual ability in gifted adults. *Journal of Gerontology, 10*, 91–107.

Bayley, N., & Schaefer, E. S. (1960). Relationships between socio-economic variables and the behavior of mothers toward young children. *Journal of Genetic Psychology 96*, 61–77.

Cameron, J., Livson, N., & Bayley, N. (1967). Infant vocalizations and their relationship to mature intelligence. *Science, 157*, 331–333.

Eichorn, D. H., & Bayley, N. (1961). Growth in head circumference from birth through young adulthood. *Child Development, 33*, 257–271.

Jones, H. E., & Bayley, N. (1941). The Berkeley Growth Study. *Child Development, 12*, 167–173.

Jones, H. E., & Bayley, N. (1950). Growth, development, and decline. *Annual Review of Psychology, 1*, 1–8.

Rheingold, H. L., & Bayley, N. (1959). The later effects of an experimental modification of mothering. *Child Development, 30*, 363–372.

Schaefer, E. S.; Bell, R. Q.; & Bayley, N. (1959). Development of a maternal behavior research instrument. *Journal of Genetic Psychology, 95*, 83–104.

Werner, E. E., & Bayley, N. (1966). The reliability of Bayley's revised scale of mental and motor development during the first year of life. *Child Development, 37*, 39–50.

Additional Representative Publications About Nancy Bayley

Cattell, J. (1973). *American men and women of science* (12th ed.). *Social and behavioral sciences*, Vol. 1, A-K. New York: J. Cattell Press.

Coe, Anthony. (1987). Nancy Bayley: A brief biography. *SRCD Newsletter*, Spring, 1–2.

O'Connell, A. N., & Russo, N. F. (1980). Models for achievement: Eminent women in psychology. *Psychology of Women Quarterly, 5*, 6–54.

Stevens, G., & Gardner, S. (1982). *The women of psychology. Volume 2: Expansion and refinement*. Cambridge, Mass.: Schenkman.

SANDRA LIPSITZ BEM (1944–   )

Vivian Parker Makosky

Sandra Lipsitz Bem's values have shaped her research and her family life, and these in turn have shaped the values of the public and the profession. Her early work on sex-biased job advertising contributed to landmark court decisions under Title VII of the 1964 Civil Rights Act. Her conceptualization and definition of androgyny changed forever the way masculinity and femininity are viewed within psychology, and her thinking has influenced the entire field of gender studies. She demonstrated that good feminist research is also good scholarship. She has received awards from the American Psychological Association, the Association for Women in Psychology, and the American Association of University Women. The creativity of her thinking has challenged both the assumptions of traditional research and theory and the nonconscious gender ideology of society. It would be difficult to overstate the impact she has had on the profession and on the American public.

FAMILY BACKGROUND

Sandra Lipsitz was born in Pittsburgh, Pennsylvania, on June 22, 1944. Her father, Peter, was a postal clerk, and her mother, Lillian, was a secretary. The first-born in her family, she has one sister, Beverly, seven years younger.

Lipsitz's parents both had high school diplomas but no college education. She described her family of origin as working class. One of the major influences in her life was the assumption that she would always work: in her family—in her social sphere—*everyone* always worked. Early in life she was attracted to the highest status occupation that seemed within her reach: she wished to be a secretary like her mother, a job for which she could go to a clean place and have a desk and telephone of her own. Lillian Lipsitz enjoyed work, hated cooking and housework in general, and certainly conveyed to her daughter that being "just a housewife" was not very desirable. The family emphasized survival and encouraged the next generation to do better than the last. Although that meant getting as much education as possible and doing as well as possible economically, going to graduate school was "eighteen steps up" from anything she had ever considered. Her family did not even know anyone in the professional classes.

EDUCATION

During elementary school she was one of three girls enrolled in a class of twelve at Hillel Academy, an Orthodox Jewish day school in Pittsburgh. There she played dodgeball and other active games and always wore pants—for which she was nearly expelled more than once. For junior high and high school, she went to public schools in Pittsburgh. Later she described herself as learning to deal with school as a good student rather than as a serious learner, and she said she never really dealt with any subject matter the way she would like her students to do. It is her belief that she "didn't really get all that much of value" out of her education at any level, although in graduate school she got a lot out of actually *doing* psychology.

She attended Carnegie-Mellon University from 1961 to 1965, where she majored in psychology. Robert Morgan, the head of the Counseling Center, urged her to consider becoming a psychiatrist. He was the first person to suggest that she had career options in the professional world. The financial demands of medical school made psychiatry impossible, but when she found that she could go to graduate school in psychology "for free" with student financial assistance, she decided to pursue child clinical psychology (Early Career Awards, 1977). It was not until the second semester of her senior year that a laboratory course in operant conditioning with John Millenson and an exciting research seminar with Al Hall changed her orientation: she liked the notion of hypothesis testing, and research began to seem more attractive than practice. Thus her move toward developmental psychology began in the context of empirical research. It was also at that time that she met a new assistant professor in the department, Daryl Bem, whom she married a few months later. It was he who suggested that there was so much variety and vitality at the University of Michigan that one could study almost anything there, and he urged her to go for the best degree program she could.

Sandra Bem entered the University of Michigan in 1965 and received her Ph.D. in developmental psychology in 1968, at the age of twenty-three. While at Michigan she worked with experimental psychologist David Birch, who was developing a research program on the ways young children develop the ability to regulate their own behavior through self-instruction. Bem's early research (1967–1970) and her dissertation dealt with cognitive processing and problem solving in young children, including such topics as verbal self-control. Birch considered her research ideas to be highly creative. Bem says that she does not feel she ever had a mentor, but she describes Birch as a potent influence. He helped her to perceive herself as someone who could "go for the gold."

CAREER DEVELOPMENT

When Sandra Bem finished her coursework, her husband (who had taken a leave of absence to be with her in Michigan) resumed his position as an assistant professor at Carnegie-Mellon University. She assumed her first professional position as an assistant professor of psychology at Carnegie-Mellon also, where she was on the faculty from 1968 to 1971.

In 1971 the Bems accepted one-year visiting positions at Stanford University, where the psychology department was interested in exploring what it would be like to have a couple in their midst. They were both offered full faculty appointments at the end of the year, and she was an assistant professor there until 1978. In spite of the unanimous endorsement of the psychology department, she did not get tenure, which was a major blow. As a result, she and her husband decided to leave. In 1978 Sandra Bem accepted a position as associate professor of psychology and director of women's studies at Cornell University. Daryl Bem received an appointment as professor of psychology. In 1981 she was promoted to professor.

In discussing her early career experiences, Bem noted that for assistant professors at Stanford there was a pervasive norm that if one did not do something really big, one might as well not do anything at all: "Seventy-two studies which do not have the capacity to fundamentally change how people think about something may buy you something in some other school, but it isn't going to buy you anything at Stanford." This fits with her own view that it is just as time-consuming to do bad research as to do good research, and that she does not have the energy to waste on second-rate work. Bem's standard of "good research" was shaped not only by the Stanford milieu, which emphasized paradigm change, theory building, and new conceptualization, but also by her husband, whose major thrust also was to generate new conceptualizations in a theory-driven model of science (as opposed to a "building block model" of science).

MAJOR CONTRIBUTIONS AND ACHIEVEMENTS

Bem lost interest in her early research soon after the completion of her Ph.D., and she decided to do work that was both personally and socially meaningful. She was interested in women's liberation as early as 1966, and in the early 1970s she turned her research skills to establishing a solid empirical basis for her feminist convictions. During that time she and Daryl Bem conducted research that established that both sex-biased wording in job advertisements and sex-segregated help-wanted ads in newspapers discourage people from applying for "opposite-sex" jobs for which they might well be qualified (Bem & Bem, 1973). This research was the first of its kind and resulted in Equal Employment Opportunity Commission actions against AT&T and the *Pittsburgh Press*. Later she worked with the California Highway Patrol devising, developing, and evaluating selection, training, and assessment procedures for recruiting women. The general thesis of her research has always been that traditional sex roles are restrictive to both women and men, and have negative consequences for individuals and society.

In the early 1970s the field of psychology shared with the larger culture the assumption that being sex-typed (as feminine girls and women, masculine boys and men) was normal, desirable, and a natural outcome of human development. Research on sex roles was conducted primarily with children, but no one asked whether the outcome of sex-typing (i.e., the nature of the specific characteristics acquired) was positive or negative. In 1971 her research program on psychological androgyny began, with the development of the Bem Sex Role Inventory (BSRI) (Bem, 1972, 1974), and this continued to be the focus of her research for several years. She made two basic assumptions in this research. The first was that masculinity and femininity are complementary domains, defined by positive traits and behaviors, each of which can be present independently in the same individual. The second assumption was that a truly effective and well-functioning person must have both masculine and feminine traits, be both agentic and communal, instrumental and expressive. Such a person would have an androgynous personality.

Bem was first in the field with the methodological innovation of the BSRI, at a time that was ripe for questioning the psychometric and conceptual assumptions about masculinity and femininity. For example, at about the same time, Block (1973) began publishing on androgyny and Constantinople (1973) criticized the bipolarity assumptions of the traditional scales of masculinity/femininity. Spence, Helmreich, and Stapp (1975) published another measure of androgyny, the Personal Attributes Questionnaire (PAQ). Bem credited the *zeitgeist* for the rapid and broad popularity her work received.

Bem's greatest contribution to the methodological armamentarium was the construction of a new sex-role inventory that contained separate scores for masculinity and femininity and also yielded a score for androgyny. In addition to constructing an appropriate measure for androgyny, Bem also was instrumental in translating her theoretical assertions about androgyny into testable hypotheses. Using independence and nurturance as exemplars of masculinity and femininity, she pioneered early laboratory studies to demonstrate that the most flexible and effectively functioning individuals possess both masculine and feminine characteristics, that is, are androgynous.

Bem's work made explicit the assumptions underlying the bipolar measures of sex roles and challenged the oppositional nature of masculinity and femininity. The value of these contributions was recognized early in her career. In 1976, at the age of thirty-one, she received the American Psychological Association Distinguished Scientific Award for an Early Career Contribution to Psychology, ''For her studies of sex roles, androgyny, and the ontogeny of psychosexual identity and maturity'' (Early Career Awards, 1977). She also received the

Distinguished Publication Award of the Association for Women in Psychology (1977) and the Young Scholar Award of the American Association of University Women (1980).

Bem often said that her work was not derived from formal theory, but rather from strong intuitions. Perhaps that is why her work often took surprising turns. At the height of her work with androgyny, when psychology had demonstrated its receptiveness to the tenet that androgyny is a cornerstone of mental health, she decided that androgyny was *not* a desirable model to set against sex-typing. Androgyny assumes that masculinity and femininity exist within us all and that these concepts have an independent reality. Bem has come to doubt this. She believes that society should be gender aschematic, and the goal of her work became to reduce the scope, function, and effects of things associated with gender.

In the late 1980s, Bem continued to develop gender schema theory, a combination of cognitive developmental theory (as exemplified by Lawrence Kohlberg) and social learning theory (as exemplified by Walter Mischel) (Bem, 1984). Gender schema theory is a theory of process, not content. The basic assumption is that for sex-typed people—for masculine males and feminine females—gender is a very salient characteristic: gender is salient in their own self-concepts; the gender of others is salient in assumptions about their characteristics; and gender is one of the major categories used to organize objects and actions. Although gender for these people is a category that is readily applied and of high priority, a further assumption of gender schematic theory is that sex-role typing is a cultural product that is not necessarily inevitable. Bem's work in the late 1980s focused on how people come to use gender as a primary category, when they use it, and why. Going back to her roots in developmental psychology, she sees the study of children as the means of understanding the development of gender schema.

CRITICAL EVALUATION OF CONTRIBUTIONS AND ACHIEVEMENTS

From the outset, many of the criticisms of Bem's work have derived from its explicit political base. She saw virtually no separation between theory, empirical work, politics, and the real world: they all combine and speak to each other. She has often declared that her major purpose was a feminist one:

Someday I'd like to bring into people's minds the idea that maybe even little children don't need to treat what sex they are as the be all and end all important aspect of their identity. I think that's something the culture does to them. Getting those less gender-typed visions of humanity—of being human—into consciousness as a legitimate way of viewing what we're like, that I consider my greatest achievement. I don't see it as done, but that's what I see myself as about.

Within the scientific establishment the role of values is often denied (Makosky & Paludi, 1989), and the politics of research is often such that work based on the status quo is not perceived to be political, whereas anything contrary to the status quo is. In addition, gender psychology is a relatively new field and does not fit precisely into any one recognized specialty. These were major issues when the administration denied her tenure at Stanford.

Apart from these global bases for dismissing the significance of Bem's contributions, criticisms of her work generally fall into two categories: criticisms of the operational methodology used to test hypotheses derived from her theories, and criticisms of the basic theoretical formulations themselves.

The first category of criticisms is represented by Spence and Helmreich (Spence, 1984; Spence & Helmreich, 1981). These authors contended that the BSRI is a measure of instrumentality and expressiveness, as directly represented by the content of items in the scale. As such, it cannot be claimed to measure anything as general as masculinity or femininity, sex-role orientation, or gender schematicity. These authors claimed the same limitations for their own measure, the Personal Attributes Questionnaire. One of the major foundations of their criticisms seems to be the large number of studies in which scores on the BSRI (or the PAQ) do not predict other gender-related attitudes or behaviors.

Although Bem (1984) agreed that it is unreasonable to expect a single paper-and-pencil measure to relate to the entire array of factors involved in an individual's gender psychology, she also asserted that the BSRI can be used to predict specific useful and theoretically meaningful relationships. She maintains that the basic assumption of gender schema theory is that people become sex-typed because of experiences in the culture that make gender a primary category for spontaneously organizing information into equivalent classes, that this includes information about the self, and that such individuals are thus highly motivated to act sex-appropriately by the standards of their culture in order to evaluate themselves positively as persons. She then concluded that the bulk of the literature that reports no relationship between scores on the BSRI and other variables is irrelevant to gender schema theory because the studies were not designed to test hypotheses that flow from the theoretical assumptions.

Disagreements relating to Bem's theoretical formulations are themselves of two sorts. First, there are theories of sex-typing that are different in kind from Bem's formulations. Three particularly influential theories have been psychoanalytic theory (as represented by Sigmund Freud and others), social learning theory (as represented by Walter Mischel), and cognitive-developmental theory (as represented by Lawrence Kohlberg) (Bem, 1983).

More direct theoretical disagreements are exemplified by Markus, Crane, Bernstein, and Siladi (1982) and Crane and Markus (1982). These authors assert that sex-typed individuals have masculine *or* feminine self-schemata and that only information relevant to their own self-schemata is highly available when processing gender-relevant information. According to these authors, androgynous individuals are the only ones who might be properly called gender schematic because they are the only ones for whom masculine information and feminine information are equally available. The empirical support for these assertions comes from such measures as the speed and confidence of participants when judging masculine, feminine, or neutral stimuli. Bem's response to these assertions is to outline the differences between what it means to be schematic in gender schema theory and what this means in self-schema theory. Gender schema theory is the more encompassing theory. Thus, for example, a masculine man would have a masculine self-schemata as part of his gender schematic functioning in the world (Bem, 1982; Frable & Bem, 1985).

Regardless of whether one agrees with Bem's conceptual definitions, operational definitions, or theoretical formulations, the value of her contributions to psychology cannot be denied. In challenging the bipolarity of masculinity and femininity, she has been a leader in getting psychology to examine the "obvious" and the implicit in much of the theory and research. By developing the concept of androgyny, she has moved people in the direction of fewer restrictions and limitations in their lives. Although by the early 1980s Bem had come to view androgyny in a much less positive light, at the time she developed the BSRI it was an example of creating an operational definition of an abstract ideal. In developing gender schema theory, she forces psychology to examine the centrality and independence that have always been assumed to characterize masculinity and femininity, and has forced attention to the question of whether these might be cognitive constructs derived from gender-schematic processing within a particular cultural context. Her explicit blending of the personal, the political, and the scholarly have called into question many of the assertions traditionally made about the "objectivity" of science. There can be no doubt that she is approaching her own goal of making a difference in the way people view the world, both personally and empirically. For these reasons, her contributions are among the most important in the field of gender psychology.

INTEGRATION OF PERSONAL AND PROFESSIONAL LIFE

Bem describes herself as a "social failure" in her teen years because she was not popular with boys, who always seemed to be "friends but not boyfriends." At the time she was very unhappy about that, but in retrospect it seems to her to have been one of her saving graces because it was the foundation of her commitment to having a career in which she could do what she wanted to do. She expected never to marry, and thus never worried about how she would integrate marriage and career. However, soon after she applied to the University of Michigan for graduate work, in the summer of 1965, after two months of friendship and a six-week engagement, she and the then-new Carnegie-Mellon assistant professor Daryl Bem were married. During this time it became apparent that others expected her to cancel her plans for graduate school or at least to modify them by remaining in Pittsburgh for her graduate training. The realization that being an about-to-be-married woman had totally changed the way family and friends thought of her and her priorities was the single most potent event in fostering and crystallizing her interest in gender issues.

What actually happened was that Daryl Bem took a leave of absence from his job to be with her while she did her coursework, with the understanding that she would return to Pittsburgh to do her dissertation and to finish the degree in absentia. This was the beginning of a totally and consciously egalitarian marriage: they both worked, they took turns cooking and cleaning, and neither individual's needs or preferences dominated the couple's actions. They rejected the option of a commuter marriage and only considered jobs that best met the needs of the two of them as a couple, even if those jobs were not the best for either of them as individuals. Their lives were so much at variance with those around them that the Bems attracted a great deal of attention from both print and broadcast media, were interviewed both individually and together, and gave dozens of public lectures—not on their research, but on their lifestyle! Their marriage became a model that has influenced the perceptions and expectations of young women and men all over the country.

Their experiences of being "social deviants" was a major factor that led to the development of their thesis that there is a powerful nonconscious ideology operating to limit women's vision and aspirations and to keep them in restricted roles (Bem & Bem, 1970).

When they decided to have children, both agreed that the children would be central in their lives and that they would spend a great deal of time with them. Since they were born (Emily in 1974 and Jeremy in 1976), the Bems have shared childcare. Sandra Bem refused to label time pressures as conflicts between family and work demands. In her opinion, there are always more things one wants to do than can be done: sometimes they are two work things, sometimes two family things, and sometimes a work thing and a family thing. Having chosen the commitments, she did not experience competing demands on her time as conflict. In addition, watching her children grow and develop was an intellectual experience and a fertile ground for ideas, insights, and questions on the development of gender identity.

In addition to being married, Sandra and Daryl Bem have combined the personal and political. They have published articles together dealing with stereotyping and sex discrimination (Bem & Bem, 1970, 1973). Sandra Bem considers her husband to be both her closest friend and her most valued colleague, and at the conceptual stages of thinking, discusses ideas with him in great detail. She is eager to acknowledge the importance of those discussions in the evolution of her thinking on scholarly topics.

Bem's family, work, personal, political, and professional lives are so intertwined that there is no clear separation. There seems to be no part that does not flow into the others. She enjoys her work and it has helped shape her views on childrearing. Her children are a constant source of questions and hypotheses relevant to her research. Her theoretical formulations are an ongoing part of her interactions with her husband. Her political commitments have shaped both her work and her family life. She continues to surprise the world in her personal and professional evolution, and psychology is richer for it.

NOTE

All quotations and biographical information not otherwise referenced are drawn from an interview with S. L. Bem conducted by the author on April 26, 1984.

REFERENCES

Bem, S. L. (1972). Psychology looks at sex roles: Where have all the androgynous people gone? Paper presented at the U.C.L.A. Symposium on Sex Roles.

Bem, S. L. (1974). The measurement of psychological androgyny. *Journal of Consulting and Clinical Psychology, 42,* 155–162.

Bem, S. L. (1982). Gender schema theory and self-schema theory compared: A comment on Markus, Crane, Bernstein and Siladi's "Self-schemas and gender." *Journal of Personality and Social Psychology, 43,* 1192–1194.

Bem, S. L. (1983). Gender schema theory and its implications for child development: Raising gender-aschematic children in a gender-schematic society. *Signs, 8,* 598–616.

Bem, S. L. (1984). Schema theory. In T. B. Sonderegger (Ed.), *Nebraska Symposium on Motivation: Psychology and Gender*, Vol. 32. Lincoln: University of Nebraska Press.

Bem, S. L., & Bem, D. J. (1970). Case study of a nonconscious ideology: Training the woman to know her place. In D. J. Bem, *Beliefs, attitudes, and human affairs.* Belmont, Calif.: Brooks/Cole.

Bem, S. L., & Bem, D. J. (1973). Does sex-biased job advertising "aid and abet" sex discrimination? *Journal of Applied Social Psychology, 3,* 6–18.

Block, J. (1973). Conceptions of sex role: Some cross-cultural and longitudinal perspectives. *American Psychologist, 28,* 512–526.

Constantinople, A. (1973). Masculinity-femininity: An exception to a famous dictum. *Psychological Bulletin, 80,* 389–407.

Crane, M., & Markus, H. (1982). Gender identity: The benefits of a self-schema approach. *Journal of Personality and Social Psychology, 43*(6), 1195–1197.

Early career awards for 1976. (1977). *American Psychologist,* 88–91.

Frable, D. E., & Bem, S. L. (1985). If you are gender schematic, all members of the opposite sex look alike. *Journal of Personality and Social Psychology, 49,* 459–468.

Makosky, V. P., & Paludi, M. A. (1989). Feminism and women's studies in the academy. In M. A. Paludi and G. Steuernagel (Eds.), *Images of women in the academy.* New York: Haworth Press.

Markus, H.; Crane, M.; Bernstein, S.; & Siladi, M. (1982). Self-schemas and gender. *Journal of Personality and Social Psychology, 42,* 38–50.

Spence, J. T. (1984). Gender identity and its implications for concepts of masculinity and femininity. In T. B. Sonderegger (Ed.), *Nebraska Symposium on Motivation: Psychology and Gender*, Vol. 32. Lincoln: University of Nebraska Press.

Spence, J. T., & Helmreich, R. L. (1981). Androgyny versus gender schema: A comment on Bem's gender schema theory. *Psychological Review, 88,* 365–368.

Spence, J. T.; Helmreich, R.; & Stapp, J. (1975). Ratings of self and peers on sex-role attributes and their relations to self-esteem and conceptions of masculinity and femininity. *Journal of Personality and Social Psychology*, *32*, 29–39.

Additional Representative Publications by Sandra Bem

Bem, S. L. (1967). Verbal self-control: The establishment of effective self-instruction. *Journal of Experimental Psychology*, *74*, 485–491.

Bem, S. L. (1970). The role of comprehension in children's problem solving. *Developmental Psychology*, *2*, 351–358.

Bem, S. L. (1975). Sex role adaptability: One consequence of psychological androgyny. *Journal of Personality and Social Psychology*, *31*, 634–643.

Bem, S. L. (1977). On the utility of alternative procedures for assessing psychological androgyny. *Journal of Consulting and Clinical Psychology*, *45*, 196–205.

Bem, S. L. (1981). Gender schema theory: A cognitive account of sex typing. *Psychological Review*, *88*, 354–364.

Bem, S. L. (1984). Reply to Morgan and Ayim. *Signs*, *10*, 197–199.

Lewittes, H. J., & Bem, S. L. (1983). Training women to be more assertive in mixed-sex task-oriented discussions. *Sex Roles*, *9*, 581–596.

Additional Representative Publications About Sandra Bem

Bruck, C. (1977). Professing androgyny. *Human Behavior*, 22–31.

Servan-Schreiber, C. (1972). Marriage of equals. *Ms.*, *1*(1), 91–93, 122–123.

JEANNE HUMPHREY BLOCK
(1923–1981)

Jack Block

During her lifetime, the scientific contributions of Jeanne Humphrey Block ranged widely. She investigated delay of gratification in young children; the parents of schizophrenic children; the factors predisposing to childhood asthma; cross-cultural differences in socialization practices; student activism; various cognitive styles; the effects of family stress; creativity; and the many long-term implications of ego control and ego resiliency for the way behavior is organized and manifested, *inter alia*. She also planned, implemented, and for many years nurtured a longitudinal study of personality and cognitive development of unprecedented scope, achievement, and continuing implication that, by itself, justifies her distinguished reputation. Her work on childhood asthma received the American Psychiatric Association Hofheimer Prize (1974), and she was elected to the status of Fellow in four divisions of the American Psychological Association. She also served on various significant editorial and national research review committees. But perhaps the primary basis for her recognition derives from the influential and thoughtful analytic essays she wrote during the 1970s and early 1980s on sex role development, culminating in the publication of *Sex Role Identity and Ego Development* (1984).

FAMILY BACKGROUND AND EDUCATION

Jeanne Lavonne Humphrey was born in Tulsa, Oklahoma, on July 17, 1923. Her father was Charles Joseph Humphrey, a building contractor earlier from Cleveland, Ohio; her mother was Louise Lewis Humphrey, originally from Rolla, Missouri, in the Ozark foothills. Her father was a moral, quietly warm person whose consistency and concern were important to his daughter's development. He became well known as a meticulous and scrupulous builder of finely crafted homes. Her mother was a firm instiller of traditional values, a believer in self-improvement, and with high intelligence, energy, and social concerns. Active in church and community affairs, when her children reached a sufficient age, she went on to become a tax analyst and a respected lobbyist of principled convictions with the state legislature.

When Jeanne Humphrey was four months old, the family wended its way to Portland, Oregon, and settled near Reed College. As a child, she played and swam at Reed and came to know several neighboring Reed professors. After the birth of a brother, Richard, in 1931, the family moved to a large house on several acres in Clackamas County, near the small town of Milwaukee and about ten miles outside Portland.

The depression period was a hard one for the Humphrey family. But with an affectionate milk cow, a productive garden, and some chickens, the family was in many immediate ways self-providing. Things eased up after several years and, overall, it seems fair to say that Humphrey lived what might be called an All-American, small-town life. Through elementary, junior high, and high school, there was the same set of chums. Humphrey was bright, vivacious, enterprising, and popular, but in adolescence she was also turning over in her own mind the various sets of values she was encountering and constructing a sense of who she was and who she wanted to be. She was powerfully upset by the absence of local community reaction when a longterm Nisei girlfriend and her family were removed from town and sent to an internment camp a few days after Pearl Harbor; she was realizing that she was smarter than she was supposed to be. A minister, Tom Shannon, was important to her thinking on self.

Upon graduation from high school in 1941, Humphrey went to Oregon State College for a year, majoring in home economics but also taking courses in architecture. She achieved the unusual distinction of failing in home economics while still making the Dean's List for academic achievement. In 1942, with America at war, college seemed insignificant. She quit school and took a job at Meier Frank, the leading department store in Portland, working as a buyer's assistant. In 1943 she accompanied a girlfriend to the recruiting office, and returned having herself enlisted in the SPARS, the women's unit of the Coast Guard. Jeanne Humphrey was commissioned an ensign in 1944 and served with distinction. In 1945, during her service, she was scalded over much of her body and almost died from the subsequent plasma loss. Coast Guard servicemen responded with blood donations (she was told at the time that she held the record for number of blood transfusions). After many painful skin grafts, Humphrey returned to active service, earning a commendation for facilitating at the end of the war, the demobilization of military men seeking rapid return to civilian life.

Demobilized in 1946, Humphrey continued her education at Reed College, near where she had lived as a young child, majoring in psychology. Her major influences there were Fred Courts and Monte Griffith, both interesting and supportive individuals as well as good psychologists, and she graduated with honors in 1947. She had applied to several graduate schools in the East and been accepted at Harvard, but during a summer visit to the San Francisco Bay area to see a friend, she used the opportunity for a spontaneous visit to Stanford University to see what the Psychology Department was like. Ernest Hilgard happened to be available to meet her, liked the verve of the eager, obviously intelligent young woman that he saw, and invited her to become a graduate student that fall. Humphrey liked Stanford, far enough and yet close enough to Portland, and so her choice was made.

At Stanford, Jeanne Humphrey majored in clinical psychology, then a field seeking to define and transform itself after the war. During these years, clinical psychology at Stanford was represented by Maud Merrill James, who had worked with Lewis Terman in revising the Stanford-Binet intelligence test and by Howard Hunt, neither of whom would be considered clinicians given later conceptions of the term. But Maud Merrill James was a quietly shrewd, elegant, and gentle person with much experience with young problem children; she became a significant mentor for Humphrey both professionally and personally. Becoming a Veterans Administration clinical psychology intern in 1948, Humphrey encountered the full range of psychopathology among the patients there and, as a personal project, for three years undertook prolonged psychotherapy with a young schizophrenic veteran, a significant learning experience. Concurrently, she served in the Stanford Child Guidance Clinic, first as a psychometrician and then as a therapist with children and with parents.

Jeanne Humphrey also took nonclinical psychology courses at Stanford: on learning with Ernest Hilgard, on statistics with Quinn McNemar (at a personal level, a significant mentor), on comparative psychology with Calvin Stone, on experimental methods with Donald Taylor, on the history of psychology with Paul Farnsworth, among others. The clinical graduate students at Stanford at the time were both clinically oriented and also bent on academically outdoing the psychology graduate students focusing on "hard-nosed, experimental" psychology. Jeanne Humphrey was a successful exemplar of this orientation.

An unusually good group of graduate students was at Stanford during the late 1940s, partly because of the return of veterans keen to renew their education: Fred Attneave, Gerry Blum, Charles Ericksen, Wayne Holtzman, Paul Mc-Reynolds, Harold Rauch, Paul Secord, among others. Intellectual discussions were intense and informal; the possiblities for psychology seemed, if not boundless, at least to extend in many alluring directions. Jeanne Humphrey had become impressed by Lewinian psychology and by psychoanalytic theory, and so had her fellow graduate student Jack Block. They talked, they argued, they formulated some theoretical conceptions regarding concepts they called ego-control and ego-resiliency that led to joint theses, they danced well together, and in 1950 they married, shortly after he completed his doctorate.

CAREER DEVELOPMENT AND ACHIEVEMENTS

Jeanne Humphrey Block completed her own doctoral thesis in 1951, already pregnant with her first child. For the academic year 1951–1952, she was invited by Stanford to be an instructor in the Psychology Department and, with a brief hiatus for the birth of Susan Dale on February 12, 1952, completed that responsibility and left Stanford with high recommendations. Jack Block had a position at the University of California's Institute of Personality Assessment and Research across San Francisco Bay in Berkeley. Susan was a small baby, more children were anticipated, the era was the 1950s—it was time to leave the academic life for a period of child-having, child-rearing, and homemaking. Through the 1950s, Jeanne Block bore three more children, Judith Lynne on December 31, 1953, David Lewis on March 20, 1956, and Carol Ann on April 15, 1959.

She continued part-time professional and scientific work, when and where it could be fitted into an often uncontrollable schedule. She was the prime mover of a study in the Department of Psychiatry at the University of California Medical School in San Francisco comparing the parents of schizophrenic children with the parents of neurotic children. For the California Medical Association, she interviewed a group of physicians who had been sued for malpractice; she wrote a fascinating report on their personalities that could never be publicly released because of its explosive implications for the medical profession. She served as a clinical psychologist and consultant at a mental health clinic, and she began her insightful and subsequently influential work on allergic predisposition and psychopathology in childhood asthma at the Children's Hospital of the East Bay. Her formal publications during this decade were relatively few: articles on ethnocentrism and intolerance of ambiguity (J. Block & J. H. Block, 1951), on reactions to authority (J. H. Block & J. Block, 1952), on the reactions of young children to frustration (J. H. Block & Martin, 1955), on psychiatrists' conceptions of schizophrenogenic parents (Jackson, J. Block, J. H. Block, & Patterson, 1958), and on the comparison of the parents of neurotic children with the parents of schizophrenic children (J. H. Block, Patterson, J. Block, & Jackson, 1958). Concurrently, she also created a well-organized and aesthetic home, became a gourmet cook, was president of the local parent-teachers association, and underwent a useful personal psychoanalysis.

During the 1960s, as the children became more self-sufficient, Jeanne Block was able to become more involved with psychology. She continued and extended her important work on factors predisposing toward asthma in childhood (J. H. Block, Jennings, Harvey, & Simpson, 1964; J. H. Block, Harvey, Jennings, & Simpson, 1966; J. H. Block, 1968), albeit still on an opportune, nonscheduled, part-time basis. In 1963 she received a Special Research Fellowship from the National Institute of Mental Health (NIMH), and the entire family spent her husband's sabbatical year in Oslo, Norway. During this time, Jeanne Block held an appointment at the Norwegian Institute for Social Research and again became a full-time psychologist. She carried out several studies comparing the socialization practices of the four Scandinavian countries, America, and England, and in the process evolved her widely used assessment instrument, the Child Rearing Practices Report (1965). Shortly after her return to Berkeley in 1964, the student Free Speech movement erupted and for the next several years the campus was preoccupied by its moral fallout. She was a passionate but still scientific observer of the ever-changing scene and received a 1965 Rosenberg Grant through the Institute of Human Development at Berkeley to conduct studies of the personalities, the moral orientations, and the parenting of different types of student activists. Her papers (Haan, J. H. Block, & Smith, 1968; J. H. Block, Haan, & Smith, 1969; Smith, Haan, & J. H. Block, 1970; J. H. Block, 1972) on these matters were widely read and remain highly influential.

Although she was becoming known as a bright, productive, thoughtful psychologist, at Berkeley Block was still without a stable or fulfilling position, and so she took, concomitantly, a part-time job as a "specialist" involved in the graduate training of teachers who had returned to the university. This was the time of the Vietnam War; Jeanne Block marched in protest of that effort, walked the precincts to muster support for Eugene McCarthy, and helped start the Committee for Social Responsibility (which later was transformed into Physicians for Social Responsibility).

In 1968 two significant events permitted a fundamental career transition. Jeanne Block received a National Institute of Mental Health Research Scientist Development Award, sited within the Institute of Human Development, and, together with her husband, started an ambitious longitudinal study of personality development. The career development award for the first time provided secure support for a long enough period so that she could explore her own thinking and pursue her own interests. The initiation of the Block and Block longitudinal study was a deliberate career investment intended to permit the developmental study of ego control and ego resiliency, the study of sex role development and of gender differences, the study of self percepts over time, and the study of parenting styles and their consequences, among other concerns. The powerful logic of the longitudinal method had impressed her as incontestable; the psychological issues that could be studied were intellectually exciting and personally meaningful; previous longitudinal projects were unable to respond to these contemporary concerns; and the idea of a jointly nurtured, complementarily managed research enterprise with her husband was reinforcing. And so the effort was begun.

In central ways, the longitudinal study, once embarked upon, shaped (indeed, controlled) Jeanne Block's subsequent life as a psychologist. She wholeheartedly contributed her intelligence, energy, and diverse talents to the enterprise, which otherwise would have foundered along the way. In return, the longitudinal study of 130 children at ages three, four, five, seven, eleven, and fourteen (later assessed at ages eighteen and twenty-three as well) provided empirical recognitions that greatly influenced her theoretical perspective. Many research articles by Jeanne Block or decisively influenced by her flowed from the study: on sex role and socialization patterns (J. Block, von der Lippe, & J. H. Block, 1973), on sex-role typing and instrumental behavior (J. H. Block, 1976b), on the many implications of ego control and ego resiliency for the way behavior is organized and manifested (J. H. Block, & J. Block, 1980), on intolerance of ambiguity in young children (Harrington, J. H. Block, & J. Block, 1978), on sex differences in cognitive functioning (J. H. Block, 1981), on activity level (Buss, J. H. Block, & J. Block, 1980), on the implications of parental disagreement regarding child-rearing (J. H. Block, J. Block, & Morrison, 1981), on various cognitive styles (J. Block, J. H. Block, & Harrington, 1974; J. Block, Buss, J. H. Block, & Gjerde, 1981), on delay of gratification (Funder, J. H. Block, & J. Block, 1983), on the effects of family stress (J. Block, J. H. Block, & Gjerde, 1988), on creativity (Harrington, J. Block, & J. H. Block, 1983), on the continuity and changes in parents' childrearing practices (Roberts, J. H. Block, & J. Block, 1984), on the personality of children prior to divorce (J. H. Block, J. Block, & Gjerde, 1986), and on the early antecedents of low self-esteem in adolescence, among others. An influential public television program, "The Pinks and the Blues," by NOVA (1980) focusing on sex role development featured Block, her thoughts, and the longitudinal study. It became widely used in college classes in the psychology of women.

However, her primary contribution—and the basis for her rapid and widespread influence—is to be seen in the series of integrative, theoretically oriented, thoughtfully analytic essays she wrote during the 1970s and early 1980s on sex role development (J. H. Block, 1973, 1976a, 1976b, 1979, 1983), culminating in her posthumously published book, *Sex Role Identity and Ego Development* (1984). In these writings, she presented her own conception of sex role based on cross-cultural and longitudinal recognitions; described the ways in which the interweaving of biological and cultural factors has historically influenced sex role development; showed how societal and technological developments have in significant ways made previously understandable sex role shapings no longer valid; documented the differential premises ingrained in little girls and little boys by their differential socialization; and radically but constructively revised previous understandings of the empirical literature on gender differences in behavior. Although an engaged feminist, Jeanne Block was also a scientist, and her unique conjoining of these identity-expanding values with sober and incisive scientific analyses struck a responsive chord in many and gave her words wide influence. Her personal presence also enhanced her effectiveness; she was womanly, energetic, warmly connecting, funny, artful in the nonpejorative sense, attractive to both women and men.

Jeanne Block was diagnosed in 1972 as having ulcerative colitis. The illness was an oppressive one, but Block remained remarkably spirited and productive. Recognizing that she no longer needed "development," NIMH gave her a Research Scientist Award in 1973, renewed in 1978. She served on numerous professional committees of the American Psychological Association (APA), was a Fellow of APA Divisions 7 (Developmental Psychology), 8 (Personality and Social Psychology), 9 (Psychological Study of Social Issues), and 35 (Psychology of Women), and was elected president of the Division of Developmental Psychology in 1980. She was a member of the National Institute of Mental Health Personality and Cognition Research Review Committee (1972–1975) and the National Institute of Child Health and Development Maternal and Child Health

Research Review Committee (1977–1981), chairing the latter committee her last two years. She received the American Psychiatric Association Hofheimer Prize for Research in 1974 because of her work on childhood asthma. She served on many editorial boards and was frequently called upon as an editorial consultant. She gave many special invitational lectures, including an APA Master Lecture in 1979 on socialization influences on personality development of males and females, was widely sought as a research consultant, and was a scholar-in-residence at the Rockefeller Foundation Study Center, Bellagio, Italy, in 1979. In belated recognition of her intensive work with many graduate students and her significant educational influence, she was appointed adjunct professor of psychology at Berkeley in 1979. And her national visibility caused her to be elected a Fellow of the American Association for the Advancement of Science in 1980. Block had realized her self, was where she wanted to be, with ideas and energy and possibilities stretching ahead when, in May 1981, she was found to have pancreatic cancer.

Jeanne Block was graceful during her last months; she fought bravely, continuing to be a model to family and friends and to strangers who knew her only from her writings but now wrote to her. She mustered her inner resources for a glorious but understood to be final Thanksgiving dinner surrounded by family and a few friends, and died on December 4, 1981.

The joint longitudinal study has been continued by her husband. Sadly, although Block was so centrally involved in the seeding and nurturing of this prolonged effort, she did not live to see the abundant harvest of implicative relations the study consequently was enabled to discern. Of her children, Susan is a psychiatrist, Judith is a registered nurse, David is a computer engineer, and Carol is a university administrator. Radcliffe College has initiated the Jeanne Humphrey Block Fellowship which, each year, supports two graduate students studying gender-related issues.

REFERENCES

Block, J. H. (1965). *The child-rearing practice report*. Berkeley Institute of Human Development, University of California. (Mimeographed)

Block, J. H. (1968). Further considerations of psychosomatic predisposing factors in allergy. *Psychosomatic Medicine*, *30*, 202–208.

Block, J. H. (1972). Generational continuity and discontinuity in the understanding of societal rejection. *Journal of Personality and Social Psychology*, *22*, 333–345.

Block, J. H. (1973). Conceptions of sex role: Some cross-cultural and longitudinal perspectives. *American Psychologist*, *28*, 512–526.

Block, J. H. (1976a). Assessing sex differences: Issues, problems, and pitfalls. *Merrill-Palmer Quarterly*, *22*, 283–308.

Block, J. H. (1976b). Sex-role typing and instrumental behavior: A developmental study. *Resources in Education*, February (Abstract no. 113 014).

Block, J. H. (1979). Another look at sex differentiation in the socialization behaviors of mothers and fathers. In F. L. Denmark & J. Sherman (Eds.), *Psychology of women: Future directions for research*. New York: Psychological Dimensions.

Block, J. H. (1981). Gender differences in the nature of premises developed about the world. In E. Shapiro & E. Weber (Eds.), *Cognitive and affective growth: Developmental interaction*. Hillsdale, N.J.: Lawrence Erlbaum Associates.

Block, J. H. (1983). Differential premises arising from differential socialization of the sexes: Some conjectures. *Child Development*, *54*, 1335–1354.

Block, J. H. (1984). *Sex role identity and ego development*. San Francisco: Jossey-Bass.

Block, J., & Block, J. H. (1951). An investigation of the relationship between intolerance of ambiguity and ethnocentrism. *Journal of Personality*, *19*, 303–311.

Block, J. H., & Block, J. (1952). An interpersonal experiment on reactions to authority. *Human Relations*, *5*, 91–98.

Block, J. H., & Block, J. (1980). The role of ego-control and ego-resiliency in the organization of behavior. In W. A. Collins (Ed.), *The Minnesota Symposia on Child Psychology* (Vol. 13, pp. 39–101). Hillsdale, N.J.: Lawrence Erlbaum Associates.

Block, J. H.; Block, J.; & Gjerde, P. F. (1986). The personality of children prior to divorce. *Child Development*, *57*, 827–840.

Block, J.; Block, J. H.; & Gjerde, P. F. (1988). Parental functioning and the home environment in families of divorce: Prospective and concurrent analyses. *Journal of the American Academy of Child and Adolescent Psychiatry*, *27*, 207–213.

Block, J.; Block, J. H.; & Harrington, D. M. (1974). Some misgivings about the Matching Familiar Figures test as a measure of reflection-impulsivity. *Developmental Psychology*, *10*, 611–632.

Block, J. H.; Block, J.; & Morrison, A. (1981). Parental agreement-disagreement on child-rearing orientations and gender-related personality correlates in children. *Child Development*, *52*, 965–974.

Block, J.; Buss, J. H.; Block, J. H.; & Gjerde, P. F. (1981). The cognitive style of breadth of categorization: Longitudinal consistency of personality correlates. *Journal of Personality and Social Psychology*, *44*, 1198–1213.

Block, J. H., & Christensen, B. (1966). A test of Hendin's hypotheses relating suicide in Scandinavia to child-rearing orientations. *Scandinavian Journal of Psychology*, *7*, 1–22.

Block, J. H.; Haan, N.; & Smith, M. B. (1969). Socialization correlates of student activism. *Journal of Social Issues*, *25*, 143–177.

Block, J. H.; Harvey, E.; Jennings, P. H.; & Simpson, E. (1966). Clinicians' conceptions of the asthmatogenic mother. *Archives of Psychiatry*, *15*, 610–618.

Block, J. H.; Jennings, P. H.; Harvey, E.; & Simpson, E. (1964). The interaction between allergic predisposition and psychopathology in childhood asthma. *Psychosomatic Medicine*, *4*, 307–320.

Block, J. H., & Martin, B. (1955). Predicting the behavior of children under frustration. *Journal of Abnormal and Social Psychology*, *51*, 281–285.

Block, J. H.; Patterson, V.; Block, J.; & Jackson, D. D. (1958). A study of the parents of schizophrenic and neurotic children. *Psychiatry*, *21*, 387–459.

Block, J.; von der Lippe, A.; & Block, J. H. (1973). Sex role and socialization patterns: Some personality concomitants and environmental antecedents. *Journal of Consulting and Clinical Psychology*, *41*, 321–341.

Buss, D. M.; Block, J. H.; & Block, J. (1980). Preschool activity level: Personality correlates, sex differences and developmental implications. *Child Development*, *51*, 401–408.

Funder, D. C.; Block, J. H.; & Block, J. (1983). Delay of gratification: Some longitudinal personality correlates. *Journal of Personality and Social Psychology*, *44*, 1198–1213.

Haan, N.; Block, J. H.; & Smith, M. B. (1968). The moral reasoning of young adults: Political-social behavior, family background, and personality correlates. *Journal of Personality and Social Psychology*, *10*, 183–201.

Harrington, D. M.; Block, J.; & Block, J. H. (1983). Predicting creativity in preadolescence from divergent thinking in early childhood. *Journal of Personality and Social Psychology*, *45*, 609–623.

Harrington, D. M.; Block, J. H.; & Block, J. (1978). Intolerance of ambiguity in preschool children: Psychometric considerations, behavioral manifestations, and parental correlates. *Developmental Psychology*, *14*, 242–256.

Jackson, D. D.; Block, J.; Block, J. H.; & Patterson, V. (1958). Psychiatrists' conceptions of schizophrenogenic parents. *Archives of Neurology and Psychiatry*, *79*, 448–459.

Roberts, G. C.; Block, J. H.; & Block, J. (1984). Continuity and change in parents' child rearing practices. *Child Development*, *55*, 586–597.

Smith, M. B.; Haan, N.; & Block, J. H. (1970). Social-psychological aspects of student activism. *Youth and Society*, *1*, 262–288.

CHARLOTTE M. BÜHLER (1893–1974)

Eileen A. Gavin

Charlotte Bühler made ground-breaking contributions to life-span developmental and humanistic psychology. She identified purposeful, uniquely patterned activity in infants, young children, adolescents, and adults and held that viewing the human person as a continually developing totality encourages fruitful exploration. To clarify the developmental process she devised naturalistic techniques that buttressed her motivation-based theory of personality. During the 1960s Bühler collaborated with like-minded psychologists, such as Abraham Maslow, in founding, publicizing, and strengthening the humanistic psychology movement. In her latter years she consolidated humanistic theory with pertinent research findings and clinical observations.

FAMILY BACKGROUND AND EARLY CAREER DEVELOPMENT

Charlotte Malachowski, the first of Walter and Rose Malachowski's two children, was born December 20, 1893, in Berlin, Germany. Her father, a gifted architect, and her mother, an accomplished musician, encouraged her to pursue her intellectual and artistic interests. During early adolescence Malachowski identified with a gifted and inspiring teacher, Hedwig von Probst.

From an early age Charlotte Malachowski demonstrated broad academic interests and a bent for investigating psychological processes. As she wondered about the existence of God and the purpose of human existence (Bühler, October 11, 1967), she began to explore human thought processes in the hope of casting light on such ultimate issues (Schenk-Danzinger, 1974, p. 205). As a high school student she conducted an original study of human thought processes that presaged her doctoral research.

University studies from 1913 to 1918 at Freiburg, Kiel, Berlin, and Munich put her in touch with excellent teachers. As early as 1913 she longed to meet Karl Bühler, whose published work on human thought seemed to parallel her own. Because he served as an army medical doctor at the beginning of World

War I, their first meeting occurred only after Oswald Kulpe, her esteemed advisor at the University of Munich, died suddenly. Karl Bühler was recalled to supervise Kulpe's graduate students. A whirlwind courtship led to the marriage of Karl Bühler and Charlotte Malachowski in 1916. Charlotte Malachowski Bühler received her Ph.D. from the University of Munich in 1918. A year earlier she had given birth to a daughter, Ingeborg; a son, Rolf, was born in 1919.

From 1920 to 1922 Charlotte Bühler assisted the Prussian government and school board with a project on adolescence. She also lectured in Dresden at the Technische Hochschule (Bühler, October 25, 1967). In 1923 she moved to Vienna, where Karl Bühler had accepted a university appointment. She accepted an appointment as lecturer at the Vienna Psychological Institute in 1923 and attained the rank of associate professor in 1929.

During her Vienna period (1923–1938) Charlotte Bühler's research focused on psychological development from infancy through adolescence. In addition to her research and teaching in Vienna, she studied, traveled, taught, and consulted (Schenk-Danzinger, 1974, p. 206) in various parts of Europe and the United States. From 1924 to 1925 Bühler attended Columbia University on a Laura Spelman Memorial Rockefeller Fellowship. That opportunity put her in touch with American scholars, including Edward Thorndike, Larry Frank, and Arnold Gesell. Her early observations had convinced her that infant development follows a predictable course. Bühler shared her research-based definition of progressive maturation with Arnold Gesell, who promptly incorporated the steplike process into his own developmental work (Bühler, October 25, 1967).

At the completion of her year at Columbia in 1925, Bühler received a ten-year grant from the Rockefeller Foundation to support her developmental research at the Vienna Psychological Institute (Bühler, October 25, 1967). In 1929 she returned to the United States for an additional year, serving as guest professor of psychology at Barnard College. Although she maintained her intellectual home and research program in Vienna until 1938, consultative and supervisory responsibilities at child guidance centers in England, Holland, and Norway sometimes called her away. At the time the Nazis invaded Vienna in 1938, she was in England.

BÜHLER'S SECOND CAREER: FROM EUROPE TO AMERICA

Immediately after her felicitous Viennese period, Charlotte Bühler embarked on a decade that was at first life-threatening and that later temporarily impeded her creative efforts (Bühler, 1972, p. 34). Because of vocal anti-Nazi sentiments, Karl Bühler was sent to prison. In 1939 Charlotte Bühler successfully negotiated her husband's release and transport to Norway. He moved to the United States that same year. She joined him in 1940, leaving Norway just ten days before the Nazis invaded that country.

During her first year as a refugee (1940–1941), Charlotte Bühler served as professor of psychology at the College of St. Catherine in St. Paul, Minnesota. In 1941 she went to Worcester, Massachusetts, where she established and directed a child guidance clinic. She returned to Minnesota in 1943 and served as clinical psychologist at Minneapolis General Hospital for the next two years. Acculturation was not easy for the Bühlers. In fact, Bühler described their first ten years after immigration as so difficult that they were unable even to write (Bühler, 1972, p. 34). She attributed what she appraised as a "cold" reception to her being viewed by American scholars as a "star" who might be a professional threat (Bühler, 1972, p. 34).

The Bühlers moved to California in 1945. From 1945 to 1953 Charlotte Bühler served as clinical psychologist at the Los Angeles County Hospital. For part of that period she held the title assistant professor of psychiatry at the University of Southern California Medical School. From 1953 to 1972 Bühler maintained a private practice in Los Angeles. She also experienced the return of her creative energies. She became a naturalized American citizen. Gradually, she met congenial colleagues, such as Abraham Maslow and Carl Rogers. She grew to like her collegial associations in the United States very much. After ill health resulted in her return to Germany in the early 1970s to be near her son Rolf, she wished to return to California to resume work with her American colleagues (Association for Humanistic Psychology Archives, H12).

ACHIEVEMENTS AND CONTRIBUTIONS

Bühler is best known for her contributions to humanistic and life-span developmental psychology. Throughout her career, the humanistic perspective of purposefulness marked her research findings, techniques, theory, and practice. In fact, she has been described as "the first humanistic psychologist" (Krippner, 1977, p. 16). She was without doubt a very early humanistic psychologist. In fact, she adopted a humanistic orientation considerably earlier than her good friend and associate, Abraham Maslow. Bühler became convinced of the centrality of human purposes in the early 1920s as she probed 135 adolescent diaries. These documents revealed that by late adolescence people often raise questions such as What am I here for? What is my purpose in life? (Bühler, 1922). Evidence of purposes in adolescence raised questions about their origins, and she turned her gaze to the activity of infants.

Long before intentional activity and distinctive personal styles became commonly recognized in developmental psychology, Bühler found evidence of curiosity, social interest, delight in achievement, and distinctive individual styles in activity of infants no older than a few months (Bühler & Hetzer, 1927; Bühler, 1930). Her observations convinced her that infants do not settle for a quiescent existence. Later clinical observations of adults (Bühler & Massarik, 1968) consolidated her long-standing belief that healthy human beings live purposeful, active lives. As evidence accumulated, Bühler devised techniques to study the functioning of the human person viewed as a continually developing totality.

Methods for Investigating the Human Person as a Totality

Bühler believed that case studies and other naturalistic techniques, not experimentation, are most needed to clarify and detail how persons seen as purposeful totalities develop continually as they interact with the environment (Bühler, 1971, p. 379). Observations of very young persons (i.e., infants) first inspired her to develop naturalistic techniques, such as situation tests, to study the developmental process. For instance, she noted the responses that two five-month-old infants placed in the same room make to each other (Bühler, 1935). Bühler believed that investigations of this kind, conducted in natural social settings, clarify individual differences and similarities that characterize infants at particular developmental levels and the ongoing development of specific individuals (Bühler, 1935).

Questions about how social interactions occur in natural settings stimulated her to devise additional research techniques. One of the techniques focused on what goes on in the natural social settings that family members experience (Bühler, 1940). She utilized trained observers to code the activity that occurred in family settings during a timed period. The technique and coding system revealed stable personality characteristics as well as characteristics that environmental conditions readily modify. Bühler's biographical technique, another naturalistic contribution, tapped information from various sources, traced over a span of time (1933). She later applied the biographical technique to clinical settings. The Life Goal Inventory, prepared with the help of Andrew Comrey and William E. Coleman (Bühler & Marschak, 1968, pp. 99–101), was an additional major methodological contribution.

Bühler's Theory of Personality Development

Bühler's observations and methods are closely related to her theory of personality development, which emphasizes personal fulfillment. According to Bühler, fulfillment results from living constructively and thoughtfully, in ways consistent with the person's best gifts. Living constructively implies profiting even from misfortune. Living thoughtfully involves creative use of one's potential, which is aided by periodic assessment of life course. Such assessment enables the person to progress toward achieving responsible, personally elected goals. The major conceptual components of Bühler's theory include four basic human tendencies and a core self.

Bühler's hypothesized basic human tendencies include need satisfaction, self-limiting adaptation, creative expansion, and upholding an internal order. She held that harmonious balance of the four basic tendencies fosters "self-development, the establishment of contacts, the mastering of reality, and the fulfillment of life through an integrated actualization of the individual's potentials" (Bühler & Marschak, 1968, p. 93). Only need satisfaction as Bühler saw it favors quiescence. The remaining tendencies orient the person toward activity.

Bühler defined self as the subconscious core system that integrates, directs, and actualizes the four basic tendencies. The self is the source of unique personality patterns. She acknowledged heredity and environment as partial causes that also modify the expression of personality patterns. According to Bühler, the core self of a healthy person is necessary, however, to integrate the individual's four basic tendencies into a unique pattern, organized to achieve coordinated action and to fulfill personal capabilities. She sees the core self as essential to continuing personal development throughout life. Because the core self is uniquely related to individual gifts, a goal that is valid for one person may not be so for another. Someone whose life is oriented toward fulfillment of valid goals, that is, toward goals that suit development of that person's best gifts, experiences meaning. Bühler realized that a person who has elected valid goals may not always follow them consistently. Moreover, some individuals fail to adopt life-ordering goals. She acknowledged that healthy persons (that is, persons whose lives are organized to achieve valid goals) may at times face challenges that threaten integration of the postulated four basic tendencies. For instance, a person may experience conflict when faced with a decision over whether to opt for secure adaptation or instead to elect "daring creative struggles" (Bühler, 1971, p. 381). For Bühler, adaptation becomes valid and useful "if the given reality is positive and favorable" for that person (Bühler, 1971, p. 382). Sometimes, however, adaptation spawns "failure in situations in which creative renewal and the effort of creative self-development are required" (Bühler, 1971, p. 382).

According to Bühler, positive reality does not hem people in. Instead it invites them to experience "the expectation and anticipation of their being able to extend themselves and to do things" (Bühler, 1971, p. 382). Although healthy people express varied styles of life, they resemble each other whenever they elect what involves them in the give and take of love and dedicated creative accomplishment (Bühler, 1971, p. 382). Healthy people may differ in choice of goals and way of life, but will be alike in sharing goal orientations that do not tend toward quiescence. In fact, "the creatively active person finds elation in . . . creative tension" (Bühler, 1971, p. 383). Bühler holds that healthy people, whatever their goals may be, generally elect growth over maintenance. They follow life paths that foster personal enrichment and relationships with others.

Latter Years

At mid-century, Bühler's observations and theory meshed with those of Abraham Maslow and Carl Rogers. Although Maslow is ordinarily acknowledged as principal founder of the American Association for Humanistic Psychology in 1962, Bühler collaborated with him and with others in inaugurating, publicizing, and strengthening the humanistic movement, the Third Force, as it came to be called. During her latter years Bühler worked to improve and sharpen humanistic psychological theory and to establish its connections with scientific findings. She continued to pursue her lifelong interest, the study of personal purposes and goals as they develop throughout the course of life. She remained alert to discover ways to apply the best insights of humanistic psychology to everyday life. She tried to encourage the most capable scientists to contribute to humanistic psychology (Association for Humanistic Psychology, Archives of the History of American Psychology, H3). She died at the age of eighty in Stuttgart, West Germany, on February 3, 1974.

EVALUATION OF ACHIEVEMENTS AND CONTRIBUTIONS

Bühler's close early collaborator, Hildegard Hetzer, believed that Charlotte Bühler's contributions involved a team effort with her husband, Karl Bühler. According to Hetzer, the Bühlers together established an outstanding research center for child and adolescent development at the University of Vienna. The Bühlers (once again cooperatively) developed highly original methods, especially in the area of infant development. Their research in the area of infant and adolescent development incorporated a real-life orientation that focused analytically on a number of important developmental issues (Hetzer, 1982).

Another close associate within the same time frame, Lotte Schenk-Danzinger, also addressed Charlotte Bühler's contributions to psychology. Schenk-Danzinger felt that Bühler's theoretical and research work has progressively illuminated, perhaps even captured, how the entire span of human life is integrated, how it comes together (Schenk-Danzinger, 1984, p. 92). Schenk-Danzinger reflected positively on the rigorous "natural science" methods that Bühler utilized (1984, p. 89). She applauded Charlotte Bühler's attention to neurophysiological and hormonal factors that influence the life course (Schenk-Danzinger, 1984, p. 89). Writing late in the twentieth century, Schenk-Danzinger reported that Bühler's detailed, systematic work in life-span development has continued to stimulate research on the continent of Europe (Schenk-Danzinger, 1984, p. 89).

Bühler presided over the First International Conference on Humanistic Psychology in Amsterdam, the Netherlands, in 1970, a fact that testifies to her international psychological perspective and to the high regard many professional colleagues had for her. Her colleagues in the American Association for Humanistic Psychology had already honored her previously, electing her to serve as president in 1965–1966. From time to time her pioneering contributions to life-span developmental psychology have been acknowledged as forerunners (Howard, 1977) of contemporary work. Nevertheless, the full range of Bühler's contributions seems poorly appreciated in mainstream American psychology, perhaps because some of her important early research is not available in English. Whatever history finally decides, Charlotte Bühler has certainly provided a mine of findings and insights for anyone willing to pursue them.

REFERENCES

Association for Humanistic Psychology Papers, Boxes H3 and H12; Archives of the History of American Psychology, Bierce Library, University of Akron, Akron, Ohio.

Bühler, C. (1922). *Das Seelenleben des Jugendlichen* (Psychology of adolescence). Jena: Gustav Fischer.

Bühler, C. (1930). *Personality types based on experiments with children.* Report of Ninth International Congress of Psychology, New Haven, Conn.

Bühler, C. (1933). *Der menschliche Lebenslauf als psychologisches Problem* (The course of human life as a psychological problem). Leipzig: Hirzel.

Bühler, C. (1935). *From birth to maturity.* London: Kegan Paul, Trench, & Trubner.

Bühler, C. (1940). *The child and his family* (H. Beaumont, Trans.). London: Kegan Paul, Trench, & Trubner (Original work published 1937).

Bühler, C. (1967 October 11). [Interview with James Birren]. Archives of the American Psychiatric Association, Washington, D.C., 37 pp.

Bühler, C. (1967 October 25). [Interview with James Birren]. Archives of the American Psychiatric Association, Washington, D.C., 26 pp.

Bühler, C. (1968). The integrating self. In C. Bühler & F. Massarik (Eds.), *The course of human life: A study of goals in the humanistic perspective* (pp. 330–350). New York: Springer.

Bühler, C. (1971). Basic theoretical concepts of humanistic psychology. *American Psychologist, 26,* 378–386.

Bühler, C. (1972). Charlotte Bühler. In L. J. Pongratz, W. Traxel, & E. G. Wehner (Eds.), *Psychologie in Selbstdarstellungen* (pp. 9–42). Bern: Hans Huber.

Bühler, C., & Hetzer, H. (1927). Inventar der Verhaltenweisen des ersten Lebensjahres. In C. Bühler, H. Hetzer, & B. Tudor-Hart (Eds.), *Soziologische und psychologische Studien uber das erste Lebensjahres: Quellen und Studien zur Jugendkunde* (pp. 125–150). Jena: Fischer.

Bühler, C., & Marschak, M. (1968). Basic tendencies of human life. In C. Bühler & F. Massarik (Eds.), *The course of human life: A study of goals in the humanistic perspective* (pp. 92–102). New York: Springer.

Bühler, C., & Massarik, F. (Eds.). (1968). *The course of human life: A study of goals in the humanistic perspective.* New York: Springer.

Hetzer, H. (1982). Kinder- und jugendpsychologische Forschung im Wiener Psychologischen Institut von 1922 bis 1938. *Zeitschrift fur Entwicklungspsychologie und Padagogische Psychologie, 14*(3), 175–224.

Howard, G. (Ed.). (1977). *Development of the adult* [Film]. New York: Harper & Row.

Krippner, S. (1977). Humanistic psychology: Its history and contributions. *Journal of the American Society of Psychosomatic Dentistry and Medicine, 24*(1), 16.

Schenk-Danzinger, L. (1974). In memoriam Charlotte Bühler. *Erziehung und Unterricht, 3,* 205–208.

Schenk-Danzinger, L. (1984). Werk und Bedeutung von Charlotte Bühler. *Proceedings of the Thirty-Fourth Congress of the German Psychological Society* (pp. 88–93). Vienna.

Additional Representative Publications by Charlotte Bühler

Bühler, C. (1918). *Das Marchen und die Phantasie des Kindes* (Fairy tales and the child's fantasy). *Zeitschrift fur angewandte Psychologie, 17.*

Bühler, C. (1919). *Uber Prozesse der Satzbildung* (On processes of sentence formation). *Zeitschrift Psychologie, 81.*

Bühler, C. (1954). The reality principle. *American Journal of Psychotherapy, 8,* 561–581.

Bühler, C. (1962). *Values in psychotherapy.* New York: Free Press of Glencoe.

Bühler, C., & Allen, M. (1972). *Introduction to humanistic psychology.* Belmont, Calif.: Brooks/Cole.

MARY WHITON CALKINS (1863–1930)

Laurel Furumoto

A long, extraordinarily productive, and distinguished career qualifies Mary Whiton Calkins as one of the most eminent women psychologists. A member of the first generation of women to enter psychology, she overcame obstacles to graduate education for women in the 1890s, gaining access to Harvard seminars and the psychological laboratory there. Her professors acknowledged Calkins as one of their most outstanding doctoral students, but the Harvard authorities refused to award her the Ph.D. because she was a woman. In 1891 Calkins founded one of the earliest psychological laboratories in America at Wellesley College, where she served on the faculty for over forty years, retiring in 1929. Her contributions to psychology include the invention of the paired-associate technique for studying memory, pioneering research on dreams, and the development of a system of self-psychology. She was elected to the presidency of both the American Psychological Association and the American Philosophical Association, the first woman to be accorded this honor by either organization.

FAMILY BACKGROUND, EDUCATION, AND CAREER

Mary Calkins was born in Hartford, Connecticut, in 1863, the eldest of five children, and grew up in Buffalo, New York, where her father was a Protestant minister. In 1881 the family moved to Newton, Massachusetts, a city about twelve miles west of Boston where the Reverend Wolcott Calkins had accepted the pastorate of a Congregational church. Calkins' closeness to her family and especially to her mother Charlotte was a dominant theme throughout her life. This lifelong attachment to family was not unusual for a nineteenth-century American middle-class woman; rather, as recent scholarship in women's history reveals, it was the norm (Smith-Rosenberg, 1975).

Despite her strong familial attachment, Calkins left home in 1882 to attend Smith College in an era when higher education for women was still an unproven experiment (Solomon, 1985). Upon completion of her undergraduate studies at Smith, where she concentrated in philosophy and the classics, the entire Calkins family embarked on a European sojourn of more than a year, during which Calkins continued her study of languages. Returning to New England in September 1887, she had plans to earn her livelihood by tutoring students in Greek. However, an unexpected opportunity arose to teach Greek at Wellesley College, a women's college located just a few miles from her family home in Newton. Calkins accepted the position, thus beginning a more than forty-year association with that institution, where she would spend her entire career.

After she had been at Wellesley a little over a year, Calkins' talent as a teacher and her expressed interest in philosophy prompted a faculty member in that department to recommend to the college president that Calkins be appointed to a newly created position in experimental psychology. The appointment was made contingent upon Calkins studying the subject for a year, an undertaking that required petitions and special arrangements, since neither Clark University, where she was tutored by Edmund C. Sanford, nor Harvard, where she attended seminars of William James and Josiah Royce, was willing to admit women as students at the time (Scarborough & Furumoto, 1987).

Upon her return to Wellesley in the autumn of 1891, Calkins established a psychological laboratory and introduced the new scientific psychology into the curriculum. Feeling the need for additional study, Calkins returned to Harvard a year later to work in the psychological laboratory of Hugo Münsterberg. There, pursuing research on factors influencing memory, she invented what has come to be known as the paired-associate technique. Although she completed all the requirements for the Ph.D., and her Harvard professors enthusiastically recommended her for the degree, the institutional authorities refused to award it because she was a woman (Scarborough & Furumoto, 1987).

Calkins spent her entire career at Wellesley College, teaching, publishing prolifically in both psychology and philosophy, and achieving eminence in both fields. By 1903, when James McKeen Cattell (1906) asked ten leading psychologists to arrange their American colleagues in order of merit with respect to the importance of their work, Calkins appeared twelfth in a listing of fifty top-ranked psychologists (Cattell & Cattell, 1933). She was elected president of the American Psychological Association in 1905 and of the American Philosophical Association in 1918, the first woman to be thus recognized by either society. Honorary degrees were bestowed on Calkins by Columbia University in 1909 and her alma mater, Smith, in 1910, and in 1928 she became the first woman elected to honorary membership in the British Psychological Association.

ACHIEVEMENTS AND CONTRIBUTIONS

Psychological Laboratory

When the psychological laboratory at Wellesley College got under way in September 1891, there were only a dozen others, none more than a few years old, currently in operation in all of North America. And, with the exception of the laboratory at McLean Asylum outside of Boston, the others were located in major universities (Garvey, 1929). The Wellesley College laboratory began in one attic room with $200 worth of furnishings and apparatus (Furumoto, 1975). Calkins consulted closely with her professors of the previous year as she went about setting it up. Lessons on dissecting and information on storing sheep's brains came from William James. Edmund C. Sanford gave help and technical advice on apparatus, providing Calkins, for example, with detailed instructions on how to get a color mixer working properly.

The fifty-four students who elected the year-long course in experimental psychology at Wellesley in 1891–1892 dissected sheep's brains and conducted studies on sensation, association, attention, space perception, memory, and reaction time. At the invitation of G. Stanley Hall, editor of the *American Journal of Psychology*, Calkins (1892) wrote an article describing her new experimental psychology course "in which simple experiments provided first-hand material for the study of a number of topics" (Calkins, 1930, p. 36). That first account was followed up over the next several years by a series of articles reporting the results of research that she and her students carried out in the Wellesley laboratory (Calkins, 1893a, 1894, 1895a, 1895b, 1895c, 1896b, 1896c, 1898, 1900). The studies covered a broad range of topics including dreams (1896c), psychological aesthetics (1900), synesthesia (1893a), and children's emotional life, moral consciousness, stories, and drawings (1895a; 1895b).

This remarkably productive period of empirical research ended around 1900 as Calkins' interests turned toward psychological theory and philosophy. In less than a decade, she had set up a laboratory, trained hundreds of students in the then current techniques of psychological research, and communicated to journals a wealth of findings collected by many of these students under her direction. From 1900 onward her contributions to psychology would be of a different kind.

Dream Research

The invention of the paired-associate technique and her pioneering dream research predate Calkins' turn toward theoretical and philosophical pursuits and, more precisely, were products of the period during which she was pursuing graduate training in psychology. While Sanford was tutoring Calkins in laboratory work, he started her on a research project that involved studying the contents of their dreams recorded during a seven-week period in the spring of 1891. In describing the investigation Calkins observed: "Its method was very simple: to record each night, immediately after waking from a dream, every remembered feature of it. For this purpose, paper, pencil, candle and matches were placed close at hand" (Calkins, 1893b, p. 311).

In this fashion, Calkins recorded 205 dreams and Sanford 170, "an average of nearly four dreams a night in each case" (p. 313). Subjecting the contents of these dreams to analysis, Calkins' major conclusion was that there existed a "close connection between the dream-life and the waking-life" (p. 315), that is, "the dream will reproduce, in general, the persons, places and events of recent sense perception" (p. 334).

In 1892 Sanford reported Calkins' study, along with five others done under his direction by students at Clark University, to the first annual meeting of the American Psychological Association (Sokal, 1973). The following year Calkins (1893b) published an extensive account of her investigation. Commenting nearly forty years later on this early study of hers, she noted wryly that its main conclusion "is almost ludicrously opposed to the nowadays widely accepted Freudian conception of the dream" and went on to admit, "In fact, my study as a whole must be rather contemptuously set down by any good Freudian as superficially concerned with the mere 'manifest content' of the dream" (Calkins, 1930, p. 32). Yet Freud (1900/1953) himself cited both Calkins' (1893b) dream research and that of her students Florence Hallam and Sarah Weed (Calkins, 1896c) without a hint of criticism. Presenting Calkins' findings on the proportion of dreams having content traceable to either external or organic stimuli and Hallam and Weed's findings on the relative proportions of disagreeable and pleasurable dreams, Freud noted approvingly that both provided statistical evidence in support of his subjective impressions.

In the 1980s Calkins' dream investigations took on new import as Freudian dream analysis, with its emphasis on hidden meanings, came under increasing attack by dream researchers in the neurosciences. One of them, J. Allan Hobson (1988), who is coauthor along with Robert W. McCarley of the activation-synthesis theory of dreaming, claims that Freud was wrong about dreams being "opaque," that is, about having disguised meanings. For Hobson, dreams are more correctly viewed "as transparent, their significance available to the dreamer unaided by prophet or psychoanalyst" (p. 3). Dubbing Mary Calkins the "dream accountant," Hobson cites her work as one of the significant pioneering empirical studies of dreaming and credits her with developing a "formal characterization of dreams . . . of direct relevance to . . . modern dream science" (p. 74).

Paired-Associate Technique

More significant than the results of her doctoral research was the research method she employed. This was the opinion Calkins (1930) voiced in the autobiography she wrote very near the end of her life. The method consisted of showing a series of colors paired with numerals, followed by testing for recall of the numerals when the colors with which they had previously been paired were again presented (Calkins, 1896a). Calkins revealed that it came as a great surprise to her when, subsequently, she discovered that she "had originated a technical memorization method" (p. 34). Far removed from experimental work by then, yet still appreciating its value, she admitted to taking "unaffected pleasure" in the thought of what she modestly termed her "one slightly significant contribution to experimental psychology" (p. 34). Writing of Calkins' place in the history of the experimental study of associative learning, Hernnstein and

Boring noted in 1966, "She was one of the first in this new field, and she created an experimental technique that is now called the method of paired-associates, which has survived to the present time" (p. 530). Perusal of even the most recently published textbooks in the psychology of learning and memory (e.g., Gordon, 1989) indicates that the method survives still.

Self-Psychology

Of all her noteworthy contributions, the one that Calkins displayed the most personal commitment to, by far, was her system of self-psychology. A newspaper account of Calkins' career published on the occasion of her retirement from Wellesley College in 1929 described her achievements and disclosed some of the resistance she encountered in promoting her system: "By her books and by her many published papers on points of view in psychology, she has not only gained international reputation but has founded a school of thought in psychology—the school of the 'self-psychologists,' which however slowly in these days of militant behaviorism, is gaining measurable ground" (E.F.K., 1929, p. 531). Today, some sixty years later, the days of militant behaviorism are past and psychologies that emphasize the self abound. Yet, curiously, current approaches to self-psychology (e.g., Kohut, 1985; Mischel, 1977; Suls & Greenwald, 1983; Yardley & Honess, 1987) fail to acknowledge Calkins' system as a forerunner.

Attempting in her autobiography to trace the origin of the idea of "the self" in her own work, Calkins encountered some difficulty. There she confessed to her reader, "I wish that I could recall more completely the sources of this personalistic doctrine of psychology" (p. 38). Calkins credited her emphasis on the social nature of the self to the influence of James Baldwin and Josiah Royce, and she felt confident that her self-doctrine must also have been influenced by the work of William James and that of James Ward. Finally, she acknowledged the influence of Hugo Münsterberg on her conception of the double standpoint in psychology—the theory that every experience may be treated alike from the atomistic and from the self-psychological standpoint—a position she was eventually to abandon in favor of a single-track self-psychology.

Calkins' two textbooks of psychology highlight her transition from the dual to the single standpoint. In the earlier, titled *An Introduction to Psychology*, first published in 1901, psychology is conceived as a science of succeeding mental events *and* of the conscious self. In the later work, first published in 1909 and titled *A First Book in Psychology*, the double treatment is dropped, as Calkins explains in her preface, "not because [she] doubt[ed] the validity of psychology as study of ideas, but because [she] question[ed] the significance and the adequacy, and deprecate[d] the abstractness, of the science thus conceived" (p. vii). "This book," she confides to her reader, "has been written in the ever strengthening conviction that psychology is most naturally, consistently, and effectively treated as a study of conscious selves in relation to other selves and to external objects—in a word, to their environment, personal and impersonal'' (p. vii).

In her autobiography, published in 1930, Calkins revealed that her psychological activities from the time the fourth and last edition of *A First Book in Psychology* appeared in 1914 to the present consisted ''in attempts to elucidate, to enrich, and to defend self-psychology'' (p. 41). In harmony with this characterization, in the second half of that work she turned from what she termed her ''autobiographical outpouring'' (p. 41) to set forth and to argue the essentials of a personalistic of self-psychology. Thus, until the very end of her life, Calkins tried to convert her psychological brethren to the point of view of the self-psychologist. In attempting this at a time when a shift was under way in academic psychology from the study of consciousness to the goal of prediction and control of behavior, Calkins was clearly swimming against the ideological current. What compelled her to do so?

Edna Heidbreder (1972), an authority on systems and theories of psychology, has argued that Calkins embarked on her crusade because of her dissatisfaction with the classical Wundtian-and-Titchenerian system then dominant in American psychology. Calkins' disagreement with the classical school was not about its usefulness in research. Rather, she questioned its insistence that the empirical contents of psychology should be limited to elemental sensations, emotions, and images.

In the 1890s, Heidbreder points out, Calkins became convinced ''that selves— persisting, complex, unitary, unique selves—are phenomenally, observably present in ordinary, conscious experience, and that they are therefore among the empirical facts with which psychology as a natural science must come to terms'' (p. 63). Calkins thus came to regard the classical system as inadequate because it excluded from its subject matter psychological phenomena that she considered basic. Moreover, Calkins came to see the classical experimental psychologists ''as out of touch—as deliberately and on principle out of touch—with important portions and aspects of that subject matter as it presents itself in ordinary experience: in ordinary experience as she herself observed it and as she believed, by checking with others, that they too observed it'' (p. 63).

Calkins' first presentation of her self-psychology in 1900 was, then, a departure from the classical school, and, as Heidbreder (1972) notes, ''Though she kept developing her system throughout the remaining thirty years of her life, she did not in any essential way alter her initial position'' (p. 57). Rather, she devoted her efforts to ''clarifying it at points, modifying it occasionally, defending it against attack'' (p. 57), and confronting it with one after another of the rival systems of her day—structuralism, functionalism, behaviorism, hormic psychology, Gestalt psychology, and psychoanalysis.

From the time Calkins came to Wellesley College in 1887 until her death in 1930, her personal and professional life was closely intertwined with those of her friends and colleagues there. This community of academic women who had so much in common has been described by one historian (Palmieri, 1983) as ''very much like an extended family . . . in this milieu no one was isolated, no one forgotten'' (p. 203). Although trained in mainstream academic, laboratory psychology of the 1890s by her male professors at Harvard and Clark, Calkins soon thereafter began to question the atomistic, impersonal conception of the subject matter characteristic of this approach, and later she rejected it outright. As noted above, Calkins came to view classical experimental psychologists as out of touch with important portions of the subject matter of psychology. Her proposed alternative to the classical view reflected the institutional context from which it emerged, calling attention to something highly salient in Calkins' communal academic world, namely, the reality and importance of selves in everyday experience.

REFERENCES

Calkins, M. W. (1892). Experimental psychology at Wellesley College. *American Journal of Psychology*, 5, 260–271.

Calkins, M. W. (1893a). A statistical study of pseudo-chromesthesia and of mental forms. *American Journal of Psychology*, 5, 439–464.

Calkins, M. W. (1893b). Statistics of dreams. *American Journal of Psychology*, 5, 311–343.

Calkins, M. W. (1894). Wellesley College psychological studies. *Educational Review*, 8, 269–286.

Calkins, M. W. (1895a). Minor studies from the psychological laboratory of Wellesley College. *American Journal of Psychology*, 7, 86–107.

Calkins, M. W. (1895b). Wellesley College psychological studies. *Pedagogical Seminary*, 3, 319–341.

Calkins, M. W. (1895c). Wellesley College psychological studies. *Psychological Review*, 2, 363–368.

Calkins, M. W. (1896a). Association: An essay analytic and experimental. *Psychological Review Monograph Supplement Number 2*, 1–56.

Calkins, M. W. (1896b). Community of ideas of men and women. *Psychological Review*, 3, 426–430.

Calkins, M. W. (1896c). Minor studies from the psychological laboratory of Wellesley College. *American Journal of Psychology*, 7, 405–411.

Calkins, M. W. (1898). Short studies in memory and association from the Wellesley College psychological laboratory. *Psychological Review*, 5, 451–462.

Calkins, M. W. (1900). Wellesley College psychology studies: An attempted experiment in psychological aesthetics. *Psychological Review*, 7, 580–591.

Calkins, M. W. (1901). *An introduction to psychology*. New York: Macmillan.

Calkins, M. W. (1909). *A first book in psychology*. New York: Macmillan.

Calkins, M. W. (1915). The self in scientific psychology. *American Journal of Psychology*, 26, 495–524.

Calkins, M. W. (1930). Mary Whiton Calkins. In C. Murchison (Ed.), *A history of psychology in autobiography: Volume 1* (pp. 31–62). Worcester, Mass.: Clark University Press.

Cattell, J. McK. (Ed.). (1906). *American men of science*. New York: Science Press.

Cattell, J. McK., & Cattell, J. (Eds.). (1933). *American men of science* (5th ed.). New York: Science Press.

E.F.K. (1929). Notes and news. *Journal of Philosophy*, 26, 531–532.

Freud, S. (1953). *The interpretation of dreams*. In J. Strachey (Ed. and Trans.), *The standard edition of the complete psychological works of Sigmund Freud* (Vols. 4–5, pp. xi–632). London: Hogarth Press. (Original work published 1900)

Furumoto, L. (1975, June). The college laboratory: Promoting the scholarly and scientific ideal. In M. M. Sokal (Chair), *The American psychological laboratory as a scientific institution: 1885–1930*. Symposium conducted at the meeting of Cheiron: The International Society for the History of Behavioral and Social Sciences, Ottawa, Canada.

Garvey, C. R. (1929). List of American psychology laboratories. *Psychological Bulletin, 26*, 652–660.

Gordon, W. C. (1989). *Learning and memory*. Pacific Grove, Calif.: Brooks/Cole.

Hawkins, H. (1960). *Pioneer: A history of the Johns Hopkins University, 1874–1889*. Ithaca, N.Y.: Cornell University Press.

Heidbreder, E. (1972). Mary Whiton Calkins: A discussion. *Journal of the History of the Behavioral Sciences, 8*, 56–68.

Hernnstein, R. J., & Boring, E. G. (Eds.). (1966). *A source book in the history of psychology*. Cambridge, Mass.: Harvard University Press.

Hobson, J. A. (1988). *The dreaming brain*. New York: Basic Books.

Kohut, H. (1985). *Self psychology and the humanities: Reflections on a new psychoanalytic approach*. (C. B. Strozier, Ed.). New York: Norton.

Mischel, T. (Ed.). (1977). *The self: Psychological and philosophical issues*. Oxford: Basil Blackwell.

Palmieri, P. A. (1983). Here was fellowship: A social portrait of academic women at Wellesley College, 1895–1920. *History of Education Quarterly, 23*, 195–214.

Scarborough, E., & Furumoto, L. (1987). *Untold lives: The first generation of American women psychologists*. New York: Columbia University Press.

Smith-Rosenberg, C. (1975). The female world of love and ritual. *Signs, 1*, 1–29.

Sokal, M. M. (1973). APA's first publication: Proceedings of the American Psychological Association, 1892–1893. *American Psychologist, 28*, 277–292.

Solomon, B. M. (1985). *In the company of educated women*. New Haven: Yale University Press.

Suls, J., & Greenwald, A. G. (Eds.). (1983). *Psychological perspectives on the self* (Vol. 2). Hillsdale, N.J.: Erlbaum.·

Yardley, K., & Honess, T. (Eds.). (1987). *Self and identity: Psychosocial perspectives*. New York: Wiley.

Additional Representative Publications by Mary Whiton Calkins

Calkins, M. W. (1892). Experimental psychology at Wellesley College. *American Journal of Psychology, 5*, 260–271.

Calkins, M. W. (1893). Statistics of dreams. *American Journal of Psychology, 5*, 311–343.

Calkins, M. W. (1900). Psychology as science of selves. *Philosophical Review, 9*, 490–501.

Calkins, M. W. (1906). A reconciliation between structural and functional psychology. *Psychological Review, 13*, 61–81.

Calkins, M. W. (1926). Converging lines in contemporary psychology. *British Journal of Psychology, 16*, 171–179.

Additional Representative Publications About Mary Whiton Calkins

Furumoto, L. (1979). Mary Whiton Calkins (1863–1930): Fourteenth president of the American Psychological Association. *Journal of the History of the Behavioral Sciences, 15*, 346–356.

Furumoto, L. (1980). Mary Whiton Calkins (1863–1930). *Psychology of Women Quarterly, 5*, 55–68.

In memoriam: Mary Whiton Calkins 1863–1930 (1931). Boston: Merrymount Press.

Onderdonk, V. (1971). Mary Whiton Calkins. In E. T. James, J. W. James, & P. S. Boyer (Eds.), *Notable American women, 1607–1950: A biographical dictionary* (Vol. 1, pp. 278–280). Cambridge, Mass.: Belknap Press.

MAMIE PHIPPS CLARK (1917–1983)

Robert V. Guthrie

It has been said that each generation must find its destiny or betray it. Mamie Phipps Clark fulfilled her destiny by pioneering developmental studies that helped remove race barriers in education. Her alma maters, Howard and Columbia universities, recognized these contributions by presenting her with distinguished alumni awards. Williams College and the Pratt Institute awarded her with honorary doctorate degrees, and the American Association of University Women presented its noted fellowship award, all citing her landmark research on the psychological effects of racism and segregation.

Mamie Clark fulfilled another aspect of her destiny when she founded the Northside Center for Children in New York (1946). Throughout her life, Clark blended her intellect, insight, and humanism in an effort to enhance the lives of children who often were misinterpreted, misjudged, or neglected because of environment or prevailing psychological theories. Her contributions to an evolving field, developmental psychology, were all the more significant during the changing social and political climate of the late 1940s and 1950s. An independent thinker and a devoted wife and mother, she combined her commitment to scientific research and social advancement throughout her life.

FAMILY BACKGROUND AND EDUCATION

Mamie Katherine Phipps, the eldest of two children born to Harold H. and Katie F. Phipps, was born in Hot Springs, Arkansas. Her father, a native of St. Kitts, British West Indies, was a self-made individual with high standards who financed his education through medical school. Her mother shared Harold Phipps' drive for achievement and assisted him in his medical practice. Mamie Phipps' brother, Harold, is now a retired dentist living in Pine Bluff, Arkansas.

Her elementary and secondary education in the small, racially segregated town was, by her own accounting, deficient in substantive areas. She later commented, however, that in retrospect this experience, together with the security of a warm and protective extended family, appeared to have been the near ideal for later career satisfaction. Upon graduation at age sixteen from Pine Bluff's Langston High School in 1934, she enrolled at Howard University with the intent of majoring in mathematics and physics (Guthrie, 1976).

Shortly after enrolling at Howard she met her future husband, Kenneth Bancroft Clark, and, through his later suggestion, decided to change her major to psychology. Francis C. Sumner, Kenneth Clark's mentor and head of the psychology department, arranged for her enrollment as a student. Since she was an academic scholarship awardee, provisions were made for her to work part-time in the psychology department. In 1938 she was awarded the B.S. degree, magna cum laude, in psychology; during the summer of that year she took a job as a secretary in the law office of William Houston. This office was the nucleus of early planning for the civil rights cases that challenged the laws requiring and permitting racial segregation in the United States. During the course of work there she witnessed the legal strategizing that would lead to the repeal of laws enacted as a result of the *Plessy v. Ferguson* decision. This high-paced, socially conscious work environment made a profound impression on her. She had the opportunity to witness the exhilaration when such legal giants as William Houston and Thurgood Marshall would confer with the Washington-based lawyers. Through experiences such as these she began to develop a sensitivity for research that could assist in providing better understanding of psychological effects of racial segregation.

CAREER DEVELOPMENT AND ACHIEVEMENTS

In the fall of 1938, Mamie K. Phipps enrolled in Howard University's graduate school under the tutelage of Max Meenes. Her interest in developmental psychology grew. She was given the opportunity to work with children in an all-black nursery school in Washington while still a graduate student. During this time she married Kenneth Clark; he suggested that she go to New York and talk to Ruth and Gene Horowitz (later Ruth and Gene Hartley) because they were pursuing interesting research studies with preschool children using line drawings of white and black children. Her discussion with the Hartleys underscored the need to expand on their studies and to utilize more black children in the sample. Clark's access to the nursery school in Washington, D.C., and her inquisitiveness led her to undertake the research that would culminate in her master's thesis, entitled "The Development of Consciousness of Self in Negro Pre-school Children." It is of historical note that this research into the importance of self in black children, completed fifteen years before the *Brown v. Board of Education of Topeka* decision, paved the way for an increase in psychological research into the areas of self-esteem and self-concept. Clark's initial research intensified the scientific enthusiasm of her husband, and they began to publish research findings that heightened professional awareness in these areas. In 1939 they submitted a research proposal to the Julius Rosenwald Fellowship program, which funded their research for a total of three years. This made it possible for Clark to enter

Columbia University to study for her Ph.D. degree. (Her husband had received his Ph.D. in psychology from Columbia in 1940.)

As her husband gathered research data in selected northern and southern states, she completed her first year at Columbia and began rearing their first child, Kate, who was born in 1940. Clark later recalled that being a graduate student in the psychology department at Columbia was a most satisfying experience. As the only black student in the department, she did not consider this a problem, nor did she feel that it was an encumbrance to her progress. With characteristic determination, she was eager to learn and selected Henry E. Garrett, an outstanding statistician, as her sponsoring dissertation professor. It was indeed fateful that years later the Clarks became political adversaries of Garrett, confronting him in a federal courtroom where a school desegregation case regarding Prince Edward County, Virginia, was being tried. Garrett opposed desegregation of the public schools on the grounds that black and white children had different talents and abilities, which he felt justified separate schools.

In 1943, when her research on identity in black children was completed, she was awarded the Ph.D. degree from Columbia. That same year her second child, Hilton, was born. The findings from her studies on black children's awareness of their racial identity between the ages of three and four were published in several articles and textbooks (M. P. Clark, 1944; K. B. Clark & M. P. Clark, 1947; K. B. Clark & M. P. Clark, 1950; Swanson, Newcomb, & Hartley, 1952; Maccoby, Newcomb, & Hartley, 1958).

In exploring the language of consciousness of skin color in children three to seven years of age the Clarks, who had joined forces in their research, gave children a coloring test and a dolls test. Children were given a sheet of paper with the drawings of a leaf, an apple, an orange, a mouse, a boy, and a girl, plus a box of twenty-four crayons including brown, black, white, yellow, pink, and tan. Each child was asked to color the leaf, orange, apple, and mouse. If the child responded correctly, the child was tested further: "See this little boy? Let us make believe he is you. Color this little boy the color you are." After the child responded, he was told, "Now this is a little girl. Color her the color you like little girls to be." These questions were also, appropriately, asked of girls. In the coloring test, all black children with very light skin color colored the child accurately; a significant portion of the children with medium-to-dark-brown skin colored their own figure with either white or a yellow crayon or with some bizarre color like red or green. These children's choice of an inappropriate color for themselves is "an indication of emotional anxiety and conflict in terms of their own skin . . . because they wanted to be white, they pretended to be" (K. B. Clark, 1988).

These findings supported those of the dolls test in which over one-half of the children preferred a white doll or rejected the brown doll. The children were shown four dolls made from the same case and dressed alike; the only difference in the dolls was that two were brown and two were white. The children were asked to make several distinctions and to choose among the dolls in answer to the instructions:

1. "Give me the white doll."
2. "Give me the colored doll."
3. "Give me the Negro doll."

The children were then asked:

1. "Which doll do you like?"
2. "Which doll is ugly? Pretty?"
3. "Which clothes belong on which doll?"

These studies showed that black children include racial group identity as part of their self-concept and when asked questions about racial identification they react with uneasiness and with tense and evasive behavior.

Results from these studies provided data for expert testimony in the federal courts. During the early 1950s under the leadership of Kenneth Clark, a prestigious group of social scientists prepared a social science brief that summarized the expert testimony and major findings on the effects of racial segregation ("The effects of segregation," 1953). This brief was submitted to the United States Supreme Court by the National Association for the Advancement of Colored People (NAACP) lawyers as a supplement to their legal brief. The importance of the negative self-image studies in black children was affirmed by the one-sentence statement in the 1954 Supreme Court decision ordering the integration of America's schools:

To separate them from others of similar age and qualifications solely because of their race generates a feeling of inferiority as to their status in the community that may affect their hearts and minds in a way unlikely ever to be undone.

The findings of the Clarks' research had reached a quintessential high-water mark as a result of the Court's 1954 ruling and its new desegregation policy.

Following Mamie Phipps Clark's graduation from Columbia University, the impact of being black and a woman in New York during the mid-1940s hit home: job offerings were few. She did manage to secure a minor position in 1944 analyzing research data, a position she later described as a humiliating and distasteful first employment experience. But she persevered and gleaned knowledge and experience. In 1945, as World War II was being waged, she was employed for a year by the United States Armed Forces Institute (USAFI) as a research psychologist. Reminiscent of her chance employment in the Washington, D.C., nursery, which helped shape the direction of her research work, she was offered a job at the Riverdale Home for Children in New York as a psychologist. She conducted psychological tests and counseled homeless black girls. This experience provided her with clear perceptions of the insufficiencies of psychological services for blacks and other minority children in New York City and laid the foundation for her life's work and significant contributions in the field of developmental psychology.

Since there were practically no resources for referring these girls in New York City, the Riverdale Home evolved into a center dedicated to helping minority youngsters. She felt that children in similar situations across the country were being destroyed by an unseen and little-recognized "ingrained frustration" ("Problem Kids," 1947). Her description of the manifestations of this "disease" ranged from enuresis to gang warfare to poor academic/scholarship performance to running-away behavior. Mamie Phipps Clark felt that the worries that plagued these youngsters were the direct outgrowth of a racially segregated society. While Clark was a strong advocate of basic research, she felt that applied psychology would provide the needed avenue to guide children to a more productive lifestyle and ambition.

In 1946 she and her husband established the Northside Center for Child Development (originally named the Northside Testing and Consultation Center) in a Harlem apartment basement that provided a homelike environment for the children. She assumed directorship of the center, and her program provided a wide array of services, ranging from medial reading to examinations by pediatricians, psychologists, psychiatrists, and social workers. A psychosocial approach rather than an isolated clinical or sterile analytic view became her modus operandi. The center's voluntary staff included her husband as well as interdisciplinary, interracial professionals, including psychiatrist Stella Chess. Occasionally, staff conflicts would arise concerning divergent approaches and clinical practices among the various professionals, but Clark was adamant in maintaining an approach that would comprehensively consider child and environmental issues.

The establishment of a psychologically oriented clinic for children was especially problematic in the 1940s due to the stigma often attached to anyone who needed or sought the help of a mental health professional, even if the "patients" were children. However, the Harlem community's acceptance of the Northside Center was enhanced because of the "acute frustration" parents felt about having their children in the New York public schools. The school system regularly used IQ tests to identify the "mentally retarded." Parents were disturbed because many children—often without parental permission—were being assigned to the Class for Children of Retarded Mental Development (CRMD) and thereby stigmatized by such placement. The Clarks and the Northside Center frequently reevaluated the school system's testing and placement process. Mamie Clark later commented, "Following psychological testing we found that most of the children were in fact above the intelligence level for placement in CRMD classes (IQ = 70) and that actions on the part of public school personnel were illegal in those schools located in minority and deprived areas'' (M. P. Clark, 1983).

As the center grew, current events regarding desegregation became increasingly important. With the problem of negative self-image and its impact through segregated schools beginning to be addressed, frustrations escalated from the fallout of restrictive housing covenants, segregated public accommodations, and barriers to equitable employment and economic opportunity. The issue of negative self-image remained unresolved in black communities until the mood shifted toward adopting ''Black Pride'' and the concept of ''Black is Beautiful'' during the 1960s. Black parents began to motivate their children to assert themselves and to pursue previously denied goals. For example, during this time numerous black professionals felt a need for a child-care book oriented toward blacks on the order of Benjamin Spock's *Common Sense Book of Baby and Child Care* (1946) to guide black parents through the problems they faced rearing children in a racist society. These adherents wanted a book geared to help parents cope with identity problems and development needs of their children. Mamie Clark responded that there were no differences between the way black and white parents reared their children other than factors of their means and resources; she felt that white parents had the same concerns and fears for their children as black parents did. She did feel, however, that there were variations in child-rearing practices, but no more than could be expected because of the diversity of groups living in the United States. Years later, her research continued to support the view that the verbalizations of pride and self-acceptance often mask ambivalence and racial identity problems. She felt that this pretense would be best remedied by unqualified racial justice in this country (Clark, as quoted by Parker, 1971).

Political differences of opinion were not new to Clark, for much of the criticism of the ''Doll Test'' was made within the context of partisan consideration: southern politicians, in particular, were upset by the *Brown* decision and decried the use of psychological theories as a ''substitute'' for the law. Although their arguments could not be seriously considered from a scientific point of view, they nonetheless constituted a vocal dispute. Probably the most noted scholarly criticism along these lines was voiced by the late professor of jurisprudence Edmond Cahn (1955), who argued that the *Brown* decision was ''caused by the testimony and opinions of scientists'' and that the right of any American should not ''rest on any such flimsy foundation as some of the scientific demonstrations in these records.'' Also, van den Haag (1957) supported Cahn's contention by iterating:

Whether humiliation leaves deep and lasting traces and whether it increases the incidence of personality disorders among Negroes, we do not know . . . [The United States Supreme Court depended on] such evidence . . . so flimsy as to discredit the conclusion.

There were also public statements by Bruno Bettelheim of the University of Chicago, who declared that "there is no scientific evidence that racial segregation damages the human personality" (K. B. Clark, 1988).

Clark's doll research paradigm continues to be discussed and replicated in colleges, universities, and research centers. Her views on self-esteem of youngsters continue to be of major importance. For example, Cook (1984) stated that "the view that black self-esteem has changed since the pre–1954 period is entirely plausible"; however, he further noted, "some writers have suggested that what the self-report questionnaires actually reflect is a new norm of racial pride rather than internalized self-esteem." Clark, in commenting on whether real change has taken place in the black child's self-esteem, indicated: "From my general observation the children's perceptions of themselves as black, and all the negatives that connotes, have not changed significantly since my first studies in the 1930s and 1940s" (Poussaint, 1974.)

Forty years following her research studies on the development of racial identification and preferences of black children, the Clarks (1980) noted that

the most poignant aspect of the struggle for a positive self-image among Blacks is to be found in their stated aspirations for their children . . . in spite of the many indications of the residues of negative self-image, self-rejection, ambivalence and conflicts in self-esteem and racial identification, Blacks persist in their desire for a better world and a more positive experience for their children.

INTEGRATION OF PERSONAL AND PROFESSIONAL LIFE

Clark's position as executive director of the Northside Center for Child Development (1946–1979) was clearly an extension of her values and ideals. She was intensely active in a variety of other roles: she was on the Board of Directors for the American Broadcasting Company, Mount Sinai Medical Center, Union Dime Savings Bank, Museum of Modern Art, Teachers College of Columbia University, Phelps Stokes Fund, New York Mission Society, Institute of Museum Services, and the New York Public Library, and she was president of the Museum Collaborative. It was in this latter capacity that she was quite vocal articulating the need for a federal presence in the funding of American cultural institutions, not only to affirm the importance of the arts themselves, but for the preservation of America's shared past.

Mamie Phipps Clark served with several advisory groups including Harlem Youth Opportunities Unlimited (HARYOU) and the National Headstart Planning Committee. She lectured at many colleges and universities and was a visiting professor of experimental methods and research design at Yeshiva University.

Her husband, Kenneth Bancroft Clark, was the seventy-ninth president of the American Psychological Association (1971). Their daughter, Kate, is the director of the Northside Center for Child Development, and her son, Hilton, is a New York City councilman.

This active, shy, somewhat introverted woman with a wonderful sense of humor died on August 11, 1983. Besides leaving her husband of forty-five years, two children, and three grandchildren, Mamie Katherine Phipps Clark left a legacy of contributions that has enriched American society through the science of psychology. To the world, she leaves the importance of the sense of self.

NOTES

The author gratefully acknowledges Kenneth B. Clark for providing invaluable information.

REFERENCES

Brown v. Board of Education of Topeka, 347 U.S. 483 (1954).

Cahn, E. (1955). Jurisprudence. *New York University Law Review, 30,* 150–159.

Clark, K. B. (1953). Desegregation: An appraisal of the evidence. *Journal of Social Issues, 9,* 1–75.

Clark, K. B. (1988). *Prejudice and your child.* Middletown, Conn.: Wesleyan University Press.

Clark, K. B., & Clark, M. P. (1947). Racial identification and preference in Negro children. In T. M. Newcomb & E. L. Hartley (Eds.), *Readings in social psychology* (pp. 169–178). New York: Holt.

Clark, K. B., & Clark, M. P. (1950). Emotional factors in racial identification and preference in Negro children. *Journal of Negro Education, 19,* 341–350.

Clark, K. B., & Clark, M. P. (1980, November). What do blacks think of themselves? *Ebony,* 176–182.

Clark, K. B., et al. (1953). The effects of segregation and the consequences of desegregation: A social science statement. Appendix to appellants' briefs: Brown v. Board of Education of Topeka (1953). *Minnesota Law Review, 37,* 427–439.

Clark, M. P. (1944). Changes in primary mental abilities with age. *Archives of Psychology, 291.* New York: Columbia University.

Clark, M. P. (1983). [Autobiography]. In A. N. O'Connell & N. F. Russo (Eds.), *Models of achievement: Reflections of eminent women in psychology* (pp. 266–277). New York: Columbia University Press.

Cook, S. W. (1984). The 1954 social science statement and school desegregation. A reply to Gerard. *American Psychologist, 39*(8), 819–832.

Guthrie, R. V. (1976). *Even the rat was white.* New York: Harper & Row.

Maccoby, E. E.; Newcomb, T. R.; & Hartley, E. (Eds.). (1958). *Readings in social psychology* (3rd Ed.). New York: Henry Holt.

Parker, A. (1971, November 14, Sec. 5). Black parents. *Chicago Tribune,* 1–3.

Plessy v. Ferguson, 163 U.S. 537 (1896).

Poussaint, F. F. (1974, August). Building a strong self-image in the black child. *Ebony, 29,* 138–143.

Problem Kids (1947, July). *Ebony, 45,* 24.

Proshansky, H., & Seidenberg, B. (1966). *Basic studies in social psychology.* New York: Holt, Rinehart & Winston.

Spock, B. (1946). *Common Sense Book of Baby and Child Care*. New York: Hawthorn Books.

Swanson, G. E., Newcomb, T. M., & Hartley, E. L. (Eds.). (1952). *Readings in social psychology* (2nd Ed). New York: Holt.

The effects of segregation and the consequences of desegregation: A social science statement. Appendix to appellants' briefs: *Brown v. Board of Education of Topeka, Kansas* (1953). *Minnesota Law Review, 37*, 427–439.

van den Haag, E. (1957). Prejudice about prejudice. In R. Ross & E. van den Haag (Eds.), *The fabric of society*. New York: Harcourt, Brace & World.

Additional Representative Publications by Mamie Phipps Clark

Clark, K. B., & Clark, M. P. (1939a). The development of consciousness of self and the emergence of racial identification in Negro pre-school children. *Journal of Social Psychology, 10*, 591–599.

Clark, K. B., & Clark, M. P. (1939b). Segregation as a factor in the racial identification of Negro preschool children. *Journal of Experimental Education, 8*, 1961–1965.

Clark, K. B., & Clark, M. P. (1940). Skin color as a factor in racial identification of Negro preschool children. *Journal of Social Psychology, 11*, 159–169.

Clark, K. B., & Clark, M. P. (1947). Racial identification and preference in Negro children. Reprinted in H. Proshansky & B. Seidenberg (1966), *Basic studies in social psychology* (pp. 308–317). New York: Holt, Rinehart & Winston.

Clark, K. B., & Clark, M. P. (1950). Emotional factors in racial identification and preference in Negro children. *Journal of Negro Education, 19*, 341–350.

Clark, M. P. (1939). The development of consciousness of self in Negro pre-school children. *Archives of Psychology*. Washington, D.C.: Howard University.

Clark, M. P. (1970). Changing concepts in mental health: A thirty-year view. Conference Proceedings, Thirtieth Anniversary Conference. New York: Northside Center for Child Development.

Clark, M. P., & Clark, K. B. (1980, November). What do blacks think of themselves? *Ebony*, 176–182.

FLORENCE L. DENMARK (1931–   )

Michele A. Paludi and Nancy Felipe Russo

Florence L. Denmark has been internationally recognized for her scholarly, administrative, educational, and leadership contributions to psychology, especially in the field of the psychology of women. She has more than ten books, sixty articles, and one hundred presentations as well as numerous media appearances to her credit. Her research encompasses prejudice and discrimination, leadership styles, power and achievement, and the status and contributions of women psychologists. As faculty member and former head of the largest psychology graduate program in the United States, she has influenced the education, training, and careers of numerous psychologists, including a large number of women and minorities. A prominent leader, in addition to being the fifth woman to serve as president of the American Psychological Association (APA), she has held presidential offices in two APA divisions (General Psychology and the Psychology of Women), the Eastern Psychological Association, the New York State Psychological Association, Psi Chi, and the International Council of Psychologists. Recipient of numerous awards and honors, Florence Denmark has been elected Fellow in seven APA divisions and was the first winner of APA's Award for Distinguished Contributions to Education and Training in Psychology. Denmark received one of the first Distinguished Leadership Awards given by APA's Committee on Women in Psychology (CWP), a Leadership Recognition Award from the Division of the Psychology of Women, and a career award from the Association for Women in Psychology.

FAMILY BACKGROUND, EDUCATION, AND CAREER DEVELOPMENT

Florence Harriet Levin was born on January 28, 1931, in Philadelphia, Pennsylvania. She grew up in a large extended family that included her parents, an older sister, grandparents, two uncles, and an aunt. Her mother, Minna Freiman Sharkis, was a musician; her father, Morris Levin, an attorney. Her sister became a physician. She credits much of her career inspiration to her mother, whom she described as the driving force behind her accomplishments (Denmark, 1988, p. 281).

She went to Roxborough High School in Philadelphia, where she was active in many extracurricular activities and excelled in her academic work. She wrote a sports column for the school paper and considered a career as a sports writer, but was discouraged by the lack of opportunity for women in that field at the time. She continued her interest in sports, describing herself as an avid sports fan (Denmark, 1988, p. 283). She was admitted to the National Honor Society and in 1948 was high school class valedictorian.

Levin entered the Women's College of the University of Pennsylvania in the fall of 1948, majoring in history. Upon discovering psychology in a laboratory course in her sophomore year, she embarked on a double major. When she graduated in 1952, she became the first student in the history of the University of Pennsylvania to earn an A.B. degree with honors in two majors—history and psychology. She also earned election to Phi Beta Kappa. She wrote her history honors thesis on Amelia Bloomer and the rise of Bloomerism. Her honors project for psychology involved research on gender and leadership styles. Later she was told that she was used as an example at the University of Pennsylvania to give the admissions committee a reason to admit more women into the program (Denmark, 1988, p. 290).

She married orthodontist Stanley Denmark in 1953 and continued her graduate training at the University of Pennsylvania, where she earned both an A.M. in psychology (1954) and a Ph.D. in social psychology (1958). Although she began her doctoral program as a clinical student, a research course in social psychology taught by Albert Pepitone led to her changing her doctoral specialty to that field.

After graduate school, Denmark lived in New York City, where she had three children, Valerie (1959), and twins, Pamela and Richard (1960). She held an adjunct teaching position at Queens College of the City University of New York (CUNY) while working in the college's counseling center sixteen hours a week. At Queens College she met Marcia Guttentag, another young mother in a part-time position who also became a well-known social psychologist. They supported each other and collaborated on many joint projects, including research on the effect of college attendance on mature women (Denmark & Guttentag, 1966), dissonance in the self and educational concepts of college and noncollege oriented women (Denmark & Guttentag, 1966, 1967), effects of racial integration in preschool programs (Denmark & Guttentag, 1969), and psychiatric labeling of immigrants (Guttentag & Denmark, 1964, 1965). The latter work was presented at the First International Congress of Social Psychiatry in London, which was the beginning of Denmark's contributions to the international literature. In addition to publishing and teaching several different courses, Denmark also supervised students in honors and independent research.

During this period, Mary Reuder, head of the Queens College evening session program in psychology, worked to obtain a full-time position for Denmark at Queens. When none was forthcoming, she recommended that Denmark apply for a position she learned was open at CUNY's Hunter College, Bronx Campus. Denmark did so, and in 1964, with six years of postdoctoral experience, she was appointed to the position of instructor.

Upon arriving at Hunter College, Denmark met Virginia Staudt Sexton, whom Denmark credits with being an important "political" mentor (Denmark, 1988, p. 290). Sexton involved Denmark in college committees and encouraged Denmark to join and become active in the many state, national, and international organizations in which she herself participated.

Denmark remained at Hunter, becoming an assistant professor in 1967, an associate professor in 1970 (with an appointment to CUNY's Graduate Center faculty), and professor in 1974. In 1984 she was named Thomas Hunter Professor in the Social Sciences, a distinguished professorship. In 1988–1989 Denmark became the first Robert Scott Pace Professor of Psychology at Pace University, an endowed chair. At the same time, she also became chair of the Pace Department of Psychology.

At Hunter, Denmark continued to conduct research related to prejudice and discrimination against women (Denmark, 1974; Starer & Denmark, 1974) and other groups (Denmark, 1971, 1972; Trachtman & Denmark, 1974), and she began to expand her research on questions relating to the psychology of women, a field just beginning to emerge (Denmark, 1976b, 1977b). She traced her involvement in this field to three sources: her early research interests in leadership styles and reentry women; the women's movement; and her teaching commitments, which required her to stay abreast of the field. In 1971 she initiated the first doctoral-level seminar on the psychology of women in the United States, a major curriculum innovation (Denmark, 1988, p. 289). The reading list of the syllabus was so comprehensive that APA's Women's Programs Office distributed it in response to inquiries from individuals who sought help in developing new courses at that time.

In addition to teaching and research Denmark chaired Hunter's Department of Academic Skills (1968–1970) and served as the first director of the SEEK program (1968–1970). SEEK (Search for Education, Elevation, and Knowledge) was created to help high school graduates from poverty areas who did not meet the usual entrance criteria to attend college. The SEEK program was a source of information about possible roles for psychologists in similar programs across the country (Denmark & Trachtman, 1974).

In 1972, as an associate professor, she became executive officer of psychology doctoral programs at CUNY's Graduate Center, a post she held until 1979. This program was the largest in the nation, with approximately 450 doctoral students and 150 faculty members. She later headed the doctoral program in personality and social psychology at the Graduate Center (1986–1987).

As Denmark's career progressed, her first marriage deteriorated, ending in separation and divorce. In 1973 she married her second husband, Robert Wesner, a publisher with Aldine Publishing Company, who was also divorced with three children: Kathleen, Michael, and Wendy. He became an important source of encouragement and support throughout her career. Her new son, Michael Wesner, became interested in psychology, earning his Ph.D. and beginning his career at the University of Chicago.

ACHIEVEMENTS AND RECOGNITION

Florence L. Denmark's career has had a significant impact on psychology through her scholarly and professional contributions in research, education, teaching, and mentoring, and through her professional leadership and advocacy. These activities have been intertwined throughout her career.

Scholar and Leader in the Psychology of Women

Denmark's scholarship and professional leadership have played a seminal role in establishing the psychology of women as a recognized and legitimate scholarly field, stimulating curriculum change as well as new research. In 1975 Florence Denmark and Julia Sherman co-chaired the first research conference specifically devoted to psychological research on women. The conference participants critically reviewed existing literature, dealt with bias in psychological theory and method, and charted future research directions for the field. The book that developed out of the conference (Sherman & Denmark, 1978) was described by E. Mavis Hetherington on the dust jacket as "an important resource for all scholars" working on the study of women. Denmark, Tangri, and McCandless' chapter on affiliation, achievement, and power motivation was identified as among the most outstanding contributions in the book (Davidson, 1980). Consideration of power and status have continued to be a defining feature of feminist psychology (Wallston, 1986).

Also in 1975, Denmark coedited *Women: Dependent or independent variable* (Unger & Denmark, 1975), which contained overviews of empirical research in seven areas relating to the psychology of women. Essays by Unger and Denmark that introduced the topics were critically reviewed as significant contributions in themselves (Pleck, 1976). The book was highly recommended as an integrated interpretive reader for both students and professionals.

Denmark documented the disadvantaged status of women in psychology (Denmark, 1979), providing evidence needed to argue for change. She wrote about the history of women's contributions to psychology to ensure that they would be preserved and serve as inspirational models for succeeding generations (Denmark, 1980a; Russo & Denmark, 1987). She also traced the emergence and legitimization of the psychology of women as a field (Denmark, 1976a, 1977a, 1979, 1981, 1987). By identifying such things as the advances, growth indicators, and contributions of the field, she validated and legitimized the field as well as individuals working in it.

Denmark's vision of the psychology of women was one of a distinct field that had separate and unique contributions to make to knowledge about women's experiences, knowledge that could then be used to enhance their status and better their lives. She saw the field as also informing other areas of psychology, challenging traditional theories and methods, and enriching the curriculum: "Even though the study of 'women' will be integrated into traditional areas, . . . both in terms of stimulating research and enriching existing courses, the psychology of women will also continue to be viable as a distinct, albeit interdependent, field" (Denmark, 1977a, p. 365).

Denmark worked to create and transform institutions of psychology so that the separate identity of psychology of women as a field would be recognized and the contributions of psychologists in it would be understood and appreciated. She was a charter member of the Association for Women in Psychology (AWP), founded in 1969. She helped found and develop Division 35 (Psychology of Women) of APA, which was established in 1973. She served as its third president from 1975 to 1976, using her negotiating and mediating skills to unify diverse feminist constituencies behind the division, broaden its scholarly base, and enhance its prestige. In the fall of 1976, the first issue of the division's new journal, the *Psychology of Women Quarterly,* was published, with Denmark among its first group of consulting editors. She also served on the editorial board of *Sex Roles,* which first appeared in 1975. Thus, she was involved in the early development of the two peer-reviewed journals in the field that gave researchers respected outlets for their work.

Denmark's contributions to the psychology of women have crossed interdisciplinary and international boundaries. As a member of the Women in Science Committee of the New York Academy of Sciences, she contributed to a conference that documented the status of women across the sciences and proposed strategies to enhance their roles (Denmark, 1979).

Denmark helped establish the International Interdisciplinary Congress on Women, first held in Israel in 1981. This was the first scholarly meeting of its kind. In her keynote address, "Women's Worlds: Ghetto, Refuge, or Power Base?," she set forth the issues involved in separation and integration of women's scholarship across the disciplines, suggesting strategies for empowering the field and the people in it internationally (Denmark, 1984). She has served on the advisory boards for subsequent congresses, which by 1987 had grown to more than 1,200 participants from fifty countries. As a result of her negotiating ability, Hunter College was chosen as the site of the fourth Congress (1990), with Denmark as co-coordinator.

Denmark has encouraged psychologists to become involved in public policy-making issues, particularly women's issues (Russo & Denmark, 1984), and she herself served on the Board of Trustees of the Association for the Advancement of Psychology, an advocacy organization representing psychology to the U.S. Congress. She also made research on the psychology of women accessible to policy makers in New York City, advocating day care as essential for women's participation in the workplace (Denmark & Rubinstein, 1976a, 1976b).

Educator, Teacher, Mentor

Invited to give a G. Stanley Hall Lecture on the psychology of women, Denmark pointed out the need for and ways of integrating such information into the introductory course (Denmark, 1983). In 1985 she published *Social/Ecological Psychology and the Psychology of Women,* which contained three papers presented at the XXIIIrd International Congress of Psychology in 1984 that examined the integration of the psychology of women into social (Denmark & Fernandez, 1985), developmental (Russo, 1985), and clinical (Kaschak, 1985) psychology courses.

Denmark helped establish both the Women's Studies Program at Hunter and the Center for the Study of Women and Society, affiliated with CUNY's Graduate Center. In 1977 she became a member of Hunter's Women's Studies Policy Committee. She participated in the Hunter College Women's Studies Collective, which developed *Women's Choices, Women's Realities* (1983), one of the first introductory texts designed for women's studies courses. The book was widely used, leading to a second edition.

Denmark recognized that her visibility made her an important role model. Her belief in the importance of role models for students, particularly students who do not fit a traditional mold, has been an important part of her professional identity: "They can see, 'Here's a woman who has made it and who has made it in research in the psychology of women.' I want students to know that, if they want to do the same, there's nothing wrong with it and they can get ahead doing it. Those who have been successful have a responsibility to reach out to others" (Denmark, 1988, pp. 290–291).

As director of the SEEK program for undergraduates, as well as faculty member of one of the largest graduate programs in the United States, Denmark has been an important role model, supporter, mentor, and research collaborator for numerous students who were members of underrepresented groups, including women, ethnic minorities, gays, and lesbians. One of the most visible of her black students was Gwen Puryear Keita, who became the third women's programs officer of the American Psychological Association. One of Denmark's high-achieving reentry students was Kathleen Grady, 1986 recipient of APA's CWP Leadership Citation in the Emerging Leader category. In addition to influencing students through her undergraduate and graduate courses, she has sponsored a multitude of honors and independent research projects. She has also chaired or been a member of more than seventy-five doctoral committees and sponsored more than twenty master's theses.

Denmark served as a mentor and role model through her participation in Psi Chi, the national honor society for psychology. She served as Hunter's Psi Chi

faculty advisor for more than twenty-five years, organizing the Hunter College
Psi Chi convention, which became an important regional meeting for the organization. Denmark held concurrent presidencies in Psi Chi and the American
Psychological Association, the only person ever to do so, which led to increased
support and exchange between the two organizations. During her Psi Chi presidency, she promoted the visibility and participation of women and ethnic minorities as members of the organization and in its programs at the APA
convention. She was instrumental in arranging its continued sponsorship of an
APA convention symposium devoted to autobiographical presentations by eminent women psychologists. Psi Chi sponsorship of those panels has continued
for more than a decade, and the panel presentations became the basis for two
books by the panel organizers (O'Connell & Russo, 1983, 1988). As a result
of her many contributions, in 1980 Denmark received Psi Chi's first national
Distinguished Service Award.

In 1987 Florence Denmark was the recipient of APA's Award for Distinguished
Contributions to Education and Training in Psychology. The language of her
citation recognizes her innovations in the curriculum and her role in the widening
opportunities for education in psychology:

Florence Denmark has been an innovator and leader in influencing education and training
so that psychology's curriculum reflects the true cultural diversity of human experience.
. . . She has played a particularly critical role in programs and activities designed to include
the new scholarship on women in both the education and training of psychologists. She
has been an advocate for changes in education and training that increase the cultural
diversity of the curriculum and open opportunity for members of all underrepresented
groups. (P. 258)

In her award address at the 1988 convention, Denmark discussed education
and training issues at undergraduate and graduate levels. She proposed a revision
of the undergraduate curriculum to include a new introductory psychology course
on the applications of psychology to oneself and to society, a course that would
recognize the fact that psychologists do important and valued work outside of
academic classrooms and laboratories. She set out her vision of a graduate
education in psychology designed to reduce schisms in knowledge across psychology's subfields and between psychology and other sciences. She advocated
a curriculum that would reflect the diversity of human experiences and be responsive to the needs of students, including ethnic minority and women students
as well as students from other nations (Denmark, 1989).

Professional Leadership

Denmark's leadership has been reflected in election to a remarkable number
of prominent positions in state, regional, national, and international organizations. As president of the New York State Psychological Association (NYSPA),

Denmark served as an important advocate for changing education and training
in psychology to increase flexibility and opportunities for students who because
of economic circumstances or family responsibilities could not attend graduate
school full time. She supported Psy.D. programs in addition to the Ph.D.,
programs for reentry students at the graduate level, and structured part-time
graduate study. Under her presidency, NYSPA established its first Committee
on Women, which later became the NYSPA Division of Women.

In 1975 the New York State Psychological Association elected Denmark to a
three-year term on the APA Council of Representatives, APA's policy-making
body. She was elected by the council to APA's Board of Directors (1977–1979).
Her impact was such that she was elected APA president—only the fifth woman
to achieve that high office—serving in 1980–1981. Denmark became the first
APA president to serve on the Executive Board of the Council of Scientific
Society Presidents (1982), where she was elected to the position of secretary
(1983–1984).

Thus, for more than seven consecutive years (1975–1982), Denmark was an
effective voice for ethnic minority and women's issues in scientific and professional psychology at APA's highest policy-making levels. During this period
APA's Women's Programs Office was established, which provided a voice,
source of expertise, and tangible resource base for women's issues in APA's
central office. APA's ethical standards were revised to specifically prohibit sexual
intimacy between client and therapist. Accreditation criteria underwent significant revision, and courses in the psychology of women were explicitly recognized
as fulfilling accreditation requirements. The critical educational role of gender
and ethnic diversity in faculty, students, and curriculum was also recognized in
these requirements, giving advocates a lever to promote change in the training
of clinical, counseling, and school psychologists. The Board for Ethnic Minority
Affairs was created, providing a voice and power base for ethnic minorities in
APA. The relationship of APA to public policy makers was reconceptualized,
and the organization carved out new roles as an active participant in policy-
making discussions of the legislative, executive, and judicial branches of government, roles that included advocating public policies that would benefit socially
and economically disadvantaged groups in American society.

At the end of her term as APA president in 1981, Robert Perloff, APA
treasurer, wrote to Denmark: "I do not recall when a Council has accomplished
so many critical items of business as this Council has done. . . . I must, in all
truth, attribute the great achievements of this Council to your desire to be fair,
your love of psychology, and your effectiveness as President and Chair of the
Council. You have left an awesome legacy."

The psychology of women attained highly visible validation in Denmark's
APA presidential address, in which she highlighted the roles and contributions
of women in psychology and linked women psychologists' invisibility and devaluation to the stereotyping and devaluation of females in the culture at large
(Denmark, 1980a).

After her APA presidency, Denmark continued to work on behalf of women's issues at APA, serving on APA's Committee on Women in Psychology (1982–1985). Among her accomplishments was the development of guidelines for eliminating sex bias in research (Denmark, Russo, Frieze, & Sechzer, 1988), which were endorsed by APA's Board of Scientific Affairs and approved as APA policy by its Council of Representatives. The guidelines were intended to help psychologists and students in psychology to develop the skills needed to identify sex bias at all stages of the research process, including question formulation, research design, data analysis and interpretation, and conclusion formulation.

Denmark also became a member of APA's Committee on International Relations (1982–1986), which sponsored programs to foster cross-cultural research on women's issues at APA conventions. She was one of two officials elected by the APA Council of Representatives to represent the United States in the International Union of Psychological Sciences (1984–1986). During this period (1983–1986) she also served on the Board of Directors of the International Council of Psychologists. She became president of that organization in 1989.

As president of the Eastern Psychological Association in 1985–1986, Denmark used her outgoing president's discretionary funds to finance an ongoing award to recognize faculty advisors who have made outstanding contributions to Psi Chi and to psychology. Under Virginia Staudt Sexton's presidency of Psi Chi, the Florence L. Denmark Faculty Advisor Award was established.

Although primarily known for her contributions in sex roles and the psychology of women, Denmark maintained her involvement in a diversity of social and public interest issues, within psychology and across the disciplines. For fourteen years (1971–1984) she was associate editor of the *International Journal of Group Tensions*. She has been named to the editorial boards of *Mind and Behavior* and *Professional Psychology* and has served as a reviewer for many other journals. From 1985 to 1988 Denmark served on the Committee on Lesbian and Gay Concerns, using her leadership skills and knowledge of the APA system to enhance the committee's effectiveness and to promote its projects, particularly to increase the participation of gays and lesbians in research and in the APA publications process.

Denmark's interdisciplinary involvement has included prominent leadership roles in the New York Academy of Sciences, which included chairing the Psychology Section (1975–1976) and serving on the Board of Governors (1977–1980). She also edited several annals published by the academy (Denmark & Salzinger, 1978; Denmark, 1980b). Denmark has continued her leadership in that organization and was elected as vice president for 1984–1987.

Her worldwide recognition is demonstrated in the more than sixty lectures and colloquia she has presented in academic institutions across the United States and internationally, including Beijing University, Hamburg University, the University of Heidelberg, and Hebrew University in Israel.

In recognition of her outstanding and sustained contributions to psychology,

Florence Denmark has been elected Fellow in seven APA Divisions: Divisions 1 (General Psychology), 2 (Teaching), 8 (Society for Personality and Social Psychology), 9 (Society for the Psychological Study of Social Issues), 31 (State Association Affairs), 35 (Psychology of Women), and 44 (Society for the Psychological Study of Lesbian and Gay Issues). She is also a Fellow of the New York Academy of Sciences and a member of the Society for Experimental Social Psychology, where membership is by invitation only and based on research performance.

Denmark is the recipient of the 1978 NYSPA Kurt Lewin Award for her accomplishments in combining research and social action, and of a 1981 Distinguished Contribution Award from the International Organization for the Study of Group Tensions. Her biography was selected for inclusion in the *Encyclopedia of Psychology,* where she is identified as a pioneer in the psychology of women and a widely recognized researcher on public interest issues (Corsini, 1984, p. 353).

Denmark is also recipient of honorary doctorates of humane letters from the Massachusetts School of Professional Psychology (1985) and from Cedar Crest College (1988). The award language of the latter paid special tribute to Denmark's mentoring contributions: "[She] brings to her relationships, personal and professional, a genuine love of people, and a sincere wish to mentor them. She gives her expertise and caring to many people; she only asks in return that these people pass on the caring and support to others."

Denmark has been recognized as an outstanding leader by APA's Division 35 (1983) and as a foremother by AWP (1984). In 1985 she and Carolyn R. Payton were the first persons to receive Distinguished Leadership Citations given by APA's Committee on Women in Psychology (CWP) in the senior awards category. In 1986 she received AWP's Distinguished Career Award for her contributions to policy, mentoring, and scholarship in the field of psychology of women. The Association for Women in Science identified her as an Outstanding Woman in Science (1980), and the Federation of Organizations for Professional Women (1980) honored her for contributions to equality for present and future women scholars.

The wording of Denmark's CWP Distinguished Leadership Citation captured her special leadership qualities and commitment to women's issues:

With genuine appreciation for her tireless commitment to the advancement of women and to teaching, research, and writing on the psychology of women. She has offered practical help and inspiration to students and colleagues through professional guidance and supportive friendship. She has used exceptional organizational skills, administrative expertise, political acumen, and humanitarian leadership to promote equality for women and ethnic minorities and to create new visions for psychologists.

REFERENCES

Corsini, R. J. (Ed.). (1984). *Wiley encyclopedia of psychology,* Vol. 1. New York: John Wiley.

Davidson, C. V. (1980). From politics to method in the psychology of women. *Contemporary Psychology, 25,* 902–903.

Denmark, F. L. (1971). Does school integration contribute to the reduction of group tensions? *International Journal of Group Tensions, 1,* 186–187.

Denmark, F. L. (1972). The effect of ethnic and social class variables on semantic differential performance. *Journal of Social Psychology, 86,* 3–9.

Denmark, F. L. (Ed.). (1974). *Who discriminates against women?* Sage Contemporary Social Science Issues Series. Beverly Hills, Calif.: Sage Publications.

Denmark, F. L. (1976a). The psychology of women: Definition and development of the field. Invited Address, Eastern Psychological Association, New York.

Denmark, F. L. (Ed.). (1976b). *Woman,* Vol. 1. New York: Psychological Dimensions.

Denmark, F. L. (1977a). The psychology of women: An overview of an emerging field. *Personality and Social Psychology Bulletin, 3,* 356–367.

Denmark, F. L. (1977b). Styles of leadership. *Psychology of Women Quarterly, 2(2),* 99–113.

Denmark, F. L. (1979). Women in psychology in the United States. In A. M. Briscoe & S. M. Pfafflin (Eds.), *Expanding the role of women in the sciences. Annals of the New York Academy of Sciences, 323,* 65–78.

Denmark, F. L. (1980a). Psyche: From rocking the cradle to rocking the boat. *American Psychologist, 35,* 1057–1065.

Denmark, F. L. (Ed.). (1980b). *Psychology: The leading edge into the unknown.* Annals of the New York Academy of Sciences. New York: New York Academy Press.

Denmark, F. L. (1981, May). Changing trends in research in the psychology of women. Paper presented at the New York Psychological Association, Monticello, N.Y.

Denmark, F. L. (1983). Integrating the psychology of women into introductory psychology. In C. J. Scheier & A. Rogers (Eds.), *The G. Stanley Hall Lecture Series, 31,* 33–75. Washington, D.C.: American Psychological Association.

Denmark, F. L. (1984). Women's worlds: Ghetto, refuge, or power base? In M. Safir, M. T. Mednick, D. Israeli, & J. Bernard (Eds.), *Women's worlds: The new scholarship.* New York: Praeger.

Denmark, F. L. (Ed.). (1985). *Social/ecological psychology and the psychology of women. Selected/revised papers. Proceedings of the XXIIIrd International Congress of Psychology, 7.* Amsterdam: North Holland.

Denmark, F. L. (1987, March). Two steps forward, one step back: A thirty year personal perspective of the psychology of women. Denver, Colo.: Association of Women in Psychology.

Denmark, F. L. (1988). Autobiography. In A. N. O'Connell & N. F. Russo (Eds.), *Models of achievement: Reflections of eminent women in psychology, Volume 2* (pp. 279–294). Hillsdale, N.J.: Erlbaum.

Denmark, F. L. (1989). Back to the future in the education and training of psychologists. *American Psychologist, 44,* 725–730.

Denmark, F. L., & Fernandez, L. C. (1985). Integrating information about the psychology of women into social psychology. In F. L. Denmark (Ed.), *Social/ecological psychology and the psychology of women* (pp. 355–368). Amsterdam: North Holland.

Denmark, F. L., & Guttentag, M. (1966). The effect of college attendance on mature women: Changes in self-concept and evaluation of student role. *Journal of Social Psychology, 69,* 155–158.

Denmark, F. L., & Guttentag, M. (1967). Dissonance in the self-concepts and educational concepts of college and non-college oriented women. *Journal of Counseling Psychology, 14*(2), 113–115.

Denmark, F. L., & Guttentag, M. (1969). Effect of integrated and non-integrated programs on cognitive change in pre-school children. *Perceptual and Motor Skills, 29,* 375–380.

Denmark, F. L., & Rubinstein, N. J. (1976a). Day care in New York City. Prepared for the Mayor's Commission on the Status of Women.

Denmark, F. L., & Rubinstein, N. J. (1976b). Resources for women in New York City. Prepared for the Mayor's Commission on the Status of Women.

Denmark, F. L.; Russo, N. F.; Frieze, I.; & Sechzer, J. (1988). *American Psychologist, 43,* 582–585.

Denmark, F. L., & Salzinger, K. (Eds.). (1978). *Psychology: The state of the art.* Annals of the New York Academy of Sciences. New York: New York Academy Press.

Denmark, F. L.; Tangri, S. S.; & McCandless, S. (1978). Affiliation, achievement, and power. In J. Sherman and F. L. Denmark (Eds.), *The psychology of women: Future directions in research.* New York: Psychological Dimensions.

Denmark, F. L., & Trachtman, J. (1974). The psychologist as a counselor in college "High Risk Programs." *Counseling Psychologist, 4*(2), 87–92.

Guttentag, M., & Denmark, F. L. (1964). The effect of Rorschach normative assumptions of the diagnostic assessment of in-migrants. Paper presented at the First International Congress of Social Psychiatry, London.

Guttentag, M., & Denmark, F. L. (1965). Psychiatric labeling: Role assignment based on the projective test performance of in-migrants. *International Journal of Social Psychiatry, 11*(2), 131–137.

Hunter College Women's Studies Collective (1983). *Women's choices, women's realities.* New York: Oxford University Press.

Kaschak, E. (1985). Integrating information about the psychology of women into the curriculum: The case for clinical psychology. In F. L. Denmark (Ed.), *Social/ ecological psychology and the psychology of women* (pp. 379–388). Amsterdam: North Holland.

O'Connell, A. N., & Russo, N. F. (Eds.). (1983). *Models of achievement: Reflections of eminent women in psychology.* New York: Columbia University Press.

O'Connell, A. N., & Russo, N. F. (Eds.). (1988). *Models of achievement: Reflections of eminent women in psychology, Volume 2.* Hillsdale, N.J.: Erlbaum.

Perloff, R. (1981). Letter to F. L. Denmark, January 26, 1981.

Pleck, J. H. (1976). Review of *Women: Dependent or independent variable?* R. K. Unger & F. L. Denmark (Eds.). *Sex Roles, 2,* 204–205.

Russo, N. F. (1985). Integrating information about the psychology of women into the teaching, research and practice of psychology: Developmental psychology. In F. L. Denmark (Ed.), *Social/ecological psychology and the psychology of women* (pp. 369–378). Amsterdam: North Holland.

Russo, N. F., & Denmark, F. L. (1984). Women, psychology and public policy: Selected issues. *American Psychologist, 39,* 1161–1165.

Russo, N. F., & Denmark, F. L. (1987). Contributions of women to psychology. *Annual Review of Psychology, 38,* 279–298.

Sherman, J. A., & Denmark, F. L. (Eds.). (1978). *The psychology of women: Future directions in research.* New York: Psychological Dimensions.

Starer, R., & Denmark, F. L. (1974). Discrimination against aspiring women. *International Journal of Group Tensions, 4,* 65–70.

Trachtman, J., & Denmark, F. L. (1974). Self-esteem and other motivational variables: Some black-white comparisons. *International Journal of Group Tensions, 4*(1), 65–70.

Unger, R. K., & Denmark, F. L. (1975). *Women: Dependent or independent variable?* New York: Psychological Dimensions.

Wallston, B. S. (1986). What's in a name revisited: Psychology of women versus feminist psychology or feminist psychology: Evolution of psychology of women. Invited address, Annual Meeting of the Association for Women in Psychology, Oakland, Calif.

ELSE FRENKEL-BRUNSWIK (1908–1958)

M. Brewster Smith

Else Frenkel-Brunswik came to the United States as part of the Jewish intellectual immigration of the Hitler years. She brought a rich European education with special qualifications both in the logical positivist philosophy of science and in psychoanalysis—both cultural gifts from her home in Vienna. Since personality and clinical psychology were just emerging in an American psychology dominated by neobehaviorism, the time was right for her contributions toward legitimizing psychoanalytic ideas. She was central to the classic research on the authoritarian personality. Her related concept of intolerance of ambiguity is a permanent contribution to the psychology of personality.

FAMILY BACKGROUND

Else Frenkel was born on August 18, 1908, in Lemberg, a Polish town that was part of the Austro-Hungarian empire. She was the second daughter of Abraham and Helene (Gelernter) Frenkel, who moved to Vienna in 1914 to escape the pogrom of that year in which Jews were randomly attacked. In Vienna Abraham Frenkel became a bank director, then owner of a private bank. Else Frenkel was educated there, graduating from the gymnasium in 1926 and in quick sequence taking her doctorate in psychology from the University of Vienna in 1930. She remained at the University of Vienna as the equivalent of assistant professor in the Psychological Institute until the *Anschluss* of 1938 that incorporated Austria into Nazi Germany.

A middle child and considered by members of her family the plainest of three sisters, Else Frenkel later attributed her intellectual achievements to her older sister's extraordinary beauty. She also referred cryptically to her "Cordelia complex" as it emerged in her psychoanalysis (Frenkel-Brunswik, 1940). Their mother was especially proud of the beautiful oldest sister and tended to baby the youngest. Else Frenkel was closest to their father, who regretted the lack of a son and appreciated her intellectual accomplishments. When she later shocked her observantly Jewish parents by her attachment and subsequent marriage to her psychologist teacher and colleague Egon Brunswik, who came from a gentile family of minor Hungarian nobility, it was her father who forgave her and maintained contact.

EDUCATION AND CAREER DEVELOPMENT

The Psychological Institute during the decade of Else Frenkel's participation was a benign but absolute monarchy presided over by Karl and Charlotte Bühler. Her dissertation with Karl Bühler sought a rapprochement between the older theories of psychological associationism and the newer Gestalt doctrines. She also assisted Charlotte Bühler in her biographical studies, which foreshadowed later research on personality in life-course perspective (see Frenkel, 1936; Frenkel & Weisskopf, 1937). A severe attack of rheumatic fever in 1932 interrupted her first venture in personal psychoanalysis after eight months and left her with a lifelong concern about her heart. It did not interfere with her subsequent capacity for assiduous work.

Frenkel-Brunswik's career as a psychologist was influenced by two of the currents that made interwar Vienna a center of European intellectual culture. One was psychoanalysis. She resumed analysis in 1937 with the renowned psychoanalytic ego psychologist Ernst Kris, terminating only when she emigrated. The other was logical positivism and the Unity of Science movement as expounded by Moritz Schlick, Rudolph Carnap, and other members of the "Vienna Circle," in which her husband-to-be also participated. Logical positivism sought a firm basis for knowledge on the basis of physicalistic observation linked to logical-mathematical deduction and elaboration. More than the ideas of the Bühlers, these intellectual sources, together with the experience of being a Jew during the Hitler years, underlay the research questions that she addressed during her two very productive decades in the United States.

Egon Brunswik had gone to the University of California at Berkeley in 1937. A philosophically and historically oriented scholar who was alien to the mechanistically behaviorist style that predominated in America, he was attractive to the cognitive behaviorist Edward Tolman, who recruited him. After the *Anschluss* that absorbed Austria into Nazi Germany, Else Frenkel joined him; they were married in New York on June 9, 1938. Nepotism rules prevented her from being considered for a tenured appointment in psychology or for any appointment on the tenure track. Instead, in 1939 she became a research psychologist in the Institute of Child Welfare (later the Institute of Human Development) at Berkeley, which remained her principal employment thereafter. As a lecturer, she often taught seminars in the psychology department, where she had devoted students, including Daniel J. Levinson, a collaborator in her work on *The Authoritarian Personality* and later a major theorist of life-span personality development.

MAJOR CONTRIBUTIONS AND THEIR IMPACT

Soon after arriving in the United States, Frenkel-Brunswik published "Mechanisms of Self-Deception" (1939), work that she had done in Vienna when first influenced by psychoanalysis. For many of its American readers, this supposedly minor paper brought the doctrines of psychoanalysis home to everyday life. In 1940 there followed her first major discussion of the bearing of psychoanalysis on the psychology of personality, her contribution to an influential symposium in which prominent psychologists commented on their own psychoanalyses (Frenkel-Brunswik, 1940). This was at the inception of the heyday of psychoanalysis in American academic psychology. That publication, which included her statement, along with those of Henry A. Murray (a founder of modern academic personality psychology) and Edwin G. Boring (the famous historian of psychology and rather hostile Harvard colleague of Murray), was a major illumination for eager acolytes who were still waiting on the outside of this attractive, arcane territory.

The time was ripe. Frenkel-Brunswik had arrived in the United States just as a new, self-conscious psychology of personality was emerging, led by Gordon Allport (Allport, 1937), Henry A. Murray (Murray et al., 1938), and Gardner Murphy (Murphy, 1947), and a new profession of clinical psychology was beginning to take form. Frenkel-Brunswik participated centrally in these developments, both very much influenced by psychoanalysis, which was and continues to be very difficult for American psychologists to assimilate. Her sophistication in both psychoanalysis and the logical positivism of the Vienna Circle enabled her to champion the scientific respectability of psychoanalytic constructions. American positivism in psychology (behaviorism) had come forth with a crass "operationism" that insisted upon limiting psychological concepts to ones closely tied to operations of measurement, thus rejecting the "speculative" and "mentalistic" formulations of psychoanalysis and other nonbehaviorist psychology. Frenkel-Brunswik (1954) was in a strong position to counter this attack.

After publishing an important monograph from the Oakland Growth Study (Frenkel-Brunswik, 1942), one of three classical longitudinal studies at the Institute of Child Welfare, showing how clinical ratings of adolescents' underlying drives could bring discrepant data from self-reports and ratings of social behavior into congruence, she joined forces with Nevitt Sanford and Daniel Levinson (then their student) in designing and launching major studies of anti-Semitism. In 1945 the American Jewish Committee supported an expansion of these studies if Theodor Adorno, a prominent emigré scholar of the Frankfort School, could join the group. Publication in 1950 of the resulting book, *The Authoritarian Personality* (Adorno, Frenkel-Brunswik, Levinson, & Sanford, 1950), was a major event in psychology and the social sciences.

The California investigators, to put it figuratively, set out to track a jackal and found themselves at grips with behemoth. They found, first of all, that anti-Semitism, far from being an isolated though unrespectable psychological phenomenon, is an integral component of a general "ethnocentric ideology." Ethnocentrism, when they pursued it, turned out to be the expression of a distinctive "authoritarian personality structure" whose unadmitted needs and defenses it serves. The central contribution of the book was the thorough empirical elucidation of this pattern of personality organization, along lines that converge strikingly with the more speculative formulations of Erich Fromm and Jean-Paul Sartre.

Briefly, the authoritarian personality syndrome that emerged characterizes the basically weak and dependent person who has sacrificed his or her capacity for genuine experience of self and others in order to maintain a precarious sense of order and safety. In the type case, authoritarians confront with a facade of spurious strength a world in which rigidly stereotyped categories are substituted for the affectionate and individualized experience of which they are incapable. Such persons, estranged from inner values, lack self-awareness and shun intraception. Their judgments are governed by a punitive conventional moralism, reflecting external standards in which they remain insecure since they have failed to make them really their own. Their relations with others depend on considerations of power, success, and adjustment, in which people figure as means rather than as ends, and achievement is not valued for its own sake. In their worlds, the good, the powerful, and the in-group stand in fundamental opposition to the immoral, the weak, the out-group. For all that they seek to align themselves with the former, their underlying feelings of weakness and self-contempt commit them to a constant and embittered struggle to prove to themselves and others that they really belong to the strong and good. Prejudice against out-groups of all kinds and colors is a direct corollary of this personality structure (Smith, 1950).

In addition to her central role in the conception of the studies, Frenkel-Brunswik contributed to the book the systematic analysis of clinical interviews that distinguished between highly prejudiced and unprejudiced persons. The research was widely acclaimed for bringing the clinical insights of psychoanalysis and the empirical methods of American social psychology jointly to bear on the study of prejudice and proto-fascist attitudes, and for presenting a well-developed model of the relations between childrearing, character structure, and ideology. It was sharply criticized for overplaying the characterological roots of prejudice as compared with class- or situation-based sources, for focusing on authoritarianism of the right to the neglect of left authoritarianism (the Cold War was just beginning), and for a variety of technical flaws (see especially Christie & Jahoda, 1954). Identifying and correcting the latter so preoccupied psychologists in the ensuing decade that the prevailing focus of research turned elsewhere before the substantive issues raised by the research had been adequately clarified. Yet the book had been firmly established as a classic of American social science.

Almost four decades later the issues dealt with by Frenkel-Brunswik and her colleagues were resurrected. A lone researcher in Canada, Bob Altemeyer (1981, 1988) did the hard work to put the measurement of right-wing authoritarianism on a firm basis. His work is cast in terms of Albert Bandura's social learning theory (Bandura, 1986) rather than of Frenkel-Brunswik's psychoanalysis, yet most of the syndrome of authoritarianism displayed by Frenkel-Brunswik and her colleagues at Berkeley is confirmed. There *are* some people who tend to kowtow to those whom they regard as their superiors, to lord it over their inferiors, and to stand rigidly and punitively for conventional morality. Else Frenkel-Brunswik's concerns once again have drawn attention.

In addition to her major part in *The Authoritarian Personality*, Frenkel-Brunswik conducted related research on prejudice in children (Frenkel-Brunswik, 1948), wrote on intolerance of ambiguity as a cognitive style of personality that emerged saliently in her studies of prejudice (Frenkel-Brunswik, 1949), and began a major study of aging in the postwar years before her life crumbled.

PERSONAL TRAGEDY

Else and Egon Brunswik were devoted to each other in a childless marriage. On July 7, 1955, near the end of her year as a Fellow of the Center for Advanced Study in the Behavioral Sciences at Stanford, Egon Brunswik ended a long and painful experience of severe hypertension by suicide. The loss to Else Frenkel-Brunswik was heartbreaking and permanently disruptive. A year as Fulbright Fellow at the University of Oslo did not put her world back together. Her husband's death coincided with profound mid-life doubts about both psycho-analysis and logical positivism as pillars of her intellectual life. She had continued for several years to mine the rich ore of *The Authoritarian Personality*; now an inner intellectual crisis became an integral aspect of her personal crisis.

Meanwhile, with the nepotism barrier removed, her colleagues in psychology at Berkeley sought to obtain a full professorship for her in recognition of her eminence in child and developmental psychology, psychoanalytic theory, and personality and cognition; the appointment was endorsed unanimously by the full professors on December 4, 1957. The recognition (which would have taken effect the following July) came too late, and although she welcomed her col-leagues' support, it in no way compensated for her sense of loss—nor, indeed, did it assuage her bitterness about aspects of her career that were attendant upon her female role. Despondent over the death of her husband and discouraged over her career, Else Frenkel-Brunswik died of an overdose of barbital on March 31, 1958, in her fiftieth year.

SIGNIFICANCE OF ACHIEVEMENTS

Else Frenkel-Brunswik was a major figure in the post–World War II emergence of personality and clinical psychology. Her chapter (Frenkel-Brunswik, 1951) in a mainstream presentation of "new look" perceptual theory (Blake & Ramsey, 1951) was a solid contribution to that passing wave relating personality to pro-cesses in what later became cognitive psychology. Her enduring significance in psychology is attested by her inclusion in the biographies of *Notable American Women* (Sicherman & Green, 1980) and by the publication of a selection of her major papers by Heiman and Grant (1974), who also provide her full bibliography and biographical material. In the introduction to their collection, one of the great American integrators of psychology at mid-century, Gardner Murphy (1974), commented as follows about Else Frenkel-Brunswik as "a person intensely loved by those who knew her, and reverently admired by thousands who knew her work":

First, she was a vital and vigorous expression of the cultural science tradition of the German-speaking world as known since the eighteenth century, richly expressive of the belief that there is a kind of science that is truly science, which is concerned with thought and aspiration as well as with the movement of bodies in space. Her writings on psychoanalysis move early and naturally into writings on politics and value systems, for she is at home in them all. She belonged to the Vienna that harbored and nourished these writings to an extraordinary development in the period between the two world wars, and she brought valuable seedlings to our American intellectual soil.

Second, she was profoundly concerned with bringing this powerful scientific tool, in which child development, psychoanalysis, history, and the social sciences all played their part, into contact with the great social illnesses of the day that are related to the irrationalities and hatreds characteristic of our time. She will probably be best known for her role in the study of the authoritarian personality. The fact remains, however, that this was merely one expression of an overriding, personal, and moral concern which lived in her all the years of her Viennese, and especially all the years of her Berkeley existence.

Thirty years after her early death, Else Frenkel-Brunswik remains an inspiring figure whose contributions to psychology are major, and whose intellectual and social commitments provide a model for her successors.

NOTE

This chapter is revised and expanded from Smith (1980). As that source indicates, I draw on correspondence and other communication with Frenkel-Brunswik's sisters, Johanna Urabin and Marta Fischler, when they were alive, and with Hedda Bolgar, Donald T. Campbell, Norma Haan, Nanette Heiman, Murray Jarvik, Marie Jahoda-Albu, Daniel J. Levinson, Read Tuddenham, Ann Vollmar, and Edith Weisskopf-Joelson, and from personal acquaintance. My correspondence is on file at the Arthur and Elizabeth Schlesinger Library on the History of Women in America, Radcliffe College, and in duplicate at the Archives of the History of American Psychology, University of Akron.

REFERENCES

Adorno, T. W.; Frenkel-Brunswik, E.; Levinson, D. J.; & Sanford, R. N. (1950). *The authoritarian personality*. New York: Harper.

Allport, G. W. (1937). *Personality: A psychological interpretation*. New York: Holt, 1937.

Altemeyer, B. (1981). *Right-wing authoritarianism*. Winnipeg, Manitoba: University of Manitoba Press.

Altemeyer, B. (1988). *Enemies of freedom: Understanding right-wing authoritarianism*. San Francisco: Jossey-Bass.

Bandura, A. (1986). *Social foundations of thought and action*. Englewood Cliffs, N.J.: Prentice-Hall.

Blake, R. R., & Ramsey, G. V. (Eds.). (1951). *Perception: An approach to personality*. New York: Ronald Press.

Christie, R., & Jahoda, M. (1954). *Studies in the scope and method of "The authoritarian personality."* Glencoe, Il.: Free Press.

Frenkel, E. (1936). Studies in biographical psychology. *Character and Personality, 5,* 1–34.

Frenkel, E., & Weisskopf, E. (1937). Wunsch und Pflicht in Aufbau des Menschlichen Lebens. *Psychologische Forschungen über den Lebenslauf,* Vol. 1. C. Bühler & E. Frenkel (Eds.). Vienna: Gerold.

Frenkel-Brunswik, E. (1939). Mechanisms of self-deception. *Journal of Social Psychology, 10,* 409–420.

Frenkel-Brunswik, E. (1940). Psychoanalysis and personality research. In Symposium on Psychoanalysis as Seen by Analyzed Psychologists. *Journal of Abnormal and Social Psychology, 35,* 176–197.

Frenkel-Brunswik, E. (1942). Motivation and behavior. *Genetic Psychology Monographs, 26,* 121–265.

Frenkel-Brunswik, E. (1948). A study of prejudice in children. *Human Relations, 1,* 295–306.

Frenkel-Brunswik, E. (1949). Intolerance of ambiguity as an emotional and perceptual personality variable. *Journal of Personality, 18,* 108–143.

Frenkel-Brunswik, E. (1951). Personality theory and perception. In R. R. Blake & G. V. Ramsey (Eds.), *Perception: An approach to personality*. New York: Ronald Press.

Frenkel-Brunswik, E. (1954). Psychoanalysis and the unity of science. *Proceedings of the American Academy of Arts and Sciences, 80,* 273–347.

Heiman, N., & Grant, M. (Eds.). (1974). *Else Frenkel-Brunswik: Selected papers. Psychological Issues, 8(3)*. New York: International Universities Press.

Murphy, G. (1947). *Personality: A biosocial approach to origins and structure*. New York: Harper.

Murphy, G. (1974). Foreword. In N. Heiman & M. Grant (Eds.), *Else Frenkel-Brunswik: Selected papers. Psychological Issues, 8(3)*. New York: International Universities Press.

Murray, H. A., et al. (1938). *Explorations in personality*. New York: Oxford University Press.

Sicherman, B., & Green, C. H. (Eds.). (1980). *Notable American women: The modern period. A biographical dictionary*. Cambridge, Mass.: Harvard University Press.

Smith, M. B. (1950). Review of T. W. Adorno, E. Frenkel-Brunswik, D. J. Levinson, & R. N. Sanford, *The authoritarian personality. Journal of Abnormal and Social Psychology, 45,* 775–779.

Smith, M. B. (1980). Else Frenkel-Brunswik. In B. Sicherman & C. H. Green, *Notable American women: The modern period* (pp. 250–252). Cambridge, Mass.: Harvard University Press.

Additional Representative Publications by Else Frenkel-Brunswik

Frenkel-Brunswik, E. (1952). Interaction of psychological and sociological factors in political behavior. *American Political Science Review, 46,* 44–65.
Frenkel-Brunswik, E. (1954). Environmental controls and the impoverishment of thought. In C. J. Friedrich (Ed.), *Totalitarianism* (pp. 171–202). Cambridge, Mass.: Harvard University Press.

Additional Publications About Else Frenkel-Brunswik

Levinson, D. J. (1968). Frenkel-Brunswik, Else. In D. L. Sills (Ed.), *International encyclopedia of the social sciences, 5,* 559–562. New York: Macmillan and Free Press.

ANNA FREUD (1895–1982)

Reuben Fine

In a survey of psychiatrists and psychoanalysts conducted to identify outstanding colleagues, Anna Freud was the name most often mentioned by both groups (Rogow, 1970). Although she never obtained a formal degree other than a teacher training diploma, she made pioneer contributions to psychoanalysis, child analysis, ego psychology, and research methodology and was a leader in both the Vienna and British psychoanalytic societies. She was instrumental in the relocation of her psychoanalytic colleagues from Nazi Germany and in the post–World War II reconstruction of psychoanalysis. She founded the influential Hampstead Center for the Psychoanalytical Study and Treatment of Children, where she explored innovative research techniques to complement classical psychoanalytic methods. She was the recipient of numerous honors, including ten honorary doctorates. Her work continues to be the foundation of one of the three current schools of thought in child psychoanalysis.

FAMILY BACKGROUND AND EDUCATION

Anna Freud, the youngest of six children, was born to Sigmund and Martha Bernays Freud in Vienna, Austria, on December 3, 1895. Little is known about the details of her childhood. She attended the Cottage Lyceum, but did not distinguish herself at school and did not pursue a formal academic education. As the youngest child in the family, she acquired a special position next to her father. She was the only child in the family who took an interest in her father's work. By the time Anna Freud was fourteen, she was "sitting on a 'little' library ladder in the corner" at the regular meetings of the Vienna Psychoanalytic Society (Young-Bruehl, 1988). After her sister, Sophie, married in 1913, Anna Freud remained as the only unmarried daughter at home and became her father's secretary.

Stimulated by the contributions of Maria Montessori, she trained to be an elementary school teacher (Solnit, 1983). Before World War I she studied in

England, which helped to equip her for her later mastery of the language. In 1918 she took her final teacher's examination.

Then, in 1918 at age twenty-two, came the decisive turning point: analysis by her father, Sigmund Freud. Just as his self-analysis was the turning point in his own career, analysis by him became the turning point for Anna Freud. As her father's daughter, secretary, and later nursemaid, her personal and professional life was intertwined with his (Dyer, 1983).

In her autobiography, written in 1964 on the occasion of being granted an honorary Sc.D. from Jefferson Medical College, Anna Freud wrote:

I share, in fact, with all other lay analysts the lack of medical education. . . . We were trained by our personal analysis, by extensive reading, by our own, unsupervised efforts with our first patients, and by lively interchange of ideas and discussions of problems with our elders and contemporaries. At the time, my own analytic apprenticeship seemed a haphazard affair to me, following no clear line.

Anna Freud's first attendance at a psychoanalytic meeting was in 1918, at Budapest. Then she began attending the weekly scientific meetings of the Vienna Psychoanalytic Society. She stated that her teaching career lasted from age nineteen to twenty-four, with about eighteen months between her decision to become a psychoanalyst and giving up her position as a school teacher. She was involved in the "children's trains" that took starving Austrian children abroad under the auspices of international aid agencies. She played a role in translating the early work of Sigmund Freud into English (S. Freud, 1954), and later his complete psychological works (S. Freud, 1976).

Her interest in child analysis began in The Hague in 1920, when Hermine Hug-Hellmuth, the first child analyst, read a paper entitled "On the Technique of Child Analysis" (Hug-Hellmuth, 1921). Both Anna Freud and Melanie Klein gave credit to Hug-Hellmuth for her early contributions (Dyer, 1983; Peters, 1985).

Anna Freud's first professional contact outside her father's immediate circle was with Lou Andreas-Salome, in 1920. Sigmund Freud sent her to Andreas-Salome for analysis, and this relationship developed into a lifelong correspondence (Peters, 1985). Anna Freud had begun to show a tendency to asceticism, which her father commented on at one point (Dyer, 1983; Peters, 1985).

From 1930 to her death, Anna Freud's closest friend and constant companion was Dorothy Burlingham, a wealthy American woman who arrived in Vienna in 1925 from the United States, bringing her son for a consultation with Anna Freud. Her son became one of Anna's first patients. Burlingham herself trained with Sigmund Freud and became one of the earliest and staunchest members of Vienna's "Child Analysis School." Anna Freud and Dorothy Burlingham lived together and devoted their lives to the cause of psychoanalysis (Dyer, 1983).

In 1922 Anna Freud applied and was accepted for membership to the Vienna Psychoanalytic Society. Her membership paper, "Beating Fantasies and Daydreams" (A. Freud, 1922), derived from Freud's 1919 paper, "A Child Is Being Beaten." The paper consisted of a detailed presentation of an elaborate daydream and its numerous variants, together with an analytic demonstration of the roots of the daydream in a masochistic beating fantasy.

That same year, Sigmund Freud wrote his revolutionary paper on ego psychology, "The Ego and the Id," published in 1923. Later Anna Freud was to contribute substantial innovations in ego psychology (A. Freud, 1936).

In 1923 Freud contracted cancer of the palate, which became terminal. Even though her mother was still alive and apparently well, it was Anna Freud who helped her father physically by adjusting his dental prosthesis and tending to other personal chores for the next sixteen years. In spite of the inextricability of their lives, Anna Freud withheld all public display of emotion when her father died in 1939 (Dyer, 1983).

CAREER AND CONTRIBUTIONS

Anna Freud's career has two parts, the first in Vienna, the second in London. In 1923 she established her private practice of psychoanalysis in Vienna. In 1924, two years after acceptance into the Vienna Psychoanalytic Society, Anna Freud replaced Otto Rank on its Executive Committee; by 1925 she chaired the society, a position she held until 1938. In 1925 she also joined the Vienna Psychoanalytic Training Institute, which was headed by Helene Deutsch, where she served as secretary. In 1926 she became the general secretary of the International Psychoanalytic Association; and in 1938 its vice president. In 1955 she was nominated for president of that organization but declined to accept it (Dyer, 1983; Peters, 1985).

From the very beginning, Anna Freud specialized in the treatment of children. In 1926 she and Dorothy Burlingham opened a small private school in Vienna, which operated until the rise of Hitler. Her Seminar on Children, given in 1926 and 1927, was attended by a variety of intellectuals, including members of Montessori's group from Germany and Austria. In 1926 she presented her first series of lectures on child psychoanalysis at the Vienna Psychoanalytic Institute. There were four lectures, dealing with (1) preparation for analysis; (2) methods of child analysis; (3) the role of transference in child analysis; and (4) child analysis and child upbringing (A. Freud, 1927). Her book on child analysis, published in 1926, was translated into English under the title *Introduction to the Technique of Child Analysis* (A. Freud, 1929). In 1975 it was reprinted as a series of classics in child development. For the rest of her life Anna Freud honed and refined her ideas and her techniques, thus advancing considerably the understanding of the child's development that can come out of the therapeutic situation.

The publication of that book was a personal, professional, and public milestone for her as well as for the development of child analysis as a prominent subspecialty of psychoanalysis and of child psychology and child study generally. It was later reviewed and revised by Joseph Sandler and reissued in the form of a discussion with Anna Freud and Joseph Sandler (Sandler, Kennedy, & Tyson, 1980).

In 1936 Anna Freud published her classic work *The Ego and the Mechanisms of Defense,* in which she set forth the important facets of the psychology of the ego. The book was immediately hailed as a major contribution and translated into a number of languages. It is still one of the core works on psychoanalytic ego psychology. Anna Freud herself compared her work to Heinz Hartmann's, indicating that their works marked the transition from the earliest psychoanalytic observations on the repression of the body and allied pleasures, to an emphasis on an orderly lifestyle in which the human being can find greatest fulfillment (Dyer, 1983). It was also later reviewed and revised by Joseph Sandler and reissued in the form of a discussion between Anna Freud and Joseph Sandler as *The Analysis of Defense: The Ego and the Mechanisms of Defense Revisited* (Sandler & A. Freud, 1985).

With the advent of Hitler and the world crisis culminating in World War II, another convulsion in her life had to be surmounted. In 1938 the Nazis invaded Austria, and Vienna was no longer safe for Jews. A day of Gestapo interrogation of Anna Freud persuaded her father to consent to leave Austria, despite his age and terminal illness. With Marie Bonaparte's help, the family relocated to England, where they settled in Marsefield Gardens, in Hampstead. Anna Freud lived to see four of her aunts perish at Auschwitz and the entire psychoanalytic establishment of Europe destroyed.

After World War II she was to play an important role in rebuilding that establishment. She joined the British Psychoanalytic Society and continued her scientific work. First there was the matter of getting as many analysts out of Europe as possible. She succeeded in helping to save a great many, and the initial postwar reconstruction of psychoanalysis was based largely on the work of these refugees in England and America. These were her *sorgenkinder,* whose travails took up much of her energy.

Then she devoted herself to the disturbed children in England. There were two aspects of her work here. One was the continuation of her therapeutic work with children. At the site of the family house at Marsefield Gardens, she and Dorothy Burlingham established the Hampstead Wartime Nursery for Homeless Children, which also served as a child research laboratory. This work is described in *Young Children in War-Time* (Burlingham & A. Freud, 1942), *War and Children* (A. Freud & Burlingham, 1943), and *Infants Without Families* (A. Freud & Burlingham, 1944). These important books challenged preconceptions about younger children's reactions to the destruction around them, emphasizing the greater importance of the effect of separation from loved ones.

The Hampstead Child Therapy Clinic was the descendant of the Hampstead nurseries. The clinic was established to study children and to train therapists in child psychoanalysis (out of deference to the American obsessive rejection of the term "lay analysis" she maintained the word "therapy" in the clinic title, however). Its first course was offered in 1947, and with the acquisition of a suitable building in London, the clinic formally opened five years later (Kennedy, 1978).

Organizationally, the Hampstead Clinic became an analytic training institute where most of the patients were children. Accordingly, application was made in 1972 to secure study group status for Hampstead. An agreement on shared courses was made with the British Psychoanalytic Society, and the Hampstead Clinic became known as the Hampstead Center for the Psychoanalytical Study and Treatment of Children, offering facilities for treatment, research, analytic training, and education. Research was enhanced by its detailed categorization and classification system of psychoanalytic material in therapists' reports called the Hampstead Index (Sandler, 1962). She remained the director of the clinic until her death.

After Anna Freud's arrival in England, where psychoanalysis had been dominated for twenty years by Ernest Jones, three schools of thought evolved. One was the Anna Freud School, the second Melanie Klein's, and the third the middle or eclectic group. This division remains in effect at the writing of this biography. It is a tribute to the British that these three disparate schools of thought, which involved sharp differences in technique, could remain united in one society. The kindliness, lack of disputatiousness, and nonauthoritarian personality of Anna Freud played a major role in the maintenance of one undivided national body. This was in itself a considerable achievement. Continuing in her father's humanistic tradition (Fine, forthcoming; Gedo & Pollock, 1976), she wrote in 1948 in the Introduction to Hans Sachs' book *Masks of Love and Life*, "Psychoanalytic psychology meant, above all, the means to inquire into the daily behavior of human beings, into their relations with each other and with their chosen love-objects, as well as into their attitudes toward the inevitable problems of life and death."

After the war, she also helped found and subsequently served as editor of *The Psychoanalytic Study of the Child*. This highly prestigious series of annuals encouraged the development of ego psychology and reported work on psychoanalytic theory, therapy, and research.

With the resumption of peacetime "harmony" she began traveling and made a number of trips to the United States. In 1960 she gave a series of lectures, "Four Contributions to the Psychoanalytic Study of the Child," in which she examined (1) the assessment of normality; (2) the assessment of pathology; (3) the therapeutic possibilities; and (4) the status of child analysis. These lectures eventually led to the publication of another great work, *Normality and Pathology in Childhood* (1965), which continued her earlier lines of thought. In this book she distinguished six "developmental lines," implying that such developmental lines could be given for all normal functions, such as eating, sleeping, sexual growth, love, and learning. Although her theorizing paid relatively little attention to the conflict that arises between mother and child, she described developmental lines and a normal developmental profile, laying the basis for a normal life. This concept, together with Sandler's (1962) elaboration of the Hampstead Index, marked a significant step in developing psychoanalytic theory about childhood based on actual observation. In the early 1960s she became involved with students of the law in the study and teaching of family law and conflicts regarding child placement (Goldstein, A. Freud, & Solnit, 1979a, 1979b; Goldstein, A. Freud, Solnit, et al., 1986).

EVALUATION OF ACHIEVEMENTS AND CONTRIBUTIONS

The collected works of Anna Freud have been published in eight volumes titled *The Writings of Anna Freud* by International Universities Press from 1965 through 1981. A number of works have always been available in single form as well. A signal contribution of Anna Freud was to systematize an approach to the therapy of children, parallel to the analysis of adults, but with variations that made allowance for the child's immaturity. One basis for her historical battle against Melanie Klein is related to this approach, which specifically revolved around the question of whether the child developed a true transference. Anna Freud felt that children were too young to shift away from the original family members, whereas Klein held that they could be analyzed through their transference-resistance reactions in much the same way as adults were analyzed. Freud also believed in the use of educational devices with both child and parent, while Klein stuck strictly to analytic methods. Among Freud's interesting innovations were using play materials and visiting the child at home.

Anna Freud's classic work *The Ego and the Mechanisms of Defense* (1936), mentioned above, was described by Harvard scholar Robert Coles as "one of the most important psychoanalytic books ever written" (*New York Times,* 1982, p. 1301), and it continues to be one of the core works on psychoanalytic ego psychology.

Among her most important contributions after 1936 was her concept of developmental lines, in which she elaborated more fully the basic theory of psychosexual development, and her discussions of normality and pathology in childhood. But she remained interested in all aspects of classical analysis and wrote extensively on a wide variety of subjects, including difficulties in psychoanalytic training and assessment (1971).

Her honors include the Dolly Madison Award for Outstanding Service to Children and Austria's Grand Decoration of Honour of Gold. She was awarded ten honorary doctorates, including the LL.D. (from Clark University and the University of Sheffield), the Sc.D. (from the University of Chicago, Harvard University, Jefferson Medical College, and Yale University), and the M.D. (from the University of Vienna). In 1978, on the occasion of being awarded an honorary D.Sc. by Columbia University, President Will J. McGill proclaimed that "from her observations have come an extraordinary series of scientific contributions." Despite such recognition, her American psychoanalyst colleagues did not regard her as a true psychoanalyst because she did not have a medical degree.

Anna Freud died on October 9, 1982, not long before her eighty-seventh birthday. She was universally mourned, and numerous tributes poured forth. That year, in a special issue of the *International Journal of Psychoanalysis,* Clifford Yorke wrote that her death

brought to a close the distinguished career of one of the great scientific leaders of our time, and one whose impact and influence will continue to be felt as long as a science of the mind survives. . . . Both father and daughter shared the same rigorous honesty and dedication to the pursuit of truth. . . . It is sad to reflect that many of our younger readers will never have met the remarkable woman whose work we commemorate today. Perhaps these contributions will convey something of the legacy they have been lucky enough to inherit, and on which they themselves may hope to build.

NOTE

The editors would like to thank Melinda Deacon, Nora Villagomez, and Brenda Lee, and Deborah Blouin of Hayden Library of Arizona State University for assistance in obtaining materials in the revision and editing of this manuscript.

REFERENCES

Anna Freud, Psychoanalyst, Dies at 86. (1982). *New York Times Biographical Service,* October, 1301–1302.

Burlingham, D., & Freud, A. (1942). *Young children in war-time: A year's work in a residential war nursery.* London: Allen & Unwin.

Dyer, R. (1983). *Her father's daughter: The works of Anna Freud.* New York: Aronson.

Fine, R. (forthcoming). *The history of psychoanalysis* (2nd ed.). New York: Continuum Press.

Freud, A. (1922). "Beating fantasies and daydreams." In Vol. 1 of *The writings of Anna Freud.* New York: International Universities Press, 1974.

Freud, A. (1926). *Introduction to psychoanalysis for teachers.* London: Allen & Unwin.

Freud, A. (1927). "Four lectures on psychoanalysis." In Vol. 1 of *The writings of Anna Freud.* New York: International Universities Press, 1974.

Freud, A. (1929). *Introduction to the technique of child analysis.* Nervous and Mental Disease Monograph Series, No. 48. New York: Nervous and Mental Disease Publishers. Reprinted as A. Freud (1975), *Classics in child development: Translation of "Einfuhrung in die technik der kinderanalyses."* New York: Arno Press.

Freud, A. (1936). *The ego and the mechanisms of defense.* (rev. ed.). Vol. 2 of *The writings of Anna Freud.* New York: International Universities Press, 1966.

Freud, A. (1965–81). *The Writings of Anna Freud.* Vols. 1–8. New York: International Universities Press.

Freud, A. (1965). *Normality and pathology of childhood.* Vol. 6 of *The writings of Anna Freud.* New York: International Universities Press, 1965.

Freud, A. (1971). *Problems of psychoanalytic training, diagnosis and the technique of therapy, 1966–1970.* New York: International Universities Press.

Freud, A., & Burlingham, D. (1943). *War and children.* New York: Medical War Books.

Freud, A., & Burlingham, D. (1944). *Infants without families: The case for and against residential nurseries*. London: Allen & Unwin.

Freud, S. (1923). *The ego and the id. Standard edition, 19*, 3–66.

Freud, S. (1954). *The origins of psychoanalysis: Letters to Wilhelm Fliess, drafts and notes, 1887-*. New York: Basic Books. Edited by M. Bonaparte, A. Freud, & E. Kris, in German; translated by E. Mosbacher & J. Strachey.

Freud, S. (1976). *The complete psychological works: Standard edition*. Vols. 1–24. New York: W. W. Norton, 1976. Edited and translated by J. Strachey in collaboration with A. Freud, and assisted by A. Strachey & A. Tysson.

Gedo, J. E., & Pollock, G. H. (1976). Freud, the fusion of science and humanism: The intellectual history of psychoanalysis. New York: International Universities Press.

Goldstein, J.; Freud, A.; & Solnit, A. (1979a). *Beyond the best interests of the child*. New York: Free Press.

Goldstein, J.; Freud, A.; & Solnit, A. (1979b). *Before the best interests of the child*. New York: Free Press.

Goldstein, J.; Freud, A.; Solnit, A., et al. (1986). *In the best interests of the child*. New York: Free Press.

Hug-Hellmuth, H. von (1921). On the technique of child analysis. *International Journal of Psychoanalysis, 2*.

Kennedy, H. (1978). The Hampstead Centre for the Psychoanalytic Study and Treatment of Children. *Bulletin of the Hampstead Clinic, 1, 7*.

Peters, U. H. (1985). *Anna Freud: A life dedicated to children*. New York: Schocken Books.

Rogow, A. (1970). *The psychiatrists*. New York: Putnam's.

Sachs, H. (1948). *Masks of love and life: The philosophical basis of psychoanalysis*. Cambridge, Mass.: Sci-ART.

Sandler, J. (1962). The Hampstead Index as an instrument for psychoanalytic research. *International Journal of Psychoanalysis, 43*, 287–291.

Sandler, J., & Freud, A. (1985). *The analysis of defense: The ego and the mechanisms of defense revisited*. New York: International Universities Press.

Sandler, J.; Kennedy, H.; & Tyson, R. L. (1980). *The technique of child psychoanalysis: Discussions with Anna Freud*. Cambridge, Mass.: Harvard University Press.

Solnit, A. J. (1983). Anna Freud, 1895–1982. *American Journal of Psychiatry, 140*(12), 1632–1633.

Young-Bruehl, E. (1988). *Anna Freud*. New York: Summit Books.

ELEANOR JACK GIBSON (1910–   )

Fairfid M. Caudle

Eleanor Jack Gibson is widely recognized for her studies with the visual cliff that demonstrated the primacy of depth perception (E. J. Gibson & Walk, 1960; Walk & Gibson, 1961), one of a long list of achievements. Gibson's early work influenced the study of verbal learning through modifying a Hullian perspective to encompass human learning. She has made substantive theoretical and empirical contributions to the psychology of reading, defined the field of perceptual learning, and stimulated the study of perceptual development. Through extending the concepts of ecological psychology to the study of perceptual development in infancy, she has established an entire field.

Her numerous awards include the Distinguished Scientific Contribution Award (1968) and the Gold Medal Award (1986) from the American Psychological Association, and the Distinguished Scientific Contribution Award (1981) from the Society for Research in Child Development. She was elected to the National Academy of Education (1972) and the American Academy of Arts and Sciences (1977) and is one of the few women elected to the National Academy of Sciences (1971).

FAMILY BACKGROUND AND EDUCATION

Gibson has described her childhood as occurring in "an atmosphere of middle-class respectability" and has wondered herself how she "managed to break away so far from this background and emerge as an intellectual" (E. J. Gibson, 1980, p. 239). She was born December 7, 1910, in Peoria, Illinois. Her father, William Alexander Jack, was a businessman specializing in wholesale hardware. Her mother, Isabel Grier Jack, was not employed outside the home. While her father did not complete college, her mother was a graduate of Smith College, as were three aunts. Her only sibling, Emily Jack, was born five years after her on September 27, 1916, and also went on to a career.

After finishing grade school at age twelve, Eleanor Jack went on to high school, where she found it beneficial to conceal her high grades from boyfriends

(E. J. Gibson, 1980). This exemplified a pattern that would often be followed in later years: minimizing her accomplishments while continuing to pursue them.

Jack continued the family tradition of attending Smith College, in Northampton, Massachusetts, where she majored in psychology and received a B.A. in 1931. The challenging atmosphere and intellectual stimulation of Smith College, a woman's college, were very important in her development. At Smith she was encouraged to become a scholar, to think independently, and to act on her own initiative. She was encouraged to follow any intellectual pathway that interested her.

Several of Jack's teachers at Smith had studied with originators of major schools or perspectives in psychology or were instrumental in defining central problems, and their influence on Jack would later become evident. Margaret Curti, Jack's teacher in courses on animal psychology and child psychology, had completed her own Ph.D. under Harvey Carr, a founder of the functionalist school, while Harold Israel, Jack's professor for a course on history and systems of psychology, had been a student of Edwin Boring, the eminent historian of psychology (E. J. Gibson, 1980). Throughout her career Eleanor Jack Gibson's work has exhibited a strong functionalist flavor, focusing on perception during development as an adaptive process, and she has addressed contemporary issues so as to demonstrate their continuity with issues important in the history of psychology.

One of the luminaries on the Smith faculty at that time was Kurt Koffka, a founder of Gestalt psychology. He taught a course on dynamic factors in perception and also taught a seminar, attended by both students and faculty, which Eleanor Jack later attended as a graduate student. Smith psychology faculty who were interested in what are today called cognitive topics attended as much for the opportunities for discussion among themselves as for contact with Koffka. Koffka's influence on Jack stemmed not from his prowess as a teacher but rather from the breadth of his theory and the fact that it seemed to approach the way "people really perceived things" (E. J. Gibson & Levin, 1979, p. 238).

By far the most influential mentor during Jack's studies at Smith was the experimental psychologist James J. Gibson, whom she met at the end of her junior year. Her interest in him was both personal (she later married him) and academic, in that his course on advanced experimental psychology led her to conclude that she wanted to do graduate work in psychology (E. J. Gibson, 1980).

Eleanor Jack's pursuit of a Ph.D. in psychology was tempered by the financial realities of the Great Depression, and, in order to continue toward this goal, she employed a strategy that she would eventually use a number of times, namely, accepting a lesser short-term goal so that she could continue, uninterrupted, toward long-range objectives. Smith College gave a master's degree (but not a Ph.D.) in psychology and also needed teaching assistants. She became a teaching assistant as well as a graduate student, enrolling in James J. Gibson's seminar on William James. She married Gibson on September 17, 1932, after completing a year of graduate work, and then became his teaching assistant, completing her master's thesis on retroactive inhibition under his supervision and receiving her degree in 1933 (E. J. Gibson, 1980).

Early publications included one resulting from Gibson's undergraduate course with J. J. Gibson, which was published under the name Eleanor G. Jack (J. J. Gibson, Jack, & Raffel, 1932). In later publications she assumed her husband's name. As James J. Gibson later noted, "No married woman kept her own name in those days. A wife's career was identified with her husband's" (J. J. Gibson, 1979, p. x). Her master's thesis was also published (E. J. Gibson & J. J. Gibson, 1934).

Further graduate study was postponed because of the financial difficulties stemming from the depression as well as Gibson's willingness to schedule her own work according to her husband's professional commitments, a pattern that had considerable influence on her own career development. In 1935, however, Gibson left to spend a year at Yale University with the objective of experimental work with Robert Yerkes and his chimpanzee population. Among the obstacles she encountered before her husband later joined her was Yerkes' adamant refusal to allow women in his laboratory, and the fact that both an important interdisciplinary seminar as well as graduate school living, dining, and recreational quarters were off limits to women. Undaunted, Gibson explored the offerings of the medical school, where she found anatomists and physiologists to be "far more tolerant of women students than the psychiatrists" (E. J. Gibson, 1980, p. 247).

At Yale, Gibson decided to study with Clark Hull, a decision somewhat influenced by a proseminar that explored numerous areas of psychology in rapid succession and by discussions among the students attending the seminar, who had formed a closely knit group among themselves (E. J. Gibson, 1980). Although Hull was interested primarily in studying learning in rats, Gibson persuaded him to allow her to study verbal learning and forgetting, thereby extending his theoretical perspective to human subjects. She received her Ph.D. in 1938, and publications based on her dissertation included a theoretical paper (E. J. Gibson, 1940) as well as several experimental studies (E. J. Gibson, 1939, 1941, 1942). Although Hull had required her to work within his system, Gibson nevertheless managed to refashion key concepts so that they became her own and began to develop ideas concerning differentiation that would influence her later work in perceptual learning. Her sojourn with Hull convinced her that an associationistic perspective was wrong. Much of her later work in perceptual learning and development was presented as an alternative to an associationistic view.

CAREER DEVELOPMENT

Except for the single year spent in residence at Yale, Gibson continued to be employed as an instructor at Smith College. She was promoted to assistant professor in 1940. At Smith both she and her husband were employed by the same institution, and faculty were evenly distributed between women and men.

The Gibsons' son, James Jerome Gibson, Jr., a physician, was born February 9, 1940, and a daughter, Jean, a Ph.D. economist, was born June 29, 1943. With the birth of her son, Gibson found that she had little opportunity for original research. Her time was fully occupied with teaching, advising, and supervising graduate students. Although she directed occasional master's or honor's theses that tested theoretical predictions growing out of her dissertation research, she did not carry out this research herself (E. J. Gibson, 1980).

When the entry of the United States into World War II created a role for psychologists, her husband's work required relocation to Texas and then to California. Placing the importance of her own career concerns secondary to those of her husband, Gibson gave up her own work to join him (E. J. Gibson, 1980), although at the time she did not view this as a sacrifice (E. J. Gibson, personal communication, August 10, 1988). For four years she held no academic position and had no contact with research other than discussing it occasionally with her husband and his colleagues. At the end of the war, both Gibsons returned to the academic life at Smith College, where they remained until J. J. Gibson accepted an offer from Cornell in 1949. There was no corresponding position for her, since Cornell's antinepotism rules did not permit both members of a married couple to hold salaried positions within the same school. Instead, Eleanor Gibson was given the title of research associate; the absence of a faculty position insured that any funds expended on her research could be obtained only through her own efforts (E. J. Gibson, 1980).

One consequence of this was that she participated in research on the barest fringes of the issues that concerned her. She became involved in a project studying conditioned responses of sheep and goats to electric shock (E. J. Gibson, 1952), which was cited at the time as an "important" study (Underwood, 1953, p. 39). While conducting this study she began to make ethological observations of maternal-infant interaction in goats. This both reawakened her earlier interests in developmental studies of animals and children and resulted in a serendipitous observation made during her research on olfactory bonds between maternal goats and newborn kids. While attending the birth of twin kids, it was necessary to put the first-born kid somewhere while the second kid was born. Gibson placed the first-born kid on a high camera stand that was handy and, when placed there, the newborn infant remained motionless (E. J. Gibson, 1980). Not until Gibson's comparative studies of depth perception with the visual cliff (E. J. Gibson & Walk, 1960; Walk & Gibson, 1961) would the significance of the newborn kid's response be understood. Clearly, since the kid had been born moments before, there had been no opportunity for the depth perception it exhibited to have been learned.

Through colleagues at an air force laboratory, Gibson received an opportunity in 1952 to initiate her own research, with ample funding provided by the United States Air Force. The air force grant was signed by Gibson's husband since

Gibson's lack of faculty status prevented her from doing so herself. However, it was her research that led to the opportunity (E. J. Gibson, personal communication, February 10, 1989). For the first time, Eleanor Gibson could develop her own projects and define the direction of her own research. This led to a fruitful period in which the field of perceptual learning began to be defined through studies of problems such as the effects of practice upon adults' judgments of distance (e.g., E. J. Gibson & Bergman, 1954; E. J. Gibson, Bergman, & Purdy, 1955). Gibson and her husband later collaborated in exploring the interaction of practice effects during perceptual learning with developmental influences (which would also become a central theme for her) in a study of children's ability to differentiate among scribble-like figures (J. J. Gibson & E. J. Gibson, 1955).

During this period, the developmental and comparative contexts of perceptual learning were expanded through experiments that explored the effects on perception of such variables as early experience (E. J. Gibson, & Walk, 1956) and deprivation of stimulation (E. J. Gibson, Walk, & Tighe, 1959), in addition to the visual cliff studies cited earlier. The field of perceptual learning was further delineated through several chapters (E. J. Gibson & Olum, 1960; E. J. Gibson, 1963a, 1963b).

Despite ever-increasing prominence and recognition in the academic world, Gibson remained an unpaid research associate at Cornell until 1965, when her husband won a Career Professorship from the National Institute of Mental Health. Once Cornell no longer paid his salary, Eleanor Gibson was appointed professor of psychology, on a half-time basis (E. J. Gibson, 1980).

MAJOR ACHIEVEMENTS AND CONTRIBUTIONS AND THEIR EVALUATION

In the 1950s Gibson was cited primarily in conjunction with her work in learning. Frequently cited was her 1940 article in the *Psychological Review,* which had grown out of her doctoral dissertation with Hull, in which she developed the concept of differentiation as it applied to verbal learning. Early recognition of Gibson's influence upon the concept of differentiation, and of the increasing importance of the then-emerging field of perceptual learning, was provided by Estes (1956). Referring to a paper in which the Gibsons had collaborated to propose perceptual differentiation as an alternative to associative learning (J. J. Gibson & E. J. Gibson, 1955), Estes noted:

In giving a new analysis of the role of differentiation in perceptual learning, Gibson & Gibson take a notable step toward narrowing the gap between the vocabularies of perception and discrimination learning. The Gibsons raise the question whether improvement in perception must be regarded as the accrual of meanings, associations, etc., rather than simply as a type of discrimination learning whereby the response becomes dependent upon more and finer aspects of the stimulating situation. (P. 29)

The first *Annual Review* chapter devoted entirely to perceptual learning (Drever, 1960) continued the debate between associationistic and differentiation viewpoints, extensively citing the Gibsons' views as well as their "cogent and ingenious" (p. 135) experiments.

In addition to Gibson's own *Annual Review* chapter on perceptual learning (E. J. Gibson, 1963b), the same volume contained indications of her expanding sphere of influence. In the chapter on developmental psychology (Rheingold & Stanley, 1963), a detailed description was given of Walk and Gibson's 1961 monograph on depth discrimination in which the "simple but ingenious" (p. 1) visual cliff was employed, noting that "the experiments of Walk & Gibson represent a major substantive and methodological achievement in developmental psychology" (p. 2).

A third *Annual Review* chapter on perceptual learning (Wohlwill, 1966) cited a number of studies by Gibson and her colleagues, including several concerned with perceptual learning as it pertained to the reading process (e.g., E. J. Gibson, Bishop, Schiff, & Smith, 1964; and E. J. Gibson, Pick, Osser, & Hammond, 1962). This was an area to which Gibson would later devote considerable attention. During the 1960s, in addition to citations concerning perception, perceptual learning, and development, Gibson's work was noted in chapters on verbal learning and memory, emotional aspects of learning, motivation and performance, and psycholinguistics, among others, demonstrating the value and relevance of her work to a far broader scope of psychology than she studied directly.

In 1969 Gibson's book *Principles of Perceptual Learning and Development* was published; it served both to summarize the past and then-current status of this emerging field as well as to indicate her own theoretical views. Gibson was awarded the Century Psychology Prize for this book and, with her inclusion in the Century series, she joined a list of authors that included her mentor Hull and other figures important in her development. One review of this book began by stating, "It will not be possible to teach or even discuss the topic of perception for many years to come without bringing in the name Gibson" (Garner, 1970, p. 958). After referring to contributions made by J. J. Gibson, the reviewer went on to note that "Eleanor J. Gibson has produced a book about perceptual development, a book which is much broader in scope than her husband's . . . which just as clearly makes its own theoretical contribution" (p. 958). In their *Annual Review* chapter on perceptual development, Aslin and Smith (1988) referred to this book as a classic.

In the 1970s, perception and development continued to be major concerns for Gibson; however, much of her work was applied toward the problem of reading, an area in which Gibson and several colleagues accepted an invitation to conduct extensive research. This research was carried out from an interdisciplinary perspective combining theories and empirical studies of perceptual learning, cognitive development, and linguistic development, an approach that was revolutionary at the time. The results were summarized in the 1975 book *The*

Psychology of Reading, in which Gibson collaborated with Harry Levin (E. J. Gibson & Levin, 1975).

The significance of this book was reflected in the broad, multidisciplinary spectrum of publications in which it was reviewed, including periodicals concerned with education, reading, language, psychology, and science. Indeed, one review was itself eighty pages in length (Calfee, Arnold, & Drum, 1976). Reactions to the book might be summarized as giving high praise to its comprehensiveness while noting that it had not succeeded totally in providing a model of the reading process that generated specific instructional strategies. Baron (1976) noted that "this book is without doubt the best available introduction to the study of reading" (p. 263), and Ruddell (1977) predicted that "*The Psychology of Reading* will undoubtedly have a substantial effect on the field of reading" (p. 443). This book provided a major impetus that stimulated a fresh reappraisal of the relevance of psychology to the study of reading, which, as the authors pointed out in their preface, had largely been shunned by experimental psychologists caught up in the influence of the stimulus-response (S-R) psychology that had dominated research for the preceding sixty years.

In 1979 *Perception and Its Development: A Tribute to Eleanor J. Gibson* was published, edited by Anne D. Pick. In the introduction, Pick stated:

We have acquired important new knowledge about the nature and development of perception in recent years, and the insights of Eleanor Jack Gibson have had a prominent role in guiding the search for that knowledge. The purpose of this volume is to honor her continuing contribution to our understanding of perception. (P. 1)

Papers were included across five broad areas, each of which has been influenced by Gibson's own work, including learning and generalization (a reminder that, in her early work, Gibson made substantive contributions to learning theory and that her views continue to be influential), development of spatial perception, perception of pattern and structure, perception of meaning, and exploration and selectivity in perceptual development.

After J. J. Gibson died in 1979, Eleanor Gibson continued to develop his concept of affordance, a term referring to properties of the environment relevant to the ecological niche of a particular animal which evolution has equipped the animal to detect (see E. J. Gibson, 1982). This concept has been central to much of the work that she and her students and colleagues have done during the 1980s, particularly with regard to the study of perceptual development in infants. Gibson has not revised *Principles of Perceptual Learning and Development* (1969) because, in her view, the field of perceptual *learning* was thoroughly explored at that time. In contrast, the field of perceptual *development* has moved very fast and importantly since that time, and that is the area in which Gibson concentrated her efforts in the late 1980s (E. J. Gibson, personal communication [recorded telephone interview], April 16, 1988).

Among the fascinating avenues that Gibson and her associates have explored in perceptual development have been the ability of infants to differentiate between the motions of objects that were rigid and those that could be deformed (E. J. Gibson, Owsley, & Johnston, 1978), and intermodal perception (for example, the ability to detect that something is hard by looking at it, an example of an affordance of the substance; E. J. Gibson & Walker, 1984). The ability of infants to utilize the optical flow, information from the environment detected as they walk, has been explored (Stoffregen, Schmuckler, & E. J. Gibson, 1987), as has the ability of infants to detect whether or not a surface may readily be traversed (E. J. Gibson, G. Riccio, et al., 1987). These studies have employed characteristically ingenious methods and apparatus (e.g., moving rooms and water beds) to study the ability of infants and children to detect and utilize information from environmental affordances.

Although a student or colleague has sometimes developed views diverging from Gibson's own (e.g., see Spelke, 1987), it is nevertheless the case that Gibson's work, both cumulative and recent, has generated a substantial body of theory and research that challenges and reinterprets the most cherished and ingrained concepts of major developmental theorists such as Jean Piaget. Gibson's explorations of perceptual development have earned her recognition as a major developmental theorist.

The editor of the *Journal of Experimental Psychology: Human Perception and Performance,* William Epstein, chose to devote his final issue to the ontogenesis, or development, of perception. In the introductory essay that Gibson was invited to prepare for this issue (E. J. Gibson, 1987), she summarized a number of conclusions drawn from research on perception with infants that are broadly relevant to theories of perception. Among the eight conclusions that she drew are the following: perception is active, exploratory, and motivated, even in the neonate (p. 515); infant perception not only uses but depends on information given in motion (p. 516); perception in infancy detects structure (p. 517); and perceptually guided actions are organized and flexible, not reflexive or mechanical S-R sequences (p. 518). Rather than emphasizing her own point of view, Gibson placed these conclusions within the context of traditional and current theories of perception and characteristically went on to tackle the "big issues" such as the nature-nurture question, the continuity-discontinuity issue, and, "at the risk of some raised eyebrows" (p. 521), the mind-body problem.

This article, together with the other studies in this issue that in some way have been influenced by Gibson's work, illustrates the consistent artistry with which she has succeeded in meshing the development of theory with the formulation of methodology and the implementation of laboratory studies to define and to further an entire field. She has done this throughout her professional career, most recently in a prefatory chapter for the 1988 *Annual Review of Psychology* (E. J. Gibson, 1988) entitled "Exploratory Behavior in the Development of Perceiving, Acting, and the Acquiring of Knowledge." The final paragraph of this chapter provides an integrative summary of the major themes that Gibson has explored throughout nearly sixty years of an extraordinarily productive professional life:

The young organism grows up in the environment (both physical and social) in which his species evolved, one that imposes demands on his actions for his individual survival. To accommodate to his world, he must detect the information for these actions—that is, perceive the affordances it holds. How does the infant creature manage this accomplishment? Has evolution somehow provided him with representations of the world, and rules for how to act? I doubt this very much. But I think evolution has provided him with action systems and sensory systems that equip him to discover what the world is all about. He is "programmed" or motivated to use these systems, first by exploring the accessible surround, then acting on it, and (as spontaneous locomotion becomes possible) extending his explorations further. The exploratory systems emerge in an orderly way that permits an ever-spiraling path of discovery. (P. 37)

Since Gibson's belated promotion to professor of psychology at Cornell in 1965, honors and recognition have steadily accumulated. From 1972 to 1979 she was the Susan Linn Sage Professor of psychology at Cornell and, since 1979, professor emeritus. She has been a visiting professor at the Massachusetts Institute of Technology (1973), the University of California at Davis (1978), the Salk Institute (1979), the Institute of Child Development at the University of Minnesota (1980), the University of South Carolina (1981), the Institute of Psychology in Beijing, China (1982), the University of Pennsylvania (1984), Dartmouth College (1986), and Emory University (1988).

In addition to the medals and awards that Gibson has received, a number of honorary degrees have recognized her achievements. These have included Doctor of Science degrees from Smith College (1972), Rutgers University (1973), Trinity College (1982), Bates College (1985), and the University of South Carolina (1987), as well as the degree of Doctor of Humane Letters from the State University of New York at Albany (1984).

INTEGRATION OF PERSONAL AND PROFESSIONAL LIFE

Although Gibson's career development was less direct than it might have been, in part because of family responsibilities and events growing out of her husband's professional life, Gibson has noted in retrospect that the "direct route . . . is not necessarily the most desirable." Noting parallels between the course of her own career and that of Mary Cover Jones (see Mussen & Eichorn, 1988), Gibson has pointed out, "I doubt that she, like myself, ever thought that she was making compromises, but only being realistic about priorities and as flexible as possible in using her professional education and talent" (E. J. Gibson, personal communication, November 22, 1988).

In examining her publications, one notes the frequency with which Gibson has collaborated with others, including her husband. She has collaborated with students and colleagues throughout her professional life and has been generous in crediting others for their ideas and contributions.

Professional networks have been important to her throughout her career, beginning with the seminar with Koffka at Smith College, social groups during her time at Yale, and her subsequent involvement in various professional societies. In 1989 Gibson was actively involved with the International Society for Ecological Psychology, which promotes a functional, ecological approach, rooted in evolution, as an alternative to an information-processing perspective. It promotes studies of the perception of *events* rather than traditional objects or printed alphanumeric characters.

Gibson's interests away from the laboratory have included reading and travel, and she has integrated both into her work. Apt quotations from literature and poetry have often found their way into her papers. After the death of James J. Gibson on December 11, 1979, Gibson traveled widely in conjunction with her visiting professorships.

Throughout her career, Gibson has demonstrated a gift for identifying problems and clarifying theoretical controversies as well as for motivating her students to explore them. Many of her students have gone on to become prominent researchers and teachers themselves. The insights, inspiration, and stimulation that Eleanor Gibson has given to psychology will continue to influence theory and research for many decades to come.

REFERENCES

Aslin, R. N., & Smith, L. B. (1988). Perceptual development. *Annual Review of Psychology, 39,* 435–473.

Baron, J. (1976). The psychology and pedagogy of reading, updated [Review of *The psychology of reading*]. *Contemporary Psychology, 21,* 261–263.

Calfee, R. C.; Arnold, R.; & Drum, P. (1976). [Review of *The psychology of reading*]. *Proceedings of the National Academy of Education, 3,* 1–80.

Drever, J. (1960). Perceptual learning. *Annual Review of Psychology, 11,* 131–160.

Estes, W. K. (1956). Learning. *Annual Review of Psychology, 7,* 1–38.

Garner, W. R. (1970). Processing sensory information [Review of *Principles of perceptual learning and development*]. *Science, 168,* 958–959.

Gibson, E. J. (1939). Sensory generalization with voluntary reactions. *Journal of Experimental Psychology, 24,* 237–253.

Gibson, E. J. (1940). A systematic application of the concepts of generalization and differentiation to verbal learning. *Psychological Review, 47,* 196–229.

Gibson, E. J. (1941). Retroactive inhibition as a function of degree of generalization between tasks. *Journal of Experimental Psychology, 28,* 93–115.

Gibson, E. J. (1942). Intra-list generalization as a factor in verbal learning. *Journal of Experimental Psychology, 30,* 185–200.

Gibson, E. J. (1952). The role of shock in reinforcement. *Journal of Comparative and Physiological Psychology, 45,* 18–30.

Gibson, E. J. (1963a). Perceptual development. In H. W. Stevenson et al. (Eds.), *Child psychology* (Sixty-second yearbook of the National Society for the Study of Education, pp. 144–195). Chicago: University of Chicago Press.

Gibson, E. J. (1963b) Perceptual Learning. *Annual Review of Psychology, 14,* 29–56.

Gibson, E. J. (1969). *Principles of perceptual learning and development.* New York: Appleton-Century-Crofts.

Gibson, E. J. (1980). Autobiography. In G. Lindzey (Ed.), *The history of psychology in autobiography* (pp. 239–271). San Francisco: W. H. Freeman.

Gibson, E. J. (1982). The concept of affordances in development: The renascence of functionalism. In W. A. Collins (Ed.), *The concept of development: The Minnesota Symposia on Child Psychology* (Vol. 15, pp. 55–81). Hillsdale, N.J.: Erlbaum.

Gibson, E. J. (1987). Introductory essay: What does infant perception tell us about theories of perception? *Journal of Experimental Psychology: Human Perception and Performance, 13,* 515–523.

Gibson, E. J. (1988). Exploratory behavior in the development of perceiving, acting, and the acquiring of knowledge. *Annual Review of Psychology, 39,* 1–41.

Gibson, E. J., & Bergman, R. (1954). The effect of training on absolute estimation of distance over the ground. *Journal of Experimental Psychology, 48,* 473–482.

Gibson, E. J.; Bergman, R.; & Purdy, J. (1955). The effect of prior training with a scale of distance on absolute and relative judgments of distance over the ground. *Journal of Experimental Psychology, 50,* 97–105.

Gibson, E. J.; Bishop, C. H.; Schiff, W.; & Smith, J. (1964). Comparison of meaningfulness and pronunciability as grouping principles in the perception and retention of verbal material. *Journal of Experimental Psychology, 67,* 173–182.

Gibson, E. J., & Gibson, J. J. (1934). Retention and the interpolated task. *American Journal of Psychology, 46,* 603–610.

Gibson, E. J., & Levin, H. (1975). *The psychology of reading.* Cambridge, Mass.: MIT Press.

Gibson, E. J., & Levin, H. (1979). Afterword. In A. D. Pick (Ed.), *Perception and its development: A tribute to Eleanor J. Gibson.* Hillsdale, N.J.: Erlbaum.

Gibson, E. J., & Olum, V. (1960). Experimental methods of studying perception in children. In P. H. Mussen (Ed.), *Handbook of research methods in child development* (pp. 311–373). New York: Wiley.

Gibson, E. J.; Owsley, C. J.; & Johnston, J. (1978). Perception of invariants by five-month-old infants: Differentiation of two types of motion. *Developmental Psychology, 14,* 407–415.

Gibson, E. J.; Pick, A. D.; Osser, H.; & Hammond, M. (1962). The role of grapheme-phoneme correspondence in the perception of words. *American Journal of Psychology, 75,* 554–570.

Gibson, E. J.; Riccio, G.; Schmuckler, M. A.; Stoffregen, T. A.; Rosenberg, D.; & Taormina, J. (1987). Detection of the traversability of surfaces by crawling and walking infants. *Journal of Experimental Psychology: Human Perception and Performance, 13,* 533–544.

Gibson, E. J., & Walk, R. D. (1956). The effect of prolonged exposure to visually presented patterns on learning to discriminate them. *Journal of Comparative and Physiological Psychology, 49,* 239–242.

Gibson, E. J., & Walk, R. D. (1960). The "visual cliff." *Scientific American, 202,* 64–71.

Gibson, E. J.; Walk, R. D.; & Tighe, T. J. (1959). Enhancement and deprivation of visual stimulation during rearing as factors in visual discrimination. *Journal of Comparative and Physiological Psychology, 52,* 74–81.

Gibson, E. J., & Walker, A. S. (1984). Development of knowledge of visual-tactual affordances of substance. *Child Development, 55,* 453–460.

Gibson, J. J. (1979). Foreword: A note on E.J.G. by J.J.G. In A. D. Pick (Ed.), *Perception and its development: A tribute to Eleanor J. Gibson.* (pp. ix-xiii). Hillsdale, N.J.: Erlbaum.

Gibson, J. J., & Gibson, E. J. (1955). Perceptual learning: Differentiation or enrichment? *Psychological Review, 62,* 32–41.

Gibson, J. J.; Jack, E. G.; & Raffel, G. (1932). Bilateral transfer of the conditioned response in the human subject. *Journal of Experimental Psychology, 15,* 416–421.

Mussen, P., & Eichorn, D. (1988). Mary Cover Jones (1896–1987). *American Psychologist, 43*(10), 818.

Pick, A. D. (1979). *Perception and its development: A tribute to Eleanor J. Gibson.* Hillsdale, N.J.: Erlbaum.

Rheingold, H. L., & Stanley, W. C. (1963). Developmental psychology. *Annual Review of Psychology, 14,* 1–28.

Ruddell, R. B. (1977). [Review of *The psychology of reading*]. *Harvard Educational Review, 47,* 442–444.

Spelke, E. S. (1987). Where perceiving ends and thinking begins: The apprehension of objects in infancy. In A. Yonas (Ed.), *Perceptual development in infancy: The Minnesota Symposia on Child Psychology* (Vol. 20, pp. 197–234). Hillsdale, N.J.: Erlbaum.

Stoffregen, T. A.; Schmuckler, M. A.; & Gibson, E. J. (1987). Use of central and peripheral optical flow in stance and locomotion in young walkers. *Perception, 16,* 113–119.

Underwood, B. J. (1953). Learning. *Annual Review of Psychology, 4,* 31–58.

Walk, R. D., & Gibson, E. J. (1961). A comparative and analytical study of visual depth perception. *Psychological Monographs, 75*(15).

Wohlwill, J. (1966). Perceptual learning. *Annual Review of Psychology, 17,* 201–232.

Additional Representative Publications by Eleanor J. Gibson

Gibson, E. J. (1953). Improvement in perceptual judgments as a function of controlled practice or training. *Psychological Bulletin, 50,* 401–431.

Gibson, E. J. (1965). Learning to read. *Science, 148,* 1066–1072.

Gibson, E. J. (1968). Perceptual development. In *Encyclopedia of the social sciences.* New York: Macmillan.

Gibson, E. J. (1970). The development of perception as an active process. *American Scientist, 58,* 98–107.

Gibson, E. J. (1971). Perceptual learning and the theory of word perception. *Cognitive Psychology, 2,* 351–368.

Gibson, E. J. (1984). Development of knowledge about intermodal unity: Two views.

In S. Liben (Ed.), *Piaget and the foundations of knowledge* (pp. 19–41). Hillsdale, N.J.: Erlbaum.

Gibson, E. J. (1984). Perceptual development from the ecological approach. In M. E. Lamb, A. L. Brown, & B. Rogoff (Eds.), *Advances in developmental psychology* (pp. 243–286). Hillsdale, N.J.: Erlbaum.

Gibson, E. J.; Gibson, J. J.; Pick, A. D.; & Osser, H. (1962). A developmental study of the discrimination of letter-like forms. *Journal of Comparative and Physiological Psychology, 55,* 897–906.

Gibson, E. J., & Guinet, L. (1971). Perception of inflections in brief visual presentations of words. *Journal of Verbal Learning and Verbal Behavior, 10,* 182–189.

Gibson, E. J.; Shurcliff, A.; & Yonas, A. (1970). Utilization of spelling patterns by deaf and hearing subjects. In H. Levin & J. P. Williams (Eds.), *Basic studies on reading* (pp. 57–73). New York: Basic Books.

Gibson, E. J., & Spelke, E. S. (1983). The development of perception. In J. H. Flavell & E. Markman (Eds), *Handbook of child psychology (4th ed.): Cognitive development* (Vol. 3, pp. 1–76). New York: Wiley.

Gibson, J. J., & Gibson, E. J. (1957). Continuous perspective transformations and the perception of rigid motion. *Journal of Experimental Psychology, 54,* 129–138.

Walker-Andrews, A. S., & Gibson, E. J. (1986). What develops in bimodal perception? In L. P. Lipsitt & C. Rovee-Collier (Eds.), *Advances in infancy research* (Vol. 4, pp. 171–181). Norwood, N.J.: Ablex.

LILLIAN MOLLER GILBRETH (1878–1972)

Rita Mae Kelly and Vincent P. Kelly

Lillian Gilbreth has been called the Mother of Scientific Management, the First Lady of Management, and the World's Greatest Woman Engineer. Author of eight books and numerous papers on education, management, and psychology, she became internationally renowned for her fundamental contributions to industrial and personnel management. In 1954 she became one of the founding members of the International Academy of Management and for years was its only female member. Two biographies and movies, *Cheaper by the Dozen* and *Belles on Their Toes,* written by two of her twelve children, also made her famous as a remarkable wife and mother. Her contributions to management science and engineering have been recognized by the issuance in 1987 of a commemorative postal stamp.

BACKGROUND AND EDUCATION

Lillian Moller was born in Oakland, California, on May 24, 1878, to William and Ann Moller. William Moller managed his father-in-law's hardware store, but later became the prosperous owner of several shoe stores in San Francisco and Sacramento. Ann Moller's main occupation was managing her household with its cook and gardener, and caring for her large family.

Lillian Moller, a very shy child, was terrified by the experience of going to first grade, so her parents tutored the child themselves, with the help of private teachers, at home for three years. Besides the usual academic subjects, Lillian Moller learned French and German and to play the piano. She read a great deal and had long, serious conversations with her father. While she had little experience in cooking and cleaning, as the eldest child she gradually took on responsibility for caring for her three brothers and five sisters because of her mother's delicate health.

A favorite aunt, Lillian Delger Powell, strengthened Lillian Moller's determination to attend a university and have a career. She may also have stimulated her niece's interest in psychology as well. Lillian Powell became a psychiatrist and studied psychoanalysis with Sigmund Freud. But during high school and college, Moller's interests lay mostly in music and literature. She composed the music and lyrics of her own songs and wrote poetry for the school paper. Despite her excellent grades, her parents believed that a university education was not appropriate for her social standing. They assumed that their daughter would marry a wealthy man and assume responsibility for running the family household.

Lillian Moller, however, regarded herself as quite plain. She assumed that no one would marry her, so she decided to prepare herself for a useful career: teaching. Since a cousin, Ann Florence, was already a student at the University of California at Berkeley, the Mollers agreed to allow their daughter to attend as well, on condition that she live at home and commute to the campus by streetcar. She majored in English literature and studied foreign languages and philosophy as well; science or mathematics held little interest for her at that stage in her life. To overcome her shyness, Moller took part in dramatic productions on campus. In preparation for teaching, she also took courses in psychology and was impressed by a young psychology professor, George Stratton. Because of her outstanding academic achievement, when Moller graduated in 1900, she was selected as a commencement speaker—the first woman to receive that honor at Berkeley. Her topic reflects her concern with philosophical and ethical questions: "Life—A Means or An End?"

Because the Mollers had close relatives in New York City, they consented when their eldest child announced her intention to attend Barnard College, the woman's college affiliated with Columbia University. Lillian Moller intended to study with the well-known critic and professor of English literature Brander Matthews. The professor, however, refused to allow a woman to attend his lectures. Nevertheless, she was able to study with the famous psychologist A. H. Thorndike.

Unfortunately, the new graduate student soon became seriously ill. She returned to California to recuperate and then stayed to obtain a master's degree in English literature at her old alma mater in 1902. Her thesis was on Ben Jonson's *Bartholomew Fair,* a satirical comedy about the Puritans in England.

Still intent on becoming a teacher, Lillian Moller entered the Berkeley doctoral program in English with a minor in psychology. But the following summer she decided to tour Europe with a group of young women and a chaperone. En route, the group stopped in Boston, where the chaperone introduced the twenty-five-year-old Moller to thirty-five-year-old Frank Gilbreth, a handsome, wealthy owner of a successful construction company. When she returned from Europe, Gilbreth was waiting with flowers. After her return to Oakland, Gilbreth traveled to Oakland to see Moller and meet her parents. They soon became engaged and were married on October 19, 1904.

Frank Gilbreth recognized Lillian Moller as an exceptionally intelligent, articulate woman. At his suggestion before they were married, she changed her major to psychology so that she could help him in his business: he foresaw the value of psychology to management, where the new science of psychology had as yet had little impact.

Frank Gilbreth never attended college. Although he had been accepted at the Massachusetts Institute of Technology, he decided instead to help his widowed mother by working as an apprentice in the construction field. Within three years Gilbreth mastered fifty separate construction crafts. He was appointed assistant foreman, then foreman and site manager. Finally he started his own construction business and ensured the efficiency of his workers by writing an instruction manual on the most effective ways to perform their tasks. The unpublished manual, privately printed in 1902 under the title "A Field System," presented Gilbreth's ideas on a new, systematic method of construction management. That was the year before Frederick W. Taylor, the person generally honored as "Father of Scientific Management," presented a paper entitled "Shop Management" in which he delineated the principles and techniques of his own management system. Taylor's "Shop Management" attracted little attention at the time, while Gilbreth's competitors in the construction business were printing pirated editions of his manual for their own work crews.

CAREER

The new bride immediately became her husband's apprentice and partner in the construction business. Together they visited building sites, climbed ladders, and walked across girders. Once too timid to go to school by herself, Lillian Gilbreth now seemed fearless. She became interested in the problems and techniques of the building industry and shared her husband's passion for finding the "one best way" to perform each of the myriad tasks and thus make the whole operation more efficient, economical, and productive. Lillian Gilbreth encouraged her husband to write down his ideas and, through an ongoing dialogue between equals, she critiqued, refined, and improved his management system. She assisted him in writing *Concrete System* (1908), *Bricklaying System* (1909), and the book that describes Frank Gilbreth's original experiments in scientific management, *Motion Study* (1911). The style and content clearly show Lillian Gilbreth's influence, yet the editor refused to include her name as coauthor in the belief that it would detract from the book's credibility. Lillian Gilbreth encouraged her husband to give up his construction business to become a management consultant and industrial engineer so that they could develop his original ideas and apply them in new management situations. Gilbreth agreed, but only if his wife would continue to be his partner and colleague in the new venture.

The Gilbreths were impressed with the ideas of Frederick W. Taylor and acknowledged his outstanding contributions to the progress of industrial management, particularly in machine shops and metal foundries. They incorporated many of his ideas into their own system. When the *American Magazine* in 1911 received a great number of questions in response to an article by Taylor, Taylor recommended that Gilbreth be assigned the task of responding since he was so familiar with the Taylor system. As usual, Lillian Gilbreth collaborated with her husband in writing *A Primer of Scientific Management* (1912), and, again, the editor refused to add a woman's name as coauthor of a technical article. Nevertheless, Lillian Gilbreth was gradually achieving her own reputation as an original contributor in the field of industrial management. At the first conference on scientific management at Dartmouth University in 1911, Lillian Gilbreth was singled out for special recognition by the chair of the final session, Morris L. Cooke: "We have all been watching the quiet work of one individual who has been working along lines different from those being followed by any other worker in the scientific management field" (cited by Yost, 1949, p. 194). It was true. Lillian Gilbreth's unique approach stemmed in part from her training in the humanities, in pedagogy and psychology; but her approach was also different because she was a person with strong sympathy and empathy for people, in distinction to products, profits, and machines.

Her *Psychology of Management* (1914) provided a logical, systematic explanation and defense of the new practices and principles of management. She stressed the importance of human relations and the need to recognize the individual differences among workers and their needs—psychological as well as physiological. The notions of justice and happiness were included in her unique analysis and interpretation of scientific management, published in installments during 1912–1913, before it was accepted as her Ph.D. dissertation at Brown University in 1914. The publisher, reluctant to reveal the gender of the author, ambiguously identified her simply as L. M. Gilbreth.

In the early years of the twentieth century, engineering, psychology, and management were still new disciplines for academic or scientific study. In synthesizing and integrating knowledge from these three fields, Lillian Gilbreth made a significant and unique contribution to scientific management. To appreciate her contributions fully, it might help to understand the status of industrial management at that time. For instance, in his *Principles of Scientific Management* (1911), F. W. Taylor had virtually ignored principles of psychology and pedagogy. He simply did not understand their relevance to the problems of industrial production. In Taylor's view, laborers would and should cooperate with his management system because they would be competing for greater financial rewards based on their ability to meet or surpass the production standards set by means of his time-study technique. Taylor believed that only lazy workers needed or wanted to join labor unions, which he believed willfully attempted to impede the progress that could be made with his management system. By the autocratic standards of management at the beginning of the century, Taylor viewed himself as eminently fair and democratic; yet his concept of "cooperation" meant simply that workers should essentially do what they were told promptly and without asking questions or making suggestions. He believed that workers should be required to work at the pace of which the machines were capable. Once, when describing the ideal laborer for shoveling pig iron, Taylor said that the individual should be "as stupid as an ox." Many workers and their union representatives were intimidated and offended by Taylor's mechanistic time-study methods. A number of strikes were held in plants where the Taylor method had been implemented, and Congress passed legislation specifically prohibiting the use of certain elements of the Taylor system—such as the use of stop-watches to time workers' performance—in industrial work financed by federal contracts.

While Lillian Gilbreth saw the value of much that was in Taylor's system, she was highly critical of what she considered his inhumane conception of the workers and his evident lack of concern for their individual needs and rights. As far back as her graduation speech in 1900, Lillian Gilbreth expressed her belief in the intrinsic value of human life: human beings should not be treated as mere tools of production; the goal of human life is the fulfillment and happiness of the person. Gilbreth brought to the field of scientific management a humanistic and psychological analysis of individual and group behavior. She emphasized the importance of human relations and the need to improve communication and cooperation among workers, foremen, and managers. Along with her husband, Lillian Gilbreth advocated adapting the tools and the workplace to fit the needs of workers, not vice versa. Together they also endeavored to apply the benefits of scientific management and time and motion study to broader areas of human need than industrial production, such as the surgical procedures of an operating room or in the rehabilitation of the physically handicapped. Lillian Gilbreth further believed that the additional profits accrued by the elimination of wasted effort or material and by the improved productivity of workers should be equitably shared among workers, managers, and owners. Unlike Taylor, Gilbreth believed that the workers directly involved in an operation were in a better position to understand how the operation could be improved. Thus, she advocated that workers be encouraged to critique operations and make suggestions for their improvement. The workers would receive recognition, respect, and rewards for the ideas they contributed.

Lillian Gilbreth convinced her husband of the value of instituting formal programs to train managers in the new techniques and principles of scientific management. By conducting summer workshops in their own home, the Gilbreths disseminated the new concepts and methods to representatives of business, industries, and universities throughout this country and abroad.

THE DISSOLUTION OF A PARTNERSHIP

In their twenty years of marriage the Gilbreths had twelve children. After her husband's death in 1924, Gilbreth had the sole responsibility for providing for her children's support and college expenses. She immediately undertook to continue the company's consulting business by herself, but she soon found that many of the companies she and her husband had helped for years were unwilling to continue or renew their contracts with a woman. So Gilbreth reinstituted the workshops, recruiting students from as far away as Germany, Belgium, England, and Japan. Gradually the reputation she gained as a gifted teacher of industrial management led to new requests for her consulting services. For a company that manufactured kitchen appliances, Lillian Gilbreth redesigned kitchens and household appliances to fit the needs of homemakers and to save them time and energy in performing daily chores. Among her innovations were the foot-pedal trash can and shelves inside refrigerator doors.

Macy's department store in New York City hired Lillian Gilbreth to study and improve some of their operations. Gilbreth worked in the store as a salesperson to share the experience of the workers. She met with such success that Macy's asked Gilbreth to train one of their executives to conduct similar motion studies and operational analyses. She received so many requests to train others in the new management techniques that Gilbreth began teaching regular courses in colleges and universities, including Newark College of Engineering, Bryn Mawr, Rutgers, and Purdue University. Appointed full professor at Purdue in 1935 when she was fifty-seven, she held that post until she "officially" retired in 1948 at the age of seventy. As a teacher of future industrial engineers, managers, and instructors, Gilbreth advocated and propagated her own and her husband's humanized version of scientific management in fields as diverse as personnel management, home economics, physical therapy, and agriculture.

In 1930, as the Depression worsened, President Hoover asked Gilbreth to serve on the Emergency Committee for Unemployment. Gilbreth quickly developed a nationwide program called "Share the Work" to stimulate the creation of new jobs. The committee chair, Arthur Woods, praised her successful plan as "a brilliant conception and carried through with speed and skill." The following year she served in the President's Organization on Unemployment Relief as an unpaid volunteer (Yost, 1949, p. 333).

When World War II involved the United States, Lillian Gilbreth was sixty-three. Five of her six sons were serving in the armed forces while she herself served as a management consultant in war plants and on military bases. It was the respect that she had earned in her own right that caused her government to request her services in two national emergencies.

Over the decades, Lillian Gilbreth found new areas and ways to apply the principles and techniques of scientific management. In 1924, the year her husband died, she wrote his biography, *The Quest for the One Best Way,* in which she expounded on his original contributions to scientific management. In the years that followed she turned her attention to the unique problems of women running homes, raising families, and working in offices, department stores, or factories. In 1927 she published *The Homemaker and Her Job* and, in 1928, *Living with Our Children.* In these books she combined her own philosophical views with the principles of psychology and management. She stressed her belief that homes should be happy places in which individuals can achieve fulfillment and a degree of freedom: wives and mothers are entitled to share in this freedom and fulfillment, but this happy situation can be attained only if the responsibilities of running the home are shared and efficiently handled. In other words, every housewife and mother needs to be an effective, efficient manager. To a large extent, Gilbreth had experimentally tested her views on managing a home and family during the years she and her husband raised their twelve children. Lillian and Frank Gilbreth did not simply teach scientific management, they lived it. Delightful accounts of their family life can be read in *Cheaper by the Dozen* (1948) and *Belles on Their Toes* (1954) by two of their children, Frank Jr. and Ernestine Gilbreth Carey.

Lillian Moller Gilbreth received many awards and honors during the sixty years of her professional career, including twenty honorary degrees. In 1921 she was given honorary membership in the Society of Industrial Engineers—a unique distinction for a woman at that time. Ten years later the same society awarded her the first Gilbreth Medal for distinguished contributions to management. In 1924 she was elected to membership in the American Society of Mechanical Engineers and was appointed to chair its Management Division's meeting on the psychology of management. Gilbreth was also named a Fellow of the American Psychological Association.

In 1944 the Gantt Gold Medal was awarded jointly to Lillian Gilbreth and, posthumously, to Frank Gilbreth by the American Society of Mechanical Engineers and the American Management Association. In 1952 J. W. McKenny called Lillian Gilbreth "The World's Greatest Woman Engineer" because of her impact on management, her innovations in industrial design, her methodological contributions to time and motion studies, her humanization of management principles, and her role in integrating the principles of science and management. In 1966 she received the Hoover Medal for distinguished public service by an engineer—the first woman to do so.

Lillian Gilbreth remained professionally active in the field of scientific management until the age of ninety. She died in 1972, mourned by her professional colleagues, her many former students, and her own extensive family.

REFERENCES

Gilbreth, F., with Gilbreth, L. M. (1908). *Concrete system*. Unpublished manuscript.

Gilbreth, F., with Gilbreth, L. M. (1909). *Bricklaying system*. Unpublished manuscript.

Gilbreth, F. (1911). *Motion study: A method for increasing the efficiency of the workman*. New York: D. Van Nostrand.

Gilbreth, F., & Gilbreth, L. M. (1912). *A primer of scientific management*. New York: D. Van Nostrand.

Gilbreth, F., Jr. (1970). *Time out for happiness*. New York: Thomas Y. Crowell.

Gilbreth, F., Jr., & Carey, E. G. (1948). *Cheaper by the dozen*. New York: Thomas Y. Crowell.

Gilbreth, F., Jr., & Carey, E. G. (1954). *Belles on their toes*. New York: Thomas Y. Crowell.

Gilbreth, L. M. (1914). *The psychology of management*. New York: Sturgis & Walton.

Gilbreth, L. M. (1924). *The quest for the one best way*. Chicago: Society of Industrial Engineers.

Gilbreth, L. M. (1927). *The homemaker and her job.* New York: Appleton-Century.

Gilbreth, L. M. (1928). *Living with our children.* New York: W. W. Norton.

Gilbreth, L. M. (1966). *Management in the home.* (Rev. ed.) New York: Dodd.

Gleason, R. (1981, April). Lillian Gilbreth wins international award. *Advanced Management,* 27.

McKenny, J. W. (1952, April). The world's greatest woman engineer. *CTA Journal,* 9–10, 20ff.

Yost, E. (1949). *Frank and Lillian Gilbreth: Partners for life.* New Brunswick, N.J.: Rutgers University Press.

Additional Representative Publications by
Lillian Gilbreth

Gilbreth, F., & Gilbreth, L. M. (1916). *Fatigue study.* New York: Sturgis & Walton.

Gilbreth, F., & Gilbreth, L. M. (1917). *Applied motion study.* New York: Sturgis & Walton.

Gilbreth, F., & Gilbreth, L. M. (1920). *Motion study for the handicapped.* New York: Macmillan.

Gilbreth, L., & Cook, A. R. (1947). *The foreman in manpower management.* New York: McGraw-Hill.

Gilbreth, L., & Yost, E. (1945). *Normal lives for the disabled.* New York: Macmillan.

FLORENCE LAURA GOODENOUGH (1886–1959)

Dennis N. Thompson

Florence Goodenough received her Ph.D. from Stanford University in 1924 and spent her career as a developmental psychologist at the University of Minnesota. Shortly after arriving at Minnesota, she published her Draw-a-Man test, a scale for measuring the intelligence of children by analyzing their drawings. She made numerous contributions to the methodology of studying children, including the development of time sampling and event sampling, research methods still in frequent use today. Following her work on testing and methodological issues, Goodenough turned her attention to the social and emotional development of young children. Her 1931 publication, *Anger in Young Children,* remains one of the most systematic and detailed analyses of emotional development during early childhood. During her brief career she published important works on a wide variety of additional topics including personality testing, individual differences, and maturation of human potential. Although illness forced an early retirement from the University of Minnesota in 1947, she remained active during her final years, publishing *Mental Testing* (1949), *Exceptional Children* (1956), and the third edition of her text *Developmental Psychology* (1959).

FAMILY BACKGROUND, EDUCATION, AND CAREER DEVELOPMENT

Florence Goodenough was born on August 6, 1886, in Honesdale, Pennsylvania, to Alice and Linus Goodenough. She was the youngest child in a large farm family of six girls and two boys. In her youth she attended school in Rileyville, Pennsylvania, and in 1908 received a B.Pd. (Bachelor of Pedagogy) from the Millersville, Pennsylvania, Normal School.

She completed her B.S. degree at Columbia University in 1920 and her M.A. at that institution under Leta Hollingworth in 1921. During this same period she served as director of research in the Rutherford and Perth Amboy, New Jersey, public schools. According to Dale Harris, who received his Ph.D. under her direction, this position would today be considered a school psychologist (D. B.

Harris, personal communication, June 6, 1988). It was also while serving in this capacity that she collected much of the data that led to her work on children's drawings.

In the summer of 1921, she began work under Lewis Terman at Stanford. She was a major participant with Terman's gifted study, serving one year as chief field psychologist and two years as chief research psychologist. She was listed as a contributor to the *Genetic Studies of Genius* (Terman, 1925).

After receiving her doctorate under Terman in 1924 she received an appointment at the Minneapolis Child Guidance Clinic. The following year, in 1925, she became a research assistant professor at the newly organized Institute of Child Welfare at the University of Minnesota under the directorship of John E. Anderson. By 1931 Goodenough became full professor and served until her retirement in 1947. Under John Anderson's long directorship, the Institute of Child Welfare at Minnesota became a center for test development and research on the origins of human abilities. It was in these areas that Goodenough was to focus her work.

MAJOR CONTRIBUTIONS AND ACHIEVEMENTS

Florence Goodenough's first book after arriving at Minnesota was *Measurement of Intelligence by Drawings* (1926a), in which she introduced her Draw-a-Man test. It remains one of her most significant achievements. Up until this time, nonverbal tests of the intelligence were either low in reliability and validity or were tediously long to administer. The Goodenough Draw-a-Man test presented a nonverbal test of intelligence for children aged two to thirteen that utilized the child's drawing of a man. In spite of a short administration time of approximately ten minutes, its reliability was high, and it correlated well with standard tests of intelligence of the period. The text of her book was profusely illustrated and contained detailed instructions for scoring and interpretation.

From its inception the Draw-a-Man test enjoyed widespread popularity. Twenty years after its introduction it was the third most frequently used test in clinical psychology, and as recently as 1961 it was still found to be among the top ten. This was particularly notable since the instrument was designed for use with children (Dunn, 1972). Dale Harris, following a joint publication with Goodenough (Goodenough & Harris, 1950), published the results of an extensive revision of the Draw-a-Man test. The revision featured new standardization, a companion Draw-a-Woman test, and introduced a drawing quality score. Now known as the Goodenough-Harris drawing test, considerations of scale development, standardization, reliability, and validity are treated in Harris' book, *Children's Drawings as a Measure of Intellectual Maturity* (Harris, 1963).

Following her work on the Draw-a-Man test, Goodenough turned her attention to developing more traditional verbal tests of intelligence for children. In her second book (Goodenough, 1928a) she investigated the 1922 Kuhlman revision of the Binet scale for preschool children. She reported that for most preschool children, IQ could be measured with significant stability. Exceptions were attributed to problems with some of the specific test items and to scoring errors.

Goodenough also worked on her own instrument to extend the Stanford Binet scale downward in age. Her efforts resulted in the publication of the Minnesota Preschool Scale (Goodenough, Foster, & Van Wagenen, 1932). The Minnesota Preschool Scale was largely an adaptation of items chosen from earlier Binet materials. It offered both language and nonlanguage scores and was designed to be compact and inexpensive (Ball, 1940). Though not as widely known as her Draw-a-Man Test, it remained in wide use into the 1940s.

In her early work on testing, Goodenough presented frequent reference to and detailed discussion of methodological issues and the limitations of research, especially her own. In 1928 she developed what has become known as time sampling (Goodenough, 1928b). In time sampling a particular behavior such as thumb sucking is targeted for observation. Researchers agree on a uniform series of short time intervals for observing subjects. By taking a series of observations a record is produced showing the frequency of occurrence of the behavior under observation. The technique has been used widely since her initial publication.

Goodenough was also one of the first to publish on event sampling, a technique she was to use with her own study on anger in childhood (Goodenough, 1931a). In this approach the investigator observes the behaviors of a given predefined category. A researcher working with children waits for the events to happen and then describes them if and when they occur. Goodenough argued that the technique was particularly useful when studying natural behavior that occurred infrequently. It is also useful, she believed, when lay adults are to serve as observers. A detailed analysis of the early literature on these two methodologies is presented by Wright (1960).

She was also responsible for developing innovations to testing. She was one of the first to critique use of the ratio IQ. In the 1933 edition of the *Handbook of Child Psychology* (Goodenough, 1933) she argued that the concept of mental age did not always have the same meaning for all children. Instead she advocated the use of percentages in reporting test results, arguing that interpretation is far clearer for lay people. In addition she maintained that percentages would allow the comparison of children of the same chronological age with each other. Her major statement on methodology can be found in *Experimental Child Study*, which presented an analysis of the methodologies and techniques in the field (Goodenough & Anderson, 1931). Perhaps most notably, in this volume she introduces the Minnesota Scale of Paternal Occupations, a scale widely used to measure socioeconomic status for more than two decades.

Following her work on testing and methodological issues, Goodenough turned her attention to the social and emotional development of young children. One of the first issues in the field of developmental psychology derived from Watson's (1926) claim that the newborn is capable of three basic emotions, rage, fear, and love, and that more complex emotions are learned from these. By the late 1920s a number of research efforts suggested modifications in Watson's ideas about the development of emotions in infancy. Perhaps the most notable of these were the work of Sherman (1927) and Bridges (1932). Goodenough's 1931 publication, *Anger in Young Children,* was an early attempt to extend work on the development of emotions beyond infancy. It remains one of the most systematic and detailed works concerning emotional development in childhood. In her study, Goodenough trained parents to use event sampling to observe and record anger outbursts in their children. Forty-one children from infancy through age seven served as subjects. Goodenough reported that in the case of children who were less than one year, one-fourth of all outbursts arose in connection with routine child care such as dressing or bathing. An additional one-fourth were attributed to minor physical discomforts. The remaining incidents were attributed to restriction of body movement and other causes. By age four, however, children had become social, and difficulties arising in connection with social relations were the greatest source of anger.

Goodenough's results were descriptive. While she was a strong advocate of the inherent basis of emotions, *Anger in Young Children* was designed to help parents and professionals identify trends in child development.

At about this same time, Goodenough did publish several additional papers in which she presented evidence that maturation rather than environment was the major factor in determining emotional development of children (Goodenough, 1931b, 1932). In one of these publications, Goodenough (1931b) presented sixty-eight university students with a task in which they were to match photographs of a ten-month-old infant with descriptions of the situation in which the pictures had originally been taken. The students were able to match the photographs and their descriptions correctly at a level well above chance. Goodenough used this evidence to argue that emotional states are based on inborn reaction patterns that can be identified even in early infancy.

Goodenough's most noted controversy was with the University of Iowa Research Group, headed by Beth Wellman, over the effects of environmental intervention on children's IQ scores. The controversy reached a peak when Skeels and Dye (1939) reported the results of a study in which two infants who were residents of a state orphanage were committed to an adult institution for the mentally retarded. The infants had scored poorly on intelligence tests and were judged to be seriously developmentally delayed. By the end of the first year in the new institution, both of the children were reported to have near-normal IQ scores. The authors attributed the improvement to the fact that the adult patients in the ward and the attendants had become attached to the infants and had spent a great deal of time interacting with them.

In response, Goodenough published a series of articles (e.g., Goodenough, 1939, 1940) in which she defended the concept of fixed intelligence and questioned the role that environmental intervention plays in the development of children's IQ scores. This had been a long-standing source of controversy in the field. One of the first reports of an improvement in intelligence from schooling came from Wooley in 1925 (Wooley, 1925). As early as 1928, a volume of the

Yearbook of the National Society for the Study of Education was devoted to the opposing sides of the debate. In Goodenough's entry in this volume (Goodenough, 1928c), she specifically addressed Wooley's findings. While arguing for a fixed or stable IQ across the developmental years, Goodenough presented a detailed analysis of possible reasons for discrepancy. In her conclusion she cited differences in the kind of mental stimulation offered by different schools, selective factors that made for irregularities in the original selection of the experimental and control groups, and unconscious bias on the part of the experimenter.

Goodenough remained objective regarding the limitations of her own views. By 1942 (Goodenough & Maurer, 1942) she critically examined her own work in the area and revised her views to admit that intellectual development was not as inflexible and was far more fluid than she had previously believed.

In the 1940s, as personality and projective testing became more important in the field, Goodenough turned her attention to the measurement of personality. During World War II, she developed for the Woman's Army Corps a projective test using free association with words having several meanings. She developed keys for masculinity-femininity and leadership but retired before she completed work on the test (Goodenough, 1946).

During her later years at Minnesota, Goodenough contracted an illness that brought about failing vision and hearing. This led to an early retirement in 1947. During her retirement in a rural community in New Hampshire, in spite of near-total blindness and partial loss of hearing, she produced three of her best-known works. *Mental Testing* (1949) not only presented detailed analysis of measurement, but established her as an important historian of the mental testing movement. *Exceptional Children* (1956) was her first major work on this subject and was referred to in the field for many years. She also published the final edition of her text book *Developmental Psychology* (1959), coauthored with Leona Tyler, which became the best known of the three editions of this work.

CRITICAL EVALUATION OF CONTRIBUTIONS AND ACHIEVEMENTS

Goodenough was nearly forty years old when she came to Minnesota to begin her professional career. Although failing health forced an early retirement, Goodenough's career at Minnesota was extremely productive. She published nine books, twenty-six professional articles, and numerous publications for the popular press. Among her more prominent students were Mary Shirley, Dorothea McCarthy, Leona Tyler, Dale Harris, and Ruth Howard, the first black woman in America to receive a Ph.D. in psychology.

She was highly recognized and honored in her time. She was president of the Society for Research in Child Development in 1946 and 1947 and concurrently was secretary and then president of the Division on Childhood and Adolescence of the American Psychological Association. In 1942 she became president of the National Council of Women Psychologists, a position with which she was never completely comfortable. At one point during her association with the council she resigned and refused to pay her dues of $4.00, insisting that she was a psychologist, not a "woman psychologist" (Mildred Templin, personal communication, June 15, 1988).

Throughout her career, Goodenough was an innovator of the first magnitude. Starting with the first edition of *Developmental Psychology* (1934), she was one of the first in her field to argue for a life-span approach to human development. But while Goodenough argued for an integrative approach to the life span, she was also one of the first to focus on the integrative and adaptive implications of young children's behavior. Up to the time of her work, most developmental psychologists were interested in studying norms of child development, such as those for motor development or speech, as isolated units of behavior. Goodenough was one of the first to focus on the necessity of studying the interrelationships among human behaviors. She maintained that proper understanding of development of one function or activity is impossible without simultaneous data on the development of other behaviors.

Her interest in testing gave her an appreciation for the differences that exist among children. Throughout her work, frequent references are made to socioeconomic, ethnic, racial, cultural, and particularly sex differences.

She was, however, also a product of her time. Lewis Terman, her advisor, had been a student of G. Stanley Hall. Goodenough was in a sense part of the third generation of developmental psychologists who fell heavily on the nature side of the nature-nurture continuum. In her early years, the fact that there were economic and cultural differences in intelligence test scores was assumed to be evidence of innate differences in educability. In an early paper, for example, Goodenough (1926b) wrote that a person of limited intelligence tends to gravitate to "those neighborhoods where the economic requirement is minimal. . . . His children inherit his mental characteristics" (p. 391).

A thorough and exhaustive scholar, Goodenough was more open than most to change. By the mid 1930s, in a paper presented before the American Association for the Advancement of Science, she argued against the classification of cultures as superior and inferior (Goodenough, 1936). In a still later paper she argued that the search for a culture-free intelligence test, suitable for all groups of people, was not possible (Goodenough & Harris, 1950). In a footnote in the same article she apologized for her early statements on cultural superiority.

INTEGRATION OF PERSONAL AND PROFESSIONAL LIFE

Goodenough is remembered not only as a distinguished research psychologist and a rigorous and exacting teacher, but also as a friend who was a delightful companion, sharing her fondness for music, nature study, and photography. She was very generous with her students. Choosing to focus on a successful professional career, she never married.

Upon her retirement she moved to New Hampshire, where she lived in a duplex with other members of her family. She adapted to her deteriorating health by learning braille and even took a trip around the world in the mid-1950s. She died of a stroke on April 4, 1959, in Lakeland, Florida, while visiting a sister.

REFERENCES

Ball, R. S. (1940). The Minnesota Preschool Scale. In O. K. Buros (Ed.), *The 1940 mental measurements yearbook* (pp. 231–232). Highland Park, N.J.: Gryphon Press.

Bridges, K.M.B. (1932). Emotional development in early infancy. *Child Development, 3*, 324–341.

Dunn, J. A. (1972). Goodenough-Harris drawing test. In O. K. Buros (Ed.), *The seventh mental measurements yearbook* (pp. 671–673). Lincoln, Nebr.: Buros Institute of Mental Measurement.

Goodenough, F. L. (1926a). *Measurement of intelligence by drawings*. Yonkers-on-Hudson, N.Y.: World Book Co.

Goodenough, F. L. (1926b). Racial differences in the intelligence of school children. *Journal of Experimental Psychology, 9*, 388–397.

Goodenough, F. L. (1928a). *The Kuhlman-Binet tests for children of preschool age: A critical study and evaluation*. Minneapolis: University of Minnesota Press.

Goodenough, F. L. (1928b). Measuring behavior traits by means of repeated short samples. *Journal of Juvenile Research, 12*, 230–235.

Goodenough, F. L. (1928c). A preliminary report on the effect of nursery-school training upon the intelligence test scores of young children. *Yearbook of the National Society for the Study of Education, 27*(1), 361–369.

Goodenough, F. L. (1931a). *Anger in young children*. Minneapolis: University of Minnesota Press.

Goodenough, F. L. (1931b). The expression of emotions in infancy. *Child Development, 2*, 96–101.

Goodenough, F. L. (1932). Expressions of the emotions of a blind-deaf child. *Journal of Abnormal and Social Psychology, 27*, 328–333.

Goodenough, F. L. (1933). The measurement of mental growth. In C. Murchison (Ed.), *Handbook of child psychology* (2nd ed., pp. 303–328). Worcester, Mass.: Clark University Press.

Goodenough, F. L. (1934). *Developmental psychology*. New York: Appleton-Century.

Goodenough, F. L. (1936). The measurement of mental functions in primitive groups. *American Anthropology, 38*, 1–11.

Goodenough, F. L. (1939). Look to the evidence! A critique of recent experiments on raising the I.Q. *Educational Methods, 19*, 73–79.

Goodenough, F. L. (1940). New evidence on environmental influence of intelligence. *Yearbook of the National Society for the Study of Education, 39*, 307–365.

Goodenough, F. L. (1946). Semantic choice and personality structure. *Science, 104*, 451–456.

Goodenough, F. L. (1949). *Mental testing: Its history, principles, and applications*. New York: Rinehart.

Goodenough, F. L. (1956). *Exceptional children*. New York: Appleton-Century-Crofts.

Goodenough, F. L., & Anderson, J. E. (1931). *Experimental child study*. New York: Appleton-Century-Crofts.

Goodenough, F. L., Foster, J. C., & Van Wagenen, M. J. (1932). *The Minnesota preschool tests: Manual of instructions. Forms A and B*. Minneapolis: Educational Testing Bureau.

Goodenough, F. L., & Harris, D. B. (1950). Studies in the psychology of children's drawings: II. 1928–1949. *Psychological Bulletin, 47*, 369–433.

Goodenough, F. L., & Maurer, K. M. (1942). *The mental growth of children from age two to fourteen years: A study of the productive value of the Minnesota Preschool Scales*. Minneapolis: University of Minnesota Press.

Goodenough, F. L., & Tyler, L. E. (1959). *Developmental psychology* (3rd ed.). New York: Appleton-Century-Crofts.

Harris, D. B. (1963). *Children's drawings as measures of intellectual maturity: A revision and extension of the Goodenough Draw-a-Man test*. San Diego: Harcourt Brace Jovanovich.

Sherman, M. (1927). The differentiation of emotional responses in infants: I. Judgements of emotional response from motion picture views and from actual observation. *Journal of Comparative Psychology, 7*, 265–284.

Skeels, H. M., & Dye, H. B. (1939). A study of the effects of differential stimulation on mentally retarded children. *Proceedings of the American Association of Mental Deficiency, 44*, 114–136.

Terman, L. M. (1925). *Genetic studies of genius: The mental and physical traits of a thousand gifted children*. Stanford, Calif.: Stanford University Press.

Watson, J. B. (1926). Experimental studies of the growth of the emotions. In C. Murchison (Ed.), *Psychologies of 1925* (pp. 37–57). Worcester, Mass.: Clark University Press.

Wooley, H. T. (1925). The validity of standards of mental measurement in young childhood. *School and Society, 21*, 476–482.

Wright, H. F. (1960). Observational child study. In P. Mussen (Ed.), *Handbook of research methods in child development* (pp. 71–139). New York: John Wiley.

Additional Representative Publications by Florence Goodenough

Goodenough, F. L. (1926). A new approach to the measurement of intelligence of young children. *Journal of Genetic Psychology, 33*, 185–211.

Goodenough, F. L. (1927). The consistency of sex differences in mental traits at various ages. *Psychological Review, 34*, 440–462.

Goodenough, F. L. (1927). The relationship of the intelligence of preschool children to the education of their parents. *School and Society, 26*, 54–56.

Goodenough, F. L. (1928). The relation of the intelligence of preschool children to the occupation of their fathers. *American Journal of Psychology, 40*, 284–294.

Goodenough, F. L. (1929). The emotional behavior of young children during mental tests. *Journal of Juvenile Research, 13*, 204–219.

Goodenough, F. L. (1930). Interrelationships in the behavior of young children. *Child Development, 1*, 29–47.

Goodenough, F. L. (1934). Trends in modern psychology. *Psychological Bulletin, 31,* 81–97.

Additional Representative Publications About Florence Goodenough

Harris, D. B. (1959). Florence L. Goodenough, 1886–1959. *Child Development, 30,* 305–306.

Stevens, G., & Gardner, S. (1982). Florence Laura Goodenough. In G. Stevens & S. Gardner (Eds.), *The women of psychology, Volume 1: Pioneers and innovators* (pp. 193–197). Cambridge, Mass.: Schenkman Publishing.

Watson, R. J. (1974). Florence Laura Goodenough. In R. J. Watson, (Ed.), *Eminent contributions to psychology, Volume 1: A bibliography of primary references* (pp. 157–158). New York: Springer.

Watson, R. J. (1976). Florence Laura Goodenough. In R. J. Watson (Ed.), *Eminent contributions to psychology, Volume 2: A bibliography of secondary references* (pp. 365–368). New York: Springer.

Wolf, T. H. (1980). Florence Laura Goodenough, August 6, 1886-April 4, 1959. In B. Sicherman and C. Green (Eds.), *Notable American women: The modern period* (pp. 284–286). Cambridge, Mass.: Belknap Press of Harvard University Press.

JACQUELINE JARRETT GOODNOW
(1924–   )

Richard D. Walk

Jacqueline Jarrett Goodnow has had a long and distinguished career as a cognitive and developmental psychologist. She began her cognitive studies at Radcliffe with a dissertation on adult two-choice learning that sparked collaborative research that resulted in the classic *A Study of Thinking* (Bruner, Goodnow, & Austin, 1956). Thus, early in her career she helped change the course of psychology toward the study of cognitive science.

She was also a pioneer in the study of the influence of culture on thinking with her monograph on the use of Piagetian tasks with schooled and unschooled children in Hong Kong (Goodnow, 1962). At George Washington University she studied intersensory topics with children and began her studies of children's drawings viewed as cognitive, problem-solving productions, resulting in the influential book *Children Drawing* (Goodnow, 1977). At Macquarie University she continued studies with children and broadened her interest in children to topics of social policy. This is represented in the books *Children and Families in Australia: Contemporary Issues and Problems* (Burns & Goodnow, 1979), *Home and School: A Child's Eye View* (Goodnow & Burns, 1985), and *Women, Social Science and Public Policy* (Goodnow & Pateman, 1985).

Jacqueline Goodnow's career has been devoted to an understanding of cognitive processes, of thinking in a broad sense, with a focus on children. Recipient of the 1989 G. Stanley Hall Award of the American Psychological Association's Division on Developmental Psychology, she is internationally known as a developmental psychologist who focuses on cognition, pushing to understand ''the links between schemas and actions'' (Goodnow, 1988b).

FAMILY BACKGROUND AND EDUCATION

Jacqueline Jarrett Goodnow was born November 25, 1924, in Toowoomba, a middle-sized town about fifty miles west of Brisbane, in Queensland, Australia. Her parents were George Bellingen Jarrett and Florence Bickley Jarrett. The second oldest of six children, she is a fifth-generation Australian with ''convict'' as well as ordinary citizen forebears on her father's side. Her family moved to Sydney by the time she was ready for high school, and she attended a girls' high school that was oriented toward the humanities but offered no physics, chemistry, or biology. She credited her mother, a former secretary, with developing her drive to achievement.

At the age of sixteen Jarrett went to the University of Sydney, graduating in 1944 with first class honours in Psychology and a University Medal. She stayed at the University of Sydney as a laboratory instructor, teaching fellow, and temporary lecturer until 1948. The university offered no Ph.D., the opportunities for women were limited, and a senior staff member, Cecil Gibb, recommended that she go to the United States, his first recommendation being Harvard's new Department of Social Relations. She received a two-year Sydney traveling scholarship, and she was at Harvard from January 1949 to March 1951, receiving a Ph.D. from Radcliffe in clinical psychology but with a dissertation on two-choice learning. She spent the summer of 1949 as a clinical psychology intern at St. Elizabeth's Hospital in Washington, D.C.

At Harvard she was a research assistant to Jerome Bruner, the statistician Frederick Mosteller, and Leo Postman. She also became acquainted with fellow graduate students Robert Goodnow (whom she later married), William Lambert, Barbara Norfleet, James Olds, Edgar Schein, Renato Tagiuri, and Richard Walk.

CAREER DEVELOPMENT AND ACHIEVEMENTS

After Harvard she went briefly to England and in 1951 accepted a job offer from Robert Goodnow, who was working near Munich, Germany, developing psychometric tests for testing Europeans, mainly refugees, who might work for the army. They married in October 1951.

In 1953 the couple returned to Cambridge, Massachusetts. She worked with Jerome Bruner and George Austin as a research associate while her husband finished his dissertation. Her husband returned to Washington after one year, while she stayed on to see the research prepared for publication. The product was *A Study of Thinking* (Bruner, Goodnow, & Austin, 1956).

From 1956 to 1959 she was a research scientist at the Walter Reed Army Institute of Research, where she worked on two-choice learning problems. She also collaborated with Harold Williams and Ardie Lubin on a large-scale study of the effect of sleep loss on performance, pursuing her interest in the effect of sleep loss on cognitive performance (Williams, Lubin, & Goodnow, 1959).

In 1959 she moved to Hong Kong, where she had an honorary appointment at the University of Hong Kong for two years and carried out a large study with Piagetian tasks on Hong Kong's diverse ethnic population (Goodnow, 1962). This period began her long interest in the cultural determinants of cognition. Her two children, Christopher and Katherine, were born in Hong Kong. Returning to the United States, Goodnow was a research associate and lecturer at George Washington University from 1962 to 1964. She continued to work on

Piaget's tasks (Goodnow & Bethon, 1966), expanding Piaget's interest in activity to research on the effects of activity on cognitive growth.

The next year she went to Rome, where her husband's position took him. In the year in Italy she read Duncker in German, took care of the children, and prepared a proposal for a five-year National Institute of Child Health and Human Development (NICHHD) Early Career Award to study cross-modal integration of information.

On returning from Rome, she joined the faculty of George Washington University, where she went from assistant to associate to full professor from 1966 to 1972. She received the NICHHD career development award and began a series of studies with children on the integration of the sense modalities (e.g., Goodnow, 1969a). She also began research on children's graphics that culminated in a book on children's drawings (Goodnow, 1977).

Jacqueline Goodnow returned to Australia in 1972. Her husband, Bob, took early retirement, and they moved to Sydney. She became a senior lecturer and associate professor at the School of Education, Macquarie University, in Sydney, from 1972 to 1976. At this time she developed an aversive reaction to sunlight that meant wearing hats and long-sleeved clothing. During this period she worked on training teachers for preschool centers and became more interested in child care and social policy. Three books, Burns & Goodnow (1979), Goodnow & Burns (1985), and Goodnow & Pateman (1985) represent this interest.

In 1976 Goodnow became professor of psychology at the School of Behavioural Sciences, Macquarie University. She is one of the few female members of the Australian Academy of Social Sciences. She retained her interest in developmental issues, in cross-cultural topics related to thinking, in families, and in social policy. In 1988 she wrote:

I was surprised to find no attention to the cognitive underpinnings of family life. What did parents think they were doing? What concepts of children and development did they hold? Where did these come from? How did change come about? What effects did these ideas have on their actions and their satisfaction with family life? I am still working on family topics as a content area, and expect to use that as a continuing empirical base. It is a topic that continually pushes me toward understanding more thoroughly the links between schemas and actions. It also brings out continually the social shaping of the frameworks and expectations we bring to tasks and situations in either laboratory or everyday settings. (Goodnow, 1988b)

While at Macquarie, she has held visiting appointments at the Institute of Child Development, University of Minnesota (Spring Quarter, 1981), and as a Fellow at the Center for Advanced Study in the Behavioral Sciences at Stanford (1984–1985). She has frequently visited the United States for conferences and meetings.

During her career Goodnow interacted with a number of psychologists, maintaining contact with many of them after returning to Australia. In addition to the Harvard graduate students previously mentioned, she became acquainted at

Harvard with George Austin (who died in 1955), Lotte Bailyn, Jean Mandler, Molly Potter, and Bob Seymour. At George Washington, Richard Walk and Lila Ghent Braine were colleagues, and she worked with students Stuart Appelle, Marcia Bernbaum, Gloria Bethon, Philip Davidson, Sarah Friedman, Elyse Lehman, Rochelle Levine, Jacqueline Samuel, Joan Shagan, and Peggy Stevenson. At Macquarie she has worked with colleagues John Antill, Ailsa Burns, Carole Pateman, and Graeme Russell along with graduate students Judith Cashmore and Rosemary Knight.

ACHIEVEMENTS AND CONTRIBUTIONS

The main themes of Goodnow's contributions to psychology are the following: (1) the two-choice learning studies, (2) research on thinking, (3) culture and thought, (4) the effect of perceptual activity on different modalities, (5) studies of children's drawings and what she terms "the grammar of action," and (6) an interest in social policy and broad developmental issues.

Two-Choice Learning Studies

Goodnow's studies beginning with Jerome Bruner at Harvard were important forerunners of cognitive psychology and helped set the stage for her later collaboration with Bruner on studies of thinking. In the view of the dominant behaviorism of the time, rewards were important determinants of behavior. But Goodnow showed that, when reward is kept constant, behavior differs depending on how the subject defines the situation (Goodnow, 1955a, 1955b). In a "gambling" situation the tendency was to maximize reward, but in a problem-solving situation the subject considered longer runs of behavior, looking for a pattern, and an individual choice, win or lose, was not so important. Strategies, that is, how the subject defined the situation, were also important in studies of concept attainment.

Research on Thinking

In experiments on thinking, subjects picked their own strategies and reward was not so important. In a typical experimental situation the subject sat facing a table with a number of cards on it. For example, the cards might vary in form (cross, square, or circle), number of forms (1, 2, or 3), color of form (green, red, or black), and border (none, 1, or 2). The task of the subject was to find the correct concept (example: all red figures with one border). The subject might be given a positive instance and told to find the concept. Subjects differed in the strategies they employed. A "focus" strategy was slow but sure, while a "scanning" strategy put many requirements on memory and was more risky. Or the subjects might be given one instance at a time, starting with a positive concept, told to write a hypothesis, given another instance (which might be a positive or negative instance), told to write a hypothesis again, and so on, until the subject could define the concept. While subjects could, in theory, learn as much from negative as positive instances, the subjects mainly learned from the positive instances.

Wessells expressed the boost this work gave to the study of cognition as follows: "In the 1950s, Bruner, Goodnow and Austin (1956) argued that people learn concepts by actively planning a method or strategy that guides their performance. These strategies were beyond the scope of associationistic theory and encouraged the development of active, cognitive theories" (Wessells, 1982, p. 216). Thus, early in her career, Jacqueline Goodnow helped change the course of psychology.

Culture and Thought

Goodnow's trip to Hong Kong (1959–1961) extended her interest in thinking from one in adult thinking processes to those of children in different cultures. She used Piaget's conservation tasks and two combinatorial tasks.

Goodnow gave the Piagetian tasks of conservation of weight, volume, and space, along with Raven's Progressive Matrices task and Piaget's factorial problem, to over 500 Chinese and European boys aged ten to thirteen. The school environment of the boys ranged from schools restricted to Europeans, to highly select schools for Chinese, to schools for those of low socioeconomic status, to "semi-schooling" of about a year or more of informal schooling. The conservation tasks were not affected by schooling—those relatively unschooled did as well as those with more education—but the factorial problem (making as many pairs of colors from six colors as possible) and the Progressive Matrices task were (Goodnow, 1962).

On return to the United States, she gave the same tasks to a sample of "average" (IQ 101–120) and "dull" (IQ 64–88) boys in Montgomery County, Maryland (Goodnow & Bethon, 1966). U.S. boys of average intelligence were similar to both schooled and semi-schooled Chinese boys on the conservation tasks and like the schooled Chinese boys on the combinatorial tasks. But the "dull" U.S. sample was inferior to both groups of Chinese on the conservation tasks and similar to the semi-schooled Chinese on the combinatorial tasks. Thus, the Piagetian tasks were not affected by cultural milieu, but they were affected by intelligence. The combinatorial tasks, on the other hand, were affected by both schooling and intelligence.

In using Piaget's approach as a paradigm to study thinking, Goodnow was ahead of her time. Interest in Piaget in the United States, as shown by references in *Psychological Abstracts,* did not take off until the publication of John Flavell's book on Piaget in 1963 (Flavell, 1963).

The research with Piagetian tasks, along with her earlier research on thinking, placed her at the forefront of those interested in developmental and cultural aspects of thinking. Her interest has been lifelong, and she has contributed to many books on cross-cultural psychology (Goodnow, 1969c, 1970, 1979, 1980). As Elkind and Flavell wrote in their introductory essay: "Conservation and other Piagetian tasks have been administered to children in virtually every corner of the globe. . . . Goodnow's paper is a model of how to exploit the potential of this sort of research" (Elkind & Flavell, 1969, p. xviii).

Perceptual Activity and Modality Perception

Goodnow next conducted a series of studies that showed the importance of tactual activity as well as comparing vision with active touch and visual with auditory matching. The importance of active manipulation for development is shown when children can think of more nonstandard uses for objects they handle and view as compared to objects they only view (Goodnow, 1969a). Kindergartners and second graders noticed changes in curvature visually but had difficulty noticing it with touch, and upside down and left-right reversals were easily noticed by touch, but not differentiated visually. Thus, each sense modality provided different properties of cross-modal figures (Goodnow, 1969b). Goodnow also found that tactual form properties were much less stable in memory than visual properties for both kindergartners and adults (Goodnow, 1971a). A last study of this series (Goodnow, 1971b) used an auditory-visual match. Kindergarten children could reproduce simple auditory patterns, but they could not equate a larger space between visual dots with a longer auditory interval, though first graders could. Thus, "correspondence rules may provide new leverage on problems in perceptual development in much the same way that a rules approach has been productive in studying linguistic development" (Goodnow, 1971b, p. 1198). The study of children's drawings would provide the vehicle for her developing interest in rules.

Children's Drawings and the "Grammar of Action"

Goodnow's work on the topic of children's drawings revealed certain basic principles. Many books (Lowenfeld & Brittain, 1970) have catalogued the progression of the child from scribbling to simple figures until, around age twelve, the child begins to draw by adult rules and usually loses the spontaneity that makes the early drawings so fascinating.

Prior research tended to classify the drawings by age and to write of the different stages the child went through in progressing from early awkward stages to the more realistic. Goodnow's method was to give the child a more pared down situation, often with constraints, then see how the child handled the problem. A child might be given a circle with two dots ("eyes") low in the circle and be asked to complete it. Some might draw the body above the circle with an upside-down mouth; a more creative child might connect the two dots (a "mouth") and draw two eyes above (Goodnow & Friedman, 1972). The research on the "grammar of action" (Goodnow & Levine, 1973) gave the children simple figures, such as a plus sign or a square, and asked the children to draw them. With age, the child used more drawing sequences from top to bottom and from left to right; squares were drawn counterclockwise with a diminishing number, with age, going clockwise. Such drawing habits suggest that the child would have more trouble drawing d's and q's than b's and p's. Basic research could predict classroom performance.

Certain principles summarize children's drawings: "to each its own space," and "to each its own boundary." A child asked to add hair and arms to a circle with two vertical lines ("legs") never has the hair cross the arm lines; given such a figure with long hair, the child tends to add the arms to the "legs." Thus, the child's drawing is viewed as a problem-solving task with the child continually solving problems with drawings while adhering to certain rules, with the result that every new way of doing things creates its own problems, or, as Goodnow expresses it, "a problem solved is a problem created" (Goodnow, 1977).

A review of her book *Children Drawing* (1977) in *Contemporary Psychology* concluded, "It well may become a classic in its field" (Ives, 1979, p. 316). The influence of the book is shown in an edited book on children's artistic products, *Visual Order* (Freeman & Cox, 1985), where children are often given drawing problems to solve that are similar to those she used.

Social Policy and Developmental Issues

In the period since the mid-1970s Goodnow's focus has changed toward broader social issues, and, with this, to a broader definition of the interaction of culture and thought.

The broader interest in social policy is represented by *Children and Families in Australia* (Burns & Goodnow, 1979) and *Women, Social Science and Public Policy* (Goodnow & Pateman, 1985). The first book is a historical and contemporary view of family life in Australia. The special problems of family life in the convict period and of the aborigines are those of a continent isolated from the rest of the world, but the problems of modern Australia, of one-parent households, migrants, violence against children, are those of modern industrialized societies. A *Contemporary Psychology* review termed the book "a sophisticated and carefully researched volume" (Martin, 1980, p. 942). Goodnow & Pateman (1985), an edited book, includes Goodnow's chapter, "Topics, Methods and Models: Feminist Challenges in Social Science." Lynette Friedrich-Cofer, writing in *Contemporary Psychology,* described the book as "well-written, provocative and timely," and termed Goodnow's chapter an "impressive introductory essay" (Friedrich-Cofer, 1988, pp. 425–426).

In the 1980s Goodnow's scholarly output includes a book based on 2,000 interviews with children in the primary grades (Goodnow & Burns, 1985), a research article on children's drawings (Goodnow, Wilkins, & Dawes, 1986), and a *Psychological Bulletin* review of the distribution of household tasks (Goodnow, 1988a).

The Goodnow & Burns (1985) volume asked the children about their family life, their school life, and their friendships. It is a child's perspective, and one can sense that much research on the perspective of the child might be inspired by the book. The Goodnow, Wilkins, & Dawes (1986) study found that children produced more detailed but less spontaneous and action-oriented drawings if asked to make a "good" drawing. It is as if they recognize that the culture wants regularity, not spontaneity and creativity. The review of household tasks (Goodnow, 1988a) found that age, sex, and type of household (single or dual parent) can influence the distribution of household tasks.

Goodnow (1988b), weighing her career, wrote, "All problem solving takes place in a context: a context of action and a social context." The action context means "the weighing of goals and the effort or rewards of various moves (a 'functional' view)." The social context means that the surrounding culture influences "worthwhile goals, significant errors and reasonable degrees of effort."

In a long and distinguished career, Jacqueline Goodnow has retained a broad view of the thinking process. She has studied concept formation, children in Hong Kong, children performing perceptual tasks, the drawings of children under different conditions, and the meaning of this for the study of cognition. She has focused on the social policy implications of the problems of modern society for child development. Her research and eloquent writing have made her, deservedly, one of the leaders of her generation in the study of child development whose broad views on the thinking process cannot help but influence those who follow in her footsteps.

REFERENCES

Bruner, J. S.; Goodnow, J. J.; & Austin, G. A. (1956). *A study of thinking*. New York: Wiley. Reissued 1986 by Transaction Books, New Brunswick, N.J.

Burns, A., & Goodnow, J. J. (1979). *Children and families in Australia: Contemporary issues and problems*. Sydney: Allen & Unwin, Rev. ed., 1985.

Elkind, A., & Flavell, J. H. (Eds.). (1969). *Studies in cognitive development: Essays in honor of Jean Piaget*. New York: Oxford University Press.

Flavell, J. H. (1963). *The developmental psychology of Jean Piaget*. Princeton, N.J.: Van Nostrand.

Freeman, N. H., & Cox, M. V. (Eds.). (1985). *Visual order: The nature and development of visual representation*. Cambridge, Eng.: Cambridge University Press.

Friedrich-Cofer, L. K. (1988). Review of J. Goodnow & C. Pateman (Eds.), *Women, social science and public policy*. Contemporary Psychology, *33*, 425–426.

Goodnow, J. J. (1955a). Determinants of choice-distribution in two-choice situations. *American Journal of Psychology, 68*, 106–116.

Goodnow, J. J. (1955b). Response sequences in a pair of two-choice probability situations. *American Journal of Psychology, 68*, 624–630.

Goodnow, J. J. (1962). A test of milieu effects with some of Piaget's tasks. *Psychological Monographs, 76*, No. 555.

Goodnow, J. J. (1969a). Effects of active handling, illustrated by uses for objects. *Child Development, 40*, 201–212.

Goodnow, J. J. (1969b). Eye and hand: Differential sampling of form and orientation properties. *Neuropsychologia, 7*, 363–373.

Goodnow, J. J. (1969c). Problems in research on culture and thought. In D. Elkind & J. J. Flavell (Eds.), *Studies in cognitive development: Essays in honor of Jean Piaget* (pp. 439–462). New York: Oxford University Press.

Goodnow, J. J. (1970). Cultural variations in cognitive skills. In J. Hellmuth (Ed.), *Cognitive studies*, Vol. 1. New York: Brunner/Mazel.

Goodnow, J. J. (1971a). Eye and hand: Differential memory and its effect on matching. *Neuropsychologia, 9,* 89–95.

Goodnow, J. J. (1971b). Matching auditory and visual series: Modality problem or translation problem? *Child Development, 42,* 1181–1201.

Goodnow, J. J. (1977). *Children drawing.* Cambridge, Mass.: Harvard University Press.

Goodnow, J. J. (1979). Conventional wisdom: Everyday models of cognitive development. In L. Eckensberger, Y. Poortinga, & W. Lonner (Eds.), *Cross cultural contributions to psychology.* Amsterdam: Swets & Zeitlinger.

Goodnow, J. J. (1980). Concepts of intelligence and development. In N. Warren (Ed.), *Studies in cross-cultural psychology.* London: Pergamon.

Goodnow, J. J. (1988a). Children's household work: Its nature and functions. *Psychological Bulletin, 103,* 5–26.

Goodnow, J. J. (1988b, September 14). Personal communication.

Goodnow, J. J., & Bethon, G. (1966). Piaget's tasks: The effects of schooling and intelligence. *Child Development, 37,* 573–582.

Goodnow, J. J., & Burns, A. (1985). *Home and school: A child's eye view.* Sydney: Allen & Unwin.

Goodnow, J. J., & Friedman, S. (1972). Orientation in children's drawings: An aspect of graphic language. *Developmental Psychology, 7,* 10–16.

Goodnow, J. J., & Levine, R. (1973). The grammar of action: Sequence and syntax in children's copying of simple shapes. *Cognitive Psychology, 4,* 82–98.

Goodnow, J. J., & Pateman, C. (Eds.). (1985). *Women, social science and public policy.* Sydney: Allen & Unwin.

Goodnow, J. J.; Wilkins, P.; & Dawes, L. (1986). Acquiring cultural forms: Cognitive aspects of socialization illustrated by children's drawings and judgments of drawings. *International Journal of Behavioral Development, 9,* 485–505.

Ives, S. W. (1979). Review of J. J. Goodnow, *Children drawing. Contemporary Psychology, 24,* 315–316.

Lowenfeld, V., & Brittain, W. (1970). *Creative and mental growth* (5th ed.). New York: Macmillan.

Martin, B. (1980). Review of A. Burns & J. Goodnow, *Children and families in Australia. Contemporary Psychology, 25,* 942.

Wessells, M. G. (1982). *Cognitive psychology.* New York: Harper & Row.

Williams, H. L.; Lubin, A.; & Goodnow, J. J. (1959). Impaired performance with acute sleep loss. *Psychological Monographs, 73,* No. 484.

EDNA HEIDBREDER (1890–1985)

Robert S. Harper

Edna Heidbreder made major contributions in three general areas: psychometrics, systematic psychology, and concept formation. She was one of the developers of the Minnesota Mechanical Abilities Tests, which established new levels of excellence in test construction. Her *Seven Psychologies*, a detailed analysis of seven systems of psychology, is a timeless book. Her thirty years of research on concept formation provided new insights into the cognitive processes during thought. All of her research is characterized by careful, systematic, and detailed study.

FAMILY BACKGROUND AND EDUCATION

Edna Frances Heidbreder was born on May 1, 1890, in Quincy, Illinois. Her parents, William Henry Heidbreder and Mathilda Emelie Meyer, both of German immigrant parents, were born and raised in Quincy. When they were married in 1882, William Henry was employed by a wholesale drug firm. Twelve years later, in partnership with August and George Heidbreder, he became head of the retail drug business of W. H. Heidbreder & Company in Quincy. William and Tillie had five children—Bertha, Louise, Edna, Helen, and Ralph.

After graduating from Quincy High in 1907, Edna Heidbreder entered Knox College in Galesburg, Illinois. In 1911, with an official major in Latin, but with almost as many courses in biology, she graduated with general honors and with special honors in both Latin and biology. In addition, she was elected to Phi Beta Kappa and was selected as one of the commencement speakers. Regarding her psychology experience at Knox, she wrote:

When I was at Knox, ψ [psychology] was taught, as in many places, in the dept. of philosophy and philosophy was a one-man department. Prof. Raub, the one man, was an excellent teacher. . . . He gave a single, one-semester course in ψ *without* a laboratory of any kind. A few exercises with tuning forks and equipment for color contrast, after images and the like were as close as we came to experimental ψ. (Heidbreder, 1971)

Edna Heidbreder returned to Quincy following graduation and, for five years, taught history in various high schools in the Quincy area. Sometime before her matriculation in 1917 at the University of Wisconsin in a Master of Arts program, she spent part of a summer reading a recently published English translation of one of Freud's books, probably *Psychopathology of Everyday Life*. From her undergraduate days with William Raub, she had been increasingly preoccupied with the question, How do we know? (Onderdonk, 1985). Perhaps her reading of Freud pushed her toward graduate study in psychology, but her choice of Wisconsin and Joseph Jastrow, America's fourth Ph.D. in psychology, resulted from a senior year conference with Raub, who told her that Wisconsin had "a very rigorous, intellectual atmosphere" and that Jastrow was "a good, solid, sound psychologist" (Furumoto, 1980). She received her master's degree, with a thesis on "The Real and the Ideal in the Philosophy of Santayana," in 1918, at the end of her sojourn on what she once referred to as "an island in my academic life" (Heidbreder, 1969).

One event that she recalled from her Wisconsin days had apparent significance for some of her later activities. She was recalling that in her required experimental course, Jastrow gave the lectures and Clark Hull, later the renowned learning theorist but then a graduate assistant, ran the labs. Hull prepared instruction sheets for each experiment, including a few relevant references, and after the experiment was completed would discuss it with the lab pair.

One conference I remember with special distinctness. It was on an experiment, entitled on our instructions-sheet "The evolution of Concepts." My partner and I both thought it an unusually ingenious feat of experimental control and were surprised that no publications on that subject had been listed. When we asked Hull about the omission, he told us that he had invented the method and apparatus himself, that he had used them in his research for the dissertation he was presenting for his Ph.D., and that no account of his invention had as yet been published. (Heidbreder, 1969)

This lab exercise was a direct takeoff from Hull's doctoral dissertation (Hull, 1920). Hull's novel method in the study of concept formation, contrary to earlier studies in which subjects had been instructed to look for common elements, was to instruct the subjects simply to learn the names of a set of Chinese characters by a paired-associate technique. Evolution of the concept was demonstrated by an increasing number of correct anticipations with successive packs of figures. A variant of this procedure was utilized by Heidbreder in her doctoral dissertation, and variants of the procedure and the topic of concept formation remained an important research area for her throughout her life.

Edna Heidbreder's 'island' sojourn was followed by a two-year academic hiatus preceding her entrance to a doctoral program at Columbia. On a 1937 alumni information form, she reported going to Columbia in 1922. Two years later, in 1924, she received her Ph.D.

CAREER DEVELOPMENT

Upon completion of her doctorate, Heidbreder went to the University of Minnesota as an instructor. She left there in 1934 as an associate professor, after sandwiching in a year of postdoctoral study at the University of London (1930–1931).

She moved to New England in 1934 when she became professor of psychology at Wellesley College, a position she retained until becoming professor emerita in 1955. She chaired the department for ten of those years, 1936 to 1946. There she distinguished herself as "a brilliant and stimulating teacher" (Onderdonk, 1985), became an active participant in the northeastern psychological establishment, and took up again her active research in the area of concept attainment.

The war years and immediate postwar years were the ones of Heidbreder's most active involvement in psychology as a profession. She was concerned with women, and with women's curricular needs, in the war. She served as one of the six members of the American Psychological Association (APA) Council of Directors for one year in 1939–1940, and again for three years in 1941–1944; she was president of the APA Division of General Psychology for the years 1949–1950, and represented APA on the National Research Council during the years 1944–1947 and 1952–1955. She was president of the Eastern Psychological Association for a year in 1943–1944, and on its Board of Directors during 1944–1947. She was elected to chair Section I (Psychology) of the American Association for the Advancement of Science (AAAS) for the year of 1947, after serving three years, 1943–1946, as its secretary; that same year she also served as a vice president of the AAAS. During these years she was an associate editor of both the *Journal of Abnormal and Social Psychology* and of *Psychological Monographs*. She had been for many years a member of Phi Beta Kappa and of Sigma Xi, and during these active professional years she added a fellowship in the New York Academy of Sciences. Prior to her retirement from Wellesley, she spent the summer of 1950 as a visiting professor at the University of California, Berkeley.

Retirement from Wellesley did not mark an end to her active career. For the next six years, 1955–1961, she served as a member of Radcliffe College's seminar staff. Her post-Wellesley years were also ones of personal recognition for her contributions. Earlier, in 1941, she had received her undergraduate college's Alumni Achievement Award for "her distinguished contribution to higher education, particularly of American women." In September 1961, on the occasion of its seventy-fifth anniversary, the APA awarded Edna Heidbreder, along with thirty-six others, a certificate for "a distinguished lifetime's contribution to psychology as a science and as a profession" (Ceremonial session, 1967). Knox College awarded her an honorary Doctor of Laws degree in 1964. Heidbreder was the first Knox graduate to earn a doctorate in psychology, and at the time she entered graduate study, only twenty women held doctorates in psychology. In 1971, when the Knox psychology department moved into facilities in the new Science Mathematics Center, the laboratories were officially identified as the Edna Heidbreder Laboratories of Psychology. Later that same year, on May 1, she was elected the first honorary member of Cheiron, the International Society for the History of the Behavioral and Social Sciences. *Historical Conceptions of Psychology* (Henle, Jaynes, & Sullivan, 1973), a book published under the auspices of Cheiron, being a collection of papers selected from the first four annual meetings of the society, was dedicated to her. In addition to several papers by Heidbreder, this volume also contains a complete bibliography of her publications.

PROFESSIONAL CONTRIBUTIONS

Edna Heidbreder's publications fall into three general categories: a psychometric group, a systematic group, and a cognitive-thinking group. In Heidbreder's dissertation study, published as "An Experimental Study of Thinking" (Heidbreder, 1924), subjects initially learned a characteristic check mark that would identify each of what were essentially nonsense figures. The figures were then presented in pairs and the subject would write down the check mark he thought was correct. After recording the check mark, but before being told if it was "right" or "wrong," each subject was asked to report "everything that went on in his mind" during the trial. This introspective supplement to what was essentially the Hullian procedure proved significant. According to Robert S. Woodworth, Columbia's greatly respected general psychologist:

Her outstanding result was the demonstration of *spectator behavior*. The more usual *participant behavior* consists in trying out hypotheses. In spectator behavior O [observer] has no hypothesis; all his guesses have been proved erroneous, and he can only make some random response and remain on the watch for some new hypothesis to emerge. (Woodworth, 1938)

Robert Leeper, an early student of cognitive processes, referring to this and others that followed her early study, pointed out that

these studies indicate not merely that responses may be governed by sets or determining tendencies, initially established by conscious processes and later dropped from consciousness, but also that complex guiding processes can be formed, retained, and used without the person's being aware of the process at any step. (Leeper, 1951)

"An Experimental Study of Thinking" marked the beginning of a topic of research, and to a large extent a procedure of research, that Heidbreder was to carry on for years. But before continuing on this line, there was a diversion.

Her work in the psychometric area coincides with her early years at the

University of Minnesota. The most significant product of this facet of her career was her involvement in the development of the *Minnesota Mechanical Ability Tests* (Patterson, Elliott, Anderson, Toops, & Heidbreder, 1930). This project involved the construction of several batteries of mechanical tests, validated against multiple criteria, and took into consideration such variables as sex, culture, environment, and past experiences. A contemporary evaluation of this project asserted:

The most thorough investigation of mechanical abilities has been conducted at the University of Minnesota, and has been described by Patterson, Elliott, *et al.* . . . In fact, this investigation gives an excellent picture of the best available techniques used in present-day test construction. (Garrett & Schneck, 1933)

Heidbreder was obviously proud of her participation in this endeavor, for she listed it as one of her two major publications on both a 1937 and a 1963 alumni biographical information sheet for her undergraduate college.

The other of the two major publications that she listed on those biographical sheets was *Seven Psychologies*, written during her latter years at Minnesota. In this book she made a careful analysis of seven systems of psychology. More psychologists probably associate her with this book than with any one of her other efforts. With the possible exception of some introductory texts, more psychologists probably have read this book than any other single book in the history of psychology. It has been used as a text by more generations of psychologists than any other never revised book and has been in continuous print since 1933.

Reviews of the book at its initial publication were laudatory. Edwin G. Boring, writing just four years after the publication of his *History of Experimental Psychology*, which established him as the historian of psychology, said:

This is no ordinary book. The depth of insight, the accuracy of information and the facility of expression set it off from most of the psychological composition that we are all obliged to read. There is in the book one joke, tinged with irony: the title page calls the volume a "Student's Edition," a statement which can be literally true only if the word *student* means *scholar*. (Boring, 1934)

Boring, always a man greatly concerned with writing style, went on to say about *Seven Psychologies*:

The author disposes of these systems by getting enthusiastically expository about each in turn. She enters the stage from the wings of history as champion of Titchenerism, and then, presently, the scene shifts, and she is a keen and appreciative Jamesian; and thus on through other metamorphoses. . . . for range, clarity, and lack of bias, this book is without peer among the very few that exist. (Boring, 1934)

Another contemporary reviewer commented:

It stands as one of the most finished, bright, and effective expositions that we possess. Professor Heidbreder has done with wit, insight, and the fluency that distinguishes competence from pedantry, what she hoped to do for the elementary student. She deserves his warmest thanks; and the gratitude will undoubtedly be shared enthusiastically by those who are long since beyond his pedagogical needs. (Chapman, 1934)

The timelessness of *Seven Psychologies* was addressed by Mary Henle and John Sullivan in their review written in 1973, forty years after its initial publication.

No one can say that psychology has stood still since 1933: its empirical foundation and its methodologies have changed drastically, as have its theories and, indeed, its attitude toward theory building and its own history. And yet the astonishing thing about reading this volume today is the impression that one is reading a *contemporary* book. In a period in which we consider our factual knowledge outdated in the course of a decade or less, how is this possible? (Henle & Sullivan, 1974)

It is possible because Heidbreder began by characterizing what a system was, and then applied this to the seven systems she explored. This approach led her to get to the core of each system, so that where a system has persisted since 1933, such as Gestalt and psychoanalysis, even though the surface structure in 1973 differed from that of forty years earlier, her exposition of the deep structure of the system still pertained. Henle and Sullivan speculate that, in addition to its readability and sensitive analyses, the book is still being read ''because of a growing sense that the fragmentation of psychology needs to be corrected,'' a condition that Edna Heidbreder probably did not prophesy forty years earlier.

Heidbreder's return to research in the area of concept formation is contained in a series of nine articles published between 1946 and 1955. Harry Harlow, best known for his studies of mother love in monkeys, in reviewing this series said:

The most intensive investigations of stimulus variables in concept formation are those of Heidbreder and associates studying systematically the relative speed of formation of color, form, object, and number concepts by several hundred college students.

. . .

. . . the Heidbreder studies indicate the complexity of the operation of stimulus variables in concept formation. Changes in the context in which the types of concepts appear, changes in the type of response required of the subject, and changes in the concreteness of the materials have been demonstrated to alter the difficulty value of the same categories of concepts. The entire series of studies raises many questions that might well be pursued by the workers who would integrate into a general theory the research findings on concept formation. (Harlow, 1951)

This ten-year research program shows the same commitment to accuracy and detail of information noted by E. G. Boring earlier in his review of *Seven Psychologies* and seen even earlier in *Minnesota Mechanical Ability Tests*.

In 1964, when Edna Heidbreder was presented with her honorary degree by

Knox College and was exhausting her hosts with her exuberance and vitality, she was publicly identified as "America's outstanding woman psychologist." Today that might be modified a bit. She was an outstanding person. She died February 19, 1985, two and a half months short of her ninety-fifth birthday. Her wit, her charm, her commitment to friends never left her, although her hearing did deteriorate in her later years. She celebrated her ninetieth birthday with a conference telephone call with a Knox College history and systems class—which had to be prearranged so as not to interfere with her daily mile walk. An outstanding psychologist, her attention to detail and thoroughness in research is a model for all psychologists. Her discoveries in psychometrics and in concept formation furthered our understanding of human cognition. Her major impact undoubtedly has been through her systematic treatise *Seven Psychologies*, which has been studied by students for more than a half century.

REFERENCES

Boring, E. G. (1934). Seven psychologies. *American Journal of Psychology, 46*, 157–159.

Ceremonial session celebrating the seventy-fifth anniversary of the American Psychological Association with honored guests. (1967). *American Psychologist, 22*, 1144.

Chapman, D. W. (1934). Seven psychologies. *Psychological Bulletin, 31*, 207–210.

Furumoto, L. (1980). Edna Heidbreder: Systematic and cognitive psychologist. *Psychology of Women Quarterly, 5*, 94–102.

Garrett, H. E., & Schneck, M. R. (1933). *Psychological tests, methods, and results*. New York: Harper.

Harlow, H. (1951). Thinking. In H. Helson (Ed.), *Theoretical foundations of psychology* (pp. 452–505). New York: Van Nostrand.

Heidbreder., E. (1924). An experimental study of thinking. *Archives of Psychology, 11*, 1–65.

Heidbreder, E. (1933). *Seven psychologies*. New York: Century.

Heidbreder, E. (1969). Jastrow and Hull. Unpublished manuscript.

Heidbreder, E. (1971). Personal communication to RSH, November 22.

Henle, M., Jaynes, J., & Sullivan, J. J. (Eds.). (1973). *Historical conceptions of psychology*. New York: Springer.

Henle, M., & Sullivan, J. (1974). Seven psychologies revisited. *Journal of the History of the Behavioral Sciences, 10*, 40–46.

Hull, C. (1920). Quantitative aspects of the evolution of concepts. *Psychological Monographs, 28*, No. 123.

Leeper, R. (1951). Cognitive processes. In S. S. Stevens (Ed.), *Handbook of experimental psychology* (pp. 731f.). New York: Wiley.

Onderdonk, V. (1985, Spring). Edna Heidbreder, 1890–1985. *Wellesley Alumni Magazine, 31*, 51.

Patterson, D. G.; Elliott, R. M.; Anderson, L. D.; Toops, H. A.; & Heidbreder, E. (1930). *Minnesota Mechanical Ability Tests*. Minneapolis: University of Minnesota Press.

Woodworth, R. S. (1938). *Experimental psychology* (p. 806). New York: Holt.

Additional Representative Publications by
Edna Heidbreder

Heidbreder, E. (1946). The attainment of concepts: I. Terminology and methodology. *Journal of General Psychology, 35*, 173–189.

Heidbreder, E. (1946). The attainment of concepts: II. The problem. *Journal of General Psychology, 35*, 191–223.

Heidbreder, E. (1947). The attainment of concepts: III. The process. *Journal of Psychology, 24*, 93–138.

Heidbreder, E.; Bensley, M. L.; & Ivy, M. (1948). The attainment of concepts: IV. Regularities and levels. *Journal of Psychology, 25*, 279–329.

Heidbreder, E., & Overstreet, P. (1948). The attainment of concepts: V. Critical features and contexts. *Journal of Psychology, 26*, 45–69.

Heidbreder, E. (1948). The attainment of concepts: VI. Exploratory experiments on conceptualization at perceptual levels. *Journal of Psychology, 26*, 193–216.

Heidbreder, E. (1949). The attainment of concepts: VII. Conceptual achievements during card-sorting. *Journal of Psychology, 27*, 3–39.

Heidbreder, E. (1949). The attainment of concepts: VIII. The conceptualization of verbally indicated instances. *Journal of Psychology, 27*, 263–309.

Heidbreder, E., & Zimmerman, C. (1955). The attainment of concepts: IX. Semantic efficiency and concept-attainment. *Journal of Psychology, 40*, 325–335.

RAVENNA HELSON (1925–   )

Harrison G. Gough

Ravenna Helson is one of the world's acknowledged authorities on the psychology of creativity. In addition, she has made basic theoretical and empirical contributions to the study of creativity among female and male mathematicians, and to the understanding of life-span accomplishments among women nominated in college for their superior creative potential. She has also conducted important studies of writers and critics of books for children, systematically tracing the interactions of gender, imaginative processes, and the individuation of self as they are expressed in stories characterized by heroic, comic, or tender themes. In the late 1980s she continued to direct a major longitudinal analysis of a sample of more than one hundred women first studied as college seniors in the 1950s, then reassessed in the early 1960s and again in the 1980s. Among the key findings emerging from this work are the discoveries that personality factors play a vital role in predicting the realization of potential for women following either traditional or nontraditional life pathways, and that ego resilience sufficient to permit an unrepressive integration of both positive and negative personal experiences is crucial as a determinant of fulfillment in adulthood. In all of her writing she has made use of a distinctive methodology that combines intuitive case evaluations with the exactitude of nomothetic quantification.

FAMILY BACKGROUND AND EDUCATION

Ravenna Mathews Helson was born on February 13, 1925, in Austin, Texas. Her father, Edward Jackson Mathews, was the registrar and dean of admissions of the University of Texas. Her mother, Ravenna Wakefield Mathews, was a teacher of French at the university before she became a housewife. Both parents had earned master's degrees. Twin brothers, Edward J. Mathews, Jr., and Reed Wakefield Mathews, were born in 1929. The former earned a medical degree and became a psychiatrist; the latter received a master's degree in biology and became a college teacher.

Both parents were supportive, but Helson refers to her father as her "first mentor," and remarked: "He read Robinson Crusoe to me and then taught me to read. We walked to school together the year I was in first grade, and he taught me the names of all the wonderful subjects I would study year by year. Also, I found out from him what you could do by reasoning—but this was later, maybe sixth grade, when I had to debate that Franklin was greater than Washington." Both parents were active in church affairs. Helson reported that she went to many revival meetings as a child, and that by age eight she was convinced of her sinfulness and had accepted religious teachings.

Helson attended the University of Texas, Austin, from 1941 to 1945, graduating with a B.A. degree summa cum laude, and being elected to Phi Beta Kappa. She served on the staff of the *Daily Texan*, where she learned to write descriptive prose that told an accurate story. The faculty advisor for the newspaper was mentioned by Helson as a second major mentor or role model. After graduation she took a job as a newspaper reporter in Corpus Christi, Texas, but found it unrewarding. In 1947 she returned to the university, where she received a master's degree in psychology in 1949.

Her thesis advisor was Hugh Blodgett, who had earned his doctorate in 1925 under Edward C. Tolman at Berkeley, and whose specialty was latent learning. Helson described Blodgett as "a lovely man, gentle, and intelligent," and as having a suitable skepticism about psychology and about academic achievement if pursued too vigorously. Her first publication (Blodgett, McCutchen, & Mathews, 1949) stemmed from this period. With Blodgett's blessing, she then went on to Berkeley in the fall of 1949. She had expected to work with Tolman, but it was the "Year of the Oath" there, and Tolman's time and energy were fully taken up by his opposition to the Regents' demand that all members of the faculty must sign a declaration of loyalty to the government. Because of this, Helson's doctoral research was carried out under the supervision of Warner Brown and Leo Postman of psychology and Edward Barnhart of journalism. Her dissertation was titled "Recall of Items as a Function of the Number of Categories into Which They Have Been Classified," and led later to her first individually authored publication (Mathews, 1954).

The year that Helson came to Berkeley was also the year that the Institute of Personality Assessment and Research (IPAR) was established there, with Donald W. MacKinnon as director and Nevitt Sanford as associate director. MacKinnon had taught for a number of years at Bryn Mawr College, where one of his colleagues was Harry Helson, the originator of the psychological theory of adaptation level (H. Helson, 1964). Ravenna Helson met MacKinnon in 1949, but neither of them then suspected that in 1954 she would marry Henry Helson, the son of Harry, and would in 1957 become a member of MacKinnon's staff.

CAREER DEVELOPMENT

From 1952 to 1955 Helson was on the faculty of Smith College, where she taught experimental psychology and continued her studies of memory. In 1953 she met Henry Helson, then a Jewett Fellow in mathematics, and they were married in June 1954. Henry received an invitation to come to the University of California, Berkeley, in the fall of 1955. To accept meant that Ravenna would need to leave her tenure-track position at Smith and to seek whatever post she might find in Berkeley. In spite of this uncertainty, she encouraged her husband to accept the offer and helped to persuade him that California was not quite the intellectual and cultural backwater that his eastern life and roots had suggested it might be.

The psychology theme ran strong in the Helson family in still another way. Henry Helson's sister Martha was to earn a Ph.D. degree in psychology and marry William A. Wilson, who would earn both a Ph.D. degree in psychology and a doctorate in medicine. In regard to these family ties, Ravenna Helson remarked: "Certainly, being in the family was important. Harry Helson knew lots of people I considered famous. I loved talking with him, and probably it was easier to feel a member of the profession as his daughter-in-law during my marginal years."

On her return to Berkeley in 1955, she took a position as a junior public health analyst in the Bureau of Maternal and Child Health of the California State Department of Health. She observed that "the job kept me alive professionally, and gave me experience in research conducted in non-academic settings."[1] In 1956 her first child, David, was born, and the bureau chief promptly gave her a half-time appointment to develop her own project. A second child, Ravenna, was born in 1957, and a third and last child, Harold, was born in 1960.

In 1957 Donald MacKinnon invited Helson to join his staff at IPAR. She accepted the invitation, beginning an affiliation that continues down to the present day. This appointment allowed her to become fully associated with personality psychology, something that she desired, but it also brought clearly to the fore the problem of developing her identity as a personality psychologist. Helson recalled this problem and her ways of coping with it in the following words:

My problem now was to become a personality psychologist worthy of IPAR. I didn't know what was involved in a career, I just wanted to do good work, and I knew I should get it published. This was a big problem because personality was a new field for me; I had three little children; there was a lot of work to do, weekends included, in assessing the various groups of creative people we were studying at IPAR, and in starting the studies of creativity in women in the samples that I assembled (women mathematicians and the Mills College seniors). It was also difficult because the people whose standards I accepted as my own were very talented and active males. Also, I tried to do something general too soon. I'm not sure where the idea came from, but I felt I should write a monograph or book right away. Part of the pressure of becoming a worthy personality psychologist was that I had a wonderful assignment (to study creativity in women), yet one that aroused all kinds of conflicts and resistances, and feelings of lonely isolation. These were the years before the Women's Movement.

These problems and the feeling of working more or less alone led Helson to adopt certain specific strategies of coping. At the institute there was a mix of theory and empiricism that she found congenial, and also an abundance of individual case material pertaining to the inner, imaginative life of the assessees. In her work then and since, case illustrations have been prominently featured, and one of her papers (Helson, 1984) consists entirely of a penetrating psychological analysis of a single author at a single point in time.

The monograph Helson mentioned above turned out to be a difficult problem, in that it was twice rejected, in part for what seemed to be rather doctrinaire beliefs about how psychological research should be conducted. Helson's style was, and is, to move back and forth between case and theory, evolving hypotheses as understanding deepens, and then checking back into earlier and ahead into later events to see how they might fare. To a formalist, this mode of research may seem improvisational and even opportunistic, but when practiced in an insightful and responsible way it can be enormously fruitful. In any case, an article (Helson, 1966) on masculinity, originality, and other characteristics as factors in the creativity of women that embodied this method was accepted as submitted, giving Helson the feeling that she was on the proper track.

But trouble still loomed ahead on the monograph, which was rejected for a third time. The impact of this blow can best be described in Helson's own comments:

After the third rejection of my monograph I had a period of what Jung called *abaissement du niveau mentale*. There were other factors, too, of course. But all this came to a dramatic end in a dream which was almost electrocuting in the terror it invoked. The next day I was a new person. I had enormous energy. I reconceptualized the monograph so that it would include both the original Mills College data and recently acquired follow-up data from these women at age 27. It was to be lean and empirical, though still containing hypotheses. I carried out my plan section by section.

There was only one place left that might publish a monograph. I wrote to Robert R. Sears, then an advisory editor for *Genetic Psychology Monographs*, and he sent the manuscript on to the Editor-in-Chief with a friendly letter. There it was accepted, and published in 1967. It isn't one of my favorite works, because it took such an effort. However, the terrible dream led to an interest in symbolism, and a new appreciation of Jungian psychology along with an expanded personal awareness for which I am very grateful.

From this time on, Helson had found her niche and was moving ahead in a creative and productive program of research, including her studies of female and male mathematicians (Helson, 1971, 1980b; Helson & Crutchfield, 1970a, 1970b), writers and critics of books for children (Helson, 1973a, 1973b, 1974b, 1977, 1978a, 1978b, 1980a), and more general discussions of personality (Helson & Mitchell, 1978), creative styles (Helson, 1968), creativity among women (Helson, 1978c), images of the career woman (Helson, 1972), and women's work patterns as related to adolescent personality (Helson, Elliott, & Leigh, 1989).

In spite of this, there were still problems in that intrauniversity recognition of her merit was slow to develop. Part of this may have been due to her affiliation with a small research institute rather than a teaching department with a doctoral program. Part of it may have been due to the fact that until 1970 her appointment, usually half-time, was funded almost entirely by extramural grants, most of which she secured herself. And, in retrospect, the delay was partly due to insufficient initiative by the IPAR staff in recommending advancements for her. For reasons such as these, but clearly not because of any inadequacies in her research performance, far more than the usual number of years elapsed before she was promoted from the associate to the full research level, and to an adjunct professorship in the Department of Psychology. Helson's observations on these years, and on the slow and almost grudging support for her work within the university, are worth quoting:

Because I was paid so little and intermittently for many years, I had taken what seemed a course not alien to the aims of IPAR, to study what seemed intensely interesting and beautiful to me, without worrying about what other people in personality were doing. I felt free to go traveling with my family on my husband's sabbaticals, and have always found those periods good for working. I made friends with persons having common psychological interests, and they led me into activities that were increasingly possible as my children grew up. One friend told me that I should teach a course in summer school on the psychology of women. I suggested it, and in fact did teach what I think was the first class in women's studies on the Berkeley campus. It was very good for me.

MAJOR CONTRIBUTIONS AND ACHIEVEMENTS

The year 1980 saw promotion to full status, as just mentioned, and also the receipt of a research grant to conduct a follow-up study of the Mills College seniors first assessed in the late 1950s. It was also a year in which Helson's professional identity began to shift from personality psychology in general to the specific topic of adult development. One of the major contributions deriving from this new emphasis was a paper with Mitchell and Moane (1984) on the social clock.

Embedded within any culture at any given time are sequential expectations, describable as a social clock, for instance starting college in the late teens, but not getting married until after graduation; then having children soon after marriage, with no delays for further education or for work. Any career plans, according to the clock, must await the growing up of children, at least into the junior or senior high school years. For a young woman brought up in the 1940s or 1950s, these expectations exerted a powerful influence. In her longitudinal study of the Mills College seniors of the 1950s, Helson and her colleagues were able to classify subjects as having lived in compliance or noncompliance with these expectations. Each path has its own problems and potentialities, of course. Threats of conventionality and suppression of independent interests go with compliance, threats of rejection by others and feelings of alienation with noncompliance. On the positive side, feelings of normative virtue are associated with compliance, and a sense of self-realization with noncompliance. Through a mixture of case analyses and adroit use of quantitative data, the ways in which each lifestyle was lived out were depicted.

Another major theme in Helson's longitudinal work has dealt with the issue of stability versus inconsistency of personality over time. She found clear evidence for change, but change that was lawful and related to life events (Helson, Mitchell, & Hart, 1985; Helson & Moane, 1987). For instance, from ages twenty-one to twenty-seven, changes were associated with heightening of self-control, greater introspectiveness, and increased sensitivity to sex-role demands. From ages twenty-seven to forty-three, sex-role concerns diminished, internal complexity increased, and coping skills improved. All of these later changes were associated with more active participation in work and in the general culture; this trend was apparent for all subjects, irrespective of their adherence or nonadherence to the social clock.

A third emphasis has been on the identification of internal and experiential factors related to the adult realization of creativity potential among women judged earlier to have considerable promise (see Helson 1985, 1987). In regard to qualities observable at the time of college attendance, she found that a combination of personal force—good ego strength and faith in self—and symbolic reach or imaginative scope would identify those young women who subsequently went on to fulfill their potentiality. The Rankian notion (Rank, 1945) that creative motivation is a force integrating and directing the personality, including separation from both parents but particularly from the mother, was highly compatible with the empirical findings. Many of the creative nominees who went on to successful careers had turned from their dependent mothers as role models to the autonomy and assertiveness of their fathers. A negative parental background factor was the presence of a strong and capable, but at the same time dominating, mother.

More should also be said about Helson's research style as it has now fully evolved, that is, on the conjoint use of nomothetic and idiographic data. In our interview (Spring 1988), she remarked: "I combine the tough and the tender. I like broad theories about the individual in society and about the intrapsychic life of the individual. My research is usually person-centered rather than variable-centered, and I like to combine the concrete with the abstract, to test and give meaning to each other." Work like this is not common, and it is hard to do. Helson's success with the method, including having her manuscripts accepted and published in refereed journals, has been admirable, and should encourage others who have felt frustrated by prevailing nomothetic conventions.

Another distinguishing feature of Helson's research is her use of Jungian concepts and theory. In the 1950s the Jungian analyst John Weir Perry (see Perry, 1974) introduced her to Erich Neumann's treatment of patriarchal and matriarchal character patterns (1954). One consequence of this reading was Helson's analysis of matriarchal and patriarchal modes in the work of women mathematicians (1980b). Certain dreams and personal experiences at about age forty led her to view the Jungian concept of individuation with increased seriousness, and to the idea that the phenomenon of individuation could be studied in imaginative literature for children. This was followed by two grants from the Frances Wickes Foundation (Wickes was a Jungian analyst) and the launching of Helson's work on critics and writers of books for children. Then, in 1975, along with James Jarrett, who was at that time dean of the School of Education at Berkeley, she established an informal Jungian discussion group composed of both on-campus and off-campus persons that even now continues to hold regular meetings.

CRITICAL EVALUATION OF CONTRIBUTIONS

In recent years, explicit recognition of the importance and high quality of Helson's work has begun to appear. For example, in 1984 she received the Henry A. Murray Award from the Division of Personality and Social Psychology of the American Psychological Association. In 1984 Rae Carlson, in a survey of all of the papers in the 1982 *Journal of Personality and Social Psychology* in regard to the criteria of use of noncollege subjects, examination of biographical and personal data, retention of the individual as the unit of analysis, and extension over at least two months of the subjects' lives, found that "only a single study (Helson, 1982) achieved the maximum possible score."

In 1985 Hogan and Jones described Helson's work as always characterized by theoretical richness and attention to quantitative detail. And in 1987, in their perusal of research trends in personality for the *Annual Review of Psychology*, Singer and Kolligian described Helson's studies as "imaginative and challenging."

In addition to these research accomplishments, Helson has served as president of the Division of Psychology and the Arts of the American Psychological Association in 1979–1980 and is currently that division's representative to the association's council. In 1978–1980 she was chair of the Committee on Personality for the Division of Personality and Social Psychology, in 1982–1983 she was a member of the Executive Committee for the Section of Personality of that division, and since 1984 she has been a member of the Executive Committee of the Society for Personology. She was an advisory editor for *Contemporary Psychology*, 1978–1983, and has served or is serving as a consulting editor for other journals, such as *Experimental Studies of the Arts, Journal of Personality and Social Psychology, Psychology of Women Quarterly*, and *Women's Studies*. In 1978, with Valory Mitchell, she wrote the chapter on personality for the *Annual Review of Psychology*.

In the late 1980s, Helson continues to explore hypotheses rich in meaning, possesses unmatchable data archives, and is assisted by a number of very talented and resourceful young colleagues. One example is her systematic survey of theoretical and empirical studies of the creative personality (Helson, 1988), and another is her analysis with Mitchell (Mitchell & Helson, 1988) of the manifestations of object relations and social interaction in short stories. In their schema, Mitchell and Helson propose four levels of world and self views, going from the most primitive, in which negative affect is projected outward, to a second, in which an insecure self nonetheless seeks attachments to others, to a third, in which the self is stronger but still distanced from others, and culminating in a fourth stage, in which an individuated self can accommodate to relational themes. Twenty short stories were intensively analyzed and coded on themes of autonomy, level of object relationships, centrality of the self, and emotional closeness between protagonist and others, for instance "Omelette à Woburn" by Dezsö Kosztolanyi (see Illés, 1979), "February 1999" by Ray Bradbury, "Leader of the People" by John Steinbeck, and "My Old Man" by Ernest Hemingway.

In her 1977 paper on the creative spectrum and in her 1973 article in *Psychology Today*, Helson probed the relationships among the stylistic patterns of a story, the gender of its author, and the degree to which creative symbolizations were utilized in its telling. This set of topics is one about which Helson would like to write a fuller account. Another story not yet told in full is Helson's (1974a) conception of the creative woman as "a company of friends," in her own case first visualized as "an owl and a dwarf in front, a maiden at the center, and a serpent and a bear behind." Each such constellation has a certain vulnerability, but also incorporates the dynamic tensions and symbolic meanings out of which individuated creativity may emerge.

Finally, in her paper with Wink (1987) on integration and competence as two of the key facets in psychological maturity, Helson has introduced a provocative conceptualization that awaits further elaboration, in particular the fulfillment of self as this requires going beyond the social clock and the contextual constraints of one's personal environment. Data from the Mills women, now in their fifties, may provide the basis for this work. Even as this biography is being written, Ravenna Helson, a creative and perspicacious scholar, continues in her seminal analyses of root issues in the lives of women and men.

NOTE

1. This comment, and others cited later, come from several interviews the author conducted with Ravenna Helson in the Spring of 1988, and from personal documents she prepared for those meetings.

REFERENCES

Blodgett, H. C.; McCutchen, K.; & Mathews, R. (1949). Spatial learning in the T-maze: The influence of direction, turn and food location. *Journal of Experimental Psychology, 39*, 800–809.

Carlson, R. (1984). What's social about social psychology? Where's the person in personality psychology? *Journal of Personality and Social Psychology, 47*, 1304–1309.

Helson, H. (1964). *Adaptation-level theory*. New York: Harper & Row.

Helson, R. (1965). Childhood interest clusters related to creativity in women. *Journal of Consulting Psychology, 29*, 352–361.

Helson, R. (1966). Personality of women with imaginative and artistic interests: The role of masculinity, originality and other characteristics in their creativity. *Journal of Personality, 34*, 1–25.

Helson, R. (1967). Personality characteristics and developmental history of creative college women. *Genetic Psychology Monographs, 76*, 205–256.

Helson, R. (1968). Generality of sex differences in creative style. *Journal of Personality, 36*, 33–48.

Helson, R. (1971). Women mathematicians and the creative personality. *Journal of Consulting and Clinical Psychology, 36*, 210–220.

Helson, R. (1972). The changing image of the career woman. *Journal of Social Issues, 28*(2), 33–46.

Helson, R. (1973a). The heroic, the comic, and the tender: Patterns of literary fantasy and their authors. *Journal of Personality, 41*, 163–184.

Helson, R. (1973b). Heroic and tender modes in women authors of fantasy. *Journal of Personality, 41*, 493–512.

Helson, R. (1973c). Through the pages of children's books and what a psychologist found there. *Psychology Today, 7*(6), 107–122.

Helson, R. (1974a). The inner reality of women. *Arts in Society, 11*(1), 25–36.

Helson, R. (1974b). The psychological origins of fantasy for children in mid-Victorian England. *Children's Literature, 3*, 65–76.

Helson, R. (1977). The creative spectrum of authors of fantasy. *Journal of Personality, 45*, 310–326.

Helson, R. (1978a). Psychological dimensions and patterns of writing in critics. *Journal of Personality, 46*, 348–361.

Helson, R. (1978b). Writers and critics: Two types of vocational consciousness in the art system. *Journal of Vocational Behavior, 12*, 351–363.

Helson, R. (1978c). Creativity in women. In J. Sherman & F. Denmark (Eds.), *The psychology of women: Future directions in research* (pp. 553–604). New York: Psychological Dimensions.

Helson, R. (1980a). Challenger and upholder syndromes in critics. *Journal of Personality and Social Psychology, 38*, 825–838.

Helson, R. (1980b). The creative woman mathematician. In L. Fox, L. Brody, & D. Tobin (Eds.), *Women and the mathematical mystique* (pp. 23–54). Baltimore, Md.: Johns Hopkins University Press.

Helson, R. (1982). Critics and their texts: An approach to Jung's theory of cognition and personality. *Journal of Personality and Social Psychology, 43*, 409–418.

Helson, R. (1984). E. Nesbit's forty-first year: Her life, times and symbolizations of personality growth. *Imagination, Personality, and Cognition, 4*(1), 53–68.

Helson, R. (1985). Which of those young women with creative potential became productive? Personality in college and characteristics of parents. In R. Hogan & W. H. Jones (Eds.), *Perspectives in personality* (Vol. 1, pp. 49–80). Greenwich, Conn.: JAI Press.

Helson, R. (1987). Which of those young women with creative potential became productive? College graduation to midlife. In R. Hogan & W. H. Jones (Eds.), *Perspectives in personality* (Vol. 2, pp. 51–82). Greenwich, Conn.: JAI Press.

Helson, R. (1988). The creative personality. In K. Gronhaug & G. Kaufman (Eds.), *Innovation: A cross-disciplinary approach* (pp. 29–64). Oslo: Norwegian University Press.

Helson, R., & Crutchfield, R. S. (1970a). Creative types in mathematics. *Journal of Personality, 38,* 177–197.

Helson, R., & Crutchfield, R. S. (1970b). Mathematicians: The creative researcher and the average Ph.D. *Journal of Consulting and Clinical Psychology, 34,* 250–257.

Helson, R.; Elliott, T.; & Leigh, J. (1989). Adolescent personality and women's work patterns. In D. Stern & D. Eichorn (Eds.), *Adolescence and work: Influence of social structure, labor marketing, and culture* (pp. 259–289). Hillsdale, N.J.: Lawrence Erlbaum Associates.

Helson, R., & Mitchell, V. (1978). Personality. *Annual Review of Psychology, 29,* 555–585.

Helson, R.; Mitchell, V.; & Hart, B. (1985). Lives of women who became autonomous. *Journal of Personality, 53,* 169–197.

Helson, R.; Mitchell, V.; & Moane, G. (1984). Personality and patterns of adherence and non-adherence to the social clock. *Journal of Personality and Social Psychology, 46,* 1079–1096.

Helson, R., & Moane, G. (1987). Personality change in women from college to midlife. *Journal of Personality and Social Psychology, 53,* 176–186.

Helson, R., & Wink, P. (1987). Two conceptions of maturity examined in the findings of a longitudinal study. *Journal of Personality and Social Psychology, 53,* 531–541.

Hogan, R., & Jones, W. H. (1985). Preface. In R. Hogan & W. H. Jones (Eds.), *Perspectives in personality* (Vol. 1). Greenwich, Conn.: JAI Press.

Illés, L. (1979). *44 Hungarian Short Stories* (pp. 121–130). Budapest: Corvina.

Mathews, R. (1954). Recall as a function of the number of classificatory categories. *Journal of Experimental Psychology, 47,* 241–247.

Mitchell, V., & Helson, R. (1988). Object relations and social interaction in short stories. *Poetics, 17,* 367–384.

Neumann, E. (1954). On the moon and matriarchal consciousness. *Spring,* 83–100. Analytical Psychology Club of New York.

Perry, J. W. (1974). *The far side of madness.* Englewood Cliffs, N.J.: Prentice-Hall.

Rank, O. (1945). *Will therapy and truth and reality* (Translated by J. Taft). New York: Knopf.

Singer, J. L., & Kolligian, J., Jr. (1987). Personality: Developments in the study of private experience. *Annual Review of Psychology, 38,* 533–574.

MARY HENLE (1913–   )

Michael Wertheimer

Mary Henle, Gestalt psychologist, experimental psychologist, historian of psychology, and incisive critic of psychological theory, has been publishing influential works steadily for a period of half a century. A champion of the approach of the Berlin school of Gestalt psychology, she edited several major books on Gestalt thought and wrote many critical articles that helped to dispel misconceptions about Gestalt psychology. Her contributions to the history of psychology transcend the Gestalt approach; she coedited a major volume on the history of psychology, published an anthology of the most important papers of the Gestalt psychologist Wolfgang Köhler, and was instrumental in the posthumous publication of a widely used text on the history of psychology by a colleague, Robert B. MacLeod. Her 1986 book, *1879 and All That*, a selective collection of her essays on the history of psychology and on psychological theories, reprints some of her best works and has received highly favorable reviews. An incisive thinker and precise and elegant writer, she set a standard in scholarly work for her students and colleagues—and herself—that is rarely met by others in the field. Her career has served as an inspiring example to many colleagues, male and female alike. In the year of her retirement, the New School for Social Research, where Henle had spent most of her career, awarded her the L.H.D. degree in recognition of her outstanding achievements.

Noteworthy about her distinguished career is that she has always been a psychologist, an academic, and a scholar, first and foremost. In her autobiography, Henle (1983, p. 229), after raising the question of what, if any, legacy her generation left to the contemporary psychology of women, writes that she believes there is indeed such a legacy: ''We have done it quietly by doing our jobs, not as women psychologists, but as psychologists. We were not thinking much about being women in psychology. We simply took it for granted that women can function well in psychology in all kinds of settings, and we showed that they could by doing our work.''

FAMILY BACKGROUND AND EDUCATION

Mary Henle was born July 14, 1913, in Cleveland, Ohio. All three of the children of Leo Henle and Pearl Hahn Henle ended up in academic careers: her older brother Paul as a professor of philosophy and Mary as a professor of psychology; her twin sister Jane's field was classical archaeology. Leo Henle had immigrated to the United States in 1880 at the age of fifteen from Stuttgart, Germany, where he had already completed his Abitur at the Gymnasium at a precocious age. Forced by economic necessity to go to work, he became a businessman, but continued his education all his life, reading, attending adult education classes, and seeking out cultural opportunities in Cleveland; Henle (1983, p. 222) writes that "he had always wanted to be a scientist. . . . The stories he told us were Greek myths; and, through him, we made the early acquaintance of telescopes, microscopes, stereoscopes, and other instruments." Mary Henle's maternal grandfather had summarily enrolled Mary Henle's mother in medical school; her mother "graduated at the head of her class" (Henle, 1983, p. 221). Henle goes on to make the point that her mother strove "to be a good physician, not to be a woman physician." Clearly Mary Henle's orientation to her own career paralleled that of her mother. Mary Henle's family tried to persuade her older brother Paul to enter law school, hoping he would enter the law firm founded by the same grandfather who had enrolled his daughter, Mary Henle's mother, in medical school. But after one semester at Harvard Law School Paul switched to graduate work in philosophy, eventually becoming a professor of philosophy. As a result, Mary Henle writes (1983, p. 221), she and her sister "were free to pursue any career we chose." With her physician mother, her father's lifelong pursuit of education, and her siblings' strong academic interests (and independent choice of specialization), Mary Henle grew up in an environment that encouraged and valued academic achievement and independence of thought.

Mary Henle enrolled at Smith College in Northampton, Massachusetts, in 1930, and majored in French, although she also took some work in psychology. She graduated with an A.B. degree in 1934, but had been so stimulated by the faculty of the psychology department that she decided to stay to pursue a master's degree in psychology. Among the members of the psychology faculty at Smith at that time were James and Eleanor Gibson, prominent contributors to the psychology of perception and developmental psychology; Harold Israel, a general psychologist; Hanna Faterson and Elsa Siipola, both specialists in personality; and Kurt Koffka, one of the founders of the Berlin school of Gestalt psychology. As Henle reports (1983, p. 222):

I had been a member of the undergraduate class to whom Koffka read his manuscript as he was writing the *Principles of Gestalt Psychology* (1935). At the end of the term, he went to his laboratory to read the final chapters. Exciting times for an undergraduate! From Harold Israel, I had learned enough about systems of psychology to know that something great was happening, that we students had been privileged to read a classic before it was available to the psychological profession.

After completing her master's degree in psychology at Smith College in 1935, Mary Henle stayed on for an additional year as an assistant in the department; her brother Paul came to Smith in 1935 to teach philosophy there. Henle (1983, p. 223) describes her time at Smith as "stimulating, mind-opening years. The psychology department members were young and sociable and liked one another. As the only graduate student in the department, I was included in the group, as was my brother, when he came to Smith the next year to teach philosophy." Koffka's influence on Henle continued; she assisted him in some perceptual experiments. The contact with Koffka, she writes (1983, p. 223), was of decisive importance for her subsequent development. By the time she went to Bryn Mawr College in Pennsylvania to study for the doctoral degree, she "was already committed to Gestalt psychology." She reports that it was almost by chance that she went to Bryn Mawr: Harry Helson was visiting a number of women's colleges, looking for an assistant. "We liked each other immediately, he respected my department, and I got the job" (Henle, 1983, p. 223). Helson had written his own doctoral dissertation on Gestalt psychology a decade before (published only a few years after Koffka's 1922 introduction of Gestalt thinking to American psychologists), and must have been impressed both by Koffka and by his bright student.

At Bryn Mawr, Mary Henle worked and studied with Helson, and then wrote her dissertation under the supervision of Donald W. MacKinnon, who introduced her to the psychology of Kurt Lewin. MacKinnon also took her along to annual meetings of the Topological Psychologists, the Lewin group. He had studied at the Psychological Institute of the University of Berlin during the time it was directed by Wolfgang Köhler and was the major world center of Gestalt psychology, but had worked there mainly with Lewin. Bryn Mawr was close to Swarthmore College, at which Köhler had recently arrived, and there were occasional meetings with the Swarthmore psychologists; while the Bryn Mawr psychologists were not themselves Gestalt psychologists, they were friendly to the approach and knowledgeable about it (Henle, 1983, p. 224). No wonder that Henle could write about her doctoral years (1983, p. 223) that "Bryn Mawr was a good place for a developing Gestalt psychologist, in a way in which few graduate schools in the country would have been."

Mary Henle spent the years 1936 to 1939, then, at Bryn Mawr, obtaining her Ph.D. in psychology in 1939. In childhood, her major mentors and role models were her parents and brother. As an undergraduate student, she was influenced significantly by her teachers Harold E. Israel, James J. Gibson, and especially Kurt Koffka. Wolfgang Köhler's work had influenced her earlier too, but he was to become her major personal mentor during her career. She was also profoundly influenced by the ideas of Max Wertheimer, Kurt Lewin, and Edna Heidbreder long before she had any personal contact with them.

CAREER DEVELOPMENT

The country had not yet recovered from the Great Depression when Henle obtained her doctorate in 1939, and jobs were not easy to find. She did succeed in obtaining a two-year position as a research associate (analogous to a post-doctoral fellowship today) at Swarthmore College. She indicated (1983, p. 224) that there was no place in the world she would rather have gone. With her enthusiasm for Gestalt psychology, this was the ideal place for her at that time. Köhler had recently arrived there as a result of the efforts of the then psychology department chair, Robert B. MacLeod, who had himself studied at the University of Berlin a few years earlier. The Swarthmore psychology faculty also included Richard Crutchfield, Edwin B. Newman, Karl Duncker, and Hans Wallach, whom, like Köhler, MacLeod had managed to bring from Germany. It was even more a center of Gestalt psychology than Smith College had been. Henle attended Köhler's seminars and collaborated with him and with Hans Wallach on experimental work. Köhler supported Henle in every way, including helping improve the content and style of her papers before she submitted them for publication. She was awed by his knowledge, skill, and precision, and by his willingness to devote time to the endeavors of his younger colleagues. She writes (1983, p. 224), "To him I owe my greatest intellectual debt. And my friendship with the Köhlers lasted over the years, . . . we chopped down trees together; my first ride in a Jeep was with Köhler at the wheel; he named my cat."

During Henle's second year at Swarthmore, Newman left to do work related to the war effort, and Henle took over his introductory psychology course. It was her first opportunity to give a full undergraduate psychology course, and she greatly enjoyed it. Her next job was as instructor of psychology at the University of Delaware in 1941–1942. At that time, many psychologists were recruited for war work, so that the job market opened up to some extent. Henle was invited by Harry Helson to return to Bryn Mawr, which she eagerly did, serving as instructor of psychology there from 1942 to 1944. Helson and MacKinnon were soon also recruited to contribute to the war effort, so she was left largely in charge of the department, teaching a graduate seminar and supervising a master's thesis in addition to her undergraduate teaching. As she describes it (1983, p. 225): "My schedule of work was very simple: I taught my class, shut myself up in my office to prepare the next one; finished preparation just in time to meet it, and so it continued. At the time I thought there was just enough time—but not a minute more—to do what one had to do. Now I know better: there is never enough time." While at Bryn Mawr, Henle also did some teaching at Swarthmore College, in exchange for some of Hans Wallach's time at Bryn Mawr.

From 1944 to 1946 Henle was a member of the psychology faculty of Sarah Lawrence College. Since the college strongly emphasized teaching, including individual instruction, Henle had little time to devote to research. While she was enthusiastic about the Sarah Lawrence educational philosophy, she was glad to accept an invitation from Solomon E. Asch to join the graduate faculty of political and social science of the New School for Social Research in New York in 1946. She was to remain there for the remainder of her career, as assistant professor from 1946 to 1948, associate professor from 1948 to 1954, and professor from 1954 to her retirement in 1983, when she became professor emeritus—except for two productive years (1951–1952 and 1960–1961) as a Fellow of the John Simon Guggenheim Memorial Foundation and one year (1963–1964) as a Research Fellow in cognitive studies and lecturer on social relations at Harvard University; she also spent the fall semester of 1981 as a visiting professor at Cornell University. She has remained productive in her scholarly work since her "retirement" from the New School in 1983.

MAJOR CONTRIBUTIONS AND ACHIEVEMENTS

Mary Henle's major academic foci have been Gestalt psychology, the psychology of thinking, experimental psychology, systematic psychology, and the history of psychology. In all her work, she has striven for impeccable standards of scholarship; she has shown a capacity for brilliance, erudition, knowledgeability, and whimsy, and a capability for clean, crisp writing as well as for incisive, scathing criticism.

She has been involved in a significant way with eight books. Her first, written with Donald W. MacKinnon, *Experimental Studies in Psychodynamics: A Laboratory Manual* (1948), was widely used. Also widely used was *Documents of Gestalt Psychology* (1961), a major source book on Gestalt theory that she edited; it contains significant and basic papers by such Gestalt psychologists as Max Wertheimer, Wolfgang Köhler, Solomon E. Asch, Rudolf Arnheim, and Henle herself, arranged into sections on general theory, cognition, social psychology and motivation, and expression and art; an Italian translation of the book appeared in 1970. With Asch and Edwin B. Newman she prepared for posthumous publication in 1969 Wolfgang Köhler's *The Task of Gestalt Psychology*, the last published work by any of the founders of the school. *The Selected Papers of Wolfgang Köhler* (1971c), for which Henle was editor, translator, and compiler, culminates Köhler's voluminous and distinguished corpus of contributions to psychology and to philosophy of science. A significant volume, dedicated to the systematic psychologist Edna Heidbreder, *Historical Conceptions of Psychology* (1973), which Henle edited with Julian Jaynes and John S. Sullivan, contains historiographic contributions as well as papers devoted to selected topics in the history of psychology. She was instrumental in getting published, and wrote a preface for, Robert B. MacLeod's posthumous *The Persistent Problems of Psychology* (1975), considered by many psychologists as the best analysis to date of how modern psychology emerged from philosophy and how its origins fit in with eighteenth- and nineteenth-century political, social, and intellectual developments. She also edited *Vision and Artifact* (1976a), a volume based on a symposium in honor of Rudolf Arnheim for his seventieth birthday in 1974. In

1986 her book *1879 and All That: Essays in the Theory and History of Psychology* was published. A culmination of her earlier scholarly work, it is a selective collection of her own writings in areas as diverse as "knowing what one is talking about," "analysis," "primary sources," "history as problem solving," "historical/systematic approaches to an empirical problem: thinking," and "people." This book displays her talent for sophisticated organization of complex material and above all her outstanding capacity for clear and convincing critical analysis of significant theoretical issues in psychology.

Just as her books came out under the imprint of prestigious publishers, including several university presses (Harvard, California, Princeton, Columbia), her papers were published in top-level journals such as the *Journal of Experimental Psychology*, the *Psychological Review*, and the *American Psychologist*. The standards of these journals are stringent; that her papers appeared in them provides silent but impressive testimony to the quality of her work.

Some of Henle's earliest papers were coauthored by Marian B. Hubbell (1938) and by Hans Wallach (1941, 1942); they concerned, respectively, egocentricity in adult conversation and experimental studies of Thorndike's law of effect. She published an experimental study of past experience as a determinant of visual form perception in 1942 and two articles on Lewinian themes in 1944. During the 1950s she published several landmark articles in the *Psychological Review*, most of them on Lewinian issues (Henle & Aull, 1953; Henle, 1955, 1956), and one on eclecticism (1957b), which pointed out that efforts to combine the best features of competing positions generally succeed only in obscuring the major theoretical issues that led to controversy in the first place. Works on the psychology of thinking appeared over a twenty-year period (Henle & Michael, 1956; Henle, 1962, 1971a, 1971b, 1975), in which her main themes were that the reasoning engaged in by participants in experiments on problem solving is usually remarkably logical—if the investigator takes the trouble to discover what assumptions the participants are making; that the most creative aspect of creative thinking is posing the right question, because a well-formulated question may carry its answer, as it were, on its back—much like a snail carries its shell; and that it is ludicrous to believe that mere chance associations and reinforcement can account for creativity. Most of her published papers since the 1960s (e.g., 1977a, 1977b, 1978a, 1978b, 1980, 1984b) have dealt with a variety of themes in the history of psychology, many attempting to return some semblance of veridicality to contemporary accounts of Gestalt psychology. She has also contributed articles to numerous encyclopedias and other reference works, such as on Gestalt psychology (1965, 1977b), on her mentor Wolfgang Köhler (1968), and on Max Wertheimer (1973). She has written tributes of Kurt Lewin (1978b), Wolfgang Köhler (1968), Max Wertheimer (1980), Robert M. Ogden (1984a), and Edna Heidbreder (Henle & Sullivan, 1974; Henle, 1987b), as well as many other works. The total corpus of her published writings is very substantial, and continuous over a period of fifty years.

But Henle's contributions are not limited to her impressive publications. She has had a profound influence on her undergraduate and graduate students. Many of her students have gone on to active and productive careers in a variety of fields and settings. Her graduate students report that she required adherence to the highest standards of scholarship in everything they did, from reports in seminars through comprehensive examinations: she expected them to have read, understood, and mastered an enormous amount of primary literature relevant to their interests; superficial knowledge or knowledge of only secondary source material would not do. She set a strict example in her own writings, and in her own behavior: she could be seen reading primary sources in the library for many hours each week.

She has also contributed her time and wisdom to various institutions in American psychology. She was senior scholar (1964–1965) and then consultant (1965–1967) for Educational Services, Inc., of Cambridge, Massachusetts. She served as a staff member for a 1971 summer institute in the history of psychology at Lehigh University funded by the National Science Foundation. She has been a member of the Board of Advisors of the Archives of the History of American Psychology in Akron, Ohio, since 1969. She served two terms as a member of the Board of Directors (1976–1979 and 1980–1983) of the Eastern Psychological Association. She has given innumerable invited addresses at educational institutions and at professional and scientific conventions. And she served as president of APA's Division of the History of Psychology in 1971–1972, of APA's Division of Philosophical Psychology in 1974–1975, and of the Eastern Psychological Association (EPA) in 1981–1982.

CRITICAL EVALUATION OF CONTRIBUTIONS AND ACHIEVEMENTS

Henle's presidencies of two APA divisions and of EPA provide evidence of the esteem in which she is held by her colleagues. A biography of her is included in the prestigious *American Men and Women of Science: Social and Behavioral Sciences* (Cattell, 1978). She was selected for inclusion in a volume of seventeen eminent women in psychology asked to provide autobiographies (O'Connell & Russo, 1983). There are entries on her in Wolman's *Dictionary of Behavioral Science* (1973) and in Corsini's *Encyclopedia of Psychology* (1984, vols. 2–3) and his *Concise Encyclopedia of Psychology* (1987).

Henle is also cited in many books on the history of psychology. For example, Lundin (1985, p. 132) refers to her 1957 paper criticizing functionalism for being too eclectic. The same paper is dealt with at length by Marx and Hillix (1973, p. 159), who also (p. 238) write that Henle's *Documents of Gestalt Psychology* "provides a useful source for many of the basic Gestalt writings," and who point out (pp. 238–239) that Henle's collection of Köhler's papers contains "two that were previously unpublished, seven translated into English from German for the first time, and one newly translated from the French." Henle's 1976 paper, "Why Study the History of Psychology?" is featured repeatedly in Brozek and Pongratz (1980, pp. 11–18) as well as in Eckardt and Sprung (1983, pp. 17–22); its closing paragraph provides a typical taste of her crisp writing (p. 20):

I have a final and most important reason for studying the history of psychology: it is fascinating. It not only, if properly used, helps keep our thinking straight, serves as a source of problems and of knowledge, gives us perspective, but it is intrinsically interesting. It is not just something to be taken because it is good for you—like vitamin pills—although it *is* very good for you. It is a gourmet dish to be enjoyed for itself. It is high adventure, like the history of all [human] intellectual pursuits—perhaps the highest adventure of all because it is the story of [humanity itself].

There are fifteen references to Mary Henle's historical writings in a selective major annotated reference work on the history of psychology (Viney, Wertheimer, & Wertheimer, 1979). Benjamin (1988) reprinted three of Henle's articles in his anthology on the history of psychology. The widely used Schultz (1981) text cites Henle five times. Murray (1988, p. 290) writes that Köhler's "ideas about isomorphism were not always properly understood, and Henle (1984[b]) is essential reading for a clarification of this difficult issue." Kendler (1987) refers to three of Henle's works and (p. 223) calls her *Documents of Gestalt Psychology* (1961) "an interesting [collection] of important papers in Gestalt psychology." Hilgard (1987) refers approvingly to five of Henle's works in his mammoth volume on psychology in America. Heider (1983, p. 107) wrote that Henle is "best known for her publications about Gestalt psychology, especially about the work of Köhler." And in their history of the New School, Rutkoff and Scott (1986, p. 199), while they erroneously claim that Henle completed her doctoral work at the New School and that she had been a graduate student of Köhler's at Swarthmore, present a brief summary of Henle's distinguished career.

In a review of Henle's 1986 book, the present writer (1988, pp. 135–142) provided a lengthy and laudatory analysis of Henle's work; among the assertions about the book and about Henle are the following:

This unassuming, unpretentious, wide-ranging book contains some of the best thinking of one of psychology's most articulate writers and critics. . . . All psychologists should strive to express themselves with the clarity, precision, and frugality characteristic of Professor Henle's prose. . . . A large proportion of the 20 essays in this collection, originally written from 1957 through 1985, are exquisitely cut gems of intellectual analysis. Many of them provide the highest esthetic and intellectual pleasure. Several of them concern issues about which much has been written before, but this particular diamond cutter knows exactly what to retain and what to cut away to yield a finished product unmatched in clarity and purity. Most of the essays contain not a single excess word, yet say everything about their topic that needs to be said. But to continue the metaphor, perfect cutting and polishing of a diamond's facets can yield keen, sharp edges between them. And Professor Henle's prose can be scathing, indeed devastating, when she reveals others' shortcomings. She does not hesitate to use her razor-sharp wit on giants as well as on lesser figures in the field; she uses it wherever she finds error or sloppiness, including ... Edwin G. Boring and Sigmund Freud, among others. ... Her felicitous style is so sparse, so admirable, so carefully wrought; yet it never becomes salient, never obscures the subject (that is, the medium never becomes the message, as is sometimes the case with a few prominent contemporary writers in psychology who shall, of course, remain nameless—although Professor Henle, if she were to make this point, would name them; her courage and intellectual honesty never flinch). ... Many thousands should read [her book]. It is refreshing, disturbing, entertaining, challenging, and inspiring. It is a model of historical, intellectual, and critical analysis at its very best.

REFERENCES

Benjamin, L. T., Jr. (Ed.). (1988). *A history of psychology: Original sources and contemporary research.* New York: McGraw-Hill.

Brozek, J., & Pongratz, L. J. (Eds.). (1980). *Historiography of modern psychology: Aims, resources, approaches.* Toronto: Hogrefe.

Cattell Press (Ed.). (1978). *American men and women of science: Social and behavioral sciences* (13th ed.). New York: Bowker.

Corsini, R. J. (Ed.). (1984). *Encyclopedia of psychology,* 4 vols. New York: Wiley.

Corsini, R. J. (Ed.). (1987). *Concise encyclopedia of psychology.* New York: Wiley.

Eckardt, G., & Sprung, L. (Eds.). (1983). *Advances in historiography of psychology.* Berlin: VEB Deutscher Verlag der Wissenschaften.

Heider, F. (1983). *The life of a psychologist: An autobiography.* Lawrence: University Press of Kansas.

Helson, H. (1925, 1926). The psychology of *Gestalt. American Journal of Psychology, 36,* 342–370, 494–526; *37,* 189–223.

Henle, M. (1942). An experimental investigation of past experience as a determinant of visual form perception. *Journal of Experimental Psychology, 30,* 1–22.

Henle, M. (1944a). The influence of valence on substitution. *Journal of Psychology, 17,* 11–19.

Henle, M. (1944b). An examination of some concepts of topological and vector psychology. *Character and Personality, 12,* 244–255.

Henle, M. (1955). Some effects of motivational processes on cognition. *Psychological Review, 62,* 423–432.

Henle, M. (1956). On activity in the goal region. *Psychological Review, 63,* 299–302.

Henle, M. (1957a). On field forces. *Journal of Psychology, 43,* 239–249.

Henle, M. (1957b). Some problems of eclecticism. *Psychological Review, 64,* 296–305.

Henle, M. (Ed.). (1961). *Documents of Gestalt psychology.* Berkeley: University of California Press. Translated into Italian: *Documenti sulla Psicologia della Forma.* Milan: Bompiani, 1970.

Henle, M. (1962). On the relation between logic and thinking. *Psychological Review, 69,* 366–378.

Henle, M. (1965). On Gestalt psychology. In B. B. Wolman (Ed.), *Scientific psychology* (pp. 276–279). New York: Basic Books.

Henle, M. (1968). Wolfgang Köhler. *Year book of the American Philosophical Society,* 139–145.

Henle, M. (1971a). The snail beneath the shell. *Abraxas, 1,* 119–133.

Henle, M. (1971b). Of the Scholler of Nature. *Social Research, 38,* 93–107.

Henle, M. (Ed.). (1971c). *The selected papers of Wolfgang Köhler.* New York: Liveright.

Henle, M. (1973). Max Wertheimer. *McGraw-Hill encyclopedia of world biography* (Vol. 11, pp. 319–320). New York: McGraw-Hill.

Henle, M. (1974). E. B. Titchener and the case of the missing element. *Journal of the History of the Behavioral Sciences, 10,* 227–237.

Henle, M. (1975). Fishing for ideas. *American Psychologist, 30,* 795–799.

Henle, M. (Ed.). (1976a). *Vision and artifact.* New York: Springer.

Henle, M. (1976b). Why study the history of psychology? *Annals of the New York Academy of Sciences, 270,* 14–20.

Henle, M. (1977a). The influence of Gestalt psychology in America. *Annals of the New York Academy of Sciences, 291,* 3–12.

Henle, M. (1977b). Gestalt psychology. In B. B. Wolman (Ed.), *International encyclopedia of psychiatry, psychology, psychoanalysis, and neurology* (vol. 5, pp. 209–213). New York: Van Nostrand Reinhold.

Henle, M. (1978a). Gestalt psychology and gestalt therapy. *Journal of the History of the Behavioral Sciences, 14,* 23–32.

Henle, M. (1978b). Kurt Lewin as metatheorist. *Journal of the History of the Behavioral Sciences, 14,* 233–237.

Henle, M. (1978c). One man against the Nazis: Wolfgang Köhler. *American Psychologist, 33,* 939–944. Also translated into German and published in *Psychologie Heute* and translated into Italian and published in *Psicologia Contemporanea.*

Henle, M. (1980). A tribute to Max Wertheimer: Three stories of three days. *Psychological Research, 42,* 295–304.

Henle, M. (1983). Mary Henle. In A. N. O'Connell & N. F. Russo (Eds.), *Models of achievement: Reflections of eminent women in psychology* (pp. 221–232). New York: Columbia University Press.

Henle, M. (1984a). Robert M. Ogden and Gestalt psychology in America. *Journal of the History of the Behavioral Sciences, 20,* 9–19.

Henle, M. (1984b). Isomorphism: Setting the record straight. *Psychological Research, 46,* 317–327.

Henle, M. (1986). *1879 and all that: Essays in the theory and history of psychology.* New York: Columbia University Press.

Henle, M. (1987a). Koffka's *Principles* after fifty years. *Journal of the History of the Behavioral Sciences, 23,* 14–21.

Henle, M. (1987b). Edna Heidbreder (1890–1985). *American Psychologist, 42,* 94–95.

Henle, M., & Aull, G. (1953). Factors decisive for resumption of interrupted activities: The question re-opened. *Psychological Review, 60,* 81–88.

Henle, M., & Hubbell, M. R. (1938). ''Egocentricity'' in adult conversation. *Journal of Social Psychology, 9,* 227–234.

Henle, M.; Jaynes, J.; & Sullivan, J. J. (Eds.). (1973). *Historical conceptions of psychology.* New York: Springer.

Henle, M., & Michael, M. (1956). The influence of attitudes on syllogistic reasoning. *Journal of Social Psychology, 44,* 115–127.

Henle, M., & Sullivan, J. J. (1974). *Seven psychologies* revisited. *Journal of the History of the Behavioral Sciences, 10,* 40–46.

Hilgard, E. R. (1987). *Psychology in America: A historical survey.* San Diego: Harcourt Brace Jovanovich.

Kendler, H. H. (1987). *Historical foundations of modern psychology*. Chicago: Dorsey.

Koffka, K. (1922). Perception: An introduction to the *Gestalt-Theorie*. *Psychological Bulletin, 19*, 531–585.

Koffka, K. (1935). *Principles of Gestalt psychology*. New York: Harcourt Brace.

Köhler, W. (1969). *The task of Gestalt psychology*. Princeton, N.J.: Princeton University Press.

Lundin, R. W. (1985). *Theories and systems of psychology* (3rd ed.). Lexington, Mass.: Heath.

MacKinnon, D. W., & Henle, M. (1948). *Experimental studies in psychodynamics: A laboratory manual*. Cambridge, Mass.: Harvard University Press.

MacLeod, R. B. (1975). *The persistent problems of psychology*. Pittsburgh: Duquesne University Press.

Marx, M. H., & Hillix, W. A. (1973). *Systems and theories in psychology* (2nd ed.). New York: McGraw-Hill.

Murray, D. J. (1988). *A history of Western psychology* (2nd ed.). Englewood Cliffs, N.J.: Prentice-Hall.

O'Connell, A. N., & Russo, N. F. (Eds.). (1983). *Models of achievement: Reflections of eminent women in psychology*. New York: Columbia University Press.

Rutkoff, P. M., & Scott, W. B. (1986). *New School: A history of the New School for Social Research*. New York: Free Press.

Schultz, D. (1981). *A history of modern psychology* (3rd ed.). New York: Academic Press.

Viney, W.; Wertheimer, M.; & Wertheimer, M. L. (1979). *History of psychology: A guide to information sources*. Detroit: Gale.

Wallach, H., & Henle, M. (1941). An experimental analysis of the law of effect. *Journal of Experimental Psychology, 28*, 340–349.

Wallach, H., & Henle, M. (1942). A further study of the function of reward. *Journal of Experimental Psychology, 30*, 147–160.

Wertheimer, M. (1988). Review of *1879 and all that: Essays in the theory and history of psychology*. *American Journal of Psychology, 101*, 135–142.

Wolman, B. B. (Ed.). (1973). *Dictionary of behavioral science*. New York: Van Nostrand Reinhold.

Additional Representative Publications by Mary Henle

Henle, M. (1941). The causes and the prevention of war: A reply to Professor Dunlap. *Psychologists' League Journal, 4*, 38–41.

Henle, M. (1942). An experimental investigation of dynamic and structural determinants of substitution. *Contributions to Psychological Theory*, (3), v, 112.

Henle, M. (1960). On error in deductive reasoning. *Psychological Reports, 7*, 80.

Henle, M. (1973). On controversy and its resolution. In M. Henle, J. Jaynes, & J. J. Sullivan (Eds.), *Historical conceptions of psychology* (pp. 47–59). New York: Springer.

Henle, M. (1979). Phenomenology in Gestalt psychology. *Journal of Phenomenological Psychology, 10*, 1–17.

Henle, M. (1984). "What is iso and what is morphic in isomorphism?": A rejoinder to Pribram. *Psychological Research, 46*, 333–335.

Henle, M. (1984). Episodes in the history of interactionism: On knowing what one is talking about. *Revista de Historia de la Psicología, 5,* 153–161.

Henle, M., & Baltimore, G. (1967). Portraits in straw. *Psychological Review, 74,* 325–329.

LETA STETTER HOLLINGWORTH (1886–1939)

Ludy T. Benjamin, Jr., and Stephanie A. Shields

Commenting on her origins in Nebraska, Leta Stetter Hollingworth wrote: "I shall never cease to rejoice that I was born on the limitless prairies. To grow up on their expanse means to see in long stretches, to scorn boundaries, to go free all one's life" (H. L. Hollingworth, 1943, p. 52). That statement is descriptive of her life and of her work, which pressed beyond boundaries that she saw as artificial. Leta Stetter Hollingworth, whose career spanned twenty-six brief years, made major contributions to the psychology of women and sex differences, clinical psychology, and educational and school psychology. Her personal values were unapologetically the foundation of her approach to research, and her strong belief in opportunity for the individual guided her work. She was among the first to challenge scientifically the assertions of a biologically based female intellectual inferiority, was active in the first movement to professionalize clinical psychology, wrote textbooks that became classics in the psychology of adolescence and of intellectually exceptional children, and was internationally renowned for her work concerning the educational and emotional needs of gifted children. Two significant themes emerge from a consideration of her career, and each is first evident in research on the psychology of women that she undertook as a graduate student. The first of these is that Leta Hollingworth was explicitly concerned with righting wrongs. This disposition, which she attributed to her prairie upbringing and which is manifested in her activism, impelled her to bring to light issues that stood outside the canon of experimental psychology. The second theme is that she recognized the great cost to society in mistaking the customary for the natural or desirable. The questions Leta Hollingworth posed are as important today as they ever were, for example, her concern with a woman's right to choose career, maternity, or both; yet they are still considered "special interest" questions by mainstream psychology (Denmark, Russo, Frieze, & Sechzer, 1988).

CHILDHOOD YEARS AND MARRIAGE

Leta Hollingworth was born Leta Anna Stetter on May 25, 1886, on her maternal grandparents' farm near the pioneer community of Chadron, Nebraska. She was the eldest of three daughters born to Margaret Elinor Danley and John G. Stetter, whose marriage in July 1885 is purported to be the first recorded in the newly organized Dawes County. During the first year of Leta Stetter's life her mother kept a diary of her infant's development written in the first person as if authored by the infant. When Leta was three years old, her mother died giving birth to her youngest sister, Margaret. The infant biography, written in her mother's hand in a small red leather-covered notebook, became one of Leta Stetter's prized possessions. Her father, described as a "rollicking cowboy minstrel," was irresponsible and ill-suited to caring for his daughters. The task of raising Leta Stetter and her sisters passed to her maternal grandparents, with whom she lived for about ten years. She was especially attached to her grandmother, admiring her kindness and patience.

The important relationship came to an abrupt end when, at age thirteen, she and her sisters were reclaimed by their father (H. L. Hollingworth, 1943). His new wife, Fanny Curtis, forbade any contact with the Danley family, especially Leta Stetter's beloved grandparents. Stetter would later recall, with considerable shame, how she would pass her grandmother on the way to school, yet not speak for fear of reprisal from her stepmother. The three sisters were awakened at 5:00 A.M. on school days to complete their chores before school. The most minor misbehaviors could be the source of a vicious scolding. Many nights Leta Stetter went to bed wondering what the next day "would bring forth in the way of strife and turmoil" (H. L. Hollingworth, 1943, p. 50). This turmoil led her to become a mother to her younger sisters, protecting them as best she could. At fourteen she published a poem titled "Lone Pine" in the local newspaper, and its imagery ("Beaten and scarred and crippled, By the winds and rain made old") suggests her lonely struggle to grow and to nurture her sisters (Roweton, 1987).

Her escape came in 1902 when, at age fifteen, she graduated from high school in Valentine, Nebraska, and traveled to Lincoln to attend the University of Nebraska. There she found the opportunity to stretch and refine her native talents, especially her abilities in creative writing. She hoped to make a career as a writer, but acquired teaching credentials as a safeguard for employment. She also began taking psychology courses as a sophomore. In her junior year she was a grader in the elementary psychology course for Thaddeus Lincoln Bolton, who had earned his doctorate under G. Stanley Hall at Clark University. Harry Levi Hollingworth was a student in that class, and he recalled being attracted to her from the moment he saw her (H. L. Hollingworth, 1940). In 1905, at the beginning of their senior year, they were engaged to be married. They both graduated in 1906, Leta Stetter earning Phi Beta Kappa honors.

While she waited to be discovered as a writer, submitting her short stories to magazines, she taught high school. Harry Hollingworth, unsuccessful in his attempt to secure an assistantship for graduate study, also took a high school position. But three months later he received a telegram from James McKeen Cattell inviting him to be Cattell's assistant at Columbia. Harry Hollingworth left several months later to begin his doctoral work in psychology.

Their separation had lasted about two and one-half years when Leta Stetter journeyed to New York City on December 31, 1908, to be married. Harry Hollingworth graduated a few months later and accepted a faculty job at Barnard, Columbia University's college for women. She hoped to get a job teaching school, only to discover that married women were prohibited by law from such employment. She turned her energies to writing, and again found herself thwarted when her stories were rejected for publication. Concerning these years Harry Hollingworth (1943) wrote:

During the earlier years of married life Leta Stetter Hollingworth's time and energy were chiefly consumed by housework, cooking, dressmaking, mending, washing, ironing, making her own hats and suits and endless other domestic duties in the frugal apartment home. Almost always she effectually stifled her own eager longing for intellectual activity like that of her husband. Day after day, and many long evenings, she led her solitary life in the meagerly furnished quarters. . . . "Staying at home eating a lone pork chop" was the way she sometimes facetiously described her experience in those days. There were occasional periods of discouragement. . . . These slips from her customary determined and courageous procedure she could hardly explain then, even to herself. Later she was able to make it clear that it was because she could hardly bear, with her own good mind and professional training and experience, not to be able to contribute to the joint welfare more than the simple manual activities that occupied her. (Pp. 98–99)

EARLY RESEARCH ON THE PSYCHOLOGY OF WOMEN AND SEX DIFFERENCES

Her husband pursued consulting opportunities beyond his academic job, and after three years they had enough money saved for Leta Hollingworth to begin her graduate study. She enrolled in the educational psychology program at Columbia's Teachers College, where she decided to look critically at the status of women. Claims for the intellectual inferiority of women were found in many published scientific works, yet her reading revealed no scientific data to support these claims. One claim was that "women, by virtue of their menstrual functions, experience regularly recurring interferences with the use of all their abilities, and must be considered for a considerable part of each lunar period as invalids, or semi invalids" (H. L. Hollingworth, 1943, p. 114). That topic would be the subject of her dissertation research, for which she received a Ph.D. in 1916.

Of more immediate concern to her was the variability hypothesis: the assertion that "women as a species are less variable among themselves than are men; all women are pretty much alike but men range enormously in their talents and defects" (H. L. Hollingworth, 1943, p. 114). The variability hypothesis (see Shields, 1982) flourished in the early 1900s principally through "armchair dogma'' in the literature of psychology, education, medicine, and sociology. This hypothesis was used to explain the greater frequency of men on lists of distinction as well as their greater number on lists of immorality and criminality. It was also used to explain a wider range of intelligence for men—more male geniuses, but also more males in institutions for the feebleminded. At the time she began to work with him, Leta Hollingworth's major professor, Edward L. Thorndike, was a proponent of the variability hypothesis.

After receiving her M.A. and a Master's Diploma in Education in 1913, Hollingworth continued her graduate studies supported by work at the Clearing-House for Mental Defectives, where she was employed to administer Binet tests. Here she had the opportunity to conduct her first study on the variability hypothesis. She examined 1,000 cases diagnosed during 1912 and 1913. In absolute terms, males did exceed females, but there was a most interesting bias in those data. For individuals over sixteen years of age at the time of admission, 78 were males, while 159 were females. And for individuals over thirty years of age upon admission, 9 were males and 28 were females (Hollingworth, 1913). Concerning those data she wrote:

At present it suffices to point out that the fact that females escape the Clearing-House till beyond the age of thirty years three times as frequently as males fits very well with the fact that more males than females are brought to the Clearing-House, on the whole. The boy who cannot compete mentally is found out, becomes at an early age an object of concern to relatives, is brought to the Clearing-House and directed toward an institution. The girl who cannot compete mentally is not so often recognized as definitely defective, since it is not unnatural for her to drop into the isolation of the home, where she can ''take care of'' small children, peel potatoes, scrub, etc. . . . Thus they survive outside of institutions. (L. S. Hollingworth, 1914a, pp. 515–516)

A later study (L. S. Hollingworth, 1922) of institutional admissions supported a similar interpretation of bias.

The variability hypothesis was also studied by Leta Hollingworth in relation to physical traits. Asking the question, Are males more variable in anatomical traits than females?, Helen Montague and Hollingworth (1914) analyzed the data from 2,000 infants (1,000 males and 1,000 females) in the New York Infirmary for Women and Children. In brief, they found that male infants were slightly larger than female infants on all anatomical variables in the study. However, there were no differences in variability between the sexes.

As mentioned earlier, Hollingworth's dissertation research, titled ''Functional Periodicity: An Experimental Study of the Mental and Motor Abilities of Women During Menstruation'' (1914b), grew out of work that she had done for her master's and was completed under the direction of Thorndike. The introduction paints an appalling picture of superstition and prejudice dominating the medical and educational opinion on menstruation. She believed that objective data could exert a much-needed correction. In the first of two studies, six women and two male controls were tested daily for three months on a series of perceptual motor and mental ability tasks, such as the tapping test, color naming, and naming opposites. In addition, the progress of three of the women in learning to type was monitored over the three months of testing. In a second study, seventeen women were tested on similar tasks for one month. She found no adverse performance effects, a finding consistent with that of more sophisticated contemporary research on the topic.

Hollingworth persistently argued that a fundamental reexamination of women's social role in industrial society was needed. The crux of the problem was obvious to her: women bear children and, for centuries, had been trained to, expected to, and if need be, coerced to devote themselves to the care of their offspring (L. S. Hollingworth, 1916a). Women's many and varied talents had traditionally been channeled away from social achievement and into childrearing and housekeeping, fields "where eminence is impossible" (L. S. Hollingworth, 1914a, p. 526). Or, as she noted elsewhere, "No one knows who is the best housekeeper in America. Eminent housekeepers do not and cannot exist" (L. S. Hollingworth, 1940, p. 16). Careful to caution that her criticism of law and social convention should not be "construed as an attack on maternity," she emphasized that the real problem was "a social order that has been built up on the assumption that there is and can be little or no variation in tastes, interests, and abilities within the female sex" (1914a, pp. 526, 528; see also 1916b, 1918, 1927b, 1928). To make her point more clearly, she relied on a simple thought experiment. She asks the reader to "imagine a man and a woman of exactly equal ability, allowed to compete intellectually for a given social prize, on the condition that each shall become the parent of two or three children. Under the prevailing economic and social order, there is no question as to which will win" (1916c, p. 933). She believed that scientific study of the important issues facing women was essential to overcome the custom of bias that hampered much-needed social change. In the meantime, each woman who deviated from the norms of the accepted role was faced with unique problems and was forced to produce unique solutions to them. It was the sum of these "experimental lives" (her choice of words is noteworthy given the high value she placed on scientific data) that would eventually produce new, broader, and more suitable guidelines for the courses that a woman's life could take.

Leta Hollingworth's actual research on the psychology of women ended shortly after she received her doctoral degree, but her interest in these issues continued throughout her life. According to Harry Hollingworth (1943), his wife had long planned a book on the social psychology of women titled *Mrs. Pilgrim's Progress*. Leta Hollingworth's work was among the first scientifically to challenge the assertions of the biological inferiority of women. Hollingworth's data and arguments against the variability hypothesis and for a consideration of social factors ultimately had an impact on several influential individuals. By the 1920s Edward Thorndike no longer referred to the variability hypothesis as either a potent discriminator between the abilities of women and men or as an explanatory concept. Somewhat later, Lewis Terman began to allow that social discrimination may be an important impediment to women's intellectual and social achievement. During her life Hollingworth was hailed as the "scientific pillar" of the women's movement, and today her work is well known among psychologists who study the social psychology of gender.

CLINICAL PSYCHOLOGY

When Leta Hollingworth was hired at the Clearing-House in 1913, she took the position as a temporary replacement for Emily T. Burr, one of the earliest workers in the field. Leta Hollingworth was kept on with Burr after her return. In 1914 the psychological examiners giving mental tests were put under Civil Service supervision, and after competitive exams Hollingworth was at the top of the list. The first opening was at Bellevue Hospital. Later she was offered the position of chief of a psychological lab to be established at the hospital. At about this time she completed the Ph.D. and was offered the late Naomi Norsworthy's position in educational psychology at Columbia's Teachers College (see Higgins, 1918) which she "reluctantly" accepted (H. L. Hollingworth, 1943). She remained in that position for the rest of her life: she was promoted from instructor to assistant professor in 1919, to associate in 1922, and to full professor in 1929.

She continued part-time work as a clinical psychologist until 1920. "Clinical psychology" was, at that time, a grab-bag term applied primarily to the field of mental testing. Her job was to test "mentally inferior" individuals for commitment by the courts. She was active in the controversy surrounding who was properly fitted to give and interpret psychological tests and was a leader in the move to build professionalism and raise the standards of mental examiners in universities and in the Civil Service (Poffenberger, 1940). During this period her research centered upon the characteristics of mental deficiency and of special mental disabilities. Her research in this area appeared in two books, *The Psychology of Subnormal Children* (1920) and *Special Talents and Defects* (1923). In working with these "mentally defective" children, she soon realized that many of them were of normal intelligence but suffered from emotional and attitudinal problems due to adjustment difficulties, especially during adolescence, so she began to focus more directly on that age group (Poffenberger, 1940). She developed courses on mental adjustments and adolescence and published *The Psychology of the Adolescent* (1928). The book became a standard in the field for the next two decades.

A particularly good example of Leta Hollingworth's activism can be found in her efforts to professionalize clinical psychologists. World War I had given tremendous impetus to the testing movement and clinical psychology, and during the postwar years there was an increasing demand for psychologists in all areas of industry and education. In the American Psychological Association (APA), which had repeatedly raised its requirements for membership, nearly half of the 300-plus members were involved in some type of applied work. Many involved in applied work believed that the organization did not meet their professional needs. The APA had done little toward establishing standards for practitioners and, in general, seemed to have no interest in psychology outside of the academy. The first organized effort of applied psychologists to correct this situation came in 1917 at the annual meeting when a group of clinical psychologists, headed by Leta Hollingworth, attempted to form an independent professional organization, the American Association of Clinical Psychology. Argument and controversy postponed action, and the following year APA did set up a committee to consider certification of "consulting psychologists" and to establish a Clinical Section within APA.

EDUCATIONAL PSYCHOLOGY AND THE GIFTED CHILD

In her capacity as a clinical psychologist, Hollingworth became more and more frequently asked to help out with mentally gifted children who were experiencing educational or emotional problems. Most psychologists and educators of her day were of the opinion that "the bright can take care of themselves." It was in this field that she established her reputation on an international basis. In the 1920s there were less than a half-dozen individuals doing research on gifted education. Her work with a seven-year-old boy who was placed in the fifth grade, but was still insufficiently challenged, led her to meet Jacob Theobald, then a school principal (P.S. 165) and later a member of the Board of Superintendents of New York City. Their consideration of the particular problems of this boy ultimately led to her first experiment with the gifted.

Hollingworth worked intensively with gifted children in two major projects. One of her Ph.D. students, Miriam Pritchard (Pritchard, 1951), described these two educational experiments in detail and summarized Hollingworth's contributions to the study of the gifted. During the course of each project she observed the children almost every school day. She maintained contact with the children in her first experimental group for the rest of her life. She repeatedly emphasized the importance of identifying gifted children early in life, believing that these children could greatly benefit from supplemental educational experience. She believed that it was children at the extremes of intelligence who most needed ability grouping, because it was at the extremes that the regular school structure failed to meet the individual child's needs. In the rest of the child's life she thought that exceptional children should not be isolated from other children.

The first of her educational experiments began in 1922 with the formation of two special opportunity classes at P.S. 165. The children, identified through a citywide search, were seven to nine years old when the classes were established. The special classes were continued for three years. During the experiment, and even in the years after they graduated, she studied all aspects of the children's lives, including gifted children's size and strength, sibling relations, musical sensitivity, play behavior, and personality characteristics. *Gifted Children* (1926) described some of this work, and like her book on adolescence, it served as a standard reference work in schools of education for many years.

Her second experiment involved children at a specially established school, Speyer School (P.S. 500), to study the special educational problems of the slow learner and of the gifted learner. Leta Hollingworth was to be the advisor for the two gifted classes and W. B. Featherstone that for the two slow learner classes. The goal was to optimize learning for the individual limits and talents of the child. Hollingworth, adopting the philosophy of her graduate school mentor, E. L. Thorndike, believed that the education of the best thinkers should be an "education for initiative and originality," and so not just an accelerated version of the normal curriculum, but a program specially geared to help these children develop attitudes, understandings, and appreciations that would enhance their childhood and help them become more effective adults (Pritchard, 1951).

She was also quite interested in the exceptionally gifted child who tests at greater than IQ 180. Her interest in high intelligence was first stimulated by a classroom demonstration of individual testing that she conducted for one of her classes in 1916. The child, who had been recommended to her as exceptional, achieved the impression IQ of 187. She continued to follow Child E——'s development to adulthood (Garrison, Burke, & Hollingworth, 1917; L. S. Hollingworth, Garrison, & Burke, 1922; L. S. Hollingworth, 1927a). Her book *Children Above 180 I.Q.* (1942), which was completed by her husband after her death, summarizes her longitudinal study of twelve exceptionally gifted individuals. Among the things she found out about these exceptionally gifted children was that many of them, from the time of their entry into school, experienced adjustment problems because of inept treatment by adults and lack of intellectual challenge. Hollingworth's work did much to dispel the notion that very bright children were fragile, clumsy, and eccentric.

Leta Hollingworth's concern with righting wrongs is especially evident in her writing on education late in her career. She was disturbed by the false egalitarianism of American education that refused to acknowledge individual differences in intellectual capacity and make allowances for them in children's education. One recurrent theme in her commentaries on education is that by enforcing rigid programs, education had succeeded only in ensuring widespread mediocrity, resulting in a loss of talent that would inevitably have negative consequences for society. She believed that, overall, IQ tests were the most equitable means of identifying highly gifted children (and given the alternatives in the 1930s, she was probably right). She argued that assertions about race differences in intelligence had not been objectively or adequately studied to support any conclusion and, in reprising her earlier observations regarding sex differences, that the social context of development must be a factor in any such research. If science could develop ways of identifying the child who would become the high-achieving adult, "we should then be able to select and cherish human genius without regard to race, sex or condition of economic servitude" (Garrison, Burke, & Hollingworth, 1917, pp. 102–103). Hollingworth was particularly concerned with the needs of families who could not afford to support the education of their gifted child. She frequently approached foundations and philanthropic agencies with proposals to set up scholarship funds, but the prevailing belief was that bright children would succeed on their own. Pritchard (1951) believes that one memorandum to the American Council on Education written shortly before Hollingworth's death finally stimulated a national conference that paved the way for recommendations regarding federal scholarship support.

Leta Hollingworth was only fifty-three years old when abdominal cancer ended her life on November 27, 1939. Her accomplishments belie the fact that she was professionally active for less than half of that abbreviated life span. Five years after receiving her doctorate, she was listed in *American Men of Science*. Her importance in psychology is evidenced by her inclusion in Robert Watson's *Eminent Contributors to Psychology* (1974, 1976), one of only fourteen women to be so recognized. In her lifetime she received a number of honors, principally for her work in gifted education, but the award of which she was proudest was the honorary doctorate conferred by the University of Nebraska the year before her death.

The boundaries that she battled in the search for equality of opportunity for women and education for gifted children are still boundaries today. However, they are far less formidable in contemporary society, a fact that is surely due in some measure to the force of her work. Leta Hollingworth enjoyed a close relationship with her husband, who was very supportive of her efforts throughout her career. Harry Hollingworth was himself a distinguished applied psychologist, and president of APA in 1927. After her death he published her public addresses and a collection of her poetry (1940) as well as her biography (1943). In 1944 he founded a graduate fellowship in her name at Columbia University that is still awarded annually. The fellowship is but one of many ways her presence is still being felt.

REFERENCES

Denmark, F.; Russo, N. F.; Frieze, I. H.; & Sechzer, J. A. (1988). Guidelines for avoiding sexism in psychological research: A report of the Ad Hoc Committee on Nonsexist Research. *American Psychologist, 43*, 582–585.

Garrison, C. G.; Burke, A.; & Hollingworth, L. S. (1917). The psychology of a prodigious child. *Journal of Applied Psychology, 1*, 101–110.

Higgins, F. C. (1918). *The life of Naomi Norsworthy*. New York: Houghton Mifflin.

Hollingworth, H. L. (1940). Years at Columbia (Vol. 2 of an unpublished autobiography). Nebraska State Historical Society Archives, Lincoln, Nebraska.

Hollingworth, H. L. (1943). *Leta Stetter Hollingworth*. Lincoln: University of Nebraska Press.

Hollingworth, L. S. (1913). The frequency of amentia as related to sex. *Medical Record, 84*, 753–756.

Hollingworth, L. S. (1914a). Variability as related to sex differences in achievement. *American Journal of Sociology, 19*, 510–530.

Hollingworth, L. S. (1914b). Functional periodicity. *Teachers College Contributions to Education*, No. 69. New York: Columbia University Press.

Hollingworth, L. S. (1916a). Social devices for impelling women to bear and rear children. *American Journal of Sociology, 22,* 19–29.

Hollingworth, L. S. (1916b). The vocational aptitudes of women. In H. L. Hollingworth (Ed.), *Vocational psychology* (pp. 222–224). New York: D. Appleton.

Hollingworth, L. S. (1916c). Phi Beta Kappa and women students. *School and Society, 4,* 932–933.

Hollingworth, L. S. (1918). Comparison of the sexes in mental traits. *Psychological Bulletin, 15,* 427–432.

Hollingworth, L. S. (1920). *The psychology of subnormal children.* New York: Macmillan.

Hollingworth, L. S. (1922). Differential action upon the sexes of forces which tend to segregate the feeble-minded. *Journal of Abnormal and Social Psychology, 17,* 35–57.

Hollingworth, L. S. (1923). *Special talents and defects: Their significance for education.* New York: Macmillan.

Hollingworth, L. S. (1926). *Gifted children.* New York: Macmillan.

Hollingworth, L. S. (1927a). Subsequent history of E——: Ten years after the initial report. *Journal of Applied Psychology, 11,* 385–390.

Hollingworth, L. S. (1927b, October). The new woman in the making. *Current History, 27,* 15–20.

Hollingworth, L. S. (1928). *The psychology of the adolescent.* New York: D. Appleton.

Hollingworth, L. S. (1940). *Public addresses.* Lancaster, Pa.: Science Press.

Hollingworth, L. S. (1942). *Children above 180 I.Q.* Yonkers, N.Y.: World Book Co.

Hollingworth, L. S.; Garrison, C. G.; & Burke, A. (1922). Subsequent history of E——: Five years after the initial report. *Journal of Applied Psychology, 6,* 205–210.

Lowie, R. H., & Hollingworth, L. S. (1916, September). Science and feminism. *Scientific Monthly, 3,* 277–284.

Montague, H., & Hollingworth, L. S. (1914). The comparative variability of the sexes at birth. *American Journal of Sociology, 20,* 335–370.

Pearson, K. (1897). Variation in man and woman. In *The chances of death* (Vol. 1). London: Edward Arnold.

Poffenberger, A. T. (1940). Leta Stetter Hollingworth: 1886–1939. *American Journal of Psychology, 53,* 299–301.

Pritchard, M. C. (1951). The contributions of Leta S. Hollingworth to the study of gifted children. In P. Witty (Ed.), *The gifted child,* Chapter 4. Boston: D. C. Heath.

Roweton, W. E. (1987). Leta Stetter Hollingworth: Her childhood years in northwest Nebraska. Unpublished manuscript, Chadron State College, Chadron, Neb.

Shields, S. A. (1982). The variability hypothesis. *Signs, 7,* 769–797.

Watson, R. I. (1974, 1976). *Eminent contributors to psychology. Volume 1: A bibliography of primary references. Volume 2: A bibliography of secondary references.* New York: Springer.

Additional Representative Publications by Leta Stetter Hollingworth

Hollingworth, L. S. (1931). The adolescent child. In C. A. Murchison (Ed.), *Handbook of child psychology.* Worcester, Mass.: Clark University Press.

Hollingworth, L. S. (1931). Special gifts and special deficiencies. In C. A. Murchison (Ed.), *Handbook of child psychology*. Worcester, Mass.: Clark University Press.

Hollingworth, L. S. (1936). The development of personality in highly intelligent children. *Fifteenth yearbook of the Department of Elementary School Principals of the National Education Association, July, 1936*.

Hollingworth, L. S. (1936). The founding of Public School 500: Speyer School. *Teachers College Record, 38*, 119–128.

Hollingworth, L. S., & Lorge, I. (1936). Adult status of highly intelligent children. *Journal of Genetic Psychology, 49*, 215–226.

Hollingworth, L. S., & Montague, H. (1914). The comparative variability of the sexes at birth. *American Journal of Sociology, 20*, 335–370.

Additional Representative Publications About
Leta Stetter Hollingworth

Benjamin, L. T., Jr. (1975). The pioneering work of Leta Hollingworth in the psychology of women. *Nebraska History, 56*, 493–505.

Rosenberg, R. (1984). Leta Hollingworth: Toward a sexless intelligence. In M. Lewin (Ed.), *In the shadow of the past: Psychology portrays the sexes* (pp. 77–96). New York: Columbia University Press.

Shields, S. A. (1975). Ms. Pilgrim's progress: The contributions of Leta Stetter Hollingworth to the psychology of women. *American Psychologist, 30*, 852–857.

Shields, S. A., & Mallory, M. E. (1987). Leta Stetter Hollingworth speaks on "Columbia's Legacy." *Psychology of Women Quarterly, 11*, 285–300.

KAREN HORNEY (1885–1952)

Agnes N. O'Connell

Karen Horney, a pioneering theorist in personality, psychoanalysis, and "feminine psychology," often has the distinction of being the only woman whose theory is included in personality textbooks. In her personality theory, Horney reformulated Freudian thought and presented a holistic, humanistic perspective that emphasized cultural and social influences, human growth, and the achievement of self-realization. The first woman to present a paper on feminine psychology at an international meeting, she pioneered and developed a feminine psychology that provided a new way of thinking about women. The insightful conceptualizations contained in her books and articles and her method of psychoanalysis opened new frontiers and influenced the works of theorists and practitioners of diverse persuasions, including self-psychologists, humanists, cognitive therapists, psychoanalysts, feminists, and existentialists. She was a founder of the Association for the Advancement of Psychoanalysis, the American Institute of Psychoanalysis, and the *American Journal of Psychoanalysis*. An extraordinary theorist, leader, teacher, and therapist, Horney made "immense" contributions (Ingram, 1985) that have been highly significant in shaping and advancing psychological thought.

FAMILY BACKGROUND AND EDUCATION

Karen Clementine Theodore Danielsen was born in a suburb of Hamburg, Germany, on September 15, 1885. Her father, Berndt Henrik Wackels Danielsen, a widower with four teenage children, was a Norwegian sea captain and a naturalized German citizen; her mother, Clotilde Marie van Ronselen (affectionately known as Sonni), was of noble Dutch-German ancestry and her husband's second wife.

Karen Danielsen was the second child born into the new family. The first was her brother, Berndt (1881), her parents' favorite. At Karen Danielsen's birth, her father was approximately fifty years of age, her mother approximately thirty-two. At this time in her parents' marriage, differences in age, temperament, and class had begun to erupt into marital discord (Horney, 1980; Quinn, 1987; Rubins, 1978).

Although her father, described as "stern, repressive and demanding" (Rubins, 1978, p. 12), was away at sea for long periods of time, his emotional presence and the anxiety it created remained. While Danielsen greatly admired and respected her father as a captain-commodore and reported that she accompanied him on one or more sea voyages, she also found him intimidating and rejecting (Horney, 1980; Kelman, 1971; O'Connell, 1980; Quinn, 1987; Rubins, 1978). Her father's derogatory comments about her looks and intelligence were a particular source of anguish. Even as an adult she shuddered at the memory of the gaze of his blue eyes (Cherry & Cherry, 1973). In later years, the anxiety that Danielsen experienced as a child would contribute to the basic tenets of the personality theory she would develop.

Danielsen chose her intellectual style of life at a young age. The psychiatrist Jack Rubins (1978) quotes her as saying, "If I couldn't be beautiful, I decided I would be smart" (p. 14). In her diaries (1980) she wrote, "School is the only true thing after all" (p. 22). Her intellectual abilities impressed her mother, who encouraged her, but not her father, who disapproved of extended education for women (Cherry & Cherry, 1973).

After completing the local Volkschule (kindergarten and elementary school), Danielsen went to the Klosterschule (a private parochial school) in Hamburg. At about age twelve (1897), she reportedly made the decision to study medicine because of a favorable impression made by a "nice country doctor" (Rubins, 1978). Studying medicine did not become a realistic possibility until both preparatory education and university admittance became available to women in Germany a few years later (around 1900). To achieve her now attainable goal to become a physician, Danielsen needed to attend the newly available Realgymnasium for girls (comparable to high school and two years of college). Her father refused the necessary permission and tuition. Through the intercession of her mother, teachers, brother, an aunt, and her own promise that, if her father would grant this request, "she would ask nothing more of him," her father relented (Rubins, 1978, p. 21). In 1901 Danielsen became one of the first women students at the Realgymnasium in Hamburg.

During her years there, her mother left her father, although they were never divorced. When Danielsen graduated in 1906 and entered medical school at the University of Freiburg, her mother relocated to be with her. Freiburg was one of the first universities in Germany to admit women as matriculated students. Of 2,350 students at the University of Freiburg in 1906, 58 were women; 34 of these chose to study medicine (Horney, 1980; Quinn, 1987). Although women's presence in medical schools was officially sanctioned, there remained strong reservations on the part of some faculty concerning the place of women. Danielsen was the only woman among seven students who passed the preclinical examination in her class in 1908 (O'Connell, 1980).

Danielsen excelled at Freiburg academically and socially. In 1906 she met

Oskar Horney, who was majoring in economics at Germany's University of Brunswick and preparing for a career in law. For the next year and a half, they were in continuous correspondence while he completed his work at Brunswick. In 1908 they both went to the University of Göttingen to continue their studies.

The years that followed were marked by a series of significant beginnings and endings. On October 31, 1909, at twenty-four years of age and in the midst of her medical studies, Karen Danielsen married Oskar Horney. In less than a year (1910–1911), Karen Horney experienced the deaths of her father and mother (May 1910 and February 1911, respectively) and the birth of her first child, Brigitte (March 1911). With her daughter still a newborn, Horney successfully completed the state medical examinations—consisting of several weeks of oral and practical tests—while returning home periodically to nurse her infant daughter (Rubins, 1978; O'Connell, 1980). She graduated from the University of Berlin (opened to women in 1908) on December 28, 1911, having followed the continental custom of studying at several universities—Freiburg, Göttingen, and Berlin. In 1913 and 1916, respectively, Horney gave birth to her second and third daughters, Marianne and Renate. In 1915 she was awarded a medical degree by the University of Berlin after completion of her dissertation, "A Casuistic [Clinical] Contribution to the Question of Traumatic Psychoses" (Kelman, 1971, pp. 2–3). The impact of the losses she endured and the strain and conflict she experienced in balancing her multiple roles were manifested in constant fatigue (Horney, 1980; Quinn, 1987; Rubins, 1978).

CAREER DEVELOPMENT

During Horney's early career years, she gained professional experience by working at the Urban Hospital in Berlin and at the Lankwitz-Kuranstalt, a neuropsychiatric hospital (1911–1912); with Herman Oppenheimer at Charite, his neurological institute (1912–1913); and with Karl Bonhoeffer also at the Charite on her dissertation (1913–1914). She returned to work at the Lankwitz-Kuranstalt in 1914 and continued there until 1918.

Meanwhile, she had become a member of the Berlin Psychoanalytic Society, headed by Karl Abraham. She entered and remained in therapy with Abraham for about two years. Abraham considered her one of "his most gifted analysands" and praised her to Sigmund Freud (Rubins, 1978). Horney, however, found Freud's basic mechanistic concepts at odds with her own observations. In her first formal psychoanalytic paper, "The Technique of Psychoanalytic Therapy" (1917), she spoke of the potential for lifelong growth, a view that differed substantially from Freud's. In 1919 Horney began her private practice as a "specialist in psychoanalysis." She taught at the Berlin Psychoanalytic Institute until 1932, when she emigrated to the United States.

Horney came to the United States at the invitation of Franz Alexander to become his assistant at the Chicago Institute of Psychoanalysis. At forty-seven years of age she left the recognition she had earned at the Berlin Psychoanalytic

Institute and established herself once again in a new country. Two years later she moved from Chicago to New York to continue teaching, writing, and training analysts. Her work at the New School for Social Research and at the New York Psychoanalytic Institute provided the material for her books (Horney, 1937, 1939). These books challenged orthodox psychoanalysis and revealed the evolution of her theories.

MAJOR CONTRIBUTIONS AND ACHIEVEMENTS

Karen Horney's contributions to psychology occurred in two major periods differentiated by time and place: (1) her early work in Germany reinterpreting and refining psychoanalytic concepts and pioneering and developing a "feminine psychology"; and (2) her later work in the United States concluding her major contributions to a feminine psychology, developing a theory of personality, and outlining neopsychoanalytic approaches and techniques. Underlying and unifying these two periods are themes that recur in her work, themes related to the description, analysis, and interpretation of the psychology of women; the influence of culture and society on the psyche and its development; the antecedents, development, and treatment of "neurosis"; human growth; and the achievement of self-realization.

Toward a Social and Cultural Feminine Psychology

Karen Horney wrote her most significant papers on feminine psychology between 1922 and 1937 while she was in Germany and shortly after she moved to the United States. In these papers she provided a new way of thinking about women (Williams, 1977). If she had written nothing else, these fourteen papers, compiled posthumously into a volume titled *Feminine Psychology* (1967), would have earned Horney a place of importance in the history of psychology and psychoanalysis (Quinn, 1987).

Horney presented her first substantial work on feminine psychology at the Seventh International Psychoanalytic Congress held in Berlin in 1922 in a paper titled "On the Genesis of the Castration Complex in Women" (published in 1924). She was the first woman to present a paper on feminine psychology at an international meeting (Quinn, 1987). In this paper she challenged some of Sigmund Freud's concepts. Ironically, Freud himself chaired the session. As Horney grew more confident and more dissonant in her disagreement with Freud's concepts, especially those on the castration complex, penis envy, female sexuality, and man as the measure of woman, he began to refute and denigrate her work (e.g., Freud, 1925, 1931, 1949).

As Horney lectured to professional and nonprofessional organizations on issues relating to women and taught such courses as Psychoanalysis and Gynecology, she developed a reputation for being "too outspoken" (Rubins, 1978). Although she did not regard herself as such, she was regarded by her audiences "as a living symbol of the new emancipated female'' (Cherry & Cherry, 1973). She compared the shortcomings of psychoanalysis with those of ''our entire masculine civilization'' in her work ''The Flight from Womanhood'' (1926). She found psychoanalysis and those who developed its tenets androcentric, overly concerned with men's sexual apparatus, and insufficiently appreciative of women's capacity for ''pregnancy, childbirth, and motherhood.'' Horney paralleled a young boy's ideas on male/female sexual organs with those held by psychoanalysts. Based on her clinical data, she would eventually assert that womb envy was at least as likely to present a problem for men as penis envy did for women. She emphasized in 1926 and in her later work the importance of cultural and societal factors on women's ''inferior position,'' and that what women envy is not the penis but the superior position of men in society (O'Connell, 1980).

Her concern with feminine psychology stemmed from her feeling that psychology was androcentric and that as a woman it was her task to ''work out a fuller understanding for specifically female trends and attitudes in life'' (Kelman, 1971). She objected to the development of a psychology of women based on the psychology of men.

It was toward this end that Horney, in ''The Problem of Feminine Masochism'' (1935), refuted previous theories about female masochism and challenged the belief in the pervasiveness of this phenomenon. She effectively demonstrated that cultural and societal factors encourage women to be dependent upon men for love, prestige, wealth, care, and protection. This dependence resulted in overemphasis on pleasing men, on the feminine ''cult of beauty and charm,'' and on the ''overvaluation of love'' (1934) (O'Connell, 1980). This emphasis also led to an ''overvaluation'' of men (Westkott, 1986) and is consistent with the ideology that a woman's life is given meaning through others, for example, husband, children, and family. Horney wrote:

Culture factors exert a powerful influence on women; such in fact that it is hard to see how any woman may escape becoming masochistic to some extent, from the effects of the culture alone without any appeal to contributory factors in the anatomophysiological characteristics of women and their psychic effects. There may appear certain fixed ideologies concerning the ''nature'' of women; that she is innately weak, emotional, enjoys dependence, is limited in capacity for independent work and autonomous thinking. *It is obvious that these ideologies function not only to reconcile women to their subordinate role, but also to plant the belief that it represents a fulfillment they crave, or an ideal for which it is desirable to strive.* (1935; italics added)

In examining the social role of women in a patriarchal society, Horney wrote:

Woman's efforts to achieve independence and enlargement of her field of activities are continually met with a skepticism which insists that such efforts should be made only in the face of economic necessity, and that they run counter to her inherent character and natural tendencies. Accordingly, all efforts of this sort are said to be without any vital significance for women, whose every thought should center upon the male or motherhood. (1934, p. 605)

Horney postulated in "The Distrust Between the Sexes" (1930) that the relationship between men and women was similar to that between children and parents. The marital relationship was based on the expectation that each partner would fulfill all the needs of the other, an impossible feat. In 1926 Horney's own marriage became no longer viable; she separated from and, years later, divorced her husband.

Analysis of Horney's life and work indicates that her experiences and observations and her professional interests often converged. Horney made personal conflicts the focus of her theoretical work. For example, "The Problem of the Monogamous Ideal" (1928) was presented shortly after she and Oskar Horney had separated. In fact, she published six papers on marital problems between 1927 and 1932 illuminating this aspect of feminine psychology. She also focused on the problems of raising adolescents at this time, for example, "Maternal Conflicts" (1933) was published when her youngest daughter was seventeen and attempting to adjust to American culture (O'Connell, 1980).

Theory of Personality and Neopsychoanalysis

Horney's transition across continents sharpened her awareness of the role of cultural factors and set the stage for her challenge of orthodox psychoanalysis through the development of her own theory. Her view of human nature was reflected in her refutation of "Freud's instinct-based metapsychology" and in her emphasis on the "person-in-context" (Ingram, 1985, p. 306). Horney's evolving theory stressed cultural and interpersonal factors, while orthodox psychoanalysis stressed biological and intrapsychic factors. The grounding of her theory and methodology in the cultural and interpersonal opened "a new frontier" (Ingram, 1985, p. 307) in understanding of the self, her "central construct" (van den Daele, 1981, p. 328). Horney observed that as a consequence of childhood anxiety and conflicting messages in the culture, an individual's self-image is easily distorted. A distorted self-image (pathology of the self) contributes to the development of neurosis and disturbed interpersonal relationships (O'Connell, 1980; van den Daele, 1981).

In *New Ways in Psychoanalysis* (1939) Horney desexualized the oedipal complex, interpreting the process as symptomatic of disturbed interpersonal relationships. Horney theorized that the "passionate clinging to one parent and jealousy toward the other" (p. 83) is the result of basic anxiety produced by a disturbed parent-child relationship, and not by the oedipal complex. In *Our Inner Conflicts* (1945) Horney reaffirmed that "neuroses are brought about by cultural factors—which more specifically meant that neuroses were generated by disturbances in human relationships" (p. 12). In *Neurosis and Human Growth* (1950) she again confirmed that neurosis is "a disturbance in one's relation to self and to others" (p. 386).

In *The Neurotic Personality of Our Time* (1937) and in her later books (1942, 1945, 1950), Horney identified and defined the causes of neurosis and "the character structure which recurs in nearly all neurotic persons of our time in one or another form" (1937, p. vii). Horney found that a childhood marked by lack of warmth and security and a feeling of isolation and helplessness in a potentially hostile world can lead to neurosis in both men and women. The underlying cause is not different for women and men, as orthodox psychoanalysts believed, but the same: basic anxiety produced by a disturbed parent-child relationship and the repression of basic hostility in the interest of survival and security. Anxiety and hostility are interlocking components of neurotic character structure.

To combat anxiety and in an effort to gain security, the child develops coping strategies. These strategies become permanent parts of the personality. The child may choose to (1) "move toward others" in a "self-effacing" solution of love and compliance; or (2) "move against others" in an "expansive" solution of mastery and aggression; or (3) "move away from others" in a "resignation" solution of freedom and detachment (Horney, 1942, 1945, 1950).

Moving well beyond Freudian concepts, Horney outlined "ten neurotic needs" or trends. With some redundancy, these needs are the components of the three solutions designed to reduce anxiety. Clustered around the "moving toward others" solution are the neurotic needs for affection and approval; for a partner to take control of one's life; and for restriction of life to narrow borders. Central to the "moving against others" solution are the needs for power, omnipotence, and perfection; for exploitation of others; for social recognition and prestige; for personal admiration; and for personal achievement. At the core of the "moving away from others" solution are the needs for restriction of life to narrow borders; for self-sufficiency; and for perfection and unassailability (1942, 1945, 1950).

In the first solution the child (or the neurotic) is saying, "If you love me, you will not hurt me"; in the second, "If I have power, I shall not be hurt"; and in the third, "If I withdraw, nothing can hurt me" (Monte, 1987). The neurotic *rigidly* uses one solution almost exclusively regardless of whether or not it is adaptive and denies or represses the other two solutions.

The healthy person, on the other hand, is able to integrate the three solutions appropriately depending upon the situation. The healthy person can be trusting, open, and loving; self-asserting and achieving; or happily alone in occasional solitude. The differences between healthy values and the neurotic trends are that the neurotic trends are compulsive, extreme in intensity, indiscriminate in application, and unrealistic. "The difference is one between 'I wish to be, and enjoy being, loved,' and 'I must be loved at any cost' " (Horney, 1937, pp. 99–100). Horney observed that the "moving toward others" solution is more typical of women and the "moving against others" solution more typical of men.

Horney theorized that nonhealthy functioning resulted in alienation from the real self (the true person, including potentialities and the urge for self-realization) and "a devil's pact" (the adoption of an unrealistic idealized self) (1950, pp. 17, 87). In an attempt to regain security, the neurotic attempts to mold the self into something valued by the culture.

He feels what he should feel, wishes what he should wish, likes what he should like. In other words, the tyranny of the should drives him frantically to be something different from what he is or could be. And in his imagination he is different—so different, indeed, that the real self fades and pales still more. (Horney, 1950, p. 159)

In examining Horney's contributions it becomes apparent that "it would be difficult to find another personality theorist with whom to compare her lucid and brilliant descriptions" (Monte, 1987, p. 431). Horney's "extremely valuable," "well-reasoned," and "profound" insights into the meaning and dynamics of neurosis "contribute significantly to a better understanding of human personality" (Ewen, 1988, p. 178). Horney has provided "a major reframing of how we comprehend personality and its disorders . . . [many of her] contributions have been assimilated into American psychology and psychoanalysis" (Ingram, 1985, p. 308).

Horney's insights and concepts have been used by theorists and practitioners of diverse persuasions. Her concept of the "tyranny of the should" has been used by cognitive therapists in their descriptions of the etiology and maintenance of various forms of neurosis (e.g., Albert Ellis in his descriptions of the cognitive element in depression [1987, p. 123]). The "tyranny of the should" and secondary defenses such as externalization, compartmentalization, and blind spots described by Horney (1950) have been widely adopted and incorporated in numerous theories of personality to the point where they have become folk wisdom. The "tyranny of the should" speaks to women who feel that they "should" be "feminine" and men who feel that they "should" be "masculine" (according to society's restricted definitions) but who at the same time have strong needs for both achievement and affiliation. These conflicts can restrict spontaneous personal growth if the focus is upon the idealized socially accepted images, that is, the images of the "should," and not upon the real self.

In reviews of theoretical concepts on narcissism, "the malady of our times," Horney emerges as one of the earliest contributors (Cooper, 1981; Quinn, 1987). Her concepts relating to "the pride system" (the idealized self, self-hatred, and self-contempt); the splitting of the self into omnipotent and self-devaluative attitudes; pathological self-esteem; and the structure and integration of the self have become incorporated in the formulations of the psychoanalyst Heinz Kohut (1977) on the self and the narcissistic personality. Horney's work foreshadowed the conceptualizations of later "self" theorists:

Roughly speaking, a person builds up an idealized image of himself because he cannot tolerate himself as he actually is. The image apparently counteracts this calamity; but having placed himself on a pedestal, he can tolerate his real self still less and starts to rage against it, to despise himself and to chafe under the yoke of his own unattainable demands upon himself. He wavers then between self-adoration and self-contempt, between his idealized image and his despised image, with no solid middle ground to fall back on. . . . [Neurotic] pride and self-hate belong inseparably together; they are two expressions of one process. . . . The godlike [self] is bound to hate his actual [self] . . . [and this is] the central inner conflict. (Horney, 1945, p. 112; 1950, pp. 109, 112, 368; Ewen, 1988, p. 170).

Horney's (1950) insights into the forces that work toward and away from the realization of the self are apparent in the theories of the giants of humanistic psychology, Abraham Maslow and Carl Rogers. The person seeking self-realization in Horney's theory of personality is someone who has unlimited potential for growth and positive interpersonal relationships but who needs security and a strong sense of self. Abraham Maslow's ideas on "self-actualization" and Carl Rogers' concept of the "fully functioning person" are indebted to Horney's concept of self-realization. All three recognized the importance of the "real self." Horney's view that survival and security needs could warp the person's concept of self was shared by Rogers. Maslow, too, recognized the importance of the attainment of basic needs such as survival and security before self-actualization could occur.

Horney's influence on therapeutic practice reached beyond neopsychoanalysts to cognitive, client-centered, and Gestalt therapists. The procedures of Ellis' rational-emotive therapy (a cognitive approach) are in many respects based on "Horney's formulations and recommendations" regarding the treatment of patients (Ryckman, 1989, p. 144). Horney (1942) believed that "self-awareness" was as crucial as awareness of other factors in the environment: "to search for truth about the self is as valuable as to search for truth in other areas of life." She favored introspection in the pursuit of becoming "a better, richer, and stronger human being" (1942). Rogers' client-centered therapy and Fritz Perls' Gestalt therapy are indebted to Horney's emphasis on the importance of "awareness" of one's feelings and emotions in addition to one's thoughts and cognitions for mental health and self-realization. (Horney briefly analyzed and then supervised Fritz Perls [Rubins, 1978, p. 316]).

In 1986 the sociologist Marcia Westkott proposed that *The Feminist Legacy of Karen Horney* extended beyond her writing on feminine psychology to her theory of personality and her approach to psychoanalysis. Westkott perceived Horney's theory of personality as a feminist statement that "specifically explains women's psychology" (p. 4) and therefore is not gender neutral. In reviewing Westkott's book in *Contemporary Psychology*, Kelman (1989) wrote that this perspective underestimated Horney's theoretic and analytic contributions to male personality development and therapy, concluding that Horney's "interest in growth, in self, in pride, and in the Devil's Pact has no gender orientation" (p. 167).

Although Horney's theoretic and analytic contributions are seen as formidable, her "revolutionary approach which implied the repudiation of so many of Freud's fundamental concepts'' (Alexander, 1969) had its critics. Horney's reinterpretation of, and deviation from, Freudian concepts and her views as expressed in *New Ways in Psychoanalysis* (1939) resulted in an uproar at the New York Psychoanalytic Society and her resignation in 1941. Horney had been removed as a training analyst because she was disturbing the students with her ''deviationist'' ideas. In the same year she became one of the founders of the Association for the Advancement of Psychoanalysis, a founder and the dean of the American Institute for Psychoanalysis, a training institute, and a founder and the editor of the *American Journal of Psychoanalysis*. In 1943, as a result of an administrative clash over ideological differences, Harry Stack Sullivan, Erich Fromm, and Clara Thompson left the new institute to form the William Alanson White Psychiatric Foundation in New York (Cherry & Cherry, 1973; Rubins, 1978). Although she was ''saddened'' by these departures (Rubins, 1978, p. 267), these were productive and rewarding years for Horney. She was active as a teacher who could simplify the most ''complex and difficult'' concepts (Rubins, 1978, p. 3), as an ''expert'' therapist with deep human involvement, and as a regular contributor to the psychoanalytic literature and to scientific sessions, especially sessions of the American Psychiatric Association (she was a Fellow of that organization).

Around 1950 Horney became interested in Zen Buddhism through her friendship with D. T. Suzuki, a Zen monk, teacher, and lecturer. After completing what would be her last book, she traveled to Japan and stayed at a series of Zen monasteries in search of further development of her concept of the real self (Kelman, 1971; O'Connell, 1980).

In 1952 Horney's friends and former patients suggested opening a clinic in her name. She wrote, ''I consider this to be the most meaningful honor I ever received or might receive in my life'' (Rubins, 1978, p. 329). She died on December 4, 1952, of cancer. The Karen Horney Clinic, a research, training, and low-cost treatment center, was opened on May 6, 1955, in New York City (Cherry & Cherry, 1973).

As noted above, Horney is often the only woman whose theory is included in textbooks on personality (e.g., Ewen, 1988; Hall & Lindzey, 1978; Ryckman, 1989). She is described as neoanalytic or neo-Freudian for her reformulation of Freudian thought, a social psychologist for her emphasis on cultural and social influences, and a humanist for her holistic view and her emphasis on self-realization.

In memory of Karen Horney, Medard Boss, the world renowned existential psychiatrist, wrote, ''From her I received my first impulses which led me to overcome mechanistic thinking and to replace it with a holistic view which since has developed in[to a] daseins [being-in-the world] analytic concept'' (1954, p. 48).

Karen Horney's humanistic qualities were captured in her eulogy by Paul Tillich:

She knew the darkness of the human soul, and the darkness of the world, but believed that what giveth light to any one suffering human being will finally give light to the world. The light she gave was not a cold light of passionless intellect, it was the light of passion and love. She wrote books but loved human beings. She helped them by insights into themselves which had healing power. (Rubins, 1978, pp. 338–339)

After reviewing Karen Horney's "immense" contributions and their influences on the occasion of the centennial year of her birth, Ingram (1985) concluded that the frontiers that Horney opened with her "profound contributions" have enabled the field "to move forward with vigor" (p. 308). The "continuing power and importance of her mature theory" (Paris, 1989, p. 568) are integral parts of her rich and seminal legacy.

NOTE

Thanks to Thomas D. O'Connell, Nancy Felipe Russo, Ira Sugarman, and Brian T. O'Connell for their comments on earlier versions of this chapter.

REFERENCES

Alexander, F. (1969). Neurosis and creativity. *American Journal of Psychoanalysis, 29*, 116.

Boss, M. (1954). Mechanistic and holistic thinking in modern medicine. Karen Horney Memorial Issue. *American Journal of Psychoanalysis, 14*(1), 14.

Cherry, R., & Cherry, L. (1973, August 26). The Horney heresy. *New York Times Magazine*, pp. 11ff.

Cooper, A. (1981). Narcissism. In S. Arieti, H. Brodie, & H. Keith (Eds.), *American handbook of psychiatry, 7: Advances and new directions* (pp. 297–316). New York: Basic Books.

Ellis, A. (1987). A sadly neglected cognitive element in depression. *Cognitive Therapy and Research, 11*, 121–145.

Ewen, R. B. (1988). *An introduction to theories of personality* (3rd ed.). Hillsdale, N.J.: Erlbaum.

Freud, S. (1925/1961). Some psychical consequences of the anatomical distinction between the sexes. *The standard edition, XIX*. London: Hogarth Press.

Freud, S. (1931/1961). Female sexuality. *The standard edition, XXI*. London: Hogarth Press.

Freud, S. (1949). *An outline of psychoanalysis*. New York: Norton.

Hall, C. S., & Lindzey, G. (1978). *Theories of personality* (3rd ed.). New York: Wiley.

Horney, K. (1917/1968). The technique of psychoanalytic therapy. *American Journal of Psychoanalysis, 28*, 3–12.

Horney, K. (1924). On the genesis of the castration complex in women. *International Journal of Psychoanalysis, 5*, 50–65. Also in H. Kelman (Ed.), *Feminine psychology* (hereafter FP). New York: Norton.

Horney, K. (1926). The flight from womanhood. *International Journal of Psychoanalysis, 7*, 324–329. Also in FP.

Horney, K. (1928). The problem of the monogamous ideal. *International Journal of Psychoanalysis, 9*, 318–331. Also in FP.

Horney, K. (1930). The distrust between the sexes. *Psychoanalytische Bewegung, 2,* 521–537. Also in FP.

Horney, K. (1933). Maternal conflicts. *American Journal of Orthopsychiatry, 3,* 455–463. Also in FP.

Horney, K. (1934). The overvaluation of love: A study of a common present-day feminine type. *Psychoanalytic Quarterly, 3,* 605–638. Also in FP.

Horney, K. (1935). The problem of feminine masochism. *Psychoanalytic Review, 22,* 241. Also in FP.

Horney, K. (1937). *The neurotic personality of our time.* New York: Norton.

Horney, K. (1939). *New ways in psychoanalysis.* New York: Norton.

Horney, K. (1942). *Self-analysis.* New York: Norton.

Horney, K. (1945). *Our inner conflicts.* New York: Norton.

Horney, K. (1950). *Neurosis and human growth.* New York: Norton.

Horney, K. (1967). *Feminine psychology.* H. Kelman, Ed. New York: Norton.

Horney, K. (1980). *The adolescent diaries of Karen Horney.* New York: Basic Books.

Ingram, D. H. (1985). Karen Horney at 100: Beyond the frontier. *American Journal of Psychoanalysis, 45,* 305–309.

Kelman, H. (1971). *Helping people: Karen Horney's psychoanalytic approach.* New York: Science House.

Kelman, H. (1989). The legacy of a nonfeminist analyst. [Review of M. Westkott, *The feminist legacy of Karen Horney.* New Haven, Conn.: Yale University Press]. *Contemporary Psychology, 34,* 166–167.

Kohut, H. (1977). *The restoration of the self.* New York: International Universities Press.

Monte, C. (1987). *Beneath the mask* (3rd ed.). New York: Holt, Rinehart & Winston.

O'Connell, A. N. (1980). Karen Horney: Theorist in psychoanalysis and feminine psychology. *Psychology of Women Quarterly, 5,* 81–93.

Paris, B. J. (1989). The importance of Karen Horney [Review of S. Quinn, *A mind of her own: The life of Karen Horney.* New York: Summit]. *Contemporary Psychology, 34,* 568–569.

Quinn, S. (1987). *A mind of her own: The life of Karen Horney.* New York: Basic Books.

Rubins, J. L. (1978). *Karen Horney: Gentle rebel of psychoanalysis.* New York: Dial Press.

Ryckman, R. M. (1989). *Theories of personality* (4th ed.). Pacific Grove, Calif.: Brooks/Cole.

van den Daele, L. (1981). The self psychologies of Heinz Kohut and Karen Horney: A comparative examination. *American Journal of Psychoanalysis, 41,* 327–336.

Westkott, M. (1986). *The feminist legacy of Karen Horney.* New Haven, Conn.: Yale University Press.

Williams, J. H. (1977). *Psychology of women.* New York: Norton.

Additional Representative Publications by Karen Horney

Horney, K. (1935). Conceptions and misconceptions of the analytical method. *Journal of Nervous and Mental Disease, 81,* 399.

Horney, K. (1936). Culture and neurosis. *American Sociological Review, 1,* 221.

Horney, K. (1936). The problem of negative therapeutic reaction. *Psychoanalytic Quarterly, 5,* 19.

Horney, K. (1946). *Are you considering psychoanalysis?* New York: Norton.

Horney, K. (1946). The future of psychoanalysis. *American Journal of Psychoanalysis,*
      6, 66.
Horney, K. (1947). Maturity and the individual. *American Journal of Psychoanalysis,*
      7, 85.
Horney, K. (1952). The paucity of inner experiences. *American Journal of Psycho-*
      analysis, 12, 3.

BÄRBEL INHELDER (1913–   )

Howard E. Gruber

Bärbel Inhelder was Jean Piaget's student and then chief collaborator for forty-eight years. Together, within the framework of genetic epistemology, they produced a series of five volumes of research on stage theory and the development of operational thought, two volumes on the development of figurative thought, and one work of synthesis. Working alone or in other collaborations, Inhelder pioneered the application of genetic epistemology to the study of mental deficiency, to cross-cultural research, and to the field of learning. She and her team of collaborators have also produced a series of studies of the development of cognitive strategies. Her work has played an essential role in the "cognitive revolution" in psychology, in assuring that developmental research and theory would be a fundamental part of that movement.

Inhelder is the author or coauthor of twelve books and about 150 other publications. She was professor of child and adolescent psychology at the University of Geneva from 1948 to 1971 and from 1971 to 1983 was Piaget's successor in the chair of genetic and experimental psychology. In 1974 she established the Fondation Archives Jean Piaget. For many years she was the director of the important journal *Archives de Psychologie*. She has served as president of the Société Suisse de Psychologie (1965–1968) and of the Association de Psychologie Scientifique de Langue Française (1968–1970). She has received many honors, including visiting professorships and other invitations, and at least six universities have named her *Docteur honoris causa*.

FAMILY BACKGROUND AND EDUCATION

Bärbel Inhelder was born April 15, 1913, in St. Gall, a small city in northern Switzerland. Her father, Alfred, of an old Swiss family, had a doctorate in zoology and taught natural history at the local Gymnasium (academic high school) at St. Gall and at nearby Rorschach, and did some university teaching as well. Her mother, Elisabeth, was part German, part Swiss, and had become a British subject by virtue of a previous marriage to an English artist. The family were liberal Protestants. Religion did not play a major role in their lives, although the mother did make a point of Christmas festivities. Later, Inhelder became and remained an atheist.

An only child, Bärbel Inhelder was given a mixture of public and private education. Her father was a major influence in her intellectual development. They went for many walks in the woods and fields, and he taught her natural history. She liked tracking and observing animals. He also invoked an early interest in philosophy. Her mother was the literary figure in the family, writing stories and plays for children, often on family themes. At home, the family read Greek and German classics and Shakespeare. Her father taught her about the evolutionary theories of Lamarck, Darwin, and Haeckel.

The primary school she attended in St. Gall was attached to the local Ecole Normale (teacher-training college), with the result that the classes were small, the school was coeducational, and Inhelder was exposed to experimental teaching and novice teachers. Her secondary education was divided between St. Gall and the nearby town of Rorschach.

The secondary schools she attended were oriented toward teacher preparation, which did not entail any university education. Since the young Inhelder wanted to keep the university option open, and her parents concurred, she had private courses in Latin, in the arts, and in science and mathematics.

Inhelder's parents were hesitant about granting permission for university education, partly because her health was delicate, partly because these were the years of the Great Depression and it was important to have a livelihood. For a young woman this meant teaching. Nevertheless, in 1932 Inhelder went to Geneva for a summer course, with no set plan, mainly to improve her French. Her background in psychology was minimal. She had disliked a course in experimental psychology, but had enjoyed reading, on her own, Freud and whatever she could find about adolescence.

At the University of Geneva, she soon found that the Institute of Educational Sciences, also known as the Institut Jean-Jacques Rousseau, was a congenial place, matching her interests. Among the senior faculty were professors Edouard Claparède and Pierre Bovet. Among the younger ones was Jean Piaget, soon to become director of the institute. The summer scheme quickly expanded into full student status. There were intense seminars, admission to private libraries, and companionable hikes with the faculty and other students. Although there was great interest in what we now call "cognition," the Geneva tradition included concern for perception and imagery, moral development, and the history of science. Geneva provided an attractive ambiance—intellectually stimulating and friendly, with broad interests and an international atmosphere. Inhelder studied the history of science, neurology, and evolutionary theory; she learned about Gestalt psychology, did some clinical work with Professor André Rey, and flourished intellectually.

CAREER DEVELOPMENT

In 1935 she earned her *Diplome général de psychologie de l'enfant.* She became Piaget's volunteer assistant for two years. Then economic reality, the need to earn her living, combined with opportunity. First she returned home to St. Gall and began to collect data for her dissertation. Then she was offered a position as school psychologist in her home canton of St. Gall. Regretfully leaving thoughts of a university career behind, she took the job. But she continued and extended her Genevan research by examining the retarded children who now would be part of her charge. Even before taking up the post, she had collected over half of the data for this project, which became her doctoral dissertation, completed in 1943. By that time she had already published her first book in collaboration with Piaget (Piaget & Inhelder, 1974/1971).

In 1943 she was invited back to Geneva as *Chef de travaux* (laboratory instructor). She has stayed at the University of Geneva ever since, having been appointed professor of child and adolescent psychology in 1948. In 1971, upon Piaget's retirement from teaching, she became his successor in the chair of genetic and experimental psychology, which she held until her retirement from teaching in 1983. In 1974 she created the Archives Jean Piaget, which has become an important center for international conferences as well as a valuable library and research center.

MAJOR CONTRIBUTIONS AND ACHIEVEMENTS

Inhelder's contributions can be organized under five main headings: conservation and concrete operations; formal operations; functional studies of learning, memory, and mental imagery; cognitive strategies; and more general work on stage theory and genetic epistemology.

Conservation and Concrete Operations

Conservation

Although they focus on developmental periods five to ten years apart, Piaget's work (1955/1937) on the development of object permanence in the first two years of life is closely connected with his work with Inhelder (1974/1941) on the idea of the conservation of matter—a development spanning roughly the years six to twelve.

On her twentieth birthday, Piaget suggested to Inhelder that she drop a cube of sugar into a glass of water and ask watching children about what happens as the cube dissolves and disappears. Three years later this investigation became Inhelder's first publication (1936) and the first article ever published devoted entirely to the question of conservation. During those years three women at the

Institut des Sciences de l'Education, Piaget's collaborators, produced three pioneering papers (Szeminska, 1935; Inhelder, 1936; Meyer, 1935) on different aspects of concrete operational thought.

Inhelder hoped to make conservation the subject of her doctoral dissertation, but before she could do that Piaget invited her to collaborate on the research project that became *The Child's Construction of Quantities: Conservation and Atomism* (Piaget & Inhelder, 1974/1941). Although the theme of invariance and conservation is the main subject of the book, there is an important second theme, the growth of the child's ideas about the atomic structure of matter. This is important because invisible transformations (such as the dispersion of "atoms") play an important role in comprehending many invariances.

Piaget and Inhelder found that the idea of conservation develops in a regular sequence: first, the conservation of matter in general; second, the conservation of weight; and finally, the conservation of volume. As Inhelder and Piaget often stressed, the important diagnostic question in determining a child's developmental stage is not whether the child gives a correct answer (e.g., same amount or different amount), but the reasons given to justify the answer.

In this work Inhelder and Piaget discuss three major findings about concrete operational thought: (1) *Decentration* or abandonment of egocentrism. The immature response is characterized by seizing on one or another directly perceived aspect of the situation; the more mature response takes several dimensions into account and composes them in a mental structure liberated from direct perception. (2) *Mental action.* An operation is not a passive registering of a situation but an action upon it. (3) *Reversibility.* The set of possible actions is grouped into structures so that the thinker can move, mentally, from one to another among the set of permissible states. The elaboration of this concept of operational thought was to take Inhelder and Piaget about twenty years.

It is not always remembered that Inhelder's doctoral dissertation (1968/1943) was, in its own way, a sequel to the previous work on conservation and the construction of quantities. In her work with the retarded, Inhelder rejected conventional intelligence tests. Instead, she worked out methods for applying the clinical method to retardates, using problems drawn from the previous work: the transformation of a ball of clay, the dissolution of sugar, and logical-mathematical composition.

Thus Inhelder's dissertation was a pioneering application of Piagetian methods to a special population. She found that, in general, retardates follow the same developmental sequence as normal children, but take much longer. However, she did not accept the conclusion that retardation is simply a slowing down of normal development. There were certain qualitative and structural differences between normal and retarded children on which she laid great stress, especially a tendency for the retarded individual to oscillate between distinctly different levels of performance. These studies had a characteristic that was to become a hallmark of Inhelder's later work: an intense interest in the process taking place.

The Representation of Space

The literature on the psychology of space is vast, almost all of it about space perception. Only a small fraction of it deals with the conception and representation of space, and that was either done by or is directly traceable to two works: Piaget & Inhelder (1956/1948), and Piaget, Inhelder, and Szeminska (1960/1948). In their replication study, Laurendeau and Pinard (1970) remark that the Geneva investigators seem to be the only ones "to have systematically studied the development of representational space in the child" (p. 13). For the most part, this remains true today. The only part of this Genevan work that has gained wide recognition is the idea of perspective-taking, especially as represented in the celebrated "three-mountain problem," the basic idea of which appeared first in an experiment in Geneva reported by Edith Meyer (1935). There were numerous intermediate publications, and then in 1948 two fundamental works appeared: *The Child's Conception of Space* (Piaget & Inhelder, 1956/1948) and *The Child's Conception of Geometry* (Piaget, Inhelder, & Szeminska, 1960/1948).

In the numerous follow-ups of this work, attention has been given one-sidedly to the three-mountain problem, which demonstrated the child's developing ability to conceive of the appearance of a scene from another perspective than her own. The basic point that Inhelder and Piaget make is that the young child has not yet mastered the set of transformations and coordinations necessary to understand the coherence of the space she inhabits. From this limitation many consequences flow, among them various levels of immature performance in the three-mountain problem. In her autobiography Inhelder sums up this work as follows:

The experiments I designed with the help of my students showed that topological relations of contiguity, separation and envelopment are more elementary as representations, closer to sensorimotor exploratory actions, than Euclidean and projective structures into which the topological relations are slowly integrated. (p. 219)

Formal Operations

Inhelder and Piaget (1958/1955) have described their work on the period of formal operations as entailing a surprise in which their two independent lines of effort almost unintentionally converged to produce their discovery of a previously unrecognized stage of development. Inhelder has enlarged upon this account in her autobiography, and in an interview in which she said of this work:

I wanted to understand the role of the object in determining the subject's behavior, the influence of the context; and I hoped to demonstrate the general laws of an experimental method. I thought that there was an evolution in the strategies, the interpretation of experience, the conception of proof, the empirical attitude. I wanted to know more about the subject's methods. But I also dreamed, a little naively, of describing the genesis of the scientific method. . . . [I had] the idea that there may be different roads, but after all certain optimal and parsimonious moves. I remember our excitement at realizing that there was also something that corresponded to a certain system. It was a little discovery: after eleven years, a new stage! (Gillièron and Coll, 1981; translation from French transcript by H.E.G.)

How far apart were Inhelder and Piaget during the gestation of this project? There is great continuity in the elaboration of themes throughout the work of Inhelder and Piaget. The later book on learning (Inhelder, Sinclair, & Bovet, 1974) takes up the theme of conservation. The books on space and geometry explicitly foreshadow the work on formal operations.

In spite of this continuity, it seems safe to say that the work on the transition from child to adolescent thinking was initiated by Inhelder and was very far along when Piaget became involved in it. In 1954, in an article entitled "The Experimental Attitudes of the Child and the Adolescent," Inhelder gave a summary of the work, which had then been in progress for several years. The title itself suggests how different her concerns were from the logical-structural preoccupations of Piaget (Inhelder, 1954).

In her article the emphasis is on the functional aspects of thought, how mental structures are put to work. This could best be studied, not by asking the subject questions, but by observing how he or she attacks a problem. Eleven problems are described, all of which appear in the later book (Inhelder & Piaget, 1958/1955), along with four others. Inhelder groups the problems as follows: discovery of invariants, equilibrium of forces, proportionality, and experimental verification (this last might well be called "isolation of variables"). The major result she describes is the emergence of experimental or inductive thinking in the adolescent: changes in strategy and tactics, in the way of "reading" experience (or representing the data), and in the concept of proof. The movement of thought, from about age five to about age fifteen, is from (a) relatively passive observing, to (b) looking for particular relationships, to (c) searching for more general truths.

The adolescent engages in a "dialogue with experience," takes account of the entire set of possibilities in setting up a plan for necessary experiments, and aims at moving toward a systematic statement of the relationships involved. Here and there appear suggestions that this picture of the adolescent as an emerging scientist is somewhat idealized, and only applicable to some of the subjects. The book ends with a chapter about the general nature of adolescent thought. Here Inhelder and Piaget discuss, among other things, how romantic and utopian thought can be understood as expressing the adolescent's pleasure in his or her new found ability to consider the real as a special case of the possible.

This work has come in for two kinds of criticism. On the empirical side, it is not clear that all adolescents attain the stage of formal operations, and it is not clear in what sense this stage is final (see, for example, Gruber & Vonèche, 1976). On the theoretical side, logicians have questioned the success of Piaget's attempt to formalize Inhelder's empirical findings (see, for example, Parsons, 1960). Nevertheless, the work stands as a landmark in our understanding of the growth of thought in adolescence. The vigorous discussion of what lies "beyond" formal operations shows that most investigators recognize that there indeed exists something to go beyond (Basseches, 1984; Commons, Richards, & Armon, 1984). The profound transformation in thought between childhood and adolescence permits both the appearance of youthful idealism and the beginning of serious consideration of life goals.

Functionalism in Genetic Psychology

For Inhelder the work on adolescent thought, culminating in 1955, was a determined step toward the reinsertion of a functional aspect into genetic epistemology. This feature of the work was somewhat lost from view in the synthesis of her experimental efforts with Piaget's formalizations. Fortunately, in 1961–1962, during a period spent at Harvard, buttressed by her fellow traveler and collaborator, Magali Bovet, Inhelder began her work on learning. This interest stemmed in part from the inner requirements of genetic epistemology: the need to understand transitions from stage to stage had become critical. The work was also a response to the provocation (as she called it) of her host at Harvard, Jerome Bruner. The book, *Learning and the Development of Cognition*, reported the collaborative work of three principal authors, all women—Inhelder, Sinclair, and Bovet (1974)—and fourteen other collaborators. In a series of eight groups of experiments, the project explored the possibility of accelerating cognitive development.

Notably, no reinforcements or corrections were introduced; instead attention was given to exposing the children to situations inducing cognitive conflict, or disequilibria. This was about the same time that Piaget and his group were studying children's resolutions of contradictions.

The experiments were generally successful in showing that "transitional" children—those whose pretest performances indicated that they were ripe for change—responded positively to the training. Inhelder displayed some ambivalence about this finding, since one of the most hallowed tenets of genetic epistemology had been the slow and spontaneous development of cognitive structures.

But for Inhelder the experimental acceleration of the acquisition of concepts was not the central issue. Rather, she hoped to clarify the mechanisms of transition from stage to stage. From this point of view, a key result of this work was its preparation of the ground for its sequel, the studies of cognitive strategies, conducted under Inhelder's direction.

Cognitive Strategies

The turn toward process, long implicit in Inhelder's work, became more pronounced and more explicit in the 1970s. Together with a group of collaborators, a series of studies was undertaken on the development of problem solving in the child. At first, the orientation of this work was to look for relatively broad strategies and to remain attuned to their connection with previously established structures and stages. But early in the work it became clear that rather than a few grand strategies it would be more appropriate to speak of the child solving problems as having available a fairly large number of procedures (specific action sequences that he knows how to do). The question then becomes, How does each child *marshal* the procedures available to him? Thus the turn toward process also became an accentuated concern with the individual, the "psychological subject," as contrasted with Piaget's overriding interest in the epigenesis of the universal or "epistemic subject." Only a few articles have appeared describing this work (Inhelder, 1978, 1983; Inhelder, Ackermann-Valladao, et al., 1976).

In some ways, the strategy of intense concentration on a few cases is comparable to the work with adult subjects of Newell and Simon (1972) or Gruber (1981/1974; Wallace & Gruber, 1989). On the other hand, Inhelder has certainly never rejected the developmental stage-structural approach, and correspondingly, the work of her team has been about children and has remained sensitive to developmental changes in children and adolescents.

As Inhelder sees this work, it is an approach to the development of heuristics in problem solving. Needless to say, she emphasizes the link between this development of functional knowledge (know-how) and the development of structural knowledge (know that) that has been the main concern of the Geneva school (Inhelder, 1983). Discussing these two inseparable poles of their work, Inhelder and Piaget (1979) characterize their relationship as "a happy marriage, subject to conflicts always surmounted" (p. 165).

Developmental Stages

Inhelder played a key role in promoting the seemingly central Genevan concept of stages. She organized and led international symposia on the subject, and she expounded the empirical findings about stages of intellectual development. Nevertheless, she now readily admits certain limitations of the stage concept, which was mainly a tool for organizing the diverse descriptions and analyses of cognitive development generated by the Geneva school.

Moreover, and perhaps paradoxically, Inhelder also played a key role in the research on figural factors in mental functioning, especially memory and imagery (Piaget & Inhelder, 1969/1966; Piaget, Inhelder, et al., 1973/1968): in these domains, according to their findings, there is no clear stage-wise development.

Inhelder's emphasis on transitions changed the focus from the generalized "epistemic" subject to the individualized psychological subject. In so doing, Inhelder constructed her own intellectual individuality. At the same time, as she and others have stressed repeatedly (e.g., Bresson, 1983; Frey, 1983), the two approaches are *deux indissociables*—not to be separated.

REFERENCES

Basseches, M. (1984). *Dialectical thinking and adult development.* Norwood, N.J.: Ablex.

Bresson, F. (1983). En guise d'introduction. *Archives de psychologie, 51,* xxv–xxviii.

Commons, M. L.; Richards, F. A.; & Armon, C. (Eds.). (1984). *Beyond formal operations: Late adolescent and adult cognitive development.* New York: Praeger.

Frey, L. (1983). Deux indissociables. *Archives de psychologie, 51,* 1–8.

Gillièron, C., & Coll, C. (1981). Entrevista con Bärbel Inhelder. *Estudios de psicologia, 7,* 3–13. (Original interview in French)

Gruber, H. E. (1981). *Darwin on man: A psychological study of scientific creativity* (2nd ed.). Chicago: University of Chicago Press. (Original work published 1974)

Gruber, H. E., & Vonèche, J. J. (1976). Réflexions sur les opérations formelles de la pensée. *Archives de psychologie, 44,* 45–55.

Inhelder, B. (1936). Observations sur le principe de conservation dans la physique de l'enfant. *Cahiers de pédagogie expérimentale et de psychologie de l'enfant,* No. 9.

Inhelder, B. (1954). Les attitudes expérimentales de l'enfant et de l'adolescent. *Bulletin de psychologie, 7,* 272–282.

Inhelder, B. (1968). *The diagnosis of reasoning in the mentally retarded.* New York: John Day. (Original work published 1943)

Inhelder, B. (1978). De l'approche structurale à l'approche procédurale: Introduction à l'étude des stratégies. In *Actes du 21ᵉ Congrès international de psychologie* (pp. 99–118). Paris: Presses universitaires de France.

Inhelder, B. (1983). On generating procedures and structuring knowledge. In R. Groner, M. Groner, & W. F. Bischof (Eds.), *Methods of heuristics.* Hillside, N.J.: Erlbaum.

Inhelder, B. (1989). Autobiography. In G. Lindzey (Ed.), *History of psychology in autobiography.* Stanford: Stanford University Press.

Inhelder, B.; Ackermann-Valladao, E.; Blanchet, A.; Karmiloff-Smith, A.; Kilcher-Hagedorn, H.; Montangero, J.; & Robert, M. (1976). Des structures cognitives aux procédures de découverte. *Archives de psychologie, 44,* 57–72.

Inhelder, B., & Piaget, J. (1958). *The growth of logical thinking from childhood to adolescence: An essay on the construction of formal operational structures.* New York: Basic Books. (Original work published 1955)

Inhelder, B., & Piaget, J. (1979). Procedures and structures. *Archives de psychologie, 47,* 181–197.

Inhelder, B.; Sinclair, H.; & Bovet, M. (1974). *Learning and the development of cognition.* Cambridge, Mass.: Harvard University Press. (Original work published 1974)

Laurendeau, M., & Pinard, A. (1970). *The development of the concept of space in the child.* New York: International Universities Press.

Meyer, E. (1935). La représentation des relations spatiales chez l'enfant. *Cahiers de pédagogie expérimentale et de psychologie de l'enfant,* No. 8.

Newell, A., & Simon, H. A. (1972). *Human problem solving.* Englewood Cliffs, N.J.: Prentice-Hall.

Parsons, C. (1960). Inhelder and Piaget's *The growth of logical thinking,* II. A logician's viewpoint. *British Journal of Psychology, 51,* 75–84.

Piaget, J. (1955). *The construction of reality in the child*. New York: Basic Books. (Original work published 1937)

Piaget, J., & Inhelder, B. (1956). *The child's conception of space*. London: Routledge & Kegan Paul. (Original work published 1948)

Piaget, J., & Inhelder, B. (1969). *The psychology of the child*. New York: Basic Books. (Original work published 1966)

Piaget, J., & Inhelder, B. (1971). *Mental imagery in the child*. New York: Basic Books. (Original work published 1966)

Piaget, J., & Inhelder, B. (1974). *The child's construction of quantities: Conservation and atomism*. New York: Basic Books. (Original work published 1941)

Piaget, J.; Inhelder, B.; & Szeminska, A. (1960). *The child's conception of geometry*. London: Routledge & Kegan Paul. (Original work published 1948)

Piaget, J., & Inhelder, B., in collaboration with Sinclair-de Zwart, H. (1973). *Memory and intelligence*. New York: Basic Books (Original work published 1968)

Szeminska, A. (1935). Essai d'analyse psychologique du raisonnement mathématique. *Cahiers de pédagogie expérimentale et de psychologie de l'enfant*, No. 7.

Wallace, D. B., & Gruber, H. E. (Eds.). (1989). *Creative people at work*. New York: Oxford University Press.

Additional Representative Publications by Bärbel Inhelder

Piaget, J., & Inhelder (1969). *The psychology of the child*. New York: Basic Books. (Original work published 1966)

Tanner, J. M., & Inhelder, B. (Eds.). (1971). *Discussions on child development: A consideration of the biological, psychological, and cultural approaches to the understanding of human development and behavior*. London: Tavistock. (Original works published 1956–1960)

Additional Representative Publications About Bärbel Inhelder

Bang, V., Bovet, M., Sinclair, H., Gillièron, C., & Kilcher, H. (Eds.). (1983). Hommage à Bärbel Inhelder à l'occasion de son soixante-dixième anniversaire. *Archives de psychologie*, *51*, 1–187. [Special issue of *Archives de psychologie*, celebrating Inhelder's seventieth birthday. 28 articles, 55 authors.]

MARIE JAHODA
(1907–   )

Stuart W. Cook

While most women who entered psychology before the gender enlightenment of recent years encountered major obstacles in their professional careers, few have faced less promising circumstances than did Marie Jahoda. She was born into a Jewish family in a country and at a time when anti-Semitic discrimination was widespread. She was a leader in an Austrian socialist youth movement and an active Social Democrat when Social Democrats in Austria were suppressed— and some were hanged. She served a prison term for her political opinions. Most of the copies of the book reporting her first major research were burned because its authors were Jewish. She lived through World War II under the Nazi aerial bombardment of London. Persecution, war, and family imperatives forced her to compartmentalize her professional life into four distinct time periods, three countries, and two languages.

Despite these circumstances, Jahoda built a distinguished scientific career. She served as a tenured faculty member at three universities in two nations. In two of these universities she had the responsibility of initiating and developing psychology departments. Her vita lists eighty-six publications; she authored or coauthored eight books and coedited five more. She received major honorary awards from both the American and British psychological societies as well as the Commander of the British Empire medal, personally bestowed by Queen Elizabeth. She became internationally famous as a pioneer and leading scholar on the psychological consequences of unemployment, the psychodynamics of ethnic and racial prejudice, and the psychology of positive mental health.

FAMILY BACKGROUND AND EDUCATION

Jahoda was born of Jewish parents in Vienna, Austria, on January 26, 1907. Against the background of anti-Semitic discrimination of the period and Austrian fascism of the mid-1930s, this became a significant factor in the early part of her life. The family was middle-class, with a liberal political orientation. Her father, Carl Jahoda, was a businessman, her mother, Betty Jahoda, a homemaker.

She had two brothers and one sister. Jahoda recalls that Karl Krauss, social critic and satirist, and Joseph Popper Lynkeus, a mathematician and social philosopher, were family idols.

After completing Realgymnasium in 1926, she entered both the Pedagogical Academy of Vienna and the doctoral program in psychology at the University of Vienna. She received a teaching diploma in 1928 and her Doctor of Philosophy in psychology in 1933.

The leading faculty members in psychology at the University of Vienna were Karl and Charlotte Bühler. Although Freud was also attached to the university, he had no part in the training of psychology students. Despite the fact that psychoanalysis was taboo for psychology students, interest in it was strong. Jahoda was among those who were secretly analyzed. She regards her analyst, Heinz Hartmann, as a significant factor in her intellectual development. She became impressed by the potential of the psychoanalytic method for studying unconscious processes and throughout her career retained an interest in the scientific and applied implications of psychoanalytic theory.

In 1923 the Bühlers established the Psychological Institute at the university. This, plus their own international reputations, attracted many foreign psychologists, including Americans, to Vienna. Their presence contributed considerably to the breadth of Jahoda's training.

In 1926 Paul Lazarsfeld, then a young instructor in the Psychological Institute and later an internationally renowned sociologist, established, under the institute's wing, a research unit for social psychology and market research, Wirtschaftspsychologische Forschungsstelle. Jahoda, although still in her last year of Gymnasium—but already anticipating the beginning of her university work in psychology—had become acquainted with the members of the Forschungsstelle staff. An anecdote from the period provides an early indication of her intellectual competence. She went to the Forschungsstelle one afternoon and found the place in turmoil. A report, not yet written, had to be delivered the following day. All that was ready were the statistical tables. The staff enlisted her aid. She was given three of the tables and asked to supply the descriptive text and interpretations. Along with the other staff members, she worked into the night until the report was finished.

As a college student, Jahoda maintained her contact with the Forschungsstelle. She and Lazarsfeld were married in 1927. Their daughter, Lotte Bailyn, born in 1930, is professor of organizational psychology and management, Sloan School of Management, at the Massachusetts Institute of Technology.

Paralleling these educational and personal events were political developments that were to have drastic consequences. As noted, Jahoda had been a leader in the Austrian socialist youth movement and was a member of the Social Democratic party. These affiliations antedated her choice of psychology as a field of study. She traces that choice to her youthful aspiration to become the minister of education in a hoped-for Austrian socialist government. She believed that psychology would be the best preparation for such a post.

In 1933 Austrian elections resulted in a Parliament of eighty Social Democrats and eighty-one right-wing Christian Democrats. Thereupon, Prime Minister Engelbert Dollfuss, from the Christian Democratic party, dissolved Parliament and instituted a number of repressive measures. Tension grew; the opponents armed themselves. In February 1934 Dollfuss' armed forces stormed the Social Democratic party headquarters in Linz. Shooting started. A general strike was called. The armed forces of the Christian Democrats bombarded working-class housing developments. Civil war continued for five days. Many Social Democrats were captured, and thirteen were hanged. Thereafter, Jahoda operated as a member of the underground opposition.

CAREER AND CONTRIBUTIONS

Austria, 1933–1937

Jahoda and Lazarsfeld were separated in the early 1930s. He left for the United States in 1933, and she succeeded him as director of the Wirtschaftspsychologische Forschungsstelle, serving in that post for the next three years.

In November 1936 Jahoda was arrested and imprisoned for her activities in the underground movement. She was subjected to nightly interrogations by the Austrian state police. Some of these dealt with the political implications of her research. Foreign intervention led to her release and expulsion from Austria in July 1937.

During the years prior to her political difficulties, Jahoda, in collaboration with a research team of fifteen members, conducted a study that achieved world fame and was the starting point of her career-long interest in the psychological consequences of unemployment. It was conducted in a small village that for many years had been supported by a single textile company. In 1929, during the Great Depression, the company failed. Within a year, in 77 percent of the families no one was employed. In 1931 a team of research workers from the Forschungsstelle studied the village in detail. Jahoda described the results in a book titled *Die Arbeitslosen von Marienthal* (Paul Lazarsfeld prepared an introduction, and Hans Zeisel a historical appendix) (Lazarsfeld, Jahoda & Zeisel, 1933; Jahoda, Lazarsfeld, & Zeisel, 1972). Most of the copies of the book were burned because its authors were Jewish. The conclusions of the study were surprising: unemployment and its accompanying economic deprivation led to resignation and passivity rather than to revolutionary tendencies. As the quality of material life deteriorated, the residents contracted their wants and lowered their expectations, presumably lessening the psychological stress that their unemployment and physical deprivation might otherwise have caused.

England, 1937–1945

When Jahoda was expelled from Austria she was invited to England by Alexander Farquharson, general secretary of the British Institute of Sociology. Farquharson had coordinated the efforts of a number of people (including a well-known British prison reformer, Margery Fry) in securing her release and was concerned that she and other refugees find work in England. He knew of a large-scale project for supplementary unemployment relief that had been initiated by an order of Friends (Quakers) in a mining community in South Wales. The key feature of the project was that it called for the unemployed to work as part of an organization that produced goods for their own consumption. Farquharson suggested to the originators of the project that Jahoda make a study of its operations, and they agreed. Her participation was supported by funds from the privately supported Society for the Protection of Science and Learning, whose objective it was to help professional emigrés get reestablished.

For Jahoda, the opportunity to study this relief project offered a valuable follow-up to her Marienthal research on the psychological consequences of unemployment. In Marienthal, the loss of work had led to resignation and inactivity. Conceivably, the regular, scheduled work called for in the Wales project might remove some of unemployment's negative effects.

The unemployed men in the Wales project continued to receive their normal unemployment allowance. They received no wages for their work in the project, but had the privilege of purchasing the cooperatively produced goods at a relatively low cost, that is, the cost of the raw materials plus a 20 percent overhead charge. A wide range of goods was produced: bread, bricks, shoe repair, meat, milk, clothing, furniture, agricultural products.

Jahoda spent four months in the mining community. She lived with the families of the unemployed miners and worked in each of the project's twelve production units. Her findings, while disappointing to the project sponsors, added considerably to her growing understanding of the meaning of employment and the consequences of its deprivation.

With respect to enforced idleness and the psychological distress that accompanied the loss of time structure formerly provided by employment, the project's results depended on the age of the workers. Older men who had resigned themselves to spending the rest of their lives on unemployment relief tended to benefit from the reinstitution of time structure associated with their thirty hour work week in the production organization. This was less true for men under age forty-five, as indicated by their high rate of absenteeism. With respect to the restoration of the regular social contacts that had characterized working in the mines, the Wales project appeared successful for most of the unemployed.

In her later theoretical analyses, Jahoda identified two other psychological burdens of unemployment (Jahoda, 1979a, 1979b, discussed below): the undermining of social status and identity, and exclusion from the purposes of the larger society. On these counts she concluded that the Wales project not only failed to relieve psychological discomfort, but may have intensified it. She attributed this to the fact that, through long-established traditions, the miners unthinkingly accepted their identity as workers in an occupation that had a purpose in the larger society. When unemployment threatened this identity it could not be restored by substitute subsistence work that, to the miners, had no societal function.

Although the report on her research was completed in the summer of 1938, Jahoda withheld its publication for many years. Her reasons for doing so reflect her concern for the feelings of a person for whom she had great respect (Jahoda, 1981a). While Jahoda was engaged in her field work in Wales, Hitler's troops occupied Austria. Her mother and siblings, as well as many of her friends—Jewish and non-Jewish—still lived in Vienna. Jahoda felt distraught and helpless. The Quaker in charge of the Wales project, Lord Forrester, immediately left for Vienna, where he contacted the Jahoda family. He arranged a code in which Jahoda and her family could correspond. In addition, he provided other support that helped them control their fear and despair. Jahoda herself operated an Austrian self-help-for-refugees organization in London. This group organized English sponsorships that were necessary to get people out of Austria. Just before the outbreak of war, Jahoda's family escaped in this way.

A few months after this visit, Lord Forrester read Jahoda's disappointing evaluation of the project he had managed. He saw it as undercutting the ideals to which he had made a lifelong commitment. Realizing this, Jahoda decided that she would not add to Forrester's distress by making the report public, but instead would distribute it only to those who had organized and administered the project. Shortly thereafter, World War II revived Great Britain's need for coal from the Wales mines, bringing that period of unemployment in the area to a close.

In the fall of 1938, in recognition of her study of the unemployed in Marienthal, Jahoda was awarded a prestigious three year Pinsent-Darwin Studentship at Cambridge University. This enabled her to conduct a study of factory workers in which she graphically documented the adoption of the social norms of factory life by newly employed teenage workers; to collect the data she worked as an unskilled laborer (Jahoda, 1941).

In 1940 Jahoda became affiliated with the British Ministry of Information and began a period of work as a member of the Wartime Social Survey, an organization established to study civilian morale. One of the causes of poor morale found by the survey team was the emphasis by government planners on carrots as the everyday available vegetable. When the ministry refused to accept the finding as valid, the twenty-person survey team (including Jahoda) resigned in indignation. So did the team's cleaning women.

A later wartime assignment was to make daily radio broadcasts to Austria. Jahoda and two other Austrians prepared materials during the day, and in the evening Jahoda broadcast for twenty minutes from a secret radio station. (She had to sign a commitment not to divulge her activities or the station's location for thirty years.) She completed the war years, 1943–1945, as a research assistant at the National Institute for Social and Economic Research. Here she assisted in research on the British economy.

United States, 1945–1958

As the war neared its end, Jahoda's main concern became reunion with her daughter, who had spent the war years in the United States. Along with a few others in similar circumstances, she managed to secure passage on a troop ship carrying wounded Canadians. The ocean voyage included a close encounter with German submarines.

Jahoda's first position in the United States was in the Research Department of the American Jewish Committee. The major American Jewish organizations had responded to the Holocaust by funding research that they hoped would guide their efforts to reduce prejudice and discrimination in the United States. The research unit at the American Jewish Committee was headed by the German social philosopher Max Horkheimer, for whom Jahoda had written an article while still in Vienna. He was happy to have her on his American staff. Among the research topics Jahoda dealt with while at the American Jewish Committee were efforts to reduce prejudice through persuasive communications (e.g., Jahoda & Cooper, 1947), and the identification of a personality type, the authoritarian personality, that was predisposed to prejudice (e.g., Christie & Jahoda, 1954). During this period she also coauthored a book on the relation between emotional disorders and prejudice (Ackerman & Jahoda, 1950).

After three years, Jahoda moved for one year to the Bureau of Applied Social Research at Columbia University. Here, at the initiative of the sociologist Robert Merton, she participated in a study of the role of interracial contact in improving race relations in interracial housing (Jahoda & Salter-West, 1951).

In 1949 Jahoda moved to New York University as associate professor (later professor) of social psychology and associate director (later director) of the Research Center for Human Relations. Her research and writing in this setting made her one of the best-known social psychologists in the nation. Three lines of work contributed to this.

The first was the publication of a book, *Research Methods in Social Relations*, that she coauthored (Jahoda, Deutsch, & Cook, 1951). This was the first textbook to describe research procedures appropriate to topics of everyday social significance. It filled the need being experienced by the rapidly developing field of social psychology and was widely used.

The second was a pair of field studies, plus several theoretical analyses, of reactions (conformity, resistance, morale) to the suppression of political opinion by loyalty oaths and employment "black listing" (e.g., Jahoda & Cook, 1952; Jahoda, 1956). This was the period of Senator Joseph McCarthy's anticommunist crusade. Jahoda's papers introduced the concept of anticipatory ideological compliance and were among the most prominent efforts by social scientists to help people understand events of the times (Jahoda & Cook, 1953). Her last paper in this series challenged social scientists to repeat their laboratory research on the topic of conformity using issues in which research subjects have an emotional and intellectual involvement (Jahoda, 1959). She predicted that when this was done it would be found that conformity is much more difficult to induce than current research had suggested.

The third line of work was a trio of publications devoted to a conceptual clarification of the idea of mental health, or as it is sometimes called, positive mental health. A growing interest in the possibility of promoting mental health—in contrast to curing and preventing mental illness—was reflected in the 1950 Mid-Century White House Conference on Children and Youth and the subsequent creation of a federal commission, the Joint Commission on Mental Illness and Health. As part of the source materials for the White House conference, Jahoda was asked to prepare a review of available knowledge on the topic of community influences on mental health (Jahoda, 1950). She followed this with a second paper (Jahoda, 1953) and, at the request of the Joint Commission on Mental Illness and Health, a book on the distinguishing criteria of mentally healthy people, called *Current Concepts of Positive Mental Health* (Jahoda, 1958).

In 1953, only eight years after she came to America unknown to the majority of American social psychologists, Jahoda was elected president of the Society for the Psychological Study of Social Issues, a division of the American Psychological Association.

England, 1958–Late 1980s

In 1958 Jahoda embarked on her ''second life'' in England, the fourth distinct period in her scientific career. The occasion for the move was marriage to Austen H. Albu, engineer and prominent Labour party member of the British Parliament. Shortly after her arrival Jahoda was appointed Research Fellow at Brunel College in London. In 1962 she was advanced to the rank of professor and given the responsibility of developing a new psychology department.

Her scientific work at Brunel represented, in part, a continuation of her efforts to develop a meaningful conception of positive mental health. The Brunel period also saw the beginning of a series of analyses of the relationship of psychoanalysis to psychology and to some of the topics psychologists study. These included an assessment of the influence of psychoanalytic ideas on American psychology (Jahoda, 1963a), and a paper and a book giving a psychoanalytic interpretation of the development of prejudice and race relations (Jahoda, 1960a, 1960b). In the latter, she discusses the psychological functions served by prejudice and its consequent resistance to modification by relevant evidence. Prejudice is seen as a defense against inner weakness.

Among the things Jahoda accomplished at Brunel were two that she considers innovative and hopes will be put to use by others in the future. One of these, the design and introduction of a new four-year program for training psychologists, was influenced by her book-length study of the integration of academic and industrial experiences in Brunel's education of engineers and technologists (Jahoda, 1963b). The key feature of the program was that six months of each year was devoted to academic study and six months to work assignments, including such social settings as factories, schools, hospitals, and research organizations. This program gave expression to Jahoda's belief that sophisticated psychological training should make students aware of the weighty factors in real-life social behavior and alert them to the interactions and circular cause-and-effect relationships to be found in complex social groups.

The second accomplishment, based on an idea first conceived while working with R. K. Merton, had to do with a new approach to characterizing the dominant culture of a community or other social organization (Jahoda, 1961). She noted that a subgroup of the participants in any social setting can often be found to feel more at ease, at home, and under less strain than the other participants. These are people who "fit" the community. By discovering the social characteristics shared by this subgroup—but not by other community participants—it becomes possible to characterize the community culture as one hospitable to these characteristics. Examples of social characteristics are social practices, such as activity in community organizations, and demographic characteristics, such as age and socioeconomic status. For example, analysis of one community found that the best fit was manifested by a subgroup who shared the following characteristics: they were pioneers in the community, they had chosen the community over other equally available communities, they were thirty-five years old or older, and they participated actively in community affairs.

While at Brunel, Jahoda coedited the first edition of a book of readings on attitudes (Jahoda & Warren, 1966). A second edition appeared some years later.

In 1965, seven years after her return to England, the University of Sussex invited Jahoda to undertake a unique and challenging assignment. She was to develop and chair a department of social psychology, the first such department in the United Kingdom. (A second candidate for this distinction is the London School of Economics, which had a department of social psychology before 1965, but did not have a professor in the department until later.) She accepted, and chaired the new department for eight years. By 1973 she had gathered a departmental faculty of nine members.

Jahoda's formal retirement in 1973 (at the age of sixty-six) unleashed an extraordinary burst of scholarly activity. In the succeeding fifteen years, she authored two books, coedited three others, and published twenty-three articles and book chapters (an output to give pause to one who believes that creativity and productivity peak early in a professional career).

After her move to the University of Sussex, Jahoda worked primarily in two problem areas with which she had been concerned in the past and one to which she was a newcomer. The areas of past interest were psychoanalysis and unemployment. The new area was that of forecasting world futures.

In 1963 (while still at Brunel) Jahoda had written what was to be the first of several analyses of the relation of psychoanalysis to the field of psychology. In that article she carefully documented the extensive influence of psychoanalytic ideas on American psychology (Jahoda, 1963a). In a subsequent article during the Brunel period she described the conditions favoring U.S. receptivity to psychoanalysis—in both the scientific and popular cultures—as well as various attempts to reconcile psychoanalysis and behaviorism (Jahoda, 1969). At Sussex she continued her writing on this theme, extending it to what she saw as the mutual challenges facing psychoanalysis and social psychology (Jahoda, 1972). In 1977 she capped this line of work with her book *Freud and the Dilemmas of Psychology* (Jahoda, 1977). In this remarkable work, she undertakes not only a description and critique of psychoanalytic theory, but also a discussion of the ways in which psychological research and theory have been influenced by psychoanalysis. In addition, as the book's title suggests, she calls attention to the persistent dilemmas that psychoanalysis and psychology share. Among these are the scientific status of the unconscious, the impact of method on the subject matter of investigation, the effect of temporal and cultural context on research results, and the choice between efforts to develop comprehensive and small-scale theory.

The second research area to which Jahoda returned at Sussex was the psychological consequences of unemployment. In 1971, two years before her formal retirement, Jahoda was appointed a senior research consultant to the university's multidisciplinary Science Policy Research Unit (SPRU). The primary aim of this unit is to contribute to the advancement of knowledge of the relations between scientific and technological developments, on the one hand, and economic, social, and political processes, on the other, and to assess their implications for public policy. Jahoda became an active participant in SPRU, coediting three of its books and contributing chapters in a number of others. In 1984 she became a visiting professor at SPRU, and in 1989 she continued to participate in its work.

Beginning in 1979, Jahoda focused on SPRU's Program on Technology and Employment Opportunities, an assignment happily congruent with her longtime interest in employment and unemployment. Following completion, in 1938, of her study of unemployed miners in Wales (Jahoda, 1987b) and, in 1941, of the psychology of employment in an English factory (Jahoda, 1941), the career circumstances described earlier had drawn her away from research on employment and unemployment to work on other problems (for two exceptions, see Jahoda, 1963b and 1966). In contrast, from 1979 through 1987, Jahoda published nine articles and a book on employment and unemployment and became a sought-after speaker and consultant on this topic in European scientific and government circles. The vigor of this renewed concern with the topic on which she had begun her research career was due to the recurrence of mass unemployment in Great Britain, a development that also stimulated initiation of the SPRU program on Technology and Employment Opportunities.

In the early articles of this period, Jahoda concentrated on two tasks. The first was a presentation of her thinking on the latent psychological, as distinct from the manifest economic, consequences of loss of employment. (In drawing the latent-manifest distinction, Jahoda followed Merton's functional analysis approach to research on social science questions [Merton, 1957].) The latent psychological burdens of unemployment, according to Jahoda's analysis, are five in number (Jahoda, 1979a, 1979b). One is the loss of time structure provided by a job; without a job there is little to shape the passage of time for the day, the week, or longer periods. The second is a narrowing of the social horizon through loss of contacts beyond the family and close friends. Third is a loss of the experience of participation in the collective efforts of a workforce to produce something valued by others. Fourth is the loss of one's social identity as a useful member of society, and the substitution of a sense of being discarded, of being on the "scrap heap." Fifth is the absence of a compelling force to engage in some activity on a regular basis.

The second task was a comparison of the consequences of unemployment in the 1970s with those of the 1930s. In comparing unemployment in these two periods, Jahoda saw the opportunity of separating the consequences of the physical deprivation that results from loss of work from the consequences of unemployment per se, that is, its psychological consequences (Jahoda, 1979a, 1979b). Government grants to the poor, while still borderline in the 1970s, were higher than those to the unemployed in the 1930s, when the dole was not only insufficient but time-limited. Jahoda concluded that even though the more adequate financial assistance to the unemployed in the 1970s removed the terror of starvation and loss of shelter, the psychological burdens of unemployment were still evident. While the evidence was scanty, she did find, in studies of long-term unemployed, indications of phenomena similar to those she had observed in her original study of the village of Marienthal, for example, a sense of resignation, a loss of time structure for the waking day, a narrowing of the social horizon due to the loss of contact with people beyond family and close friends.

In subsequent papers (e.g., Jahoda, 1981b), as well as in her 1982 book, *Employment and Unemployment: A Social-Psychological Analysis*, Jahoda broadened her approach in several directions (Jahoda, 1982). One of these was the experience of alienation from work, due to routinized tasks, unchallenging activities, and lack of opportunity for self-direction. She undertook a review of approaches to the reduction of alienation that involved the "humanization" of work. Among other things, she presented a critical analysis of successes (e.g., increased satisfaction, reduced absenteeism) and failures (no increase in productivity) of humanization experiments.

In 1973 Jahoda published the first of a series of contributions on the topic of forecasting world futures (Jahoda, 1973). It appeared in a book that she coedited, called *Thinking About the Future: A Critique of "The Limits to Growth"* (Cole, Freeman, Jahoda, & Pavitt, 1973). As indicated in the title, the book raised questions about the pessimistic conclusions of an earlier, quite famous analysis of the world's future. In the book's final chapter, Jahoda calls attention to the failure of earlier forecasters to consider the human potential for behavior change, and argues that such change could greatly alter the outcomes of the computer simulations that generated doomsday predictions.

In 1976 and 1978 Jahoda coedited and contributed to two additional books on social forecasting (Freeman, Jahoda, & Miles, 1976; Freeman & Jahoda, 1978). In her concluding chapter to the 1978 book, *World Futures: The Great Debate*, Jahoda summarizes the many considerations, other than the familiar material problems of population growth, energy supply, natural resources, rate of use, and so on, that will influence the future (Jahoda, 1978). These include such nonmaterial matters as the effectiveness of international organizations, resource distribution problems, value choices regarding the use to which scarce materials are put, the military versus nonmilitary use of scientific creativity.

As noted above, the initiation of the SPRU Program on Technology and Employment Opportunities created a context in which Jahoda could contribute simultaneously to her long-term interest in employment and unemployment and her more recent concern with futures forecasting. An example was a chapter discussing the probable psychological barriers to and consequences of alternative societal adaptations to future technological unemployment (Jahoda, 1987a).

A by-product of Jahoda's expertise in forecasting is a unique familiarity with the possible contributions of psychology to interdisciplinary forecasting efforts. Although she has written an analysis of this potential, it is not yet available in published form (Jahoda, 1980).

Jahoda's scientific activity following her return to England was paralleled by an equally impressive record of public service on high-level scientific committees of the British government. A few years after her arrival from the United States she was appointed to the Home Office Committee on Mass Media Research (1963–1966). This was followed by a five-year period of disbursing scientific grants as a member of the Social Science Research Council (1965–1970). Soon thereafter came service on the Advisory Committee to the Home Secretary on Race Relations Research, which she chaired. Next were appointments to the Council for Science Policy (1970–1971) and to the Genetic Manipulation Advisory Committee (1976–1978), both government committees at the national level. On the former she participated in the distribution of research funds among the different research councils and provided advice on science to government officials.

In 1978 Jahoda was honored by election to the presidency of Section X (Social Sciences) of the British Association for the Advancement of Science. Her scientific eminence has been recognized on numerous other occasions. She has received honorary degrees from the universities of Leicester and Sussex, in England, the University of Bremen, in Germany, and the University of Stirling, in Scotland. Her scientific peers, both in England and the United States, have honored her work. In 1979 the American Psychological Association presented her its Award for Distinguished Contributions to Psychology in the Public Interest. In 1980 the Society for the Psychological Study of Social Issues gave her the Kurt Lewin Memorial Award, "for furthering in her work, as did Kurt Lewin, the development and integration of psychological research and social action." In 1978 the Council of the British Psychological Society elected her to the special status of Honorary Fellow, an honor limited to a select few of its members.

A paragraph from the ceremony at which the American Psychological Association award was presented captures the essence of Jahoda's scientific career:

The inspiring model that Marie Jahoda has set for many—of socially concerned, empirically competent, responsible, and psychoanalytically enriched psychology brought to bear on the important issues of freedom, justice, and equality in the contemporary world, as they touch the lives of real people—continues to serve psychology and the public interest.

REFERENCES

Ackerman, N. W., & Jahoda, M. (1950) *Anti-Semitism and emotional disorder: A psychoanalytic interpretation*. New York: Harper.

Christie, R., & Jahoda, M. (Eds.). (1954). *Studies in the scope and methods of the authoritarian personality*. Glencoe, Ill.: Free Press.

Cole, H.S.D.; Freeman, C.; Jahoda, M.; & Pavitt, K.L.R. (Eds.). (1973). *Thinking about the future: A critique of "The Limits to Growth."* London: Chatto & Windus.

Freeman, C., & Jahoda, M. (Eds.). (1978). *World futures: The great debate*. London: Martin Robertson.

Freeman, C.; Jahoda, M.; & Miles, I. (Eds.). (1976). *Problems and progress in social forecasting: Disciplinary contributions to an interdisciplinary task*. London: Social Science Research Council.

Jahoda, M. (1941). Some socio-psychological problems of factory life. *British Journal of Psychology, 31* (Part 3), 193–206.

Jahoda, M. (1950). Toward a social psychology of mental health. In M.J.E. Senn (Ed.), *Problems of infancy and childhood*. New York: Josiah Macy, Jr. Foundation.

Jahoda, M. (1953). The meaning of psychological health. *Social Case Work*, October, 349–354.

Jahoda, M. (1956). Anti-communism and employment policies in radio and television. In J. Cogley (Ed.), *Blacklisting* (Vol. 2). New York: Fund for the Republic.

Jahoda, M. (1958). *Current concepts of positive mental health*. New York: Basic Books.

Jahoda, M. (1959). Conformity and independence: A psychological analysis. *Human Relations, 12*, 99–120.

Jahoda, M. (1960a). Prejudice: A psychoanalytic interpretation. In S. M. Cole (Ed.) *Races of Man*. London: British Museum (Natural History).

Jahoda, M. (1960b). *Race relations and mental health*. Paris: UNESCO.

Jahoda, M. (1961). A social-psychological approach to the study of culture. *Human Relations, 14*, 23–30.

Jahoda, M. (1963a). Some notes on the influence of psychoanalytic ideas on American psychology. *Human Relations, 16*, 111–129.

Jahoda, M. (1963b). *The education of technologists*. London: Tavistock.

Jahoda, M. (1966). Notes on work. In R. M. Lowenstein, L. M. Newman, M. Schur, & A. J. Solnit (Eds.), *Psychoanalysis: A general psychology*. New York: International Universities Press.

Jahoda, M. (1969). The migration of psychoanalysis: Its impact on American psychology.

In D. Fleming & B. Bailyn (Eds.), *The intellectual migration: Europe and America, 1930–1960*. Cambridge, Mass.: Harvard University Press.

Jahoda, M. (1972). Social psychology and psychoanalysis: A mutual challenge. *Bulletin of the British Psychological Society, 25*, 269–274.

Jahoda, M. (1973). Postscript on social change. In H.S.D. Cole, C. Freeman, M. Jahoda, and K.L.R. Pavitt (Eds.), *Thinking about the future: A critique of "The Limits to Growth."* London: Chatto & Windus.

Jahoda, M. (1977). *Freud and the dilemmas of psychology*. London: Hogarth Press.

Jahoda, M. (1978). Introduction. Conclusions. In C. Freeman & M. Jahoda (Eds.), *World futures: The great debate*. London: Martin Robertson.

Jahoda, M. (1979a). The impact of employment in the 1930s and the 1970s. *Bulletin of the British Psychological Society, 32*, 309–314.

Jahoda, M. (1979b). The psychological meanings of unemployment. *New Society, 49* (883), 492–495.

Jahoda, M. (1980). Some comments on the role of social psychology in forecasting. Unpublished manuscript. Science Policy Research Unit, University of Sussex, Sussex, England.

Jahoda, M. (1981a). To publish or not to publish. *Journal of Social Issues, 37*, 208–220.

Jahoda, M. (1981b). Work, employment and unemployment: Values, theories, and approaches in social research. *American Psychologist, 36*, 184–191.

Jahoda, M. (1982). *Employment and unemployment: A social-psychological analysis*. Cambridge, Eng.: Cambridge University Press.

Jahoda, M. (1987a). Unemployment: Facts, experience and social consequences. In C. Freeman & L. Soete (Eds.), *Technical change and full employment*. New York: Basil Blackwell.

Jahoda, M. (1987b). Unemployed men at work. In D. Fryer & P. Ullah (Eds.), *Unemployed people: Social and psychological perspectives*. Philadelphia: Open University Press.

Jahoda, M., & Cook, S. W. (1952). Security measures and freedom of thought: An exploratory study of the impact of loyalty and security programs. *Yale Law Journal, 61*, 295–333.

Jahoda, M., & Cook, S. W. (1953). Ideological compliance as a social-psychological process. In C. J. Friedrich (Ed.), *Totalitarianism*. Cambridge, Mass.: Harvard University Press.

Jahoda, M., & Cooper, E. (1947). The evasion of propaganda: How prejudiced people respond to anti-prejudice propaganda. *Journal of Psychology, 23*, 15–25.

Jahoda, M.; Deutsch, M.; & Cook, S. W. (1951). *Research methods in social relations*. New York: Holt, Rinehart & Winston.

Jahoda, M.; Lazarsfeld, P. F.; & Zeisel, H. (1972). *Marienthal: The sociography of an unemployed community*. London: Tavistock.

Jahoda, M., & Salter-West, P. (1951). Race relations in public housing. *Journal of Social Issues, 7*, 132–139.

Jahoda, M., & Warren, N. (Eds.). (1966). *Attitudes*. Baltimore: Penguin Books. (2nd ed., 1973)

Lazarsfeld, P.; Jahoda, M.; & Zeisel, H. (1933). *Die Arbeitslosen von Marienthal*. Leipzig: Hirzel.

Merton, R. K. (1957). *Social theory and social structure*. Chicago: Free Press of Glencoe.

CHRISTINE LADD-FRANKLIN (1847–1930)

Thomas C. Cadwallader and Joyce V. Cadwallader

Christine Ladd-Franklin was the pioneer American woman psychologist, logician, and mathematician. After graduating from Vassar College in 1869, she taught science and mathematics at the secondary level until 1878, when she began graduate work in mathematics at Johns Hopkins University. She earned a Ph.D. in logic and mathematics by 1882, but the degree was not granted until 1926. In 1892 she formulated the Ladd-Franklin color-sensation theory, which almost a century later is still cited. She was the coeditor of the important *Dictionary of Philosophy and Psychology* (1901–1905). She was a part-time lecturer at Johns Hopkins University from 1904 to 1909 and at Columbia University from 1915 until her death. Ladd-Franklin published on logic, psychology of vision, and on women's and other issues throughout her entire adult life. Among her honors are an 1887 Vassar College LL.D. degree and a ranking as one of the fifty most important psychologists in the first *American Men of Science* in 1906.

FAMILY BACKGROUND AND EARLY EDUCATION

Christine Ladd was born December 1, 1847, to Eliphalet Ladd, a merchant, and Augusta Niles Ladd at Windsor, Connecticut. In 1853 the family returned to Windsor after some years in New York City. Following her mother's death in 1860, her father remarried in 1862. From about then Ladd lived with her paternal grandmother in Portsmouth, New Hampshire. She had a brother, Henry (born 1850); a sister, Jane Augusta Ladd McCordia (born 1854); a half-sister, Katharine (born 1865); and a half-brother, George (born 1867). Ladd was a distant relative of the psychologist George Trumbull Ladd (1842–1921); their common ancestor died in 1693.

Ladd graduated from the coeducational Welshing Academy in Wilbraham, Massachusetts, in 1865 as valedictorian. She entered Vassar College in 1866, but due to a shortage of funds she withdrew at the end of the year. She taught public school during part of the 1867–68 year; and with aid from an aunt, she reentered Vassar and graduated in 1869. At Vassar Ladd studied with the astronomer Maria Mitchell, then the leading American woman scientist, who inspired Ladd. Ladd's primary interest at Vassar was physics, but she recognized the impracticality of a woman's interest in a laboratory science at that time and so focused her attention on mathematics, a field that required no laboratory for original investigation.

EARLY CAREER DEVELOPMENT

Following graduation from Vassar, Ladd taught science and mathematics at the secondary level in several locations, including Washington, Pennsylvania. She began to submit both mathematical problems and solutions to the *Educational Times* of London; some seventy-seven were published from 1873 to 1885 in the semiannual cumulative versions (Miller, 1873–1885). Ladd also published six items in *The Analyst: A Journal of Pure and Applied Mathematics* from 1875 to 1880 (e.g., 1877) and three in the *American Journal of Mathematics*, 1879–1881.

GRADUATE EDUCATION (1878–1882)

During the period when she taught at Washington, Ladd studied mathematics with George B. Vose, professor of mathematics and mechanics at Washington and Jefferson College.

Although no support for Ladd's claim for having studied mathematics at Harvard during the early 1870s has been found in the university archives (J. Zukowski, personal communication, November 17, 1978), private study with Harvard faculty is possible (Woody, 1929/1974). Ladd was a student in botany in the Harvard Summer School in 1875 (Harvard University, 1899, p. 46).

In the fall of 1876, Johns Hopkins University opened as the nation's first institution primarily focused on graduate education and research. The granting of earned Ph.D.s in the United States had begun at Yale in 1861, and most "graduate" offerings were simply undergraduate elective courses opened to graduate students.

Ladd applied directly to the most distinguished of the Hopkins faculty, the brilliant English mathematician James J. Sylvester, for admission. He remembered some of her London *Educational Times* contributions and urged her admission. Although some of the Hopkins trustees opposed coeducation, Ladd was admitted to Sylvester's courses. Ladd's work during the 1878–1879 year was recognized as outstanding. For the following year the restriction to Sylvester's classes was removed, and Ladd was awarded the stipend, but not the title, of a Fellow.

Starting in 1879–1880, Ladd began to take courses with Charles S. Peirce, who, although a full-time physicist with the U.S. Coast and Geodetic Survey, had just joined the Johns Hopkins faculty as a half-time lecturer in logic (Ladd-

Franklin, 1916a). He was the first American to become involved in symbolic logic and was the first American experimental psychologist (Cadwallader, 1975). Under his influence, Ladd became the first American of her gender to become involved in these disciplines. Ladd contributed a chapter (1883) to a volume on logic edited by Peirce. At this point, Ladd virtually abandoned mathematics for logic and was soon to embrace psychology.

Although Ladd had completed all requirements for a Ph.D. in mathematics and logic by 1882, she did not then receive a degree because Hopkins did not grant degrees to women. Ladd-Franklin finally received her Ph.D. at the Johns Hopkins University semicentennial, February 22, 1926, when she was age seventy eight.

After completing graduate work in 1882, Ladd married one of her instructors (previously a fellow graduate student), Fabian Franklin, and thus she became Christine Ladd-Franklin. Fabian Franklin had received his Ph.D. in mathematics from Johns Hopkins in 1880, stayed on, and became professor in 1892. He resigned in 1895 to become editor of the Baltimore *News*.

After leaving Johns Hopkins, Ladd-Franklin had two children, one of whom died in infancy. A daughter, Margaret Ladd Franklin (1884–c. 1961), later became active in the women's suffrage movement (Franklin, 1913).

LATER CAREER DEVELOPMENT (1882–1930)

After Ladd-Franklin left Johns Hopkins in 1882, she continued to publish in logic until near her death. In 1887 she published her initial vision paper (1887) in the first issue of the *American Journal of Psychology*. This article, and three reviews of work on visual processes in the same volume, constitute the basis for considering Ladd-Franklin the pioneer American woman psychologist. Ladd-Franklin's entry into psychology was soon followed by other women. Mary W. Calkins began the study of psychology with William James in 1890 and established a psychology laboratory at Wellesley College in 1891. In 1894 Margaret F. Washburn received the first Ph.D. in psychology awarded to a woman; the degree was awarded by Cornell University and was the first granted under the direction of E. B. Titchener.

By the start of the new century, Ladd-Franklin was well known both in logic and psychology. Although their connection is unknown, Ladd-Franklin was asked by James Mark Baldwin, then professor of psychology at Princeton University, to become associate editor for logic and psychology for the *Dictionary of Philosophy and Psychology* (Baldwin, 1901–1905).

In 1903 Baldwin was called to Johns Hopkins as professor of philosophy and psychology to revive those moribund subjects. For the 1904–1905 year, among the seven new department members was Ladd-Franklin. At Johns Hopkins Ladd-Franklin typically taught a course in symbolic or mathematical logic in the fall semester and a course on some facet of vision in the spring. Her yearly appointments as lecturer were renewed through 1909–1910, but prior to the 1909–1910 academic year, she moved to New York. Fabian Franklin had resigned as editor of the Baltimore *News* to become associate editor of the New York *Evening Post* and its sister publication, the important weekly, *The Nation*.

After moving to New York, Ladd-Franklin published with her institutional address as Columbia University (e.g., 1911). Her first appointment of record did not take effect until the spring of 1915, however. She received annual appointments for the rest of her life; all were "without salary" (Columbia University, 1914–1929).

MAJOR CONTRIBUTIONS AND ACHIEVEMENTS

Ladd-Franklin Theory of Color Sensation

Ladd-Franklin's major contribution has become known as the Ladd-Franklin theory of color sensation. In 1891–1892 Fabian Franklin's sabbatical leave from Johns Hopkins permitted a trip to Europe. Ladd-Franklin used this opportunity to work in the laboratories of G. E. Müller at Göttingen and of H. v. Helmholtz at Berlin, where she also attended the lectures of Arthur König. The exposure to rival color theories, that of Ewald Hering as championed by Müller, and that of Helmholtz (also advocated by König)—usually termed the Young-Helmholtz theory after Thomas Young who first formulated such a position—led Ladd-Franklin to a theory of color sensation that was, on the one hand, an evolutionary one and, on the other, a synthesis of the Young-Helmholtz and the Hering theories. Ladd-Franklin's theory had the advantage of simultaneously drawing upon the strengths of both the Young-Helmholtz and the Hering theories while at the same time avoiding their most glaring defects. She first presented her theory at the Second International Congress of Psychology, held in London in 1892 (1892a, 1892b). Soon after Ladd-Franklin's theory was published, it began to draw critical international attention, for example in the British journal *Nature* ("The new theory," 1894).

Around the turn of the century a number of theories of color vision were formulated. All fell into competition for the third position behind the Young-Helmholtz and Hering theories. Boring (1942, p. 210) listed nine theories proposed between 1880 and 1910. By about 1920, Ladd-Franklin's theory began to be the only one other than the Young-Helmholtz and Hering theories to be included in most discussions. Starting about 1960, the Ladd-Franklin theory was replaced by, most notably, that of Hurvich and Jameson (1957), but there was renewed interest during the 1970s. During the 1980s interest again waned.

Ladd-Franklin's last major statement of her theory was presented as an appendix to volume two of the English translation of the third edition (1909–1911) of Helmholtz's *Treatise on Physiological Optics*. Ladd-Franklin noted that if Helmholtz's book "were to be brought out now for the first time it would undoubtedly be called Psychological Optics instead of Physiological Optics"

(1924, p. 455). Reviewers of volume two generally gave much attention to Ladd-Franklin's contribution (e.g., Allen, 1925).

In 1929 Ladd-Franklin published *Colour and Colour Theories*; it contained twenty of her previously published papers and five papers concerning her theory. At least seven reviews appeared in the United States and abroad; Harry Helson, then a leading vision researcher, considered Ladd-Franklin as "probably one of the five or six people in the world competent to discuss the facts and theories of vision with a proper grasp of the numerous problems involved." He said, "Certainly in the field of color and color theories she has no peer" (Helson, 1929, p. 1190).

Ladd-Franklin Theory of "Blue Arcs"

During the 1920s Ladd-Franklin turned her attention to another visual phenomenon often called the blue arcs of Purkinje. First described by the physiologist-psychologist Jan Purkinje about 1825, it remains an unsolved problem. The phenomenon is the brief experience of an arc (sometimes two) of a bluish-violet light extending upward and downward in the direction of the blind spot when a small light-source is viewed monocularly. The phenomenon has been discovered and rediscovered several times (see Amberson, 1924, and Judd, 1927, for brief histories).

In her explanation of blue arcs, Ladd-Franklin posited that when stimulated, nerve fibers themselves gave off light and this light was what was perceived as the blue arcs. Although Drualt (1914; cited in Judd, 1929) had earlier offered a similar explanation, his paper went unnoticed on this side of the Atlantic, and thus Ladd-Franklin's hypothesis was independently formulated (Judd, 1929, p. 443). There were nine blue-arc papers by Ladd-Franklin from 1926 through 1928 (e.g., 1927).

Ladd-Franklin's blue-arc papers quickly sparked discussion and research both for (Judd, 1927, 1929) and against (e.g., Amberson, 1924) her position. The matter has been reexamined by Rudolf and Chamberlin (1965), who did not find support for Ladd-Franklin's position.

Dictionary of Philosophy and Psychology

Another of Ladd-Franklin's major contributions was as associate editor for logic and psychology for the *Dictionary of Philosophy and Psychology* (1901–1905), edited by the psychologist J. M. Baldwin. The *Dictionary* was then and is today regarded as having been a major contribution to both psychology and philosophy (vide, e.g., Gerber, 1967, p. 183).

Ladd-Franklin also contributed to the *Dictionary*. She wrote or coauthored much of the long (34–page) section on vision. She was sole or first author of about four dozen articles or parts of articles and second or third author of another dozen.

Logic

Ladd-Franklin has some claim as a historical figure in logic in America. She was the pioneer American woman logician. Her views influenced Charles S. Peirce's logic (Fisch, 1978). Shen (1927, 1929) recognized her views as important, and Prior (1967, p. 548) called her a logician "of some distinction." Her logical notation drew the attention of Cajori (1929). Zellweger (1982, 1987) has devised a new set of signs for the propositional calculus which, through some of Peirce's later ideas, draws on some of Ladd-Franklin's suggestions (1883, 1890) concerning notation building.

Mathematics

Ladd-Franklin appears to be the pioneer American woman mathematician on the basis of publications. No paper by a woman in a mathematical journal earlier than Ladd's 1877 *Analyst* paper has been identified. She also contributed mathematical problems and solutions to the *Educational Times* from at least 1873. Ladd-Franklin also appears to be the first American woman to have earned a Ph.D. in mathematics and logic—in 1882, as noted above. She is the earliest American included in the volume on women mathematicians in the series of which this volume is a part (Grinstein & Campbell, 1987; see Green, 1987), although no claim for Ladd-Franklin's (or anyone's) priority is made generally nor in the article on Ladd-Franklin (Green, 1987).

Although Ladd-Franklin's publications were largely concentrated in visual processes and logic, her reading notes and manuscripts show her as being interested in a broad spectrum of psychological and philosophical topics.

Professional Involvement

Ladd-Franklin was involved in professional organizations throughout her career, and she often presented papers at meetings, including the International Congress of Psychology in London, 1892; Paris, 1900; Geneva, 1909; and Groningen, 1927. She also read a paper at the 1908 International Congress of Philosophy at Heidelberg.

Along with Mary W. Calkins, Ladd-Franklin was elected to the American Psychological Association at its second annual meeting, held in December 1893. She presented ten papers at APA meetings from 1894 to 1925. Ladd-Franklin was one of ninety-eight charter members of the American Philosophical Association and remained a member until her death in 1930; she presented five papers at the philosophical meetings from 1905 to 1917.

The Optical Society of America (OSA) was founded in 1916, and Ladd-Franklin became the first female member about 1919 and remained a member until her death. Between 1922 and 1928 she presented six papers and two exhibits at OSA meetings.

Ladd-Franklin on occasion presented papers elsewhere, including the American Physiological Society, 1894; American Mathematical Society, 1918; British Association for the Advancement of Science, 1924, in Toronto; National Academy of Sciences, 1926 and 1929; also, a paper was presented for her at a 1927 meeting of the French Academy of Sciences.

In all, Ladd-Franklin presented at least thirty-two papers and two exhibits; thirteen of these were during the period 1924–1928, when she was between seventy-seven and eighty-one years of age.

Productivity

Although no complete bibliography of Ladd-Franklin's published works exist, those known are impressive in quantity as well as in quality. In addition to her book (1929), Ladd-Franklin is known to have written 31 major papers (five or more pages), 33 smaller papers, 28 notes, 57 reviews of literature, at least 77 items in *Educational Times* (Miller, 1873–1885), or at least 245 professional items. She wrote at least 49 items in *The Nation* (Haskell, 1953) and many in the New York *Times* (Falk & Falk, 1976–1983). *Science Citation Index* lists 25 citations by 18 authors from 1965 to 1986.

Ladd-Franklin defended her work from being appropriated without citation. She criticized the psychologist Hermann Ebbinghaus about color: "While [his] discovery of the fact is therefore doubtless independent of mine, I allow myself to point out that mine is prior to his in point of time" (1893, p. 517). She also defended her logic: "I take it very ill of Mr. W. E. Johnson that he has robbed me, without acknowledgment, of my beautiful word 'antilogism' " (1928a, p. 532).

Ladd-Franklin became involved in a number of public controversies over professional matters. For example, she criticized the views of E. B. Titchener, later the leader of the structuralist school of psychology, on color vision (Titchener, 1898a, 1898b; Ladd-Franklin, 1898a, 1898b).

Ladd-Franklin had strong opinions, which she often expressed in no uncertain terms, for example "the absurdities of the Freudian doctrine—[or] better . . . the Freudian mythology" (1916b, p. 373).

Ladd-Franklin contributed many items to periodicals on a wide range of social issues—many focusing on women's issues, especially equality of opportunity (e.g., 1904, February). She also advocated adoption of an international language. Initially she favored Espranto, but later Ido (1918, July 20).

She was also personally involved in the women's rights movement. When the forerunner of the American Association of University Women, the Association of Collegiate Alumnae, was established, Ladd-Franklin joined and remained an active member at the national level throughout her life.

In 1887 Vassar College awarded Ladd-Franklin an LL.D. degree, the only honorary degree Vassar has awarded. She was included in *Who's Who in Amer-*

ica, 1901–1902 (second edition). She was fond of saying (e.g., 1928b, p. 141) that Fabian Franklin and she were the only married couple both of whom were "starred" in the first *American Men of Science* in 1906. She was included in *Woman's Who's Who of America, 1914–1915*, in the 1914 edition of *Who's Who in Science (International)*, and in Watson's (1974–1976) *Eminent Contributors to Psychology*. Her entry (1928b) in *Biographical Cyclopaedia of American Women* is essentially autobiographical, as shown by a manuscript in her unmistakable hand and four progressively polished typescripts among the Franklin Papers at Columbia University.

Ladd-Franklin's life spanned a period of history that witnessed notable changes. She played a role in effecting some of those changes—in logic, color theory, academia, and society at large. The full magnitude of her role is yet to be assessed.

NOTE

We thank Kenneth A. Lohf, Librarian for Rare Books and Manuscripts, Butler Library, Columbia University; Julia Morgan, Archivist, Ferdinand Hamburger, Jr., Archives, and Carolyn Smith, Department of Special Collections, The Milton S. Eisenhower Library, Johns Hopkins University; and Harley P. Holden, Curator, Harvard University Archives and their respective staffs for their great help and many courtesies during our research on Ladd-Franklin and other matters.

REFERENCES

Allen, F. (1925). Helmholtz's treatise on physiological optics. *Journal of the Optical Society of America, 11*, 369–374.

Amberson, W. R. (1924). Secondary excitation in the retina. *American Journal of Psychology, 69*, 354–370.

Baldwin, J. M. (1901–1905). *Dictionary of philosophy and psychology* (3 vols.). New York: Macmillan.

Boring, E. G. (1942). *Sensation and perception in the history of psychology*. New York: Appleton-Century.

Cadwallader, T. C. (1975). Peirce as an experimental psychologist. *Transactions of the Charles S. Peirce Society, 11*, 167–186.

Cajori, F. (1929). *History of mathematical notations* (Vol. 2). Chicago: Open Court.

Columbia University (1914–1929). Ladd-Franklin, Mrs. Christine. Personnel Records. Office of the Secretary of the Faculty.

Falk, B. A., & Falk, V. R. (1976–1983). *Personal name index to the New York Times Index, 1851–1974* (Vols. 7 & 12). Succasunna, N.J.: Roxbury Data Interface.

Fisch, M. (1978). Peirce's general theory of signs. In T. A. Sebeok (Ed.), *Sight, sound, and sense*. Bloomington: Indiana University Press.

Franklin, M. L. (1913). *The case for woman suffrage: A bibliography*. New York: National College Equal Suffrage League.

Gerber, W. (1967). Philosophical dictionaries and encyclopedias. In P. Edwards (Ed.), *Encyclopedia of philosophy* (Vol. 6, pp. 170–199). New York: Macmillan.

Green, J. (1987). Christine Ladd-Franklin (1847–1930). In L. S. Grinstein & P. J. Campbell (Eds.), *Women of mathematics* (pp. 121–128). New York: Greenwood Press.

Haskell, D. C. (1953). *The Nation, volumes 1–105, New York, 1865–1917: Vol. 2. Index of contributors.* New York: New York Public Library.

Harvard University (1899). List of students of the Harvard University-Summer School: 1875–1898. Cambridge, Mass.: Privately printed.

Helson, H. (1929). A theory of color. *Saturday Review of Literature, 5*, 1190.

Hurvich, L., & Jameson, D. (1957). An opponent-process theory of color vision. *Psychological Review, 64*, 384–404.

Judd, D. B. (1927). A quantitative investigation of the Purkinje after-image. *American Journal of Psychology, 38*, 507–533.

Judd, D. B. (1929). Least retinal illumination by spectral light required to evoke the "blue arcs" of the retina. *Bureau of Standards Journal of Research, 2*, 441–451.

Ladd, C. (1877). Quaternions. *Analyst, 4*, 172–174.

Ladd, C. (1883). On the algebra of logic. In C. S. Peirce (Ed.), *Studies in logic by members of the Johns Hopkins University* (pp. 17–71). Boston: Little, Brown.

Ladd-Franklin, C. (1887). The experimental determination of the horopter. *American Journal of Psychology, 1*, 99–111.

Ladd-Franklin, C. (1890). Some proposed reforms in common logic. *Mind,* o.s. *15*, 75–88.

Ladd-Franklin, C. (1892a). A new theory of light sensation. *Proceedings of the International Congress of Experimental Psychology, London* (pp. 103–108).

Ladd-Franklin, C. (1892b). Eine neue Theorie der Lichtempfindungen. *Zeitschrift für Psychologie, 4*, 211–221.

Ladd-Franklin, C. (1893). Hering's theory of colour vision. *Mind, 48*, 517.

Ladd-Franklin, C. (1898a). Color vision. *Science, 7*, 832–833.

Ladd-Franklin, C. (1898b). Color vision. *Science, 8*, 23.

Ladd-Franklin, C. (1904, February). Endowed professorships for women. *Association for Collegiate Alumnae Bulletin,* Series 3 (No. 9), 53–61.

Ladd-Franklin, C. (1911). The foundations of philosophy: Explicit primitives. *Journal of Philosophy, Psychology, and Scientific Method, 8*, 708–713.

Ladd-Franklin, C. (1916a). Charles S. Peirce at the Johns Hopkins University. *Journal of Philosophy, Psychology, and Scientific Method, 13*, 715–722.

Ladd-Franklin, C. (1916b). Freudian doctrines. [Letter to the Editor]. *The Nation, 103*, 373–374.

Ladd-Franklin, C. (1918, July 20). For Ido and Usona [Letter to the Editor]. *New York Times*, p. 10.

Ladd-Franklin, C. (1924). The nature of the colour sensations. In J.P.C. Southall (Ed.), *Helmholtz's treatise on physiological optics* (Vol. 2, pp. 455–468). Ithaca, N.Y.: Optical Society of America. (Reprinted by Dover, 1962)

Ladd-Franklin, C. (1927). Visible radiation from excited nerve fiber: The reddish blue arcs and the reddish blue glow of the retina. *Science, 66*, 239-241.

Ladd-Franklin, C. (1928a). The antilogism. *Mind, 37*, 532–534.

[Ladd-Franklin, C.] (1928b). Ladd-Franklin, Christine. In E. C. Lee & H. C. Wiley (Comp.), *The biographical cyclopaedia of American women.* New York: Williams-Wiley.

Ladd-Franklin, C. (1929). *Colour and colour theories.* New York: Harcourt, Brace.

Miller, W.J.C. (1873–1885). *Mathematical questions and solutions from the "Educa-*

tional Times," with many additional papers and solutions not published in the *"Educational Times."* London: Francis Hodgson.

The new theory. . . . (1894). *Nature, 49,* 394.

Prior, A. N. (1967). Peirce [part of the section on "Logic, history of"]. In P. Edwards (Ed.), *Encyclopedia of philosophy* (Vol. 4, pp. 546–549). New York: Macmillan.

Rudolf, N. de M., & Chamberlin, L. W. (1965). A test of the hypothesis of bioluminescence in the human eye. *Experimental Eye Research, 4,* 87–94.

Shen, E. (1927). The Ladd-Franklin formula in logic: The antilogism. *Mind, 36,* 54–60.

Shen, E. (1929). The 'complete-scheme' of propositions. *Psyche, 9,* 48–59.

Titchener, E. B. (1898a). Color vision. *Science, 7,* 603–605.

Titchener, E. B. (1898b). Color vision. *Science, 7,* 832–833.

Watson, R. I. (Ed.). (1974–1976). *Eminent contributors to psychology* (2 vols.). New York: Springer.

Woody, T. (1974). *A history of women's education in the United States* (Vol. 2). New York: Octagon. (Originally published 1929)

Zellweger, S. (1982). Sign-creation and man-sign engineering. *Semiotica, 38,* 17–54.

Zellweger, S. (1987). Notation, relational iconicity, and rethinking the propositional calculus [Summary]. In *Program Abstracts, Eighth International Congress of Logic, Methodology, and Philosophy of Logic, Moscow, USSR, August 17–22* (vol. 1, pp. 376–379).

ELEANOR EMMONS MACCOBY (1917–   )

Agnes N. O'Connell

In a highly productive career that has spanned more than fifty years, produced six books, two monographs, and more than one hundred chapters and papers, Eleanor Emmons Maccoby stands as one of the most prominent and influential psychologists in developmental and social psychology. Her research and methodological contributions have illuminated the study of the socialization of young children and the critical dimensions of their social behavior. Her reviews of research and theory, particularly in the area of gender differences, have significantly influenced the direction and content of subsequent research. A professional leader, Maccoby has served as president of the Society for Research in Child Development and of the American Psychological Association's (APA) Division on Developmental Psychology, and has been the recipient of numerous awards including the APA Distinguished Scientific Contributions Award.

FAMILY BACKGROUND, EDUCATION, AND EARLY CAREER DEVELOPMENT

Eleanor Emmons, the second of four daughters, was born in Tacoma, Washington, on May 15, 1917. Her father, Eugene Emmons, owned a small millwork business, and her mother, Viva Johnson Emmons, was a musician and singer (Maccoby, 1989). As a child, Eleanor Emmons read at age four, sang and played the guitar at age eleven, formed a trio with two of her sisters, briefly had a weekly program on a local radio station, and engaged in tomboyish behavior (Maccoby, 1989).

During her childhood her parents became members of the Theosophical Society, adopting the required vegetarian diet. She grew up sharing her family's theosophical interests in spiritualism and extrasensory perception and their strong inclination to act on their principles. While in high school, however, her confidence in the doctrines of the Theosophical Society began to erode following unsuccessful attempts to replicate J. B. Rhine's experiment at Duke University on extrasensory perception (Maccoby, 1989).

In the fall of 1934, Eleanor Emmons went to Reed College in Portland, Oregon, on a one-year scholarship. Unable to continue because of financial reasons, she took a secretarial course during the following summer and worked as a secretary for a year while living at home. Having saved enough money for her second year's tuition, she returned for her sophomore year at Reed, where she took her first course in psychology. William Griffith, a behaviorist and former student of Edwin Guthrie, taught the course, and Emmons was impressed with the psychological perspective that Griffith presented. Emmons transferred to the University of Washington in Seattle for her junior and senior years (1937–1939) to study with Guthrie, assimilating his stimulus-response contiguity theory of learning. In the fall of her senior year (September 16, 1938), she married Nathan Maccoby, a graduate student in social psychology, whom she had met the year before. She earned her B.S. in 1939, declining a teaching fellowship at Washington when her husband, who had finished his M.A., accepted an instructorship at Oregon State College in Corvallis.

In 1940, when Nathan Maccoby got a job at the U.S. Civil Service Commission, they moved to Washington, D.C. Eleanor Maccoby first took a job at the State Technical Advisory Service of the Social Security Board, where she wrote test items. Later she joined the luminous staff of Rensis Likert's Division of Program Surveys of the Department of Agriculture. His staff included the psychologists Jerome Bruner, Angus Campbell, Richard Crutchfield, Ernest Hilgard, Robert Holt, and David Krech, among others. Maccoby engaged in public opinion field studies on the impact of various wartime programs (e.g., fuel oil rationing and the sale of war bonds). First as an assistant and later as study director, she learned "to organize and carry out large-scale studies in field settings and gained experience in applied psychology work" (Maccoby, 1989, p. 305). "The idea of applying psychological concepts and methods to policy-relevant issues took root and had a lasting impact on her subsequent career" ("Eleanor E. Maccoby," 1989, p. 621).

At the end of the war, Likert decided to move his organization to the University of Michigan-Ann Arbor, where he and some core personnel established the Institute for Social Research. Eleanor Maccoby remained in Washington, D.C., carrying on the work of the organization for a year until the move was completed. In 1947 she joined her husband, who had preceded her, in working for the Survey Research Center at the University of Michigan-Ann Arbor and in pursuing graduate study. As a Ph.D. candidate Maccoby specialized in learning theory, studying with Donald Marquis and Edward Walker, but she also studied social psychology with Theodore Newcomb and personality with Urie Bronfenbrenner.

By the fall of 1949, Maccoby had finished her doctoral work except for her dissertation. Her husband had earned his Ph.D. and accepted an offer from Boston University. They moved to Boston. For her dissertation, Maccoby was conducting a conditioning study on partial reinforcement, exploring some of B. F. Skinner's hypotheses. Skinner offered her space in his laboratory in the Psychology Department at Harvard University, and she completed her experimental work there ("Eleanor E. Maccoby," 1989). Meanwhile, she was recruited by Jerome Bruner (whom she had met while working in the Division of Program Surveys) to do some pilot work on political surveys in the Boston area for the Department of Social Relations. There were major contrasts between the "hard science" atmosphere in the Psychology Department (experimental, physiological, sensory, and perceptual psychology) and the science and practice atmosphere in the Social Relations Department (social, clinical-personality psychology, social anthropology and sociology) at Harvard. These contrasts extended to concepts and methodology. Maccoby was strongly committed to a rigorous, experimental, learning theory approach, but she also was interested in the theoretical and applied issues and ideas of social relations (Maccoby, 1989).

CAREER AFTER DOCTORATE: ACHIEVEMENTS AND CONTRIBUTIONS

In 1950 Maccoby finished her dissertation, returned to Ann Arbor for her final orals, and was ready for a full-time position in Boston. An ideal opportunity to join her two kinds of interests occurred when Robert Sears, the new head of the Laboratory of Human Development at Harvard University, needed a research associate to supervise the field work for mother interviews for a large-scale socialization study on child-rearing practices. Before the study was completed, Sears accepted the position of Psychology Department chair at Stanford University. Robert Sears, Eleanor Maccoby, and Harry Levin, a postdoctoral researcher, collaborated at long distance to write the book *Patterns of Child Rearing* (1957) on the mother interview part of the study. When Sears left the Social Relations Department, Maccoby inherited the course on child psychology first as instructor then as lecturer. To train her graduate students in a seminar on field research methods, she conducted some of the first studies on the impact of television on the lives of children and families (1951, 1954) and on the social control of juvenile delinquency (Maccoby, Mathews, & Morton, 1954). At the same time, she conducted several film studies on viewer identification with filmed fictional characters (Maccoby & Wilson, 1957; Maccoby, Wilson, & Burton, 1958). Although she was clearly an active researcher and teacher, her situation at Harvard was influenced by the fact that she was a woman. She could not enter the Faculty Club by the front door or borrow a book from Lamont Library (Maccoby, 1989).

In 1952 the Maccobys adopted a ten-year-old girl, Janice, and in 1956 they adopted a seven-month-old girl, Sarah. With the arrival of the second daughter, Eleanor Maccoby, wanting to spend more time with the children, began to work half-time at her career. During this time, however, she worked on chapters for *Patterns of Child Rearing* (Sears, Maccoby, & Levin, 1957) and did most of the organizational and editorial work for the new edition of *Readings in Social Psychology* (Maccoby, Newcomb, & Hartley, 1958).

In 1958 the Maccobys went to Stanford at the invitation of Robert Sears to work with him on a research project for a year. Through Sears' efforts both were subsequently offered and accepted faculty appointments (Maccoby, 1989). An antinepotism rule at Stanford prevented their being appointed in the same department. Eleanor Maccoby joined the Psychology Department as an associate professor half-time, teaching courses in child psychology, and her husband joined the program in communications, which he helped build into a department. During that first year, a seven-month-old boy, Mark, was adopted.

Although Eleanor Maccoby continued to do research and write during this period, she reported in her autobiography (1989) that she felt "intellectually adrift," unable to find a "satisfying focus for a new research program." She was undergoing "intellectual reorientation" and needed to experience a "fallow phase" (Maccoby, 1989, p. 316). She began to find the stimulus-response theoretical framework more and more constricting, and by the 1960s, influenced by John Flavell, the Piagetian scholar, and others, she had moved strongly toward a cognitive developmental position. She began to believe that it was important to describe, explain, and understand sequences and their variations in development. She wrote a chapter on the "Effects of Mass Media" for Hoffman and Hoffman's *Review of Child Development* (Maccoby, 1964a) and the "Developmental Psychology" section for the *Annual Review of Psychology* (Maccoby, 1964b), and conducted a series of studies on developmental changes in selective attention from her new perspective (e.g., Maccoby, 1967, 1969; Maccoby & Hagen, 1965; Maccoby & Konrad, 1966, 1967).

In the 1960s Maccoby was a member of a Social Sciences Research Council Committee on Socialization (1962–1967). This membership led to her reviewing and organizing the work on moral development (1968) and to her serving as editor of a book on the differential development of male and female children, *The Development of Sex Differences* (1966) (Maccoby, 1989). She wrote the chapter on "Sex Differences in Intellectual Functioning," exploring the possible explanations for differences in performance on intellectual tasks by boys and girls. Among the chapter contributors were Lawrence Kohlberg and Walter Mischel. Roberta M. Oetzel compiled an annotated bibliography and a "Classified Summary of Research in Sex Differences," which appeared at the back of the book. Published the same year that Maccoby was promoted to full professor, this influential book made clear the different perspectives held by social learning and cognitive developmental theories in explaining the process of "sex" typing and the difficulties in distinguishing biological from social determinants of roles and characteristics.

In an attempt to bring objectivity in research to the issue of gender-related studies, Eleanor Maccoby and Carol Jacklin, a research associate, began assembling material for their monumental book, *The Psychology of Sex Differences* (1974), a sequel to the earlier work. This landmark book portrayed the development of gender-typed behavior as a joint product of biological predispositions, social shaping, and cognitive self-socialization processes. It contained a comprehensive literature review of approximately 1,600 studies (most published between 1966 and 1973) in a 233–page annotated bibliography, eighty-six tables summarizing analyses of studies on "sex" differences, discussion of each table, and discussion regarding alternative interpretive viewpoints. In the final summary chapter, the authors assessed the validity of the most widely held beliefs about "sex" differences. They concluded that there were four differences that were "fairly well established": "girls have greater verbal ability than boys"; "boys excel in visual-spatial ability"; "boys excel in mathematical ability"; and "males are more aggressive" (Maccoby & Jacklin, 1974, pp. 351–352).

The book was immediately controversial, and the reactions of professional colleagues varied widely. The book was praised for generating new and provocative hypotheses and moving "the study of sex differences toward the necessary next stage of scientific investigation" (Block, 1976). It was also criticized for its assumptions, methodology, and conclusions (e.g., Block, 1976; Tiger, 1980). The book was extremely influential in shaping the field of gender studies. It was frequently cited by scholars and the media, and the summary chapter was reprinted in a leading textbook for psychology of women courses (Cox, 1981). With *The Psychology of Sex Differences* as a point of departure, the debates on the basis of gender differences continued (e.g., the basis of gender differences in aggression [Tiger, 1980; Maccoby & Jacklin, 1980]), as did the debates on the explanatory theories for these differences.

Responding to these ongoing matters and reflecting the evolution of the field in gender studies, Maccoby wrote in her autobiography that if she were to write the book again, she "would be more explicit about the fact that neither biological predispositions, socialization pressures, nor self-regulated cognitions can alone account for gender differentiation, but that the three processes are intricately interwoven" (Maccoby, 1989, p. 327). In a review article on research on "sex-segregation" and free play of children, she elaborated on this position (Maccoby, 1988).

Maccoby's continuing interests in children's socialization and the development of gender differences now focused on a longitudinal study of gender differentiation involving three cohorts of children from birth to age six. Observational studies of parent-child interactions supported an interactionist perspective, revealing circular processes and mutual influences between parent and child (Maccoby & Jacklin, 1983; Martin, Maccoby, Baran, & Jacklin, 1981). Maccoby's book *Social Development* (1980), her chapter on middle childhood (Maccoby, 1984a), and her presidential address to the Society for Research in Child Development (1984b) contained an interactionist theme: family socialization processes influenced, and were influenced by, the sequences of the children's developmental changes. The children's developmental functioning was partially related to prior socialization, but also limited the nature and effect of parent-child interactions. In these works, and particularly in a chapter on parent-child interactions (Maccoby & Martin, 1983) and a study on reciprocal compliance (Parpal & Maccoby, 1985), Maccoby emphasized the importance of the willingness of partners in a relationship (including parent-child relationships) to be influenced by the other.

In the late 1980s her interest in family functioning prompted her to embark on another longitudinal study: a study on the functioning of a large group of divorcing families (Maccoby, Depner, & Mnookin, 1990). Maccoby is working with Robert Mnookin, a law professor, and Charlene Depner, a social psychologist, on this interdisciplinary, policy-relevant study located in the Center for the Study of Families, Children, and Youth.

IMPACT, LEADERSHIP, AND RECOGNITION

Eleanor Emmons Maccoby's contributions to psychology and society as presented in this chapter are just a few of her highly productive career. With over one hundred publications to her credit, she has been most influential in developmental and social psychology. "Her substantive discoveries on the socialization of young children have been paralleled by equally important contributions to the methodology of interviewing and the measurement of critical dimensions of social behavior in both infants and preschool children" ("Eleanor E. Maccoby," 1989, p. 621).

Maccoby has served as president of the Society for Research in Child Development (1981–1983), APA's Division on Developmental Psychology (1971–1972), and the Western Psychological Association (1974–1975) and as vice chair of the Committee on Child Development and Public Policy of the National Research Council (1977–1983). She was the first woman to serve as chair of the Psychology Department at Stanford University (1973–1976).

Her work has been recognized by election to Fellow status in APA's Division on Developmental Psychology and by various prestigious awards. She is the recipient of the Stanford University Walter J. Gores Award for Excellence in Teaching (1981), the American Educational Research Association Award for Distinguished Contributions in Educational Research (1984), the Society for Research in Child Development Award for Distinguished Scientific Contributions to Child Development (1987), the G. Stanley Hall Award of APA's Division on Developmental Psychology (1982), and the APA Distinguished Scientific Contributions Award (1988). In 1979 she was named Barbara Kimball Browning Professor at Stanford University.

NOTE

Information not otherwise referenced is based on personal communications with Eleanor Emmons Maccoby, 1989.

REFERENCES

Block, J. H. (1976). Debatable conclusions about sex differences. *Contemporary Psychology, 21*, 517–522.

Cox, S. (Ed.). (1981). *Female psychology: The emerging self* (2nd ed.). New York: St. Martin's Press.

Eleanor E. Maccoby [Biography; no author]. (1989). *American Psychologist*, 621–623.

Maccoby, E. E. (1951). Television, its impact on school children. *Public Opinion Quarterly, 15*, 421–444.

Maccoby, E. E. (1954). Why children watch television. *Public Opinion Quarterly, 18*, 239–244.

Maccoby, E. E. (1964a). Effects of mass media. In M. L. Hoffman & L. W. Hoffman (Eds.), *Review of child development research*. New York: Russell Sage Foundation.

Maccoby, E. E. (1964b). Developmental psychology. *Annual Review of Psychology, 15*, 243–253.

Maccoby, E. E. (Ed.). (1966). *The development of sex differences*. Stanford, Calif.: Stanford University Press.

Maccoby, E. E. (1967). Selective auditory attention in children. In L. P. Lipsitt & C. C. Spiker (Eds.), *Advances in child development and behavior* (Vol. 3, pp. 99–125). New York: Academic Press.

Maccoby, E. E. (1968). The development of moral values and behavior. In J. A. Clausen (Ed.), *Socialization and society* (pp. 227–269). Boston: Little, Brown.

Maccoby, E. E. (1969). The development of stimulus selection. In J. P. Hill (Ed.), *Minnesota Symposia on Child Psychology* (Vol. 3, pp. 68–96). Minneapolis: University of Minnesota Press.

Maccoby, E. E. (1980). *Social development: Psychological growth and the parent-child relationship*. New York: Harcourt Brace Jovanovich.

Maccoby, E. E. (1984a). Middle childhood in the context of the family. In W. A. Collins (Ed.), *Development during middle childhood: The years from six to twelve* (pp. 184–239). Washington, D.C.: National Academy Press.

Maccoby, E. E. (1984b). Socialization and developmental change. *Child Development, 55*, 317–328.

Maccoby, E. E. (1988). Gender as a social category. *Developmental Psychology, 24*, 755–765.

Maccoby, E. E. (1989). Eleanor E. Maccoby [Autobiography]. In G. Lindzey (Ed.), *A history of psychology in autobiography* (Vol. 8, pp. 290–335). Stanford, Calif.: Stanford University Press.

Maccoby, E. E.; Depner, C.; & Mnookin, R. (1990). Co-parenting after divorce: Communication, cooperation and conflict. *Journal of Marriage and Family, 54*, 141–155.

Maccoby, E. E., & Hagen, J. (1965). Effects of distraction upon central versus incidental recall: Developmental trends. *Journal of Experimental Child Psychology, 2*, 280–289.

Maccoby, E. E., & Jacklin, C. N. (1974). *The psychology of sex differences*. Stanford, Calif.: Stanford University Press.

Maccoby, E. E., & Jacklin, C. N. (1980). Sex differences in aggression: A rejoinder and reprise. *Child Development, 51*, 964–980.

ELEANOR EMMONS MACCOBY 237

Maccoby, E. E., & Jacklin, C. N. (1983). The "person" characteristics of children and the family as environment. In D. Magnussen & V. Allen (Eds.), *Human development: An interactional perspective*. New York: Academic Press.

Maccoby, E. E., & Konrad, K. W. (1966). Age trends in selective listening. *Journal of Experimental Child Psychology, 3*, 113–122.

Maccoby, E. E., & Konrad, K. W. (1967). The effect of preparatory set on selective listening: Developmental trends. *Monographs of the Society for Research in Child Development, 32*(4).

Maccoby, E. E., & Martin, J. A. (1983). Socialization in the context of the family: Parent-child interaction. In E. M. Hetherington (Ed.), *Manual of child psychology: Volume 4. Social development* (pp. 1–102). New York: Wiley.

Maccoby, E. E.; Matthews, R. E.; & Morton, A. S. (1954). Youth and political change. *Public Opinion Quarterly, 18*, 23–29.

Maccoby, E. E.; Newcomb, T. R.; & Hartley, E. (Ed.). (1958). *Readings in social psychology*. New York: Henry Holt.

Maccoby, E. E., & Wilson, W. C. (1957). Identification and observational learning from films. *Journal of Abnormal and Social Psychology, 55*, 76–87.

Maccoby, E. E.; Wilson, W. C.; & Burton, R. V. (1958). Differential movie-viewing behavior of male and female viewers. *Journal of Personality, 26*, 259–267.

Martin, J. A.; Maccoby, E. E.; Baran, K.; & Jacklin, C. N. (1981). Sequential analysis of mother-child interaction at eighteen months: A comparison of microanalytic methods. *Developmental Psychology, 17*, 146–157.

Parpal, M., & Maccoby, E. E. (1985). Maternal responsiveness and subsequent child compliance. *Child Development, 56*, 1326–1334.

Sears, R. R.; Maccoby, E. E.; & Levin, H. (1957). *Patterns of child rearing*. Evanston, Ill.: Row-Peterson.

Tiger, T. (1980). On the biological basis of sex differences in aggression. *Child Development, 51*, 943–963.

Additional Representative Publications by Eleanor E. Maccoby

Maccoby, E. E., & Feldman, S. S. (1972). Mother-attachment and stranger-reactions in the third year of life. *Monographs of the Society for Research in Child Development, 37*(1).

Maccoby, E. E., & Jacklin, C. N. (1987). Gender segregation in childhood. In H. Reese (Ed.), *Advances in child behavior and development* (Vol. 20, pp. 239–287). New York: Academic Press.

Maccoby, E. E., & Masters, J. C. (1969). Attachment and dependency. In P. Mussen (Ed.), *Carmichael manual of child psychology* (Vol. 3, pp. 73–158). New York: Wiley.

Maccoby, E. E., & Zellner, M. (1970). *Experiments in primary education*. New York: Harcourt Brace Jovanovich.

Additional Representative Publications About Eleanor E. Maccoby

Stevens, G., & Gardner, S. (1982). *The women of psychology: Volume 2: Expansion and refinement* (pp. 21–220). Cambridge, Mass.: Schenkman.

CLARA MAYO
(1931–1981)

Marianne LaFrance

Clara Mayo was a social psychologist who conducted important research into the processes of social perception and nonverbal communication with the primary purpose of understanding prejudice and stereotyping. The work on nonverbal communication and particularly that concerned with gender relations and race relations helped evolve research in that area from a focus on individual behaviors to an exploration of how nonverbal behaviors mediate important social processes. From her research in the 1960s on busing through her role in the 1970s and 1980s as scholar, teacher, trainer, and expert witness, she articulated the form that applied social psychology could and should take, thus helping to formalize and legitimize the field. She was elected to the presidency of both the Society for the Psychological Study of Social Issues from the American Psychological Association (APA) and the New England Psychological Association (NEPA).

FAMILY BACKGROUND

Clara Alexandra Weiss, the first and only child of Joseph and Maria Weiss, was born in Linz, Austria, on September 13, 1931. The setting for her childhood was comfortable, almost bucolic, and on weekends there would be drives in a fancy Packard to Vienna.

But then things changed. Hitler and Nazism were on the move, and in 1938, while Clara Weiss' father was in England on a business trip, her mother decided that it was time to leave—and to leave immediately. Everything was to be left behind. The familiar and the predictable had become precipitously freakish and unhinged. No matter that her mother was Catholic or that her father was himself the product of a "mixed marriage." To have a surname such as Weiss was sufficient stigma.

Mother and daughter settled for a bit in Paris, where Joseph Weiss managed to catch up with them, traveling next out of danger's way to Marseille. There in southern France they became refugees attempting to elicit help from strangers so that they could emigrate to the United States.

Clara Weiss started school in Austria speaking German, quickly acquired French in order to continue in school in France, and subsequently learned English upon arrival in the United States in 1939. Her method of learning her third language involved reading her way from A to Z around the Children's Room of the New York Public Library. She felt herself akin to Joseph Conrad, who, though born in Poland, wrote in English, and said about his life, "My nationality is the language that I write in."

EDUCATION

Once settled in New York City, Clara Weiss attended public school, then was accepted into Hunter High School. From Hunter High School, she went directly to Cornell University in Ithaca, New York. Although her major was philosophy, she was introduced to psychology by Urie Bronfenbrenner, for whom she served as a research assistant in 1952. The specific project involved observing family interaction *in situ*, and the task entailed keeping track of whole stretches of interaction without benefit of recorder. Even though proficiency in observation came easily to her, she continually practiced the skill and promoted its importance. Moreover, her later research, which focused on the capacity to detect small behavioral cues, demonstrated that women especially are good at reading others' nonverbal cues (LaFrance & Mayo, 1978; Mayo & Henley, 1981).

After graduating with an honors bachelor's degree in philosophy from Cornell in 1953, she was faced with choosing a graduate school and field of research. Being newly married to James P. Mayo, Jr., in January 1953, and living in southern New Hampshire, she decided to explore psychology through the master's degree program at Wellesley College in Wellesley, Massachusetts. The program held an important benefit in addition to location. It was "applied" in a way different from most clinical programs at the time, being associated with the Human Relations Service, a demonstration and research community mental health program that had been inaugurated by the Harvard School of Public Health in 1948.

Mayo received her master's degree from Wellesley in 1955 and acceptance into the social psychology doctoral program at Clark University in Worcester, Massachusetts. The experience at Wellesley cemented her commitment to psychology, and Clark University offered an intellectually compelling version of it. According to Walter Crockett, who served as Clara Mayo's dissertation advisor, the intellectual tone of the psychology department at Clark at the time was keyed to the organismic developmental theory of Heinz Werner. In addition, she was exposed to the theoretically congenial applied social emphasis provided by Tamara Dembo, who was the director of a research project on which Mayo worked (Crockett, 1982).

Clara Mayo received her Ph.D. from Clark University in 1959 with a dissertation that examined the impressions that people form from inconsistent information about others (Mayo & Crockett, 1964). The dissertation had its conceptual roots in G. A. Kelly's (1955) personal construct theory and J. Bieri's (1955) conception of "cognitive complexity." Its purpose was to explore the degree to which first impressions could be altered in the face of subsequent discrepant information. The aim was to determine whether individual differences in cognitive complexity would moderate the degree to which people can incorporate the contradictory input. The larger concern was to understand how social stereotypes might be amended.

CAREER DEVELOPMENT

After leaving Clark, Mayo took a postdoctoral position as a social psychology trainee at the Veterans Administration Hospital in Brockton, Massachusetts, during 1959–1960 and then moved to the Veterans Administration Hospital in Boston as a research social psychologist, where she stayed from 1960 to 1964. In both locations, she conducted research on the hospital as a social system with emphasis on perceptions of and attitudes toward mental illness.

Mayo was a born teacher, and after graduate school the search was on for an academic position so that she could have contact with both undergraduate and graduate students. While at the Boston Veterans Administration Hospital, she became a lecturer in the psychology department at Boston University in 1961, achieving a full-time position as assistant professor there in 1964. Four years later she was promoted to associate professor with tenure. She served as director of the graduate program in social and personality psychology from 1970 to 1974 and was promoted to full professor in 1974. In 1978 she also became acting director of the graduate program in what was then called Afro-American studies at Boston University.

MAJOR CONTRIBUTIONS AND ACHIEVEMENTS

The fundamental principle guiding Clara Mayo's work was that knowledge must produce usable findings. In a publication entitled "Toward an Applicable Social Psychology," she argued that a relevant and worthy social psychology would consist of three interlocking elements: a concern with improving the quality of life, a commitment to knowledge building, and active involvement in intervention (Mayo & LaFrance, 1980). Although this chapter was published only a year before she died, it reflected principles that guided her work from the beginning. Social perceptions are important to study not just because they are intellectually interesting but because the perceptions of one group are frequently at odds with those of other interested groups, and hence become implicated in sustaining discord among them. For example, Mayo and her colleagues contrasted the attitudes toward mental illness between hospital personnel and patients (Mayo & Havelock, 1970) and between male psychiatric patients and their wives (Mayo, Havelock, & Simpson, 1971).

Mayo strongly believed in the potential of applied social psychology to redress social problems, and her own work addressed ways to deal with racism and sexism. She was involved in one of the first studies of school busing to effect racial integration (Teele, Jackson, & Mayo, 1967; Teele & Mayo, 1969). The busing program, "Operation Exodus," began in 1965 and involved black families paying to bus their own children to predominantly white Boston schools. The central research question was to examine why black families chose to bus their children and what the effects were of having made this decision. She also did research that examined subtle nonverbal differences in how blacks and whites manage conversational interaction (LaFrance & Mayo, 1976). She later took what she knew about racial attitudes and behaviors into the courtroom, where she consulted with the National Jury Project and provided expert testimony on racism and jury selection.

Understanding and doing something about racism was not a short-term or risk-free concern for Clara Mayo. From the inception of the Afro-American Studies Center at Boston University, she, a white woman, taught "The Psychology of Racism" to a predominantly black audience; she also taught a course called "Prejudice, Sexism and Racism" in the psychology department. Her last research on the connection between racism and sexism, pursued by examining the oral histories of older black women, was cut short by her untimely death.

The study of nonverbal behavior, specifically its racial and gender aspects, was also undertaken to explore the conditions under which apparently small cues could act as powerful barriers to or facilitators of social change. In the book *Moving Bodies: Nonverbal Communication in Social Relationships*, LaFrance and Mayo (1978) showed that nonverbal communication operates according to a complex set of overlearned rules and at a number of levels from individual action to social scripts. In the book *Gender and Nonverbal Behavior*, Mayo and Henley (1981) assembled a collection of empirical studies that addressed the role that nonverbal behaviors play in creating gender distinctions and maintaining power discrepancies.

The alliance with application extended beyond social psychology. Begun while at Wellesley College, the tie to community mental health and particularly to training professionals was a sustaining one. In an early contribution to the *Handbook of Community Psychiatry*, Mayo and Klein (1964) foreshadowed the subsequent research in community psychology on the impact of life events by calling for a "broad appraisal of predicament situations" and by showing how the community could be used "as a laboratory for social change." In one of her last publications, entitled "Training for Positive Marginality," she redefined the training issue not as being one of how to help the professional expel marginality but how to exercise it (Mayo, 1982). Specifically, she saw a number of benefits accruing to the marginal position, among them freedom from orthodoxy, occupancy in a boundary-spanning position, multiple bases of support, and a fresh perspective. Professional marginality also entails taking on a particular kind of responsibility. In 1968 she wrote, "This seems to me to constitute a mandate for stating a dissident opinion" (Mayo, 1968, p. 29). In addition to training social psychologists in positive marginality at Boston University, Mayo taught part-time in the interdisciplinary community mental health training program at Massachusetts General Hospital.

The "boundary-spanning" orientation extended to research methodology. In a text titled *Evaluating Research in Social Psychology*, Mayo and LaFrance (1977) paired laboratory and field studies addressing the same question with the aim of demonstrating the close connection between method adopted and results acquired. There was no easy resolution here, that is, that laboratory experiments or naturalistic field investigations are necessarily superior as research tools. Nor was there any simple summation about the state of the art of social psychology, for no one method is "inherently better suited to answer every question," and no one study "provides the final and definitive answer" but perplexing, new questions (p. 298).

In many ways Mayo represented establishment social psychology, yet she felt herself to be an outsider. She was a tenured full professor. She was listed in several national and international directories. She had the credentials to render her an expert witness in the courtroom. She had been elected to the presidency of the New England Psychological Association for 1976–1977 and invited to join the Society for Experimental Social Psychology. She was a Fellow of the American Psychological Association from Division 9 and had been elected to the presidency of the Society for the Psychological Study of Social Issues (SPSSI) for 1981–1982. If this is not the inner circle of psychology, it is difficult to imagine what is.

Yet there can be no doubt that she identified in her scholarly and applied work with outsiders. Concern with understanding racism and sexism were there from the beginning, and it was to the issue of the links between these two isms that she was working at the time of her death. Moreover, she saw, as did Carolyn Heilbrun (1979), that the condition of femaleness, in contrast to the condition of being foreign, was impossible to deny or change and comparable to Yeats' description as being "the greatest obstacle to achievement one might confront without despair" (p. 22).

She understood tokenism and knew that the promotion of any one woman did not necessarily mean that other women would be able to follow suit (Mayo, 1975). Moreover, she personally rejected the press that comes with being an accomplished woman to disengage from others and to see achievement solely as an individual matter.

CRITICAL EVALUATION OF CONTRIBUTIONS AND ACHIEVEMENTS

As is the case with any scholar, assessing Clara Mayo's contribution to psychology is no simple task. On the one hand, one can look to the visible record, that is, the publications and papers, the professional activities and awards. On the other hand, a full evaluation is only possible when the tacit record is taken into account, containing such aspects as impact on students and associates, colleagues and collaborators. In terms of the latter, participants at memorial services for Clara Mayo at Boston University in December 1981 and at the American Psychological Association in August 1982 repeatedly described the profound impact she had on their aspirations to become first class professors and first-rate practitioners of psychology in the real world.

With respect to the visible record, Mayo's published work is characterized by a remarkable seriousness of purpose. The publications on busing were among the first to be done on that complex topic; in addition, the research took the unusual step of focusing on the black parents rather than on the white community. The work on nonverbal communication, and particularly that concerned with gender relations and race relations, helped to move that field beyond the study of small though fascinating individual cues to that of exploring how important social processes are mediated by nonverbal messages.

Clara Mayo helped formalize and legitimize the budding field of applied social psychology. This was to be no adjunct activity but a mainstay of psychology, and her death cut short a planned volume on this issue. As an intellectual psychologist, Mayo was vitally concerned with the ways in which ideas affect psychological research, and her coauthored text contrasting laboratory and field research methods provided a way to examine the relation between theoretical ideas and methodological choices.

Finally, as an applied social psychologist, Mayo's expert testimony on the nature and expression of prejudice in court cases involving black defendants showed how basic research on racial beliefs and behaviors could be translated into more valid ways to quiz potential jurors as to their racial attitudes.

INTEGRATION OF PROFESSIONAL AND PERSONAL LIFE

At the 1982 meeting of the American Psychological Association in the time slot that would have been Clara Mayo's presidential address to Division 9 (SPSSI) had she not died suddenly on November 21, 1981, a number of colleagues spoke on her contribution to their professional and personal lives. On that occasion in describing her, Lawrence Wrightsman paraphrased George Orwell to the effect that "all people are complex, but some are more complex than others."

Some facts about her personal life are straightforward: she was married in 1953 and divorced in 1978; there were no children. There were also some paradoxes in Clara Mayo's life. She was in many ways a private person, an intimate to few yet a confidante to many. She also recognized the truth behind the feminist maxim that the personal is political. She cited Virginia Woolf, who recognized that one major function of the woman's movement would be to redefine marginal status as deliberate rather than imposed. Specifically, Woolf (1938) called for a Society of Outsiders, clearly defined and intentionally outside.

Having recognized their stance as outsiders they could then bond for independence and support.

Whatever else accrued by virtue of being marginal, Clara Mayo's life showed that the position can entail new ways of being flexible, of expanding one's repertoire, of gaining strength without the adventitious help of belonging by virtue of birth or gene. She knew the outsider's role from the inside and saw potential therein. Clara Mayo began her chapter on marginality with a quote from *As You Like It* that reflects this spirit: "I do desire we may be better strangers."

REFERENCES

Bieri, J. (1955). Cognitive complexity-simplicity and predictive behavior. *Journal of Abnormal and Social Psychology, 51*, 263–268.

Crockett, W. (1982). Some memories of Clara Weiss Mayo. Paper presented at the Meeting of the American Psychological Association, Washington, D.C., August.

Heilbrun, C. (1979). *Reinventing womanhood.* New York: Norton.

Kelly, G. A. (1955). *The psychology of personal constructs.* New York: Norton.

LaFrance, M., & Mayo, C. (1976). Racial differences in gaze behavior during conversations: Two systematic observational studies. *Journal of Personality and Social Psychology, 33*, 4547–4552.

LaFrance, M., & Mayo, C. (1978). *Moving bodies: Nonverbal communication in social relationships.* Monterey, Calif.: Brooks/Cole.

Mayo, C. (1968). Not only an individual but a member. *Zygon, 3*, 21–31.

Mayo, C. (1975). Achievement and self concept in women. In E. T. Nickerson & E. S. Williams (Eds.), *Women, today! Tomorrow?* Dubuque, Iowa: Kendall/Hunt.

Mayo, C. (1982). Training for positive marginality. In L. Bickman (Ed.), *Applied social psychology annual*, Vol. 3. Beverly Hills, Calif.: Sage.

Mayo, C., & Crockett, W. H. (1964). Cognitive complexity and primacy-recency effects in impression formation. *Journal of Abnormal and Social Psychology, 68*, 335–338.

Mayo, C., & Havelock, R. G. (1970). Attitudes toward mental illness among hospital personnel and patients. *Journal of Psychiatric Research, 7*, 291–298.

Mayo, C.; Havelock, R. G.; & Simpson, D. L. (1971). Attitudes toward mental illness among psychiatric patients and their wives. *Journal of Clinical Psychology, 27*, 128–132.

Mayo, C., & Henley, H. (Eds.). (1981). *Gender and nonverbal behavior.* New York: Springer-Verlag.

Mayo, C., & Klein, D. C. (1964). The role of group dynamics in community psychiatry. In L. Bellak (Ed.), *Handbook of community psychiatry.* New York: Grune & Stratton.

Mayo, C., & LaFrance, M. (1977). *Evaluating research in social psychology.* Monterey, Calif.: Brooks/Cole.

Mayo, C., & LaFrance, M. (1980). Toward an applicable social psychology. In R. Kidd & M. Saks (Eds.), *Advances in applied social psychology.* Hillsdale, N.J.: Lawrence Erlbaum Associates.

Teele, J.; Jackson, E.; & Mayo, C. (1967). Family experiences in Operation Exodus:

The bussing of Negro children. *Community Mental Health Journal*, Monograph No. 3.

Teele, J. E., & Mayo, C. (1969). Racial school integration: Tumult and shame. *Journal of Social Issues, 25*, 137–155.

Woolf, V. (1938). *Three guineas*. New York: Harcourt, Brace.

Wrightsman, L. (1982). Some comments on Clara Mayo. Paper presented at the Meeting of the American Psychological Association, Washington, D.C., August.

MARIA MONTESSORI (1870–1952)

Nancy M. Rambusch

Maria Montessori, the first woman granted a medical degree in Italy, devised "psychopedagogy," an educational method for young children. To the tradition of Jean-Jacques Rousseau, Johann Pestalozzi, and Friedrich Froebel, Montessori joined a scientific spirit, exemplified by her clinical experience and expressed by her as an impressionistic developmental psychology. Montessori worked first with deficient, and then with ordinary children with startling results. The work done in her Children's Houses brought her international acclaim. Montessori developed a worldwide network of schools and societies devoted to her "method." After her death, Montessori's ideas reentered the free market of educational theory and practice. Montessori's interactionist thought anticipated many contemporary developmental constructs.

FAMILY BACKGROUND AND EDUCATION

Maria Montessori was born August 31, 1870, in Chiaravalle, Italy, the only child of Alessandro Montessori, a civil servant in the state-run tobacco industry, and Renilde Stoppani, a homemaker.

Montessori, an unexceptional student except in mathematics, intended originally to become an engineer. While attending a technical secondary school, she decided to become a physician. Since no Italian woman had ever done this, only Pope Leo XIII's extraordinary support gained her admission (1892) to the University of Rome medical school, from which she graduated in 1896. In 1897 she audited university courses in pedagogy and in 1901, intent on further integrating her medical training and her emergent educational interests, she reenrolled in the university to study physical anthropology, experimental psychology, and educational philosophy.

CAREER DEVELOPMENT

In 1895 Montessori won a competitive post as assistant doctor (*aggiunto di medecina*), studying pediatrics and attending a psychiatric clinic. In 1896 she became an assistant at Rome's San Giovanni Hospital and entered private practice. In 1897, as part of her work, she visited local insane asylums, selecting suitable subjects for clinic treatment. There she saw feebleminded children for whom no other social provision had been made, locked up with catatonics and the criminally insane. During this period Montessori became convinced that mental deficiency was not a medical but a pedagogical problem. She studied the work of two French medical predecessors dealing with "defective" children, Jean Marc Gaspard Itard and Eduoard Seguin. She also studied the educational theories of Jean-Jacques Rousseau, Johann Pestalozzi, and Friedrich Froebel, linking their focus on sense training to a curriculum of direct experience with concrete objects. Montessori shared the belief of her mentor, Guiseppe Sergi, a pedagogical anthropologist, that observation of the individual was the starting point for social reform.

In 1899 Montessori was appointed lecturer in hygiene and anthropology at the Regio Istituto Superiore di Magistero Femminile, one of the two women's teacher training colleges in Italy, remaining associated with that institution until 1916. In 1900 she was named co-director of the Scuola Magistrele Ortofrenica, a medico-pedagogical institute training teachers of deficient children. There Montessori demonstrated her "new" pedagogy. She owed her belief in the child's natural capacities unfolding through firsthand experience to Pestalozzi and in learning as a process of stage-related self-discovery to Froebel. She owed her realization of sense-training–based education to an educator of the deaf, Jacob Pereira. Her pediatric practice had made her aware of the child's need for self-chosen purposive activity. Measurement techniques used in physical anthropology offered her a strategy for paying minute attention to individual learners. In her two years at the Orthophrenic School, Montessori's identity changed from physician to educator.

In 1901 Montessori left the school, redirecting her energies to normal children. From 1904 to 1908 she taught at the University of Rome and served as a member of its Board of Examiners.

In the decade following medical school graduation, Montessori published a number of scientific papers, reflecting her shift from medicine to pedagogy. In 1896 she wrote on the significance of Leyden's crystals in the treatment of bronchial asthma, in 1897 on bacteriological research on the cephalo-rachitic liquid in paralytic insanity. In 1904 she wrote on anthropometric characteristics in relation to the intellectual standing of school children's intellectual development, in 1905 on physical characteristics of the young women of Latium, and in 1906 on the importance of regional ethnology in pedagogical anthropology (Kramer, 1976, p. 385).

In 1907, invited by a real estate group renovating a housing project for the poor in the San Lorenzo quarter of Rome, Montessori organized her first Children's House. There she had a laboratory for normal children, while her sponsors had her assurance that the children would not "scratch the walls and foul the stairways" (Fisher, 1912, p. 233).

To this "experiment," located in a single room in an apartment building, about fifty three- to six-year-olds came daily to be cared for by an uneducated local woman following Montessori's directives. The children swept and dusted the room as well as sorting, classifying, and counting blocks and beads. Within weeks of their arrival, the children's behaviors changed. From acting sullen, listless, and withdrawn, they became sociable and communicative (Kramer, 1976, p. 148). The children's spontaneous interest in writing, and then reading, led Montessori to develop materials and strategies for the early acquisition of literacy-related skills, typically presented four years later in Italian primary school classes.

Her work at the first Children's House brought Montessori a lifelong international reputation. The European press celebrated her as an educational wonder worker (Kramer, 1976, p. 148). Visitors from all over the world came to Rome to see her, to be trained by her, and to replicate her work.

By 1910 Montessori's mission in life, the refinement and dissemination of her "method," had crystallized (Standing, 1962, p. 61). Working outside conventional teacher training channels, Montessori created an international franchise system, empowering only those teachers trained by her or her designees to open Montessori classes, and permitting no one, except those empowered by her personally, to train teachers. She also strictly controlled the sale of her "didactic apparatus," the learning materials she had devised for sensory training.

Montessori's diffusion strategies arose both from the conviction that her insights belonged exclusively to her and from her need to earn a living once she had left teaching and had stopped practicing medicine. The proceeds of her lectures, training courses, books, and didactic apparatus constituted that living. In 1929 Montessori organized the Association Montessori Internationale (AMI) to oversee the schools and societies developed as a result of her personal efforts. This group, headquartered in Amsterdam, institutionalized Montessori's psychopedagogy. The AMI continued its work after her death, when her ideas reentered the free market of educational theory and practice. National Montessori societies then promoted indigenous versions of the "method," diminishing the influence and relevance of the AMI's centralized authority.

MAJOR CONTRIBUTIONS AND ACHIEVEMENTS

Montessori's Psychopedagogy

Montessori called her work "psychopedagogy." The developmental psychology undergirding it is interactionist and "surprisingly modern in its concepts, if somewhat archaic and mystical in its terminology" (Hornberger, 1982/1984, p. 211). Montessori's theories did not develop from systematic research, but were based on her clinical observations of children in their natural settings and reflected what she thought was important in the child's interactions with the world.

The developmental character of nature, and therefore of behavior, was central to her thought (McDermott, 1970, p. xi).

Man changes as he grows; the body itself not only undergoes an increase in volume, but a profound evolution in the harmony of its parts and the composition of its tissues; in the same way, the psychic personality of man does not grow, but evolves, like the predisposition to disease which varies at different stages in each individual considered pathologically. (Montessori, 1913, pp. 17–18)

Montessori recognized the respective claims of maturation and development.

It follows that "maturation" is far more than "the net sum of the gene effects operating in a self-limited time cycle," for besides the effects of the genes there are also the effects of the environment on which they act. This environment has a dominant part to play in the process of maturation.

As regards psychological maturation, this can only occur by environmental experience, and the latter changes its form at each level of development. (Montessori, 1967, p. 95)

Montessori saw the environment as furnishing the child with the circumstances for constructing and elaborating mental structures. "The mental organism is a dynamic whole, which transforms its structure by active experience obtained from its surroundings" (Montessori, 1967, p. 80).

Montessori's theory of child development included such concepts as (a) adaptation and organization, (b) the absorbent mind, (c) developmental stages, (d) an enriched environment, and (e) a drive toward independence (Hornberger, 1982/1984, p. 8).

Adaptation and Organization

Montessori (1967) saw adaptation as "the transformation of one's self of such a kind as to make one suited to one's surroundings, which then become a part of one's being" (p. 102). The child was transformed mentally through the process of adaptation. Montessori (1971) argued that the child possessed a biologically derived natural capacity for "incarnation" or organization of cognitive structures proceeding from the child's inner life. "We can do nothing but wait for this inner life to organize itself" (p. 48).

The Absorbent Mind

Montessori (1967) characterized the first six years of life as the period of the "absorbent mind," when the child assimilated the environment involuntarily. This assimilation represented the coordination and integration of mental and physiological development. "Just as there is no complete man already formed in the original germinative cell, so there seems to be no kind of mental personality already formed in the new born child" (p. 51).

The absorbent mind operated through time-bound, irreversible "sensitive periods," during which the child was amenable, as at no other time, to personal development along certain lines (McDermott, 1970, p. xvi). These sensitivities created not the mind itself but its organs. Sensitive periods, in the various domains of development, developed separately. These periods include order, motor development, language, writing, interest in small objects, refinement of the senses, images, morality, socialization, and reading.

Each of these powers has its own special interest and this form of sensitivity is so lively that it leads its possessor to perform a certain series of actions. None of these sensitivities occupies the whole period of development. Each . . . lasts long enough for the construction of the psychic organ. Once that organ is formed, the sensitivity disappears. . . . When all the organs are ready, they unite to form what we regard as the psychic unity of the individual. (Montessori, 1967, p. 51)

Developmental Stages

Montessori (1967) saw development as occurring in a series of irreversibly traversed stages, each one qualitatively different from the others (p. 194). "We have before us at each new stage a different child who presents characteristics different from those he exhibited during preceding years" (Montessori, 1973, p. 3).

Montessori (1946) posited three developmental stages:

Stage 1: Birth to about six years of age, subdivided into birth to about three years and three to six years.

Stage 2: Six to about twelve years.

Stage 3: Twelve to about eighteen years.

An Enriched Environment

Montessori (1913) saw as the best means of promoting growth an environment rich in possibilities representing "intellectual culture, education and hygiene" (p. 254).

We had prepared a place for children where a diffused culture could be assimilated from the environment, without any need for direct instruction. . . . Education is not something which the teacher does, but . . . a natural process which develops spontaneously in the human being. (Montessori, 1967, pp. 5–6)

Through the child's interaction with an environment responsive to its developmental needs, the child can achieve full potential (Montessori, 1966, p. 35). This environment is a humanized setting, including but not limited to the parent or teacher (McDermott, 1970).

Independence

For Montessori (1965) the essential condition necessary to the child's optimal development was liberty or freedom.

In order to expand, the child, left at liberty to exercise his activities, ought to find in his surroundings something organized in direct relation to his internal organization which is developing itself by natural laws, . . . a direct correspondence between form and sustenance. (Pp. 69–70)

This liberty related to the child's need to grow and develop in harmony with the individual, spontaneous manifestations of the child's nature, as appropriate socialization was occurring (Montessori, 1964, p. 28).

All the efforts of growth are efforts to acquire independence. A matter of vital importance to an individuality is that it be able to function by itself. In order to grow and develop, the child needs to acquire independence. (Montessori, 1966, pp. 11–12)

In an optimal environment, the child acquires the ability to control intentions and actions through ordering sensorimotor and mental actions. Discipline as the inhibitor of disorder comes from within the child.

The Montessori Method

Montessori's method, the practical expression of her developmental psychology, evolved gradually. Support for her work came initially from political and educational progressives and the popular press, but not from those in America "formulating the new psychological theories nor from those formulating the philosophy of education" (Hunt, 1964, p. xiii). Although such psychologists as Howard C. Warren, 1912 president of the American Psychological Association, and Lightner Witmer, founder of the first psychological clinic at the University of Pennsylvania, supported Montessori's work, those of the functionalist school and the soon to be dominant behavioristic school did not. "Montessori's notions were too dissonant to hold their own" (Hunt, 1964, p. xiv).

Among Montessori's "dissonant" notions were these six:

1. Intentionally organized early learning experiences for three- and four-year-olds were significant for their later development.
2. Intelligence was not fixed; therefore, mental retardation, as a defect, called for pedagogical treatment.
3. Development was not predetermined.
4. All behavior was not motivated by instincts, painful stimuli, homeostatic needs, and sex, or by acquired drives based on these, as some American psychologists and Sigmund Freud maintained. Rather, Montessori placed "children's spontaneous interest in learning" at the center of her work (Hunt, 1964, p. xvi).
5. Sensory training, as described by Montessori, was out of step with stimulus-response theory, which limited the function of the brain to essentially static connections between stimulus and responses. Montessori's critics thought her hopelessly behind the times, since her use of language was reminiscent of faculty psychology, the doctrine that

mind is composed of a number of "powers" or "agencies" such as memory, will, or attention, which produce various mental activities.

6. The child, not the teacher, was center stage in the educational process. "Each individual child had a stage of his own where the didactic materials were at the center of his attention." (Hunt, 1964, p. xvii)

CRITICAL EVALUATION OF CONTRIBUTIONS AND ACHIEVEMENTS

Montessori's most vocal American critic was William Heard Kilpatrick of Teachers College, Columbia University, the immensely influential popularizer of John Dewey's thought. After visiting Rome in 1911, Kilpatrick wrote *The Montessori System Examined*. In it, he firmly assigned Montessori a place "some fifty years behind the present development of educational theory," criticizing her for failing to provide for the child's self-directing adaptation to a novel environment (Kramer, 1976, p. 228). The more sympathetic John and Evelyn Dewey dismissed Montessori as a faculty psychologist (McDermott, 1970, p. xii).

John McDermott, an explicator of Dewey and Montessori, argues that both Kilpatrick and the Deweys rendered a far too hasty verdict on Montessori's work. Their expressed attitudes, he maintains, resulted from a misreading of *The Montessori Method* and from a failure to consider Montessori's already published *Pedagogical Anthropology*. The notion of structure, so central to Montessori's thought, does not of itself preclude the variety of experiences indispensable for learning. Montessori's own disclaimers make the faculty psychology charge unfounded (McDermott, 1970, p. xii). Like Dewey, Montessori insists on the quality, not the quantity, of experience, the relationship between the potentialities of the child and the *kind* of experience offered (McDermott, 1970, p. xii). Nonetheless, Kilpatrick's perception of Montessori's work sealed her American fate for fifty years.

Contemporary psychologists have addressed Montessori's prescient thinking regarding such constructs as autonomy (Gardner, 1966; Banta, 1968); plasticity of intelligence (Hunt, 1975); the "problem of the match" (Hunt, 1964); a language acquisition device (Crain, 1980); critical periods (Crain, 1980); attention (Gardner, 1966; Jensen & Kohlberg, 1966; Kohlberg, 1968; McCormick & Schnobrich, 1971; Banta, 1969; Berger, 1969), and motivation (Morra, 1969).

In the 1960s some apparent communalities between the thought of Jean Piaget, the genetic epistemologist, and Montessori's were noted (Elkind, 1967). The role Montessori assigned to the child's own initiative and to the child's capability for self-construction is strongly suggestive of contemporary "constructivism" (Hornberger, 1982/1984, p. 211). Montessori's concept of intrinsic motivation anticipated Robert White's (1959) "competence motivation" by half a century.

In the mid-1960s, when Head Start was being organized to redress the educational inequities poor black children suffered, J. McVicker Hunt, a cognitive psychologist (1964), suggested a qualified revisitation of Montessori's pedagogy. Opining that Montessori had built pedagogically far better than her critics knew, Hunt nonetheless was cautious:

While [Montessori's] practice is no longer out of step with the conceptions emerging from recent evidence, her theory was never the kind that supplies a good guide to the observation and investigation required to settle the various issues that are still highly problematical. (pp. xxxi-xxxii)

Hunt saw in Montessori's pedagogy a compelling operational argument for breaking the lockstep of American educational practice. Observant teachers could facilitate youngsters in "matching" themselves to the most appropriate kinds of cognitive and social opportunities:

If a teacher can discern what a child is trying to do in his informational interaction with the environment, and, if that teacher can have on hand materials relevant to that intention, if he can impose a relevant challenge with which the child can cope, supply a relevant model for imitation, or pose a relevant question that the child can answer, that teacher can call forth the kind of accommodative change that constitutes psychological development or growth. This sort of thing was apparently the genius of Maria Montessori. (Hunt, 1964, p. xxxiv)

Montessori's genius was not widely recognized by academic psychology, although her work anticipated several contemporary developmental themes:

In contemporary terms, her psychopedagogy would be considered an action psychology, which basically precludes it from academic respectability. Her theory contains both strengths and weaknesses in light of present day thinking; however, on balance, Montessori's theory is quite contemporary and remarkably ahead of most psychological thinking of her time. (Hornberger, 1982/1984, p. 211)

INTEGRATION OF PERSONAL AND PROFESSIONAL LIFE

Montessori never married. She had one child, Mario Montessori, born in 1898. The reason she did not marry the child's father, Guiseppe Montesano, her co-director at the Orthophrenic School, is unknown (Kramer, 1976, p. 92). Following his marriage to another in 1901, Montessori resigned from the school.

From then on, Montessori devoted her life to her method. Her followers, led by her son, Mario Montessori, as director of the Association Montessori Internationale, saw as their work the maintenance of doctrinal purity rather than the accommodation of Montessori's ideas to changing cultural circumstances and the assimilation of those ideas into the ever expanding disciplines of psychology and education. She died on May 6, 1952, at Noordwijk aan Zee, the Netherlands.

REFERENCES

Banta, T. (1968). *The Sands School Project: First year results*. Cincinnati: University of Cincinnati. (ERIC Document Reproduction Service No. ED 054870)

Banta, T. (1969). The Montessori research project. *American Montessori Society Bulletin, 7*, 1.

Berger, B. (1969). *A longitudinal investigation of Montessori and traditional prekindergarten training in inner city children: A comparative assessment of learning outcome*. New York: Center for Urban Education.

Crain, W. C. (1980). *Theories of development*. Englewood Cliffs, N.J.: Prentice-Hall.

Elkind, D. (1967). Piaget and Montessori. *Harvard Educational Review, 37*, 535–545.

Fisher, D. C. (1912). *A Montessori mother*. New York: Henry Holt.

Gardner, R. (1966). A psychologist looks at Montessori. *Elementary School Journal, 67*, 72–83.

Hornberger, M. A. (1984). The developmental psychology of Maria Montessori (unpublished doctoral dissertation, Teachers College, Columbia University, 1982). *Dissertation Abstracts International, 44* (11), 33206A-33207A.

Hunt, J. McV. (1964). Introduction. In M. Montessori, *The Montessori method* (pp. i-xxxvi). New York: Schocken.

Hunt, J. McV. (1975). Children learn in different ways. *Proceedings of the American Montessori Society Seminar* (pp. 1–10). New York: American Montessori Society.

Jensen, J., & Kohlberg, L. (1966). *Report of a research project for culturally disadvantaged children in the Ancona Montessori School*. Washington, D.C.: DHEW National Institute of Education, Educational Resources Center. (ERIC Document Reproduction Service No. ED 015014)

Kohlberg, L. (1968). Montessori with the culturally disadvantaged: A cognitive developmental interpretation and some research findings. In R. Hess & R. M. Baer (Eds.), *Early education*. Chicago: Aldine.

Kramer, R. (1976). *Maria Montessori: A biography*. New York: G. P. Putnam's Sons.

McCormick, C. C., & Schnobrich, J. M. (1971). Perceptual motor training and improvement in concentration in a Montessori preschool. *Perceptual and Motor Skills, 32*, 71–77.

McDermott, J. J. (1970). Introduction. In M. Montessori, *Spontaneous activity in education* (pp. i-xx). New York: Schocken.

Montessori, M. (1913). *Pedagogical anthropology*. New York: Frederick C. Stokes.

Montessori, M. (1946). *Education for a new world*. Thiruvanmujar, India: Kalakshetra.

Montessori, M. (1964). *The Montessori method*. New York: Schocken.

Montessori, M. (1966). *The secret of childhood*. New York: Schocken.

Montessori, M. (1967). *The absorbent mind*. New York: Dell.

Montessori, M. (1970). *Spontaneous activity in education*. New York: Schocken.

Montessori, M. (1971). *The formation of man*. Adyar, India: Theosophical Publishing House.

Montessori, M. (1973). *From childhood to adolescence*. New York: Schocken.

Morra, M. (1967). The Montessori method in light of contemporary views of learning and motivation. *Psychology in the Schools, 4*(1), 48–53.

Standing, E. M. (1962). *Maria Montessori: Her life and work*. New York: Mentor Omega.

White, R. W. (1959). Motivation reconsidered: The concept of competence. *Psychological Review, 66*, 297–333.

Additional Representative Publications by
Maria Montessori

Montessori, M. (1965). *Dr. Montessori's own handbook*. New York: Schocken.
Montessori, M. (1967). *The discovery of the child*. New York: Ballantine.

Additional Representative Publications About
Maria Montessori

Elkind, D. (1979). Piaget and Montessori in the classroom. *American Montessori Society Bulletin, 17*.
Montessori in perspective. (1964). Washington, D.C.: National Association for the Education of Young Children.

BERNICE L. NEUGARTEN
(1916–   )

Nancy K. Schlossberg and Lillian E. Troll

Bernice L. Neugarten created the academic field of adult development and aging. She has worked on the cutting edge of several disciplines in her quest to articulate the intersection between individual choice and social, economic, and political constraints. She has perpetually challenged stereotypical views about aging, connecting the fields of sociology, psychology, and anthropology through lectures, writing, research, and policy analysis, as well as consultations with individuals, organizations, and state and federal governments. Most important, she has taught and mentored several generations of scholars and practitioners who now are teaching and conducting research across the world.

FAMILY AND CAREER INFLUENCES

Bernice Levin was born in 1916 in a small town in Nebraska, the older of two children. Her father had come to the United States from Lithuania in his early twenties and, instead of following the most common pathway for Jewish immigrants of that time, of settling into a large eastern city in an ethnic neighborhood, he chose the more adventurous route of traveling about the western prairie states selling goods to farmers and ranchers, and later buying their raw wool and shipping it to mills in New England. It was in the course of a business trip that he met his future wife, who lived in Chicago. The newlyweds moved to Norfolk, a railroad center of 4,000 to 5,000 inhabitants, thus a convenient place to locate a shipping business. Here Bernice Levin and her brother were born and raised.

Although David and Sadie Levin did not have much formal education themselves, they valued it highly and encouraged their intellectually gifted daughter. She was a voracious reader and a good student who skipped grades frequently. She carried courses in high school at the age of eleven and completed high school at the age of fifteen, too young to go away to college. She took "two years out," therefore, enrolling in courses at the local junior college for one year and reading a lot. The Norfolk superintendent of schools thought that she should go to the University of Chicago. (He had been impressed with the ferment of intellectual activity created there by its youthful president, Robert Maynard Hutchins.) But it was the Depression, and she would have been unable to go if not for a chance meeting between her father, who was on a business trip to Chicago, and a friend who lived on the north side of the city, an hour's "el" ride away from the campus. This friend suggested that Levin live with their family so that she could commute to campus with their daughter.

Thus Bernice Levin arrived in Chicago at the age of seventeen, and once there, she never left. In fact, she has even lived in the same neighborhood— Hyde Park (the area of the University of Chicago)—all but that first year. She met Fritz Neugarten on campus, when he came to Chicago from Paris, and they married in 1940. She has noted how unusual it is for somebody in academia to be so geographically stable. In part, this is attributable to Fritz. Although educated as a lawyer in Europe, he has been in business all his adult life, so they did not have to move about to accommodate two academic careers. He has been, not incidentally, totally supportive of her scholarly pursuits.

There were many inspiring teachers at Chicago during that era of the 1930s and 1940s (and since). During her undergraduate years, those who impressed Bernice Levin the most were Anton Carlson, the physiologist, and Thornton Wilder, the writer, who, she notes, had a way of "lifting you up into another world." At that time in Chicago, it was not unusual for someone majoring in English and French literature to be inspired by scholars in a variety of disciplines. Because she was fortunate to have been awarded scholarships and part-time jobs, she was able to complete her B.A. degree by age twenty and go on for an M.A. in educational psychology, which she obtained at the age of twenty-one. This should have made her eligible to teach high school, but she looked too young, and she was consequently relieved when the newly formed Committee on Child Development offered her an assistantship to study for a Ph.D. This interdisciplinary committee included psychologists, sociologists, anthropologists, biologists, and educators.

She was inspired by many of her teachers during her graduate studies. Robert Redfield, the anthropologist, "made you feel you were right there in the folk society he was describing." Charles Judd, W. Lloyd Warner, Alison Davis, Helen Koch, Robert Havighurst, and William Henry were all important influences. Her graduate assistantship with Daniel Prescott involved her with people like Ernest Hilgard, Lois Meek, Herbert Stoltz, Erik Erikson, and Fritz Redl.

She participated in a community study of Morris, Illinois (which came to be pseudonymously called alternatively Jonesville or Elmtown), which was directed by Warner and Havighurst. In the course of this study, she was able to collect data for her dissertation on the influence of social class on friendship patterns among children and adolescents. Because the committee had just been expanded from child development to human development, she became the first Ph.D. in human development, not only at the University of Chicago, but anywhere.

One of her many concepts to enrich the field of life-span development is the significance of being "off-time"—either too early or too late according to our ubiquitous age norms—and she suspects that she later became interested in that construct because she herself was so persistently off-time. Until the age of twenty-one, she was too early. After that, her marriage and the birth and rearing of two children slowed her down a bit academically, so that she finished the Ph.D. more or less on time (at age twenty-seven) and was late in joining the faculty (at age thirty-five).

It is interesting, in the light of Neugarten's groundbreaking work on grand-parenting, that for many years her household was a three-generation one. After her father's death, her mother came to live with them, a significant grandmother to their daughter, Dail, and son, Jerrold. Bernice Neugarten is the proud grand-mother of three, and her relations with her husband, her daughter, her son, and her daughter-in-law are as vital to her as those with colleagues and students. During the eight years following the Ph.D., while taking "time out" to raise their children, the Neugartens were deeply involved in local politics, including the exciting effort to create a racially integrated community in Hyde Park (the first in the country). She was also, of course, writing part-time, as well as involved in research. In fact, even when she became a faculty member, she remained part-time for another five years. Once she went on the tenure track, however, in 1960, she was awarded tenure in four years and promoted to a professorship in another four. By 1969 she was chair of the Committee on Human Development. She remained on the faculty of the University for thirty years, until her early retirement in 1980 to start a new doctoral program at Northwestern University called Human Development and Social Policy. Eight years later, when that program was flourishing, she "retired" again and returned to the University of Chicago as Rothschild Distinguished Scholar at the Center on Aging, Health, and Society, her efforts turning to new health policy related to aging.

What Neugarten is noted for, above all, is having molded the field of adult development and aging, giving it a life-span perspective and making it a part of what has come to be called life-span development (by psychologists) or life-course studies (by sociologists). In a way this was the consequence of a mixture of chance and demographic exigency. In the mid-1940s, while she was still a graduate student, the committee decided that the core sequence for the Ph.D. in human development should include a course on maturity and old age to follow a course on childhood and another on adolescence. (For many years, the University of Chicago was the only university that gave a course on the second half of life.) In 1952 a teacher was needed for that course, and Neugarten was asked. As she noted recently, if someone had been needed instead to teach either the childhood or the adolescence course, for either of which she would have been well qualified, her subsequent career would have been different. For one thing, as a child or adolescent psychologist, she might have followed the lead of earlier innovators instead of herself becoming a chief innovator. In addition to this serendipitous teaching assignment, the increase in life expectancy during the second half of the century provided a "demographic imperative" that pushed the issues of middle age and aging into national and international prominence and provided the context for exercising her impressive talents. She emerged as one of the prime experts to whom persons in the media, the government, and the academic community have consistently turned for scholarly guidance on issues of aging.

The course on maturity and old age, which she developed and renamed Adult Development and Aging, has been a model for similar courses now taught in more than 1,000 colleges and universities, although few retained its multidisciplinary nature. The 150 Ph.D.'s she has trained during her career as a professor are almost all now on university faculties, engaged in teaching and research on life-span development or directing multidisciplinary gerontological programs. Her former students produced many of the texts and other significant writing in the field. She can claim several generations of scholars as direct descendants.

MAJOR CONTRIBUTIONS

The major strands of Bernice L. Neugarten's contributions suggest why her work has influenced both the academic community and the public in general. Her early work, carried out with professors Havighurst and Warner, showed her commitment to multidisciplinary inquiry across the life span, realized in more than eight authored and edited books, over 150 articles and monographs, and countless public lectures.

Her writing and research progressed along three interrelated but distinct areas: the psychology of aging, often referred to as developmental or life-span psychology, which attends to changes that occur within the individual; the sociology of aging, which examines the social structures or cultures as they shape the individual's experience over the life course; and social policy, which examines laws, regulations, and policies that influence people's options. On the whole, she has opened up new topic areas rather than followed a single line of inquiry. Sometimes her methods have been qualitative, sometimes quantitative. She prefers exploration to replication, mapping out some of the landscape of what earlier had been the neglected territory of the second half of life.

Psychology of Aging

Bernice Neugarten's monograph with David Gutmann (1957), later elaborated in the now classic volume, *Personality in Middle and Late Life* (Neugarten & Associates, 1964), represented the first systematic studies of personality change and aging. Her findings that personality continues to develop and change throughout life contradicted long-standing assumptions that personality is formed primarily in childhood and thereafter remains relatively fixed.

The overriding themes in this area relate to diversity, timing, and change. Over the years, she has continued to look at changes in personality and age-sex roles; the diversity of patterns of aging; middle-aged parenting and grandparenting; adjustment to retirement, the empty nest, and menopause; and the changing meanings of age to the individual. For example, life events were touted in the 1950s as the significant causes of the transitions of middle age. Neugarten found that the menopause was a psychological nonevent to most women; that the empty nest was not a crisis to parents unless it occurred later than anticipated and therefore signified delayed maturity in their children; and that most middle-aged and older people had never experienced, nor had they perceived in others, a midlife crisis (Neugarten & Datan, 1973).

In her 1982 lecture, "Successful Aging," delivered to the American Psychological Association, she stated:

Perhaps the most consistent finding to emerge from the study of aging is that people grow old in very different ways. [There are] . . . striking variations between successive groups who reach old age . . . among ethnic, urban and rural, and socioeconomic groups. This is to say nothing of the idiosyncratic sequences that widen the divergence among individuals as lives are marked by an increasing number of role transitions, by the proliferation of timetables, and by the lack of synchrony among age-related roles. (1982, pp. 6, 9)

Because of the fluid life span, Neugarten concludes that age is a poor predictor of an aging individual's physical, social, or intellectual competence. She suggests that life-span psychology is not a psychology of crisis behavior but a psychology of timing (1976). Adulthood is not marked by the dramatic biological changes that trigger psychological development in childhood and adolescence, but most adults have built-in "social clocks" by which they judge whether they are "on time" or "off time." It is the unanticipated life events, not the anticipated ones, that produce stress: for example, the death of one's child before the death of one's parents. Death is always a crisis, but especially when it occurs off time.

Her findings and conclusions run counter to much of the popular writing, which suggests that adults have predictable life passages and go through expectable stages. Appealing as it is to latch on to a stage theory of the adult years, Neugarten continually points to the fact that the adult years have more variability, not less, than childhood. She reminds us that we do not yet have a theory of adult development. In fact, she has even questioned the term "development" as applied to adults since the essence of a developmental perspective is a belief that certain dimensions unfold in a predictable, sequential fashion.

Sociology of Aging

One of Bernice Neugarten's earliest and most frequently cited studies, "Age norms, age constraints, and adult socialization" (Neugarten, Moore, & Lowe, 1968), found remarkable agreement among American respondents of different ages about age-appropriate behavior, about when to marry, when to go to school, when to leave home, when to start and end careers. Such age norms are systems of social control that shift with social changes. For example, she has recently found changes in these norms associated with the lengthened life span. Each society, she concluded, has its own expectations about age-appropriate behavior, and within a given society, different subgroups have different expectations. Further, her landmark book, *Middle Age and Aging* (1968), reports a series of studies on age status and age-sex roles. More recently, she has reported that the large majority of Western older persons, although retired, are vigorous and competent. She has labeled them the "young old," seeing their large numbers as a new historical phenomenon in postindustrial societies. This term has become part of our everyday vocabulary. Neugarten reserves the term "old-old" for that minority of frail older people, regardless of age, who need special care and support.

Policy

Drawing from her studies in psychology and sociology, she moved to a consideration of their implications for ethics and public policy regarding older persons. She elucidated the notion and implications of "agism" for age-divisiveness, articulating an ideal of an "age-irrelevant" society. Ironically, it is her application to the field of social policy of what she knows about the psychology, sociology, and anthropology of aging that has aroused some controversy. Her questioning of the use of chronological age as a basis for allocating public benefits and of many of our laws, procedures, and regulations that create age distinctions has run counter to the positions taken by age advocacy groups. Since the needs of the young-old and old-old differ dramatically, she writes in her edited book *Age or Need?* (1982), the collection and reporting of data in terms of age levels rather than need levels make it impossible to monitor our progress. Her suggestion, however, that age-entitlement programs be reexamined from the perspective of need-entitlement is anathema to many who have labored to improve the economic and social status of older people. Although she accepted the appointment as one of the deputy chairs of the 1981 White House Conference on Aging and spent many hours for over a year shaping its agenda, she expressed reservations about a national policy meeting based on age rather than on more relevant dimensions of human competencies and human needs.

AWARDS AND HONORS

The significance of Bernice L. Neugarten's work is attested by the many honors she has been awarded. Among the most recent, the 1987 Sandoz International Prize for Research in Gerontology carried the following citation:

For documenting with extraordinary insight the social aspects and implications of aging over the human life course. Her distinguished work laid the basis for optimism about a society's capacity to modify the aging process beneficially, and has helped define key issues in public policy options for aging societies. . . . The insights of this articulate social scientist will be remembered and used by future generations of scholars. (*Northwestern News*, November 1987)

In the fall of 1988 Neugarten received two major academic awards: an honorary doctorate from the Catholic University at Nijmegen, the Netherlands, and the Distinguished Mentorship Award of the Behavioral and Social Sciences Section of the Gerontological Society of America. Before that, in 1982, Neugarten had won the prestigious Brookdale Award, designated for those who have made "distinguished contributions to gerontology." Mentioned were her published papers and speeches, which have been reprinted in readers and texts and quoted by most people writing in the field; her development of the most widely used inventory of life satisfaction; her development of one of the first doctoral training programs in the United States in the area of adulthood and aging; her sponsorship of over 150 students in their Ph.D. programs; and her editorial role in many journals, including *Human Development, Journal of Gerontology,* and *Psychology and Aging.*

In 1980 Neugarten was the first social scientist specializing in aging to be elected a Fellow of the American Academy of Arts and Sciences. That same year, she received an honorary degree from the University of Southern California. She is also a senior member of the Institute of Medicine, National Academy of Sciences. The American Psychological Foundation Distinguished Teaching Award (1975) celebrates her teaching achievements. Other honors include the Gerontological Society of America's Kleemeier Award for Outstanding Research Contributions in Aging (1971), the Illinois Psychological Association Distinguished Psychologist Award (1979), and the Distinguished Scientific Contribution Award from the Division on Adult Development and Aging, American Psychological Association (1980).

Active in numerous professional organizations and public service, Neugarten has been president of the Gerontological Society of America (1969), deputy chair of the 1981 White House Conference on Aging, and a member of the Federal Council on the Aging. She served as consultant to the National Institute of Child Health and Human Development, and was a member of the Council of Representatives of the American Psychological Association, the Technical Committee on Research and Demonstration for the 1971 White House Conference on Aging, the Governing Council of the International Association of Gerontology, and the National Advisory Council of the National Institute of Aging.

In 1982 the Committee on Human Development of the University of Chicago organized a two-day symposium to mark four decades of Neugarten's contributions to the study of adult life. The letters of nomination and support for these numerous awards from her students and colleagues reflect a woman of brilliance and compassion, one who challenges and stimulates. The late Nancy Datan wrote: "Bernice Neugarten was at the very forefront of what must be considered a counter-culture movement in our youth-oriented culture . . . thanks to her tireless efforts . . . to create an awareness of . . . the strengths and diversities of the aging and elderly, and the continuity of the life cycle, through which the well being of the young is bound up with the fate of their elders'' (1985).

REFERENCES

Datan, N. (1985, January 31). Letter to Elva M. D. Walker, Chairman of the Board, National Purity Soap and Chemical Co., 110 S. 5th Ave., Minneapolis, Minn. 55414.

Neugarten, B. L. (Ed.). (1968). *Middle age and aging*. Chicago: University of Chicago Press.

Neugarten, B. L. (1976). The psychology of aging: An overview. *Master Lectures on Developmental Psychology*. Washington, D.C.: American Psychological Association.

Neugarten, B. L. (Ed.). (1982). *Age or need? Public policies for older people*. Beverly Hills, Calif.: Sage Publications.

Neugarten, B. L. (1982). Successful aging [Invited address]. American Psychological Association.

Neugarten, B. L., & associates. (1964). *Personality in middle and late life*. New York: Atherton Press.

Neugarten, B. L., & Datan, N. (1973). Sociological perspectives on the life cycle. In P. B. Baltes & K. W. Schaie (Eds.), *Life-span developmental psychology: Personalities and socialization*. New York: Academic Press.

Neugarten, B. L., & Gutmann, D. L. (1957). Age-sex roles and personality in middle age: A thematic apperception study. *Psychological Monographs, 72*(17), Whole No. 470.

Neugarten, B. L.; Moore, J. W.; & Lowe, J. C. (1968). Age norms, age constraints, and adult socialization. In B. L. Neugarten (Ed.), *Middle age and aging*. Chicago: University of Chicago Press.

Northwestern News (1978, November). Evanston, Ill.: Northwestern University, University Relations.

Additional Representative Publications by
Bernice L. Neugarten

Neugarten, B. L. (1965). Personality and patterns of aging. *Gawein*, Journal of Psychology of the University of Nijmegen, *13*, 249–256. Reprinted in B. L. Neugarten (Ed.) (1968), *Middle age and aging: A reader in social psychology*. Chicago: University of Chicago Press.

Neugarten, B. L. (1967). A new look at menopause. *Psychology Today, 1*(7), 42–45, 67–69.

Neugarten, B. L. (1969). Continuities and discontinuities of psychological issues into adult life. *Human development, 12*, 121–130.

Neugarten, B. L. (1970). Adaptation and the life cycle. *Journal of Geriatric Psychiatry, 4*(1), 71–87.

Neugarten, B. L. (1971). Grow old along with me. *Psychology Today, 5*(7), 45–48, 79–81.

Neugarten, B. L. (1972). Social implications of a prolonged lifespan. *Gerontologist,* *12*(4), 437–440.

Neugarten, B. L. (1973). Personality change in late life: A developmental perspective. In C. Eisdorfer & P. Lawton (Eds.), *The psychology of adult development and aging*. Washington, D.C.: American Psychological Association.

Neugarten, B. L. (1974). Age groups in American society and the rise of the young-old. *Annals of Political and Social Sciences, 415*, 187–198.

Neugarten, B. L. (Ed.). (1975). Aging in the year 2000: A look at the future. *Gerontologist, 15*(1), Part 2. (Special issue.) The future and the young-old, 4–9.

Neugarten, B. L. (1977). Personality and aging. In J. E. Birren (Ed.), *Handbook of the psychology of aging*. New York: Van Nostrand Reinhold.

Neugarten, B. L. (1979, July). Time, age, and the life cycle. *American Journal of Psychiatry*, 887–894.

Neugarten, B. L. (1979, November). Policy for the 1980s: Age entitlement or need-entitlement. In *Aging: Agenda for the eighties* (pp. 48–52). Washington, D.C.: National Journal Issues Book.

Neugarten, B. L. (1980). Acting one's age: New rules for the old. Interview by Elizabeth Hall. *Psychology Today, 14*(4), 66–80.

Neugarten, B. L. (1982). Aging: Policy issues for the developed countries of the world. In H. Thomae & G. L. Maddox (Eds.), *New perspectives on old age: A message to decision makers*. New York: Springer.

Neugarten, B. L. (1982, May). Human behavior is malleable throughout life. *Psychology Today*, Fiftieth Anniversary Issue, 54–55.

Neugarten, B. L. (1982, June). Older Americans: A profile of social and health characteristics. In *The hospital's role in caring for the elderly: Leadership issues* (pp. 3–16). Chicago: Hospital Research and Educational Trust.

Neugarten, B. L. (Ed.). (1982). *Age or need? Public policies for older people*. Beverly Hills, Calif.: Sage Publications.

Neugarten, B. L. (1985). Interpretive social science and research on aging. In A. Rossi (Ed.), *Gender and the life course*. New York: Aldine.

Neugarten, B. L. (1988). The aging society and my academic life. In M. W. Riley (Ed.), *Sociological lives, Volume 2: Social change and the life course*. Newbury Park, Calif.: Sage Publications.

Neugarten, B. L. (1988). Personality and psycho-social patterns of aging. In M. Bergener, M. Erminie, & H. B. Stähelin (Eds.), *Crossroads in aging: The 1988 Sandoz Lectures in Gerontology*. London: Academic Press.

Neugarten, B. L., & Datan, N. (1974). The middle years. In S. Arieti (Ed.), *American handbook of psychiatry, 2nd edition, Volume 1*. New York: Basic Books.

Neugarten, B. L., & Eglit, H. (Eds.). (1981). Age discrimination. Proceedings of the National Conference on Constitutional and Legal Issues Relating to Age Discrimination and the Age Discrimination Act. *Chicago Kent Law Review, 57*(4).

Neugarten, B. L., & Hagestad, G. (1976). Aging and the life course. In J. E. Birren (Ed.), *Handbook of aging and the social sciences*. New York: Van Nostrand Reinhold. Revision by G. Hagestad & B. L. Neugarten, in E. Shanas & R. Binstock (Eds.) (1984), *Handbook of aging and the social sciences* (2nd ed.).

Neugarten, B. L., & Havighurst, R. R. (Eds.). (1977). *Extending the human life span: Social policy and social ethics*. Washington, D.C.: Government Printing Office.

Neugarten, B. L.; Havighurst, R. J.; & Tobin, S. S. (1961). The measurement of life satisfaction. *Journal of Gerontology, 16*, 134–143.

Neugarten, B. L., & Neugarten, D. A. (1986). Changing meanings of age in the aging society. In A. Pifer & L. Bronte (Eds.), *Our aging society: Paradox and promise.* New York: W. W. Norton. (An adaptation of this paper appeared in *Psychology Today*, 1987, *24*(5), 29–33.)

Neugarten, B. L., & Peterson, W. A. (1957). A study of the American age-grade system. *Proceedings*, 4th Congress, International Association of Gerontology, Merano, Italy, Vol. 3, 497–502.

Neugarten, B. L., & Weinstein, K. K. (1964). The changing American grandparent. *Journal of Marriage and the Family, 26*, 199–204.

CAROLYN ROBERTSON PAYTON
(1925–   )

Gwendolyn Puryear Keita and Tressie Muldrow

A black woman born and reared during an era of racism and sexism, Carolyn Robertson Payton became a leader in cross-cultural and ethnic minority psychology and an early pioneer in the push for special training in psychotherapy with ethnic minority clients. She has been instrumental in training hundreds of clinicians. The first psychologist to become director of the U.S. Peace Corps, she was also the first woman and the first black to hold that presidential appointment. As a mentor and advocate of social justice, she influenced the lives of numerous individuals, especially ethnic minorities, women, and the disadvantaged.

FAMILY BACKGROUND AND EDUCATION

Carolyn Robertson was born on May 13, 1925, in Norfolk, Virginia. Her parents were Leroy Solomon Robertson, a chef and restaurateur, and Bertha Flanagan Robertson, a seamstress and homemaker. There was one other child in the family, her older sister, Jean Robertson Scott, who became an elementary school supervisor. Robertson's early years were spent during the Depression. However, the nature of her parents' employment (cook and seamstress) meant that she did not experience the deprivation of food and clothing common during that period.

Though Carolyn Robertson was spared the obvious consequences of poverty in her childhood, she experienced the full effects of racism. In her later years she did not forget the unpaved streets and sidewalks in her segregated neighborhood. She also did not forget that her elementary school—a school that had been condemned for whites many years prior to her attendance there—was equipped with outdoor toilets. Nor did she forget that she was able to see the animals in the city zoo only in passing, for admission was off-limits to blacks. Chief among her early influences was the continued reinforcement of her status as a black person, with all of the slights and subtle putdowns as well as the blatant hostilities, including the "for whites only" signs that she regularly encountered. Yet, in school she learned that as an American she was guaranteed certain rights that are synonymous with equality. As a little girl and as an adult, she constantly strove to achieve those rights for herself and others.

Her education-oriented family expected that after high school she would attend college. Though her choice was Hampton Institute, her father chose Bennett College in Greensboro, North Carolina (both were predominantly black colleges). Bennett had a reputation for being the college "where discriminating parents sent their distinguished daughters." Robertson went to Bennett in 1941, where she majored in home economics. The significant influences during her undergraduate days were the upperclass women who were pursuing studies in any area of their choosing and the numerous women leaders, activists, and educators who frequently addressed the Bennett women at Sunday afternoon vespers. Her sense of well-being was enhanced by her eligibility for all leadership opportunities. Years later Carolyn Payton came to appreciate the benefit of her education at a women's college.

Willa B. Player, then professor and administrator at Bennett College and later its first female president, was a role model during Robertson's undergraduate years. Player communicated poise, commitment to excellence, and effective leadership. She conveyed that women can achieve and excel in major leadership positions.

During her years at Bennett College, Robertson met Eleanor Roosevelt, whom she held in high esteem because of her advocacy for oppressed people. Four other individuals that she met during her years at Bennett had a major impact on her: Mary McCloud Bethune, Nannie Burroughs, Mary Church Terrell, and Charlotte Hawkins Brown. These black women leaders were civil rights activists long before the movement reached its apex in the 1960s.

At the graduate level Robertson chose psychology because of practicality. In 1945 the separate-but-equal doctrine in educational institutions was in force in Virginia. In essence this meant that if a course of study was available to whites at the white state-supported institutions, but not available to blacks at the black state-supported institution, the state would pay all the expenses the student would incur by having to attain an education elsewhere. The field of psychology met this criterion. Knowing other Bennett graduates were at the University of Wisconsin in Madison, Robertson chose to go to Wisconsin. Three years were required to earn the Master of Science degree, because when Robertson enrolled at Wisconsin she had only nine credits in psychology.

In the Department of Psychology at Wisconsin, Robertson was again reminded of her ethnicity. She has vivid memories of her loneliness as a graduate student, for there were no other black students in her classes. She acutely missed the support provided by a sense of belonging and collegiality at Bennett College. She eventually moved to the "Bush," the black ghetto in Madison, and found needed support from the blacks who lived there. During this time she married Raymond Rudolph Payton, a police detective. The marriage was short-lived, ending within four years.

CAREER

Upon receiving the M.S. in clinical psychology in 1948, Payton sought a position as a college teacher in a historically black institution; this appeared to be her only career option. After reading in a newspaper advertisement that Livingstone College in Salisbury, North Carolina, was seeking an instructor in psychology, she applied for the position and was hired. Being the only psychologist on the faculty, she was afforded the opportunity to develop many skills and to venture into other areas, especially psychological testing programs and student personnel. This was an excellent opportunity for a beginning instructor.

After five years at Livingstone, the desire of her family for Payton to live closer to home and the prospect of major career advancement motivated her to respond once again to a job advertisement, this one at Elizabeth City State Teachers College in Elizabeth City, North Carolina. She applied for the position of dean of women with an appointment as a psychology instructor. Payton accepted this appointment because of the challenge of administrative responsibilities. This is the one position that Payton has held in which her gender was the deciding factor. As dean of women, she was considered the role model for students and was to serve as a substitute parental figure for them. Critical to her success was the manner in which she handled her role as a model of propriety at all times. The strict dress code, which was not in keeping with Payton's preferred casual demeanor, could have posed a conflict for someone with less self-assurance. But Payton, equal to any occasion, handled this aspect of the position with only minor trepidation as she regularly donned the required hat and gloves.

In 1956 Payton was recruited to become associate professor of psychology at Virginia State College in Petersburg, Virginia. This offer was very appealing, for she wanted the experience of being in a ''real'' psychology department as well as being near family in Virginia. The position involved teaching half-time at the undergraduate level and working half-time as clinical counselor, which involved psychological testing and providing psychotherapy to students.

Meanwhile, desiring to feel more comfortable in her work and to continue her professional development, in 1952 Payton had begun to take courses during summers at Teachers College, Columbia University, accumulating a large number of credits. In the beginning, it was not her intent to pursue a degree. However, she believed that it would be foolish to ignore credits that she had accumulated. Recognizing that she would be unable to transfer these to Wisconsin, she applied and was accepted as a doctoral candidate at Columbia University. In 1958 Payton took a leave of absence from Virginia State College to fulfill the requirements for the Ed.D. at Teachers College, receiving her degree in 1962. Her advisor, Esther Lloyd-Jones, a renowned expert in the field of student personnel, provided important support for Payton during her study at Teachers College.

In 1959 Payton became an assistant professor at Howard University in Washington, D.C. At Howard she inherited a primate laboratory and, with a three-year grant from the National Institute of Mental Health, began to explore perception. Her plan was to build on this research and study racial perception in young children. The election of John F. Kennedy intervened, however. He had promised the nation a Peace Corps, and in making good that promise, Carolyn Payton was recommended by her university to assist in the design of selection procedures for Peace Corps service. Subsequently, she became a field assessment officer for trainees preparing to serve in Togo, West Africa. Field assessment officers were responsible for the psychological evaluation and assessment of trainees at the training site; that is, the preparation of comprehensive appraisals on each Peace Corps trainee based on psychological tests, personal interviews, clinical observations, faculty grades and assessments, peer reviews, and other pertinent information. From the accumulated data, the physical, mental, and technical qualifications of each trainee for success in the overseas assignment were derived (Payton, 1988).

A year later she was afforded the opportunity to evaluate assessment procedures under conditions presented by training and living at an actual camp site with the objective of determining the feasibility of continuous programs. This assignment was undertaken at Camp Crozier in Arecibo, Puerto Rico. These successes led to full-time employment at the Peace Corps as a field selection officer. This position enabled her to travel extensively overseas and gain firsthand experience with the attitudes and behaviors of the Peace Corps volunteers. Her observations led her to request an overseas post. She wanted to determine the conditions that would lead to a more satisfying experience for the volunteers. This experience led to her appointment as deputy director for the Caribbean region in 1966, and less than a year later she was named director for the post. At the time there was only one other female country director, reflecting a reluctance to appoint women to the overseas staff. Payton's success and the success of other women demonstrated that women were effective in conducting overseas programs, thus opening the doors of opportunity for others (Payton, 1988).

In 1970 Payton returned to Howard to direct the University Counseling Service (UCS). Feeling that UCS was greatly underutilized by students and staff and was too isolated from university life, Payton expanded activities and staff. She spearheaded the growth of UCS from a small, obscure agency primarily engaged in career/vocational counseling and testing to a large, multiservice counseling and training center integrally involved in the university and the community. Payton and her staff became involved in Student Special Services and the Center for Academic Reinforcement, serving environmentally and academically underprepared students entering the university. Payton had succeeded in convincing the mainstream university and more traditional counseling staff that academic intervention is not enough—that counseling was a vital link without which the potential program success would not be realized.

Payton continued in her efforts to make UCS an integral part of the university and to destigmatize counseling/psychotherapy for the campus and the wider Washington community. Another step in this effort was achieved when she obtained permission from the vice-president for student affairs to see community clients at UCS. A number of potential clients and practitioners had been requesting UCS to see community clients since UCS was part of a highly visible and respected black institution well-known for its quality treatment. Many of the clients wanted to be seen by black therapists they could trust, and they felt confident that, if anyplace, these therapists would be found at Howard.

During this time, Payton had become increasingly impressed with the usefulness of group methods of counseling and psychotherapy. She began to use groups for counseling and psychotherapy as well as for supervision of the large number of new counselors, tutors, psychologists, and trainees brought on staff during that period. Payton, a firm believer in supervision and training, had built in training and supervision components throughout all of the new programs at UCS.

With the interest in group psychotherapy and counseling, Payton decided to increase her skills, and later those of other staff members, through enrollment in the group training program of the Psychiatric Institute Foundation, and later, the Washington School of Psychiatry. She began to see the importance of group methods for black clients whose lives are intricately connected to groups—family, community, or others. As her experience in this treatment modality increased, so did her belief in its efficacy for black clients. She sent additional staff for further training and slowly increased the number of counseling and psychotherapy groups at the agency. Later UCS began its own group training program with a focus on training for work with ethnic minority clients. Payton and her staff began to be major proponents of the group modality in work with ethnic minorities and in training therapists to work with ethnic minority clients.

INNOVATOR AND ROLE MODEL

Payton was one of the early pioneers in the push for special training and skills development for working with ethnic minority clients. Through direct individual and group supervision, speeches, and conference presentations, she has espoused this view. She has also been instrumental in making available counseling and therapy to large numbers of individuals who would otherwise have been too afraid or without financial resources to get these services. Payton has been instrumental in using short-term special focus groups at UCS to destigmatize mental health care and to make it accessible to all in need. She has trained hundreds of counselors and psychotherapists, who have continued to spread her views. Moreover, she is regularly sought out for consultations and presentations to trainees and professionals throughout the country.

Payton's interest in and concern about training led to her spearheading UCS's successful attempt to become an APA-accredited counseling psychology internship site—one of the few at a predominantly black institution.

In 1977 Carolyn R. Payton was again lured away from the university to the Peace Corps when President Carter asked her to become Peace Corps director, the first woman and first black to receive that presidential appointment. She had overall responsibility for the work of over 6,000 volunteers serving in sixty-three countries, as well as for her staff in the nation's capital and abroad. Under her tutelage, these volunteers left their marks in towns and villages around the world, enabling students to pass exams that led the way to universities and careers, training farmers to increase their crops, teaching mothers basic nutrition, and assisting researchers and government officials in the areas of business, conservation, and rural urban development.

Payton fought to preserve the apolitical identity of the Peace Corps as envisioned by its founder, President John F. Kennedy. But having served only thirteen months, she was forced to resign as director since she would not compromise her ideals. In a speech before the Conference of the Eastern Association of College Deans, she articulated her ideals, saying, "It is wrong to use the Peace Corps as a means of delivering a message to particular constituencies in the United States, or to export a particular political ideology" (Brown, 1978).

In 1979 Payton returned to Howard University as dean of counseling and career development, where she continued her earlier work, developing a major counseling/therapy and training center in ethnic minority psychology.

PROFESSIONAL INVOLVEMENT AND ACHIEVEMENTS

Carolyn R. Payton has been a leader in the American Psychological Association, the major scientific and professional society representing psychology in the United States and the world's largest association of psychologists. She was a member of the Committee on Scientific and Professional Ethics and Conduct (1971–1977; chair in 1975, 1976); the Task Force on Sex Bias and Sex Role Stereotyping in Psychotherapeutic Practice (1974–1976); the Committee on Women in Psychology (1980–1982; chair in 1981); the Committee on Lesbian and Gay Concerns (1983–1985); and the Policy and Planning Board (1985–1987). Additionally she chaired the American Psychological Foundation's National Media Awards Committee (1980–1981).

Throughout her involvement with APA, Payton has worked to increase representation and involvement of underrepresented groups (i.e., women, ethnic minorities, lesbians and gay men, and the handicapped) within the governance structure, postulating that more diverse representation will generate more diverse perspectives on social problems. She has also been a strong advocate for APA's involvement in public policy issues, serving on APA's Public Policy Committee from 1985 to 1989. In an article titled "Who Must Do the Hard Things?" she noted that psychology as a science devoid of social implications or responsibilities will not survive (Payton, 1984).

Through her writings and speeches, Carolyn Payton has advanced such causes as comparable worth for women and an end to apartheid. She is a strong proponent of the stance that psychologists must actively participate in the political process to end social injustice. She has exhorted her fellow psychologists to "place our talents, our expertise, and our energy in the service of our conscience as well as our discipline'' (Payton, 1984, p. 395).

In addition to her work within APA, Carolyn Payton has served on numerous boards and committees. She was appointed by the President of the United States to the Board of Directors of the Inter-American Foundation (1978–1982) and served as secretary of the Board of Psychologist Examiners of the District of Columbia (1980–1983).

Active in a variety of other organizations, her memberships include Pi Lamba Theta; Kappa Delta Pi; Sigma Delta Epsilon, National Association for Women Deans, Administrators and Counselors; American Group Psychotherapy Association; Society for the Psychological Study of Social Issues; and Delta Sigma Theta.

AWARDS AND RECOGNITION

Payton is a member of APA's Division of the Psychology of Women, and in 1987 first became a Fellow of APA, ''In recognition of outstanding and unusual contributions to the science and profession of psychology,'' through that division. Payton has also received two major APA awards in recognition of her professional contributions and leadership: the Distinguished Professional Contributions to Public Service Award (1982) and the Committee on Women in Psychology (CWP) Leadership Citation (1985).

In the award citation for her distinguished professional contributions to public service, it was observed that

In both public and private forums, she has worked persistently to promote world understandings through cross-cultural interactions. . . . Her work with Third World countries reflects her more pervasive belief that all of humanity, regardless of socioeconomic and political beliefs, share common goals and can form partnerships which advance the cause of people in service to one another. She is an inspiring role model to psychologists who seek to apply their professional skills to the formulation of public policy and to a commitment for peace.

APA's Committee on Women in Psychology Leadership Citation was awarded in recognition of Payton's special commitment to women, ethnic minorities, and other disadvantaged groups. The citation reads:

In recognition of her extraordinary influence on cross-cultural understanding in her work settings, in APA and internationally. She is an outstanding teacher, role model, and mentor for women and ethnic minorities. She has provided leadership on ethical and consumer issues in psychology and in eliminating sex bias in psychotherapeutic practice. She has fostered respect and forged working partnerships among persons with diverse cultural backgrounds, socioeconomic resources, and political beliefs. Her commitment to equality and justice for all oppressed peoples has made a precious difference in all our lives.

Payton has also received numerous awards from community and professional groups, including the American College Personnel Association's Silver Anniversary Recognition Award; the Howard University Armour J. Blackman Award for Dedicated Service; the National Capital Personnel and Guidance Association (NCPGA) award for recognition of commitment and concern and conquests in the field of counseling and psychology; the Peace Corps 1988 Leader for Peace Award; the Elizabeth City State College award for excellence in academic and leadership achievement; and the Big Brothers of the National Capital Area Outstanding Service Award, 1980. Additionally, Payton received the Capital Press Club's 1978 Humanitarian of the Year Award and was awarded the honorary degree Doctor of Humane Letters by Lake Erie College for Women, Lake Erie, Pennsylvania in June 1978.

Payton is an avid supporter of her undergraduate alma mater, contributing freely of her intellectual and financial attainments. She has stated on numerous occasions that her experiences at Bennett College were invaluable in her development and that she must now give something back to the college. Her achievements have been recognized by Bennett College, and in 1980 she was awarded the Bennett College Achievement Award for Outstanding Accomplishments in her chosen profession.

Carolyn Robertson Payton helped to redefine the role of women in American society and had the rare opportunity to fill leadership positions that few women and ethnic minorities had held previously. Many women and ethnic minorities, especially during the years of Carolyn Payton's early accomplishments, have had difficulty eluding the sexism and racism of the society long enough to discover themselves as persons. Not true of Payton. Believing that one's life can make a difference if the individual is willing to work and sacrifice, she availed herself of opportunities that were accompanied by responsibility and wielded as much authority as she could handle. Carolyn R. Payton discovered and effectively defined what it truly means to be a first-class citizen—making a contribution by achieving personally but also by reaching out to help others.

REFERENCES

Brown, W. (1978, December 8). "Political Activism" Peace Corps Goal, Ex-Director Asserts. *Washington Post*.

Payton, C. R. (1984). Who must do the hard things? *American Psychologist, 39*, 391–397.

Payton, C. R. (1988). Carolyn Robertson Payton. In A. N. O'Connell & N. F. Russo (Eds.), *Models of achievement* (pp. 229–242). Hillsdale, N.J.: Lawrence Erlbaum Associates.

Additional Representative Publications by Carolyn Robertson Payton

Payton, C. R. (1975). Employment qualifications and selection procedures: Library of Congress (Agreement No. A75–18). Washington, D.C.: Library of Congress.

Payton, C. R. (1981). Substance abuse and mental health: Special prevention strategies needed for ethnics of color. *National Institute on Drug Abuse Public Health Report*, *1*, 20–25.

Payton, C. R. (1985). Addressing the special needs of minority women. In N. J. Evans (Ed.), *New directions for student services, No. 29: Facilitating the development of women*. San Francisco: Jossey-Bass.

Payton, C. R., & Blake, L. (1964). Difference limen for perception of the vertical in monkeys. *Journal of Perceptual and Motor Skills, 19*, 455–461.

PAULINE (PAT) SNEDDEN SEARS (1908–   )

Judy F. Rosenblith

Pauline (Pat) Snedden Sears has made outstanding contributions in a number of areas, including level of aspiration, self-esteem, achievement motivation, mathematics learning, and sex differences in classroom behaviors including teacher-pupil interactions. The seminal nature of both her own work and joint work with her husband is widely recognized. The mutual interactions of their thinking and work are highly unusual even in the field of psychology, where there have been a number of husband-wife teams, and especially in the time period in which it occurred. The larger world's recognition of Pauline Sears' work is seen in the fact that she was elected president of the American Psychological Association's Division of Developmental Psychology, serving in 1959–1960. The collaborative contributions of Pauline Sears and her husband were recognized by their being joint recipients of the American Psychological Foundation's 1980 Gold Medal for their lifetime contributions to the field of psychology in the study of human development and applications of knowledge to the educational and social betterment of children.

FAMILY BACKGROUND AND EDUCATION

Pauline K. Snedden was born in Vermont on July 5, 1908, while her mother was vacationing there with her older children. She was the fourth child (third girl) of David Snedden and Genevra Sisson Snedden and was joined four years later by another sister. The Sneddens could be characterized as an academic family. Her father was an educational administrator early in life, then a longtime professor at Teachers College of Columbia University, a prolific author of educational works, and a frequent guest lecturer at other institutions. Her maternal grandmother, who lived with them for some years, had been a school teacher, as had her mother. Her mother had also written a book about a Santa Clara Indian boy (Docas) that was used for half a century in the California schools. Much later she wrote a book of stories about her husband's life on a cattle ranch. She also coauthored one of her husband's books on educational sociology to ensure its being more intelligible to a less specialized audience. It was expected that all of the children would go to college. But after two years in college the women were expected to leave and teach for a year, then take vocational training of some kind.

Pat Snedden started school in the public schools of Brookline, Massachusetts, where her father was commissioner of education of the Commonwealth. By the time she was eight her father became a professor at Teachers College; they moved to Yonkers, New York, where they lived for the next fourteen years. After graduating from the eighth grade in public school there, she attended the private Lincoln School in New York City.

Like her father, mother, two older sisters, and brother before her, Pat Snedden attended Stanford University; her younger sister started elsewhere, but finished at Stanford. (At the time his oldest daughter was born David Snedden had been teaching there.)

At Stanford Pat Snedden met Robert R. Sears, also from a Stanford family, his father having long been a professor in the School of Education there. Snedden and Sears took the same introductory psychology class. She credits him with being a strong factor in her decision to major in psychology, while he says that he was drawn from literature to psychology by her. Thus began their long life of mutual intellectual influence, which culminated in the joint Gold Medal award.

Pat Snedden wanted to stay and finish her degree at Stanford, a course of action that was contrary to her father's educational philosophy and to what her older sisters had done. Consequently, she told her father that her course on the Stanford-Binet had provided her with vocational training. Her father accepted that, and she was allowed to continue. An outsider might question whether, with all his education background, he was really taken in by this or merely chose to go along.

Although she did not stop to teach for a year, there was a hiatus in her undergraduate studies. She had violated a rule relating to the dean of women's stringent definitions of ladylike behavior of those times and was asked to take a leave of absence. During this period she lived with her parents in New York City, modeled dresses in the garment industry, and worked in a bank and in a real estate office. She shortly returned to Stanford and obtained her A.B. in psychology in 1930.

Pat Snedden went on to Teachers College in the clinical child psychology program under Goodwin Watson and obtained her M.A. in 1931. She then moved to New Haven (where Robert Sears was a graduate student in psychology at Yale) and took an assistantship with Catherine Cox Miles in which she did very comprehensive testing of psychiatric patients. When Robert Sears completed his Ph.D. in the spring of 1932, they were married. Yale psychophysiological papers appearing in 1932 and 1934 carried both Pauline K. Snedden and Robert R. Sears among many junior authors.

Because of nepotism rules at the University of Illinois, where her husband took a position after getting his degree, there were no job possibilities for Pat

Sears. She took graduate courses, which she enjoyed very much (especially the opportunity to study neurology). She started research on level of aspiration, a long-term thread in her research interests stimulated by contact with Kurt Lewin during an earlier summer visit to Stanford. She gave a paper in 1936 at the American Psychological Association Convention on "The Effect of Success and Failure on Level of Aspiration." In addition she gave birth to their first child, David, in 1935. It was at Illinois that Pat Sears suggested to her husband that he investigate the possibilities of translating Freud's theories into testable learning theory propositions. This approach, enriched by his extensive use of illustrative materials from classic literature, led to his great popularity as a teacher. His researches on projection and repression and his conditioning-based theory of repression, which had stemmed from her suggestion, led to his being invited to return to Yale in 1936.

Back at Yale, Pat Sears entered the psychology program with an emphasis on clinical work, a highly unusual emphasis at Yale at that time. While taking her clinical training she embarked on her classic studies on level of aspiration. Their second child, Nancy, was born in 1938, and Pat Sears received her Ph.D. and was appointed to the psychiatry faculty in 1939. A paper based on her thesis was published in 1940 with a further, more clinical, paper appearing in 1941.

EVALUATION OF MAJOR CONTRIBUTIONS AND ACHIEVEMENTS

The Level of Aspiration Classics

Pat Sears' studies on level of aspiration became classics both because of the characteristics of their subjects and because of their innovative methods. The subjects were selected from a population that enabled generalization to normal, broadly middle-class subjects who were ego-involved in their schoolwork. The tasks used to assess aspiration level were not games or artificial tasks, but real-life (school) reading and arithmetic tasks. Lifelong success and failure, not just success and failure in the experimental situation, was manipulated. This was done by choosing students (fourth, fifth, and sixth graders) whose achievement levels in these areas were either high or low on both reading and arithmetic achievement tests, or high on reading but low on arithmetic. These groups were then presented tasks under success, neutral, or failure conditions.

In addition, the clinical portion could be used to test hypotheses based on the group data. This was possible because Sears individually examined the children with measurements of intelligence, achievement, and emotional-social reactions; collected teacher ratings; developed a self-appraisal scale for the students to rate themselves; and rated the children on various traits following her experiences with them. On the self-appraisal scale students rated themselves both in comparison to their classmates and to how they wished they were themselves. Non-academic activities were found to be clearly separate for each sex: baseball, having lots of male friends, running fast, football, fist-fighting, and being very strong for boys; music, skating, having lots of female friends, drawing, and sewing for girls.

The Iowa Period

The Searses decided to go to the University of Iowa in 1942. Robert Sears had been offered the directorship of the Iowa Child Welfare Research Station. Pat Sears wrote to a colleague and was offered an appointment in the department of psychiatry. On arrival at Iowa her colleagues in psychiatry were informed that antinepotism rules forbade her appointment in psychiatry. She consequently was an unpaid research associate for the seven years that they were there.

At Iowa they embarked on a joint research program that drew upon her clinical skills and the learning and performance concepts he and his interdisciplinary associates at Yale had developed. They focused especially on those aspects of parental behavior that were expected to affect sex-typing and such interpersonal motives as dependency and aggression. As these studies took place during World War II, the effects of father absence on doll play aggression were an important focus of study. Father absence was related to decreased aggression in boys and fewer differences between boys and girls at earlier ages.

This program led to a jointly authored paper (R. R. Sears, Pintler & P. S. Sears, 1946) as well as to her classic monograph (P. S. Sears, 1951). These papers introduced the laboratory use of doll play, a technique that had been (and still is) used clinically. It is now used to assess dependent variables used in research to study the effects of developmental level and family status on the amount of aggression shown by young children. Large numbers of studies by their students and others used this technique and various modifications of it, but it has largely fallen into disuse due to its lack of reliability as a dependent variable when assessing effects of child-rearing behaviors.

The multiple-authored classic monograph on child-rearing antecedents of aggression and dependency (R. R. Sears, Whiting, Nowlis, & P. S. Sears, 1953) was also a product of this period. This work was a precursor to the major study of child rearing and its outcomes that followed in the Harvard period (R. R. Sears, Maccoby, & Levin, 1957). The dyadic relations that were explored in the Iowa monograph were outgrowths of the joint thinking of the Searses. Robert Sears' 1951 presidential address to the APA considered the mother and child as an interacting dyad, each of whom influenced the subsequent behavior of the other. This idea did not permeate developmental psychology for years. (Initially the concern was with the fact that the child influenced the behavior of the parent. Only later did the interactions themselves become the focus of attention.) In recent years the dyadic concepts he set forth in that address have dominated much research in infancy and early childhood, albeit they are no longer couched in learning theory terms.

The team at Iowa included Kurt Lewin, Tamara Dembo, and Leon Festinger, with whom Pat Sears coauthored the important theoretical chapter on level of aspiration in J. McV. Hunt's two-volume work (1944), as well as the coauthors listed on the publications mentioned in the previous paragraphs.

The Harvard Years

In 1949 the Searses moved to Harvard. She found it gratifying that Frank Keppel, the dean of the Harvard Graduate School of Education (HGSE), treated her as a full-fledged professional in seeking her agreement to an appointment at HGSE when he was in Iowa wooing her husband. She was indeed appointed lecturer and research associate, with pay. This must have seemed a great advance over no position or no pay. She was one of many such women with non–tenure-track positions at that institution.

At Harvard Pat Sears taught and was involved in the patterns of child-rearing project and the launching (with Beatrice and John Whiting, who had come via Yale and Iowa) of the cross-cultural study of socialization. Once again she did a study on levels of aspiration, this time in preschool children (P. S. Sears & Levin, 1957).

The Stanford Years

Then in 1953 the Searses returned to Stanford, where she joined the faculty of the School of Education and he chaired the department of psychology. Pat Sears was again gratified to be assured, prior to their joint decision to relocate, that she was needed in the School of Education; she was given a tenure-track position, albeit at the assistant professor level. At this point their careers diverged for a period. She embarked on a series of studies of self-esteem and achievement motivation and their relation to school performance, on mathematics learning in the gifted, and on computer assisted instruction (CAI). She administered the Elementary Teacher Training Program for several years, and she organized the program in child development in the School of Education. She became an associate professor in 1958 and professor in 1966. He had an eighteen-year administrative career, much of it as dean of humanities and sciences.

Much of her work while at Stanford is insufficiently known to the psychological community for two reasons: material in education publications is often overlooked by psychologists, and much of the research appeared only in grant reports and was not published in regular channels. Fortunately, much of it is available through ERIC, as can be seen in the listing of her representative publications.

Her work in the Program for Teaching Effectiveness covered effects on classroom behavior of accelerated math programs, computer assisted instruction, and teaching strategies for effective reinforcement of culturally different children. It was found that CAI had a significant effect on the black males in the program, though not on the females. It appeared that CAI provided more consistent rewards and was less punitive than traditional teacher-taught classes. Another finding was that first grade achievement is less related to behavior in the classroom when there is CAI. This work was methodologically sophisticated and important, but did not at that time lead to a meaningful series of follow-up studies. Indeed, even today, when computers are evident in the classroom, there is not adequate attention to this research or further research in areas identified by it as needing study.

One project, "The Effect of Classroom Conditions on the Strength of Achievement Motive and Work Output on Elementary School Children," was monumental in scope (see P. S. Sears, 1963). It was an attempt to look at the interrelations among six desired outcomes of elementary education and at the classroom conditions or situational variables associated with each. It involved an impressive number of measures of the children, the teachers, and their interactions. Standardized tests, self-reports, systematic observation, experimental tests, teacher ratings, peer nominations, and a projective test (the Thematic Apperception Test) were used.

Some 265 students from ten different self-contained classrooms and their teachers were evaluated in both the fall and spring. There were three first or second grade classes and seven fifth or sixth grade classes. Data analyses focused on the older classes. Their seven teachers had at least three years' experience and ranged in age from twenty-four to forty-three. While all could have been classified as good teachers, it is interesting to note that their teaching styles were highly varied. For example, teachers ranged from 6 percent at one extreme to 71 percent at the other in the amount of attention they directed to individual students rather than the group.

When the children were stratified into sex and ability groups and all of the variables examined, it produced a 246-by-246 variable matrix. The 346-page summary contains findings of interest to anyone concerned with the reform of education or the topic of sex differences. These data predated the strong interest in sex differences that characterized many developmental studies. Her paper (1966) with Feldman also addressed sex differences. It showed that the sex of the child was more important than the sex of the teacher in determining the effects of computer assisted instruction. Its findings and its review of the literature were much quoted and reprinted.

It was case studies from the massive project that constituted the material for *In Pursuit of Self-Esteem* by Sears and Sherman (1964). The review in *Contemporary Psychology* (Rau, 1965) noted that "for [readers] whose primary concern . . . is understanding the reactions of children to the social and intellectual environment of the classroom, this book will prove an invaluable source of information, ideas, and increased sophistication." Rau also stressed the importance of the example of "tact, sophistication and respect which this project exemplifies" and that it should add to understanding that "the child's academic learning cannot be understood or facilitated apart from the interpersonal context in which it occurs."

Shortly after the completion of that project Pat Sears was asked by the American Educational Research Association to edit a volume on intellectual development. The process as well as the product deserves mention. A group of graduate students met in a weekly seminar to discuss possible inclusions, the approach, and the field, and four of them became the editors of the four sections of the book (psychometric intelligence, cognition, problem solving, and language). The fact that the students rose to the challenge and the effectiveness of the intellectual spade work are well reflected in the book's review in *Contemporary Psychology*, "A Collection of Readings Can Be Greater than the Sum of Its Parts" (Hung, 1972). To quote briefly: "It is rich in ideas and is thought provoking because of the way in which the editors have combined these ideas into an intellectual whole."

As the Searses neared retirement they again became research collaborators. In 1972 they performed a follow-up study of the Terman sample of gifted children with Stanford professor Lee Cronbach, a distinguished specialist in measurement and former president of the American Psychological Association. Both of the Searses worked on the analyses of these data. Pat Sears and Ann Barbee published a chapter, "Career and Life Satisfactions Among Terman's Gifted Women," in a book edited by Stanley, George, and Solano (1977), and Bob Sears published a paper on the gifted men in the *American Psychologist* (R. R. Sears, 1977). Health problems curtailed Pat's further work on this project.

Pat Sears likes to point out that Terman's gifted women, when asked in their sixties what life pattern they would choose, overwhelmingly responded, "I'd choose to have a career after raising children." Her fondness for this is related to the fact that Pat Sears sees herself as a "transitional" woman—transitional between being fiercely professional (as many of today's professional women are) and being a homebody. Her mother's absorption in rearing a large family may have played a role in Sears' enjoyment of being, as she says, "a halfway volunteer and mother for a part of her life" and in her lack of a sense of frustration about being in academically peripheral positions for so long.

Pat Sears feels that next to her husband, and perhaps Kurt Lewin, her graduate students have been her most important colleagues and mentors. She was a mentor for many of them, especially at Stanford. Her critical but supportive role, which was not contingent on their working in her research area, was noted by a number of her former students. One envies the small, quiet gestures Pat Sears made that were so informative and helpful. During her Stanford years she frequently reviewed books for *Contemporary Psychology*, an honor since it is done only by invitation.

Their older child, David Sears, became a psychologist prominent in the field of political psychology, and now is a political scientist. Their daughter, Nancy Sears Barker, interrupted her Radcliffe studies to marry the son of another famous psychologist, Roger Barker. She is now an elementary school teacher in Toronto, where her husband is a political scientist. The Searses have six grandchildren.

On the occasion of the American Psychological Foundation's Joint Gold Medal Award, the biography accompanying the award citation provides an apt summary of her contributions:

[She] has applied high scientific standards and rigorous methods to "soft" but important problems; in [her] sustained interest in identification, self-concept . . . and motivational aspects of learning, [she] has kept these topics active during a period when the field . . . had turned to more exclusively cognitive concerns. [She] has been hospitable to ideas from a number of sources, . . . but has not been eclectic; rather [she] has always striven to formulate [her] own work in terms of a coherent body of behavior theory in which the origins of personality are sought in the child's affective relationships. (*American Psychologist*, 1981, p. 91)

NOTE

I am grateful to a number of Pat Sears' students and colleagues from Stanford for discussing their work there and Sears' role as a mentor in their lives with me. Susan B. Crockenberg, David H. Feldman, Lillian G. Katz, and Nancy L. Stein were generous of their time for this purpose.

REFERENCES

American Psychological Foundation (1980). Gold Medal Award citation (1981). *American Psychologist*, *36*, 88–91.

Feldman, D. H., & Sears, P. S. (1970). Effects of computer assisted instruction on children's behavior. *Educational Technology*, *10*, 11–14. An expanded version of this is found in P. S. Sears & D. H. Feldman (1968), *Changes in young children's classroom behavior after a year of computer-assisted instruction: An exploratory study, research memorandum*. Stanford, Calif.: Stanford Center for Research and Development in Teaching. (ERIC Document Reproduction Service No. ED 022 366).

Hunt, J. V. (1972). A collection of readings can be greater than the sum of its parts. [Review of *Intellectual development*. (Readings in Educational Research Series.)] *Contemporary Psychology*, *17*, 287–288.

Lewin, K.; Dembo, T.; Festinger, L.; & Sears, P. S. (1944). Level of aspiration. In J. McV. Hunt (Ed.), *Personality and the behavior disorders*, vol. 1, pp. 333–378. New York: Ronald Press.

Rau, L. (1965). The child as individual. [Review of *In pursuit of self-esteem*]. *Contemporary Psychology*, *10*, 472–473.

Sears, P. S. (1940). Levels of aspiration in academically successful and unsuccessful children. *Journal of Abnormal and Social Psychology*, *35*, 498–536.

Sears, P. S. (1941). Level of aspiration in relation to some variables of personality: Clinical studies. *Journal of Social Psychology*, *14*, 311–336.

Sears, P. S. (1951). Doll play aggression in normal young children: Influence of sex, age, sibling status, father's absence. *Psychological Monographs: General and Applied*, *65*(6), Whole No. 323.

Sears, P. S. (1963). *Achievement motivation and work output in elementary school chil-*

dren. U.S. Office of Education, Project No. OE 873. Stanford, Calif.: Stanford University. (ERIC Document Reproduction Service No. ED 001 136).

Sears, P. S. (1971). *Intellectual development*. (Readings in Educational Research Series.) New York: Wiley.

Sears, P. S. (1988, May 6&7). Personal interview. Palo Alto, Calif.

Sears, P. S., & Barbee, A. (1977). Career and life satisfactions among Terman's gifted women. In J. C. Stanley, W. C. George, & C. H. Solano (Eds.), *The gifted and the creative: A fifty-year perspective* (pp. 28–65). Baltimore: Johns Hopkins University Press.

Sears, P. S., & Feldman, D. H. (1966). *Teachers' interactions with boys and with girls*. (Report No. BR–5–0252–1) Stanford, Calif.: Stanford University. (ERIC Document Reproduction Service No. ED 011 935).

Sears, P. S., & Levin, H. (1957). Levels of aspiration in preschool children. *Child Development, 28*, 317–326.

Sears, P. S., & Sherman, V. (1964). *In pursuit of self-esteem: Case studies of ten elementary school children*. Belmont, Calif.: Wadsworth.

Sears, R. R. (1951). A theoretical framework for personality and social behavior. *American Psychologist, 6*, 476–483.

Sears, R. R. (1977). Sources of life satisfaction of the Terman gifted men. *American Psychologist, 32*, 119–128.

Sears, R. R.; Maccoby, E. E.; & Levin, H. (1957). *Patterns of child rearing.* Stanford, Calif.: Stanford University Press.

Sears, R. R.; Pintler, M. H.; & Sears, P. S. (1946). The effect of father separation on preschool children's doll play aggression. *Child Development, 17*, 219–243.

Sears, R. R.; Whiting, J.W.M.; Nowlis, V.; & Sears, P. S. (1953). Some child-rearing antecedents of aggression and dependency in young children. *Genetic Psychology Monographs, 47*, 135–254.

Snedden, D. (1949). *Recollection of over half a century spent in educational work*. Stanford, Calif.: Stanford University Press.

Snedden, G. S. (1947). *Mountain cattle and frontier people: Stories of the Snedden family 1867 to 1947*. Stanford, Calif.: Stanford University Press.

Additional Representative Publications by Pauline S. Sears

Sears, P. S. (1957). Problems in the investigation of achievement and self-motivation. In M. R. Jones (Ed.), *Nebraska Symposium on Motivation*. Lincoln: University of Nebraska Press.

Sears, P. S. (1972). *Effective reinforcement for achievement behaviors in disadvantaged children: The first year*. (Report No. TR-30) Stanford, Calif.: Stanford University, Stanford Center for Research and Development in Teaching. (ERIC Document Reproduction Service No. ED 067 422).

Sears, P. S., & Dowley, E. (1963). Research on teaching in the nursery school. In N. L. Gage (Ed.), *Handbook of research on teaching*. Chicago, Il.: Rand McNally.

Sears, P. S., & Hilgard, E. R. (1964). The teacher's role in the motivation of the learner. In *Sixty-third Yearbook of the National Society for the Study of Education* (pp. 182–209). Chicago, Il: University of Chicago Press.

Sears, P. S., & Hilgard, E. R. (1970). The teacher's role in the motivation of the learner. In H. F. Clarizio, R. C. Craig, & W. A. Mehrens, (Eds.), *Contemporary Issues in Educational Psychology*, *44*, 562–567.

Sears, P. S.; Katz, L.; & Soderstrum, L. (1966). Psychological development of children participating in a vertically accelerated mathematics program. *Psychology in the Schools*, *3*, 307–318.

Sears, R. R., & Sears, P. S. (1940). Minor studies of aggression: V. Strength of frustration-reaction as a function of strength of drive. *Journal of Psychology*, *9*, 297–300.

VIRGINIA STAUDT SEXTON
(1916–   )

Florence L. Denmark and Nancy Felipe Russo

Virginia Staudt Sexton's contributions to the history and philosophy of psychology, education, teaching and mentoring, and professional service have had a significant impact on psychology. Her numerous books and articles include landmark publications on the history of American and international psychology that have been influential in establishing this field of study and promoting courses at undergraduate and graduate educational levels. A dynamic and inspiring teacher, she has seen many of her students go on to become leaders in psychology. Her involvement in prominent positions in state, regional, national, and international organizations attests to her effective professional leadership on behalf of psychology. In addition to serving on the Board of Directors of the American Psychological Association (APA), other high offices include the position of president in four APA Divisions, the New York State Psychological Association, the Eastern Psychological Association, the American Catholic Psychological Association, Psi Chi, and the International Council of Psychologists. She has been elected Fellow in eight APA divisions. Other recognition includes numerous service awards, including a gold medal from the New York Academy of Sciences.

FAMILY BACKGROUND AND EDUCATION

Virginia Mary Staudt, the youngest of four children, was born in New York City on August 30, 1916. Her father, Philip Henry Staudt, was a special patrol officer for the Interborough Rapid Transit Company. Her mother, Kathryn Philippa (Burkard) Staudt, was a homemaker who before her marriage had been a designer and sample maker of infants' and children's wear. Sexton credits her sister, Florence (older by six years and the only other sibling to survive beyond childhood) with arousing and sustaining her intellectual curiosity, and her parents with providing a nurturing, comfortable, and enriching environment that valued academic achievement.

After graduation from Cathedral High School in New York City in 1933, Virginia Staudt majored in the classics at Hunter College of the City University of New York (CUNY), graduating in 1936. During her senior year of college, she did practice teaching at Hunter College Model Elementary School, Hunter College High School, and George Washington High School.

She obtained her B.A. cum laude and was elected to Phi Beta Kappa and to Eta Sigma Phi, the classics' honor society. When the country was in the middle of the Depression and employment was scarce, she was able to secure a teaching post in a Catholic elementary school, at a salary of $540 per year. Unable to achieve her dream of becoming a high school teacher of Latin or Greek, Staudt decided to supplement her background in classics and enrolled for her master's degree in psychology at the Fordham University Graduate School of Arts and Sciences in February 1938, receiving her degree in June 1941. She then went on to pursue her Ph.D. from September 1942 to June 1946. From 1949 to 1951, she obtained her postdoctoral training in clinical psychology at New York State Psychiatric Institute and in neuroanatomy at Columbia University.

Virginia Staudt's interest in psychology arose from two main sources: her genuine concern for the practical aspects of human behavior, which was stimulated by her studies in literature, and her preparation for the teaching profession. As a student of the classics she became intensely interested in motivation and character portrayal by Sophocles, Aeschylus, and Euripides. This led to an interest in the modern drama of Chekhov, Shaw, Ibsen, O'Neill, Pirandello, and others. Such exposure to a wide variety of personalities stimulated her to probe the puzzle of human behavior and to seek answers in the science of psychology at Fordham University. While working for a master's in psychology, she came under the tutelage and mentoring of Joseph F. Kubis, who advised her in her research, coursework, and writing.

CAREER DEVELOPMENT

On Kubis' recommendation, she obtained her first college teaching assignment in 1944, as lecturer at Notre Dame College of Staten Island. Upon completion of her doctorate in experimental psychology from Fordham University in 1946, she was promoted to assistant professor. During her tenure there (1944–1952) she worked as guidance director, opened a psychology laboratory, developed a psychology major, and was appointed associate professor and chair of the department. Staudt was able to stimulate great interest in her subject and had the rewarding experience of seeing many of her students continue for their master's and doctoral degrees and distinguish themselves as scientists and practitioners of psychology.

A Ford Foundation Faculty Fellowship awarded in 1952 enabled her to undertake postdoctoral work in neuroanatomy and clinical psychology at Columbia University. She also carried out research under the direction of Joseph Zubin at the New York State Psychiatric Institute. This association was fruitful, resulting in a widely cited *Psychological Bulletin* article with Zubin, titled "A Biometric Evaluation of the Somatotherapies in Schizophrenia" (Staudt & Zubin, 1957), that examined the data on the effectiveness of shock therapies and psychosurgery in the treatment of schizophrenia.

In 1953 she resigned from Notre Dame College to accept an instructorship (with a considerable increase in salary) at the Bronx campus of her alma mater, Hunter College. Prior to receiving tenure, and solely because she was a woman, Staudt was required each semester to teach one more course than her male counterparts. After she achieved tenure in 1956 and was elected to serve on the department's Personnel and Budget Committee, Staudt witnessed and fought against discrimination against other women. She was promoted to assistant professor in 1957, associate professor in 1961, and full professor in 1967. In 1968 Hunter's Bronx campus was renamed Herbert H. Lehman College, and she held the rank of professor at Lehman until her retirement in 1979. Subsequently, as a professor emerita, Virginia Staudt Sexton was offered and accepted a position as Distinguished Professor of Psychology at St. John's University in Jamaica, New York. On January 21, 1961, she married Richard J. Sexton, Ph.D., an English professor at Fordham University, who was a widower with four children. With this marriage Sexton faced the challenge of being a stepmother to three girls and one boy ranging from eight to twenty-one years of age. The youngest, Richard Sexton, now holds a Ph.D. in psychology; the second youngest, Mary Sexton, is a doctoral candidate in educational administration.

CONTRIBUTIONS AND ACHIEVEMENTS

Virginia Staudt Sexton's scholarly and professional contributions have had a significant impact on psychology. The remarkable quality of this impact is the close link between Sexton's intellectual interests and organizational involvement.

History and Philosophy of Psychology

Virginia Sexton's contributions in the history and philosophy of psychology— national and international—have received widespread recognition for preserving and shaping the personal and intellectual history and status of psychology around the world. This work includes more than one hundred articles, a monograph, and six books, five coauthored with her longtime friend and collaborator, Henryk Misiak (Misiak & Staudt, 1954; Misiak & Sexton, 1966, 1973; Sexton & Misiak, 1971, 1976).

Sexton's early work in the history of psychology, reflected in her book *Catholics in Psychology: A Historical Survey* (Misiak & Staudt, 1954), explored contributions of Catholics to the development of psychology. That book, which was so well received that it was translated into Spanish (Misiak & Staudt, 1955), was published at a time when it was held in some circles that psychology and Catholicism were incompatible. It was highly influential in altering that viewpoint.

Sexton became recognized as a critical link in the communication between psychology and Catholicism, serving as a bridge between the two in writings, numerous lectures to Catholic groups (including parent-teacher and alumni associations), and participation in professional organizations. In this work she drew attention to the contributions of Catholic psychologists, including Edward A. Pace, the first American Catholic and priest to study with Wilhelm Wundt (Sexton, 1962, 1980). She provided biographies of twenty-three psychologists for the *New Catholic Encyclopedia* (Sexton, 1967). She translated the research on adolescence for Catholic parents (Sexton, 1964, 1965a). She was also active in the American Catholic Psychological Association (ACPA), working to help Catholics become aware of psychology and to facilitate employment opportunities for Catholic psychologists (Staudt, 1955; Sexton, 1965b). In recognition of her prodigious contributions, service, and leadership, she was elected to the presidency of that organization (1964–1965).

In 1976, in large part due to the efforts of Virginia Sexton and William Bier (Sexton, 1980), ACPA members voted to affiliate with the American Psychological Association, and Division 36—Psychologists Interested in Religious Issues—was born, with Sexton serving as its first elected president. In 1977 that organization honored her with a special award "in recognition of dedicated service and outstanding contributions to the founding of this Division." In 1987 she was also the first recipient of a distinguished service award presented by that division.

Sexton's involvement in religious issues reflected and was reflected in efforts to preserve psychology's philosophical roots and to integrate psychology and philosophy. Her book *Phenomenological, Existential, and Humanistic Psychologies* (Misiak & Sexton, 1973) clearly explained these relatively new and frequently misunderstood topics in modern psychology and countered the view that the purview of psychology was confined to the experimental laboratory. Her interest in philosophy is also seen in *History and Philosophy of Science: Selected Papers* (Dauben & Sexton, 1983).

Sexton served as president of APA's Division of Philosophical Psychology in 1975–1976 and as president of the Division of Humanistic Psychology in 1979–1980. In her presidential address delivered for the former group (Sexton, 1978), Sexton pointed to the rise in cognitive psychology after World War II and psychology's "rediscovery of the mind," saying, "There has never been a more propitious time in the last century than at present for a reconciliation with philosophy and the development of psychology as a human science. Accordingly, psychologists in America need to rethink their definition of the subject matter, methodology, and practice of psychology" (p. 3). In what she termed "a call to arms" for philosophical psychologists, she set out her vision of psychology: one that focuses on humans, that includes inner experience as well as overt behavior, and that is guided by conceptual frameworks.

Sexton viewed herself primarily as a textbook writer and teacher, and the link between her historical interests and those related to education is found in the Misiak and Sexton text *History of Psychology: An Overview* (1966), a landmark work still widely used in psychology history courses. This text surveyed, from the time of the early Greeks to the mid-twentieth century, the development of psychology as a science and profession. It helped create the field of the history of psychology and was influential in establishing the legitimacy of courses in the history of psychology, courses that are now mandated by accreditation requirements in the core curriculum of graduate programs in clinical, counseling, and school psychology.

Commitment to the quality of teaching of the psychology history course was also expressed in the book *Historical Perspectives in Psychology: Readings* (Sexton & Misiak, 1971), which differed from the usual readings in that it presented articles by modern American psychologists, such as E. G. Boring, B. F. Skinner, and R. I. Watson, addressing theoretical and practical problems relevant to psychology.

Through the publication of brief biographies in the *Dictionary of Behavioral Science* (Sexton, 1973), Sexton has also played a role in preserving and communicating the contributions of twenty-two key contributors to psychology, including Mary W. Calkins, Christine Ladd-Franklin, Karen Horney, and Margaret F. Washburn.

In 1965, Virginia Sexton served on the first Board of Advisors for the Archives of the History of American Psychology at the University of Akron, which John Popplestone planned and implemented with the help of APA's newly formed Division of the History of Psychology (Division 26). The archives became accepted as *the* repository for papers of individual psychologists and organizations other than APA itself (Watson, 1974). Sexton's activities in Division 26 led to her election to the positions of secretary-treasurer (1972–1978), and president (1979–1980).

Believing that psychologists must develop an international vision of their field, Sexton has been a leader in promoting international issues in psychology. Her book *Psychology Around the World* (Sexton & Misiak, 1976) was the first to explore in detail the status of psychology in thirty-one countries in Africa, Asia, Europe, Latin America, and Oceania. It has served as a valuable reference source for subsequent investigators in international psychology and is now under revision. Sexton participated in the development of Cheiron, the International Society for the History of the Behavioral and Social Sciences, serving as one of the co-hosts of the third meeting of that organization in 1971. Sexton also held a number of positions in the International Council of Psychologists, including that of president (1981–1982). She served as a liaison between that organization and APA beginning in 1983 and was subsequently appointed to APA's Committee on International Relations (1985).

In her inclusion of women in the portrayal of the history of psychology, Sexton anticipated the interest in women's history in psychology that bloomed in the 1970s and 1980s (cf. Bernstein & Russo, 1974; O'Connell, Alpert, Richardson, Rotter, Ruble & Unger, 1978; Denmark, 1980; O'Connell & Russo, 1980, 1983, 1988; Russo & Denmark, 1987; Scarborough & Furumoto, 1987). In the 1960s, she drew attention to the work of early women in psychology in articles for international audiences (Sexton, 1969, 1974), highlighting such greats as Calkins, Ladd-Franklin, and Washburn. She continues to have an interest in the history and status of women psychologists around the world (Ribarich & Sexton, 1988).

At the 1967 meeting of APA Sexton presented a paper dealing with the characteristics and roles of women psychologists, the first in a number of lectures, panels, and discussions that she would present related to that topic over the years at APA, regional associations, and especially the New York State Psychological Association (NYSPA). In 1983 the NYSPA Committee on Women formally recognized Sexton's service to women in that organization.

This interest in women's issues extended to other scholarly writing and was expressed in a chapter (Sexton, 1968) on the meaning of psychological fulfillment for women, which she defined as the development and realization of one's potentialities. In that chapter she wrote: "One principle must be the enduring keystone of a woman's psychological structure: There is not *only no one role for* all women, but there is rarely, and certainly *not* necessarily, *one single role* for any given individual woman" (p. 256). In that article Sexton considered the implications of women's changing roles, pointing to the need for business to change as well: "[Women] must be given better job opportunities, opportunities in keeping with their talents and training. Perhaps even more importantly, they must be compensated on the principle of equal pay for equal talents and training" (p. 259).

Education, Teaching, and Mentoring

Sexton's view of undergraduate education went beyond lecture and textbook sources. She was among the first persons to advocate the use of films, field trips, psychology clubs, career forums, and participation in psychological research to enhance the teaching of psychology (Staudt, 1951). She also wrote a number of articles directed toward the education and training of teachers (Staudt, 1956a, 1956b, 1957) and promoted psychology's involvement in adult education (Johnson & Staudt, 1957a, 1957b) and business communication (Sexton & Staudt, 1955, 1958, 1959).

Throughout her CUNY years, Virginia Staudt Sexton encouraged and fostered the professional growth of her students and younger colleagues with boundless energy and enthusiasm. During her tenure there she taught and mentored many students who later became distinguished in diverse subfields of psychology, including Ellen Bloch, clinical psychologist; Mary Corcoran, educational psychologist; Richard Lerner, developmental psychologist; Lawrence Marks, professor of epidemiology and psychology; Raymond Millimet, director of graduate training at the University of Nebraska (Omaha); and Lenore Walker, the recipient of the 1987 APA Distinguished Contribution to Psychology in the Public Interest Award for her work on battered women.

Interest and concern for students was also expressed in her service as chair of the Middle Atlantic District of Phi Beta Kappa (1976–1979) and in her involvement with Psi Chi, psychology's undergraduate honor society, which included holding the office of national president in 1986–1987. Under her presidency, Psi Chi established the Psi Chi/Florence L. Denmark Faculty Advisor Award.

Community activities have reflected her commitment to educational issues as well. Sexton served on the Advisory Council on Psychology of the New York State Education Department (1967–1971) and on the Mayor's Advisory Committee on Appointments to the Board of Higher Education (1971–1973).

Professional Leadership and Service

Sexton's professional leadership has resulted in her election to high office in a remarkable number and variety of state, regional, national, and international professional organizations. A theme throughout her leadership activities is the understanding and application of psychological knowledge and the promotion of bridges across boundaries, whether they be of gender, ethnicity, discipline, or geography.

Sexton's international and cross-cultural experiences were reflected in her commitment to ethnic minorities in psychology, and she became known as an advocate for those issues in her university as well as nationally. At St. John's University she served on the Minority Students Advisory Committee; in the American Psychological Association she was the Board of Directors' liaison to the Board of Ethnic Minority Affairs. She supported the organization of the Society for the Psychological Study of Ethnic Minority issues, becoming one of its first members to achieve Fellow status in recognition of her contribution to ethnic minority and cross-cultural psychology, and subsequently serving on its 1989 Fellows Committee to select others.

In addition, Sexton held leadership positions in the prestigious New York Academy of Sciences, including chair of the Section on Psychology (1966–1967), chair of the Section on History, Philosophy, and Ethical Issues of Science and Technology, and vice president and member of the Board of Governors, where she worked to advance the understanding and application of psychology across scientific fields.

Recognition of her significant contributions in the history of psychology led to her appointment as editor of the History and Systems of Psychology Section of the *International Encyclopedia of Neurology, Psychoanalysis, Psychiatry, and Psychology* (Sexton, 1977), where she assigned and edited 281 articles for this fundamental reference work. Sexton also served as associate editor for *Psychological Abstracts*, as a member of the editorial boards of six journals, including the *Journal of Phenomenological Psychology*, *Journal of Mind and Behavior*, *Professional Psychology: Research and Practice*, and the *Humanistic*

Psychologist, and as a member of the Obituary Selection Committee of the *American Psychologist*.

CRITICAL EVALUATION OF CONTRIBUTIONS AND ACHIEVEMENTS

In the foreword to her first book, *Catholics in Psychology: A Historical Survey* (Misiak & Staudt, 1954), E. G. Boring, a historian of psychology, called the work

an excellent account of the contributions of Catholics to scientific psychology during the years of its inception, growth, and establishment. [Misiak and Stuadt] have worked from original sources with great care and they [have] made an important contribution to the history of modern psychology, not only by their description of the achievements of Catholic psychologists, but also by the vivid settings which they provide for the little-known work of such countries as Italy, Poland, and Spain (P. xi)

In a review of *History of Psychology: An Overview* (Misiak & Sexton, 1966), Josef Brozek (1968) singled out the book as especially important for its range of presentation of topics such as psychology in Asia and the development of new areas in clinical psychology, topics that were not covered in the available textbooks of the history of psychology at the time. In 1971 this volume was also included in the *Harvard List of Books of Psychology*, a prestigious source compiled and annotated by psychologists at Harvard University. It is described as "the broadest in scope of any of the histories" and as having "excellent complete bibliographies" (p. 10). Similarly, in 1974 Ruben Ardila, a distinguished Latin American psychologist, cited this same volume in a listing of one hundred books of psychology emphasizing works having the greatest influence on the development of the field.

Sherman Ross' review (1978) of Sexton and Misiak's book *Psychology Around the World* (1976) stated that "Sexton and Misiak have made a contribution by their organizational and editorial efforts." Ross also recommended that the volume "should be stocked by college and university libraries" and predicted that "the book will be used for the specific chapter entries by individuals seeking information on those countries . . . the book in its entirety is a positive contribution." Moreover, this volume was cited by Over (1984) as "the major source of information in the English language about national psychologies" (p. 2). In their 1987 *International Handbook of Psychology*, Gilgen and Gilgen also observed that this volume is "the most significant publication relative to the internationalizing of psychology" and "the first extensive collection of perspectives on psychology in many different countries compiled by North American psychologists" (p. 6).

As a tribute to her contributions as a psychologist, Virginia Staudt Sexton was asked to write an autobiography for the "Focus on the Psychologist" section of Richard M. Lerner, Philip C. Kendall, Dale T. Miller, David F. Hultsch, and Robert A. Jensen's book, *Psychology* (1986).

Through her writings, editorial activities, and organizational leadership, Virginia Staudt Sexton has played a critical role as gatekeeper in the definition, interpretation, and preservation of psychological knowledge in diverse subfields of the discipline. Her sustained and outstanding contributions across subfields have been recognized in her election to Fellow status in eight APA divisions: General Psychology, Teaching of Psychology, Theoretical and Philosophical Psychology, History of Psychology, State Psychological Association Affairs, Psychology of Women, Psychologists Interested in Religious Issues, and the Society for the Psychological Study of Ethnic Minority Issues. She is also a Fellow of the American Association for the Advancement of Science and of the New York Academy of Sciences.

In recognition of her many achievements, Sexton has received numerous other honors, including the Wilhelm Wundt Award from the Academic Division of the New York State Psychological Association (1987). She also received a gold medal from the New York Academy of Sciences in 1982 for service as a member of the Board of Governors (1977–1979) and vice president (1980–1982). Her autobiography has also been included in publications featuring distinguished psychologists (Sexton, 1983, 1984).

In 1980, when Sexton was awarded an honorary doctorate of humane letters by Cedar Crest College in Allentown, Pennsylvania, her ground-breaking service as a role model was captured by President Gene Caesari, who said while conferring the degree: "You never lost sight of the fact that women are capable of being thoroughly competent professionals and scientists. Before there was a self-conscious feminist movement you were living, writing, and saying that women could be mothers and active family members, and highly skilled professionals as well."

While Virginia Staudt Sexton's many contributions and achievements received formal national and international recognition, an informal communication written by Margaret E. Donnelly, a psychology faculty member at Pace University, New York, on January 4, 1989, exemplifies the personal esteem in which Sexton is held by her colleagues.

I regard Virginia Staudt Sexton as the ideal role model for students, especially women, aspiring to professional careers. Her own impressive professional accomplishments in terms of numerous publications, offices held in psychological associations, local, national, and international, all attest to "practicing what she preaches" ... her students ... find her an unfailing source of encouragement and inspiration. . . . She is truly an exemplary role model.

REFERENCES

Ardila, R. (1974). Los 100 libros de psicologia mas importantes. *Revista Latinoamerica de Psicologia, 6*, 197–227.

Bernstein, M. D., & Russo, N. F. (1974). The history of psychology revisited: Or, up with our foremothers. *American Psychologist, 29*, 130–134.

Brozek, J. (1968). History of psychology: Variations on a theme. *Contemporary Psychology, 13*(5), 246–262.

Dauben, J., & Sexton, V. S. (Eds.). (1983). *History and philosophy of science: Selected papers*, New York: Annals of the New York Academy of Sciences.

Denmark, F. L. (1980). Psyche: From rocking the cradle to rocking the boat. *American Psychologist, 35*, 1057–1065.

Gilgen, A. R., & Gilgen, C. K. (1987). *International handbook of psychology.* New York: Greenwood Press.

Johnson, L. S., & Staudt, V. S. (1957a). Let's get into adult education. *American Psychologist, 12*, 228.

Johnson, L. S., & Staudt, V. S. (1957b). Adult education is the psychologist's business. *Journal of Genetic Psychology, 91*, 147–148.

Lerner, R. M. (Ed.). (1983). *Developmental psychology: Historical and philosophical perspectives.* Hillsdale, N.J.: L. Erlbaum.

Lerner, R. M.; Kendall, P.; Miller, D.; Hultsch, D.; & Jensen, R. (1986). *Psychology.* New York: Macmillan.

Misiak, H., & Sexton, V. S. (1966). *History of psychology: An overview.* New York: Grune & Stratton.

Misiak, H., & Sexton, V. S. (1973). *Phenomenological, existential, and humanistic psychologies: A historical survey.* New York: Grune & Stratton.

Misiak, H., & Staudt, V. S. (1954). *Catholics in psychology: A historical survey.* New York: McGraw-Hill.

Misiak, H., & Staudt, V. S. (1955). *Los Catolicas y la psicologia: Anotaciones historicas* (Spanish translation of Misiak & Sexton, 1954).

O'Connell, A. N.; Alpert, J.; Richardson, M. S.; Rotter, N.; Ruble, D. N.; & Unger, R. K. (1978). Gender-specific barriers to research in psychology: Report of the Task Force on Women Doing Research—APA Division 35. *Journal Supplement Abstract Service: Catalog of Selected Documents in Psychology* (MS No. 1753) 8.

O'Connell, A. N., & Russo, N. F. (Eds.). (1980). *Eminent women in psychology.* New York: Human Sciences Press.

O'Connell, A. N., & Russo, N. F. (Eds.). (1983). *Models of achievement: Reflections of eminent women in psychology.* New York: Columbia University Press.

O'Connell, A. N. & Russo, N. F. (Eds.). (1988). *Models of achievement: Reflections of eminent women in psychology.* Vol. 2. Hillsdale, N.J.: Erlbaum.

Over, R. (1984). Psychology and psychologists in Europe: A bibliography of English language publications. *Psychological documents*, MS no. 2638.

Ribarich, M. T., & Sexton, V. S. (1988). The status of women psychologists around the world: Report of a survey. *International Psychologist, 29*, 22–24.

Ross, S. (1978). Psychology: Africa to the United Kingdom. *Contemporary Psychology, 23*, 405–406.

Russo, N. F., & Denmark, F. L. (1987). Contributions of women to psychology. *Annual Review of Psychology, 38*, 279–298.

Scarborough, E., & Furumoto, L. (1987). *Untold lives: The first generation of women psychologists.* New York: Columbia University Press.

Sexton, V. S. (1962). Pioneer priest psychologist. *Bulletin Albertus Magnus Guild*, *9*, 1–3.

Sexton, V. S. (1964). Adolescence—Perspectives for 1965. *Summary Proceedings of the Annual Meeting of the Catholic Guidance Council*, Archdiocese of New York.

Sexton, V. S. (1965a). The adolescent in the affluent society of the sixties: A sketch. *National Catholic Guidance Conference Journal*, *9*, 143–155.

Sexton, V. S. (1965b). Catholics in psychology: 1965. (Presidential Address to the American Catholic Psychological Association). *Catholic Psychological Record*, *3*, 81–86.

Sexton, V. S. (1967). Twenty-three biographies published in *The new Catholic encyclopedia*. New York: McGraw-Hill.

Sexton, V. S. (1968). Psychological fulfillment for the woman. In W. C. Bier (Ed.), *Women in the modern world*. New York: Fordham University Press.

Sexton, V. S. (1969). Women's accomplishments in American psychology: A brief survey. *Pakistan Journal of Psychology*, *2*, 29–35.

Sexton, V. S. (1973). Twenty-two biographies and one autobiographical entry in B. B. Wolman (Ed.), *Dictionary of Behavioral Science*, New York: Van Nostrand Reinhold.

Sexton, V. S. (1974). Women in American psychology: An overview. *International Understanding*, *9/10*, 66–67.

Sexton, V. S. (1977). Eight biographies in B. B. Wolman (Ed.), *International Encyclopedia of Neurology, Psychoanalysis, Psychiatry, and Psychology*. New York: Van Nostrand Reinhold.

Sexton, V. S. (1978). American psychology and philosophy, 1876–1976: Alienation and reconciliation. *Journal of General Psychology*, *99*, 3–18.

Sexton, V. S. (1980). William C. Bier, S. J. (1911–1980). *Newsletter of APA Div. 36*, *5*(2), 2–3.

Sexton, V. S. (1983). Autobiography. In B. B. Wolman (Ed.), *International encyclopedia of neurology, psychoanalysis, psychiatry, and psychology*. New York: Aesculapius (First Progress Volume).

Sexton, V. S. (1984). Autobiography. In R. Corsini (Ed.), *Wiley encyclopedia of psychology* (pp. 309–310). New York: Wiley.

Sexton, V. S., & Misiak, H. (1971). *Historical perspectives in psychology: Readings*. Belmont, Calif.: Brooks/Cole.

Sexton, V. S., & Misiak, H. (1976). *Psychology around the world*. Monterey, Calif.: Brooks/Cole.

Sexton, R., & Staudt, V. S. (1955). The communication clinic approach: A proposed solution to the business communication problem. *Journal of General Psychology*, *60*, 57–62. Reprinted in W. C. Redding & G. A. Sanborn (1964), *Business and Industrial Communication: A source book*. New York: Harper & Row.

Sexton, R., & Staudt, V. S. (1958). Can the schools help industry with communications? *Education*, *78*, 1–3.

Sexton, R., & Staudt, V. S. (1959). Business communication: A survey of the literature. *Journal of Social Psychology*, *56*, 101–118.

Staudt, V. S. (1951). The use of extracurricular training facilities in undergraduate departments of psychology. *Journal of Psychology*, *31*, 29–35.

Staudt, V. S. (1955, May). Opportunities for Catholic psychologists in research and service. *American Catholic Psychological Association Newsletter*, Supplement No. 15.

Staudt, V. S. (1956a). Graduate seminar for teachers of psychology. *Psychological Reports*, *2*, 309.

Staudt, V. S. (1956b). Character formation is the teacher's business. *Education*, *77*, 1–5.

Staudt, V. S. (1957). Graduate schools ought to train teachers of psychology. *Journal of Genetic Psychology*, *90*, 271–274.

Staudt, V. S., & Zubin, J. (1957). A biometric evaluation of the somatotherapies in schizophrenia. *Psychological Bulletin*, *54*, 171–196.

Watson, R. L. (1974). The history of psychology as a specialty: A personal view of its first fifteen years. Paper presented at the annual meeting of Cheiron, the International Society for the History of the Behavioral Sciences, Durham, N.H., May 31–June 2, 1974.

Additional Representative Publications by Virginia Staudt Sexton

Sexton, V. S. (1965). Clinical psychology: An historical survey. *Genetic Psychology Monographs*, *72*, 401–434.

Sexton, V. S. (1982a). Intimacy, a historical perspective. In M. Fisher & G. Stricker (Eds.), *Intimacy*, (pp. 1–20). New York: Plenum Press.

Sexton, V. S. (1982b). A view of contemporary psychology from the United States. In V. Pecjak (Ed.), *Znameniti psihologia psiholoji* (Psychologists about psychology) (pp. 255–256). Ljubljana: Cankarjeva Zalozba. (In Serbo-Croatian).

Sexton, V. S. (1983). Humanistic psychology in the United States. In G. Bittner (Ed.), *Festschrift in honor of Ludwig Pongratz* (pp. 72–83). Göttingen: C. J. Hogrefe.

Sexton, V. S. (1986). Psychology and religion: Some accomplishments and challenges. *Journal of Psychology and Christianity*, *5*, 78–83.

Sexton, V. S, & Misiak, H. (1984). American psychologists and psychology abroad. *American Psychologist*, *39*, 1026–1031.

CAROLYN WOOD SHERIF
(1922–1982)

Maria E. Vegega and Margaret L. Signorella

Carolyn Wood Sherif made substantive contributions to both the fields of social psychology and the psychology of women. Her approach to social psychology and to the study of social problems was distinctive in its interdisciplinary scope and its focus on significant human and scientific problems. Together with Muzafer Sherif, she conducted seminal work in the study of intergroup relations, delineating the conditions for group formation, competition, and cooperation. Sherif's social judgment/involvement approach to the study of attitudes was one of her most widely recognized contributions. This work, together with her work on the self-system, became instrumental in her contributions to the psychology of women. Her critical examination of traditional methodologies and theories in psychology and her ability to integrate scientific knowledge led to her proposals for new ways to study the complex relationships among gender, social power, and the self-system. Carolyn Sherif occupied leadership positions in the American Psychological Association (APA) and in APA's Division on the Psychology of Women (Division 35). Her many honors include the Association for Women in Psychology's Distinguished Publication Award (1980) and the American Psychological Foundation's Award for Distinguished Contributions to Education in Psychology (1982).

FAMILY BACKGROUND AND EDUCATION

Carolyn Wood, born in Loogootee, Indiana, on June 26, 1922, grew up in Indiana, the youngest of three children. In her autobiography (C. W. Sherif, 1983), she recalled that her parents expected academic achievement and encouraged her ambitions. Financial considerations limited her college options to Purdue University, where her father was a supervisor for teacher training in agricultural education. Consequently, after graduating from West Lafayette High School in 1940, toward the end of the Great Depression, Carolyn Wood entered Purdue University.

Although Wood's father had once hoped that she would have a career in home economics, she instead entered an experimental program for women science majors at Purdue. The program, which included eight semesters of specially designed classes in science and mathematics, encouraged the study of science within historical and humanist perspectives. Wood's other classes included history and literature, but little psychology. When she later asked herself how she became a social psychologist, she cited her amazement over the sudden change in attitudes from isolationism to war support at the beginning of World War II, her own desire to succeed and to better the world, and her realization that these goals could be pursued through scientific research in social psychology (C. W. Sherif, 1983, p. 282). Thus, after obtaining a B.S. in 1943 with highest distinction, Wood went to graduate school at the State University of Iowa to study social psychology.

At the State University of Iowa, Carolyn Wood was influenced by her reading of F. C. Bartlett and Muzafer Sherif. While working on a master's thesis on the effects of prejudice on serial recall, she read Muzafer Sherif's book *The Psychology of Social Norms* (1936). Years later she was to recall that, after reading the book, she went around telling anyone who would listen, "That's the kind of social psychologist I want to be" (C. W. Sherif, 1983, p. 283).

In 1944, after having completed work for her master's degree, Wood moved to Princeton to work at Audience Research, Inc., a Gallup organization. To her disappointment, the research was primarily commercial, such as collecting data about planned Hollywood movies. After a "Monday morning declaration of love" by the research director, Wood decided to leave the field of survey research. She wrote to Hadley Cantril, requesting advice on applying to graduate schools. Not long afterwards, Cantril called to ask her to apply for a research assistantship with Muzafer Sherif at Princeton. The effect of Wood's meeting with Muzafer Sherif is delightfully described in her autobiography: she was so taken up in meeting Sherif, whose work had inspired her and "who espoused social psychology and male-female equality with equal fervor," that when asked by Sherif how far she wanted to go in social psychology, she replied, "All the way" (C. W. Sherif, 1983, p. 284).

CAREER DEVELOPMENT

In December 1945, Carolyn Wood and Muzafer Sherif were married, thus embarking on a personal and professional partnership. As Princeton would not accept women as graduate students, Sherif took courses at Columbia. At the same time, she collaborated with Muzafer Sherif in their work on intergroup relations (M. Sherif & C. W. Sherif, 1953), attitudes and social judgment, and in writing a joint text (M. Sherif & C. W. Sherif, 1956). It was also during these years that their three daughters were born: Sue in 1947, Joan in 1950, and Ann in 1955. Thus, within a short period of time Carolyn Sherif assumed the roles of research collaborator, wife, mother, and student in a world and a profession that did not accept such multiple roles for women (Shaffer & Shields, 1984).

Although Carolyn Sherif held no regular academic positions between 1947 and 1958, she was actively engaged in research with her husband both during their time at Yale and, after 1949, at the University of Oklahoma in Norman. In her autobiography (1983), she describes her work during these years as among her most exciting. Despite her contributions to seminal research in social psychology, her work often went unnoticed, due in part to the eminence of Muzafer Sherif (Shaffer & Shields, 1984). In her autobiographical sketch, Carolyn Sherif poignantly described the effect this had on her:

In several instances, when Muzafer asked me to appear as co-author, instead of in footnote or preface, I declined, a tendency that persisted into the 1960s. I would not do so again. I now believe that the world which viewed me as a wife who probably typed her husband's papers (which I did not) defined me to myself more than I realized. (C. W. Sherif, 1983, p. 286)

Carolyn Sherif's lack of recognition is further illustrated by the fact that, although she is first author of *Attitude and Attitude Change*, her "authorship . . . is to be found 'corrected' in several references by listing Muzafer first" (C. W. Sherif, 1983, p. 287).

In 1958 Carolyn Sherif returned to graduate school at the University of Texas. Again, she was juggling multiple roles: full-time student, author, researcher, wife, and mother of three daughters (the youngest of whom was three years old). In her autobiography, Sherif describes, in a way that only she could do, the conflicting strains and stresses these differing roles placed upon her. In 1961 Carolyn Sherif completed her Ph.D. under Wayne Holtzman, thus obtaining her "union card," as Muzafer Sherif called it.

From 1959 to 1965 Carolyn Sherif held the position of research associate at the Institute of Group Relations at the University of Oklahoma. Between 1961 and 1965 the Sherifs published four books: *Intergroup Conflict and Cooperation: The Robbers Cave Experiment* (M. Sherif, Harvey, White, Hood, & C. W. Sherif, 1961); *Reference Groups: Exploration into Conformity and Deviation of Adolescents* (M. Sherif & C. W. Sherif, 1964); *Problems of Youth* (M. Sherif & C. W. Sherif, 1965); and *Attitude and Attitude Change* (C. W. Sherif, M. Sherif, & Nebergall, 1965). During these years following the Ph.D., Carolyn Sherif was also asked to teach on an adjunct basis, first by the Oklahoma Medical School and then by the Department of Sociology at the University of Oklahoma.

In 1965 Carolyn and Muzafer Sherif were invited to the Pennsylvania State University as visiting faculty—she in psychology and he in sociology. A year later, both assumed tenure-track positions in their respective departments. According to Sherif (1983) this was "the first and only opportunity for both of us" (p. 287). Except for a year as visiting professor at Cornell University (1969–1970) and a semester at Smith College (1979), Carolyn Sherif remained at Penn State until her untimely death.

Following her year as visiting faculty at Cornell University, Carolyn Sherif was promoted to full professor. In reflecting on the delayed recognition of her achievement, Sherif observed that she may have remained an associate professor had not the women's movement revitalized questions of inequity in women's opportunities. During these years, her interest in gender issues increased and she began to apply her social psychological framework to understanding gender in terms of the self-system, reference groups, and power, status, and role relationships.

In her final decade of life, Sherif's contributions gained long overdue recognition. In 1976 she was elected to the status of Fellow in the American Psychological Association and in 1980 was awarded the Association for Women in Psychology's Distinguished Publication Award for her book chapter on bias in psychology (C. W. Sherif, 1979). She also received a Psi Chi Certificate of Recognition in 1980 and the Pennsylvania State University College of Liberal Arts' Alumni Distinction in the Social Sciences Award in 1982. She was elected a Sigma XI National Honor Society national lecturer from 1981 to 1983, lecturing on the topic of intergroup conflict and cooperation. In 1981 she served as a G. Stanley Hall Lecturer on social psychology, and in 1982 the Association of Women in Psychology nominated Carolyn Sherif for the American Psychological Foundation's Award for Distinguished Contributions to Education in Psychology. Although she knew that she was to receive the award, she died prior to its presentation. Carolyn Sherif has been listed in *Who's Who of American Women*, *American Men and Women of Science*, *Who's Who in the Eastern United States*, and *Who's Who in America* (Mednick & Russo, 1983).

The professional community was also served by Carolyn Sherif. Her service to the American Psychological Association (APA) included participation on the Program Innovations Subcommittee of the Board of Convention Affairs and on the Subcommittee on Continuing Education of the Education and Training Board. In these capacities, she was instrumental in initiating APA's Master Lecture Series. Sherif was also a member of APA's Committee on Academic Freedom and Conditions of Employment, APA's Policy and Planning Board, and the Council of Representatives of Division 9, the Society for the Psychological Study of Social Issues. In 1982 she was appointed editor of the *Journal of Social Issues*; regrettably, she did not live to assume the position.

Carolyn Sherif made both substantive and leadership contributions to the field of the psychology of women. In addition to her research and critiques of psychology, she served as consulting editor for *Psychology of Women Quarterly* from its inception in 1977 until her death. She was a leader in APA's Division on the Psychology of Women (Division 35), serving as a member of its Executive Committee (1975–1981) and chairing the Task Force on Affirmative Action (1976–1977). She also served on both the Fellows (1976–1977) and Governance (1977–1978) committees, and served as program chair for the 1978 APA Convention. She was elected president of the division for the 1979–1980 term. As testament to Carolyn Sherif's leadership and contributions to the psychology of women, Division 35 established an award in her honor.

In terms of the university community, Carolyn Sherif taught both undergraduate and graduate courses in social psychology, social research, group processes, attitude and attitude change, and adolescent psychology. She was instrumental in the development of a course on psychology and women and in the formation of the Women's Studies Program at Penn State. Finally, Carolyn Sherif served on a myriad of university-, college-, and department-level committees (e.g., faculty search committees, women's advisory committee, curriculum and program review).

MAJOR CONTRIBUTIONS AND ACHIEVEMENTS

Together, the Sherifs developed a singular and coherent approach to social psychology and to the study of social problems. They argued that human behavior could best be understood by studying the setting in which the behavior takes place, the presence of other individuals, the tasks or activities undertaken by the individuals, and cultural values and norms. Such a conceptual framework recognized the importance of both past and present experiences, and provided a unifying thread for the study and understanding of social issues, social change, attitude change, intergroup relations, and individual behavior in times of uncertainty. Within this framework, the Sherifs preferred to study significant social and scientific problems that did not always lend themselves to quick, simple research designs. Thus, their work was interdisciplinary in scope at a time when such a perspective was not necessarily accepted in psychology.

One of Carolyn Sherif's earliest research contributions is now known as the Robbers Cave study (M. Sherif, Harvey, White, Hood, & C. W. Sherif, 1961; also described in M. Sherif & C. W. Sherif, 1969, Ch. 11, and C. W. Sherif, 1976, Ch. 5). In a series of studies conducted at boys' summer camps, the conditions associated with the formation of in-groups and out-groups and the generation and reduction of intergroup conflict were examined. The results provided hope for the elimination of intergroup conflict and prejudice by demonstrating that working toward *superordinate goals* (i.e., goals desired by members of both groups but obtainable only through the cooperation of both groups) eventually eliminated the conflicts that had arisen between groups of boys at the camp. General and social psychology texts continue to cite the Robbers Cave study twenty years later. In a poll of editors of social psychology journals, this study was among the six most frequently cited as an empirical work that had made a significant and innovative contribution to the field (Diamond & Morton, 1978).

Sherif's interest in group behavior continued with her work on adolescent groups, described in the book *Reference Groups* (M. Sherif & C. W. Sherif, 1964). In this research, participant-observers were trained to establish relationships with existing adolescent groups and to observe the role and status relationships within the groups, as well as norms regulating acceptable and unacceptable behavior within the groups. According to Shaffer and Shields

(1984), Muzafer Sherif credited Carolyn Sherif with "the leading role in planning, designing, analyzing, and interpreting the research" (p. 177). Reviewers have praised this work for its innovative methodology and interdisciplinary focus (Ausubel, 1965; Mack, 1965).

The research on attitudes from the framework of the self-system that was published in *Attitude and Attitude Change* (C. W. Sherif, M. Sherif, & Nebergall, 1965) became one of Sherif's most widely recognized contributions. Shaffer and Shields (1984) aptly summarized the contribution of this book, named a "Citation Classic" in 1970 by *Current Contents*, as follows:

This approach was the only theory of attitudes that attempted to integrate the study of specific attitudes with the overall structure of the individual's self-system. . . . The Sherifs' research demonstrated that as individuals make personal commitments, they develop their own categories for perceiving the social world. The result is usually to systematically distort others' positions on social issues by assimilating near their own and contrasting the others. (P. 177).

This book continues to be an important reference in the area of attitudes, as demonstrated by its continuing citations, having been cited forty-two times between 1984 and 1988.

Many of the issues first raised by Sherif, Sherif, and Nebergall (1965) were the focus of continued empirical work by Sherif and her students (e.g., Luis Escovar, Helen Kearney, Merrilea Kelly, Leigh Shaffer, and Margaret Signorella). The social judgment/involvement approach to the study of attitudes was also summarized by Sherif in two comprehensive chapters: "Social Values, Attitudes, and Involvement of the Self," from the prestigious Nebraska Symposium on Motivation (1980b) and "Social and Psychological Bases of Social Psychology," from the G. Stanley Hall Lecture Series (Volume 2), sponsored by the American Psychological Association (C. W. Sherif, 1982b). These invited chapters reflect the respect that Sherif's work was gaining in mainstream psychology. The irony of being invited to give a G. Stanley Hall lecture, however, was not lost on Sherif, for Hall had argued that adolescent girls were delicate and in need of special education emphasizing domestic arts (see Shields, 1975).

Aside from the contributions of the above works to the study of attitude and attitude change, Sherif was ahead of her time in her insistence on including the self in any study of individual attitudes and behavior. As she stated in her chapter for the Nebraska Symposium on Motivation, "We keep bumping into something like self in research on human cognition and . . . the encounters are critical for understanding the attitude-social value relationship" (C. W. Sherif, 1980b, p. 3). She later elaborated this position with regard to gender identity (C. W. Sherif, 1982a). It was not until the late 1970s that mainstream social psychology began to recognize the importance of the self, and Sherif's pioneering contributions to these efforts too often go unacknowledged.

Sherif's interest in gender increased greatly in the early 1970s. One result of this interest was her participation in the first graduate seminar on the psychology of women at the Pennsylvania State University. The bibliography that she and Helen Kearney (Baer) compiled (Baer & Sherif, 1974) went on to be a bestseller from the *Catalog of Selected Documents in Psychology* of the Journal Supplement Abstract Service (H. R. Kearney, personal communication, March 20, 1982). This was the start of a generation of graduate students who were inspired to continue research on gender-related issues (e.g., Helen Kearney, Stephanie Shields, Margaret Signorella, and Maria Vegega).

Several chapters that Sherif wrote and lines of research that she and her students began in the late 1970s have proved to be influential in the field of the psychology of women. Probably the most famous was the "Bias in Psychology" chapter that appeared in *The Prism of Sex* (1979). In this essay, described as written in the " 'sociology of knowledge' tradition" (C. W. Sherif, 1983, p. 289), Sherif argued that orthodoxy within psychology perpetuated myths about human behavior and women's "inferior" position. In her critique of traditional methodologies and theories in psychology, Sherif succinctly communicated how psychology has perpetuated such social myths: "Restrict the framework for study to a narrow span of time, attend only to what you think is important and ignore as much else as possible" (C. W. Sherif, 1979, p. 107). To overcome such shortcomings she drew upon her earlier research in social psychology and argued for broadening the framework within which knowledge is sought to study individuals as whole persons within the context of relationships occurring within cultural and social institutions. Reviewers of *The Prism of Sex* frequently and admiringly cited Sherif's contribution to this book (Baker, 1980; Epstein, 1982; Garfunkel, 1980).

The above themes were articulated once again in Sherif's Division 35 Presidential Address, "Needed Concepts in the Study of Gender Identity" (C. W. Sherif, 1982a). In this address, she integrated the conceptual themes employed earlier in her career in the study of attitudes and intergroup relations with the study of gender. She argued for the importance of such concepts as the self-system, reference persons, and social power in understanding gender identity. Sherif included such concepts to provide a better understanding for the study of problems associated with the subjection of women, which in turn is essential to understanding the behavior of both women and men (p. 395). Psychologists have continued to cite this paper as raising key issues in the study of gender specifically and social issues more generally (e.g., Unger, 1986).

Sherif's chapter, "A Social Psychological Perspective on the Menstrual Cycle," addressed methodological issues in conducting research on a distinctly female topic (C. W. Sherif, 1980a). Central to this chapter is a description of a study on moods in relation to the menstrual cycle, conducted by Sherif with two graduate students, Linda Wilcoxon and Susan Schrader (Wilcoxon, Schrader, & Sherif, 1976). This study was exemplary in (1) ensuring that subjects were blind to the purpose of the study, and (2) employing male subjects as a control group. The research established that, for both males and females, the events of the day had the greatest effect on moods. Sherif's critique of the body of menstrual cycle research in that chapter and her devastating summary of Dalton's work on premenstrual syndrome (PMS) is an enjoyable antidote to the publicity that misleads the public into thinking that PMS is widespread. Once again, Sherif's chapter proved to be one of those praised by reviewers of the book (Richardson, 1981; Staff, 1980).

Finally, any discussion of Sherif's contribution to the field also needs to include the social psychology texts that she wrote, first in collaboration with Muzafer Sherif (1956, 1969), and then on her own (1976).

Sherif's foresight, flexibility, and interdisciplinary approach allowed her to contribute to areas of research outside her own field, as demonstrated by her work on the menstrual cycle. In addition, her expertise in group formation and competition allowed her to contribute to the emerging field of sport psychology. Sherif was the only woman speaker at a plenary session of the Scientific Congress held before the 1972 Olympic Games in Munich (Shaffer & Shields, 1984). As a nationally renowned teacher and mentor she inspired her students and encouraged them to study issues meaningful to them rather than confining them to scientific inquiries of interest to her. For this reason, Carolyn Sherif was able to support students in such diverse research topics as leadership, gender identity, racial marginality, personal space, personal commitment to action, and attitude-communication problems. Her 1976 textbook (C. W. Sherif, 1976), her 1980 Nebraska Symposium chapter (C. W. Sherif, 1980b), and her Division 35 Presidential Address (C. W. Sherif, 1982a) are replete with examples of research by her students, testimony to her role as a mentor and her ability to acknowledge the contributions of others. When Carolyn Wood Sherif died suddenly and prematurely of cancer in 1982, the field of psychology lost a scholar and a scientist who was able to transcend the narrow scientific and methodological definitions of the day and offer psychology a more comprehensive framework with which to study human behavior and social problems.

NOTE

This Chapter represents a collaborative effort. We would like to thank Donald Gramberg, Leigh Shaffer, and Stephanie Shields for their assistance.

REFERENCES

Ausubel, D. P. (1965). [Review of *Reference groups.*] *Harvard Educational Review*, *35*, 239–242.

Baer, H. R., & Sherif, C. W. (1974). A topical bibliography (selectively annotated) on psychology of women. *Journal Supplement Abstract Service: Catalog of Selected Documents in Psychology*, *4*, 42 (MS No. 614).

Baker, G. C. (1980). [Review of *The prism of sex.*] *Journal of Higher Education*, *51*, 588–590.

Diamond, S. S., & Morton, D. R. (1978). Empirical landmarks in social psychology. *Personality and Social Psychology Bulletin*, *4*, 217–221.

Epstein, C. F. (1982). [Review of *The prism of sex.*] *Social Forces*, *60*, 1211–1213.

Garfunkel, G. (1980). [Review of *The prism of sex.*] *Harvard Educational Review, 50,* 113.

Mack, R. W. (1965). [Review of *Reference groups.*] *American Sociological Review, 30,* 143.

Mednick, M. T., & Russo, N. F. (1983). Carolyn Wood Sherif: Brilliant scholar, gifted teacher, cherished friend. 1922–1982. *Psychology of Women Quarterly, 8,* 3–8.

Richardson, L. (1981). [Review of *The psychobiology of sex differences and sex roles.*] *Contemporary Sociology, 10,* 843–844.

Shaffer, L. S., & Shields, S. A. (1984). Carolyn Wood Sherif (1922–1982) [Obituary]. *American Psychologist, 39,* 176–178.

Sherif, C. W. (1976). *Orientation in social psychology.* New York: Harper & Row.

Sherif, C. W. (1979). Bias in psychology. In J. A. Sherman & E. T. Beck (Eds.), *The prism of sex* (pp. 93–133). Madison: University of Wisconsin Press.

Sherif, C. W. (1980a). A social psychological perspective on the menstrual cycle. In J. E. Parsons (Ed.), *The psychobiology of sex differences and sex roles* (pp. 245–268). Washington, D.C.: Hemisphere.

Sherif, C. W. (1980b). Social values, attitudes, and involvement of the self. In H. Howe & M. Page (Eds.), *Values and attitudes. The Nebraska Symposium* (pp. 1–64). Lincoln: University of Nebraska Press.

Sherif, C. W. (1982a). Needed concepts in the study of gender identity. *Psychology of Women Quarterly, 6,* 375–398.

Sherif, C. W. (1982b). Social and psychological bases of social psychology. In A. Kraut (Ed.), *G. Stanley Hall Lecture Series* (Vol. 2, pp. 5–72). Washington, D.C.: American Psychological Association.

Sherif, C. W. (1983). Carolyn Wood Sherif [Autobiography]. In A. N. O'Connell & N. F. Russo (eds.), *Models of achievement: Reflections of eminent women in psychology* (pp. 278–293). New York: Columbia University Press.

Sherif, C. W.; Sherif, M.; & Nebergall, R. E. (1965). *Attitude and attitude change.* Philadelphia: Saunders.

Sherif, M. (1936). *The psychology of social norms.* New York: Harper & Row.

Sherif, M.; Harvey, O. J.; White, B. J.; Hood, W. R.; & Sherif, C. W. (1961). *Intergroup conflict and cooperation: The Robbers Cave experiment.* Norman, Okla.: Institute of Group Relations.

Sherif, M., & Sherif, C. W. (1953). *Groups in harmony and tension.* New York: Harper & Row.

Sherif, M., & Sherif, C. W. (1956). *An outline of social psychology.* New York: Harper & Row.

Sherif, M., & Sherif, C. W. (1964). *Reference groups.* New York: Harper & Row.

Sherif, M., & Sherif, C. W. (1965). *Problems of youth.* Chicago: Aldine.

Sherif, M., & Sherif, C. W. (1969). *Social psychology.* New York: Harper & Row.

Shields, S. A. (1975). Functionalism, Darwinism, and the psychology of women: A study in social myth. *American Psychologist, 30,* 739–754.

Staff (1980). [Review of *The psychobiology of sex differences and sex roles.*] *Choice, 18,* 168.

Unger, R. K. (1986). Looking toward the future by looking at the past: Social activism and social history. *Journal of Social Issues, 42,* 215–227.

Wilcoxon, L. A.; Schrader, S. L.; & Sherif, C. W. (1976). Daily self-reports on activities, life events, moods and somatic changes during the menstrual cycle. *Psychosomatic Medicine, 38,* 399–417.

Additional Representative Publications by
Carolyn Wood Sherif

Sherif, C. W. (1963). Social categorization as a function of latitude of acceptance and series range. *Journal of Abnormal and Social Psychology*, *67*, 148–156.

Sherif, C. W. (1979). What every intelligent woman should know about psychology and women. In E. Snyder (Ed.), *Women: Study toward understanding*. New York: Harper & Row.

Sherif, C. W.; Kelly, M.; Rodgers, H. L.; Sarup, G.; & Tittler, B. I. (1973). Personal involvement, social judgment, and action. *Journal of Personality and Social Psychology*, *27*, 311–328.

Sherif, C. W., & Sherif, M. (Eds.). (1967). *Attitude, ego-involvement, and change*. New York: Wiley.

Spiro, R. J., & Sherif, C. W. (1975). Consistency and relativity in selective recall with differing ego-involvement. *British Journal of Social and Clinical Psychology*, *14*, 351–361.

Young, C. J.; MacKenzie, D. L.; & Sherif, C. W. (1980). In search of token women in academia. *Psychology of Women Quarterly*, *4*, 508–525.

Young, C. J.; MacKenzie, D. L.; & Sherif, C. W. (1982). "In search of token women in academia": Some definitions and clarifications. *Psychology of Women Quarterly*, *7*, 166–169.

Additional Representative Publications About
Carolyn Wood Sherif

Evans, R. I. (1980). *The making of social psychology: Discussions with creative contributors*. New York: Gardner Press.

Shaffer, L. S., & Shields, S. A. (1984). Carolyn Wood Sherif (1922–1982) [Obituary]. *American Psychologist*, *39*, 176–178. Reprinted in R. L. Shotland & M. M. Mark (Eds.) (1985), *Social science and social policy*. Beverly Hills, Calif.: Sage.

JANET TAYLOR SPENCE
(1923–   )

Kay Deaux

Janet Taylor Spence is a major figure in contemporary American psychology, having made sustained contributions to the scientific literature and to the profession for nearly forty years. Her empirical and theoretical contributions include work on manifest anxiety, intrinsic motivation, gender-related traits, and achievement behavior. This work has introduced new concepts into the literature (e.g., manifest anxiety) and has changed the way that we think about familiar issues (e.g., masculinity and femininity, achievement motivation). Spence's professional contributions include the presidency of both the American Psychological Association and the more recently formed American Psychological Society. She has been a Fellow at the Center for Advanced Study in the Behavioral Sciences and has received honorary degrees from Oberlin College and Ohio State University. In addition she has been elected to the status of Fellow in four divisions of the American Psychological Association representing the fields of experimental, social, and clinical psychology and the psychology of women. In 1979 Spence was named Ashbel Smith Professor of Psychology and Educational Psychology at the University of Texas.

BACKGROUND AND EDUCATION

Janet Taylor Spence was born in Toledo, Ohio, on August 29, 1923, to a family in which education for women was the rule rather than the exception. Spence's mother and grandmother were both graduates of Vassar College, and her mother earned a master's degree in economics at Columbia as well. Political consciousness also permeated the Toledo household in which Janet and her younger sister, Christine, were raised. Their father, John C. Taylor, was active in the Socialist party and became a labor union business manager. Helen Hodge Taylor, an activist Republican, developed a career path that moved from the League of Women Voters to the management of several election campaigns to the head of a social service agency concerned with families and dependent children (Spence, 1988b).

Two high school years at an all-girls' school in Northfield, Massachusetts, dissuaded Janet Taylor from becoming the third generation to attend Vassar, and she chose to attend Oberlin College instead. Although not in the family tradition, the Ohio school, with its well-established liberal credentials and academic reputation, was congruent with the social consciousness of the Taylor family. Graduating from Oberlin in 1945, Taylor moved on to the clinical psychology program at Yale University, despite harboring some uncertainty about the field and her place in it.

In its 1945–1946 postwar period, the somewhat depleted Yale program did not offer Taylor the intellectual excitement and cohesion she was seeking. Administering intelligence tests under the supervision of Catherine Cox Miles proved unsatisfying, and Taylor left Yale to take a rotating internship in New York State. That experience led her to conclude that clinical practice was not the answer; yet the internship had significant consequences, as it was one of the supervisors in that program who recommended that Janet Taylor go to Iowa and work with Kenneth Spence.

Iowa in the late 1940s was an intellectually exciting place. Many of the participants in the "Yale school" were now in the Iowa psychology department, including Robert Sears, John Whiting, and Judson Brown. I. E. Farber was heading the experimental-clinical program in which Taylor enrolled, Gustav Bergmann was infusing philosophy of science into the psychological discourse, and Kenneth Spence was exciting a generation of psychologists with regard to the potential of Hull-Spence theory for understanding basic principles of behavior.

Janet Taylor entered Iowa in 1947; she left with her Ph.D. in 1949 and with a conception of the psychological research enterprise that would stay with her throughout her career. Kenneth Spence was a powerful mentor. Hull-Spence theory, though primarily a historical landmark now, was a seductive framework for young scientists at Iowa during the 1940s and 1950s and into the 1960s. Beyond formal theory, Kenneth Spence provided students with a model for thinking about psychological questions. As Janet Spence later recalled, he created a sense of what theories are and how to test one's ideas (Spence, 1988c). These general analytic principles could survive the demise of stimulus-response learning theory and could be applied, as Janet Spence has done, to other domains with equally productive consequences.

CAREER DEVELOPMENT

In 1949 Janet Taylor began her postgraduate career at Northwestern University, where she remained until 1960. Initially appointed as an instructor, a fairly standard practice at the time, she was promoted to assistant professor in 1951 and to associate professor in 1956. Taylor was the first woman on the Northwestern psychology faculty, and her hiring was considered something of an experiment—an experiment embedded in some controversy. Yet Spence (1988b) reported that she was treated well in most respects, with the exception of her rate of promotion, which lagged behind the norm of the day.

Northwestern was a productive place for Taylor's career development. During her eleven years there, she published eighteen scientific papers and coauthored the first edition of an elementary statistics textbook (now in its fifth edition). Included among those papers were the initial presentation of the Taylor Manifest Anxiety Scale (Taylor, 1953) and an important summary of the arguments for the place of manifest anxiety in contemporary drive theory (Taylor, 1956).

This scholarly record was compiled despite a teaching load that would make most contemporary academics gasp. During the first year alone, Taylor taught courses in statistics, abnormal psychology, personality theory, experimental psychology, history and systems, adjustment, and introductory psychology; in addition, she had full responsibility for undergraduate advising. Despite the heavy load, Taylor was an enthusiastic teacher, and her skills in the classroom are recalled with admiration. Doctoral students were particularly attracted to Taylor, and she devoted considerable energy and attention to their projects. Martha Mednick, an early Taylor doctoral student, offered this recollection: "She was loved by all of us—a marvelous, dedicated teacher . . . students were attracted to her like flies" (Mednick, 1988, p. 251).

On December 27, 1959, Janet Taylor and Kenneth Spence were married, and Janet Taylor Spence returned to Iowa City the following fall. Although the marriage was a happy personal resolution, it also forced Spence to face the nepotism policies that were to constrain her career for the next eight years. In Iowa, she joined the Veterans Administration Hospital as a research psychologist. Four years later, when Kenneth Spence joined the psychology department at the University of Texas, Janet Spence was, in her words, "dumped" at a state school for the retarded in a research associate position. In 1965 she was appointed to the faculty of the department of educational psychology at the university.

Only in 1967, when Kenneth Spence's untimely death made the nepotism issue moot, did Janet Spence move back to the psychology department track that she had left in 1960. The department of psychology wasted no time in capitalizing on Janet Spence's talents. In 1968 she was appointed chair of the department, a position she held for the next four years.

CONTRIBUTIONS AND ACHIEVEMENTS

The end of her term as department chair in 1972 allowed Spence to accelerate the pace of other professional activities. She served as editor of *Contemporary Psychology* from 1973 to 1979, following a four-year term as associate editor. Her numerous contributions include membership on the editorial committee of the *Annual Review of Psychology*, the Board of Governors of the Center for Creative Leadership, and the Board of Trustees of the James McKeen Cattell Foundation. Other honors have accrued. In 1978–1979 Spence was a Fellow at the Center for Advanced Study in the Behavioral Sciences. In 1979 she was named the Ashbel Smith Professor of Psychology and Educational Psychology at the University of Texas, the only named professorship in the department at the time. She was elected to membership in the American Academy of Arts and Sciences and received honorary degrees from Oberlin College and Ohio State University.

During the 1970s and 1980s, Spence was extremely prominent in professional leadership positions and committed to the health and well-being of the scientific community. Her presidencies include the Southwestern Psychological Association (1972), the American Psychological Association (1984), and the newly formed American Psychological Society (APS) (1988). In addition she has served as chair of the psychology section of the American Association for the Advancement of Science (1984) and as secretary-treasurer (1975–1977) and a member of the governing board (1978–1983) of the Psychonomic Society. Throughout these involvements, Spence has focused clearly on the research community and has committed herself to protecting and strengthening the scientific wing of the profession. In APS, she sees the possibility of ''an alternative society that preserves and advances psychology as a unified discipline'' (Spence, 1988a). Unity is a key word for Spence, linked closely to her beliefs about what psychology should be. ''The heart, the centerpiece, of the science of psychology . . . is or should be a theory of *action*, what people actually do'' (Spence, 1987). Only by keeping cognitive scientists, neuroscientists, and social scientists together, rather than isolated in their separate societies, can this vision of psychology be realized.

The Spence research record is a remarkable account of productivity, of sustained contributions to the psychological literature over nearly a forty-year period. These contributions can be divided into four fairly distinct phases: first, the pioneering work on manifest anxiety; second, concern with issues of reinforcement and intrinsic motivation; third, influential work on gender issues; and fourth, fresh looks at achievement motivation. Although these topics might appear to be quite diverse, there are constant themes that pervade the corpus.

Manifest Anxiety

The Taylor Manifest Anxiety Scale (MAS) (Taylor, 1953) was an auspicious beginning for a young investigator, an unusual instance in which a person's dissertation work becomes part of the accepted wisdom of a field. In the context of Hull-Spence theory, the MAS was considered an index of differences in drive level between individuals, and the scale was used to select subjects for experimental studies. The more general theoretical framework relating anxiety and performance began to evolve at Taylor's dissertation oral, stimulated by questions from Kenneth Spence, Judson Brown, and Gustav Bergmann (Spence, 1988c). A few years later, Taylor (1956) could review an extensive body of research that spoke to the interaction between anxiety level and task complexity.

The theoretical framework in which anxiety was embedded has been largely forgotten by the current generation of psychologists. Yet the measure of anxiety that Janet Taylor Spence developed has been remarkably durable. Although published in 1953, the MAS is still cited extensively by investigators who find it a useful gauge of levels of emotionality, arousal, or general anxiety level.

The MAS in many ways epitomizes pervasive themes in Spence's work. At this early stage, she was already concerned with the interaction between person and situation. Development of the MAS was a means of assessing a dimension of individual difference that had motivational properties. This research program, concerned with the link between personality and behavior, foreshadowed many of the subsequent trait-state analyses within personality. Thus, more than yielding one specific measure, the Spence program of research on anxiety established a research style and reflected concerns that would be evident several decades later.

Reinforcement, Feedback, and Intrinsic Motivation

In the 1960s Spence's research began to move beyond issues of anxiety to more general concepts of reinforcement and motivation. Although often dependent on schizophrenic and brain-damaged patients as subjects, Spence continued to use basic experimental analyses to probe questions of interest—questions that increasingly came to challenge the received knowledge of the time.

Still dominated by basic learning theories and without theoretical models that could handle cognitive constructs, mainstream American psychology was not ready to believe that basic reinforcement properties could be superseded. Thus concept formation studies showing superior performance by subjects reinforced overtly for wrong answers compared to those reinforced for right answers were interpreted in terms of the stronger reinforcement value of ''wrong'' versus ''right.'' Spence questioned this interpretation, suggesting that ''the performance differences among the reinforcement conditions can be attributed to the informational characteristics of blank'' (Spence, 1970, p. 322), where ''blank'' refers to the absence of overt reinforcement. Using a clever experimental design, Spence demonstrated that subjects do indeed extract information value from a ''blank'' and that this information is equivalent in its impact to experimenter-designated reinforcement.

The recognition that the dominant interpretations of learning and performance were incomplete was reflected in Spence's consideration of alternatives to extrinsically motivated behavior. Intrinsic motivation was an idea whose time had not yet come. Yet, in characteristic fashion, Spence was able to step back from the crowd, consider the accepted wisdom, and suggest an alternative perspective. As she concluded in her 1971 paper, ''Material reinforcers have effects that interfere with performance in ways that we are only beginning to understand'' (Spence, 1971, p. 1469). History has certainly proved her correct.

Gender

In the early 1970s, Spence began a highly productive collaboration with Robert Helmreich. Influenced by the feminist *zeitgeist* and piqued by curiosity, the Spence-Helmreich team first asked whether competent women and men are judged by the same standards (Spence & Helmreich, 1972b). To accompany experimental studies of this question, the Attitudes toward Women Scale (Spence & Helmreich, 1972a) was developed, the first of several scales Spence and Helmreich constructed to assess individual differences in gender-related traits and attitudes.

With the development and publication of the Personal Attributes Questionnaire (PAQ) (Spence, Helmreich, & Stapp, 1974), Spence and Helmreich found themselves to be one of several independent groups of investigators who were concerned with conceptualizing and assessing masculinity and femininity in something other than a unidimensional, bipolar mode. Although the questions these various investigative teams posed were quite similar, the assumptions they made and the answers they offered often diverged. From the beginning, Spence and Helmreich argued for the multidimensionality of gender-related attitudes and behaviors. As stated in the preface to their 1978 book, *Masculinity and Femininity*:

It will be our contention that the psychological dimensions of masculinity and femininity should not only be conceptually distinguished from masculine and feminine sex roles but the masculine and feminine attributes, while they differentiate the sexes to some degree, are not bipolar opposites but in each sex are separate and essentially orthogonal dimensions. Finally, we will argue that, at least in contemporary society, these psychological dimensions are only weakly related within each sex to the broad spectrum of sex-role behaviors. (P. 3)

Their conceptual analyses and abundant data were salutary for the field. Babladelis, reviewing the Spence-Helmreich volume, advised readers "to explore with the authors the multifaceted aspects of androgyny, masculinity, and femininity, and to comprehend the correlates of androgyny in a new and compellingly sensible framework" (1979, p. 4).

As gender-focused research increased in popularity, this sensibleness was often tested. Spence and Helmreich began to qualify their use of the terms "masculinity" and "femininity," adding "instrumentality" and "expressiveness" as critical modifiers. Through both empirical demonstrations and conceptual analyses, they argued persistently and persuasively for a multidimensional perspective (e.g., Foushee, Helmreich, & Spence, 1979; Helmreich, Spence, & Holahan, 1979; Spence, 1983b, 1984; Spence & Helmreich, 1979, 1981). The impact of their work has been substantial. As evidenced by citations in the *Social Science Citation Index*, their publications have become pivotal pieces in the literature of the field.

Still intrigued by the puzzles of gender, Spence moved beyond the specifiable dimensions of expressiveness and instrumentality to what she terms the "ineffable" constructs of masculinity and femininity. In her Nebraska Symposium contribution, Spence (1985b) offered a general theory of gender identity. In this model, she considers the basic meanings of masculinity and femininity to individuals self-definition and discusses how specific gender-linked behaviors may or may not be linked to these more primitive senses of self. Although difficult to test, this model of gender identity offers some important insights on the idiosyncratic nature of gender identity, and on the opportunistic and protective ways in which individuals define their masculinity and femininity.

Achievement Motivation

The Spence and Helmreich collaboration spawned still another productive line of research activity. Begun at the same time and initially related to the gender work, their explorations in achievement motivation and behavior soon developed into a distinct line of inquiry. In trademark fashion, Helmreich and Spence (1978) first developed an assessment tool, the Work and Family Orientation Questionnaire (WOFO), to measure separate components of achievement motivation. By their analysis, achievement can be considered in terms of three separate factors: work (a Protestant ethic kind of perseverance); mastery (tapping perceived challenges and intrinsically motivated activities); and competitiveness (reflecting direct comparisons to the performance of others).

This tripartite distinction has demonstrated its utility. For example, although competitiveness is related to sheer productivity, for example, the number of publications by academic scholars, the impact of scientific work, as gauged by citations, is more closely related to work and mastery and is suppressed by strong competitiveness (Helmreich, Bean, et al., 1978; Helmreich, Spence, et al., 1980). Not only do these studies demonstrate a link between personality and behavior, they also provide evidence for the predictability of personality to indirect indices of the behavior many years later.

Spence's interest in achievement produced at least two other important works. The first, an edited volume on achievement and achievement motives (Spence, 1983a), offered "a truly sophisticated conceptual synthesis of the major theoretical ideas and empirical results in the field over the past three decades" (Horner, 1985, p. 261). Within that volume, a chapter by Spence and Helmreich effectively sets their own work within the broad domain of achievement literature. In her presidential address to the American Psychological Association, Spence (1985a) took an even broader view, bringing humane concerns to questions of achievement and individualism in American society.

Consistent Research Themes

Across various domains, common elements of Spence's research style emerge. Characteristic of her approach from the beginning has been a tendency to look skeptically at accepted wisdom, to reject simplistic answers, to probe and ponder, and to emerge with a conceptually clearer view of phenomena. The complexity she embraces is not always appreciated, and subtle points she offers are frequently lost in ensuing debates. Yet in the final analysis her perspective generally prevails.

The conceptual glue that binds her contributions together is a persisting concern with the relationship of personality to behavior, and a recognition that behavior emerges from the interaction of persons and situations. These themes are evident in her earliest work on manifest anxiety and are equally prominent in the most recent achievement work. The central concern with behavioral, as opposed to cognitive, consequences is seen in the performance tasks of her anxiety research, again in the performance measures used to demonstrate intrinsic motivation (in contrast to the emphasis of more contemporary investigators on perceived task value), and in the citations and salaries that index achievement behavior. Within the gender domain, those links to behavior have not been quite so apparent as she and her colleagues grappled with some of the conceptual problems. Yet even here, her most recent work promises to provide some of that behavioral evidence, linking negative aspects of instrumentality and impulsiveness to sexually coercive tactics in dating relationships.

Just as Spence does not leave her models of human personality "buried in thought," neither does she delegate herself to that state. Throughout her career she has continued, with unusual steadiness and remarkable productivity, to display the kind of motivated behavior that only an individual difference analysis can adequately explain.

REFERENCES

Babladelis, G. (1979). Accentuate the positive. . . . *Contemporary Psychology*, *24*, 3–4.

Foushee, H. C.; Helmreich, R. L.; & Spence, J. T. (1979). Implicit theories of masculinity and femininity: Dualistic or bipolar? *Psychology of Women Quarterly*, *3*, 259–269.

Helmreich, R. L.; Beane, W. E.; Lucker, G. W.; & Spence, J. T. (1978). Achievement motivation and scientific attainment. *Personality and Social Psychology Bulletin*, *4*, 222–226.

Helmreich, R. L., & Spence, J. T. (1978). The Work and Family Orientation Questionnaire: An objective instrument to assess components of achievement motivation and attitudes toward family and career. *Journal Supplement Abstract Service: Catalog of Selected Documents in Psychology*, *8*, 35 (MS No. 1677).

Helmreich, R. L.; Spence, J. T.; Beane, W. E.; Lucker, G. W.; & Matthews, K. A. (1980). Making it in academic psychology: Demographic and personality correlates of attainment. *Journal of Personality and Social Psychology*, *39*, 896–908.

Helmreich, R. L., Spence, J. T., & Holahan, C. K. (1979). Psychological androgyny and sex-role flexibility: A test of two hypotheses. *Journal of Personality and Social Psychology*, *37*, 1631–1682.

Horner, M. S. (1985). A significant achievement. *Contemporary Psychology*, *30*, 261–263.

Mednick, M. T. (1988). Martha T. Mednick, 1929– . In A. N. O'Connell & N. F. Russo (Eds.), *Models of achievement: Reflections of eminent women in psychology: Vol. 2.* (pp. 247–259). Hillsdale, N.J.: Erlbaum.

Spence, J. T. (1970). Verbal reinforcement combinations and concept-identification learning: The role of nonreinforcement. *Journal of Experimental Psychology, 85*, 321–329.

Spence, J. T. (1971). Do material rewards enhance the performance of lower-class children? *Child Development, 42*, 1461–1470.

Spence, J. T. (Ed.). (1983a). *Achievement and achievement motives: Psychological and sociological approaches.* San Francisco: W. H. Freeman.

Spence, J. T. (1983b). Commentary on Lubinski, Tellegen, and Butcher's "Masculinity, femininity and androgyny viewed and assessed as distinct concepts." *Journal of Personality and Social Psychology, 44*, 440–446.

Spence, J. T. (1984). Masculinity, femininity, and gender-related traits: A conceptual analysis and critique of current research. *Progress in Experimental Personality Research, 13*, 2–97.

Spence, J. T. (1985a). Achievement American style: The rewards and costs of individualism. *American Psychologist, 40*, 1285–1295.

Spence, J. T. (1985b). Gender identification and its implications for masculinity and femininity. In T. B. Sonderegger (Ed.), *Nebraska Symposium on Motivation and Achievement: Psychology and gender* Vol. 32, (pp. 59–95). Lincoln: University of Nebraska Press.

Spence, J. T. (1987). Centrifugal versus centripetal tendencies in psychology: Will the center hold? *American Psychologist, 42*, 1052–1054.

Spence, J. T. (1988a). If reorganization fails. *As Soon as Possible, 1*, 4.

Spence, J. T. (1988b). Janet Taylor Spence, 1923– . In A. N. O'Connell & N. F. Russo (Eds.), *Models of achievement: Reflections of eminent women in psychology*: Vol. 2, pp. 191–203. Hillsdale, N.J.: Erlbaum.

Spence, J. T. (1988c, August 29). Personal communication.

Spence, J. T., & Helmreich, R. (1972a). The Attitudes toward Women Scale: An objective instrument to measure attitudes toward the rights and roles of women in contemporary society. JSAS *Catalog of Selected Documents in Psychology, 2*, 66–67 (MS No. 153).

Spence, J. T., & Helmreich, R. (1972b). Who likes competent women? Competence, sex-role congruence of interest, and subjects' attitudes toward women as determinants of interpersonal attraction. *Journal of Applied Social Psychology, 2*, 197–213.

Spence, J. T., & Helmreich, R. L. (1978). *Masculinity and Femininity: Their psychological dimensions, correlates and antecedents.* Austin: University of Texas Press.

Spence, J. T., & Helmreich, R. L. (1979). On assessing "androgyny." *Sex Roles, 5*, 721–738.

Spence, J. T., & Helmreich, R. L. (1981). Androgyny vs. gender: A comment on Bem's gender schema theory. *Psychological Review, 88*, 365–368.

Spence, J. T.; Helmreich, R. L.; & Stapp, J. (1974). The Personal Attributes Questionnaire: A measure of sex-role stereotypes and masculinity-femininity. *Journal Supplement Abstract Service: Catalog of Selected Documents in Psychology, 4*, 43–44 (MS No. 617).

Taylor, J. A. (1953). A personality scale of manifest anxiety. *Journal of Abnormal and Social Psychology*, *48*, 285–290.
Taylor, J. A. (1956). Drive theory and manifest anxiety. *Psychological Bulletin*, *53*, 303–320.

Additional Representative Publications by
Janet Taylor Spence

Helmreich, R. L.; Spence, J. T.; & Gibson, R. H. (1982). Sex-role attitudes: 1972–1980. *Personality and Social Psychology Bulletin*, *8*, 656–663.
Spence, J. T.; Deaux, K.; & Helmreich, R. L. (1985). Sex roles in contemporary American society. In G. Lindzey & E. Aronson (Eds.), *Handbook of social psychology* (3rd ed.) (pp. 149–178). New York: Random House.
Spence, J. T., & Helmreich, R. L. (1980). Masculine instrumentality and feminine expressiveness: Their relationships with sex role attitudes and behaviors. *Psychology of Women Quarterly*, *5*, 147–163.
Spence, J. T.; Helmreich, R. L.; & Holahan, C. K. (1979). Negative and positive components of psychological masculinity and femininity and their relationships to self-reports of neurotic and acting out behaviors. *Journal of Personality and Social Psychology*, *37*, 1637–1644.
Spence, J. T.; Helmreich, R. L.; & Stapp, J. (1973). A short version of the Attitudes toward Women Scale (AWS). *Bulletin of the Psychonomic Society*, *2*, 219–220.
Spence, J. T.; Helmreich, R.; & Stapp, J. (1975). Ratings of self and peers on sex-role attributes and their relations to self-esteem and conceptions of masculinity and femininity. *Journal of Personality and Social Psychology*, *32*, 29–39.
Spence, J. T., & Spence, K. W. (1966). The motivational components of manifest anxiety: Drive and drive stimuli. In C. Spielberger (Ed.), *Anxiety and behavior* (pp. 291–326). New York: Academic Press.
Spence, K. W., & Spence, J. T. (1966). Sex and anxiety differences in eyelid conditioning. *Psychological Bulletin*, *65*, 137–142.

BONNIE RUTH STRICKLAND
(1936–   )

Stephen Nowicki, Jr.

Bonnie Ruth Strickland has shaped the mainstream of psychology through her research and administrative leadership. The search for ways to improve the state of those who are underprivileged and discriminated against stems from her own struggle to overcome the barriers of poverty to attain her educational goals. The need to understand why she persisted toward her goals, while most of her peers did not, led her to undertake research with the locus of control of reinforcement construct. Strickland has received two Citation Classic awards for her research on locus of control, which has shown the important role of generalized expectancies in determining behavior, especially the behavior of the poor and disadvantaged.

Strickland has been called on to lead in many capacities, including being elected president of the American Psychological Association (APA). Her views concerning many of the salient psychological issues of our time became part of the *Congressional Record* through her testimony in the United States Senate and House of Representatives in 1985 and during her appointment to the National Advisory Council of the National Institute of Mental Health (NIMH) in 1988. She was elected to the status of Fellow in five divisions of the American Psychological Association and awarded a diplomate from the American Board of Professional Psychology.

FAMILY BACKGROUND AND EDUCATION

Bonnie Strickland's parents were from different backgrounds. Her mother, Willie Whitfield, the twelfth of thirteen children, was born and raised on the Apalachicola River in rural northwest Florida. The family ran a dry goods business, and she often traveled north to buy supplies. It was on one of her trips, this time to Birmingham, Alabama, that Willie Whitfield met and subsequently married Roy E. Strickland in 1934. Roy Strickland worked for the railroad when he could find work, which, unfortunately, was difficult during the Great Depression. Bonnie Strickland was born in Louisville, Kentucky, on November 24,

1936. A brother followed in four years. Her parents divorced when she was seven, and with her three-year-old brother, she and her mother set up housekeeping on their own in Alabama. Strickland often visited with her father during her childhood, but it was through trips to see her mother's relatives, including uncounted numbers of aunts, uncles, and cousins living in rural northwest Florida, that she experienced some of her most pleasant memories.

The experiences with her mother's family contrast sharply with the more difficult life Strickland faced on the south side of Birmingham, Alabama. Because her mother worked as a waitress, Strickland was responsible for most of the housework and took a job in the local public library to supplement the family income in her early teenage years. She was an active, curious child, and a major focus for her energy and interest was sports. An avid softball player, she was introduced to tennis by a neighbor, Eunice Foster. During high school, Strickland was good enough to play on the boys' team, win a state tennis championship, and be nationally ranked for her age. As well as being an outstanding all-around athlete, Strickland was also an excellent student. Unlike most of her female classmates, who saw high school as the last of their formal education, Strickland chose to attend college even though she had to pay for her own expenses through a combination of scholarships and outside work.

Strickland took the advice of her high school teacher, Louise Pope, and attended Alabama College for Women, a school with a well-known reputation for training physical education teachers. Strickland did not seriously consider psychology until the last two years of college. Competitive athletics remained important to her, and she even considered pursuing a professional career in tennis. She also briefly flirted with the idea of working in the theater, since she not only enjoyed acting but was well experienced with stage managing and lighting. Besides enjoying sports and dramatic activities, Strickland, through her class work, was being challenged for the first time to consider in depth social issues such as racial prejudice. She reported vividly remembering her biology instructor Gideon Nelson scraping away a thin layer of skin from a cadaver, an elderly black man, and saying to her, "Look, the color is not even skin deep."

It was during this time of self-exploration and questioning that Herbert Eber and Katherine Vickery, the only two psychology professors in the college, gave Strickland the encouragement to pursue a career in psychology. Eber became aware of Strickland's intellectual promise after she had taken an intelligence test from one of his students as part of a class project. He and Vickery took a personal interest in helping Strickland to learn the basic foundations of psychology. In 1958, her senior year, Strickland applied to graduate schools in psychology. On the advice of Eber, she accepted the offer from the clinical psychology program at Ohio State University.

Bonnie Strickland began her graduate education at the Ohio State University in 1958, a time of significant scholarly activity and production. Julian Rotter had published *Social Learning and Clinical Psychology* (1954), and George Kelly had published his two-volume set, *Psychology of Personal Constructs*

(1955). The department also included Edward Barker, Douglas Crowne, Shepperd Liverant, and Alvin Scodel. Julian Rotter, Stickland's major professor, guided her training in the scientist-practitioner model of clinical psychology, a model requiring clinical psychologists to be equally knowledgeable in both research and practice. He was dedicated to issues of social welfare and equality, holding ideas and views that Strickland found to be very close to her own.

Her clinical training was varied and included work at the Veterans Administration hospital in Palo Alto, one of the finest training facilities in the country. Here she came in contact with people like Leonard Ullman and Leonard Krasner, early theorists in behavioral therapy approaches, and Albert Bandura and Gregory Bateson, who were developing social learning theory and family therapy approaches, respectively. Strickland's clinical activities were centered in the ward Ken Kesey made famous in *One Flew over the Cuckoo's Nest*.

Bonnie Strickland received her Ph.D. in 1962 and shortly thereafter took an academic position in the department of psychology at Emory University. Strickland had returned to the South, but she was not the same person who had left four years before. Her world had grown enormously; not only had she encountered many different kinds of people, but she found that she was stimulated by her interactions with them. After two years as an assistant professor at Emory, she was offered and accepted the position of Dean of Women. Being responsible for nearly 1,800 women at Emory sensitized Strickland more intensely to the specific problems of women. Later, she would remember these experiences as she helped to clarify women's issues and to fight for women's rights through the American Psychological Association.

Toward the end of her stay as dean of women, significant changes were occurring in the department of psychology at Emory that would lead to its tripling in size. The department had hired a new chairperson, Jay Knopf, and a new clinical director, Alfred Heilbrun. New doctoral programs in clinical and educational psychology were added also. It was during this time of growth that Strickland returned again to an academic position in the department.

Strickland was one of the most popular professors at Emory. Her courses were consistently oversubscribed. One never knew who might show up in Strickland's class; it could as easily be the governor of the state as well as a radical from a student movement. Strickland was equally at home with either. She was a respected facilitator of university and community relationships. Among her friends were leaders in Martin Luther King's nonviolent movement with whom she had marched during the 1960s.

Strickland's academic reputation grew rapidly. She published a number of influential articles (e.g., Strickland, 1965; Nowicki & Strickland, 1973), and she was in demand as a speaker. After a decade in the South, Strickland accepted a position as full professor at the University of Massachusetts at Amherst, a large department with sixty faculty members. Instead of being one of few women in an entire university, Strickland found that she was one of a dozen women in a single department.

It was at the University of Massachusetts at Amherst that Bonnie Strickland's considerable organization and leadership skills began to blossom. She chaired the Faculty Senate Status of Women Committee and was director of graduate studies for the department. In 1976 she became chair of the department of psychology. During her tenure as chair both extramural funding and the average number of annual faculty publications doubled. She served in that position until 1983, when she was asked to become an associate to Joseph Duffy, the new chancellor of the university. Among her responsibilities were advising in the areas of affirmative action and university organization.

MAJOR ACHIEVEMENTS AND CONTRIBUTIONS

Research on Control Expectancies

Strickland's early research at Ohio State University signaled the beginning of her research with personality variables such as need for approval (Crowne & Strickland, 1961; Strickland & Crowne, 1962, 1963) and internal-external control beliefs (Strickland, 1970). In her dissertation (Strickland, 1970), she found that internal subjects were more likely than externals to be aware of reinforcement and extinction conditions in a "learning without awareness" paradigm. This finding alerted Strickland to the fact that possessing an internal or external orientation could potentially affect how people would behave in a variety of social situations.

Her interest in facilitating race relations led to her research study of the behavior of social activists. Since she had earned the trust and respect of the members of the Southern Student Non-Violent Coordinating Committee (SNCC), Strickland was able to get them to cooperate with her research project. Among other results, Strickland found that social activists were significantly more internal than a matched group of college students (Strickland, 1965). It was, and still remains, one of the few studies to demonstrate a relationship between a personality construct like locus of control of reinforcement and social activism. It has been cited often enough by other researchers to be designated a Citation Classic.

In the late 1960s and early 1970s, Strickland expanded her study of the locus of control construct to measurement. She had noted the lack of an acceptably reliable and valid scale to measure generalized internal-external expectancies of reinforcement in children. Strickland teamed up with Emory University colleague Steve Nowicki to construct a scale to fulfill that need, the Children's Nowicki-Strickland Internal-External Control Scale (CNS-IE, Nowicki & Strickland, 1973). Later, when Marshall Duke joined the Emory faculty, he helped to produce other forms of the Nowicki-Strickland Scale for preschool (Nowicki & Duke, 1974a), adult (Nowicki & Duke, 1974b), and geriatric populations (Duke, Shaheen, & Nowicki, 1977). As a result of this work, there are now scales to measure locus of control orientation across the entire life span, probably the only such set of instruments that can be used for cross-generational research in the area. The various Nowicki-Strickland measures have been used in over 700 studies (Nowicki, 1988) and translated into over two dozen languages. The original children's scale has been evaluated as the most valid and popular measure of locus of control of reinforcement, reprinted often in textbooks, and Strickland's 1973 article with Steven Nowicki became her second Citation Classic. For the past fifteen years, the locus of control of reinforcement scales have been used to gather an impressive amount of information on a variety of socially important variables in psychology, ranging from development of psychopathology to determinants of achievement.

Much of Strickland's other locus of control research focused on how internality served as an adaptive mediating variable for children's behavior (Strickland, 1972, 1973; Zykoskee, Strickland, & Watson, 1971). Throughout the 1970s and 1980s, Strickland often has been the one responsible for providing theoretical integration of the field of locus of control research especially in the areas of health and adaptive behaviors (Strickland, 1977a, 1977b, 1978, 1979, 1989; Strickland & Janoff-Bulman, 1980). Through these presentations, she helped clarify issues for the increasingly divergent group of investigators who are involved in locus of control of reinforcement research.

Although Strickland probably is best known for her studies of locus of control of reinforcement, she also has published on conformity (e.g., Strickland & Crowne, 1962), verbal conditioning (e.g., Crowne & Strickland, 1961), prejudice (Proenza & Strickland, 1965), psychotherapy (Strickland & Crowne, 1963; Doster & Strickland, 1971), the adjustment of gay men and lesbians (Thompson, McCandless, & Strickland, 1971), approval motivation (e.g., Strickland, 1977a), and on the impact of mood state, especially depressive mood, on behavior (Strickland, Hale, & Anderson, 1975; Hale & Strickland, 1976; Haley & Strickland, 1986). Strickland has presented evidence that there are individual sensitivities to common foods and environmental pollutants that may increase the likelihood of depression (Strickland, 1981, 1982). One of her students, David King (1981), was the first to use carefully controlled double-blind conditions to demonstrate a relationship between food and chemical sensitivities and emotional symptoms. In fact, several of her master's and doctoral students have studied depression extensively. As APA president, Strickland appointed a special Task Force on Women's Depression to advance research and increase public awareness about this topic. Strickland's own presentations in this area have emphasized the importance of mind-body interactions and women's health (Strickland, 1984, 1987; Strickland & Kendall, 1983).

Leadership Contributions

As chair of the psychology department at the University of Massachusetts at Amherst, Strickland was part of the mainstream of American psychology. She was elected first woman chair of the Council of Graduate Departments of Psychology and appointed to the Advisory Council for the National Institute of Mental Health. Because of her well-known commitment to minority and women's issues, she was asked to chair the first Equal Opportunity and Affirmative Action Committee of the Division of Clinical Psychology of the American Psychological Association. She helped to establish the section on the Clinical Psychology of Women in 1981, and in 1983 she became the second woman to be elected president of the Division of Clinical Psychology. She served as the representative from the Division of Clinical Psychology to APA's Council of Representatives for three terms and was on the editorial boards of five journals: *Cognitive Therapy and Research*, *Journal of Consulting and Clinical Psychology*, *Journal of Personality and Social Psychology: Personality Processes and Individual Differences*, *Journal of Social and Clinical Psychology*, and *Professional Psychology*. She also became heavily involved in accreditation consulting for various universities with graduate clinical psychology programs.

Strickland has been instrumental in strengthening organizations working for women's rights both inside and outside psychology. She was a member of the Conference Advisory Committee that brought fifty leaders together to develop a national agenda for women's mental health (Russo, 1985). A diplomate in clinical psychology with a longtime independent practice, she has also published and presented numerous research articles, obtained research grants, received the University of Massachusetts Distinguished Service Award, and chaired the APA Board of Professional Affairs. With the support of a variety of groups within APA, Strickland ran for and was elected president of the American Psychological Association in 1987, the seventh woman to be so honored.

Among Strickland's most notable achievements during her presidency was the improved relations between APA and various consumer groups such as the National Alliance for the Mentally Ill. She met regularly with representatives of the other major mental health professions and was particularly supportive of the new Office of Professional Practice in APA. The central office of APA was reorganized to reflect the major aims of the association, namely, science, practice, and the public interest. A Task Force on AIDS was appointed and an office for AIDS activities established. The real estate holdings of APA were sold and plans developed for a new building. After a series of financial losses, *Psychology Today* was sold. Strickland also appointed a prestigious interdisciplinary Task Force on Women and Depression, charged with developing position papers on the state of the art, knowledge of the etiology, assessment, treatment, and public policy issues related to depression in women.

Strickland was a visible and effective leader of the association through one of its most trying times, traveling thousands of miles and putting in eighteen-to-twenty hour days in her attempts to facilitate communication among the forty-five subfields of psychologists, the fifty-four state and provincial associations, and the numerous boards and committees. She worked diligently on the task forces and committees created to negotiate a reorganization plan for the APA that would meet the needs of scientists and streamline the governance structure.

When her tenure as president was over, during the fall of 1988, Strickland and others founded a new organization called the American Psychological Society, an independent multipurpose organization committed to maintaining the scientific base of psychology. Strickland continued her services to NIMH as a scientific advisor to the Depression Awareness, Recognition and Treatment Project, the first public educational campaign mounted within mental health.

Awards and Recognition

Strickland is a Fellow in five divisions of the American Psychological Association (Personality and Social Psychology, Clinical Psychology, Psychology of Women, Health Psychology, and Society for the Psychological Study of Lesbian and Gay Issues), a Fellow in the American Psychological Society, and the holder of a diplomate from the American Board of Professional Psychology. She is in *American Men and Women of Science*, *Who's Who in America*, and the *World's Who's Who of Women* and has received certificates of recognition from Psi Chi, the national honor society in psychology, from two states, New York and Ohio, and from the District of Columbia. As in her research, Strickland's leadership activities have reflected her commitment to help the less fortunate and have contributed to the evolution of psychology.

Through her research and leadership, Strickland has had and continues to have a significant impact on the study of depression specifically, and on public health in general. In the late 1980s she continued to be involved in the activities of the American Psychological Association and the newly emerging American Psychological Society.

REFERENCES

Crowne, D. P., & Strickland, B. R. (1961). The conditioning of verbal behavior as a function of the need for social approval. *Journal of Abnormal and Social Psychology*, *63*, 395–401.

Doster, J. A., & Strickland, B. R. (1971). The disclosing of verbal material as a function of information requested, information about the interviewer, and interviewee differences. *Journal of Consulting and Clinical Psychology*, *37*, 187–194.

Duke, M. P; Shaheen, J.; & Nowicki, S. (1977). The determination of locus of control in a geriatric population and a subsequent test of social learning model for interpersonal distance. *Journal of Psychology*, *86*, 735–736.

Hale, W. D. & Strickland, B. R. (1976). Induction of mood states and their effect on cognitive and social behaviors. *Journal of Consulting and Clinical Psychology*, *44*, 155.

Haley, W. D., & Strickland, B. R. (1986). Interpersonal betrayal and cooperation: Effects on self-evaluation in depression. *Journal of Personality and Social Psychology*, *50*, 386–391.

Kelly, G. A. (1955). *The psychology of personal constructs* (2 vols.) New York: Norton.

Kesey, K. (1962). *One flew over the cuckoo's nest*. New York: Viking.

King, D. S. (1981). Can allergic exposure provoke psychological symptoms? A double
    blind test. *Biological Psychiatry*, *16*, 3–19.
Nowicki, S. (1988). A manual and reference list for the Nowicki-Strickland Internal-
    External Control scales across the life-span. Atlanta: Emory University.
Nowicki, S., & Duke, M. P. (1974a). A locus of control measure for noncollege as well
    as college educated adults. *Journal of Personality Assessment*, *38*, 136–137.
Nowicki, S., & Duke, M. P. (1974b). A preschool and primary locus of control scale.
    Developmental Psychology, *10*, 874–881.
Nowicki, S., & Strickland, B. R. (1973). A locus of control scale for children. *Journal
    of Consulting and Clinical Psychology*, *40*, 148–154.
Proenza, L., & Strickland, B. R. (1965). A study of prejudice in Negro and white college
    students. *Journal of Social Psychology*, *67*, 273–281.
Rotter, J. B. (1954). *Social learning and clinical psychology*. Englewood Cliffs, N.J.:
    Prentice-Hall.
Russo, N. F. (1985). *A women's mental health agenda*. Washington, D.C.: American
    Psychological Association.
Strickland, B. R. (1965). The prediction of social action from a dimension of internal-
    external control. *Journal of Social Psychology*, *66*, 353–358.
Strickland, B. R. (1970). Individual differences in verbal conditioning, extinction, and
    awareness. *Journal of Personality*, *38*, 364–378.
Strickland, B. R. (1972). Delay of gratification as a function of race of the experimenter.
    Journal of Personality and Social Psychology, *22*, 108–112.
Strickland, B. R. (1973). Delay of gratification and a belief in internal locus of control
    among children. *Journal of Consulting and Clinical Psychology*, *40*, 338.
Strickland, B. R. (1977a). Approval motivation. In T. Blass (Ed.), *Personality variables
    and social behavior* (pp. 341–356). Hillsdale, N.J.: Lawrence Erlbaum Associates.
Strickland, B. R. (1977b). Internal-external control of reinforcement. In T. Blass (Ed.),
    Personality variables and social behavior (pp. 219–280). Hillsdale, N.J.: Law-
    rence Erlbaum Associates.
Strickland, B. R. (1978). Internal-external expectancies and health-related behaviors.
    Journal of Consulting and Clinical Psychology, *46*, 1192–1211.
Strickland, B. R. (1979). Internal-external expectancies and cardiovascular functioning.
    In L. C. Perlmuter & R. A. Monty (Eds.), *Choice and perceived control* (pp.
    221–231). Hillsdale, N.J.: Lawrence Erlbaum Associates.
Strickland, B. R. (1981). Psychological effects of food and chemical susceptibilities.
    Voices: The Art and Science of Psychotherapy, *17*, 68–72.
Strickland, B. R. (1982). Implications of food and chemical susceptibilities for clinical
    psychology. *International Journal of Biosocial Research*, *3*, 39–43.
Strickland, B. R. (1984). Levels of health enhancement: Individual attributes. In J. D.
    Matarazzo, N. E. Miller, S. M. Weiss, J. A. Herd, & S. M. Weiss (Eds.), *Be-
    havioral health: A handbook of health enhancement and disease prevention* (pp.
    101–113). New York: Wiley.
Strickland, B. R. (1987). Menopause. In A. Blechman & K. Brownell (Eds.), *Handbook
    of behavioral medicine for women* (pp. 41–47). New York: Pergamon.
Strickland, B. R. (1989). Internal and external control expectancies: From contingency
    to creativity. *American Psychologist*, *44*, 1–12.
Strickland, B. R., & Crowne, D. P. (1962). Conformity under conditions of simulated

group pressure as a function of need for social approval. *Journal of Social Psychology, 58*, 171–181.

Strickland, B. R., & Crowne, D. P. (1963). Need for approval and the premature termination of psychotherapy. *Journal of Consulting and Clinical Psychology, 27*, 95–101. Also in J. B. Rotter, J. E. Chance, & E. J. Phares (Eds.) (1972), *Applications of a social learning theory of personality*. New York: Holt, Rinehart, & Winston.

Strickland, B. R.; Hale, W. D.; & Anderson, L. K. (1975). Effect of induced mood states on activity and self-reported affect. *Journal of Consulting and Clinical Psychology, 43*, 587.

Strickland, B. R., & Janoff-Bulman, R. (1980). Expectancies and attributions: Applications for community mental health. In M. S. Gibbs, J. R. Lachenmeyer, & J. Wigal (Eds.), *Community psychology: Theoretical and empirical approaches* (pp. 97–119). New York: Gardner.

Strickland, B. R., & Kendall, K. E. (1983). Psychological symptoms: The importance of assessing health status. *Clinical Psychology Review, 3*, 179–199.

Thompson, N. L.; McCandless, B. R.; & Strickland, B. R. (1971). Personal adjustment of male and female homosexuals and heterosexuals. *Journal of Abnormal Psychology, 78*, 237–240.

Zykoskee, A.; Strickland, B. R.; & Watson, J. (1971). Delay of gratification and internal versus external control among adolescents of low socioeconomic status. *Developmental Psychology, 4*, 93–98.

Additional Representative Publications by Bonnie Ruth Strickland

Strickland, B. R. (1977). The approval motive. In B. B. Wolman & L. R. Pomer (Eds.), *International encyclopedia of neurology, psychoanalysis and psychology* (Vol. 2, pp. 86–87). New York: Human Sciences Press Periodicals.

Strickland, B. R. (1984). Psychologist as department chair. *Professional Psychology, 5*, 730–740.

Strickland, B. R. (1984). This week's Citation Classic (Prediction of social action from a dimension of internal-external control). *Current Contents, Social and Behavioral Sciences, 16*, 20.

Strickland, B. R. (1985). Over the Boulder and through the Vail. *Clinical Psychologist, 38*, 52–56.

Strickland, B. R. (1987). Apprenticeships in health psychology. In G. Stone, S. A. Weiss, J. D. Matarazzo, N. Miller, J. Rodin, G. Schwartz, C. Belar, M. Follick, & J. Singer (Eds.), *Health psychology: A discipline and a profession* (pp. 351–360). Chicago: University of Chicago Press.

Strickland, B. R. (1987). Foreword. In A. Blechman & K. Brownell (Eds.), *Handbook of behavioral medicine for women*. New York: Pergamon Press.

Strickland, B. R. (1987). On the threshold of the second century of psychology. *American Psychologist, 42*, 1055–1056.

Strickland, B. R. (1988). Clinical psychology comes of age. *American Psychologist, 43*, 104–107.

Strickland, B. R., & Calkins, B. S. (1987). Public policy and clinical training. *Clinical Psychologist, 40*, 31–34.

Strickland, B. R., & Haley, W. E. (1980). Sex differences on the Rotter IE Scale. *Journal of Personality and Social Psychology, 39*, 930–939.

Strickland, B. R., & Halgin, R. (1987). Integration of clinical, counseling, and social psychology. *Journal of Social and Clinical Psychology, 5*, 150–159.

THELMA GWINN THURSTONE (1897–)

Carolyn T. Bashaw and W. L. Bashaw

Thelma Thurstone made signal contributions to intelligence theory, reading instruction, and intelligence and personality testing. She was a charter member of the Psychometric Society and has been a prolific test author since 1924. One of her major contributions was the creation of learning materials based upon the common factor theory of intelligence. Thurstone was coauthor of the *Psychological Examinations* and the *Primary Mental Abilities* testing programs. These included many pioneering practices and were fundamental to the origins of the Educational Testing Service and to Science Research Associates, respectively. As well as contributing to test theory and practice, she produced a pioneering study concerning the mainstreaming of retarded children. Thurstone's learning materials and numerous versions of her tests are still marketed.

FAMILY BACKGROUND AND EDUCATION

Thelma Gwinn, born in Hume, Missouri, December 11, 1897, was the oldest child and only daughter of Richard Luther and Dora Buckles Gwinn, a school teacher and music teacher, respectively. Her parents expected and urged her and her two brothers to succeed, and Gwinn enjoyed a normal, active childhood and adolescence. She completed high school in Mount Vernon, Missouri, as the valedictorian of her class.

Gwinn entered the University of Missouri in 1913, graduating in 1917 with an A.B. in German. Her academic record merited her election to Phi Beta Kappa. Realizing that she must be self-supporting, Gwinn subsequently earned a second bachelor's degree, in education, from the University of Missouri. To support her studies, she simultaneously taught in public high schools in Vandalia (1917–1919) and Joplin, Missouri (1919–1920).

While pursuing her degree in education, Gwinn enrolled in her first psychology course. Her attraction to the discipline was immediate. In 1919 W. W. Charters offered her a scholarship for graduate study in psychology at Carnegie Institute of Technology. In addition to her graduate work, between 1920 and 1923, Gwinn also taught introductory courses in psychology at the Margaret Morrison College, the female annex of Carnegie Tech (T. G. Thurstone, 1985a).

While at the Carnegie Institute, Gwinn met Louis Leon Thurstone, a professor involved in the study of human intelligence. Upon completion of her master's degree in 1923, they both accepted positions at the Institute for Government Research in Washington, D.C. There she worked as a statistician in the Bureau of Public Personnel Administration. In addition to this work, she also enrolled in graduate courses at George Washington University.

In 1924, following her marriage to L. L. Thurstone and his acceptance of a faculty position at the University of Chicago, Thurstone became a full-time doctoral student, earning the Ph.D. in psychology from the University of Chicago in 1926. During their years in Chicago, 1924–1952, she held a series of full- and part-time jobs.

CAREER DEVELOPMENT

Between 1924 and 1948 Thurstone worked with her husband, creating and editing both the *Psychological Examinations* and the *Primary Mental Abilities* batteries. In addition to her professional work, she managed a household of three sons, Robert Leon (1927), Conrad Gwinn (1930), and Frederick Louis (1932). During their early years, from 1927 to 1938, she did not hold full-time employment, working instead with the American Council on Education. Such employment was considered ideal by Thurstone, since she could work at home, writing test items and performing other test development activities. As the children grew older, however, she employed full-time child care in order to continue her career (T. G. Thurstone, 1985a). Between 1942 and 1952 Thurstone held the position of research assistant at the University of Chicago.

Excluded from a full-time academic position at Chicago because of anti-nepotism regulations, she turned to the public sector for her primary employment. In 1948 Thurstone accepted the directorship of the Division of Child Study of the Chicago public schools, in which she supervised a staff of sixty-five psychologists. This, she maintained, "was the most exciting job that I ever had" (T. G. Thurstone, 1985b).

In 1952 L. L. Thurstone accepted a position at the University of North Carolina (UNC) at Chapel Hill. Again, antinepotism regulations denied Thurstone employment in the Psychology Department, so she accepted an appointment in the School of Education (T. G. Thurstone, 1985a). In addition, Thurstone worked in the Psychometrics Laboratory at UNC as project director, a title she held until 1982.

In 1955, following the death of her husband, Thurstone assumed the directorship in the Psychometrics Laboratory for two years. Although she took the position to supervise the completion of her husband's already funded research projects, Thurstone clearly wanted to continue her own independent research

(T. G. Thurstone, 1985a). She remained on the UNC faculty until her mandatory retirement in 1968.

In addition to her work in the United States, Thurstone also accepted two visiting professorships, at the University of Frankfurt in 1948 and at the University of Kabul in 1961. Despite her formal retirement from UNC in 1968, Thurstone worked actively throughout the 1970s, developing numerous curriculum materials. In 1979 the University of North Carolina awarded her an honorary doctor of laws degree.

When asked to identify a scholarly mentor in her life, Thurstone immediately cited her husband, who directed her doctoral work and with whom she worked continuously throughout their marriage (T. G. Thurstone, 1985a, 1985b). As a result of this association as well as her own work, Thurstone was an active part of the psychological network both at Chicago (Jones, 1985) and throughout the country. Her professional associations include Fellow status in the American Psychological Association and membership in various regional associations. Thurstone was also one of the nine women charter members of the Psychometric Society.

MAJOR CONTRIBUTIONS AND ACHIEVEMENTS

Thurstone's major work can be divided into two phases: her test research and development with L. L. Thurstone, and her own rather more wide-ranging research, which combined both theoretical consideration and practical classroom implementation. Throughout her long and distinguished career, Thurstone's primary scholarly concern remained not only the study of the theory and measurement of intelligence, but also the use of both in instructional materials. This work she termed her "crusade," an endeavor she intended to pursue "as long as I am able" (T. G. Thurstone, 1980a).

Thurstone's first substantial professional collaboration with L. L. Thurstone was the development of the *Psychological Examinations* for the American Council on Education, a project that dominated her career for twenty-four years. Between 1924 and 1948 the Thurstones were responsible for all annual revisions of the tests. Furthermore, they published annual reports on the *Psychological Examinations* in *Educational Record*.

In 1947 the Thurstones completed their final revision of the *Psychological Examinations*. The following year, the Educational Testing Service (ETS) assumed both the development and publication of these instruments. However, subsequent versions, prepared by the Cooperative Test Division of ETS, relied heavily on materials that the Thurstones supplied to ETS. The battery remained in circulation until 1964, when ETS discontinued its publication.

The Thurstones' second major research project was the development of the various editions of the *Primary Mental Abilities* (*PMA*) test batteries, based upon common factor theory, developed by L. L. Thurstone. Thelma Thurstone's first published contributions to measuring the primary factors of intelligence appeared in 1941 and included tests not initially credited to her. The American Council on Education had previously published commercial forms of these instruments, which became the *PMA*, credited only to L. L. Thurstone. Both names appear on all versions published since 1941, when Science Research Associates (SRA) initiated publication with the Single Booklet Edition of *The Chicago Tests of Primary Mental Abilities*. Science Research Associates published all subsequent English-language versions of the *PMA*, which also appeared in French, Italian, and Spanish versions. Revised forms of the English battery continued to appear until 1974.

Thurstone's own research can be divided into two categories: her early, theoretical work with test items and her subsequent, more practical production of curriculum materials. In her doctoral dissertation, Thurstone (1926) demonstrated that free response items, such as spelling tasks, chosen at moderate difficulty, would generate a test with optimum discrimination. She recommended that test constructors aim for an average difficulty of .5 and for a range of difficulty of .3 to .7, recommendations that are standard in contemporary texts. In her dissertation, Thurstone also employed a methodology common in current psychometric research. She obtained a large data bank of responses from which she simulated data from tests varying in difficulty level, thus utilizing "real data," which simulated test characteristics controlled to allow tests of her hypotheses.

Between 1957 and 1959 Thurstone served as principal investigator in a comparison of handicapped children in special classes with those in regular classes (T. G. Thurstone, undated). She concluded that, although the handicapped children appeared to benefit socially from special classes, they benefitted academically from regular classes. This pioneering effort predates the popular use of the term "mainstreaming" by nearly fifteen years. The Psychometrics Laboratory of the University of North Carolina continues to distribute copies of her findings (Jones, 1985).

Thurstone's interest in the application of theoretical work in the classroom resulted in the production of two sets of curriculum materials, published by SRA and updated in this decade. The first series, Learning to Think (T. G. Thurstone, 1981b), began in 1947 with *The Red Book*. Thurstone produced three subsequent volumes, *The Blue Book* (1948), *The Green Book* (1949), and *The Gold Book* (1972). In 1981 *The Rainbow Book*, a consolidated version of the four, appeared. This series taught children to perceive identities, similarities, and differences; to increase vocabulary; to reason in cause-effect and genus-species terms; and to improve hand-eye coordination.

The Reading for Understanding series (RFU) (T. G. Thurstone, 1980b) consists of six kits of reading comprehension test exercises. The first, *General Kit*, appeared in 1959. Subsequent kits include *Junior Kit* (1963), *Senior Kit* (1965), *Kit 2* (1978), *Kit 3* (1978), and *Kit 1* (1980). The RFU series emphasized reading comprehension; however, unlike the usual reading comprehension test items, RFU items require that the student find the implied answers, thus emphasizing inferential comprehension. This series ranges in difficulty from primary to college levels.

In addition to her major research and development efforts, Thurstone made a variety of other contributions. These include measures of personality, creativity, and mechanical aptitude. She also published a significant study of identical and fraternal twin differences.

CRITICAL EVALUATION OF CONTRIBUTIONS AND ACHIEVEMENTS

Critical evaluations of the Thurstones' published tests appear in numerous *Mental Measurements Yearbooks* (*MMYs*). Critics maintained that the *Psychological Examinations* represented significant advances in test data analysis, test and answer sheet layout, and scoring procedures. In the 1938 *MMY*, both Anne Anastasi and David Segal praised not only the quality of the battery, but also its technical development, including the annual norms updating the invention of a scale giving equivalent scores year to year. In *The Third Mental Measurements Yearbook*, W. D. Commins (1949, p. 297) claimed that "anyone looking for a 'good' intelligence test" should select the *Psychological Examinations*.

Reviewers generally acknowledge the *PMA* as a significant innovation in intelligence theory and testing. Despite criticism of *PMA* validity, John B. Carroll (1953, pp. 704–707) defended the test on theoretical grounds, positing that a test should be evaluated consistently with the theory upon which it was based, as the Thurstones had done. This "construct validity" point of view soon dominated validity considerations.

Most reviews of the *PMA* praised the Thurstones' contributions to intelligence theory and to the methodology of intelligence measurement. However, by the 1970s, reviewers began to compare the *PMA* negatively with newer instruments, such as the *Differential Aptitude Tests*. By this point, however, one must recognize that Thurstone herself had for some years been far more extensively involved with her own development of instructional materials.

Neither Thurstone's Learning to Think series nor the Reading for Understanding series has attracted substantial critical review. In one early review, however, John Carroll (1953, pp. 706–707) did praise Thurstone's efforts in the Learning to Think series and predicted much progress in the future. Nevertheless, continued revision and publication of both series suggests at least a tangible commercial value to SRA.

Thelma Thurstone made signal contributions to intelligence theory, reading instruction, and intelligence and personality testing. She contributed to the origins of two of the major test publishers—the Educational Testing Service and Science Research Associates, the latter of which is now part of the International Business Machines conglomerate. Perhaps the most pertinent assessment of Thurstone and her work came from her husband, who concluded his contribution to *A History of Psychology in Autobiography* with this statement:

Thelma has the outstanding achievement in our family in managing an active household at the same time she was professionally active. She has been a partner in every research project in the Psychometric Laboratory. For many years she was in the laboratory daily, helping to plan the projects, supervising most of the test construction, and participating especially in the interpretation of the results. In 1948 she left this work to become director of the Division of Child Study in the Chicago public schools. This report should really have been written as a biography of both of us. (L. L. Thurstone, 1952, p. 321)

REFERENCES

Anastasi, A. (1938). [Review of the A.C.E. *Psychological Examinations.*] In O. K. Buros (Ed.), *The 1938 mental measurements yearbook of the School of Education of Rutgers University* (p. 96). New Brunswick, N.J.: Rutgers University Press.

Carroll, J. B. (1953). [Review of the *S.R.A. Primary Mental Abilities.*] In O. K. Buros (Ed.), *The fourth mental measurements yearbook* (pp. 704–707). Highland Park, N.J.: Gryphon Press.

Commins, W. D. (1949). [Review of the A.C.E. *Psychological Examination.*] In O. K. Buros (Ed.), *The third mental measurements yearbook* (p. 297). New Brunswick, N.J.: Rutgers University Press.

Jones, L. V. (1985, August 7). Transcript of interview. Chapel Hill: Psychometric Laboratory, University of North Carolina.

Segal, D. (1938). [Review of the A.C.E. *Psychological Examinations.*] In O. K. Buros (Ed.), *The 1938 mental measurements yearbook of the School of Education of Rutgers University* (p. 96). New Brunswick, N.J.: Rutgers University Press.

Thurstone, L. L. (1952). L. L. Thurstone. In E. G. Boring (Ed.), *A history of psychology in autobiography* (Vol. 4, pp. 295–321). Worcester, Mass.: Clark University Press.

Thurstone, T. G. (1926). The relation between the difficulty of a test and its diagnostic value. Unpublished doctoral dissertation, University of Chicago. A version of this work appears as "The difficulty of a test and its diagnostic value," *Journal of Educational Psychology, 23,* 1932, 335–343.

Thurstone, T. G. (1980a). Looking back and looking forward. Presentation at the Science Research Associates fiftieth anniversary celebration, St. Louis, Mo.

Thurstone, T. G. (1980b). Reading for understanding series [Series includes *General Kit* (1959), *Junior Kit* (1963), *Senior Kit* (1965), *Kit 2* (1978), *Kit 3* (1978), and *Kit 1* (1980)]. Chicago: Science Research Associates.

Thurstone, T. G. (1981). *Learning to think series* [Series includes *The red book, The blue book, The green book, The gold book,* and *The rainbow book*]. Chicago: Science Research Associates (Original edition in 1947).

Thurstone, T. G. (1985a, June 21–22). Transcript of interview. Chapel Hill: Psychometric Laboratory, University of North Carolina.

Thurstone, T. G. (1985b, August 7–8). Transcript of interview. Chapel Hill: Psychometric Laboratory, University of North Carolina.

Thurstone, T. G. (undated). *An evaluation of educating mentally handicapped children in special education classes and in regular classes.* Final report of Cooperative Research Project No. OE-SAE-6452 of the U.S. Office of Education. Chapel Hill: University of North Carolina College of Education.

Additional Representative Publications by Thelma Gwinn Thurstone

Englehart, M. D., & Thurstone, T. G. (1938). *The "Chicago reading tests."* Chicago *School Journal, 20,* 74–81.

Englehart, M. D., & Thurstone, T. G. (1939). *Chicago reading tests.* Eau Claire, Wis.: E. M. Hale Co.

Thurstone, L. L., & Thurstone, T. G. (1929). *Personality schedule.* Chicago: University of Chicago Press.

Thurstone, L. L., & Thurstone, T. G. (1930). A neurotic inventory. *Journal of Social Psychology, 1,* 3–30.

Thurstone, L. L., & Thurstone, T. G. (1930). The 1929 *Psychological Examination. Educational Record, 1,* 101–128. [Note: A similar report appeared in *Educational Record* annually until 1947.]

Thurstone, L. L., & Thurstone, T. G. (1941). *The Chicago tests of primary mental abilities, for ages 11–17.* Chicago: Science Research Associates.

Thurstone, L. L., & Thurstone, T. G. (1941). *Factorial studies of intelligence* (Psychometric Monograph No. 2). Chicago: University of Chicago Press.

Thurstone, L. L., & Thurstone, T. G. (1943). *The Chicago test of primary mental abilities, single booklet edition.* Chicago: Science Research Associates.

Thurstone, L. L., & Thurstone, T. G. (1953). *Classification test* (Psychometric Monograph No. 2). Chapel Hill: University of North Carolina Press.

Thurstone, T. G. (1941). Primary mental abilities of children. *Educational and Psychological Measurement, 1,* 105–116.

Thurstone, T. G. (1950). Testing of primary mental abilities. *NEA Journal, 39,* 346–347.

Thurstone, T. G. (1957). The tests of primary mental abilities. *Personnel and Guidance Journal, 35,* 569–577.

Thurstone, T. G. (1961). What is intelligence? *NEA Journal, 50,* 50–54.

Thurstone, T. G. (1974, October 18). Louis Leon Thurstone and the history of the Psychometric Laboratory. Presentation to the Psychometric Laboratory of the University of North Carolina, Chapel Hill, N.C.

Thurstone, T. G. (1974). *PMA readiness level K–1.* Chicago: Science Research Associates.

Thurstone, T. G., & Lillie, D. L. (1970). *Beginning to learn: Fine motor skills.* Chicago: Science Research Associates.

Thurstone, T. G., & Lillie, D. L. (1972). *Beginning to learn: Perceptual skills.* Chicago: Science Research Associates.

Thurstone, T. G., & Mellinger, J. (1957). *CREE questionnaire.* Chicago: Industrial Relations Center.

Thurstone, T. G., & Thurstone, L. L. (1947). *Mechanical aptitude: Report of the first year of the study* (Psychometric Monograph No. 47). Chicago: University of Chicago Psychometric Laboratory.

Thurstone, T. G., & Thurstone, L. L. (1949). *Mechanical aptitude II: Description of group tests* (Psychometric Monograph No. 54). Chicago: University of Chicago Psychometric Laboratory.

Thurstone, T. G., & Thurstone, L. L. (1949). *Mechanical aptitude IV: Description of individual tests* (Psychometric Monograph No. 56). Chicago: University of Chicago Psychometric Laboratory.

Thurstone, T. G.; Thurstone, L. L.; & Strandskou, H. H. (1953). *A psychological study of twins. 1. Distributions of absolute differences for identical and fraternal twins* (Psychometric Monograph No. 2). Chapel Hill: University of North Carolina Psychometric Laboratory.

Thurstone, T. G.; Thurstone, L. L.; & Strandskou, H. H. (1955). *A psychological study of twins. 2. Scores of one hundred and twenty-five pairs of twins on fifty-nine tests* (Psychometric Monograph No. 12). Chapel Hill: University of North Carolina Psychometric Laboratory.

Additional Representative Publications about Thelma Gwinn Thurstone

Bashaw, W. L., & Bashaw, C. T. (1988). Thelma Gwinn Thurstone: Career strategies and contributions to measurement. *Psychology of Women Quarterly*, *12*, 341–356.

LEONA E. TYLER (1906–)

Suzanne M. Zilber and Samuel H. Osipow

Leona E. Tyler contributed significantly to the fields of individual differences and counseling psychology through her research, teaching, and widely respected graduate-level textbooks. Her work was at the leading edge of counseling psychology, and her ideas greatly influenced the field. Leona Tyler provided direction and definition to counseling as a specialty at a time when it was shakily emerging from the threads of other fields. More than one generation of psychologists grew to professional maturity influenced and guided by her book *The Work of the Counselor* (1969), in which she presented a theory of personality and life-span development. She was one of the early psychologists concerned with cross-cultural and sex differences, highlighting the importance of a balance between the environment and the individual. An innovator in many areas, she organized one of the first university counseling centers at the University of Oregon. She later demonstrated her remarkable professional leadership by serving simultaneously as graduate school dean and president of the American Psychological Association (APA). Her awards include the University of Minnesota Outstanding Achievement Award, the University of Oregon Distinguished Service Award, and the National Vocational Guidance Eminent Career Award. In addition, APA's Division of Counseling Psychology has recognized Tyler's work by naming its highest award the Leona Tyler Award. Tyler's prolific contributions continued into her eighties with a focus on the philosophy of science. Overall, an optimism about human development and human behavior underlies her work, which has provided a vital humanistic foundation for psychology.

FAMILY BACKGROUND AND EDUCATION

Leona Elizabeth Tyler was born on May 10, 1906, in Chetek, Wisconsin. Her father, Leon M. Tyler, worked as an accountant and later as a house restoration contractor. Her mother, Bessie J. Carver Tyler, managed their home. Both parents had graduated from high school, but there was no one in Leona Tyler's immediate or extended family who had gone to college. Nonetheless, her mother communicated strong expectations that all four of her children would go to college, and they all achieved career distinction.

Bessie Tyler believed that the Nineteenth Amendment securing the vote for women removed sexist barriers for women, and she treated Tyler as an equal to her brothers. While her mother's fundamentalist religious and moral values included more restrictions on Tyler's social activities than on her brothers', her mother's faith provided the basic foundation for Tyler's spirituality and moral principles (Tyler, 1988). In addition to her mother's social restrictions, Tyler's acceleration through her early schooling made it difficult for her to socialize with older schoolmates, so she spent her free time entertaining herself, developing a devotion to music and literature.

Three years ahead of her peers, Leona Tyler graduated at the remarkably young ages of fifteen from high school and nineteen from college. She recalled that in high school a female assistant principal insistently warned, "Don't let them send you to a teacher's college, go to a university." That advice provided significant guidance in a time when women usually went to teacher's colleges and she had thought she would too (personal communication, March 22, 1988). Consequently, Leona Tyler entered junior college in her hometown, then the University of Minnesota two years later, receiving her bachelor's degree in 1925. She was most enthusiastic about chemistry, but because she had emphasized literary studies in high school rather than mathematics and science, she found that she was not equipped for the advanced courses necessary for a chemistry major. Instead, she chose to complete a B.S. in English literature while proactively remedying her lack of math background with advanced math courses her last two years of college.

After graduation, Tyler taught English and various other subjects in junior high schools in Minnesota and Michigan. She was moved by personal accounts her students wrote, and the diversity in their themes sparked her interest in individual differences. The school administration expected her to pursue further training in the summers, so she enrolled in a course on individual differences in 1937 at the University of Southern California. Her instructor, Donald G. Paterson, a faculty member from the University of Minnesota, helped her develop a research project on the interests of adolescent girls and strongly encouraged her entry into the master's program in psychology at the University of Minnesota. Tyler, who was committed to the peace movement, found psychology appealing and hoped that studying psychology would answer her questions on how to further the goals of the peace movement.

She returned to Muskegon Heights, Michigan, to teach one more year and collect the data for her master's thesis. She found the burden of disciplining her students a terrible strain and was quite relieved to quit teaching. The next year, as a full-time graduate student, Tyler greatly enjoyed focusing her energies on reading. She minored in statistics and continued work on developing an interests test for adolescent girls for her dissertation, completing her Ph.D. in psychology in 1940.

CAREER DEVELOPMENT

In 1940 Tyler began her university teaching career in the psychology department of the University of Oregon at Eugene as an instructor. She taught a wide variety of courses, including individual differences, testing, and counseling, and less frequently, general, abnormal, child, adolescent, educational, and social psychology. The university received funds to establish a counseling service for veterans of World War II in 1941. With no examples to follow, Tyler innovatively organized that service, under the auspices of the psychology department. It later became the university counseling center at Oregon. Once the service was established, she spent about a third of her time counseling (Sundberg, 1980).

In addition to her counseling and administrative work, Tyler participated in various research projects within the university while writing *The Psychology of Human Differences*, first published in 1947 (Tyler, 1965). She found that her teaching, writing, and counseling all interacted to stimulate reevaluation and integration of ideas about human nature. Both research and writing activities provided a desirable professional balance for Tyler, for she found that research involvement alone can overly narrow one's focus, while textbook writing encourages consideration of a wide range of information.

Tyler integrated many theories in developing her own view of behavior. Her work reflects her own unique blending of the concepts of Carl Rogers, individual differences and psychometrics, psychoanalytic theory, behaviorism, developmental stage theory, and existentialism. Robert Leeper, a colleague at Oregon, influenced Leona Tyler's thinking as she shifted from a behavioristic approach to a more cognitive approach (Tyler, 1978).

Existentialism and developmental theory were the two most important conceptual influences, excluding general individual differences, on Tyler's theory of possibilities developed later in her career. Tyler was exposed to existentialism when she was on sabbatical in London in 1951. Of the existential writers, she was most influenced by Karl Jaspers, who emphasized the importance of individual choices (Gilmore, Nichols, & Chernoff, 1977). While in London, she started writing *The Work of the Counselor* (1969).

Tyler began her career focusing on interest development. She noted that interest measures reveal more through what they tell us about what people dislike or avoid rather than about what they like. Consequently, she became interested in how children developed dislikes and conducted a longitudinal study with first graders that stimulated ideas about theory and research related to interests and general development (Tyler, 1978).

In 1967–1968 she immersed herself in developmental theory to work on the latest revision of *Developmental Psychology* (1959) with Florence Goodenough. Tyler incorporated the stage theories of Piaget and Erikson into her work before these writers became influential in the United States. Tyler thought the most important developmental concept was that successive stages are qualitatively rather than quantitatively distinct.

Under the influences of existential and developmental thought, Tyler focused on the construct of organized choices as opposed to measured interests. In her 1958 presidential address to the Western Psychological Association (Tyler, 1959), she proposed that individuality is based on the choices people make and the cognitive structures people use to organize their experiences. This bold new orientation significantly changed the field's focus away from the current heavy emphasis on psychometrics and directed it more to developmental and learning processes.

In 1958, dissatisfied with her results on differences between noncareer and career oriented girls and scientifically and nonscientifically oriented boys, Tyler questioned why students make different choices. Intrigued by George Kelly's theory of personal constructs (1955), she searched for a methodology that would reveal the organizational structures underlying choices. She developed a card sort technique she called the Choice Pattern Technique, choosing occupations as the content of the cards (Tyler, Sundberg, Rohila, & Greene, 1968). Research participants sorted the occupations into piles reflecting interest or lack of interest. Participants then categorized the cards further into personally logical categories while explaining the reasons for their sorting choices. This creative work was the original card sorting technique, a procedure widely used today in career counseling. Unfortunately, the card sort technique produced diverse responses that were difficult to code, and as a result validity and reliability were difficult to determine. Tyler discounted concerns about validity and reliability as inappropriate criteria for measuring human behaviors, which by their nature are always changing (Tyler, 1978).

Tyler used the Choice Pattern Technique with Norman Sundberg to study adolescents from the United States, the Netherlands, and India, testing the assumption that environmental differences contribute to differences in cognitive organization (Tyler, Sundberg, Rohila, & Greene, 1968). Tyler received a Fulbright scholarship to work at the University of Amsterdam in 1962, where she collected a portion of the data. The results suggested that the more the environment determined vocational choice, the narrower and less differentiated the student's occupational choices. These results indicate the delicate interactive influence of environmental and individual variables on choices. This research fostered further development of Tyler's theory, which she presented as possibility theory in *The Work of the Counselor* (1969).

Tyler's organizational involvement began with the Western Psychological Association and Division 17, Counseling Psychology, of the American Psychological Association. In both organizations she served in leadership roles, eventually progressing to president in each. Division 17 has recognized Tyler's contribution by naming its highest award after her. In the mid–1960s she was elected to the APA Board of Directors, and later to the Policy and Planning Board. Tyler was appointed dean of the Graduate School of the University of Oregon in 1965 and was elected APA president in 1972, thus achieving important leadership roles both at the university and professionally. As an administrator she enjoyed observing group problem-solving processes, being involved in the decisions, and developing close professional relationships.

MAJOR CONTRIBUTIONS AND ACHIEVEMENTS

Tyler's book *The Work of the Counselor* (1969) was used extensively as a primary textbook for graduate students in counseling psychology, and in clinical psychology to a lesser extent. The book captures the essence of her major contributions in its coverage of life-span concerns, its focus on the individual in context, the "no-nonsense" applications of empirical research findings to counseling, and the concern with the real-life problems of ordinary people. She astutely covered this material while still conveying warmth and regard for her readers and their clients.

In *The Work of the Counselor* Tyler described her "theory of possibilities." Based on certain biological facts, her theory poses that all creatures are characterized by multipotentiality. At each point of development many possibilities exist for what one may become or choose to become. Development, therefore, consists of transforming a wide range of potentialities into a limited number of actualities. This development occurs over time in only one direction. As a result, some opportunities are necessarily missed and only some potentialities develop. All persons select which potentialities are actualized, whether consciously or unconsciously, driven by internal and environmental pressures.

People naturally engage in spontaneous activity, which then becomes modified by parents or other factors in the environment. Thus, parents may guide the direction of activity patterns, but do not create the activity itself. As a result of such guidance, basic organizational structures for guiding choices develop. These structures then channel future development. As an individual develops more complex organizational schemas, a new, qualitatively different individual will emerge. In addition, cognitive structures for organizing possibilities vary widely; for example, some structures guide short-term and some guide long-term decisions. People may or may not make decisions consistently over different life domains such as family or work (Tyler, 1970).

Leona Tyler applied her theory to counseling by proposing that clients seek counseling when they are confused or when a crisis occurs and their cognitive structures do not adequately guide their choices. She suggested that as society becomes more complex, it is the counselor's job to help clients survey all their possibilities. In summary, counseling is the process of examining possibility structures and facilitating choice among available options.

Tyler later applied her theory of possibilities to explore the choice behavior of scientists in *Thinking Creatively* (Tyler, 1983). She suggested that perceptions of choices for scientific inquiry are distorted or limited by professional education and discipline-based conformity (Lachman, 1984). She proposed that science would be best served if different scientific paradigms could coexist, tolerate, and inform each other's work. In her eighties she continued to work on issues in the philosophy of science (personal communication, March 22, 1988).

With creativity and persistence, Leona Tyler contributed significantly to both the science and the profession of psychology. Her vision and leadership helped shape both the Division of Counseling Psychology and the American Psychological Association. In her writing and research, she integrated ideas and communicated with astounding clarity about the complexities of human multipotentiality. She exemplified such multipotentiality, excelling in the many roles of teacher, administrator, mentor, researcher, and writer, as well as dog owner, music lover, and world traveler (Sundberg, 1980).

REFERENCES

Gilmore, S. K.; Nichols, M. E.; & Chernoff, S. P. (1977). Mountain Iron woman: A case of androgyny. *Personal and Guidance Journal, 55*, 451–459.

Goodenough, F., & Tyler, L. E. (1959). *Developmental psychology*. New York: Appleton-Century-Crofts.

Kelly, G. A. (1955). *The psychology of personal constructs*. New York: W. W. Norton.

Lachman, R. (1984). Innovative thinking about the fields of psychology [Review of *Thinking creatively*]. *Contemporary Psychology, 29*, 933–934.

Sundberg, N. (1980, May). Tribute to Leona Tyler. Paper presented at "Women Pathfinders in Psychology and Counseling" conference, Eugene, Oregon.

Tyler, L. E. (1959). Toward a workable psychology of individuality. *American Psychologist, 14*, 75–81.

Tyler, L. E. (1965). *The psychology of human differences* (3rd ed.). New York: Appleton-Century-Crofts/Prentice-Hall. (Also 1947 & 1956)

Tyler, L. E. (1969). *The work of the counselor* (3rd ed.). New York: Appleton-Century-Crofts. (Also 1953 & 1961)

Tyler, L. E. (1970). Thoughts about theory. In W. Van Hoose & J. Pietrofesa (Eds.), *Counseling and guidance in the twentieth century: Reflections and reformulations* (pp. 296–306). Boston: Houghton Mifflin.

Tyler, L. E. (1978). My life as a psychologist. In T. Krawiec (Ed.), *The psychologists: Autobiographies of distinguished living psychologists* (pp. 289–301). Brandon, Vt.: Clinical Psychology.

Tyler, L. E. (1983). *Thinking creatively: A new approach to psychology and individual differences*. San Francisco: Jossey-Bass.

Tyler, L. E. (1988). Years of my life. In A. N. O'Connell & N. F. Russo (Eds.), *Models of achievement*. Hillsdale, N.J.: Erlbaum.

Tyler, L. E.; Sundberg, N. D.; Rohila, P. K.; & Greene, M. M. (1968). Patterns of choices in Dutch, American, and Indian adolescents. *Journal of Counseling Psychology, 15*, 522–529.

Additional Representative Publications by Leona E. Tyler

Sundberg, N., Taplin, J. R., & Tyler, L. E. (1983). *Introduction to clinical psychology: Perspectives, issues, and contributions to human service*. Englewood Cliffs, N.J.: Prentice-Hall.

Tyler, L. E. (1945). Relationships between Strong Vocational Interest scores and other attitude and personality measures. *Journal of Applied Psychology*, *29*, 58–67.

Tyler, L. E. (1959). Distinctive patterns of likes and dislikes over a twenty-two year period. *Journal of Counseling Psychology*, *6*, 234–237.

Tyler, L. E. (Ed.). (1969). *Intelligence: Some recurring issues*. New York: Van Nostrand.

Tyler, L. E. (1973). Design for a hopeful psychology. *American Psychologist*, *28*, 1021–1029.

Tyler, L. E. (1978). *Individuality: Human possibilities and personal choice in the psychological development of men and women*. San Francisco: Jossey-Bass.

Tyler, L. E. (1979). *Tests and measurements* (3rd ed.). Englewood Cliffs, N.J. : Prentice-Hall. (Also 1963 & 1971)

Tyler, L. E. (1981). More stately mansions: Psychology extends its boundaries. *Annual Review of Psychology*, *32*, 1–20.

MARGARET FLOY WASHBURN (1871–1939)

Elizabeth Scarborough

Margaret Washburn of Vassar College was a leading psychologist during the first third of the twentieth century. The first woman to receive a Ph.D. in psychology, she achieved prominence in every facet of the field: research, publishing, editorial and organizational service, theory development, and teaching. Her most renowned work, *The Animal Mind*, was widely acknowledged as the first comprehensive textbook in comparative (animal) psychology. While she headed the psychology department at Vassar, she was also particularly active and influential in professional involvements that extended to regional, national, and international levels through leadership positions held in significant organizations such as the American Psychological Association, the Eastern Psychological Association, the National Research Council, and the Society of Experimental Psychologists. She was the second woman to become president of the American Psychological Association and the second woman elected to the National Academy of Sciences.

FAMILY BACKGROUND AND EDUCATION

Born July 25, 1871, in the Harlem district of New York City, Margaret Floy Washburn was the only daughter of Francis Washburn and Elizabeth Floy Davis, both of whom were natives of the city. Her father, who had little formal education, was a businessman until he entered the Episcopal ministry eight years after her birth. Her mother came from a prosperous family, completed high school, and lived her adult life as a housewife and mother, taking much satisfaction in the achievements of her competent daughter. Both parents shared with Washburn exceptionally strong literary interests and encouraged her intellectual pursuits.

For a year and a half, beginning at age seven, Washburn attended an excellent private school located in the house next to her home. Her schooling suffered when the family moved to her father's parishes in Orange and Ulster counties (New York), but she graduated from high school in 1886 and entered Vassar

College that fall, at age fifteen, as a preparatory student because of deficiencies in Latin and French. She reveled in the intellectual atmosphere there, finding special pleasure in poetry, philosophy, and science, and years later described in some detail the particular persons and experiences that influenced her (Washburn, 1932). She was introduced to psychology in a required senior course taught by the college president, who argued against materialism in an effort to preserve students' religious convictions, which Washburn had already abandoned.

Upon graduation from Vassar in 1891, Washburn sought to enroll in the graduate psychology program at Columbia University, although Columbia had not yet admitted a woman graduate student. In January she was admitted, but only as an auditor. James McKeen Cattell, however, treated her as a "regular" student and guided her first experimental work and theoretical study. She developed an early and durable respectful affection for him, her first and most influential mentor in psychology. On his advice she transferred to the newly organized Sage School of Philosophy at Cornell University, where she was eligible for degree candidacy and also a graduate scholarship, neither of which seemed possible at Columbia.

During her first year at Cornell, 1892–1893, Washburn was the first and at that time the only major graduate student of E. B. Titchener. She conducted an experimental study of the method of equivalents in tactual perception, which earned her an M.A. *in absentia* from Vassar in 1893. The following year she was joined in the graduate program by Walter B. Pillsbury, who became a lifelong friend, and completed her doctor's thesis on the influence of visual imagery on judgments of tactual distance and direction. That work was subsequently sent by Titchener to Wilhelm Wundt and published in *Philosophische Studien* (1895). In June 1894, having met all requirements for the doctoral degree, Washburn became the first woman to receive a Ph.D. in psychology. That year she was elected to membership in the newly organized American Psychological Association (APA).

CAREER

Washburn was on the point of accepting an offer to teach in a finishing school—the only position available to her—when she was unexpectedly recruited by Wells College. She was appointed chair of psychology, philosophy, and ethics and taught these subjects, plus logic, at the small women's college from 1894 to 1900. During this time she kept in close contact with her friends on the philosophy faculty at Cornell and published several articles that enhanced her visibility and reputation in the professional community. By 1900, however, she grew restless and felt that she needed a change and perhaps a more stimulating environment in which to pursue the new ideas that were emerging as her own view of psychology.

She returned to Cornell for two years, holding the title Warden of Sage College, which required functioning as residence director for the women's dormitory. She used this opportunity, however, to engage in laboratory work, further exploring the area of visual phenomena and testing the merits and limitations of introspection as a method. She also attended Titchener's seminar and began to elaborate her objections to his structural psychology. For the 1901–1902 academic year Washburn was appointed lecturer in psychology and taught two courses that involved her keen interests in social psychology and animal psychology, topics that figured prominently in later teaching, research, and writing. In 1902 Washburn left the uncongenial duties associated with being a warden and accepted an assistant professorship in psychology at the University of Cincinnati. She spent only one year in the Midwest, however, and was delighted when she received an offer to return to Vassar College as associate professor of philosophy.

Remaining at Vassar for the rest of her career, Washburn soon established there one of the most significant psychological centers in the country, a most unusual achievement since she was at a women's college that provided limited support for experimental work and had no graduate students. She was promoted to professor in 1908, and when a department of psychology was organized in 1912, she became its head, the position she held until her retirement in 1937. Washburn was a campus leader in faculty governance, often playing a mediating role between opposing factions, but forceful in advocating high standards of academic performance. She steadfastly objected to efforts at Vassar to modify the liberal arts curriculum by adding applied subjects (home economics, child study, and euthenics, for example), maintaining that to do so would destroy the hard-earned intellectual gains made by and for women. President H. N. MacCracken considered her "probably [Vassar's] most famous scholar and certainly [its] best lecturer" (MacCracken, 1950, p. 73). Generations of appreciative students held her in great awe, though many learned—sometimes only after graduation—that she was warmly interested in their personal welfare and extremely supportive. Faculty colleagues valued her friendship, wit, and enthusiastic participation in academic and extracurricular activities.

MAJOR CONTRIBUTIONS AND ACHIEVEMENTS

Washburn's contributions to psychology were significant and sustained. She participated actively and effectively in the maturation of psychology as both a scientific discipline and a scholarly profession. The range of her involvements included methodological innovation, development of theory, experimental research, education and encouragement of undergraduate women students, editorial service on major journals, and responsible leadership positions in professional organizations. Her bibliography includes 134 articles and 66 book reviews and notices (see Kambouropoulou, 1940, and Mull, 1927).

A major contribution, and the most enduring of her writings, was *The Animal Mind* (1908). This work was the first textbook in comparative psychology, a pioneering effort to compile, analyze, and interpret the burgeoning literature dealing with experimental studies of animal behavior and mentality. In later editions of the book, published in 1917, 1926, and 1936, Washburn incorporated the relevant new research, but staunchly maintained her conviction that mental phenomena—for example, feelings and sensations, colors and tones—were not only legitimate but necessary topics to examine. For her, psychology was the study of behavior *and* consciousness. Here she was flying in the face of the behaviorist movement that accelerated during the 1920s and 1930s. Her subjective stance drew increasing criticism, and yet she could not be easily dismissed. Harvey Carr (1927) devoted his APA presidential address to discussing the merits and problems of her approach, and even the harshest critics of her position in later years acknowledged that her presentation of the experimental literature was exhaustive, that her methodological comments were critical, and that the book was essential reading for any serious study of comparative psychology.

In Washburn's view, the goals of psychology included description *and* explanation, both to obtain and to interpret facts. Unable to accept the formulations of any of the major schools of psychology, Washburn developed and vigorously defended her own motor theory, presented most completely in her other book, *Movement and Mental Imagery* (1916). She drew on results of numerous German and French experiments on the higher mental processes, but interpreted the data by her own motor principles, developing the doctrine that thinking requires tentative movements. She had begun working on the idea some twenty years before when she began to see the limitations of Titchener's strict structural psychology as well as some promise in Hugh Münsterberg's use of movement as an explanatory principle. Washburn had earlier published the basic outline of her motor system (1914). During the 1920s she advanced her position by demonstrating the worth of the theory for explaining the research data being produced by scientists of differing orientations.

Washburn's paper in *Psychologies of 1930* (1930) was a succinct statement that laid out clearly her position, showing how motor psychology, based on sound physiological evidence and logic, dealt with the concepts and facts of drive, emotion, learning, perception, and thinking. In a one-page statement she detailed her heterodoxy by summarizing the relation of her system to other psychologies. She both agreed and disagreed with aspects of behaviorism, structuralism, functionalism, and Gestalt psychology, but was totally opposed to purposive psychology because of its nonmechanistic bias. Her position agreed with both behaviorism and structural psychology in being mechanistic, but hers was a dualistic mechanism that regarded study of mental processes as necessary (in opposition to the behaviorists' materialistic monism). She differed from structural psychology by discounting the minute description of mental processes and focusing instead on behavior as an expression of conscious experience and using laws of bodily movement as central explanatory principles. She agreed with the Gestalt psychologists on subject matter but believed that hers was a far more adequate explanation for the phenomena. She considered her theory closer to functional psychology than to any other system, but was opposed to the interactionism implied by the functionalists. In short, Washburn was a mechanistic dualist who rejected any form of interactionism and viewed consciousness as an epiphenomenal process that accompanies the simultaneous excitation and inhibition of a motor discharge.

Washburn was given an important forum for expressing her theory in a paper (1928) delivered at the 1927 Wittenberg Conference on Feelings and Emotions, an unusual gathering of international scholars in chemistry and psychology. She was the only woman speaker and one of the few participants who were granted honorary degrees at the conclusion of the affair. This occasion clearly signified her status as a renowned experimentalist.

Throughout this time Washburn was carrying a heavy teaching and administrative load. She managed to maintain her experimental work through collaborative work with selected senior students, establishing a series of published studies that spanned a thirty-five-year period and covered a wide range of problems, including spatial perception by different senses, memory, experimental aesthetics, individual differences, animal psychology, emotion, and affective consciousness. Most of these reports were published in the *American Journal of Psychology*, on which she served in various editorial capacities from 1903 to 1937. In 1927 that journal honored her third-of-a-century of psychological work by publishing a ''commemorative volume''; all the contributing authors had been associated with her on various psychological journals. In addition to work for the *American Journal of Psychology*, she also held editorial responsibilities for *Psychological Bulletin* (1909–1915), *Journal of Animal Behavior* (1911–1917), *Psychological Review* (1916–1930), and *Journal of Comparative Psychology* (1921–1935).

Margaret Washburn served as APA president in 1921. The office then represented primarily an honorific distinction. Her reputation as an influential and respected leader, however, is buttressed by highly significant contributions to the organizational life of psychology, many of which followed her APA presidency. In addition to serving as chair of several extremely important national committees, she was a member of the APA Council (1912–1914), psychology representative to the National Research Council Division of Psychology and Anthropology (1919–1920, 1925–1928), vice president and chair of the psychology section of the American Association for the Advancement of Science (1927), member of the International Committee on Psychology (1929), chair of the Society of Experimental Psychologists (1931), and president of the New York Branch of APA, which became the Eastern Psychological Association (1931).

Washburn's highest national achievement was election to the National Academy of Sciences in 1932. She was the first woman psychologist and the second woman scientist to be so honored. Early in her career she had been identified as a leading scientist, included (along with Christine Ladd-Franklin and Mary Whiton Calkins) among the fifty top-ranked American psychologists in 1903 (Cattell & Brimhall, 1921). Her lasting influence in psychology was indicated in a 1967 study that used an international panel to rank over 1,000 contributors to psychology who lived between 1600 and 1967. The highest possible score was 27, and 583 eminent persons were identified as ranking between 11 and 27. Margaret Washburn's score was 23 (Watson, 1974).

INTEGRATION OF PERSONAL AND PROFESSIONAL LIFE

Interviews conducted with a number of her associates and examination of both published and archival sources (see especially Chapter 5 in Scarborough and Furumoto [1987] and Goodman [1980]) make it clear that Washburn's achievements represent an admirable response to her personal situation. Washburn's professional accomplishments and her widely acknowledged status in psychology resulted from several advantageous elements: early intellectual interests and ability, augmented by parental support and disciplined scholarly activity; a clear sense of self and wise career choices; social skills that encouraged cordial relations with diverse groups of colleagues, sustained over long periods; and career dedication combined with pleasurable personal pursuits. As an only child, she bore a heavy responsibility for the care of her parents, but they were strongly supportive of her aspirations, and she arranged her work so as to be near them and provide for their needs. Rather than agonizing over the career versus marriage decision that plagued many highly educated women of her generation, Washburn made an early and personally satisfying choice of career. She converted the limitations of employment at a women's college into an advantage by becoming a prominent leader on her own campus and enlisting junior faculty and students as research assistants. She escaped professional isolation and invisibility by frequent travel, regular correspondence with colleagues, and undertaking numerous professional responsibilities, all of which kept her in close touch with other psychologists. Through a facilitating blend of independence and affiliation she was able to avoid being identified with any one faction of the field and instead maintained good relations with people representing quite different points of view.

A forceful personality with a sharp sense of humor moderated by sensitivity to others' feelings, Washburn presented a reserved demeanor in social situations with acquaintances. With close friends, both men and women, she displayed great warmth. She enjoyed many extra-career activities, some private, some shared with others: piano playing, singing, ballroom dancing, amateur dramatics, oil painting, collecting memoirs of English political history. She had a lifelong fascination with animals and especially loved cats. Margaret Washburn suffered an incapacitating stroke in 1937 and died in Poughkeepsie, New York, on October 29, 1939.

REFERENCES

Carr, H. (1927). The interpretation of the animal mind. *Psychological Review, 34*, 83–97.

Cattell, J. McK., & Brimhall, D. R. (Eds.). (1921). *American men of science* (3rd ed.). Garrison, N.Y.: Science Press.

Goodman, E. S[carborough]. (1980). Margaret F. Washburn (1871–1939): First woman Ph.D. in psychology. *Psychology of Women Quarterly, 5,* 69–80.

Kambouropoulou, P. (1940). A bibliography of the writings of Margaret Floy Washburn: 1928–1939. *American Journal of Psychology, 53,* 19–20.

MacCracken, H. N. (1950). *The hickory limb.* New York: Scribner's.

Mull, H. K. (1927). A bibliography of the writings of Margaret Floy Washburn: 1894–1927. *American Journal of Psychology, 39,* 428–436.

Scarborough, E., & Furumoto, L. (1987). *Untold lives: The first generation of American women psychologists.* New York: Columbia University Press.

Washburn, M. F. (1895). Ueber den Einfluss der Gesichtsassociationen auf die Raumwahrnehmungen der Haut. *Philosophische Studien, 11,* 190–225.

Washburn, M. F. (1908). *The animal mind: A textbook of comparative psychology.* New York: Macmillan.

Washburn, M. F. (1914). The function of incipient motor processes. *Psychological Review, 21,* 376–390.

Washburn, M. F. (1916). *Movement and mental imagery: Outlines of a motor theory of the complexer mental processes.* Boston: Houghton Mifflin.

Washburn, M. F. (1922). Introspection as an objective method. *Psychological Review, 29,* 89–112.

Washburn, M. F. (1928). Emotion and thought: A motor theory of their relations. In M. L. Reymert (Ed.), *Feelings and emotions: The Wittenberg symposium* (pp. 105–115). Worcester, Mass.: Clark University Press.

Washburn, M. F. (1930). A system of motor psychology. In C. Murchison (Ed.), *Psychologies of 1930* (pp. 81–94). Worcester, Mass.: Clark University Press.

Washburn, M. F. (1932). Some recollections. In C. Murchison (Ed.), *A history of psychology in autobiography* (Vol. 2, pp. 333–358). Worcester, Mass.: Clark University Press.

Watson, R. I. (1974). *Eminent contributors to psychology: Volume 1, A bibliography of primary references.* New York: Springer.

Additional Representative Publications by Margaret Floy Washburn

Washburn, M. F. (1894). The perception of distance in the inverted landscape. *Mind,* N.S. *3,* 438–440.

Washburn, M. F. (1894). Some apparatus for cutaneous stimulation. *American Journal of Psychology, 6,* 422–426.

Washburn, M. F. (1896). The intensive statement of particular and negative propositions. *Philosophical Review, 5,* 403–405.

Washburn, M. F. (1897). The process of recognition. *Philosophical Review, 6,* 267–274.

Washburn, M. F. (1898). The psychology of deductive logic. *Mind,* N.S. 7, 523–530.

Washburn, M. F. (1899). After-images. *Psychological Review, 6,* 653.

Washburn, M. F. (1899). Recent discussions of imitation. *Philosophical Review, 8,* 101–104.

Washburn, M. F. (1899). Subjective colours and the after-image: Their significance for the theory of attention. *Mind*, N.S. *8*, 25–34.

Washburn, M. F. (1900). The color changes of the white light after-image, central and peripheral. *Psychological Review*, 7, 39–46.

Washburn, M. F. (1902). Some examples of the use of psychological analysis in system-making. *Philosophical Review*, *11*, 445–462.

Washburn, M. F. (1903). The genetic function of movement and organic sensations for social consciousness. *American Journal of Psychology*, *14*(3–4), 73–78.

Washburn, M. F. (1903). Notes on duration as an attribute of sensations. *Psychological Review*, *10*, 416–422.

Washburn, M. F. (1905). Wundtian feeling analysis and the genetic significance of feeling. *Philosophical Review*, *14*, 21–29.

Washburn, M. F. (1909). The physical basis of relational processes. *Psychological Bulletin*, *6*, 369–378.

Washburn, M. F. (1917). The social psychology of man and the lower animals. In *Studies in psychology: Titchener commemorative volume* (pp. 11–17). Worcester, Mass.: Wilson.

Washburn, M. F. (1917). Some thoughts on the last quarter century in psychology. *Philosophical Review*, *26*, 46–55.

Washburn, M. F. (1919). Dualism in animal psychology. *Journal of Philosophy, Psychology, and Scientific Methods*, *16*, 41–44.

Washburn, M. F. (1926). Gestalt psychology and motor psychology. *American Journal of Psychology*, *37*, 280–283.

Washburn, M. F. (1928). Purposive action. *Science*, *67*, 24–28.

Additional Representative Publications About Margaret Floy Washburn

Boring, E. G. (1971). Margaret Floy Washburn. In E. T. James (Ed.), *Notable American women, 1607–1950* (Vol. 3). Cambridge, Mass.: Belknap Press.

Dallenbach, K. M. (1940). Margaret Floy Washburn: 1871–1939. *American Journal of Psychology*, *53*, 1–5.

Furumoto, L., & Scarborough, E. (1986). Placing women in the history of psychology. *American Psychologist*, *41*, 35–42.

Furumoto, L., & Scarborough, E. (1987). Placing women in the history of comparative psychology: Margaret Floy Washburn and Margaret Morse Nice. In E. Tobach (Ed.), *Historical perspectives and the international status of comparative psychology* (pp. 103–117). Hillsdale, N.J.: Erlbaum.

Martin, M. F. (1940). The psychological contributions of Margaret Floy Washburn. *American Journal of Psychology*, *53*, 7–18.

Pillsbury, W. B. (1940). Margaret Floy Washburn: 1871–1939. *Psychological Review*, *47*, 99–109.

Woodworth, R. S. (1949). Margaret Floy Washburn. In *National Academy of Sciences biographical memoirs* (Vol. 25). Washington, D.C.: National Academy of Sciences.

BETH LUCY WELLMAN (1895–1952)

Marie Skodak Crissey

Beth Lucy Wellman's studies of the mental development of children in enriched and deprived environments, and follow-up observations of the same children into young adulthood, were the first to challenge the then generally held concept that intelligence was largely immune to environmental influences and that the IQ was a stable and constant measure of intelligence. The discovery that environmental influences such as parental stimulation, appropriate preschool experiences, and intellectually stimulating circumstances did indeed affect the individual's mental functioning level opened the door to programs aimed at improving the competencies of groups and individuals who were assumed to be of limited initial capability. Wellman's pioneering studies were, in a sense, the scientific foundations for many of the Great Society efforts of the 1960s. Programs such as Head Start, Home Start, early education of the mentally retarded, some aspects of mainstreaming, and various educational innovations owe their beginnings to the implications of Wellman's researches. Few studies begun in academic circles have had as much influence on public policy.

FAMILY BACKGROUND AND EDUCATION

Beth Lucy Wellman was born in Clarion, Iowa, on June 10, 1895. Her parents, Alonzo and Hannah Wellman, had two additional daughters, Rowena and Roxanne. From the small farming market town of Clarion, the family moved to the college town of Ames, Iowa, where Wellman graduated from high school. They moved again to Waterloo, a somewhat larger city, closer to Iowa State Teachers College at Cedar Falls, where Beth Wellman received a B.A. degree. During her college years, she worked part time as a secretary, and after graduation she was secretary to the administrators of the college.

While Beth Wellman was in high school (1908–1912), half a world away Alfred Binet had devised a series of test items that proved useful in estimating a child's mental age and classifying the child in relation to age peers. Brought to the United States by Henry Goddard, the test was elaborated and standardized during 1912–1916 by Lewis Terman. By the time Beth Wellman graduated from college the Stanford Binet had become a most promising tool in the psychological armamentarium. To supplement the predominantly verbal Stanford Binet, a spate of performance traits followed, first for adults, then for children (Baldwin & Wellman, 1928).

On the social-political scene, World War I and the prosperity of the early 1920s had an impact on Iowa's farm economy, but occupational channels for women were still limited largely to teaching, nursing, and secretarial work.

Her work in the administrative offices of a leading teacher training school exposed Wellman to the new movements in child development research. The studies of World War I recruits had shown that the health and education of young men varied according to the educational and social resources in their respective states, and that there were great gaps in knowledge about how children grow and how optimum development could be best facilitated.

In the early years of the twentieth century there was rising concern about the welfare of children, part of the larger social welfare and progressive reform movement. In Iowa the need for better information about the optimum care of children was especially felt by Cora Bussey Hillis (three of her children died in infancy). It was through her persistence and her influence in social and political organizations that a new research facility, functioning under the aegis of the State University of Iowa, was established in 1917. Bird T. Baldwin, released from military service with the close of World War I, became the first director of the Iowa Child Welfare Research Station. His goal was the development of a center in which all aspects of normal children's growth would be studied. The staff he carefully assembled included specialists in nutrition, physical growth and development, family relationships, and psychological development.

CAREER PATH

It was into this new arena of studies that Beth Wellman found her way by 1920. She became secretary to the director and enrolled in graduate courses when she could. From 1921 to 1924 she was appointed a research associate. In 1923 she spent several months in California, taking physical measurements of Terman's gifted children. This research, jointly under Terman and Baldwin, was analyzed at the Iowa Child Welfare Research Station. Wellman's experiences at Stanford, where she had contact with Lewis Terman, Florence Goodenough, and others, strengthened her identification with the generally accepted concept that tests were reliable measures of intelligence, which was predictably constant and largely genetic in origin.

On returning to Iowa, Wellman continued her work on the development of formboard tests and other performance measures suitable for young children. By this time the laboratory preschools for two- to four-year-old children had been established at the Iowa Child Welfare Research Station, and tests of all kinds were being given to establish a baseline of normal child growth and development.

To broaden her experience, Wellman went to the Lincoln School at Columbia in 1924–1925, but returned to Iowa for the Ph.D. degree, granted in 1925. That year she was appointed research associate professor. In 1929 she became associate professor, and in 1937 full professor. She remained active at Iowa until her death in 1952. In addition to her primary responsibilities of teaching courses at the graduate level, supervising research assistants, and advising graduate students, she had major interim leadership duties. From 1949 to 1951 she was chair of the Administrative Council, which directed the station operations between the departure of Robert Sears as director in 1949 and the appointment of Boyd McCandless in 1951. Her whole professional career was intertwined with the station. Staff and students regarded her as the one who provided stability in an academic world that saw staff and students come and go.

PERSONAL LIFE

In addition to her devotion to research and related professional activities, Beth Wellman had a private life as well. Her work as a secretary and later as research assistant brought her close to Bird Baldwin, the director. He had come to Iowa with an invalid wife and four young children. A live-in couple managed the household and provided some continuity when Mrs. Baldwin died. The youngest child was then about five, the boy twins about ten, and the oldest boy an adolescent. Wellman received her degree, marriage was planned, and a house was being built when, in 1928, Bird Baldwin developed erysipelas and died within a few days. It was left to Beth Wellman to settle the estate, sell the nearly completed house, and plan for the children. Subsequently she became the guardian of the three youngest ones and provided a loving and stable home. In this she was assisted by her mother, who brought a warm, grandmotherly atmosphere not only for the Baldwin children but for the lonely or homesick graduate students who drifted into the Wellman household. Her mother's management of the household and of the modest finances gave Beth Wellman the freedom to pursue the researches and professional responsibilities that she kept separate from her family relationships.

Characteristic of Wellman's ability to separate her personal problems from her professional activities was her casual attitude toward the breast cancer for which she had surgery in the 1940s and which eventually took her life. She returned to work soon after surgery in spite of the discomfort and inconvenience of the swollen arm which in those days inevitably followed a mastectomy.

LIFE AT THE STATION

In 1928, faced with personal loss and the expansion of her home and household responsibilities, she was also faced with a change of directors of the still fledgling research station. The choice fell on George Stoddard, who, like Wellman, was a 1925 Ph.D. from Iowa. Although his primary interests had been in college-level aptitude and achievement tests, he readily moved into the area of research in child development. For the next fourteen years Wellman had in Stoddard a staunch supporter. Not least among his qualifications was that in postwar Paris he had been a student of Theodore Simon, and through him had absorbed Alfred Binet's philosophy and psychological legacy. The congenial working relations with Stoddard resulted in two coauthored major texts: *Child Psychology* (1934) and *A Manual of Child Psychology* (1936).

Her publications began in 1926 with a study of leadership among high school students (Caldwell & Wellman, 1926). Although under Bird Baldwin there was some emphasis on field studies in the rural schools, the focus soon shifted to laboratory-type researches. For Beth Wellman this meant investigations of motor development in young children (1926, 1931) and the use of the Merrill-Palmer tests (1938a). She also collaborated in research on language development (Wellman & Bradbury, 1929).

However, it was with the evaluation of the intelligence test results of preschool enrollees that Beth Wellman found her metier. Publication of the findings began in the early 1930s and at first created no stir among her peers (Wellman, 1932). The publication of follow-up studies, tracing the mental development (as indicated by the IQ on individual tests) of children from preschool through high school aroused more attention (Wellman, 1932–1933, 1936). Although subsequent studies confirmed her findings and extended their implications, she was initially severely criticized by leaders in psychology who espoused the belief that intelligence was determined by genetic and social characteristics, and once set on course, would remain at the level assessed by properly administered tests. At the same time studies of the mental progress of children from inadequate homes, children in institutions, children in adoptive homes, and children in so-called therapeutic situations were appearing. Wellman was intimately associated with these studies, most of which were under the more immediate supervision of Harold Skeels (Skeels et al., 1938). In any case the results were discussed in detail, and their rather disconcerting implications were not at first congenial for the investigators. It must be remembered that Wellman had been influenced by Terman, with his meritocracy bias, and by Baldwin, who had a deep interest in human genetics. Skeels had a background in animal husbandry, with its emphasis on genetics, and team member Marie Skodak had been a student of Henry Goddard, with his hereditarian bias.

From the consistent results, both from studies of upper socioeconomic status children from enriched school programs (1936), and from studies of children experiencing varied environmental deprivations and advantages (1934), there developed what became known as the "Iowa point of view" (1940a, 1940b). In contrast to the general belief that intelligence was genetic in origin and impervious to environmental influence, this new position suggested the opposite (1938b). The evidence strongly suggested that children in stimulating nursery schools or homes could and did show gains in functioning or on tests of school achievement (1937). On the other hand, those who were in less stimulating situations did not show gains, indeed experienced marked losses in IQ if the environment was sufficiently stultifying (Wellman, 1945; Wellman & Pegram, 1944). Since the major journal articles, especially the early ones, were Wellman's, the criticisms and hostility were directed primarily at her as well as the research station in general. The severest criticism came from Terman and his associates at Stanford and from Florence Goodenough at Minnesota.

The director of the station, George Stoddard, not only defended the studies and their implications for social policy, but found the concept of the flexibility of intelligence and its responsiveness to environmental conditions quite in accord with his own definition of intelligence (Stoddard & Wellman, 1940). Binet's concepts, transmitted by Simon, had never been based on fixed, developmental unfolding that was free from environmental effects. Stoddard's national leadership (e.g., as editor of the twenty-seventh yearbook of the National Society for the Study of Education) enabled him effectively to interpret and defend the Iowa studies. However, it took years for the futility of the nature-nurture debate to be recognized and for the contentiousness to die down. Its most virulent form continued until the mid-1940s, when World War II brought rapid changes in priorities and concerns. After the mid-1940s there were few articles debating the issue or challenging the veracity of the Iowa studies.

Through all the acrimony that was directed at her, Beth Wellman remained calm, at least externally. She did not engage in the ad hominem attacks, and parried them by referring to the facts and the evidence (Wellman, Skeels, & Skodak, 1940). That she was saddened and hurt by the attacks on her research and her personal integrity was evident only to her close associates.

Since one of the mandates for the Iowa Child Welfare Research Station was the dissemination of knowledge, there was considerable emphasis on publication. Between 1926 and 1946, Wellman published some forty major articles, some twenty jointly authored articles, two books with George Stoddard, and numerous popular and professional service pieces. The majority appeared between 1932 and 1942 and were related to mental development and environmental influences. In addition she served on most dissertation and thesis papers in which there was some involvement with mental development. Wellman's contributions ranged from reports on motor development and hand skills of very young children to leadership in adolescent girls, with the bulk of her contributions having to do with mental test results and the emerging nature-nurture controversy. There were only a half dozen publications after 1942, reflecting both her deteriorating health and the changing milieu at the research station.

By 1942, when it seemed that all that could reasonably be said about IQ flexibility and the nature-nurture debate had appeared in print, changes occurred at the research station. George Stoddard accepted an invitation to become jointly the president of the State University of New York and the commissioner of education. Robert Sears was appointed director of the station and remained until

1949. Sears' interest in personality, projective studies, and clinical observations brought a new emphasis to the station. It was a time of many changes brought by World War II. Some staff members (Harold Skeels) and research assistants (Boyd McCandless and others) went into the services. Kurt Lewin and his associates and students became involved in war-related motivational studies. Perhaps equally important for the source of research subjects and problems was the dissolution of the close ties between the research station and the state children's agency and state institutions for children. Although Wellman had supervised many of the dissertations based on institution problems and populations, she had not been the primary liaison who tied the two facilities together. She did not have the political finesse or the kind of ruthlessness that power maneuvering requires. In a sense, she withdrew and focused her attention increasingly on the more detailed evaluation and analysis of data that had accumulated over the years.

In 1949 Robert Sears accepted a position at Harvard. There were financial problems for the research station. The support from the Rockefeller Foundation, which supplied initial funds, had long been terminated. There were some stresses with the mainstream department of psychology. The halcyon days when Stoddard simultaneously chaired the Department of Psychology and was director of the station and dean of the Graduate School had long gone (irreverently, he had been known as the Holy Trinity). In 1949, with the postwar emphasis on clinical psychology training programs, the position of director of the Child Welfare Research Station was not a particularly appealing one. It was decided that an administrative council would offer a breathing space until a permanent director was appointed. Beth Wellman, who had served as interim administrator during previous changes, was asked to be chair of this council from 1949 to 1951. In 1951 Boyd McCandless was named director of the Iowa Child Welfare Research Station. This was particularly gratifying to Wellman, as McCandless and his family had been especially close. Their eldest daughter was named Beth for Wellman. By this time Beth Wellman's health had deteriorated seriously. Her long illness was closed by death on March 22, 1952.

IMPACT OF CONTRIBUTIONS

When Beth Wellman's findings about the improvement in IQ among children who attended preschool were published, they rocked the conventional beliefs not only of psychologists and educators, but of much of society. The evidence from cross-sectional studies of IQs of children had suggested that there was little change from year to year. It had been concluded that intellectual capacity was adequately measured by a well-administered individual test and remained acceptably constant over a long period. Differences in IQ between occupational or social levels were attributed to genetic differences. This point of view was supported by "common observation" and by the influence of family studies, for example, the Kallikaks, and studies of eminent families and the eugenics movement in general. The possibility that a child could improve those capabilities defined as intelligence, and change his status from "average" to "superior," with all that that implied for education and the prediction of his future progress, was contrary to then accepted beliefs of dedicated professionals.

Wellman's research, which showed that even children from homes of above-average educational and cultural status could—and did—show marked gains in IQ, and thus reflected gains in intelligence as defined, had implications for education and social policy regarding children. Results of studies of less fortunate children than the State University of Iowa preschool students showed that not only were even spectacular gains in IQ possible, but equally spectacular losses could occur as well. The crucial factor was the intervening experience of the individual.

Beth Wellman's research and the studies that followed it—some provoked by a desire to prove the Iowa position in error—were consonant with the social developments of the 1950s and 1960s. Concern for the children of poverty, Head Start, Home Start, and day-care programs were forecast from the optimistic results of the Iowa studies. Beth Wellman could see the bright future that attention to the underprivileged child could make possible. She would have been pleased at the vindication, not for herself, but for those whose lives were improved as a result of the application of her findings.

Her influence was perhaps even greater as it was extended through the graduate students at the station. All students, not her advisees alone, regarded Beth Wellman as a role model—for integrity, for respect for facts, for careful work-manship, for clarity of expression, for personal commitment to scientific inquiry. Beth Wellman labored in the modest Iowa Child Welfare Research Station, but influenced child welfare, child development research, and generations of professionals who put into action the implications of her research.

NOTE

Special thanks for the preparation of this chapter are due to Ruth Updegraff, Emeritus Professor of ICWRS, Henry Minton, of the University of Windsor, and several former ICWRS graduates who contributed and refreshed the author's memory of Iowa City events of the Wellman years.

REFERENCES

Baldwin, B., & Wellman, B. (1928). The peg board as a means of analyzing form perception and motor control in young children. *Journal of Genetic Psychology*, *35*, 389–414.

Caldwell, O., & Wellman, B. (1926). Characteristics of school leaders. *Journal of Educational Research*, *14*, 1–15.

Skeels, H. M.; Updegraff, R.; Wellman, B.; & Williams, H. M. (1938). A study of environmental stimulation: An orphanage preschool project. *University of Iowa Studies in Child Welfare*, *15*(4), 1–191.

Stoddard, G., & Wellman, B. (1934). *Child psychology.* New York: Macmillan.

Stoddard, G., & Wellman, B. (1936). *A manual of child psychology.* New York: Macmillan.

Stoddard, G., & Wellman, B. (1940). Environment and the IQ. In G. Whipple (Ed.), Intelligence: Its nature and nurture. *Yearbook of the National Society for the Study of Education, 39,* Part I, 405–442.

Wellman, B. (1926). The development of motor coordination in young children: An experimental study in the control of hand and arm movements. *University of Iowa Studies in Child Welfare, 3,* 1–93.

Wellman, B. (1931). Physical growth and motor development and their relation to mental development in children. In C. Murchison (Ed.), *A handbook of child psychology* (pp. 242–277). Worcester, Mass.: Clark University Press.

Wellman, B. (1932). Some new bases for interpretation of the IQ. *Pediatrics Seminar and Journal of Genetic Psychology, 41,* 116–126.

Wellman, B. (1932–1933). The effect of preschool attendance upon the IQ. *Journal of Experimental Education, 1,* 48–69.

Wellman, B. (1934). Growth in intelligence under differing school environments. *Journal of Experimental Education, 3,* 59–83.

Wellman, B. (1936). The permanence of early training effects on intellectual growth: A longitudinal study of forty-one subjects from preschool through senior high school. *Proceedings of Society for Research in Child Development,* 161–162.

Wellman, B. (1937). Mental growth from preschool to college. *Journal of Experimental Education, 6,* 127–138.

Wellman, B. (1938a). The intelligence of preschool children as measured by the Merrill-Palmer scale of performance tests. *University of Iowa Studies in Child Welfare, 15,* 1–150.

Wellman, B. (1938b). Our changing concept of intelligence. *Journal of Consulting Psychology, 2,* 97–107.

Wellman, B. (1940a). The meaning of environment. In G. Whipple (Ed.), Intelligence: Its nature and nurture. *Yearbook of the National Society for the Study of Education, 39,* Part I, 21–40.

Wellman, B. (1940b). Iowa studies on the effects of schooling. In G. Whipple (Ed.), Intelligence: Its nature and nurture. *Yearbook of the National Society for the Study of Education, 39,* Part II, 377–399.

Wellman, B. (1945). IQ changes of preschool and non-preschool groups during the preschool years: A summary of the literature. *Journal of Psychology, 20,* 347–368.

Wellman, B., & Bradbury, D. (1929). Studies in language development. In G. Whipple (Ed.), Preschool and parental education. *Yearbook of the National Society for the Study of Education, 28,* Part II, 495–568.

Wellman, B., & Pegram, E. (1944). Binet IQ changes of orphanage preschool children: A re-analysis. *Journal of Genetic Psychology, 65,* 239–263.

Wellman, B.; Skeels, H.; & Skodak, M. (1940). Review of McNemar's critical examination of Iowa studies. *Psychological Bulletin, 37,* 93–111.

Part III

Awards and Recognition

SELECTED AWARD-WINNING CONTRIBUTIONS

*Nancy Felipe Russo, Agnes N. O'Connell,
and Melinda Deacon*

A critical lesson from the history of women in psychology is that women's activities and contributions in the field must be considered in their social and historical context (O'Connell & Russo, 1980, 1983, 1988; Russo & Denmark, 1987; Scarborough & Furumoto, 1987). This is not unique to women: both genders influence and are influenced by the systems in which they find themselves. The milieu affects whether innovations will be encouraged and if observers will perceive them as meaningful and valuable. Thus, recognition of contributions by awards plays a direct role in encouraging and shaping the production and preservation of theories, methods, and applications in a field. Awards create a climate that values accomplishment and inspires achievement. Labels attached through an awards process can also determine what work will be preserved and how it will be transmitted to following generations (Albert, 1975; Csikszentmihalyi, 1988; Mooney, 1963).

In 1951 Mildred Mitchell pointed out that women in psychology had not attained visibility and distinction "in proportion to their numbers and qualifications" (Mitchell, 1951, p. 200). In 1980 Russo and O'Connell reviewed the honors, awards, and historical attention to women contributors in psychology, and observed little change in the basic truth of that statement. Mitchell's statement continues to be accurate. According to the 1988 membership statistics of the American Psychological Association (APA), the major psychological association of the United States, proportionally fewer women than men have been elected to APA Fellow status "in recognition of unusual and outstanding contributions or performance." Of the 38,054 men in the member category, 9 percent are Fellows; of the 20,595 women, 3 percent are Fellows (American Psychological Association, 1988, p. vii). The biographies in this volume are strong testimony to the quantity, richness, and diversity of women's contributions throughout the history of the field. What is required to increase the visibility and recognition of women's contributions?

In response to Mitchell, psychologist-historian E. G. Boring (1951) observed that the prestige of a discovery is more than a function of its merit or social value, citing, among other things, the importance of promotion and advertisement of the discovery and the prestige of the discoverer. In his words, "prestige begets prestige" (p. 679). Thus, the power to confer honor and prestige held by psychology's award-granting organization is a force that can affect both the evolution of the field and the career development of individuals. Furthermore, making women's award-winning contributions more visible is an instrument for social change.

According to APA's Arthur W. Melton Library (1989), in the United States there are more than 220 awards, honors, and prizes in psychology given by scientific and professional organizations such as APA and APA boards, committees and divisions, state associations, Psi Chi (the National Honor Society in Psychology), and the American Psychological Foundation (APF).

The most highly visible awards in psychology are those given by the American Psychological Foundation and the American Psychological Association at the APA convention awards ceremony. These are prestigious awards, with distinguished judges, monetary value, and award citations and recipients' biographies published in the *American Psychologist*. Here too, women are underrepresented. Although in 1988 women were 36 percent of members and 18 percent of Fellows of APA, out of the 261 senior distinguished contribution awards given by APA and APF through that year, only 25, less than 10 percent, went to women.

Despite the fact that women have not received recognition in proportion to their contributions, the contributions of some women have been recognized. To **widen** the visibility and preserve knowledge of some of women's contributions, we present here, in one place, the citations of women APF and APA award winners to 1988, which appeared in the *American Psychologist* to 1989, the most recent year available.

Section 1: Awards to Established Contributors to Psychology

AMERICAN PSYCHOLOGICAL FOUNDATION

Awards by the American Psychological Foundation include the prestigious Gold Medal awards and awards for Distinguished Teaching in Psychology.

Gold Medal Award

This annual award is given by the APF Board of Trustees to up to three North American psychologists, sixty-five years of age or older, "in recognition of a distinguished and long-continued record of scientific and scholarly accomplishments." Of the forty-three Gold Medals awarded since 1956, five were to women (11.6 percent). The first woman award recipient, Pauline S. Sears, shared it with her husband, Robert R. Sears, for their lifetime collaboration. After 1980 Gold

Medals were awarded to women in 1982 (Bayley) and 1984 (Anastasi); then the awards were split into science, professional, and public interest categories. Two women (Lacey and Gibson) subsequently received the award in the science category, one, Beatrice Lacey, sharing it with her husband. Through 1989, no woman has ever won in the professional or public interest categories.

1980 Pauline Snedden Sears (with Robert Sears) *American Psychologist*, 1981, *36*(1), 88–91:

Psychologists who for decades have inspired both students and colleagues in the study of human development; whose empirical and theoretical contributions have kept the concepts of motivation and of the self in the forefront of the scientific study of developmental processes, and have given substance to the role of parent-child interaction in the formation of personality; and whose efforts have furthered the applications of knowledge to the educational and social betterment of children.

1982 Nancy Bayley *American Psychologist*, 1983, *38*(1), 61–63:

For a half century of outstanding research and professional leadership in the study of human development. Nancy Bayley has been a pioneer in longitudinal research on much of the life span; in careful psychometric assessment of the mental, motor and behavioral development of infants and young children; and in the study of interactions among behavioral and biological aspects of human development. Her collaborative spirit and interdisciplinary interests have been evident both in her research and in her professional service. The Bayley Scales of Infant Development are used around the world by scientists and professionals from a number of disciplines because they are the most carefully standardized instruments yet available for this age range. She is also known to the national and international community for her generous and wise counsel to colleagues, students, government and private agencies, and professional societies representing a variety of disciplines and many nations. Bayley's scientific findings have stood the test of time and clime. May her example of the benefits of international and disciplinary cooperation prove as durable.

1984 Anne Anastasi *American Psychologist*, 1985, *40*(3), 340–341:

As a scientist, scholar, and teacher whose career has spanned more than a half century, Anne Anastasi has stood unwaveringly for excellence. A prolific writer and exacting researcher, she has made major contributions to our understanding of psychological traits, environmental and experiential influences upon psychological development, and the construction and interpretation of tests. Her classic texts, *Psychological Testing*, *Differential Psychology*, and *Fields of Applied Psychology*, translated into many foreign languages, are models of clarity, comprehensiveness, and synthesis. They frame the very questions scientists in these disciplines ask and the manner in which research is conducted. In tackling critical controversies that confront the psychology of individual differences and their measurement, she has furthered the development of psychology as a quantitative behavioral science. A truly staggering schedule of consultantships, committee memberships, invited addresses, and publications continue to provide an ongoing forum for her probing and incisive examination of salient issues in different psychology and psychological testing.

Gold Medal Award—Psychological Science

1984   Beatrice C. Lacey (with John Lacey)   *American Psychologist*, 1985, *41*(4), 409–411:

Decade by decade this generative match of hearts and minds has developed our knowledge of the complex interplay between heart and brain. That fine intellects with a deep mutuality of goals should produce rigorously executed experiments of elegant simplicity is understandable. The paradox is that so stable and serene a personal union should so often nurture its intellectual progeny by attacking unidimensional concepts with multidimensional vigor and by providing provocative, innovative alternatives to conventional theories. From their early studies of individual differences in patterns to autonomic responses to stressors, to their recent research on information processing, the Laceys have insisted on the centrality of the organism in the integration of stimulus and response and on the necessity of understanding the physiological processes underlying behavior. This broad biobehavioral approach has extended their profound and pervasive influence and made psychophysiology central to most psychology.

1986   Eleanor Jack Gibson   *American Psychologist*, 1987, *42*(4), 327–329:

An innovator in theory and research for more than fifty years, Eleanor Gibson has combined elegant experiments with profound conceptual insights to advance our knowledge of perception. From her early research on differentiation and generalization to her present research on perceiving affordances, she has stressed the adaptive function of perception—to keep in touch with the world—and thereby focused her inquiry on fundamental questions of perception. She formulated the issues of perceptual development as a comprehensive new theory, she described general principles of that development, and she identified perceptual learning as a basic developmental process. Her strategies of scholarship and the important knowledge gained therefrom are a compelling demonstration that essential understanding of human perception depends on revealing its course of development.

Distinguished Contributions to Education in Psychology

This award is given by the APF Board of Trustees for contributions to teaching or education in psychology. Criteria include demonstrated influence as a teacher of students who become outstanding psychologists, development of effective or innovative teaching methods, materials, curricula and courses, and significant research on teaching. Of the thirty-three award recipients, five are women (15 percent).

1970   Freda Rebelsky   *American Psychologist*, 1971, *26*(1), 93–94:

Superlative teacher, creative developer of new courses, respected model for students. Her teaching makes science relevant without sacrificing rigor.

1975   Bernice L. Neugarten   *American Psychologist*, 1976, *31*(1), 83–86:

. . . a dedicated teacher, possessed of enormous energy, who spends countless hours with her students. . . . Insofar as her former students represent a population of teachers of adult development and aging, one could say that she has in large measure "created" this area of study, since PhD programs in adult development and aging are not commonly found in universities. . . . Finally, one should note the significant role that she has played in bringing women into the academic world and research. . . . One half of her PhD students have been women.

1982   Carolyn Wood Sherif   *American Psychologist*, 1983, *38*(1), 54–65:

An outstanding social psychologist and fine teacher whose role as teacher and mentor at large has contributed notably to the restructuring of teaching and research on the social psychology of gender.

1986   Ellen P. Reese   *American Psychologist*, 1987, *42*(4), 334–335:

Capturing students' interest and enthusiasm for the field of psychology through a total commitment to undergraduate education has been a passion of Ellen P. Reese. This she has accomplished by preparing numerous films, texts, workshops, and laboratory manuals on the analysis of behavior; by advocating and supporting independent student research and scholarship; by serving as a model of excellence as a writer, committed scholar and researcher; and by inspiring dedication among individual learners as they strive toward reaching their full potential. The large number of Ellen Reese's students who have elected to gain post graduate training is one measure of her many important contributions to the field as a whole. Over thirty-five have received doctoral degrees and nearly all of them, in turn, now advance our field through their own teaching and scholarly research products.

1987   Eileen Mavis Hetherington   *American Psychologist*, 1988, *43*(4), 265:

Eileen Mavis Hetherington has long been recognized as one of the finest lecturers and teachers at the University of Virginia, and has also made a singular contribution to the behavioral sciences through her investigations on the impact of divorce and remarriage on children. As a lecturer, Dr. Hetherington is absolutely brilliant. Many students have remarked that she is the best lecturer that they have ever encountered, that she is eminently well-prepared for class, and that the material is current and stimulating. Through her research projects in divorce and family adjustment, she has provided research training for a large number of undergraduate and graduate students. Her professional accomplishments and popularity among her peers and students are a tribute to Dr. Hetherington's unceasing dedication to the science of psychology.

AMERICAN PSYCHOLOGICAL ASSOCIATION

Awards in Scientific Psychology

Since 1956, APA's Committee on Scientific Awards has made awards for distinguished scientific achievements. Since 1987, the awards have been in two categories, Distinguished Scientific Contributions and Distinguished Scientific Award for the Applications of Psychology. The committee also decides the winners of the Distinguished Scientific Award for an Early Career Contribution in Psychology, which is described in Section 2 of this chapter.

Distinguished Scientific Contributions

Since 1956, of the 108 recipients receiving this award up to 1989, 6 (6 percent) have been women, two of whom (Lacey and Jameson) shared the award with their husbands. One award was shared by a two-man-team. The first woman (Bayley) received an award in 1966. Although the published citations are available only through 1988, one of the three award winners for 1989 was a woman. Mary Ainsworth shared the Distinguished Scientific Contributions Award with John Bowlby.

1966   Nancy Bayley   *American Psychologist*, 1966, *21*, 1190–1194:

For the enterprise, pertinacity, and insight with which she has studied human growth over long segments of the life cycle. With consummate skill in the use of available but imperfect instruments and with respect and sensitiveness for her subjects, she has rigorously recorded their physical, intellectual, emotional, and social development from birth to middle life. Her studies have enriched psychology with enduring contributions to the measurement and meaning of intelligence, and she traced important strands in the skein of factors involved in psychological development. Her participation in a number of major programs of developmental research is a paradigm of the conjoint efforts which are essential in a field whose problems span the generations.

1968   Eleanor J. Gibson   *American Psychologist*, 1968, *23*(12), 857–867:

For distinguished studies of perceptual learning and perceptual development. Following participation in the guidance of studies which have significantly advanced our understanding of depth perception in infants and young organisms, she has turned to the systematic analysis of reading. Her analysis and experimental study of the discriminatory and decoding aspects, as well as semantic and syntactical features of reading, have indicated what must be learned. Her analysis of the learning process itself has delineated how reading is acquired. Always the experimentalist, she has elucidated the steps that must precede application in formal instruction. By doing so, she has imaginatively shown how to bridge the gap from laboratory to classroom.

1972   Dorothea Jameson (with Leo Hurvich)   *American Psychologist*, 1973, *28*(1), 60–64:

The research team of Dorothea Jameson and Leo Hurvich has significantly advanced our knowledge of color vision through a broadly based program of conceptually sophisticated and rigorously conducted experiments. Their research has provided basic data which are essential to theory and at the same time provide a quantitative framework for physiological investigations. Their very unusual scholarship, technical skill, untiring motivation, and contagious enthusiasm for scientific discovery have set new standards of excellence against which future experimenters and theorists will be judged.

1973 Brenda Milner *American Psychologist*, 1974, *29*(1), 36–38:

For outstanding psychological study of the human brain. She and her students have elucidated the role of prefrontal lobes, previously resistant to analysis; have provided definitive data on the relation of speech localization to handedness; and have demonstrated the importance of the right temporal lobe in pattern perception (visual, auditory, tactual). Of great significance is Milner's study of the function of the hippocampus in the consolidation of memory and the devastating effect of the bilateral loss of the hippocampus on the mental aspect of the temporal lobe. The result is an inability to form new memories and an astonishing helplessness even though earlier established memories are not impaired: a dramatic demonstration of the importance of that ability we take so lightly for granted, the ability to remember what happened 10 minutes (or more) ago.

1976 Beatrice C. Lacey (with John I. Lacey) *American Psychologist*, 1977, *32*(1), 54–61:

For conceptions of automatic nervous system activity that have had an explosive impact on research in psychophysiology. In wide-ranging, eloquent, and scholarly papers, they have described complicated interactions among behavioral, autonomic, and central systems. Arguing the inadequacy of traditional views of a unitary activational system, they have described a system with central feedback and dissociable sub-systems. With superb technology and meticulous experiments, they have demonstrated that complex patterns of autonomic responses are measurable characteristics of individuals, stable across years, and predictive of individual-environment transactions. Few areas of psychology remain unaffected by the implications of their work.

1988 Eleanor E. Maccoby *American Psychologist* 1989, *44*(4), 622–623:

For her wide-ranging and authoritative contributions to developmental and social psychology. Her substantive discoveries on the socialization of young children have been paralleled by equally important contributions to the methodology of interviewing and the measurement of critical dimensions of social behavior in both infants and preschool children. Her incisive reviews of research and theory in the fields of attachment, dependency, and gender differences have broadly influenced the style and direction of subsequent research in these fields.

Distinguished Scientific Award for the Applications of Psychology

This award recognizes distinguished theoretical or empirical advances leading to the understanding or amelioration of important practical problems. Since 1973, of the seventeen winners, one (6 percent) has been a woman.

1981   Anne Anastasi   *American Psychologist*, 1982, *37*, 52–59:

For persistently seeking to clarify the nature and origins of psychological traits and facilitating their valid measurements. She has been a major force in the development of differential psychology as a behavioral science, having illuminated the ways trait measurement is affected by training and practice, cultural contexts, and language differences. Her texts, *Differential Psychology* and *Psychological Testing*, being both integrative and probing, do not simply summarize the groundwork in these fields but provide impetus for further work. Ever watchful for misleading generalizations and misconceptions, she displays unusual perceptiveness in her timely emphasis on key issues and unusual critical acumen in her timely undercutting of spurious issues.

Awards in Professional Psychology

These awards recognize contributions that have served to advance psychology as a profession. Since 1979, awards have been given for distinguished contributions in three categories: public service, professional practice, and knowledge. Up to 1989, of the forty-six recipients since the first award in 1972, five (11 percent) were women; 1981 was the first year that a woman (Kessler) received an award. Of the five women award winners, three won for public service (Kessler, Payton, Walker), one for contributions to professional practice (Lambert), and one to knowledge (Ainsworth). In 1989 one woman was among four award winners: Florence Kaslow won an award for Distinguished Contributions to Professional Practice.

Distinguished Professional Contributions—Public Service

1981   Jane W. Kessler   *American Psychologist*, 1982 *37*(1), 65:

Jane W. Kessler uniquely blends the role of accomplished scholar, teacher, sensitive clinician, and esteemed organizational leader. Jane has a profound sense of the human dilemma, balanced by hope and the belief that she should do something about it. Her outstanding contribution to services for retarded and disturbed children and her holistic and interdisciplinary orientation to child development are reflected in the Case Western Reserve Mental Development Center, of which she was the first director. She has always grasped and dealt with the total dynamics of any problem, and she has always inspired both colleagues and students to examine new ideas and programs. Jane W. Kessler's dedication and the breadth, depth, and quality of her work are testimony that she is a scholar with a commitment to solving the problems of the real world.

Distinguished Professional Contributions—Public Service

1982   Carolyn R. Payton   *American Psychologist*, 1983, *38*(1), 32–33:

Carolyn Payton has devoted many selfless years and boundless energies to helping people become the best they can be. She has served individuals and groups as a therapist, teacher, university administrator, consultant to federal and private service agencies, and official representative of our country to the peoples of the world. In both public and private forums, she has worked persistently to promote world understanding through cross-cultural interactions. Notable are her contributions to the Peace Corps for six years in Latin America and the Caribbean, and more recently as director of the Peace Corps. Her work with third world countries reflects her more pervasive belief that all humanity, regardless of socioeconomic and political beliefs, share common goals and can form partnerships which advance the cause of people in service to one another. She is an inspiring role model to psychologists who seek to apply their professional skills to the formulation of public policy and to a commitment for peace.

Distinguished Professional Contributions—Practice

1986   Nadine Lambert   *American Psychologist*, 1987, *42*(4), 307–312:

As many who have been privileged to work with her realize, for over twenty years Dr. Nadine Lambert has made numerous contributions to the professional practice of psychology. In 1960, Dr. Lambert was among the first to advocate and support multilevel legislation for children with learning and mental health problems in California. In 1965, she initiated and developed the first doctoral-level professional school program in California. She is also responsible for the adaptation, validation, and standardization of the AAMD-SE Adaptive Behavior Scale. Dr. Lambert's research on the social and the psychological antecedents of various childhood and adolescent mental health problems, as well as her work with hyperactive children, has contributed significantly to the improved treatment and understanding of many childhood and adolescent behavioral problems.

Distinguished Professional Contributions—Public Service

1987   Lenore Walker   *American Psychologist*, 1988, *43*(4), 243–244:

Until 1962 the term "battered woman" was barely known. Lenore Walker's ground-breaking book, *The Battered Woman*, and tireless lobbying efforts, have heightened awareness of domestic violence as a public health hazard, increased services for family violence victims and helped change legal and public policy to better protect battered women and their children. Dr. Walker has been a primary advocate in the identification of the problem of battered women, the development of a base of scholarly knowledge about it, and the creation of a scientifically informed public policy that has improved the lives of millions of women battered in America each year.

Distinguished Professional Contributions—Knowledge

1987   Mary D.S. Ainsworth   *American Psychologist*, 1988, *43*(4), 248–250:

For her insights into the nature and development of human security. Her exquisite observational studies of infant-mother relationships in Uganda and Baltimore, her conceptual analyses of attachment and dependency, and her contributions to methodology of infant assessment are the cornerstones of modern attachment theory and research. The patterns of attachment identified in her work have proven robust and significant in research across diverse cultures and across the human life span. Her theoretical, methodological and empirical contributions, as well as her teaching, colleagueship, and grace are a secure base from which generations of students can explore.

Awards for Psychology in the Public Interest

These awards, presented under the auspices of the APA Board of Social and Ethical Responsibility, are given in two categories: They recognize a single extraordinary achievement or a lifetime of outstanding contributions. Criteria include a courageous and distinctive contribution in the science or profession of psychology that makes a contribution to the solution of social problems, a contribution that makes psychology more accessible to a greater number of persons, or an integration of the science or profession of psychology with social action in a manner beneficial to all. One award is designated for psychologists who make their contributions in an early stage of their career who may not have held a Ph.D. for more than fifteen years. Up to 1989, of the eleven senior winners since the first award in 1978, one (9 percent) was a woman, Marie Jahoda, who won in the second year of the award. Of the two awards for senior career achievement in 1989, none went to women.

Distinguished Public Interest Contributions

1979   Marie Jahoda   *American Psychologist*, 1980, *35*(1), 74–76:

In a distinguished career in Austria, the United States, and England, Marie Jahoda has brought high psychological competence to bear on many significant human problems. As a young woman in Vienna, she went to jail for her political convictions; during the McCarthy aberration, she studied the consequences of conformity pressures and political oppression in America. Through her work, we know more about psychological aspects of unemployment, prejudice and race relations, work satisfaction, mental health, and social forecasting. We salute her as a model of humane concern and commitment, and of thoughtful application and extension of psychology in the public interest.

Distinguished Contributions to Research in Public Policy

Begun in 1988, this award recognizes a distinguished empirical or theoretical contribution to research in public policy, either through a single extraordinary achievement or a lifetime of work. The first recipient was a woman. In 1989, the second recipient was a man.

1988   Sandra Wood Scarr   *American Psychologist*, 1989, *44*(4), 652–653:

For notable scientific contributions in the public interest as the result of her willingness to seek answers to questions that few others have dared ask. Combining intellectual boldness with meticulous methodological rigor, Sandra Scarr's impressive work on Black and White twins, transracially adopted children, and racial admixture stands as an unparalleled contribution to supporting the theoretical foundation of a truly interactive nature-nurture approach to intelligence. Her accomplishments have borne out her belief that only by asking fair questions and seeking honest answers can one make a contribution to science and to one's society. Her commitment to research that fosters the human potential for better adaptation is widely recognized. Her recent work on the effects of child care environments provides a guiding light for an informed national policy on working families and child care. Throughout her career, Dr. Scarr has been an inspiring role model dedicated to advancing psychological knowledge and to creating effective solutions to the most important real-life social policy issues of our time.

Distinguished Career Contributions to Education and Training in Psychology

In 1987 APA's Education and Training (E&T) Board established its first awards in two categories: Distinguished Career Contributions to Education and Training in Psychology, and Distinguished Contribution to Education and Training in Psychology. The former recognizes a long-continued record of accomplishments, the latter, a distinguished accomplishment. In the first two years of these awards, one woman was among the total of five award winners. Florence L. Denmark was the first person and the only woman to receive a Distinguished Contribution to Education and Training Award. In 1989, three more men received awards under E&T Board auspices, bringing the total to one woman among seven men.

1987   Florence L. Denmark   *American Psychologist*, 1988, *43*(4), 258–259:

Florence Denmark has been an innovator and leader in influencing education and training so that psychology's curriculum reflects the true cultural diversity of human experience. She is recognized for her considerable contributions to psychology in the area of women's studies. She has played a particularly critical role in programs and activities designed to include the new scholarship on women in both the education and training of psychologists. She has been an advocate for changes in education and training that increase the cultural diversity of the curriculum and open opportunity for all underrepresented groups. Her publications, as well as professional activities in psychological organizations on a national and international level, and her leadership at her university have all influenced the way that knowledge in the discipline is transmitted to the next generation of psychologists.

Section 2: Awards for Early Career Contributions

DISTINGUISHED SCIENTIFIC AWARDS FOR AN EARLY CAREER CONTRIBUTION TO PSYCHOLOGY

The early career awards, given for the first time in 1974, are presented to individuals who have not held the Ph.D. for more than nine years. Nine categories are used for the early career awards, three considered each year in a three-year cycle: animal behavior and ethology, developmental, personality; human learning and cognition, physiology, psychopathology; applied research and methods, sensation and perception, and social. Up to 1989, of the forty-three winners of this award (some of them shared), 30 percent (thirteen) went to women. Women

received 20 percent (one) of the total awards in two categories, physiology/
biology and psychopathology, respectively; 33 percent (two) of the total awards
in developmental; 40 percent (two) of the awards in personality and animal
learning/behavior, respectively; 50 percent (two) of the total awards in sensation/
perception, and 60 percent (three) of the total awards in social. No women had
ever received an award in the human learning/cognition or applied research
categories. In 1989 one of the four early career awards went to a woman: Ruth
Kanfer received the award in applied research.

Developmental

1976   Rochel S. Gelman   *American Psychologist*, 1977, *32*(1), 91–94:

For her outstanding contributions to our understanding of the early development of number
knowledge and skills, of the important role of attentional processes in the child's cognitive
performance and cognitive growth, and, with Marilyn Shatz, of the young child's ability
to adapt his communication behavior to the information processing capacities of his listener
in certain situations. Her research has compelled developmental psychologists to rethink
the processes that might underlie the child's basic understanding of important concepts,
as well as the processes that might influence the child's ability to use that understanding
in specific task contexts.

Personality

1976   Sandra Lipsitz Bem   *American Psychologist*, 1977, *32*(1), 88–91:

For her studies of sex roles, androgyny, and the ontogeny of psychosexual identity and
maturity. She has both clarified and questioned long-held assumptions about the oppositional or bipolar nature of sex roles, and persuasively put forward a concept of psychological androgyny. These analytic and logical endeavors have been buttressed by the
accumulation of an impressive amount of empirical data to support the hypothesis that a
blending of so-called masculine and feminine dispositions is more adaptive than ste-
reotypic emphasis on either alone. These findings are leading her to a fundamental
reexamination of the psychological, philosophical, and ego-integrative implications of
sex role conflicts and resolutions.

Social

1977   Judith Rodin   *American Psychologist*, 1978, *33*(1), 77–80:

For major theoretical contributions to our understanding of the relationship between
obesity and general sensitivity to external stimulation, and for seminal studies on altruism,
on aging and the effects of control or helplessness, and on the consequences of overcrowding. Rodin's work, in collaboration with Stanley Schachter, places human obesity
in a broader theoretical context involving information processing correlates and potential
physiological mechanisms. Her eclectic contributions on altruism, overcrowding, and

control brilliantly combine field and laboratory procedures, illustrating the implications of social psychological principles and phenomena for an understanding of human problems and suggesting directions for their remedy.

Sensation and Perception

1980   Lynn Cooper   *American Psychologist*, 1981, *36*(1), 78–81:

For her incisive investigation of the nature and individual variation of the internal processes of visual representation, transformation, and comparison by means of which we identify, discriminate, and prepare for external objects and events. In a coherent series of chronometric experiments of extraordinary elegance and quantitative precision, she has decisively demonstrated the analog character of "mental rotation" and the existence of striking qualitative differences between individuals in holistic versus analytical processing of visual information. Her findings have a central bearing on both theoretical and practical issues concerning perceptual cognition, the underlying components of human abilities, and alternative strategies of performance.

Social

1980   Shelley Taylor   *American Psychologist*, 1981, *36*(1), 81–84:

For outstanding contributions to cognitive social psychology and its application to health related behaviors, medical care and prejudice. Her creative experiments demonstrate that an observer's perceptions of an actor are profoundly affected by momentary salience of social stimuli, by seating arrangement, visual field, and differentiating characteristics of the actor. Thus, prejudicial treatment and stereotyping result from being the token woman, the sole pregnant woman, or the lone handicapped person in a group or organization. Her health research integrates the cognitive perspective with the larger social context in delivery of services, in an effort to identify how basic perceptions and cognitions shape health behavior; her work indicates the importance of active participation of patients in health care.

Social

1980   Camille Wortman   *American Psychologist*, 1981, *36*(1), 84–87:

For providing stimulating and influential analyses of how people react to uncontrollable outcomes and cope with undesirable life events; for illuminating how causal attributions made by accident victims and rape victims influence the success or failure of their adaptation; for brilliantly clarifying how coping by victims is made more difficult by well-intentioned others who are simultaneously motivated to be supportive and threatened by the victim's status; and, in general, for enriching social psychological theory and research by bringing it to bear on an exciting range of real life problems with important clinical implications.

Psychopathology

1981   Lyn Y. Abramson   *American Psychologist*, 1982, *37*(1), 79–83:

Lyn Abramson's first word was "own-self," and accordingly her work in the fields of depression and of helplessness displays independence, persistence, and love of challenge. In reformulating helplessness theory she integrated attribution theory with learning theory. She then discovered an insidious attributional style among depressed students, patients, and children, one which may predict who is vulnerable to depression once bad life events occur. She discovered that depressed people judge reality well while nondepressed people have benign illusions of control which may protect them from depression. All these contributions combined experimental ingenuity, theoretical boldness, and clinical insight.

Animal Learning and Behavior

1982   Martha K. McClintock   *American Psychologist*, 1983, *38*(1), 57–60:

For original and broadly conceived research on the social regulation of reproductive function. Her animal research, employing unconventional testing conditions, sophisticated data analyses, and creative syntheses, has helped to place mating behavior in a functional context and thereby reinforce the links between psychobiology and sociobiology. Her groundbreaking investigations of social synchronization of the human menstrual cycle and of cyclic reproductive functions in Norway rats helped to reveal the complex—but not incomprehensible—interactive regulation of these cycles, and are important contributions to our understanding of the psychosomatics of reproduction.

Sensation and Perception

1983   Carol L. Krumhansl   *American Psychologist*, 1984, *39*(3), 284–286:

For her elegant quantitative elucidation of cognitive schemata underlying visual, auditory, and, particularly, musical perception. Since Helmholtz, tonal perception has been related to fixed physical attributes of the tones and physiological properties of the ears. However, through a dazzling interplay of experimental techniques, music theory, and multidimensional scaling, Krumhansl and her co-workers have established that in a musical context, tones are interpreted via an internal tonal schema corresponding to the musical key implied by that context. Her work is demonstrating how, by departing from the standard visual and verbal approaches, one may uncover new cognitive structures of great richness and beauty.

Physiology

1984   Marta Kutas   *American Psychologist*, 1985 *40*(3), 309–312:

For outstanding research on the physiology of human cognition and language. Her innovative studies of event-related brain potentials have clarified mechanisms of sensory-motor performance and decision making and have opened new avenues for probing the organization of language in the brain. She has shown how electrophysiological measures can reveal the timing of semantic analyses during reading and the operation of semantic priming and memory mechanisms. Using elegant experimental designs, she has elucidated the role of contextual factors in language comprehension. This work constitutes a landmark for demonstrating the value of combined physiological/behavioral approaches to the analysis of human thought and language.

Personality

1985   Nancy E. Cantor   *American Psychologist*, 1986, *41*(4), 365–368:

Beginning her career in time perception, Cantor carried the concepts and principles of cognitive psychology to the study of personality and social interaction. Her earliest work on social categorization showed how our concepts of social entities are structured probabilistically, as fuzzy sets. Continuing work on this problem showed how social concepts are employed in impression formation, psychiatric diagnosis, judgment, and planning. In her most recent efforts, she has begun to explore how we use social knowledge to solve life's mundane and monumental problems. Along the way, she has radically altered the way we think about the way we think about ourselves and others.

Developmental

1985   Linda B. Smith   *American Psychologist*, 1986, *41*(4), 371–373:

For her innovative exploration of the way humans perceive, compare, represent and think about complex objects and the relations between them; and for demonstrating clearly that a most profitable approach to acquiring an understanding of human knowledge is by studying the origins and growth of that knowledge in young children. Her early research included close examinations of how children freely classify objects and she soon discovered that children's perceptions were structured. From these beginnings her research has been leading to greatly increased understanding of the ways humans, both children and adults, mentally represent the structure of perceptually and conceptually complex objects.

Animal Learning and Behavior

1988   Barbara Boardman Smuts   *American Psychologist*, 1989, *44*(4), 632–634:

For outstanding research devoted to the analysis of social relationships among free living primates. Her exquisitely sensitive, skillful observations, which masterfully integrated quantitative and qualitative methods, have led to primate field data of extraordinary quality, setting standards of excellence in primate field studies in process. In these landmark primate studies, she has opened new vistas to understanding the nature of cooperative as well as conflictual social relationships, male-female friendships and long-term affiliations outside the mating context, and male-infant relationships—documenting their existence, describing their social dynamics, exploring their evolutionary significance, and thereby illuminating human social relationships.

DISTINGUISHED CONTRIBUTIONS TO PSYCHOLOGY IN THE PUBLIC INTEREST—EARLY CAREER STAGES

Since this award was established in 1983, up to 1989, of the seven individuals to receive it, one (14 percent) was a woman.

1988   Ellen Langer   *American Psychologist*, 1989, *44*(4), 647–649.

For her courageous, stimulating, and unique intellectual contributions towards the solution of problems associated with disadvantaged groups, particularly the elderly. Her pioneering work with nursing home residents revealed the profound effects of increasing mindful behavior and environmental control on health and longevity, significantly changed our thinking about the aging process, and offered new hope and dignity to millions whose problems were previously seen as unalterable and inevitable. The elaboration of her theory of mindfulness, together with its associated body of elegantly designed and compelling research, illustrates how science and public interest can best nourish each other. Eschewing intellectual givens and leaving no shibboleth unturned, Ellen Langer has demonstrated repeatedly how our limits are of our own making, both as individuals and scientists. She is a personal testimonial for the mindful life-style, bringing vast resources of contagious energy and exuberance to all she does. Her pioneering work has cut new theoretical paths through the forest of mindless behavior, thereby enlarging our possibilities for positive social change.

REFERENCES

Albert, R. S. (1975). Toward a behavioral definition of genius. *American Psychologist*, *30*, 140–151.

American Psychological Association (1988). *1988 APA membership register*. Washington, D.C.: American Psychological Association.

Arthur W. Melton Library (1989). Awards, honors and prizes in psychology. Washington, D.C.: American Psychological Association.

Boring, E. G. (1951). The woman problem. *American Psychologist*, *6*(12), 679–682.

Csikszentmihalyi, M. (1988). Society, culture, and person: A systems view of creativity. In R. J. Sternberg (Ed.), *The nature of creativity* (pp. 325–339). New York: Cambridge University Press.

Mitchell, M. B. (1951). The status of women in the American Psychological Association. *American Psychologist*, *6*, 193–201.

Mooney, R. L. (1963). A conceptual model for integrating four approaches to the identification of creative talent. In C. W. Taylor & F. Barron (Eds.), *Scientific creativity: Its recognition and development* (pp. 331–340). New York: Wiley.

O'Connell, A. N., & Russo, N. F. (Eds.) (1980). *Eminent women in psychology*. New York: Human Sciences Press.

O'Connell, A. N., & Russo, N. F. (Eds.) (1983). *Models of achievement: Reflections of eminent women in psychology*. New York: Columbia University Press.

O'Connell, A. N., & Russo, N. F. (Eds.) (1988). *Models of achievement: Reflections of eminent women in psychology: Volume 2*. Hillsdale, N.J.: Erlbaum.

Russo, N. F., & Denmark, F. L. (1987). Contributions of women to psychology. *Annual Review of Psychology*, *38*, 279–298.

Russo, N. F., & O'Connell, A. N. (1980). Models from our past: Psychology's foremothers. *Psychology of Women Quarterly*, *5*, 11–54.

Scarborough, E., & Furumoto, L. (1987). *Untold lives: The first generation of women psychologists*. New York: Columbia University Press.

Part IV

Bibliographic Resources

WOMEN IN PSYCHOLOGY: BIBLIOGRAPHIC RESOURCES

Agnes N. O'Connell, Nancy Felipe Russo, Melinda Deacon, and Brenda Lee

The purpose of this chapter is to enhance the reader's access to information about women contributors to psychology by identifying selected works that are especially noteworthy for their richness as sources of autobiographical, biographical, and related materials. It is divided into five sections separating sources that specifically focus on (1) women in psychology, (2) psychology in general, (3) women in general, (4) persons in general, and (5) individual women contributors to psychology.

Section 1: Works Specifically Focusing on Women's Contributions to Psychology

Note: Works included in Sections 1–4 that are used later as a reference for specific women listed in Section 5 will be subsequently identified by the code that appears in brackets after the first use of the reference.

O'Connell, A. N., & Russo, N. F. (Eds.). (1980). *Eminent women in psychology*. New York: Human Sciences Press [Special issue, *Psychology of Women Quarterly*, 5(1)]. **[O&R–80]**
Includes biographies of seven women: M. W. Calkins, S. Gray, E. Heidbreder, K. Horney, M. C. Jones, A. Roe, and M. F. Washburn, and an overview that contains material on many other women and includes thirty items to test knowledge of psychology's foremothers.

O'Connell, A. N. & Russo, N. F. (Eds.). (1983). *Models of achievement: Reflections of eminent women in psychology*. New York: Columbia University Press. **[O&R–83-I]**
Autobiographies of seventeen women born between 1897 and 1922; M.D.S. Ainsworth, T. G. Alper, K. M. Banham, A. I. Bryan, M. P. Clark, E. Hanfmann, M. R. Harrower, M. Henle, R. W. Howard, M. Ives, M. H. Jones, M. B. McGraw, M. B. Mitchell, L. B. Murphy, M. J. Rioch, C. W. Sherif, and M. J. Wright. Two additional chapters analyze the societal and historical context and similarities and differences among the women.

O'Connell, A. N., & Russo, N. F. (Eds.). (1988). *Models of achievement: Reflections of eminent women in psychology. Volume 2*. Hillsdale, N.J.: Erlbaum. **[O&R–88-II]**

Autobiographies of seventeen women born between 1891 and 1936 (twelve were born between 1915 and 1936): A. Anastasi, M. E. Bernal, M. S. Crissey, F. L. Denmark, O. E. Engelhardt, D. H. Eichorn, E. Fromm, F. K. Graham, J. Loevinger, M. T. Mednick, C. R. Payton, P. C. Smith, J. T. Spence, L.H.M. Stoltz, B. R. Strickland, L. E. Troll, and L. E. Tyler. Additional chapters consider the social and historical context and analyze educational, professional, and personal similarities and differences among these women and the women in Volume 1, providing transhistoric and time-specific profiles.

Over, R. (1983). Representation, status and contributions of women in psychology: A bibliography. *Psychological Documents*, *13*(2), MS 2473.

Partly annotated bibliography of 153 references to work concerned with the participation of women in psychology in Australia, Canada, Great Britain, New Zealand, and the United States.

Scarborough, E., & Furumoto, L. (1987). *Untold lives: The first generation of American women psychologists*. New York: Columbia University Press. **[S&F–87]**

Chapters on five women: M. W. Calkins, M. Shinn, E. Puffer (Howes), M. F. Washburn, and C. Ladd-Franklin, and "cameo" portraits of six: K. G. Moore, L. J. Martin, N. Norsworthy, F.H.R. Dewing, T. L. Smith, and H.B.T. Woolley. Two additional chapters include information on other women's education and careers.

Stevens, G., & Gardner, S. (1982). *The women of psychology*, Vols. 1 & 2. Cambridge, Mass.: Schenkman. **[S&G–82I; S&G–82-II]**

Volume 1: biographical information ranging from one paragraph to a few pages on thirty-seven "pioneers and innovators." Introductory and concluding chapters mention other women. Volume 2: biographical information ranging from one paragraph to a few pages on one-hundred women contributors to the "expansion and refinement" of psychology. Introduction and epilogue mention others.

Section 2: Some General Works on Psychologists and Social and Behavioral Scientists that Include Autobiographical or Biographical Information on Women

American Psychological Association (multiple years). *APA Biographical Directory*. Washington, D.C.: APA. **[APA]**

Contains brief biographical information on members of APA; is periodically updated. Entries below were taken from the 1985 and 1973 directories. **[APA–85; APA–73]**

Benjamin, L. B., Pratt, R., Watlington, D., et al. (1989). *A history of American psychology in notes and news, 1883–1945: An index to journal sources*. New York: Kraus International.

Approximately 5,000 main entries and 20,000 secondary entries in a cross-referenced alphabetized index covering six journals.

Guthrie, R. (1976). *Even the rat was white*. New York: Harper & Row.

Information on pioneering black women psychologists, including M. P. Clark, R. W. Howard, I. Prosser, and A. B. Turner. **[RG–76]**

Jacques Cattell Press (Ed.) *American men and women of science: Social and behavioral sciences*. (1978). 13th ed. New York: Bowker. **[AMWS]**
Brief biographical material.

Krawiec, T. S. (Ed.). (1972). *The psychologists*. Vol. 1. New York: Oxford University Press. **[TSK–72-I]**
Autobiography of A. Anastasi.

Krawiec, T. S. (Ed.). (1974). *The psychologists*. Vol. 2. Brandon, Vt.: Clinical Psychology. **[TSK–74-II]**
Substantial biographical information on R. Ansbacher.

Krawiec, T. S. (Ed.). (1978). *The psychologists*. Vol. 3. Brandon, Vt.: Clinical Psychology. **[TSK–78-III]**
Autobiographies of M. Harrower, L. B. Murphy, L. E. Rhine (with her husband J. B. Rhine), and L. Tyler.

Lewin, M. (Ed.). (1984). *In the shadow of the past: Psychology portrays the sexes: A social and intellectual history*. New York: Columbia University Press.
Information on L. S. Hollingworth.

Lindzey, G. (Ed.). (1974). *A history of psychology in autobiography*. Vol. 6. Englewood Cliffs, N.J.: Prentice-Hall.
Autobiography of M. Mead.

Lindzey, G. (Ed.). (1980). *A history of psychology in autobiography*. Vol. 7. San Francisco: W. H. Freeman. **[GL–80-VII]**
Autobiographies of A. Anastasi and E. J. Gibson.

Lindzey, G. (Ed.). (1989). *A history of psychology in autobiography*. Vol. 8. Palo Alto, Calif.: Stanford University Press. **[GL–89-VIII]**
Autobiographies of D. Jameson, B. Inhelder, and E. E. Maccoby.

Murchison, C. (Ed.). (1930). *A history of psychology in autobiography*. Vol. 1. Worcester, Mass.: Clark University Press. **[CM–30[I]**
Autobiography of M. W. Calkins.

Murchison, C. (Ed.). (1932a). *A history of psychology in autobiography*. Vol. 2. Worcester, Mass.: Clark University Press. **[CM–32a-II]**
Autobiography of M. F. Washburn.

Murchison, C. (Ed.). (1932b). *Psychological register*. Worcester, Mass.: Clark University Press.
Brief biographical material with entries in alphabetical order.

Wolman, B. B. (Ed.). (1977). *International encyclopedia of psychiatry, psychology, psychoanalysis, and neurology*. Vols. 1–12. New York: Van Nostrand Reinhold. **[BBW–77]**
Includes information on lives, views, and works of L. Bender, C. Bühler, M. W. Calkins, H. Deutsch, D. L. Dix, A. Freud, F. Fromm-Reichmann, F. L. Goodenough, K. Horney, M. Klein, C. Ladd-Franklin, M. Mahler, J. T. Spence, C. Thompson, M. F. Washburn, and B. Zeigarnik.

Zusne, L. (1975). *Names in the history of psychology*. Washington, D.C.: Hemisphere. **[LZ–75]**
Brief biographical material in alphabetical order.

Zusne, L. (1984). *Biographical dictionary of psychology*. London: Aldwych Press. **[LZ–84]**

Brief biographical information in alphabetical order on R. Benedict, C. Bühler, M. Calkins, D. Dix, J. E. Downey, E. Frenkel-Brunswik, A. Freud, F. Goodenough, L. S. Hollingworth, K. Horney, G. Kent, M. Klein, C. Ladd-Franklin, M. Montessori, and M. F. Washburn.

Zusne, L. (1987). *Eponyms in psychology.* Westport, Conn.: Greenwood Press. **[LZ–87]**
Includes brief biographical information on originators of approximately 800 discoveries and concepts as well as references to other sources.

Obituaries, award announcements, and historical pieces published in journals such as the *American Psychologist* **[AP]**, *American Journal of Psychology*, and *Journal of the History of the Behavioral Sciences* are also sources of biographical information, as is the newsletter of APA's Division of the History of Psychology. Part III of this book **[O&R–90-PTIII]** contains citations to biographical information on winners of American Psychological Association (APA) and American Psychological Foundation awards published with the award announcements in *AP*.

The Archives of the History of American Psychology at the University of Akron and the APA Archives housed in the Library of Congress contain a wealth of information. In addition, primary and secondary references are available on women contributors to psychology in the following:

Watson, R. I. (1974a). *Eminent contributors to psychology, Volume 1: A bibliography of primary references.* New York: Springer.
References for major primary publications for 538 persons including 228 psychologists living between 1600 and 1967. Women contributors represented include A. F. Bronner, M. Calkins, J. E. Downey, E. Frenkel-Brunswik, F. Fromm-Reichmann, F. L. Goodenough, L. S. Hollingworth, K. Horney, C. Ladd-Franklin, M. Klein, M. Montessori, and M. F. Washburn.

Watson, R. I. (1974b). *Eminent contributors to psychology, Volume 2: A bibliography of secondary references.* New York: Springer.
A bibliography of secondary references (i.e., references for publications about persons and their works) is included for the women listed under Volume 1.

Section 3: General Works on Women that Include Some Psychologists

Addis, P. K. (1983). *Through a woman's I: An annotated bibliography of American women's autobiographical writings, 1947–1976.* Metuchen, N.J.: Scarecrow Press.
Listed by author as well as indexed by field.

Herman, K. (1984). *Women in particular: An index to American women.* Phoenix, Az.: Oryx.
Contains reference information to a variety of biographical sources.

Ireland, N. O. (1970). *Index to women of the world from ancient to modern times.*
Westwood, Mass.: F. W. Faxon Co.
Brief biographical information and references for biographical collections on approximately 2,000 women.

Ireland, N. O. (1988). *Index to women of the world from ancient to modern times: A supplement.* Metuchen, N.J.: Scarecrow Press.

James, E. T., & James, J. W. (Eds.). (1971). *Notable American women, 1607–1950.*
Volumes 1, 2 and 3. Cambridge, Mass.: Belknap Press. **[NAW-I; NAW-II; NAW-III]**
Includes biographies of J. Addams, A. F. Bronner, M. W. Calkins, D. L. Dix,
J. E. Downey, M. P. Follett, C. P. Gilman, L. S. Hollingworth, C. Ladd-Franklin,
L. J. Martin, M. W. Shinn, M. F. Washburn, H.B.T. Woolley, and C. B. Zachry.

O'Neill, L. D. (Ed.). (1979). *The women's book of world records and achievements.*
Garden City, N.Y.: Anchor Books/Doubleday. **[LDO–79]**
Highlights significant achievements of women.

Rosenberg, R. R. (1982). *Beyond separate spheres: Intellectual roots of modern feminism.*
New Haven, Conn.: Yale University Press.
Includes information on women psychologists involved in the history of the debate
on sex differences and the psychology of women.

Rossiter, M. W. (1982). *Women scientists in America: Struggles and strategies to 1940.*
Baltimore, Md.: Johns Hopkins University Press.
Describes careers and contributions of women scientists, including a number of
psychologists.

Seigel, P. J. (1985). *Women in scientific search: An American bio-bibliography, 1724–1979.* Metuchen, N.J.: Scarecrow Press.
Chronological information organized by field in addition to name index.

Sicherman, G., Green, C. H., Kantrov, I., & Walker, H. (Eds.). (1980). *Notable American women: The modern period.* Cambridge, Mass.: Belknap Press. **[NAW-MP]**
Includes biographies of A. F. Bronner, C. B. Bühler, H. F. Dunbar, E. Frenkel-
Brunswik, F. Fromm-Reichmann, L. M. Gilbreth, F. L. Goodenough, K. Horney,
L. Levine, M. G. Rand, R. M. Strang, J. Taft, H. Taba, and C. Thompson.

Uglow, J. S. (1985). *The international dictionary of women's biography.* New York:
Continuum. **[IDWB]**
Brief biographical sketches, including some of women contributors to psychology.

Section 4: General Biographical Sources

There are numerous resources for identifying biographical information, many
of them regularly updated (see the introduction to IDWB for a more comprehensive summary). The following are particularly useful and informative:

The Annual Obituary. Chicago: St. James.
Obituaries indexed by name and by profession, psychology and psychiatry listed
separately.

Biographical books 1950–1980. New York: Bowker.
A list of over 42,000 titles.

Biographical Dictionaries and Related Works: An International Bibliography. Detroit:
Gale Research.
Updated periodically.

Biography Index. New York: H. W. Wilson.

> A quarterly index covering current books, periodicals, obituaries, etc., with annual and three-yearly cumulations, beginning in 1946.

Devine, E., Held, M., Vinson, J., & Walsh, E. (Eds.). (1983). *Thinkers of the twentieth century: A biographical, bibliographic and critical dictionary*. London: Macmillan.

> Contains one to two pages of information on R. Benedict, A. Freud, K. Horney, M. Mead, and M. Montessori.

Herbert, M. C., & McNeil, B. (1980). *Biography and Genealogy Master Index*. Detroit: Gale Research.

> Consolidated index to more than 3,200,000 biographical sketches. Cumulative updates available beginning in 1985.

Kiffer, M. E. (Ed.). (1987). *Current Biography Cumulated Index 1940–1985*. New York: H. W. Wilson.

New York Times Obituary Index.

Section 5: Selected Biographical Resources for 185 Women Contributors to Psychology

The purpose of this section is to enhance the readers' access to a representative variety of information about selected women, not to provide comprehensive coverage. While it was not possible to include all women contributors to psychology, selected bibliographic sources of information are provided for the collective list of 185 women. The women who are included reflect the combined list of contributors identified by the process described in Part I.

Each entry includes the name, and when available, date and place of birth, some areas of contribution (in alphabetical order), and selected bibliographic information. A more detailed breakdown by major fields for women whose biographies are included in Part II is found in Appendix B. Space limited the number of bibliographic sources that could be included, so recent materials containing bibliographic references to additional biographical and autobiographical sources were given greatest preference. For works that are referenced in Sections 1–4 of this chapter, the abbreviations are used that appear at the end of the full reference above. Abbreviations are derived from those used for major fields as listed in the *1988 APA Membership Register* (p. 715). In addition, areas specifically represented by APA Division 9 (Society for the Psychological Study of Social Issues), Division 44 (Society for the Psychological Study of Lesbian and Gay Issues), and Division 45 (Society for the Psychological Study of Ethnic Minority Issues) are included. A summary of the abbreviations used in the entries can be found at the end of the listing.

Theodora M. Abel Sept 9, 1899, Newport, RI, USA; Clin/Psychother/Soc
S&G-82-II, 9–16.

Lyn Y. Abramson Feb 7, 1950, Benson, MN; Clin/Dev/Persnlty/Soc
O&R-90-PTIII; Science Digest (1984). *America's brightest scientists under forty*. New
York: Hearst, 70.

Dorothy Christina Adkins Apr 6, 1912; Persnlty/Soc/Sys Meth & Tech
APA-73, 7; Thurstone, L. G. (1976). [Obit]. *Psychometrika, 41*, 435–437.

Mary D. Salter Ainsworth Dec 1, 1913, Glendale, OH; Clin/Dev/Persnlty
O&R-83-I, 201–219; O&R-90-PTIII.

Doris Twitchell Allen Oct 8, 1901, Old Town, ME; Clin/Psychother/Soc Is
AMWS, 19.

Thelma G. Alper July 24, 1908, Chelsea, MA; Clin/Dev/Soc/Soc Is/Sys Meth & Tech/
Wmn
APA-73, 15; O&R-83, 189–199.

Louise Bates Ames Oct 29, 1908, Portland, ME; Clin/Dev/Ed
APA-73, 17; Candee, M. D. (Ed.). (1956). *Current Biographies*. New York: H. W.
Wilson, 299–300; Murstein, B. I. (1974). Louise Bates Ames. *Journal of Personality
Assessment, 386*, 505–506.

Anne Anastasi Dec 19, 1908, New York, New York; Dev/Sys Meth & Tech.
GL-80-VII, 1–37; O&R-88-II, 57–66, O&R-90-PTII & PTIII; TSK-72-I, 3–37.

Rowena Ripin Ansbacher Dec 26, 1906, New York, NY; Persnlty/Soc Is
APA-85, 25; Ansbacher, H. L. (1974). Psychology: A way of living. TSK-74-II, 3–
49.

Magda B. Arnold Dec 22, 1903, Maehr-Truebau, Czechoslovakia; Dev/Exptl/His/Soc
AMWS, 38; S&G-82-II, 126–129.

Helen S. Astin Feb 6, 1932, Serras, Greece; Couns/Ed/Soc Is/Wmn
AMWS, 43; APA-85, 33; LDO-79, 423.

Carolyn Lewis Attneave July 2, 1920, El Paso, TX; Couns/Comun/Eth Min Is/Soc Is
APA-73, 32; Albin, R. (1980, Jan). Snapshot: Carolyn Attneave. *APA Monitor, II*,
11; La Fromboise, T. D., & Fleming, C. forthcoming. Keeper of the fire: A profile
of Carolyn Attneave. *Journal of Counseling and Development*.

Katharine M. Banham (Bridges) May 26, 1897, Sheffield, England; Dev/Exptl.
O&R-83-I, 27–41; S&G-II, 70.

Judith M. Bardwick Jan 16, 1933, New York, NY; Pers/Wmn
AMWS, 74; APA-73, 46; S&G-82-II, 186–187.

Franziska Baumgarten-Tramer Nov 26, 1886, Lodz, Poland; Dev/Indus/Soc
Canziani, W. (1975). Franziska Baumgarten-Tramer, I & II. *Perceptual and Motor
Skills, 41*, 479–486, 487–490; S&G-82-I, 212–215.

Diana Baumrind Aug 23, 1927, New York, NY; Clin/Dev
AMWS, 74; APA-85, 59; Baumrind, D. (1972). From each according to her ability.
School Review, 80(2), 161–197.

Nancy Bayley Sept 28, 1899, The Dalles, OR; Clin/Dev/Sys Meth & Tech
O&R-90-PTII & PTIII.

Sandra Lipsitz Bem June 22, 1944, Pittsburgh, PA; Dev/Persnlty/Soc/Soc Is/Sys Meth
& Tech/Wmn
O&R-90-PTII & PTIII.

Lauretta Bender Aug 9, 1897, Butte, MT; Exptl/Sys Meth & Tech
BBW-77, 333–336; LZ-87, 24; S&G-82-II, 22–27, 75.

Ruth F. Benedict June 5, 1887, New York, NY: Anthropologist
Gacs, U., Khan, A., McIntyre, J., & Weinberg, R. (Eds.). (1988). *Women anthropologists.* Westport, CT: Greenwood, 1–8; Mead, M. (1959). *Ruth Benedict: An anthropologist at work.* Boston: Houghton Mifflin.

Martha E. Bernal Apr 13, 1931, El Paso, TX: Clin/Eth Min Is
O&R-88-II, 261–276

Jessie Bernard June 8, 1903, Minneapolis, MN; Sociologist/Wmn
IDWB, 55; Denmark, F. (1976). Kurt Lewin Memorial Award Presentation to Jessie
Bernard. *Journal of Social Issues, 32*(4), 209–211; Mattfeld, J. A., & Van Aken, C.
G. (Eds.). (1965). *Women and the scientific professions.* Cambridge, MA: MIT Press,
163–182.

Jeanne Humphrey Block July 17, 1923, Tulsa, OK; Dev/Persnlty/Soc/Soc Is/Wmn
APA-73, 144; O&R-90-PTII.

Hedda Bolgar Aug 19, 1909, Zurich, Switzerland; Clin/Comun/Psychother
AMWS, 123; S&G-82-II, 173–174.

Yvonne Brackbill Oct 11, 1928, Modesto, CA; Dev/Exptl
AMWS, 136.

Augusta Fox Bronner July 22, 1881, Louisville, KY; Clin/Comun
LDO-79, 144, 156; Mora, G. (1972). William Healy and Augusta Bronner. *American
Journal of Psychiatry, 11*, 1–29; NAW-MP, 108–110; S&G-82-I, 198–203.

Alice I. Bryan Sept 11, 1902, Kearney, NJ; Exptl/Sys Meth & Tech
O&R-83-I, 69–86.

Charlotte M. Bühler Dec 20, 1893, Berlin, Germany; Clin/Dev/Psychoan
O&R-90-PTII; LZ-84, 64–65.

Mary Whiton Calkins Mar 30, 1863, Hartford, CT; Exptl/Persnlty
LZ-84, 72–73; O&R-80, 55–68; O&R-90-PTII; S&F –87, 17–51.

Nancy E. Cantor Apr 2, 1952, New York, NY; Soc
O&R-90-PTIII

Rosalind Dymond Cartwright Dec 30, 1922, New York, NY; Clin/Exptl/Physiol
AMWS, 194; APA–85, 159–160.

Mamie Phipps Clark Oct 18, 1917, Hot Springs, AR; Dev/Eth Min Is
RG–76; O&R-83-I, 267–277; O&R-90-PTII.

Lillian Comas-Diaz July 18, 1950; Chicago, IL; Clin/Comun/Eth Min Is/Psychother/
Wmn
APA–85, 193.

Lynn Cooper Dec 31, 1947, Toledo, OH; Exptl
O&R-90-PTIII.

Marie P. Skodak Crissey Jan 10, 1910, Lorain, OH; Comun/Sch/Sys Meth & Tech
O&R-88-II, 71–84.

Frederica Annis de Leo de Laguna Oct 3, 1906, Ann Arbor, MI; Anthropologist

Gacs, U., Khan, A., McIntyre, J., & Weinberg, R. (Eds.). (1988). *Women anthropologists*. Westport, CT: Greenwood, 37–44.

Ursula M. Delworth Oct 22, 1934, San Diego, CA; Clin/Comun/Couns/Wmn
AMWS, 289; APA–85, 236.

Tamara Dembo May 28, 1902, Baku, USSR; Clin/Dev/Soc/Soc Is
AMWS, 299; S&G-82-II, 174.

Florence L. Denmark Jan 28, 1932, Philadelphia, PA; Les & Gy Is/Persnlty/Soc/Soc Is/Wmn
O&R-88-II, 279–293; O&R-90-PTII & PTIII.

Cynthia P. Deutsch Apr 16, 1928, Chicago, IL; Clin/Dev/Soc/Soc Is/Wmn
AMWS, 294; APA–85, 241.

Helene Deutsch Oct 9, 1884, Przemysl, Galicia, Austro-Hungarian Empire (Poland); Clin/Psychoan/Wmn
Deutsch, H. (1973). *Confrontations with myself: An epilogue*. New York: Norton; BBW–77–4, 79–80; IDWB, 142; LDO–79, 413; S&G-82-I, 186–193.

Dorothea Lynde Dix Apr 4, 1802, Hampden, ME; Reformer
Tiffany, F. (1980). *Life of Dorothea Lynde Dix*. Boston: Houghton Mifflin; BBW–77–4, 131–132; IDWB, 146–147; LZ–75, 109; LZ–84, 103–104; NAW-I, 486; S&G-82-I, 51–69.

Elizabeth M. Douvan Nov 3, 1926, South Bend, IN; Dev/Soc/Soc Is/Wmn
AMWS, 313; APA–85, 256.

June Etta Downey July 13, 1875, Laramie, WY; Exptl/Sys Meth & Tech
LZ–84, 107; NAW-I, 514–515; S&G-82-I, 121–124; Uhrbrock, R. S. (1933). [Obit]. *Journal of General Psychology, 9*, 351–364.

Anke Ehrhardt Dec 20, 1940, Hamburg, Germany; Clin/Dev/Physio/Wmn
AMWS, 336; APA–85, 274; *APA Monitor*, 1986, *17*(9), 25.

Dorothy Hansen Eichorn Nov 18, 1924, Montpelier, VT; Dev/Expl/Physiol
O&R-88-II, 205–224.

Olga E. deCillis Engelhardt Aug 26, 1917, New York, NY: Exptl/Indust & Org
O&R-88-II, 119–134.

Sibylle K. Escalona July 7, 1915; Berlin, Germany; Clin/Dev/Psychoan
AMWS, 352; S&G-82-II, 194–195.

Lorraine Eyde Feb 20, 1932, New York, NY; Couns/Indust & Org/Sys Meth & Tech/Wmn
AMWS, 356; APA–85, 291.

Leah Gold Fein Dec 10, 1910, Minsk, Russia: Clin/Dev/Psychother/Soc
APA–64, 180; APA–85, 298; *Journal of Clinical Child Psychology, 4*(2), 3.

Grace Maxwell Fernald Nov 19, 1878, Clyde, OH; Ed/Sys Meth & Tech
S&G-82-I, 124–125; Sullivan, E. B., et al. (1950). *Psychological Review, 57*, 319–321; [Obit]. *School & Society, 11*, 62.

Norma Feshbach Sept 6, 1926, New York, NY; Clin/Dev/Sch/Soc/Soc Is/Wmn
AMWS, 373; APA–85, 304.

Else Frenkel-Brunswik Aug 18, 1908, Lemberg, Austro-Hungarian Empire (Poland);

Clin/Eth Min Is/Psychoan/Soc/Soc Is
LZ–84, 139; O&R-90-PTII.

Anna Freud Dec 3, 1895, Vienna, Austria; Clin/Dev/Psychoan/Psychother
BBW–77–5, 90–94; LZ–84, 139–140; O&R-90-PTII.

Erika Fromm Dec 23, 1901, Frankfurt, Germany; Clin/Dev/Psychoan/Psychother
O&R-88-II, 89–101.

Frieda Fromm-Reichmann Oct 23, 1889, Karlsruhe, Germany; Clin/Psychoan/Psy-
chother
BBW–77–5, 140–141; LZ–75, 417; NAW-MP, 252–255; S&G-82-I, 205–208.

Eleanor A.M. Gamble Mar 2, 1868, Cincinnati, OH; Exptl
American Men of Science, 1st ed.; Ruckmick, C. A. (1934). [Obit]. *American Journal
of Psychology, 46*, 154–156; S&G-82-I, 127–129.

Beatrice T. Gardner July 13, 1933, Vienna, Austria; Exptl/Physiol
AMWS, 420; S&G-82-II, 196–197.

Ann M. Garner Jan 25, 1916, Omaha, NE; Clin/Dev/Persnlty
APA–85, 348.

Rochel S. Gelman Jan 23, 1942, Toronto, Canada; Dev/Exptl
AMWS, 427; O&R-90-PTIII.

Eleanor Jack (Jackie) Gibson Dec 7, 1910, Peoria, IL; Dev/Exptl
GL–80-VII, 239–271; O&R-90-PTII & PTIII.

Lillian Moller Gilbreth May 24, 1878, Oakland, CA; Eng/Indust & Org
O&R-90-PTII.

Florence Laura Goodenough Aug 6, 1886, Honesdale, PA; Dev/Persnlty/Sys Meth &
Tech
LZ–84, 162; O&R-90-PTII.

Jacqueline Garrett Goodnow Nov 25, 1925, Toowoomba, Queensland, Australia; Dev/
Exptl
O&R-90-PTII.

Kathleen Grady July 23, 1950, Springfield, MA; Soc/Soc Is/Wmn
APA–85, 387; *APA Monitor*, 1986, *17*(9), 25.

Frances K. Graham Aug 1, 1918, Canastoga, NY; Dev/Exptl/Physiol
O&R-88-II, 169–187.

Susan W. Gray Dec 5, 1913, Rockdale, TN; Dev/Sch/Soc/Soc Is
APA–85, 391; O&R-80, 127–139.

Florence C. Halpern Jan 5, 1900; Clin/Comun/Dev/Sch
APA–73, 397.

Eugenia Hanfmann Mar 3, 1905, St. Petersburg, USSR; Clin/Couns/Persnlty
LZ–87, 111; O&R-83-I, 141–152; S&G-82-II, 161–163.

Rachel T. Hare-Mustin Apr 7, 1928, New York, NY; Clin/Psychother/Wmn
APA–85, 426.

Margaret Kuenne Harlow Aug 8, 1918, St. Louis, MO; Dev/Exptl
[Obit], 1971, *Child Development, 42*, 1313–1314; S&G-82-II, 199–201.

Lenore W. Harmon Aug 21, 1935, Minneapolis, MN; Couns/Sys Meth & Tech
APA–85, 427.

Molly R. Harrower Jan 25, 1906, Johannesburg, South Africa; Clin/Couns/Psychother/
Sys Meth & Tech
LZ–87, 112; O&R-83-I, 153–171; TSK–78-III, 85–104.

Ruth E. Hartley May 26, 1910, New York, NY; Clin/Dev/Soc/Wmn
AMWS, 516; S&G-82-II, 163–164.

Elaine (Walster) Hatfield Oct 22, 1937, Detroit, MI; Soc
AMWS, 1246; APA–85, 435.

Edna Heidbreder May 1, 1890, Quincy, IL; Exptl/His/Persnlty/Sys Meth & Tech
O&R-80, 94–102; O&R-90-PTII.

Grace Heider Nov 30, 1903, Jacksonville, FL; Dev/Soc
S&G-82-II, 175; Heider, F. (1983). *The life of a psychologist: An autobiography.*
Lawrence: University of Kansas.

Ravenna Mathews Helson Feb 13, 1925, Austin, TX; Persnlty/Wmn
O&R-90-PTII.

Mary Henle July 14, 1913, Cleveland, OH; Exptl/His/Persnlty/Sys Meth & Tech
O&R-83-I, 221–233; O&R-90-PTII.

Nancy M. Henley Oct 27, 1934, Palatka, FL; Exptl/Soc/Soc Is/Wmn
AMWS, 538; APA–85, 449.

Marguerite R. Hertz Aug 31, 1899, New York, NY; Clin/Psychother
APA–85, 453; S&G-II, 71.

Eileen Mavis Hetherington Nov 27, 1926, Ocean Falls, British Columbia, Canada;
Comun/Dev
AMWS, 546; APA–85, 454.

Gertrude Howell Hildreth Oct 11, 1898, Terre Haute, IN; Dev/Ed/Sys Meth & Tech
APA–73, 436.

Lois Wladis Hoffman Mar 25, 1929, Elmira, NY; Dev/Soc/Soc Is/Wmn
AMWS, 560; S&G-82-II, 203–204.

Leta Stetter Hollingworth May 25, 1886, Chadron, NE; Clin/Dev/Ed/Soc/Wmn
LZ–84, 194; O&R-90-PTII.

Evelyn Hooker Sept 2, 1907; Clin/Exptl/Les & Gy Is
APA–85, 472.

Karen Danielson Horney Sept 15, 1885, Hamburg, Germany; Clin/Dev/Persnlty/Psy-
choan/Psychother/Wmn
BBW–77-5, 414–420; LZ–84, 196; NAW-MP, 351–354; O&R-80, 81–93; O&R-90-
PTII; Horney, K. (1980). *The adolescent diaries of Karen Horney.* New York: Basic.

Ruth Winifred Howard (Beckham) Mar 25, 1900, Washington, DC; Clin/Couns
O&R-83-I, 55–67; RG–76.

Ethel Dench Puffer Howes Oct 19, 1872, Framingham, MA; Exptl
American men of science, 1st ed.; S&F–87, 71–90.

Thelma Hunt Nov 30, 1903, Aurora, AK; Clin/Persnlty/Physiol
APA–85, 484.

Elizabeth B. Hurlock July 4, 1898, Harrisburg, PA; Dev/Persnlty
AMWS, 586, AP–85, 486.

Bärbel Inhelder Apr 15, 1913, St. Gall, Switzerland; Dev/Exptl/Sys Meth & Tech
GL–89-VIII, 208–243; O&R-90-PTII.

Susan Isaacs 1885; Dev/Psychoan/Psychother
IDWB, 238–239; Levy, E. (1977). Susan Isaacs: An intellectual biography. *Dissertation Abstracts International, 38*(4-A), 2002–2003.

Margaret Ives Apr 10, 1903, Detroit, MI; Clin/Exptl
AMWS, 594; O&R-83-I, 109–118.

Marie Jahoda Jan 26, 1907, Vienna, Austria; Clin/Persnlty/Psychoan/Soc/Soc Is
O&R-90-PTII & PTIII.

Maud Merrill James Apr 30, 1888, Owatonna, MN; Dev/Persnlty/Sys Meth & Tech
S&G-82-I, 210–212; Sears, R. (1979). [Obit]. *AP, 34*, 176.

Dorothea Jameson Nov 16, 1920, Newton, MA: Exptl
GL–89-VIII, 156–206; O&R-90-PTIII; S&G-82-II, 206–208.

Margaret Hubbard Jones Apr 23, 1915, Fairfield, CT; Engr
O&R-83-I, 235–249.

Mary Cover Jones Sept 1, 1896, Johnstown, PA: Dev/Exptl
Jones, M. C. (1975). A 1929 pioneer looks at behavior therapy. *Journal of Behavior Therapy & Experimental Psychiatry, 6*, 181–187; O&R-80, 103–115; S&G-82-II, 39–46.

Ruth Kanfer Feb 1, 1955; Exptl/Indust & Org
APA-85, 523; O&R-90-PTIII.

Florence Whiteman Kaslow Philadelphia, PA; Clin/Psychother
ANWS, 633, APA-85, 528; O&R-90-PTIII.

Phyllis A. Katz Apr 9, 1938, New York, NY; Dev/Ed/Eth Min Is/Soc/Soc Is/Wmn
AMWS, 635; APA–85, 530.

Tracy Seedman Kendler Aug 4, 1918, New York, NY; Dev/Exptl
AMWS, 644; S&G-82-II, 210–212.

Grace Helen Kent June 6, 1875, Michigan City, IN; Sys Meth & Tech
LZ–75, 319; LZ–84, 224; LZ–87, 146; S&G-82-I, 134–135; Shakow, D. (1974). [Obit]. *Journal of the History of the Behavioral Sciences, 10*, 275–280.

Jane Kessler Mar 9, 1921, Beverly, MA; Clin/Dev/Persnlty/Psychoan/Psychother
O&R-90-PTIII.

Barbara A. Kirk Nov 26, 1906, San Francisco, CA; Clin/Couns/Soc
AMWS, 657; APA-85, 549.

Melanie Klein Mar 30, 1882, Budapest, Hungary; Clin/Dev/Psychoan
Lindon, J. A. Melanie Klein: Her view of the unconscious. In F. Alexander, S. Eisenstein, & M. Grotjohn (Eds.) (1966), *Psychoanalytic pioneers*. New York: Basic Books; BBW–77–6, 291–305; IDWP, 259; LDO–79, 414; LZ–75, 319; LZ–84, 227; Wintle, J. (Ed.). *Makers of modern culture*. New York: Facts on File, 277–278.

Carol Krumhansl Sept 17, 1947, Providence, RI; Exptl
O&R-90-PTIII.

Marta Kutas Sept 2, 1949, Fulpos, Hungary; Exptl/Physiol
O&R-90-PTIII.

Beatrice Lacey July 22, 1919, New York, NY; Dev/Physiol
O&R-90-PTIII; S&G-82-II, 213–215.

Christine Ladd-Franklin Dec 1, 1847, Windsor, CT; Exptl/Sys Meth & Tech
BBW–77–6, 321; LZ–84, 242; O&R-90-PTII, S&F–87, 109–129.

Nadine Lambert Oct 21, 1926, Ephraim, UT; Comun/Ed/Sch
APA–85, 582; O&R-90-PTIII; S&G-II, 215–216.

Ellen J. Langer Mar 25, 1947, New York, NY; Soc/Soc Is
APA–85, 586; O&R-90-PTIII.

Hannah Lerman Mar 7, 1936, New York, NY; Clin/Persnlty/Psychother/Wmn
APA–85, 603.

Esther McDonald Lloyd-Jones Jan 11, 1901, Lockport, IL; Couns/Sch/Soc
AMWS, 738; APA–85, 624; Smith, Margaret R. (1976). *The voyage of Esther Lloyd-Jones: Travels with a pioneer. Personnel and Guidance Journal, 54*, 473–480.

Jane Loevinger Feb 6, 1918, St. Paul, MN; Dev/Persnlty/Sys Meth & Tech
AMWS, 740; O&R-88-II, 155–166.

Chalsa M. Loo Mar 7, 1945, Honolulu, HI; Comun/Eth Min Is/Soc/Soc Is
APA–85, 628.

Eleanor Emmons Maccoby May 15, 1917, Tacoma, WA; Dev/Soc
O&R-90-PTII & PTIII; GL–89-VIII, 291–336.

Jean W. Macfarlane Jan 1, 1894; Clin/Dev/Soc
APA–48, 184; APA–85, 641.

Margaret Schoenberger Mahler May 10, 1897, Sopron, Hungary; Clin/Psychoan/Psychother
BBW–77–6, 459–460; S&G-82-II, 52–53; Stepansky, P. (1988). *The memoirs of Margaret S. Mahler*. New York: Free Press.

Dorothy Postle Marquis July 18, 1905, Columbus, OH; Clin/Dev
APA–73, 630.

Lillien J. Martin July 7, 1851, Olean, NY; Clin/Dev
American Men of Science, 1st ed; Deford, M.A. (1948). *Psychologist unretired: The life pattern of Lillien J. Martin*. Stanford, CA: Stanford University Press; NAW-II, 504–505; S&F–87, 189–191; S&G–82-I, 89–96; Martin, L. J. (1927). *Round the world with a psychologist*. San Francisco: J. W. Stacey.

Clara Weiss Mayo Sept 13, 1931, Linz, Austria; Eth Min Is/Soc/Soc Is/Wmn
O&R-90-PTII.

Martha K. McClintock Feb 22, 1947, Pasadena, CA; Physiol
O&R-90-PTIII; Science Digest (1984). *America's 100 brightest scientists under forty*. New York: Hearst, 71.

Myrtle B. McGraw Aug 1, 1899, Birmingham, AL; Dev/Ed
O&R-83-I, 43–53.

Margaret Mead Dec 6, 1902, Philadelphia, PA; Anthropologist
Gacs, U., Khan, A., McIntyre, J. & Weinberg, R. (Eds.). (1988). *Women anthropologists*, Westport, CT: Greenwood, 252–260; GL-VI, 293–326; IDWB, 315–316; S&G–82-II, 98–105; Mead, M. (1972). *Blackberry winter: My earlier years*. New York: Morrow.

Martha Tamara Shuch Mednick Mar 31, 1929, New York, NY; Persnlty/Soc/Soc Is/
Sys Meth & Tech/Wmn
AMWS, 813; O&R-88-II, 245–259.

Maud A. Merrill (James) Apr 30, 1888, Owatonna, MN; Sys Meth & Tech
Sears, R. R. (1979). [Obit]. *AP, 34*, 176.

Catherine Cox Miles May 20, 1890, San Jose, CA; Dev/Persnlty
S&G–82-I, 216–217.

Brenda Atkinson Milner July 15, 1918, Manchester, England; Exptl/Physiol
O&R-90-PTIII; S&G–82-II, 223–225.

Mildred B. Mitchell Dec 25, 1903, Rockford, IL; Clin/Couns/Eng
APA–73, 686; O&R-83-I, 121–139.

Maria Montessori Aug 13, 1870, Chiaravalle, Italy; Educator/Dev/Sys Meth & Tech
LZ–84, 301–302; O&R-90-PTII.

Lois Barclay Murphy Mar 23, 1902, Lisbon, IA; Clin/Dev
O&R-83-I, 89–107; S&G–82-II, 134–139; TSK–78-III, 167–180.

Bernice Levin Neugarten Feb 11, 1916, Norfolk, NE; Dev/Persnlty/Soc
O&R-90-PTII; S&G–82-II, 227–228.

Naomi Norsworthy Sept 29, 1877, New York, NY; Sys Meth & Tech
Higgins, F. C. (1918). *The life of Naomi Norsworthy*. Boston: Houghton Mifflin; S&F–
87; S&G–82-I, 135–136.

Michele A. Paludi June 13, 1954, Schenectady, NY; Dev/Soc/Wmn
APA–85, 782.

Carolyn Robertson Payton May 13, 1925, Norfolk, VA; Clin/Couns/Eth Min Is/Soc
Is/Wmn
O&R-88-II, 227–242; O&R-90-PTII & PTIII.

Helen Peak May 17, 1900, Dallas, TX; Exptl/Soc/Sys Meth & Tech
APA–73, 792; Katz, D. (1987). [Obit]. *AP, 42*, 510.

Lillien Portenier Aug 23, 1890, Guide Rock, NE; Dev/Sys Meth & Tech
APA–73, 783; Bruce, R. H. (1982). [Obit]. *AP*, 971.

Inez Beverly Prosser 1897, Yoakum, TX; Ed
RG–76, 134–135.

Marian Jeannette Radke-Yarrow Mar 2, 1918, Horicon, WI; Dev/Persnlty/Soc/Soc Is
AMWS, 1315; APA–85, 833.

Marie Gertrude Rand Oct 29, 1886, Long Island, NY; Exptl
LZ–87, 81; NAW-MP, 565; *New York Times*, July 2, 1970, 35.

Freda Gould Rebelsky Mar 11, 1931, New York, NY; Dev/Physiol/Soc/Soc Is
AMWS, 981; APA–85, 842; O&R-90-PTIII.

Ellen P. Reese Aug 20, 1926, Hartford, CT; Exptl/Sys Meth & Tech
APA–73, 807; O&R-90-PTIII.

Pamela T. Reid June 1, 1946, Bronx, NY; Dev/Eth Min Is/Soc Is/Wmn
APA–85, 846.

Harriet Lange Rheingold Feb 13, 1908, New York, NY; Dev/Exptl
AMWS, 991; APA–85, 851–852.

Louisa E. Rhine Nov 9, 1891, La Salle, NY; Exptl/Persnlty
AMWS, 991; TSK–78-III, 181–206.

Maria A. Rickers-Ovsiankina, May 3, 1898, Tschita, Russia; Clin/Comun/Psychother/
Soc/Soc Is
AMWS, 996; APA–73, 819; S&G–82-II, 73.

Margaret J. Rioch Jan 24, 1907, Paterson, NJ; Clin/Psychother
O&R-83-I, 173–186.

Florence Richardson Robinson 1885, Hiawatha, KS; Exptl/Physiol
McGeoch, J. A. (1937). [Obit]. *American Journal of Psychology, 49*, 321.

Judith Rodin Sept 9, 1944, Philadelphia, PA; Clin/Exptl/Soc/Soc Is
O&R-90-PTIII.

Anne Roe Aug 20, 1904, Denver, CO; Clin/Dev/Persnlty
O&R-80, 116–125; O&R–90-PTIII; S&G–II, 105–112; Simpson, G. G. (1978).
Concession to the improbable: An unconventional autobiography. New Haven, CT:
Yale University.

Judy F. Rosenblith Mar 20, 1921, Salt Lake City, UT; Dev/Exptl/Sys Meth & Tech
AMWS, 1019; APA–85, 876.

Nancy Felipe Russo May 3, 1943, Oroville, CA; Dev/Eth Min Is/His/Soc/Soc Is/Sys
Meth & Tech/Wmn
AMWS, 1034; APA–85, 891; *APA Monitor*, 1986, *17*(9), 25; LDO–79, 433.

Sandra Wood Scarr (Salapatek) Aug 8, 1936, Washington, DC; Dev/Ed/Eth Min Is/
Persnlty/Physiol/Soc Is
O&R-90-PTIII; S&G–82-II, 321–234.

Pauline (Pat) K. Snedden Sears July 5, 1908, Fairlee, VT; Clin/Dev/Ed/Sch/Soc
O&R-90-PTII & PTIII; S&G–82-II, 241–242.

Georgene Hoffman Seward Jan 21, 1902, Washington, DC; Clin/Comun
S&G–82-II, 139–143; AMWS, 1080.

Virginia Staudt Sexton Aug 30, 1916, New York, NY; Couns/Ed/His/Persnlty/Sys Meth
& Tech/Wmn
O&R-90-PTII.

Carolyn Wood Sherif June 26, 1922, Loogootee, IN; Persnlty/Soc/Soc Is/Wmn
O&R-83-I, 279–293; O&R–90-PTII & PTIII.

Linda Smith Dec 9, 1951, Portsmouth, NH; Dev/Exptl
O&R-90-PTIII.

Patricia Cain Smith Oct 28, 1917, Choteau, MT; Eng/Indust & Org/Soc
AMWS, 1119; O&R-88-II, 139–153.

Barbara Boardman Smuts Nov 9, 1950, New York, NY; Physiol
O&R-90-PTIII.

Janet Taylor Spence Aug 29, 1920, Toledo, OH; Clin/Exptl/Persnlty/Soc/Wmn
O&R-88-II, 189–203; O&R-90-PTII.

Lois Hayden Meek Stolz Oct 19, 1891, Washington, DC; Dev
AMWS, 1158; O&R-88-II, 33–40.

Bonnie Ruth Strickland Nov 24, 1936, Louisville, KY; Clin/Eth Min Is/Les & Gy Is/

Persnlty/Soc/Soc Is/Sys Meth & Tech/Wmn
O&R-88-II, 295–313; O&R–90-PTII.

Shelley E. Taylor Sept 10, 1946, Mt. Kisco, NY; Soc/Wmn
O&R-90-PTIII.

Clara Mabel Thompson Oct 3, 1893, Providence, RI: Clin/Psychoan/Psychother/Wmn
BBW–77-11, 171–172; NAW-MP, 680–683; S&G–82-II, 31–39.

Thelma Gwinn Thurstone Dec 11, 1897, Hume, MO; Ed/Sch/Sys Meth & Tech
O&R-90-PTII.

Ethel Tobach Nov 7, 1921, Miaskouka, USSR; Dev/Exptl/Physiol/Soc Is
AMWS, 102; APA–85, 1045.

Lillian E. Troll Sept 24, 1915, Chicago, IL; Clin/Dev/Persnlty/Sch/Soc/Wmn
O&R-88-II, 105–117.

Alberta Banner Turner Mar 7, 1909, Chicago, IL; Clin/Dev
APA–73, 1017; RG–76, 146–148.

Leona E. Tyler May 10, 1906, Chetek, WI; Couns/Persnlty/Sys Meth & Tech
O&R-88-II, 43–55; O&R–90-PTII; TSK–78-III, 289–362.

Ina C. Uzgiris Dec 2, 1937, Kaunas, Lithuania: Dev/Exptl/Persnlty
APA–73, 1022; S&G–82-II, 241–242.

Lenore Walker Oct 3, 1942, New York, NY; Clin/Les Gy Is/Psychother/Wmn
APA–85, 1082; O&R-90-PTIII.

Barbara Strudler Wallston Aug 15, 1943, New York, NY; Persnlty/Soc/Sys Meth & Tech/Wmn
APA–85, 1084; Russo, N. F. (1990). Barbara Strudler Wallston: Pioneer of contemporary feminist psychology. *Psychology of Women Quarterly*, 14 (2).

Margaret Floy Washburn July 25, 1871, New York, NY; Exptl/Physiol
LZ–84, 451; O&R-80, 69–80; O&R–90-PTII; S&F, 91–107.

Beth Lucy Wellman June 10, 1895, Clarion, IA; Dev/Sys Meth & Tech
O&R-90-PTII.

Eleanor Harris Roland Wembridge 1883, Lee, MA; Exptl
S&F–87, 134, 161, 171; Moore, K. G. (1944). [Obit]. *Psychological Review, 51*, 326–327.

Gertrude J. Williams June 8, 1927, Boston, MA; Clin
AMWS, 1287; APA–85, 1121.

Helen Bradford Thompson Woolley Nov 6, 1874, Chicago, IL; Dev/Persnlty/Wmn
NAW-III, 657–660; S&F–87, 199–201; S&G–82-I, 125–127, *AP*, 1975, 739–754. See also Rosenberg (1982).

Camille Wortman July 2, 1947, Pittsburgh, PA; Clin/Soc
O&R-90-PTIII.

Beatrice A. Wright Dec 16, 1917, New York, NY; Clin/Dev/Soc
AMWS, 1310; APA–85, 1140; B. A. Wright. Interviews with "Pioneers in Counseling and Human Development." *Journal of Counseling and Development, 67*(7), 384–393.

Mary J. Wright May 20, 1915, Strothroy, Ontario, Canada; Dev
AMWS, 1311; O&R–83-I, 251–265.

Ruth Wylie Jan 24, 1920, Beaver Falls, PA; Exptl/Persnlty/Sys Meth & Tech
AMWS, 1313; APA–85, 1143.

Bluma Zeigarnik Nov 9, 1900, Prienai, Lithuania (USSR); Exptl
S&G–82-II, 73–73; *Voprosy Psikhologii*, 1975, *20*(6), 159–160.

ABBREVIATIONS

Area

Clin	Clinical
Comun	Community
Couns	Counseling
Dev	Developmental
Ed	Educational
Eth Min Is	Ethnic Minority Issues
Eng	Engineering
Exptl	Experimental
His	History
Indust & Org	Industrial and Organizational
Les & Gy Is	Lesbian & Gay Issues
Persnlty	Personality
Physiol	Physiological and Comparative
Psychoan	Psychoanalysis
Psychother	Psychotherapy
Sch	School
Soc	Social
Soc Is	Social Issues
Sys Meth & Tech	Systems, Methodology & Techniques
Wmn	Psychology of Women/Sex and Gender Roles & Differences

Information Sources

AMWS	*American men and women of science*
AP	*American Psychologist*
APA	American Psychological Association
BBW	B. B. Wolman
CM	C. Murchison

GL	G. Lindzey
IDWB	*International dictionary of women's biography*
LDO	L. D. O'Neill
LZ	L. Zusne
NAW	*Notable American women*
NAW-MP	*Notable American women: Modern period*
O&R	O'Connell & Russo
RG	R. Guthrie
S&F	Scarborough & Furumoto
S&G	Stevens & Gardner
TSK	T. S. Krawiec

Part V

Appendices

A Chronology of Birth Years

1847	Christine Ladd-Franklin
1863	Mary Whiton Calkins
1870	Maria Montessori
1871	Margaret Floy Washburn
1878	Lillian Moller Gilbreth
1885	Karen Horney
1886	Florence Laura Goodenough
	Leta Stetter Hollingworth
1890	Edna Heidbreder
1893	Charlotte M. Bühler
1895	Anna Freud
	Beth Lucy Wellman
1897	Thelma Gwinn Thurstone
1899	Nancy Bayley
1906	Leona E. Tyler
1907	Marie Jahoda
1908	Anne Anastasi
	Else Frenkel-Brunswik
	Pauline (Pat) Snedden Sears
1910	Eleanor Jack Gibson
1913	Mary Henle
	Bärbel Inhelder
1916	Bernice L. Neugarten
	Virginia Staudt Sexton
1917	Mamie Phipps Clark
	Eleanor Emmons Maccoby
1922	Carolyn Wood Sherif
1923	Jeanne Humphrey Block
	Janet Taylor Spence
1924	Jacqueline Jarrett Goodnow

1925   Ravenna Helson
        Carolyn Robertson Payton
1931   Florence L. Denmark
        Clara Mayo
1936   Bonnie Ruth Strickland
1944   Sandra Lipsitz Bem

Places of Birth

AUSTRALIA

Toowoomba, Queensland: Jacqueline Jarrett Goodnow

AUSTRIA

Linz: Clara Mayo

Vienna: Anna Freud; Marie Jahoda

GERMANY

Berlin: Charlotte Malachowski Bühler

Hamburg: Karen Horney

ITALY

Chiaravalle: Maria Montessori

POLAND

Lemberg (Austro-Hungarian Empire): Else Frenkel-Brunswik

SWITZERLAND

St. Gall: Bärbel Inhelder

UNITED STATES OF AMERICA

Arkansas

Hot Springs: Mamie Phipps Clark

California

Oakland: Lillian Moller Gilbreth

Connecticut

Hartford: Mary Whiton Calkins

Windsor: Christine Ladd-Franklin

Illinois

Peoria: Eleanor Jack Gibson

Quincy: Edna Frances Heidbreder

Indiana

Loogootee: Carolyn Wood Sherif

Iowa

Clarion: Beth Lucy Wellman

Kentucky

Louisville: Bonnie Ruth Strickland

Missouri

Hume: Thelma Gwinn Thurstone

Nebraska

Chadron: Leta Stetter Hollingworth

Norfolk: Bernice Levin Neugarten

New York

New York City: Anne Anastasi; Virginia Staudt Sexton; Margaret Floy Washburn

Ohio

Cleveland: Mary Henle

Toledo: Janet Taylor Spence

Oklahoma

Tulsa: Jeanne Humphrey Block

OregonThe Dalles: Nancy Bayley

Pennsylvania

Honesdale: Florence Laura Goodenough

Philadelphia: Florence L. Denmark

Pittsburgh: Sandra Lipsitz Bem

Texas

Austin: Ravenna Mathews Helson

Vermont

Fairlee: Pauline (Pat) K. Snedden Sears

Virginia

Norfolk: Carolyn Robertson Payton

Washington

Tacoma: Eleanor Emmons Maccoby

Wisconsin

Chetek: Leona E. Tyler

Major Fields

Clinical/Counseling Psychology

Nancy Bayley

Charlotte M. Bühler

Else Frenkel-Brunswick

Anna Freud

Leta Stetter Hollingworth

Karen Horney

Marie Jahoda

Carolyn Robertson Payton

Pauline (Pat) Snedden Sears

Janet Taylor Spence

Bonnie Ruth Strickland

Leona E. Tyler

Developmental

Anne Anastasi

Nancy Bayley

Sandra Lipsitz Bem

Jeanne Humphrey Block

Charlotte M. Bühler

Mamie Phipps Clark

Anna Freud

Eleanor Jack Gibson

Florence L. Goodenough

Jacqueline Garrett Goodnow

Leta Stetter Hollingworth
Karen Horney
Barbel Inhelder
Eleanor Emmons Maccoby
Maria Montessori
Bernice L. Neugarten
Pauline (Pat) Snedden Sears
Leona E. Tyler
Thelma Gwinn Thurstone
Beth Lucy Wellman

Educational/School
Leta Stetter Hollingworth
Pauline (Pat) Snedden Sears
Virginia Staudt Sexton
Thelma Gwinn Thurstone
Maria Montessori
Beth Lucy Wellman

Ethnic Minority Issues
Florence L. Denmark
Mamie Phipps Clark
Else Frenkel-Brunswick
Marie Jahoda
Clara Mayo
Carolyn Robertson Payton
Bonnie Ruth Strickland

Experimental/Physiological/Comparative
Mary Whiton Calkins
Eleanor J. Gibson
Jacqueline Garrett Goodnow
Mary Henle
Barbel Inhelder
Christine Ladd-Franklin
Janet Taylor Spence
Margaret Floy Washburn

History
Edna Heidbreder

Mary Henle

Virginia Staudt Sexton

Industrial/Organizational/Engineering

Lillian Moller Gilbreth

Personality

Sandra Lipsitz Bem

Jeanne H. Block

Charlotte M. Bühler

Mary Whiton Calkins

Florence Denmark

Florence Goodenough

Else Frenkel-Brunswick

Edna F. Heidbreder

Ravenna Helson

Mary Henle

Karen Horney

Marie Jahoda

Bernice L. Neugarten

Virginia Staudt Sexton

Carolyn Wood Sherif

Janet Taylor Spence

Bonnie Ruth Strickland

Leona E. Tyler

Psychoanalysis

Else Frenkel-Brunswick

Anna Freud

Karen Horney

Marie Jahoda

Psychology of Women/Sex and Gender Roles

Sandra Lipsitz Bem

Jeanne Humphrey Block

Florence L. Denmark

Ravenna Helson

Leta Stetter Hollingworth

Karen Horney

Eleanor Emmons Maccoby

Clara Mayo

Bernice L. Neugarten
Carolyn Robertson Payton
Virginia Staudt Sexton
Carolyn Wood Sherif
Janet Taylor Spence
Bonnie Ruth Strickland

Social
Sandra Lipsitz Bem
Jeanne Humphrey Block
Florence L. Denmark
Else Frenkel-Brunswick
Leta Stetter Hollingworth
Marie Jahoda
Eleanor Emmons Maccoby
Clara Mayo
Bernice L. Neugarten
Pauline (Pat) Snedden Sears
Carolyn Wood Sherif
Janet Taylor Spence
Bonnie Ruth Strickland

Systems, Methods, and Techniques
Anne Anastasi
Nancy Bayley
Sandra Lipsitz Bem
Florence L. Goodenough
Edna Heidbreder
Mary Henle
Barbel Inhelder
Christine Ladd-Franklin
Maria Montessori
Virginia Staudt Sexton
Janet Taylor Spence
Bonnie Ruth Strickland
Thelma G. Thurstone
Leona E. Tyler
Beth Lucy Wellman

INDEX

Note: page numbers in *italics* indicate main entries in the text.

INDEX

Note: page numbers in *italics* indicate main entries in the text.

ABOUT THE CONTRIBUTORS

CAROLYN T. BASHAW is a doctoral candidate in History at the University of Georgia. Her primary research interests are women's higher education and professionalization in the early twentieth century. She has published articles in *Educational Theory* and *Psychology of Women Quarterly*.

W. L. BASHAW is Professor of Educational Psychology and the former head of the Department of Educational Psychology at the University of Georgia. His research concerns measurement theory with a particular interest in Item Response Theory. He is the author of *Mathematics for Statistics* and recently contributed chapters to *The Handbook of School Psychology* and *Educational Technology*.

LUDY T. BENJAMIN, JR., is Professor of Psychology at Texas A&M University and formerly held appointments with the American Psychological Association and Nebraska Wesleyan University. His principal research interest is in the history of American psychology. He is currently working on a biography of Harry Hollingworth, the husband of Leta S. Hollingworth.

JACK BLOCK is Professor of Psychology at the University of California at Berkeley. His principal work has been in the fields of personality psychology and developmental psychology, with an emphasis on longitudinal research. He is the author of *Lives Through Time*, *The Challenge of Response Sets*, and numerous journal articles and book chapters.

JOYCE V. CADWALLADER is Associate Professor in the Department of Science and Mathematics at Saint Mary-of-the Woods College, Indiana, and was a postdoctoral trainee in Developmental Biology at the Wisconsin Regional Primate Research Center at the University of Wisconsin. Her interests include women in science and biological views of women.

THOMAS C. CADWALLADER is Professor of Psychology at Indiana State University. His historical research has been published in the *Journal of the*

History of the Behavioral Sciences, *Transactions of the Charles S. Peirce Society*, and *Journal of Comparative Psychology*. He is a past president of APA's Division of the History of Psychology.

FAIRFID M. CAUDLE is Assistant Professor of Psychology, Sociology, and Anthropology at CUNY College of Staten Island. Her interest include psychology and the arts, consumer psychology, and the history of psychology.

STUART W. COOK is Distinguished Professor of Psychology at the University of Colorado and former Chair of the Psychology Department at Colorado and New York University. He is the recipient of SPSSI'S Kurt Lewin and Gordon Allport Research Awards, the APA Award for Distinguished Contributions to Psychology in the Public Interest, and the APF Gold Medal. He is co-author of *Research Methods in Social Relations*.

MARIE SKODAK CRISSEY retired as Director of Psychological Services and Special Education in the Dearborn Michigan Schools, and as a member of the Extension Faculty of the University of Michigan. She is currently involved in private practice as a psychologist. Her principle research interests are in mental development of children who experience major changes in environment through adoption or special education. She is co-editor of *Institutions for the Mentally Retarded: A Changing Role in Changing Times*.

MELINDA DEACON is a master's student in Family Resources and Human Development at Arizona State University. Her goal is to earn a doctorate in Clinical Psychology and pursue a research career.

KAY DEAUX is Professor of Psychology at the Graduate School and University Center of the City University of New York. Previously she taught at Purdue University. She is 1990–91 president of the Society of Personality and Social Psychology, and has received both the Gordon Allport Intergroup Relations Prize and the Carolyn Wood Sherif Award. She is the author of *The Behavior of Women and Men*, *Women of Steel*, and *Social Psychology*.

FLORENCE L. DENMARK is Professor of Psychology and Chair of the Psychology Department of Pace University. A former president of the American Psychological Association, she was the 1987 recipient of the APA Award for Distinguished Contribution to Education and Teaching in Psychology. Her biography is included in this volume.

DOROTHY H. EICHORN recently retired as Associate Director, Institute of Human Development, University of California, Berkeley, and as Executive Officer, Society for Research in Child Development. She is a developmental psychologist with particular interest in bio-behavioral interactions. Her latest publication is *Adolescence and Work*.

REUBEN FINE is Director Emeritus of the New York Center for Psychoanalytic Training, as well as visiting Professor of Psychology at Adelphi University. His many works include *The History of Psychoanalysis*, *Love and Work: The Value System of Psychoanalysis*, and *Current and Historical Perspectives on the Borderline Patient*.

LAUREL FURUMOTO is Professor of Psychology at Wellesley College. The three divisions of the American Psychological Association of which she is a Fellow—teaching, history, and psychology of women—reflect her principal areas of interest. She is co-author of *Untold Lives: The First Generation of American Women Psychologists*.

EILEEN A. GAVIN is Professor of Psychology at the College of St. Catherine in Minnesota, where she previously chaired the psychology department for twelve years. Her wide-ranging publications have dealt with the history of psychology, moral development, the psychology of religion, and the psychology of women.

HARRISON G. GOUGH is Professor of Psychology, Emeritus, at the University of California, Berkeley, where he was formerly Director of the Institute of Personality Assessment and Research, and Chair of the Department of Psychology. He is the author of the *California Psychological Inventory*, and co-author (with A. B. Heilbrun, Jr.) of the *Adjective Check List*. In 1986 he received the Bruno Klopfer Distinguished Contribution Award from the Society for Personality Assessment.

HOWARD E. GRUBER is Research Scholar of Psychology at Teachers College, Columbia University, and was formerly Professor of Psychology at the University of Geneva and Rutgers University. He is the author of *Darwin on Man: A Psychological Study of Scientific Creativity*, and co-editor and author of *Creative People at Work: Twelve Cognitive Case Studies*.

ROBERT V. GUTHRIE is a Clinical Psychologist in San Diego, California. He was formerly Associate Director, Psychological Sciences Division, Office of Naval Research and has held several university professorships. He is the author of *Even the Rat Was White: A Historical View of Psychology*, and has written extensively for scientific journals.

ROBERT S. HARPER is Professor Emeritus of Psychology at Knox College in Galesburg, Illinois, where an endowed scholarship for graduate study in psychology was established in his name. Also, the Spoon River Center Library is known as the Robert S. Harper Library. His primary research interests are in the history of psychology.

JOHN D. HOGAN is Associate Professor of Psychology at St. John's University, NY. His major interests are in life-span development, the history of psychology, and international psychology. He is co-editor, with Virginia Staudt Sexton, of the upcoming volume *Psychology Around the World*, 2nd edition.

GWENDOLYN PURYEAR KEITA is Assistant Executive Director of the Public Interest Directorate and Director of the Women's Program Office at the American Psychological Association. She has written extensively on factors affecting achievement and mental health in African-American women.

RITA MAE KELLY is Professor of Justice Studies, Political Science, and Women's Studies at Arizona State University, where she is also editor of *Women & Politics*. Her numerous books include *The Making of Political Women*, *Comparable Worth, Pay Equity, and Public Policy*, and *Gender, Bureaucracy and Democracy*.

VINCENT P. KELLY is visiting professor of Intercultural Studies, American Graduate School of International Management, and a teacher in the Tempe Elementary School System. Formerly a professor at the University of Maryland, District of Columbia Teachers' College, and Kean College of New Jersey, he has authored several articles on bilingual education and ethnic/linguistic differences.

MARIANNE LAFRANCE is Associate Professor of Social Psychology and former Director of Women's Studies at Boston College. She has also held appointments at Yale, Radcliffe, and the University of California at San Francisco. She is the author of *Moving Bodies: Nonverbal Communication in Social Relationships*.

BRENDA LEE is Site Director for the Young Women's Christian Association Shelter in Glendale, California, where she is pursuing her interest in helping battered women.

LEWIS P. LIPSITT is Professor of Psychology and Medical Science, and Director of the Child Study Center, at Brown University, and has been a Fellow of the Center for Advanced Study in the Behavioral Sciences at Stanford, as well as a Guggenheim Fellow. He is the founding editor of *Infant Behavior and Development*, and founding co-editor of *Advances in Infancy Research*.

VIVIAN PARKER MAKOSKY is Assistant Executive Director of the Institute of Scrap Recycling Industries, Washington, D. C., and former Executive Director for Educational and Public Affairs at the American Psychological Association. Her publications include *Activities Handbook for the Teaching of Psychology*, Volumes 2 and 3, and *Factbook on Women in Higher Education*.

TRESSIE MULDROW has interests in social perception and motivation, statistics, and psychology of women. In 1973 she became Personnel Research Psychologist in the Personnel Research and Development Center of the Civil Service Commission.

STEPHEN NOWICKI, JR., is Professor of Psychology at Emory University. He is co-author of the *Nowicki-Strickland Internal-External Control Scale* and numerous publications concerning social learning theory. Most recently, he is co-author of *Abnormal Psychology: A New Look*.

AGNES N. O'CONNELL is Associate Professor of Psychology and Director of the Community Psychology Program at Montclair State College. A Fellow of APA, her publications include the award-winning *Eminent Women in Psychology*, and *Models of Achievement: Reflections of Eminent Women in Psychology*, Volumes 1 and 2, and numerous journal articles and chapters on personality, adult development, mental health, the psychology of women, and the history of psychology.

SAMUEL H. OSIPOW is Professor of Psychology and former Chair of the Psychology Department at Ohio State University, Columbus. He was the 1989 recipient of the Leona Tyler Award for Distinguished Contributions to Counseling Psychology. He is the author of *Theories of Career Development*, and past editor of the *Journal of Counseling Psychology* and *The Journal of Vocational Behavior*.

MICHELE A. PALUDI is Associate Professor of Psychology at Hunter College. She was the recipient of the 1988 Emerging Leader Award from the Committee on Women in Psychology of the APA. She is author of *Exploring/Teaching the Psychology of Women: A Manual of Resources*, and co-author of *Sex and Gender; The Human Experience*.

NANCY M. RAMBUSCH is Associate Professor and Coordinator for Early Childhood Education at the State University of New York College at New Paltz. She recently authored "Montessori Methods: Eighty Years Later" in *Channel*. She is credited with the American reformation of Montessori education and the establishment of the American Montessori Society.

JUDY F. ROSENBLITH is Professor Emerita, Wheaton College, and previously held appointments at Brown and Harvard Universities. Her principal research has been on the relations of newborn behavior as assessed by the Graham/

Rosenblith Scale to later developmental outcomes. She is co-author of *In the Beginning: Development in the First Two Years of Life*.

NANCY FELIPE RUSSO, Professor of Psychology and Director of Women's Studies at Arizona State University, is editor or author of numerous books and articles related to the history of psychology and the psychology of women, including the award-winning *Eminent Women in Psychology*, and *Models of Achievement: Reflections of Eminent Women in Psychology*. A Fellow of five APA Divisions, she was the 1985 recipient of the Distinguished Leadership Award of APA's Committee on Women in Psychology.

ELIZABETH SCARBOROUGH is Professor of Psychology at the State University of New York College at Fredonia, and formerly served as Chair of the department. She is co-author, with Laurel Furumoto, of *Untold Lives: The First Generation of American Women Psychologists*.

NANCY K. SCHLOSSBERG is Professor of Counseling and Personnel Services, College of Education, University of Maryland, College Park. Her books include *Overwhelmed: Coping with Life's Ups and Downs* and *Improving Higher Education Environments for Adults*. She is a G. Stanley Hall Lecturer and recipient of numerous awards.

VIRGINIA STAUDT SEXTON is Distinguished Professor of Psychology at St. John's University, New York, and Professor Emeritus of Psychology of the University of the City of New York. Her books include *Psychology Around the World* and *History of Psychology: An Overview*. Her biography is included in this volume.

STEPHANIE A. SHIELDS is Associate Professor of Psychology at the University of California, Davis, and has served as Director of the Women's Studies Program. She is currently writing a book on gender and social meaning of emotion. Her research has been supported by the National Science Foundation and the Rockefeller Foundation.

MARGARET L. SIGNORELLA is Associate Professor of Psychology and Women's Studies at Penn State, McKeesport. She is co-editor of *Children's Gender Schemata*, and her articles have appeared primarily in *Developmental Psychology*, *Child Development*, and *Sex Roles*.

M. BREWSTER SMITH is Professor Emeritus of Psychology at the University of California, Santa Cruz. He previously taught and administered at the University of Chicago, the University of California, Berkeley (where he directed the Institute of Human Development), New York University, Vassar College, and Harvard. He is co-author of *The American Soldier* and *Opinions and Personality*. In 1987, he was president of the American Psychological Association.

DENNIS N. THOMPSON is Associate Professor of Educational Foundations at Georgia State University. He has published numerous articles on both psychology and education, and has an active research interest in the history of developmental psychology. He is currently working as co-editor of the 100th anniversary issue of the *Journal of Genetic Psychology*.

LILLIAN E. TROLL is Adjunct Professor in Human Development and Aging, and Anthropology and Aging, at the University of California, San Francisco, and Professor Emeritus of Psychology at Rutgers University. She was awarded the 1989 Distinguished Contribution Award by APA's Division on Adult Development and Aging. Her many chapters and books include *Development in Early and Middle Adulthood*, *Continuations: Development in Adulthood and Old Age*, and *Family Issues in Current Gerontology*.

MARIA E. VEGEGA is a research psychologist with the U.S. Department of Transportation. With an academic background in social psychology, her interests in public policy led her to accept a legislative fellowship, during which she worked on budget, health, and family issues. Her articles on preventing impaired driving have been published in *Evaluation and Program Planning* and *Health Education Quarterly*.

RICHARD D. WALK is Professor of Psychology at George Washington University and has previously held appointments at Cornell University, the University of California, Berkeley, the Massachusetts Institute of Technology, and the University of London. His numerous publications include *Perceptual Development*, *Perception and Experience*, and *Intersensory Perception and Sensory Integration*.

MICHAEL WERTHEIMER is Professor of Psychology at the University of Colorado at Boulder. He has been president of the American Psychological Association's Divisions of General Psychology, the Teaching of Psychology, Theoretical and Philosophical Psychology, and the History of Psychology. A recipient of the American Psychological Foundation's Distinguished Teaching in Psychology Award, his books include *A Brief History of Psychology* and *History of Psychology: A Guide to Information Sources*.

SUZANNE M. ZILBER is a doctoral candidate in Counseling Psychology at the Ohio State University and is currently an intern at the University of Texas at Austin. Her research interests include women's career development and the relationship between attributional styles and self-efficacy expectations.